Blonde On The Tracks
Dylan's Discography re-imagined and re-examined

Scot P. Livingston

Copyright © 2019 Scot P. Livingston

All rights reserved.

ISBN: 978-1545137284
ISBN-13: 1545137285

TABLE OF CONTENTS

Introduction   6

THE ALBUMS:

Bob Dylan	9
The Freewheelin' Bob Dylan	22
The Times They Are A-Changin'	48
Another Side Of Bob Dylan	62
Bringing It All Back Home	71
Highway 61 Revisited	81
Blonde On Blonde	89
The Basement Tapes	99
John Wesley Harding	122
Nashville Skyline	130
Self-Portrait	139
Dylan	160
New Morning	166
Greatest Hits, Vol. II	180
Pat Garrett & Billy The Kid	185
Planet Waves	193
Blood On The Tracks	200
Desire	209
Street Legal	219
Slow Train Coming	229

Saved	237
Shot Of Love	245
Infidels	261
Empire Burlesque	274
Knocked Out Loaded	287
Down In The Groove	295
Oh Mercy	305
Under The Red Sky	317
Good As I Been To You	326
World Gone Wrong	336
Time Out Of Mind	344
Love & Theft	354
Modern Times	364
Together Through Life	374
Christmas In The Heart	383
Tempest	391
Shadows In The Night	399
Fallen Angels	404
Triplicate	409

APPENDECIES

The Never Ending Bootleg Series	421
Dylan in Compilations	424
Dylan on Live Albums	431
Dylan on Stage	434
Dylan in Digital & Streaming Format	451
Dylan's Biggest Hits (As Covered by Others)	456
Dylan on Cassette	459
Dylan on 45 (or cassingle or MP3...)	466
Dylan on MTV/YouTube	471
Dylan on LP	480
Original or Cancelled Album Line-Ups	497
Song Index	500

INTRODUCTION

Does the world need another book about Bob Dylan?
The answer is clearly, no.

But I wanted to write one anyway. So I did. When I wrote my last book, The Monkees: A Many Fractured Image (plug plug), I knew I was writing to a fairly small audience, but one that did not have nearly enough books written for it. While Bob Dylan fans are certainly a much larger demographic, they are plenty well served literarily. There are entire publishing companies that do nothing but churn out books about Bob Dylan. Why would I want to add to this already saturated market? Because I wanted to. I had a lot of things to say on the subject, and I wanted to compile them into one simple easy-to-find place.

But why would anyone want to read another series of opinions on Dylan from another random, unrelated, and unqualified guy? Why wouldn't this be better suited to a blog or a podcast or something? I don't know. I like books. Besides, I thought I might have a take on the material that was slightly different from most: I don't like most of what most Dylan fans do like about Dylan's album. Conversely (or possibly perversely) I tend to love a lot of what most people consider Dylan's worst records. And I wanted to explore that.

Of course, this does raise a big problem, anyone who is familiar enough with the material I'm talking about most of the time is also going to disagree with me most of the time vehemently. And anyone who doesn't have an opinion yet is not going to waste their time reading about 600+ songs they are not familiar with. This book is not a good starting point for getting to know Dylan. I'm going to assume that you already know most of the biographical facts of Bob Dylan's life and have heard all of his albums as well as having managed to track down and hear quite a few illicitly obtained bootlegs of unreleased material.

So who is this book for? It's for me. I wanted to write it. This, in fact, started out as an article I wrote for *Ear Candy Mag*, an online magazine, in December 2004 entitled "A Contrarian's Guide To Bob Dylan". There's a lot of that spirit still in here – just expanded exponentially. But I wanted to add a bit more than just my uninformed opinions. So I wanted to add a little bit more to this. One less subjective feature I included was Bob's "Famous/Popular/Important Tracks" from each album. I tried to be a little scientific here, although ultimately this still could all be argued. I have included a series of appendixes at the end of the book that helped me determine which track or tracks off of each album are the quote-unquote biggest. This is followed by a list of my favorite songs. That is completely subjective. I tried to have the same number of favorite songs from each album, while clearly some of Bob's albums have a lot more "Famous/Popular/Important" material than others. Inevitably there will be some overlap between those songs and my favorites, although generally, I tend to favor the shorter, faster, and less lyrically focused songs of Bob Dylan.

In presenting this album, I have listed the albums in chronological order as they were (mainly) recorded rather than in the order they were actually officially released. It just makes more sense for to me to put *The Basement Tapes* as a bridge between *Blonde On Blonde* and *John Wesley Harding* rather than sitting uncomfortably between the wholly unrelated *Blood On The Tracks* and *Desire*. This is a little harder for the album called *Dylan* that was released in 1973 but consists of outtakes from both *Self-Portrait* and *New Morning*. I ended up just slotting it in between the other two, because it makes the most sense rather than ignoring it, or piecing it out between the other two. In constructing an overall narrative to the flow of Bob's discography, that's where *Dylan* makes the most sense.

The other, far less scientific, feature I have included in this book is a series of "album re-imaginings." This is a popular game amongst Monkees fans playing armchair Don Kirshner or Beach Boys aficionados trying to reconstruct *SMiLE*. Bob himself is somewhat noteworthy for rethinking his albums at the last minute (see *Freewhelin'*, *Blood On The Tracks*, or even *Down In The Groove*). I have included some of these almost-happened line-ups as an appendix to this book as well. I am definitely in agreement with most Dylan fans when I complain that his best stuff is often left on the cutting room floor. So I have gone through at the end of each chapter I have presented my personal re-imagining of what songs should have gone on which album. Some albums are expanded or divided or squished together into one. This is all very subjective, and I'm sure if I were going to re-write this book tomorrow would do almost all of these differently. It's fun for me to do, and hopefully, it will be enjoyable for you read. Even if you don't like what I came up with, it should at least spur you to think about these albums in different ways.

Now, I tried as hard as I could to be as accurate as I could with all the information I presented in this book. There are professionals out there whose whole job is to know more about Dylan than I. Furthermore, there thousands upon thousands of fans who have devoted a good portion of their lives to learning as much about Bob as they possibly can. I know inevitably I have made mistakes. Please know that I tried my best within my admittedly limited skill set and budget. I just hope that the reader will forgive any historical or factual errors I may have made and not use them to invalidate my opinions about the music itself.

I was initially a little hesitant to write this book, for much the same reason I don't want to start my *Simpsons* book. Namely, it's not done yet. This will never be definitive. Bob is still out there writing and recording, and I will have to update this book with each new release. Heck, even after Dylan finally rolls over and croaks (which may or may not be within my lifetime given his age and my health), Columbia Records is going to continually find and release more material which may shed some light or change my mind about these albums. It is a fear of mine that his book will never really be done. But I wanted to write it anyway.

So I did.

BOB DYLAN
Produced by: John Hammond
Recorded: Nov. 20th & 22nd, 1961
Released: March 19th, 1962

Famous/Important/Popular Track(s):
- Song To Woody

My Personal Favorite Track(s):
- House Of The Risin' Sun
- In My Time Of Dyin'
- Fixin' To Die

In the popular consciousness, Bob Dylan is first and foremost a songwriter (primarily noted for his lyrics) whose vocal abilities are, at best, an acquired test. It might surprise those with only a cursory knowledge of Dylan to know that he was actually signed to a record contract and made his first album before he began actually writing his own material in earnest. Sure, there are two self-penned compositions on his debut, but that apparently was not the reason Bob got to record for Columbia Records. Legend is that Dylan was signed primarily on his strength playing harmonica on a Harry Belafonte session.

This album is now, retrospect, seen as something of a miss. Not bad, by any respect, but it was followed up by nine albums (ten if you count *The Basement Tapes*) that range from, near-perfect at worst, to an unassailable masterpiece. In some ways, it similar to the prevailing critical opinion of *The Simpsons*, where critics may argue endlessly as to when the show jumped the shark, but generally don't consider the first season part of the show's "golden era".

But is this album really that much different or worse from the next three? Sure, the relative dearth of original material does paint it as something of an outsider. But overall this is a really good listen. Bob was already bucking the folk trends, which by this point favored the smooth collegiate sounds of groups such as The Kingston Trio or The Chad Mitchell Trio. As Bob himself put it, he "sounds like a hillbilly". And while this album is clearly part of the folk scene of the time; Dylan is already stretching his legs, incorporating Blues and Country into his sound. Hank Williams and Robert Johnson are as big of an influence on this as the oft-cited Woody Guthrie.

Sure Bob was only 20 at the time of this record, but he is desperately trying to sound so much older. The best moments on this record are where he goes really dark and gritty. In contrast, Dylan is still playing up his Charlie Chaplin-derived rascally tramp character. There is a lot of humor on this album and Bob is using this humor to help ingratiate himself with his audience. As the tenor and nature of his material got more overtly political, this more funny side of him slowly began to fade from his repertoire. He is definitely a sly mischief-stirring trickster, which somehow doesn't invalidate his more sincere blues aspirations. It is in fact on his two original songs ("Song To Woody" and "Talkin' New York") where the balance between the goofy and the deathly serious is least successful.

And when I say deathly serious, Bob means it. A surprising number of songs on this debut album are about death and dying. For a young man, he is very morbid. Maybe it is part of his attempt to mimic the older blues artists that he loved, but a lot of this songs are about Dylan's own mortality.

While the first four acoustic albums of Dylan's might be a bit hard to get into with their repetitive instrumentation throughout, they are not as boring as one might first suspect. (If you want to hear how boring just one man and his acoustic guitar can sound, check out *Good As I Been To You* and *World Gone Wrong*). Personally, I think Bob's debut easily stands up to, in some cases trounces the next three acoustic albums.

You're No Good
(written by Jesse Fuller)

A chugging upbeat tune that despite several lyrical references to "the blues" in fact has a much more complicated chord structure than your usual I-IV-V, especially in the bridge. The pace slowly increases throughout the whole tune. There's some fun quick harmonica work on here, and the whole thing almost sounds more like a parody of the blues genre than an actual attempt at it. Bob's vocal delivery leaves one wondering exactly how sarcastic we are supposed to be taking these jovial lyrics about "wanting to die."

Talkin' New York
(written by Bob Dylan)

The first song written by Bob officially released. This is another up-tempo tune with some wry observations from Bob about his early impressions of his new home city. The lyrics are surprisingly straight-forward and direct. Even more unusual is how honest and autobiographical they are. At this point, Bob was not a huge star yet and may not have been guarding his privacy and anonymity as much as he soon would be. The harmonica playing is unhinged and joyful. When *Bob Dylan* was first compiled (with the working title of *Free Wheeling*), this song traded placed with "Freight Train Blues" in the track listing. The whole thing is humorous without being jokey. Still, it's not a very deep or serious song, and it ends with a punchline about moving to East Orange before fading out with a harmonica solo. Odd that Bob hadn't figured out a real written ending for this song musically.

In My Time of Dyin'
(traditional, arranged By Bob Dylan)

As far as I know, this is the only recorded example of Bob playing slide or bottleneck guitar. It's a shame because it helps to vary the instrumental palette – particularly on these first four albums. Bob's voice is such an over-the-top blues homage it would come off as parody if it didn't feel so sincere. Bob doesn't need a full band to rock out, and this is one of the loudest, rockingest songs of the early acoustic albums. While "You're No Good" had pretensions towards suicide that never seemed plausible, this song takes its death deathly serious. It is a dark haunting performance and one of the best songs recorded for *Bob Dylan*.

Man of Constant Sorrow
(traditional, arranged By Bob Dylan)

You can't really talk about this track without also mentioning the famous rendition of "Man Of Constant Sorrow" that was the centerpiece of *O Brother, Where Art Thou?* both the film and the soundtrack. That version is a hoot with fun backing vocals and a pumping rhythm to it. Bob takes this far more seriously, although the way he elongated some of these words borders on comedic, this is not meant to be a comic version. Bob sounds hurt sing these lyrics of homelessness and hopelessness. There's no anger here, just remorse. The wailing of the harmonica echoes the haunted ache in the lyrics. An impressively wise song for one so young.

Fixin' to Die
(written by Bukka White)

Another song about death. For someone only 20 years old when he recorded this, Bob seems especially morbid. It's not nearly as cool as "In My Time Of Dyin'" but only because it doesn't have that bottleneck guitar. Bob's voice has this cool gruff affection that gives this blues song some real grit. The guitar playing is spooky and superb. The lyrics do seem to be the fleeting final thoughts of a man who is about to die. As dark as the subject matter is, Dylan makes this song rock. It may not be "fun" necessarily, but it is compelling. It's almost a shame that Bob gave up officially releasing covers songs for so long after his debut because he has a real knack for it.

Pretty Peggy-O
(traditional, arranged By Bob Dylan)

Bob Dylan at the apex of his early comic persona. He even opens this song with a joke about being unable to find "Fenario." The harmonica playing is all over the place, with the occasional pause for Dylan to let out a "woo-hoo!" This is the kind of folk tune that could be taken super-seriously (see the version on Simon & Garfunkel's *Wednesday Morning, 3 A.M.*) Bob isn't making fun of this song, per se. He is just using it as a platform to jump off of in all sorts of giddy, goofy ways. It's not to see Bo with a sense of humor about himself. While it is not nearly as funny as some of the tracks he would write for himself later, this is a fun one.

Highway 51
(written by Curtis Jones)

This song is so rocking with its faux-Bo Diddley beat, that it could've easily been transformed into an electric song on the 1966 tour. Bob sings this with a real blues growl in his voice. I think the lyrics are about a road, but I'm assuming that the road is a metaphor. In some ways "Highway 51" does feel like a precursor to "Highway 61 Revisited". While Bob has often included blues songs in his repertoire and used them as a point of influence, it's a shame he never did record a full blues album like this back when he was younger. Perhaps if he hadn't had sound songwriting, that would be something he might've ended up doing. Given the diversity just between this track and "In My Time Of Dyin'" it probably would've had more variety than your usual blues album. Particularly one that was just a single voice, acoustic guitar, and harmonica.

Gospel Plow
(traditional, arranged By Bob Dylan)

Long before Bob's born-again period of the late '70s and early '80s, Dylan was singing traditional gospel fare such as this. However, Bob hardly sounds converted here. Sure, his singing is sincere, but the goofy, puffing harmonica and frantic pace of the guitar undercut any possibility that Bob is trying to preach to us here. He is just singing the song because he likes it. And it is a great, little song. Bob's voice is almost a parody of the gruff wizened old man he was pretending to be on much of this album. Super-short (under two minutes) but makes for a pleasing diversion from some the longer and more serious tracks.

Baby, Let Me Follow You Down
(traditional, arranged by Eric Von Schmidt)

A song that Bob admits he learned from Von Schmidt during the spoken intro on the officially released version of this song. So it's somewhat surprising to hear Bob doing a version of this cover as a demo for his publishing company on *The Bootleg Series vol. 9*. The lyrics are pretty much what you would expect from a pop love song (albeit a tad more nihilistic), so it's no surprise that this one of the earliest songs Bob re-did as a rock number for his 1966 electric tour. He even revisited again for the Band's *Last Waltz*. It doesn't feel like the more traditional folk or blues tunes Dylan was doing at the time. In addition to the unexpected spoken introduction of the song on the record, every single verse on this version is separated by an entire harmonica solo. Despite this, the song still clocks in at just over two-and-a-half minutes. In this original guise, there's not much to this song. While not imbued with great depth, it also doesn't sound like on the songs Bob does humorously either. As a result, it sort of straddles a weird middle ground, being neither funny nor serious. It feels like as a solo acoustic song, Dylan isn't sure what to do with this song yet. That's probably the best way to enjoy the original *Bob Dylan* version of this song: as a hint of things yet to come.

House of the Risin' Sun
(traditional, arranged By Dave Van Ronk)

Sure, Bob may have nicked his arrangement of this song from Dave Van Ronk before he got a chance to record. And yes, The Animals did glean much of their inspiration for their hit cover from the version on *Bob Dylan*. Still, this is one of the best tracks on Bob's debut album. It's not surprising that when Bob Johnston hired the backing band to overdub on top of some Dylan tracks to see if the melding of folk and rock were viable, this is the track he had them work on. If you haven't heard the "electric" version, I would highly recommend it. It has only been officially released on the CD-ROM "Highway 61 Revisited". But even without the full band backing, this is an electrifying listening experience. In fact, it may be an even more gripping incarnation as a solo acoustic performance. Sure, the song is a garage band staple, being simple to learn (it was the first song I learned on the guitar) but this take is revelatory. I love the fact that Bob doesn't even change the pronouns here, singing it from the woman's POV. Bob and The Band also attempted re-recording this track for *Planet Waves* although I don't think they ever got a finished take. For anyone who still doubts that Dylan is a masterful and powerful singer, this is one of the tracks I usually play them to dissuade them. It is stunning and frightening. One of the best covers Dylan has ever recorded.

Freight Train Blues
(written by John Lair, Arranged By Bob Dylan)

Another goofy and less serious song. It's amazing how much variety Bob is able to create on his debut album that eludes him entirely on his mid-90s records, *Good As I Been To You* and *World Gone Wrong*. He's working with the same restricted components: just acoustic guitar, voice and harmonica playing (mostly) traditional folk tunes. Those albums are dour and humorless and could've really used the excitement of a track like this one. Sure, it's not terribly deep or meaningful. Really all Bob is trying to do here is impress you with how long he can hold that one note. And boy howdy, can he hold that note for a long time. Much like the gag of Sideshow Bob stepping on the rakes in *The Simpsons*, this goes on so long it starts as funny, gets funnier, eventually becomes annoying before finally becoming hysterical by the very end. It is fascinating. Plus it the perfect song to follow-up the harrowing "House Of The Risin' Sun" without undermining or negating it.

Song to Woody
(written by Bob Dylan)

The weaker of the two originals on *Bob Dylan*. Only Bob Dylan would write a tribute to a man by also plagiarizing him a bit as this song is a recasting of Woody's "1913 Massacre". It's a nice little folk-waltz, but nothing spectacular. Bob isn't saying much here except that he likes Woody Guthrie and we all should too. He also shows off his folk credentials by also including shout-outs to Leadbelly, Cisco Houston, and Sonny Terry in the lyrics. The song is dripping with sincerity that almost bubble over to slavish fanboy desperation. It's charming to see Bob reduced to just a normal human being quaking in awe in front of his idol. Soon Dylan will be so vaunted by other that he completely loses touch with sort of humility. Sure, becoming a legend yourself might help you be less nervous in the company of other so-called legends; still, it's a shame there is so little of Bob in this pre-fame mold.

See That My Grave Is Kept Clean
(written by Blind Lemon Jefferson)

Another dark blues song about death in the same vein as "In My Time Of Dyin'" and "Fixin' To Die". While this is not as good as those other two (possibly because it's less of a surprise by this point), it is still a haunting and gripping performance. Clearly, this was the style and theme that Bob was really into at the time that fell to the wayside once he started penning his own material. Bob's voice forces itself into a growl that would naturally have by the time he was an old man. While this may hurt its authenticity, the artifice actually bolsters its sincerity. Bob is deliberately choosing to sound like an old man even if he's only twenty. Who knows why this preoccupation with his own demise was at the forefront of his first album. Still, it makes a powerful statement, one that still resonates even after Dylan's predictions of an early grave turned out to be wildly inaccurate.

<u>Songs not on the album:</u>
Hard Times In New York Town from *The Bootleg Series vol. 1*
(written by Bob Dylan)

An earlier, less funny version of "Talkin' New York". As much as he pretended to be a world-traveler, moving to NYC was quite impactful to the young small-town Bobby Zimmerman. Three of the five chapters of his autobiography are focused on those first few months moving to New York. The home-taped version on *The Bootleg Series vol. 1* has some nice finger-picking on it. The songwriter demo on *The Bootleg Series vol. 9* feels extremely rushed as if Bob were trying to get through it as quickly as possible. Maybe by this point, he was sort of embarrassed by the tune, or felt he had done it all the better on "Talkin' New York". Both songs carry a sense of being overwhelmed by their new surroundings. And while Dylan feels lonely in this new place with all these strangers, neither song reveals any sort of homesickness or regret in moving. Bob is still trying to be funny here, although the humor is less as necessary as it would be on the re-write. Apparently there was no way he could include both on his debut, and he chose the better for the record. Still, it's a beautiful little piece of juvenilia.

He Was a Friend of Mine from *The Bootleg Series vol. 1*
(traditional, Arranged by Bob Dylan)

One of the four songs recorded for Dylan's debut that were left off the album. This is a mournful, sad song. While many of the tracks on *Bob Dylan* are about dying, usually it is about the death of the person singing the song. This song is the only one to look at mortality from the perspective of one who is left behind. It's a shame that this wasn't included on the album itself as it would've provided a good balance to songs like "In My Time Of Dyin'" and "Fixin' To Die". The heartache of the man left behind helps keep these songs from glorifying death too much. Bob does a fantastic job of showcasing the melancholy beauty of his young but rough vocals. The guitar picking on here is not deft but excellently executed. This is just a stunning song. It certainly would've bolstered the album had one of the weaker tracks been swapped out for it. Unfortunately, those weaker tracks are Dylan's original compositions, and Bob was trying to stake his claim as a songwriter (and Albert Grossman wanted his share of the publishing royalties), so they weren't going anywhere.

Man on the Street from *The Bootleg Series vol. 1*
(written by Bob Dylan)

The only original song recorded for *Bob Dylan* to end up getting cut. Bob would later come back to this concept in the much stronger track "Only A Hobo". Bob is especially nasal on this track. He sings without pity about a homeless man who died on the street and the general apathy of those who discovered his body the next day. It's a grim and gruesome scenario, but Dylan doesn't do much with it. The police come, harass the man, figure out he's dead, and take him away. The narrator seems to be surprised that he never sees the man again. I don't know what Bob was expecting. The song is done with a very flat, unaffected style that should amp up the tragedy, but somehow falls flat. The full version on *The Bootleg Series vol. 9* is a little better, although there is a second incomplete version included on that album for no good reason. I think the problem is we never really a chance to get know the policeman or the homeless man or narrator very well, so it's hard to be very invested. However, Bob does start the song by saying it's not too long and he isn't kidding. This tracks in under two minutes, so it's no wonder that we don't have time to really get to know who any of these characters are or what they're feeling. A valiant effort on Bob's part and certainly something that needs to be addressed, but this is not the best way to do it.

House Carpenter from *The Bootleg Series vol. 1*
(traditional, arranged By Bob Dylan)

An old folk tune first recorded for Bob's debut but left off the album. It was later attempted again for the *Self-Portrait* album. In the intervening eight years, Dylan had left these types of traditional songs for his own compositions, left protest-oriented songwriting for a more personal and abstract POV, plugged in, fell of his bike and hid in the basement, and then went to Nashville. It's fascinating to listen to the differences in this song between a young man steeped in this kind of music and an older man facing middle age trying to re-connect. The *Bob Dylan* version is another dark up-tempo acoustic ballad about death. It is a confident and gripping portrait. By 1970, Bob has returned to New York City and is trying his hand at playing these old songs (along with a smattering of country standards and some recent tunes by contemporary singer-songwriters). It had been a long time had since Dylan had recorded alone in a room and had enlisted David Bromberg on lead acoustic and Al Kooper on the piano to reinforce his sound even as he is initially attempting to return to this more stripped-down style. In this version, the song has become much jauntier. His voice still carries that *Nashville Skyline* croon. The latter recording is less about the feel and more focused on the particulars of the story. This version feels half-finished like you want producer Bob Johnston to take this to Nashville and overdub at least some bass and drums on here. The debut outtake version is so stunning you can easily ignore the preachy and stupid narrative of the lyrics. The *Self-Portrait* version is a little more cautious. There's certainly a sense of catharsis and relief in there as Dylan re-discovers his roots, it lacks the depth and commitment of a more focused young man who luxuriated in nothing but these types of traditional folk songs. Not a great song. I'm not sure I like the message of "If you leave your husband you are going to hell." But certainly, it would've fit in much better on the self-titled debut than on *Self-Portrait*.

When I Got Troubles from *The Bootleg Series vol. 7*
(written by Bob Dylan)

Much like the release of "That'll Be The Day" and "In Spite Of All The Danger" on *The Beatles Anthology 1*, this is far more interesting from a historical perspective than it is enjoyable as a listening experience. Recorded on amateur equipment in 1959, this is obviously a little murky.

However, if you want to hear what Bob Dylan sounded like in the fifties, this is about all you've got. When *Nashville Skyline* came out in 1969, Bob's old childhood friends remarked that he sounded more like he did when they knew him back in Minnesota than the nasally gravel-voiced sound the Dylan presented once he arrived in New York. Listening to this, it doesn't really sound similar, but you can certainly see the artifice that Bob presented both in his country croon and his electric snarl. This is Bob trying to sing pretty, without much self-awareness or control of his vocal instrument yet. Within two years, Dylan would have a distinct voice in mind for himself as well as the ability to present it flawlessly. On this track, as a mere teenager, he mostly sounds like he's trying to sound good similar the popular folk acts of the time like the Kingston Trio and future paramour Joan Baez. The song itself is unremarkable, a couple of chords clumsily strummed. It's credited to Bob, although he hadn't yet begun his songwriting in earnest by this time and may well be a cover of a tune whose author has been lost to the mists of times; either an old obscure folksinger or possibly a classmate that Dylan just nicked this tune from.

Rambler, Gambler from *The Bootleg Series vol. 7*
(traditional, arranged By Bob Dylan)

Another amateur home recording, this one a year after "When I Got Troubles". This song finds Bob far less enthralled with folk music generally and more specifically under the spell of Woody Guthrie. Bob's fascination with hopping the rails becoming a hobo is already starting to manifest themselves, although this is a cover rather than an original. The sound quality is a bit higher, showing that Dylan was hanging out with a better class of friends – or at least friends with better recording equipment. Bob's guitar playing is not much better from a technical standpoint, it does sound less hesitant than on "When I Got Troubles". Bob's voice has mutated into that faux-old man sound that he would employ in New York, but he does sound a little less preoccupied with singing "pretty", showing his moving from the more collegiate folk sound of the Chad Mitchell trio towards the more "authentic" rural sound of Woody and Leadbelly. Still, it is a track that is far more interesting for its historical import than it is a fun tune to listen to.

Dink's Song from *The Bootleg Series vol. 7*
(traditional, arranged By Bob Dylan)

One of the songs from the "Minnesota Hotel Tape", recorded in December of 1961 after *Bob Dylan* was recorded but before it was released while Dylan was home visiting family for Christmas. The sonic quality of this admittedly amateur recording is vastly improved from "When I Got Troubles" and "Rambler, Gambler". Bob is definitely deep into his well-worn "Dylan" voice by this point. This is a pleasant if unremarkable traditional tune. Unlike the previous two tracks however, this might actually be of a good enough quality to be slotted amongst Dylan's other material of the time without sticking out too badly. That being said, it's not long lost treasure unearthed here. It doesn't rock nearly as hard as some of the harder-edged songs on Bob's debut but is still trying to be a little rollicking. It could be that this is something of a restrained run-through of the song rather than a full-blooded performance; perhaps out of deference to any neighbors who may have been next door while Dylan was playing.

I Was Young When I Left Home from *The Bootleg Series vol. 7*
(*written by Bob Dylan*)
Another song from the "Minnesota Hotel Tape." This track feels even more like a casual encounter between friends than a full-blown attempt to do the song justice. While plenty of Bob's officially released tracks have spoken introductions, this sounds more like Dylan just talking rather than an official start to the song. Bob's fingerpicking is showed off quite nicely here, and luckily the home recording equipment is more than up to the task of capturing it. Bob's singing sounds truly sorrowful here. Considering that this is Bob's first real homecoming since his initial breakthrough in the New York folk scene, the lyrics to this song must've been particularly in the forefront of Dylan's mind at the time. The worry and nervousness are appropriate since Bob had managed to get a record deal and record an album at this point, he was by no point assured of success at this point in his career. In fact, given the way that *Bob Dylan* was initially received, the trepidation in Bob's voice is more than justified. At this point, Dylan's career could've still stalled out, and he could've been reduced to having to move back to Minnesota. A scary thought not just for us fans, but also a young Bob Dylan still aching to prove himself.

Poor Boy Blues from *The Bootleg Series vol. 9*
(*written by Bob Dylan*)
One of the songs demoed for copyright for Leeds Music. Considering that this recording was intended just as a guide for those transcribing his music, and not for public consumption, Dylan imbues this with a ton of personality. There's not much to the song otherwise. Pretty simple chords, nothing spectacular lyrically, long-held notes of just humming. This seems like an odd choice for Bob to try and interest other artists into covering. Still, it's a worthwhile listen of Dylan digging into his blues roots and doing a fairly convincing impression of one of the old traditional blues singers.

Ballad For A Friend from *The Bootleg Series vol. 9*
(*written by Bob Dylan*)
Another Leeds Music demo. No surprise, this is a song with lyrics about trains. Less of a blues pastiche than "Poor Boy Blues" this song seems

more likely to spur the interest of another artist looking for material to cover, with a lot more melody. Bob must've been stomping his foot something finger-picking pattern. In a real studio recording, this would've been quelled or at least muted, but it's a nice honest addition to a somewhat simple song. Also charming is Bob noting at the end that he sang the third verse last because he accidentally skipped it. This would've been useful information to whoever was transcribing this song, but honestly, the order of these verses all about leaving on a train or whatever doesn't really change the mood or the meaning of this recording. Nothing outstanding, but another nice little track.

Standing On The Highway from *The Bootleg Series vol. 9*
(written by Bob Dylan)

The last of the Leeds Music demos, it's another bluesy song. Bob clearly felt that at this point there was some money to be made writing songs for blues artists who couldn't create their own material, which doesn't seem like a particularly fertile demographic to specialize in. There's not much to this song, just a single repeated riff with some pretty typical blues lyrics. Dylan's foot-tapping is once again audible but goes in and out. While there's nothing particularly wrong with this song, it certainly feels like Bob has mined the last of this more traditional blues vein and needed to start writing something new and more challenging or he was going to repeat himself into an early career dead-end.

Rumored to have been recorded but unheard:
(As I Go) Ramblin' Round
(written by Woody Guthrie)

It's funny that Bob Dylan's debut album has a song to Woody, but no songs from Woody. I have not heard this track, but I did want to include a list of various songs that were attempted during each album's recording sessions that may illuminate what songs (and how many) it would take before Bob felt any particular record was complete. I'm sure there are more resourceful people than I who have been able to track down bootlegs of some of this stuff. There also may be some tracks listed that didn't actually happen, but I don't know for sure. I am trying to avoid being too speculative here, but I do want to list these songs at the end of each chapter. Even if I can't go into much detail about them, just to help illuminate the method and atmosphere surrounding the recording of each album. As with all things Dylan, they could be released on a future volume of *The Bootleg Series* or be refuted by some scholar, but I am working with what I've got so far.

Played live, but never recorded:
No More Auction Block from *The Bootleg Series vol. 1*
(traditional, arranged By Bob Dylan)

Bob has undoubtedly performed far more songs in concert than he has ever attempted in the studio. If I were trying to cover every cover that Dylan has played I would nearly triple the length of this book. For the most part, I will be skipping over these songs that don't have a definitive studio or home recording available. However, some tracks certainly help illuminate what Bob's songwriting process and state of mind were during the creation of each album. If there are live songs that have escaped on an official release (and not the odd one-off compilation like *Live 1961-2000* or tribute album like *Enjoy Every Sandwich* or *Stolen Roses*) than I will turn my attention to those songs and the specific rendition that was deemed worthy of release by Dylan (or Columbia Records).

The reason this song was never committed to wax or tape by Bob is fairly apparent; Dylan took the rough melody of this traditional folk song and used it as the basis for one of his most famous songs, "Blowin' In the Wind". However, this song more than stands on its own as a separate piece. Dylan does a great job of singing it, and personally, I prefer this song to the long-winded "Blowin' In The Wind". While the specifics about slavery may not be particularly relevant, the lyrics feel just as timeless. Definitely, Bob's career was boosted at a crucial point by his first big break-out hit as a songwriter, but I wish he held it back and recorded this song instead.

This Land Is Your Land from *The Bootleg Series vol. 7*
(written by Woody Guthrie)

If "Blowin' In The Wind" is Bob's one big, obvious, famous song, then this is the big, obvious, famous song of his hero Woody Guthrie. While one expects Dylan to unearth some really obscure, rare track; hearing him tackle this standard of the folk repertoire gives the listener an excellent chance to compare Bob's interpretative skills with other artists who have covered this tune over the years. Certainly this version sounds like Dylan and would not be mistaken for Woody or anyone else, it is fascinating to get a close-up examination of how much Bob was borrowing from Woody. Especially in these early years. While this is a tune that is so thoroughly embedded in our cultural DNA that I don't ever need to listen to it again, Dylan acquits himself nicely here.

"BIG BOB'S DEBUT DISC"

SIDE A:
1. Gospel Plow
2. You're No Good
3. House Carpenter
4. He Was A Friend Of Mine
5. Highway 51
6. Freight Train Blues

SIDE B:
1. See That My Grave Is Kept Clean
2. In My Time of Dyin'
3. Fixin' To Die
4. Man Of Constant Sorrow
5. Pretty Peggy-O
6. House Of The Risin' Sun

There are only four outtakes from the official sessions for this album – three of which have appeared on *The Bootleg Series vol. 1*, although I was unable to locate the fourth song, Woody Guthrie's "(As I Go) Ramblin' Round". However, there a lot of songs recorded either for radio broadcast or by enterprising amateurs. I don't want to put any live tracks on these fake albums of mine, but I am torn about using these somewhat apocryphal studio sources. Sometimes the recording quality is quite poor, but other times it matches or even surpasses the officially released material. I try to shy away from it, particularly in these early acoustic years, but don't avoid them altogether. In the end, I took off the two original songs that Bob wrote on this album and swapped in some more traditional material to give this album more of a cohesive feel.

THE FREEWHEELIN' BOB DYLAN

Produced by: John Hammond, Tom Wilson
Recorded: April 24th, 1962 – April 24th, 1963
Released: May 27th, 1963

Famous/Important/Popular Track(s):
- Blowin' In The Wind
- Girl From North County
- Masters Of War
- A Hard Rain's A-Gonna Fall
- Don't Think Twice, It's All Right

My Personal Favorite Track(s):
- Masters Of War
- Talkin' World War III Blues
- Talkin' Hava Negeilah Blues

While Bob's first album was (and still is) considered something of a "swing and a miss," his second album is the first to be hailed as a genius masterpiece. The giant artistic and critical leap from the first album is, in fact, something of an illusion. Because *Bob Dylan* stiffed commercially, he was given plenty of time to craft a worthy successor. However, since he was signed by John Hammond, Dylan knew he would get at least one more chance at bat. He may have also surmised that this could be his last opportunity if his sophomore album also flopped.

As a result, Bob recorded a lot of material before finally deciding on pairing down his second album. If his work had come out as it was being recorded from Spring of '62 to the Spring of '63, his growth and evolutionary process would've come as far less of a shock. The end result may not sound like it, but it is something of a compilation of the best moments from really three different albums worth of material.

This may surprise someone on first listen, as *Freewheelin'* sounds pretty cohesive and unified. This is probably due to the fact that the album is once again just Bob's voice, acoustic guitar, and harmonica (save for one exception). But once you know the recording history and separate out the songs by when they were done the cracks begin to show. Even the illusion of the solo artist is thrown out once you know how many songs Bob tried with much more augmented arrangements. Not only are there some proto-rock tunes with a full band, but there are other tracks where Bob adds an upright bass that would've helped distinguish this album from its predecessor.

One of the most significant changes between Bob's first and second album is that while the debut only had two originals on it, *Freewheelin'* only has one cover. Bob had obviously decided to take the task of songwriting seriously, but it was no overnight feat. With each recording session was including more and more originals and pruning away the folk and blues covers that defined his first album.

In the end, Bob curates a particular image for himself, that may be accurate but is far from complete. The songwriting is definitely spotlighted, as Dylan is definitely aspiring folkies to cover on college campuses across the country. As such "Corrina, Corrina" is definitely the outlier. It is the only track to feature additional musicians, and it is the only cover song on the album. This was all very deliberate as Dylan (and Columbia Records) were trying to put his best foot forward and not squander what may be his last chance at stardom. It's no surprise that the album was initially pressed with a slightly different track listing that was quickly recalled. Everyone involved wanted to get this right.

And they did get it right. At least from a commercial and critical standpoint. *The Freewheelin' Bob Dylan* is the album that put Bob squarely on the map. But for me personally, the album feels like a bit of a cheat or compromise. While individual songs on it are great, overall the record doesn't hang together. For all of its political ambition, the album feels a little like a compromise to sell-out as some of Dylan's more interesting diversion and evolutionary step are axed in favor of presenting this monolithic view of Bob as the songwriting voice of a generation. Ironically enough, as hard as Dylan worked to display this image on this album and the subsequent one; he would spend the remainder of his career fighting hard to refute it.

Blowin' in the Wind
(written by Bob Dylan)

An undeniable anthem. For a song that is supposed to be so revolutionary, it is surprisingly resigned. There are several questions posed which illustrate various inequities and injustices that need to be righted. But there is no call to action. There isn't any real certainty when or even if these problems will ever be addressed. Having the answer stuck within the wind instead of the actions of the people takes the imperative to cause change out of our hands. I think a lot of this ambiguity was overlooked during this song's heyday. At this point, however, Bob is not entirely sure if the times are a-gonna change, much less who is going to do the changing and if that will be a change is for the better.

Girl from the North Country
(written by Bob Dylan)

Some beautiful finger-picking on the acoustic guitar by Bob on this song. The tune is heart-breaking and lovely. The first harmonica solo is an understated variation on the vocal melody. The song ends with a second harmonica solo that is even more simple and in fact, is mostly just one note. The effect is fantastic yet mournful. The lyrics are wistful and sad. No mention of why he isn't with the girl in question anymore other than he doesn't live there anymore. But he wishes her well and still holds a warm part in her heart for her. There's no regret expressed, but it's obvious that he is still in love with her. He still remembers her well, but he knows that those memories will fade – and may already have faded for her. This is one of the best songs Bob ever recorded.

Masters of War
(written by Bob Dylan)

Another stone-cold classic from Bob Dylan. This one takes aim at the military industrial complex that profits (and profiteers) from the perpetuation of war. Rarely have Dylan sounded angrier than he has here. The proclamation that he'd stand over the graves of his foes to ensure that they're really dead not only speaks to his intense dislike of them, but also to his distrust that they are even normal mortal human beings and not some sort of supernatural demon or monster. Bob accuses these corporations and the men who run them of making him not want to have children; but the masterstroke is then phrasing it as "threatening my baby, unborn and unnamed." Dylan even condemns their crimes as unforgivable by Jesus. That is harsh. The guitar playing matches the venom in Bob's words and voice. While not a terribly complicated song, it is simply too furious to try any tricks like a key change or a bridge or a solo or anything like that. As angry as Bob is here there is a certain resignation to hopeless in his singing that belies how little one man can do in the face of such large industrialized institutions of evil. It is a great song.

Down the Highway
(written by Bob Dylan)

A pretty standard blues song based around a single riff. Given the free-form nature of Bob's playing and the lack of anyone else he needs to sync up with, that central riff can stay on the high notes at the beginning for as long as he wants and it ends up coming down at some random and unexpected intervals. Bob's young voice is trying its best to add some blues gristle to its timbre, and for the most part, it works. He even jumps up to that weird blues falsetto at one point. It's probably a good thing Dylan is strumming a lot of full chords here as his guitar sounds like it is going out of tune. Surprisingly, there's no blues harmonica on here. The lyrics are simple I miss my baby / walking down the road-style blues clichés. Still, it's a pretty accurate pastiche and somewhat shocking to find that this is an original tune and not some obscure cover of an old blues tune.

Bob Dylan's Blues
(written by Bob Dylan)

While comprised of three simple chords, this song doesn't actually follow the traditional blues formula. In fact, it is more of a folk or pop song in format. Sure there's plenty of harmonica on here, but it doesn't even sound like it's attempting to be bluesy. The lyrics are not your typical blues fare either. Bob opens this song by announcing that this song wasn't written in Tin Pan Alley, but rather in America. The words are surreal goofy images with lots of jokes and some irreverent behavior. I'm not sure why Bob would title this "Bob Dylan's Blues", it seems more of a piece with "I Shall Be Free", "I Shall Be Free no. 10" and "Motorpsycho Nitemare". People tend to forget just how funny Bob could be, particularly in these early ragamuffin days. While these songs might get overshadowed by the more ominous classics like "A Hard Rain's A-Gonna Fall", but I think this more puckish nature is what helped first endear him to the crowds in Greenwich Village and make him stand out when he first arrived in New York City.

A Hard Rain's a-Gonna Fall
(written by Bob Dylan)

One of the more famous songs that Bob has ever written. To me, it just feels like Dr. Seuss's <u>And To Think That I Saw It On Mulberry Street</u>, only not as a good. It just goes on and on. None of it adds up to much to me. It all seems startling and disturbing, but it doesn't make any impression. The instrumentation – like all songs in this period – is minimal, but Bob doesn't even vary the strumming throughout the song. Dylan's vocals are fine, but not enough to compel me to think about what all these various things mean. Each verse runs as long as Bob thinks it does and then is capped off with another repetition of the chorus. There's not even a harmonica solo to break everything up. Maybe if it weren't so long and so overplayed, I might be able to get into this. This song appears on *The Bootleg Series vol. 5, 6, 7, & 9*. It's not that great of a song. Clearly, I am in the minority in that opinion, however.

Don't Think Twice, It's All Right
(written by Bob Dylan)

For a guy whose career started out as a solo acoustic act, Bob Dylan doesn't really do a lot of fingerpicking. But when he does, like on this song, it is always great. This is an odd love song. It's undoubtedly the dismissal of an unsuitable paramour, but instead of being harsh, Bob comes across as very understanding here. There's a tinge of feeling love for the person in question that is subtly shaded in the background while Dylan stands firm and does what he's got to do for both himself and her. A lot of people latch onto the line about her wanting his soul and the remark about goodbye being too good of a word and twist the whole song to mean that Bob is somehow angry or disgusted by the object of the song's affection. Yet the gentle way Bob sings it makes it plain that he isn't trying to hurt the woman in question with that line as much as he is trying to minimize their past relationship to help her move on and heal faster. Thanks in no small part to the Turtles cover of this song, it has always been one of the big hits in Bob's canon. Still, I think this is one of his sweetest most lovely recordings, even if it is one that I feel gets frequently misinterpreted. Certainly, Bob himself as leaned into the more harsh reading of the lyrics when he's played it live over the years. Just compare the accusatory tone on *The Bootleg Series vol. 6* to the more forgiving version only two years prior on *Live At The Gaslight 1962*. But this original release on *The Freewheelin' Bob Dylan* is the kindest and the best. A great song.

Bob Dylan's Dream
(written by Bob Dylan)

Here Bob is bidding farewell to some clique that he used to hang out with. The song seems to really be about the sad realization that all friendships will inevitably fall apart as he continues his meteoric rise to stardom. It is hard to say what group Bob is leaving here. Is it his friends and family that he already abandoned in Minnesota? Or is it the traditional Greenwich folksingers he was going to surpass and then dispose of? Either way, Bob sounds genuinely hurt by the loss that is either happening or had already happened. The guitar playing throughout is steady but straightforward. Dylan's got a lovely harmonica solo. The melody helps push the message of the song, and Bob's vocals do a great job of adding an extra sadness to the proceedings. The version released on *The Bootleg Series vol. 9* is nearly identical. Maybe a touch more nasal, but pretty unnecessary. It is not a stand-out track by any stretch, and pales when compared to "Restless Farewell", but still this is an excellent addition to Bob's repertoire.

Oxford Town
(written by Bob Dylan)

A song somewhat obliquely about the murder of University of Mississippi student James Meredith. For a song with such a tragic and horrific subject matter in the lyrics, the music itself is a little bouncy. Not enough to be insulting to the memory of the slain student, but enough to make the song catchy. It's an interesting tactic with which to tackle the issue. I'm not sure how effective it is, but it does help keep this incident in the public consciousness. The key to the song isn't who the two men who died are, or even why they died as much as it that someone needs to investigate soon. Indeed that is all Bob is trying to say here, and so the song sneaks in under two minutes. The music is minimal, but Dylan's guitar playing is consistent. Bob doesn't add any inflection to his vocal delivery, delivering this straight like a newspaper report. There's a different version on *The Bootleg Series vol. 9*, but it sounds nearly identical, just not as good. Either way this a good song, you just wish with a story like this it had managed to become a great song.

Talkin' World War III Blues
(written by Bob Dylan)

A song fully playing up to Bob's early (and quickly discarded) persona as a prankster and a humorist. The song here is all about the words. The music is a simple three-chord pattern with no variations. The melody, as is expecting in a "talking" blues song, nearly non-existent. The lyrics here are almost like a stand-up comedy bit. It's definitely designed first and foremost to elicit laughter, even if there is a secondary message about the futility of war that is layered underneath it. The set-up here is Bob recounting a post-apocalyptic dream to his psychiatrist. Nearly every verse ends with a punchline of sorts. It's a good bit, that holds up even after the specific Cold War nuclear fears that inspired it have long since passed (or mutated into even more slippery and scarier terrors). The song coasts by as much on Bob's charisma as the actual jokes themselves. This may be the funniest of all of Dylan's humorous song. Sure, it doesn't really work that much as a song, but it still is one of my favorite tracks from the early acoustic albums.

Corrina, Corrina
(traditional, arranged By Bob Dylan)

Other than the quickly withdrawn single "Mixed-Up Confusion", this is the first chance most people got to hear what Dylan would sound like with a backing band. The backing here is some minimal and light that most people forget about it and assume that *The Freewheelin' Bob Dylan* is another all-solo album. It's doesn't interrupt or feel as jarring as the piano does in "Black Crow Blues" on *Another Side Of Bob Dylan*. With just lightly brushed drums and an upright, there is nothing terribly radical here. You would have just as much instrumentation on a traditional folk tune by the Chad Mitchel Trio or Peter, Paul, & Mary. However in its own way "Corrina, Corrina" points the way to the softer rock band songs on *Bringing It All Back Home,* songs like "Love Minus Zero / No Limit" and "She Belongs To Me". It is also one of the few non-originals that Bob allowed on his sophomore album. While he is committing to being the songwriter here that he wasn't on his debut album, Dylan doesn't want you to think he has given up covering others' songs entirely. It's a simple enough song, pleasant but mild. Bob's young voice sounds lovely here. If it weren't for its historical importance as the first signpost to where Dylan was heading, this song might be forgotten entirely. As it is, the song is a delightful little hint and a nice change of pace for the album.

Honey, Just Allow Me One More Chance
(written by Henry Thomas)

Another tune in the early puckish rapscallion mode that Dylan arrived in Dylan with. This is the other non-original that ended up on the official *Freewheelin'*. While the lyrics could be read as a desperate plea from a scorned lover, Bob using this as a springboard for all sorts of absurd flights of fancy. I particularly enjoy the line about looking for a girl like you, but not finding her, that you'd have to do. It's a clever bit of wordplay that I don't if it was in Henry Thomas's original or an invention of Dylan's. It sounds like something he'd make up. There's very little in the original recording that makes its way into Bob's arrangement, and it is surprising that Henry Thomas managed to retain any of the songwriting credit for this song. Bob is going for broke blowing his harmonica and even letting out a "woo-hoo!" in the midst of it. This is a sprightly good time that Bob would indulge in less and less frequently before abandoning it all together shortly after plugging in and going full rock'n'roll.

I Shall Be Free
(written by Bob Dylan)

Bob winds up his second album firmly in his stand-up comic mode. While "Honey, Just Allow Me One More Chance" is a gentle mocking and an exaggeration of a typical folk song, this is Bob making jokes. Some of the punchlines are a little dated and require some research to get the more obscure references. There are jokes about two-faced politicians and jokes about TV commercials and jokes about his relationship and jokes about segregation. There's a whole stand-up special's worth of material here. He kids about Joan Baez's patronage in a somewhat ballsy and self-aware move. Still, it's great to hear Bob not just telling a funny story, but rattling off a bunch of one-liners (or one-versers). There's a slightly different version of this song on *The Bootleg Series vol. 9*. The essence of the jokes are all still there, but some of the ad-libs have changed, and the energy of the delivery is ever so slightly off. Plus there's a gag about moving to Reno to divorce a horse to lose weight or something that wisely got cut. Sure, comedy generally doesn't have the timelessness or replayability of a record that wouldn't be considered novelty. I really enjoy it that after a full, heavy album like *Freewheelin',* Bob wants to end things on a light, goofy, humorous note.

Songs not on the album:
Mixed-Up Confusion A-side of a non-album single
(written by Bob Dylan)

The first indication of Bob's rock'n'roll aspirations turned out to be a blink-and-you-missed-it moment as the single was withdrawn as quickly as it was released. This brings up two perplexing questions that have never really been answered: Why was it withdrawn and why was it released in the first place? Maybe Dylan wanted to make sure he got this out before his career and public persona were too frozen in the folk music milieu. Bob wasn't a big enough star at this point for an artistic left turn to seem like career suicide yet. Whatever the reason, this shows just how certain Dylan was in how his particular brand of rock would sound even if he wouldn't venture into that territory again for another couple of years. Really, it's no surprise that when this track started appearing on bootleg in the late 60s, it was often mislabeled as an outtake from *Bringing It All Back Home*. Sure the lead guitar is acoustic, the bass is upright, and the organ is missing; but otherwise, this sounds like the kind of music he would be making. The song itself is super-simple, just two chords. The lyrics are obscure dumb fun; two-line verses with mildly clever turns. The best part of the song is the way Bob stretches out that one note at the beginning of each verse to such ridiculous lengths. There's no consistency to it, just a matter of Bob's breath control each time around. As a result, the band has to lay back and listen for when he's done and it's time to switch chords. A couple of different versions are floating out there, such as the original single take and mix got replaced with an alternate when it was first released on CD on the 1978 Australian box-set, *Masterpieces* and as a result that version sometimes appears on *Biograph* depending on where and when you got it. Ultimately it doesn't matter much as all the various takes of the song sound about the same. There was rumored to be a Dixieland version attempted, but no tapes of that have surfaced, unfortunately. Any way you slice it, this is not only a vital track historically, but a fun song to listen to as well.

Baby, I'm In the Mood For You from *Biograph*
(written by Bob Dylan)

A goofy fun song in the vein of "Honey, Just Allow Me One More Chance". In fact, it is so similar I can see why the album didn't contain both. It also shares a lot in common with Bob's winking version of "Pretty Peggy-O". While this song is deliberately designed to be slight and shallow, Bob is having a lot of fun with it. The version of this song that appeared on *The Bootleg Series vol. 9* has a few lyrical alterations that don't really alter the crux of the song much. I understand that those songwriter demos weren't meant to be preserved for prosperity, the fidelity on that version detracts from your ability to enjoy it. At this point in his career, Dylan was fluctuating from a dire serious mode pointing out society's ills and this lighter silly folk-satirist. With the popularity of "Blowin' In The Wind" and others, Bob would abandon this path and concentrate on the protest songs, but I can't help but wonder what would've happened had he got his first success with songs like this if he would've ended up taking a whole different career trajectory. Maybe he would've ended up with his own variety show on TV, beating the Smother Brothers to the punch in his combination of satire and social consciousness. Probably not, but it is fun to think about. He certainly had enough humorous material to sustain himself solely in that mode at this point.

Talkin' Bear Mountain Picnic Massacre Blues from *The Bootleg Series vol. 1*
(written by Bob Dylan)

Like many of Bob's songs with titles that start with "Talkin'", this another stand-up routine in the form of a song. Much like "Talkin' John Birch Paranoid Blues" Bob still seems to be getting the hang of doing these songs in the studio without the interaction and laughter from the audience. Doing a funny song in the studio is tough. Comedy is all about timing, but the rhythm dictates to a certain degree where the jokes and punchlines land. You also have to leave pauses for the audience to laugh without seeming too needy or desperate if the song fails to elicit the same guffaws on subsequent re-listens. I think Dylan does a fine job, but you can tell he was concerned about this because he left both of these tracks off of the final album. He also recorded this song as songwriting demo which was released on *The Bootleg Series vol. 9*. It's amusing to listen as he stops the song to correct a lyric, but it keeps the track from really working as a listening experience. It's also clear on that version of this song that Bob isn't really putting his all into performing this song as he doesn't expect it will ever really be heard. There's a live version put out on *In Concert – Brandeis University 1963* that are far more engaged and livelier, but the audience laughter actually gets a little distracting from the song's flow. While the main goal of the song is to evoke laughter, apparently this is based on a real incident where scalper's sold counterfeit tickets to a cruise on the Hudson River to Bear Mountain. While not as obvious as "Talkin' John Birch Paranoid Blues", there is an element of decrying social injustice in this song. At least a protest against those who put making money above the well-being of those who are being swindled. But Dylan doesn't dwell on those aspects of the song. Ultimately it's all about his (or his character's) cluelessness about what was going on and how in the end it all just ruined his "picnic spirit." It's another fun goofy little song of the type that I adore from Dylan.

Let Me Die in My Footsteps from *The Bootleg Series vol. 1*
(written by Bob Dylan)

A song about proudly choosing to die in a nuclear holocaust rather than hide in the safety of a fallout shelter. Kind of an odd thing to find heroic. However, if you expand it out to a more general sense of being willing to risk things a live life instead of acting with cowardice throughout one's life, it does feel a lot more noble. The song is pretty much just three chords in a basic strummed waltz pattern. It's perfectly serviceable, but not one of Bob's stronger melodies. The chorus is slightly better, but this is pretty close to a talking blues without the blues part. The song is only three-and-a-half minutes but feels a lot longer for some reason. The version on *The Bootleg Series vol. 9* is much shorter as Bob stops to ask if he really wants to record it. I like hearing Bob agree with me that the song is "long" and "a drag," but this recording so muffled as to make it almost unlistenable. As Bob was quickly writing better and more popular material, it is now a big surprise that this minor work got left in the dust.

Rambling, Gambling Willie from *The Bootleg Series vol. 1*
(written by Bob Dylan)

As someone who finds watching poker on TV silly, even for ESPN, I have no idea why this gambler who was really good at taking other people's money is the type of person who needs to be idolized like this. Maybe for Dylan, this is a throwback to an earlier time that he admires. Willie does pay his child support, avoids ostentatious jewelry and gives to charity, but he doesn't seem terribly admirable or even moral. Heck, other than his expertise at poker, we don't really learn much about who Willie was. The guitar playing on this track is competent but undistinguished. The vocals on the original version are pretty uninvolved. Oddly, Bob gives a more passionate performance on the songwriter demo that appeared on *The Bootleg Series vol. 9*. In either guise though, this is not a very memorable or engaging song. This song was initially supposed to appear on *Freewhelin'* but got axed after the album was released then recalled. I definitely think that was the right decision.

Talkin' Hava Negeilah Blues from *The Bootleg Series vol. 1*
(written by Bob Dylan)

Bob's shortest song by a long shot; already it is winning points with me. Obviously this song is trying to be funny, but I'm not exactly sure what the joke is. Is it just that the Hebrew words sound funny to English speakers? Or that those words kind of sound like yodeling? Is the joke that Bob has stretched just this one line into a nearly one-minute talking blues that doesn't reference the melody of the Israeli folk song at all? Who knows? I can't imagine that Dylan put a lot of thought or effort into this song, but I appreciate that Bob doesn't drag this out. Although I don't quite get the joke, I still find the song pretty funny. And even if you don't like the song, it's at least over too quickly to really get worked up by it.

Quit Your Low Down Ways from *The Bootleg Series vol. 1*
(written by Bob Dylan)

Another typical blues song over a repetitive guitar lick. With the jumps up to a falsetto voice, this is as close as Bob has ever gotten to writing a

Robert Johnson song. The lyrics are somewhat religious with its references to sinning but is much more relatable in scope. Dylan here is imploring some unknown person to refrain from some unspecified "low down ways." It's never explicit whether he is talking about some politician enacting evil on a large scale or if he is merely asking a personal acquaintance to knock off some annoying behavior that is just irking Bob personally. There's another version of this song recorded as a publishing demo that ended up on *The Bootleg Series vol. 9* that sounds about the same, only done with much less high-fidelity equipment. It's not a particularly interesting or memorable song, but as a Robert Johnson pastiche, it's as good as Dylan gets.

Worried Blues from *The Bootleg Series vol. 1*
(traditional, Arranged by Bob Dylan)

It takes a worried man to sing a worried song. But this song is not that particular worried song. Despite the title, it's not really a blues song either. It's a lovely little folk tune with some excellent fingerpicking from Dylan. The lyrics are pretty repetitive and simplistic, with each verse starting with its first line repeated like five times. The melody is quite pretty, and the way that Bob's voice cracks a little on the line "I got trouble in my mind" is heartbreaking. Bob seems a little uncertain of this song, accidentally venturing into a whole new chord for "I hear the cold wind blow" verse, which sounds as surprising to him as it is to the listener, but he quickly but smoothly backs out of it and finishes the song with one last repeat of the first verse. It's not very long, and probably could've used a harmonica solo, but is a quick a pleasant little diversion.

Kingsport Town from *The Bootleg Series vol. 1*
(traditional, Arranged by Bob Dylan)

There's a second guitar playing some lovely little acoustic fills on this recording that are easy to miss if you're not listening for them. Even though this is no electric strong by any stretch, this does point the way to the way to arrangements like "She Belongs To Me" and "It's All Over Now Baby Blue" from *Bringing It All Back Home*. The songs itself is a gentle, lilting waltz. It's quite charming, if nothing surprising from Bob by this point. The idea of Dylan slowly sneaking extra musicians into his music instead of just coming out full-guns a-blazing is an intriguing idea. I wonder if Pete Seeger and the other hardline folkies would've been less surprised by Dylan's electric transformation if he had worked his way up to it gradually. It may have been easier for them to swallow but may have made less of an impact outside of the insular folk genre. This would've been an interesting transitional step if he had chosen to go that route. Otherwise, it's just another pretty ballad that Bob does quite ably.

Walkin' Down the Line from *The Bootleg Series vol. 1*
(written by Bob Dylan)

A semi-upbeat song with an appropriately ambling tempo. As usual for Dylan at this period, the lyrics involve a lot of repetition. Bob is complaining here about heavy-headed gals, money going and clothes with holes in it, but he doesn't let it bother him. Instead, Bob just chooses to walk away from his problems. It's a good message that seems stretched to the point of irresponsibility. There is a good joke about Bob seeing the sunrise not from waking up early but rather staying up late. There's a lot of harmonica in here, filling in between each verse to try and lengthen this to regular song length. There's also a second version that is song publishing demo on *The Bootleg Series vol. 9* that sounds pretty indistinguishable. Clearly *The Bootleg Series vol. 9* is the least essential of the official bootleg releases as most of the songs have already been released before, usually in fairly similar versions only recorded better. Sure, there are a few songs on the collection that can't be found elsewhere, but for the most part, this is not a particularly useful or exciting entry in the Bootleg Series. This song, for instance, didn't need to be released twice. It's perfunctory at best, and Dylan's half-hearted vocal doesn't work very hard to sell it.

Walls of Red Wing from *The Bootleg Series vol. 1*
(written by Bob Dylan)

A tune about the abusive and unsanitary conditions at a juvenile corrections facility. Like many of Bob's protest songs, it's unsure if he is singing about a place in the 1600s Scotland, or 1800s Appalachia, or 1930s Dust Bowl, or if it's something that was actually happening in New York City while Dylan was writing it. Dylan sings from the perspective of a former inmate of the titular prison, helping engender sympathy from the listener. The point of the song doesn't seem to be asking for prison reform, but rather cautioning against being prejudiced against those who might have gone to such institutions. Dylan sings about how one might be surprised to find out what currently successful adults may have spent time there more than he laments those who never break out of that system and spend their lives insane or otherwise incarcerated. It's an interesting tack to take. Unfortunately, the song itself is far less complicated. A simple basic strummed waltz with only a few chords, Bob sings plainly. This might make the most sense in attempting to show how average and ordinary the "graduates" of Red Wing might seem, it doesn't make it any easy to feel sorry for their plight. Everything about this song screams "plain," and while that is a bold artistic choice, it makes for a rather dull recording.

Talkin' John Birch Paranoid Blues from *The Bootleg Series vol. 1*
(written by Bob Dylan)

A goofy character sketch with a keen social edge. The song is sung from the point-of-view of a member of the conservative advocacy group, which during this time was known for their anti-communism focus. Rather than attacking the institution directly Bob inhabits the skin of a paranoid member and lets the hypocrisy show through indirectly by his thoughts and actions. Despite the relative marginalization of the JBS since the sixties, this song has been released on *The Bootleg Series, vols. 1, 6,* and *9* as well as on the album *In Concert – Brandeis University 1963*. Still, the official studio take of this song for this album has not yet been released. Each version of this song contains some ad-libbing and extemporizing, but they all are about the same. While Dylan is crucifying this entirely fictional character, he does show a bit of sympathy for him as well, humanizing him a bit. Yet, there's no mistaking Bob's feelings of disgust for the titular group. He sees them far more as hopelessly foolish than possibly insidious. Perhaps he makes a bit of a straw man of this extremist rather than tackling the more intricate ways in which this sort of thinking does permeate the larger society. But it does make for much funnier jokes. And even now, when the political climate may be similar, if none of the specifics remain relevant, this song is still funny. Maybe not as uproarious as we hear some of the contemporary audiences reacting to it, but a funny little character sketch worthy of Randy Newman.

Sally Gal from *The Bootleg Series vol. 7*
(written by Bob Dylan)

Another one of Dylan's few pre-electric songs to feature guest musicians. The upright bass in here is pretty mellow and doesn't add much, but it is a nice touch. This is another upbeat fun toe-tapping song like "Pretty Peggy-O" from the debut album. More than half of the song is occupied by Bob's frenzied harmonica work-out. The lyrics are pretty much just "I'm going to get you Sally gal" repeated over and over, so it's going to need a ton of harmonica to stretch it out to normal song length. Bob even lets out a nice little whoo-hoo in this song. For those who like their Dylan more energetic and excited as opposed to sedate and portentous, this is one of the better songs of Dylan's early acoustic years. Sure, it's slight, but I am always in favor of Bob being more humble in scale and joyous in his intent.

Long Ago, Far Away from *The Bootleg Series vol. 9*
(written by Bob Dylan)

Another muddy recording from the publisher's demos that ended up on *The Bootleg Series vol. 9*. This is an ironic song that talks about the evils that men used to do, with the wrap-up at the end of each verse proudly proclaiming that "things like that don't happen no more these days" with the clearly implied joke being that these sorts of injustices are still quite prevalent in the world. Bob even sings of Jesus on the cross, but again it is not personally religious as much as it is just coming from the tradition of spirituals that Dylan's music was wrapped up in. Despite the somewhat murky recording, Bob gives a tremendous performance with some extra grit in her voice. This is good, because a lot of the intent in this song is subtextual, and if you had a performing singing this straight, they might not convey they joke. They may even give the impression that things have improved and we should all relax and celebrate and stop worrying about social causes and civil liberty. It's a jumping blues number, without any substantial musical surprises, but that works well for conveying the ironic tone of the lyrics. Maybe not a song Dylan needed to revisit in a high-quality recording studio, but definitely worth having preserved.

Tomorrow Is A Long Time from *The Bootleg Series vol. 9*
(written by Bob Dylan)

A song that Bob didn't officially record back when he wrote it but seems to be regretting ever since. Perhaps Bob was inspired by the fact that Elvis Presley himself covered this song for the 1966 soundtrack to *Spinout*. During the *New Morning* sessions in 1970, Bob finally attempted his own studio version of the song, but ended up not including it on that album. When his 1971's *Greatest Hits vol. II* came out, Bob scrounged up a live version from April 12th, 1963, to include as a bonus track. Unlike the *Basement Tapes* songs that were included on that compilation, this wasn't a re-recording. The live version is quite stunning and as much as I dislike live recordings, tends to be my go-to version of this song. The publisher demo from *The Bootleg Series vol. 9* is pretty close, but he throws in a couple extra words and syllables in there, interrupting the general flow of the melody. The fingerpicking is more intricate, but he unnecessarily repeats the final verse to extend the song. The 1970 studio version is clearly informed by, if not modeled after, the Elvis version. Lots of the standard *New Morning* backing vocalists adding their "aah-oops." Nonetheless, this is an amazingly touching and heartbreaking song that almost any arrangement cannot completely destroy. It's a short song, but it doesn't need much. Why this was never even attempted in the studio at the time, much less actually included on *Freewheelin'* is entirely beyond me. One of the best songs he wrote during this period.

The Death Of Emmett Till from *The Bootleg Series vol. 9*
(written by Bob Dylan)

The 1955 murder and mutilation of 14-year old Emmett Till, and the subsequent acquittal of the perpetrators is one of the more grotesquely embarrassing moments in American history. Needless to say, his story is a galvanizing catalyst for the civil rights movement of the early sixties. That's a lot of pressure on Bob to get any song about Emmett Till right. And he certainly could've avoided writing about it altogether. Luckily, Dylan is up to the task and writes a darkly compelling song. While, it might not be nearly as powerful as something Bob made up whole cloth like "Ballad Of Hollis Brown" or "North Country Blues", but Dylan did have to confine himself to the actual facts of the case somewhat. One of the most powerful moments in the song is the way Bob describes his stomach turning when he saw the pictures of the freed murders. His disgust in this song seems as much aimed at those who weren't sickened by this atrocity as much as it is intended for the actual perpetrators of the crime (and the criminal justice system that failed to punish them). The unreleased version recorded for *Freewheelin'* and the demo that released on *The Bootleg Series vol. 9* and both given a terrifyingly flat vocal inflection that makes it harder to ignore or dismiss the gruesomeness of Emmett's fate, although the real studio version is much easier to listen to. It's a shame that it wasn't released at the time, and it's still disappointing that this version is available more widely. Bob may have seen this tragedy as somewhat timely, and afraid that its time might've passed he decided against releasing the song by the time *Freewheelin'* was finally done, even the story was only six years old by then. While the specifics of this story may be aging into the historical, this anecdote still sadly apropos in the racial tensions in this country today. It would be nice to have a clear, clean sounding recording of this tune officially available to help continually remind people of this horrible crime.

Bound To Lose, Bound To Win from *The Bootleg Series vol. 9*
(written by Bob Dylan)

A super-short upbeat little ditty. Bob mentions that he doesn't remember all the verses and that he will write them out for the publisher later. So about all we have here is the chorus. I haven't gone back and read the lyrics, but this seems like an early precursor to songs like "When The Ship Comes In". The performance is muted, ending well before it has a chance to take flight. It's not surprising considering the circumstances. What we do have here is pretty inconsequential.

All Over You from *The Bootleg Series vol. 9*
(written by Bob Dylan)

Bob blurts out "let's just put this one down for kicks" before tuning up and finding the right starting key. This is a goofy, affectionate love song somewhere along the lines of "All I Wanna Do". The lyrics are no more meaningful than that songs, but this tune is a lot less repetitious. The offhand manner Dylan uses to intro this publisher's demo show a tinge of disdain the author has for this particular piece of work. That is a shame because this is a fun little piece of fluff. Despite the disinterest Bob seems to have in singing this song, he gives it a joyous performance full of personality even as it peters out towards the end. Having a full recording on decent equipment would be nice. This seems like the type of song that a harmonica solo would definitely need to be injected into if it were being attempted for an official release. Even by this early point, Dylan seems a little wary of his more humorous persona and seems to want to steer things towards his more important/serious side, even if he wasn't completely willing to give up "funny" songs like this entirely for another couple of years.

I'd Hate To Be You On That Dreadful Day from *The Bootleg Series vol. 9*
(written by Bob Dylan)

Another pre-"Born Again" song with religious overtones and imagery. Again Bob casts himself as the superior person compared to the subject of his song. I'm not sure who the specific "you" is in this song, but it's probably the same one who needs to quit his low down ways or will be drowned when the ship comes in (or the times a-change). This is a well that Dylan has drawn from often enough. Oddly enough Bob remarks that this is his calypso type number at the end of the publisher's demo. Not much in the delivery or the arrangement of this tune differs from his usual acoustic folk stylings of this period. It's too bad because I would love to hear Bob try out something very Harry Belafonte-styled with steel drums and everything. As it is, this is well-worn territory for Dylan, so it's no real shame that we don't have a better recording of this.

Long Time Gone from *The Bootleg Series vol. 9*
(written by Bob Dylan)

Another song perpetrating Bob's myth of having a spent his childhood and adolescence spent as a rail-riding transient. Certainly if he was going to maintain this facade of a "ramblin'" upbringing Dylan was going to need to make sure that no one ever seriously delved into his past since it is pure fabrication. For whatever reason, this did not deter Bob from seeking fame and fortune, the attention of which was bound to uncover the truth behind this hard-luck veneer. That being said, Dylan does a very convincing job of portraying this fictional character that he's created for himself. This tune aims for some sort of haunting pathos, and while it's not bad, he has done this type of song better. The tune is simple, but the vocal performance goes a long way towards selling the song. The guitar is badly out of tune, but since this is only a publisher's demo and not a real recording, it can be forgiven. However, it does detract from my ability to enjoy this otherwise standard Dylan tune.

Hero Blues from *The Bootleg Series vol. 9*
(written by Bob Dylan)

This song must be something of a personal favorite of Bob's. Not only did he record it for both *Freewheelin'* and *The Times Are A-Changin'* but he opened with it a couple of times on the 1974 comeback tour despite its relative obscurity. Although it has been professional attempted a number of times, the only version that has been officially released so far is the truncated publisher's demo on *The Bootleg Series vol. 9*. Lyrically this song treads the same territory as "It Ain't Me, Babe" only in a much more sarcastic and comedic vein. In some ways, it also mirrors "John Brown" condemning not the titular characters, but rather the women behind them who are looking to live vicariously through their narrators' martyrdom. While the context frames the issue in terms of a romantic relationship, it could be that Dylan is writing about the folk music scene that was pushing him towards the role of generational spokesman and civil rights hero that Bob was already chafing against. While the song is clearly trying to be funny, it is not nearly as humorous as some of Bob's better funny songs of times. It may just be a matter of being too mean-spirited, but the jokes just aren't really there. The *Freewheelin'* version of this song is based on a cool acoustic guitar riff. While it is blues-based, it still has a lot more going for it than the usual three chords. The piano version attempted for *The Times They Are A-Changin'* loses that, making it the weaker of the two. Bob clearly is not as accomplished of a pianist, and as a result, he stretches the song from three minutes to four as he has trouble ending the lines and getting through the turnaround. Bootlegs of the 1974 tour show this song reduced to a pretty bland blues-rock number with the addition of The Band. The central riff is missing, but still it's nice to hear this acoustic song get an electric version. *The Bootleg Series vol. 9* version is cut off at the very beginning, and the guitar swaps the single note riff for some simple chord strumming. While this is not a great song, it deserves better than having this be the only official version out there.

What'cha Gonna Do? from *The Bootleg Series vol. 9*
(written by Bob Dylan)

Another song like "I'd Hate To Be You On That Dreadful Day" or "When The Ship Comes In" about the price that is going to be paid by those who stand in Bob's way. Either in this life or on Judgment Day. Even "The Times They Are A-Changin'" contains bits of this weird type of threatening. Dylan's schadenfreude turns this song into a celebratory hoedown. Again this is a song that was recorded in the studio for *Freewheelin'*, but only the publisher demo has been released. Due to an odd loophole in copyright law, some of these songs technically squeaked out in 2012 on a limited edition of 100 on vinyl only, just so that Columbia Records can retain the rights to these songs. But really those releases are so negligible and impossible to find, or afford, or copy to a digital medium that they might as well not exist for most of us. The song starts out as more of a slow blues tune, with each subsequent take giving it a bit more devilish glee.

The publisher's demo has a distracting cough from Bob punctuating the song. The song is adequate, but considering the rate at which Dylan was writing at this time, it's hardly something worth taking time out for.

Roll On John from *There Is No Eye: Music For Photographs*
(traditional, arranged By Bob Dylan)

Bob starts the song by mentioning someone named Ralph, whom he learned the song from. He then proceeds to tune his guitar. This clearly is not a formal studio session. Apparently, this was recorded for some radio show and then used by Smithsonian in 2001 for their accompanying soundtrack to John Cohen's book of photographs. The sound quality is notably higher than most of the publisher's demos on *The Bootleg Series vol. 9* which is nice. Bob in fact recorded a lot of tunes during these early years for various radio shows that have leaked out over the years. These songs I usually treat in the same manner as I would with live recordings; there may be some interesting stuff there, but to keep the scope of the book from reaching over 2,000 pages, I am just going to have to ignore them. I am only including this particular radio performance since it did see an official release on an album. The song itself heavily leans on Bob's "old man" voice. It is a quick but effective little traditional song. What it is definitely not, is a song Dylan wrote under the same title about John Lennon nearly fifty years later for *Tempest*. This song is a little harder to find but it is a sweet little treasure if you can unearth it. However, if you can't find it, it won't be the end of the world. This is pretty typical of Bob's early folk tunes of the period.

Talking Devil from *Broadside Ballads, Vol. 1*
(written by Bob Dylan)

Broadside Magazine was a publication that would print the latest musical "hot takes" from the folk music scene at the time. Bob (using the contractually obligated pseudonym Blind Boy Grunt) contributed a number of songs for the magazine. A couple of these tracks would later be recorded and released by the Smithsonian Folkways label. "Talking Devil" is one of these tracks. An extremely short song – under one minute – still manages to have a spoken introduction. The song is just a lark about how the devil seems like a regular guy, who may not even be recognized as evil by his own children. As Dylan himself sheepishly admits at the end, there are only two verses to it. It sounds like the start of something that has yet to be followed up on. Another funny/angry screed about the military-industrial complex most likely. Maybe Bob was hoping to inspire others to finish the song for him. As it stands now, it is amusing and charming, but unfinished.

Train A-Travelin' from *Broadside Ballads, Vol. 6: Broadside Reunion*
(written by Bob Dylan)

Another traditional sounding blues song, although credited to Dylan. Who knows where it came from. It certainly seems disconnected from the struggles of the day, which tend to be Broadside Magazine's bread-and-butter. The recording quality here is much closer to the publisher's demos than an official studio recording. Bob also seems to be fishing around for the correct note before he starts singing in earnest. While this obscurity might have increased the value of *Broadside Ballads, Vol. 6*, it doesn't seem like Dylan put a lot of effort into this particular song. Pretty typical of early Bob blues, this one isn't worth going to too much trouble to hunt down.

The Ballad Of Donald White from *Broadside Ballads, Vol. 6: Broadside Reunion*
(written by Bob Dylan)

This topical song seems far more within Broadside's wheelhouse. The music derives from an old folk tune. The lyrics are ripped from the headlines as Bob had just watched a TV special about murderer Donald White. The words tell the sad, tragic story of White who seems to have killed merely because he felt far more comfortable in prison and didn't know how to cope with life on the outside. According to the song Donald White asked to be kept in jail but was refused because the prison was overcrowded. This might be a glib simplification of Donald's real motives, but it makes for a gripping and heart-rending tale. Donald White is one of a handful of actual persons who got immortalized during Bob's run of current event songwriting along with Willam Zanzinger, Emmett Till, Medgar Evars, etc. One can't help but wonder how many of these people during this relatively small slice of the civil rights timeline would've been much more forgotten if it weren't for Dylan's pen. The song is sung with Bob's typical flat, deadpan delivery he uses for inhabiting the personas of various lowlifes. The tune is pretty, although not remarkable. Maybe Bob should've gone to the trouble of writing a new melody for these lyrics, although this might be part of why this song never made it into an official Columbia recording studio. An fascinating history lesson, but not one of Dylan's better recordings of the period.

Baby, Please Don't Go from iTunes' *Exclusive Outtakes from No Direction Home* EP
(written by Big Joe Williams)

Some of Bob's most masterful blues guitar picking. Alternating a throbbing bass part with his thumb and some nifty blues riffs with the rest of his fingers this may be Dylan's finest hour as a guitar player. The energy and excitement of this record show Bob straining at the limits of recording as a solo artist. This might not quite be rock'n'roll, but it is straining towards it. The vocals are fiery, and the harmonica is superb. In just over two minutes, Dylan leaves us out of breath. This may be one of Bob's finest hours in these early acoustic sessions. It's a shame that it never even made it on an official volume *Bootleg Series*, instead of languishing as a bizarre bonus track on a digital-only EP.

Rocks and Gravel from the soundtrack to *HBO's True Detective*
(written by Bob Dylan)

This is a song attempted during that mythical first electric session that also produced "Mixed-Up Confusion". Like that song, this one shares the long held-out notes sung by Bob to end of his breath. Bob also recorded this song a number of times as a solo acoustic track. Bob Johnston took some of these outtakes and overdubbed a band on top of them (as he did with Bob's version of "House Of The Risin' Sun" as well as inadvertently starting Simon & Garfunkel's career by creating the hit version of "Sounds Of Silence"). Truth is, this song works well in both the solo acoustic and full electric band settings. It is a blues-based song with some of the haunting falsetto leaps of a Robert Johnson. While this might not quite be the rocket explosion of "Mixed Up Confusion" this song certainly shows that Bob knew how to use a rock band to do more than rock. While Dylan certainly still had more to say in the solo acoustic vein, he clearly was already capable of skipping straight to the next step in his career had the "Mixed-Up Confusion" single taken off as it should.

Milk Cow Blues officially unreleased
(written by James "Kokomo" Arnold)

Second only to "Baby, Please Don't Go" as Bob's best blues guitar playing. Once again her emulates the Robert Johnson style falsetto leaps, which is appropriate as this song is probably best known at this point for Robert Johnson's version. Bob thoroughly inhabits the persona of an old blues singer on this track. It is both haunting and haunted. If Bob had never written an original song himself, he would still be worthy of all the accolades based on this one tune alone. There's no way a middle-class Jewish twenty year old from Minnesota should be able to play the blues this well. It is quite amazing, so needless to say, this recording has never been officially released. Some things in life just don't make no sense.

Wichita (Going To Louisiana) officially unreleased
(traditional, arranged by Bob Dylan)

A much less impressive blues song than "Milk Cow Blues". Bob is just giving the three chords a rudimentary up-and-down strum as opposed to the impressive fretwork of "Baby, Please Don't Go". He does stretch out to the blues yodel at one point, but it feels a bit forced, and Dylan doesn't go back to it. The best part of this song is probably harmonica. This is kind of thing Bob can do in his sleep. While there are ample examples of him doing it superbly, this almost sounds like he is doing it in his sleep. The fact that this has been left off *Freewheelin'* as well as any subsequent volume of *the Bootleg Series* is not worth losing sleep over.

(I Heard That) Lonesome Whistle officially unreleased
(written by Hank Williams and Jimmie Davis)

One of the most obviously country songs from Dylan pre-*Nashville Skyline*. A lot of the songs recorded with the stand-up bass have the bass mixed so low as to be easily mistaken for a solo performance. Not so much on this track, where the upright bass is giving us the traditional I-V backbeat of an early country tune. Bob once again is yodeling here, but the falsetto is far more Hank Williams than Robert Johnson. Had this track come out on *Freewheelin'* it might have caused tonal whiplash. While the folkies might not have seen it as the blasphemy of going electric, it still might have raised more than a few eyebrows. Had more people been as aware of Dylan's country proclivities as they were of his blues leanings, his move to rock'n'roll might have been a little more predictable. While *Nashville Skyline* and *Self-Portrait* used the trappings of the country sound (fiddles and pedal steel) as signposts that these were supposed to be country songs, there's no way to deny it on this track, even without those accouterments. Not just because Hank Williams wrote this tune, but because it just sounds so undeniably country. A bravura performance.

Going To New Orleans officially unreleased
(traditional, arranged by Bob Dylan)

Another track, along with "Sally Gal" and "Lonesome Whistle" with an upright bass accompanying Bob. This is old-school blues number, which Dylan plays with more than a little joviality. It's not quite the off-the-rails performance of "Pretty Peggy-O", but it is a lot of fun, despite having lyrics about owning a large enough gun for killing. This is more like Bob's self-titled debut in its warm, relaxed atmosphere than most of the more world-weary material of *Freewheelin'*. Bob has done plenty of acoustic blues songs in this period. Some of them are a lot better than this, but this one isn't bad by any stretch. This is certainly easier to listen to than "Bob Dylan's New Orleans Rag". Dylan was doing a lot of songs with place names in them at this time, probably to bolster his image as a train-hopping world-traveling hobo. The foundation of the stand-up bass gives the song a much fuller sound than some of Bob's less successful blues covers. But there is really nothing new with this song.

That's Alright, Mama officially unreleased
(written by Arthur Crudup)

Recorded during the first band sessions of Bob's that also produced

"Mixed-Up Confusion" and "Rocks And Gravel". This song is most likely known as the first single by Elvis Presley. While Dylan has done plenty of Elvis over the years, this is the Presley song closest to the early blues that Bob was primarily mining during these years. As a result, it comes off as less of one icon tipping his hat to another, and more like just a typical early rock song. Bob also tried this song again during the session for *Another Side* playing the song solo at the piano. That version makes the tune's essence as a blues song even more clear. Dylan's piano playing here is much better than he employed for "Black Crow Blues", but the song still comes off a bit stiff. The early full-band version is much better. It's got all the swagger that the song requires. The older, fatter, Vegas version of Elvis can sometimes make it hard for modern audiences to realize just how threatening Elvis was when he first strode onto the scene. Bob's version is a little more acoustic than you would think for his first full band session. The bass is upright, and the drums are mostly just brushes on a snare. Still, the song rocks in the original sense of the word. The piano and acoustic lead guitar are all fighting for space, knowing that Dylan's harmonica was going to take the solo spotlight. The song ends with Bob calling out that he wants to do it again fast. Truer words have not been spoken. While it took him a couple years after this to fully plug-in, there was ultimately no stopping Dylan from going down this path. This song is ample evidence of that.

Played live, but never recorded:
Who Killed Davey Moore? from *The Bootleg Series vol. 1*
(written by Bob Dylan)

Another ripped from the headlines song from Bob that had probably grown cold before it got a chance to be recorded in the studio. The song is a list of various parties denying culpability for the death of boxer Davey Moore. Dylan never has to interject on how flimsy these excuses are. Nor does he ever been the blame more squarely on any one group or another. Instead he just lists all the people who could've done something to avert this tragedy, but didn't. Musically the song is as exciting as a list of various excuses could, or should, be. While this song does achieve its goal of making you think about the brutality of the sport of boxing, it's not terribly enjoyable. Whatever your opinion is on the sport itself, this song doesn't do much. A little tedious even if it's heartfelt.

You've Been Hiding Too Long officially unreleased
(written by Bob Dylan)

A song that is sadly still relevant fifty-plus years later. This is Samuel Johnson's aphorism about patriotism being the last refuge of a scoundrel turned into a full-length song. This short song was apparently played live only once, on April 12th, 1963 and never made it into the studio. Musically it is pretty simple, but catchy. Lyrically it is angry and strident, and Bob's voice projects that. Yes, there are plenty of horrible people in the world who get away with all numbers of atrocities while hiding behind the excuse that it's "patriotic." It's a shame that this song didn't receive more of a chance to reach a larger audience. Its official obscurity is probably due to Bob dropping the n-word, albeit in the guise of a hypocritical politician. It is jarring to hear, and still would be thirteen years later in the song "Hurricane". Dylan himself may have felt uncomfortable with it because of that as he never performed it again. I can understand that, but it's a shame that Bob couldn't just re-write that line as this is a message that still needs to be heard.

"BOB DYLAN MAKES YOU LAUGH"

SIDE A:
1. Bob Dylan's Blues
2. Talkin' John Birch Paranoid Blues
3. Talkin' Hava Nageilah Blues
4. Talkin' Bear Mountain Picnic Massacre Blues
5. Talkin' World War III Blues
6. Hero Blues

SIDE B:
1. Hero Blues
2. I Shall Be Free
3. What'cha Gonna Do?
4. Honey, Just Allow Me One More Chance
5. Baby, I'm In The Mood For You
6. Rambling, Gambling Willie

"BOB DYLAN MAKES YOU DANCE"

SIDE A:
1. Mixed Up Confusion
2. Sally Gal
3. Rocks and Gravel
4. Going Down To New Orleans
5. That's Alright, Mama
6. Lonesome Whistle Blues
7. Corrina, Corrina

SIDE B:
1. Kingsport Town
2. Worried Blues
3. Wichita
4. Quit Your Low Down Ways
5. Down The Highway
6. Milk Cow Blues
7. Baby Please Don't Go

"BOB DYLAN MAKES YOU THINK"

SIDE A:
1. Blowin' In The Wind
2. Don't Think Twice, It's Alright
3. A Hard Rain's A-Gonna Fall
4. Girl Of The North Country
5. Masters Of War

SIDE B:
1. Death Of Emmett Till
2. Oxford Town
3. Let Me Die In My Footsteps
4. Walls Of Red Wing
5. Ballad Of Hollis Brown

With the relative failure of Bob's first album, producer John Hammond knew that the record company wasn't going to give Dylan a lot more chances and he was going to have to really deliver with his sophomore effort. As a result, Columbia gave Bob nearly a year exactly (April 24th, 1962 – April 23rd, 1963) in the studio to craft his follow-up. In this time period Bob recorded a total of 36 songs in the studio, not counting all the songs written and performed live but only recorded as publishing demos, home recordings, or live radio appearances. Of those 36 studio tracks, one-third was selected for *The Freewheelin' Bob Dylan*. Certainly, I could've just picked my dozen or so favorites from that list as well.

But imagine instead an alternate timeline where Dylan's debut was a big smash, and Columbia was hankering for more product as quickly as they could get it. There are three albums worth of material here. While that might seem like a lot, keep in mind that between October 1st, 1962 and October 7th, 1963, The Beach Boys released four albums: *Surfin' Safari*, *Surfin' U.S.A.*, *Surfer Girl*, and *Little Deuce Coupe*. So this kind of pace wasn't unexpected at the time.

On April 24th and 25th 1962, Bob recorded 14 tracks. Two of these ("Corrina, Corrina" and "Rocks & Gravel") were later re-recorded with a full band so we can assume that Dylan was dissatisfied with how they turned out and they would've been left off of the next album. While his first album was completely solo, Bob did employ a stand-up bassist named Bill Lee on several of these songs, making a first tentative start into expanding his sound. Now if we take the remaining twelve tracks from these sessions and re-arrange then, we would have more than enough for an adequate follow-up for Dylan's debut had Columbia wanted product on the store shelves sooner rather than later, although who knows if they would've needed four months between recording the album and releasing it as they did for Dylan's first album

Only July 9th, 1962, Bob laid down another seven songs for what could've been his third album. As usual Dylan recorded solo and acoustic, but clearly, he was itching to stretch out and experiment more for this album. Two more sessions (October 26th and November 1st, 1962) would give him the chance to finish off four "electric" tracks. While not quite enough for a split album rock/folk album alá *Bringing It All Back Home*, these eleven tracks would've been sufficient for Columbia to crank out a new Dylan in time for the holiday shopping season.

At this point Dylan admits that he isn't quite ready for the challenge of leading a full band and resorts to recording solo again starting on November 14th, 1962; although he does have Bruce Langhorne provided a second acoustic guitar on this session; usually he is mimicking Bob's playing so closely you would assume there's only one guitar. With another session on December 6th, 1962 and a final recording date on April 24th, 1963 gives Bob and Columbia another thirteen songs from which to create a third and final album out of the *Freewheelin'* sessions and outtakes.

While arranging the songs like this makes for an intriguing alternate history; these three hypothetical albums suffer a bit from the same patchwork inconsistency that plagues the actual *Freewheelin'* disc. So instead of going through the effort of finalizing the track order for *Bob Dylan II-IV*, I decided to break the 36 songs into three albums by theme rather than chronology.

The first group (*Laugh*) is the most obvious, as this is Bob's comedy record. I even thought about swapping out "Rambling Gambling Willie", "Bob Dylan's Dream", and "What'cha Gonna Do?" with the otherwise anachronistic "I Shall Be Free, no. 10" and "Motopsycho Nitemare" from *Another Side* as well as maybe the acoustic version of "Bob Dylan's 115th Dream" from *The Bootleg Series, vol. 12* but decided that I had played with the timeline too much as it is and filled out Dylan's all-funny records with a handful of tunes that were at least story-songs of some sort.

The second group (*Dance*) features as many tracks with multiple musicians playing as possible – even if it's just the upright bass on songs like "Sally Gal". While there's not enough to make a full pre-*Bringing It All Home* rock record, I tried to make the first side a little heavier than the second. This was also a good home for all the darker blues covers that Bob had recorded during this period.

The last group (*Think*) would probably be the most commercially successful and critically lauded of the three; although personally, I find it the least interesting. Sure it has all of the biggest classics from this period on here, but the songs are all so long, that in order to even the running times out, this disc only has ten songs on it as opposed to twelve or fourteen. While nine of the ten tracks are centered on politics and current events, even the lone romantic number, "Don't Think Twice, It's Alright" shares the same angry and dour outlook as the rest of the album, with just a glimmer of hope reserved for the future. While it's not as fun as *Dance* or as funny as *Laugh*, these are the songs that were going to push Bob Dylan into superstardom. And encourage Columbia Records to allow him to continue to use their resources to make further albums in the future.

THE TIMES THEY ARE A-CHANGIN'

Produced by: Tom Wilson
Recorded: August 6th – October 31st, 1963
Released: January 13th, 1964

Famous/Important/Popular Track(s):
- The Times They Are A-Changin'
- With God On Our Side

My Personal Favorite Track(s):
- Ballad Of Hollis Brown
- Boots Of Spanish Leather
- Moonshiner

While the relative success of *Freewheelin'* meant that Bob would need to come up with a follow-up sooner rather than later, Dylan did again take his time recording an abundance of tunes to trim down into the statement he wanted to make. With the sales of "Blowin' In The Wind", Bob consciously decided to focus on the more grim, serious, and political fare.

In some ways, this is just as disingenuous as the façade Dylan presented on his last album. Because of the overall gloomy feel of this record, most fans nowadays see this album as (slightly) inferior to the breakthrough of *Freewhelin'*. Personally, I actually like this third album better. I feel it holds together much better. And while there are many tracks on *The Times They Are A-Changin'* which annoy me in a way that nothing on the first two LPs do, there are a number of some of my all-time favorites from early acoustic Bob on this particular record.

The music inside is a grim and gritty as the black-and-white cover. The humorous rapscallion of "I Shall Be Free" is nowhere to be heard here, although he would return on "I Shall Be Free, no. 10" on the next record. Despite the overly political nature of many of the lyrics on this album, it never feels dated. This may be because Bob also chose to focus on more universal rather than specific themes, even if the inciting incidents have become dusty memories.

Oddly enough the more protest-oriented material is much less dour than the romantic songs on this album. While Bob is optimistic that the times are changing and the ship is coming in, he seems far less hopeful about his own relationships. Songs like "One Too Many Mornings", "Restless Farewell", and "Boots Of Spanish Leather" give the whole album a despondent aftertaste that bleeds onto the more political material.

Still, this feels like a more honest representation of where Dylan's head was at throughout the Fall of 1963. There's not a lot of comedic material written or attempted at this time. Bob was thoroughly an angry young man at the time, and as much as he later dismissed this period as deliberately writing socially aware songs in a calculated move to appease his main fan base at the time, even in his more introspective and personal songs, Dylan sounds particularly depressed.

While this all works better for me as a single piece than the last album, it is a lot harder to love unreservedly. There's a couple of real clunkers released on this album. After this album, Bob would never again be these thoroughly engaged with the news of the day. I'm just glad we did get one album that is primarily nothing but a full broadside of Dylan's ideas of the day.

The Times They Are A-Changin'
(written by Bob Dylan)

This song is certainly more proactive than "Blowin' In The Wind." However, instead of preaching to the choir who will be causing the time to a-change, these song is more of a warning to those who are going to be pushed out of their positions of power when this change comes. It's hard to say whether Bob is sympathetic to these soon-to-be-deposed. It doesn't sound like he actually expects them to heed his warnings. Furthermore, he's not really saying anything about whether this change is necessarily a change for the better – or just a chance for the oppressed to get be the oppressors for a change. It's also somewhat vague, meaning almost everyone can see themselves on the side of change while imagining those who stand against them as the ones who will be overturned in the coming revolution. This lack of specificity allows the songs to become a standard that stands the test of time but does become troubling when the wrong side takes this as a signifier that things are going to change in their favor. Don't forget that in Tim Robbin's satirical *Bob Roberts*, one of the title character's screeds is entitled "The Times They Are A-Changin' Back."

Ballad of Hollis Brown
(written by Bob Dylan)

Bob's acoustic guitar sounds especially olden on this track. The main guitar pattern that makes up the majority of this song becomes almost hypnotic. Bob's vocal delivery is exceptionally flat and emotionless making it the perfect vehicle to convey these words. The lyrics tell a story about a desperately poor man. His children are crying, his family is starving, his horse is dead, and he doesn't even have any safe water to drink. Instead of seeking solace in others in the same plight, he assumes that because he is so destitute, no one would want to be his friend. As the guitar keeps pounding away, we can see that the man is slowly going mad. He wants to do right by his family, but the only solution he can find is a grisly murder-suicide. The song ends noting that although this family died, somewhere else in the world others are being bored. Dylan's vocal inflection hide whether this is a hopeful ending or just another tragedy waiting to recur. This is one of Bob's most haunting and compelling songs ever. The version he recorded for (and left off of) *The Freewheelin' Bob Dylan* is still pretty effective, but isn't nearly as harrowing. Bob's singing is a little too affected and animated. The tempo is taken a tad fast for what needs to be a slow burn. The harmonica bursts, absent from the officially released version, are almost happy thereby undercutting the mood of the recording. But either way "Ballad Of Hollis Brown" is a masterfully written song.

With God on Our Side
(written by Bob Dylan)

Bob is completely undecided on what kind of strumming pattern he is going for on this track. This indecisiveness is supremely distracting. While I don't mind that Bob doesn't play with a strict click track ensuring a consistent tempo throughout any of his songs, the way this track is continually speeding up and slowing down is slightly nauseating. While I appreciate the message of the lyrics: that the self-righteousness that America uses to justify its warmongering is baseless at best. I do love that among the multiple accusations of being too militaristic Dylan muddies the waters by also being upset at the USA for forgiving the Germans so quickly after the Holocaust. Bob's vocal performance here is flat and unaffected. He is playing the role of the uninformed Midwesterner who blindly follows his government's orders rather than questioning them, but this performance makes the song even less pleasant to listen to musically. As much as I agree with Bob's sentiments here, I have to say that I have never had much love for this song.

One Too Many Mornings
(written by Bob Dylan)

A mournful tune with some really lovely fingerpicking by Dylan. Bob's voice is especially heartbreaking, and his harmonica is perfectly subdued here. There's a lot of sorrow in this song, so it's surprising to find that this is one of the old acoustic tunes that Bob turned into a barnstormer during his first electric tour in 1966. Hearing Bob and The Band remove all the sorrow from this song on *The Bootleg Series vol. 4* is almost enough for me to scream "Judas" as well. *The Basement Tapes* version is a little closer to the impact of the original... or would be if they didn't have one of the guys from The Band singing the first verse. Again, I'm not sure why that version was recorded, other than an excuse to get Dylan out of his house while he didn't have anywhere to really go. This is a song that Bob has returned to often in concert, but none of these live versions hold a candle to the pang that the original version evokes. The Isle Of Wight rendition from 1969 released on the deluxe edition of *The Bootleg Series vol. 10* is way too jaunty; the *Hard Rain* arrangement is too accusatory. But the studio version is the only one that contains all the pathos this song deserves.

North Country Blues
(written by Bob Dylan)

A sad, mournful tale of the effects of outsourcing as told from a woman's POV. The story here is heartbreaking as the depressed conditions of the rural community are wholly devastated as the company moves out of town. Rather than trying to sing about the entire population from a macro level, Bob provides anecdotal evidence giving little gestures that hint at the broader consequences of corporate greed at the heart of this tale. While not nearly as frenzied as "Ballad Of Hollis Brown" this song is equally as mesmerizing and tragic. The music feels like an old folk tune (and probably was borrowed from one). Bob doesn't put on any affections or try to distance himself from the female narrator of this tale. It's a bold choice. Bob doesn't even outright announce that he's not singing as himself, but just lets it be revealed naturally through the course of the song. The small, relatable scale of this song makes it far more potent as a protest song than one of his grand sloganeering epics. Another favorite track of mine.

Only a Pawn in Their Game
(written by Bob Dylan)

Looking at the murder of Medgar Evers, the slain civil rights activist, Bob refuses to demonize the assassin; refusing even to name him in the song. While not forgiving the killer, he explains his behavior and places the burden of guilt for this and many other crimes at the feet of the institutions and politicians who benefit from maintaining the status quo. Sadly this is an accusation that is still as timely as it was back in 1964. Perhaps even more so. That is a tricky line to walk, because if you don't want to make the actual killer here blameless. That might come off as heartless or self-serving. Dylan does a great job threading that needle with these lyrics. While the music may not be as powerful as a message like this deserves, at least it isn't hampered by it. The tempo and rhythmic loose-ness are as loose and unpredictable as "With God On Our Side", but not nearly as bad. It still feels like occasionally the stop trips forward rushing for a few seconds before catching itself and getting back to the previously established pattern. I think this song could've been a much more effective method for progress if it was given a straightforward reading. This was way too idiosyncratic to be embraced by the masses, which is a shame.

Boots of Spanish Leather
(written by Bob Dylan)

Sure, it's pretty much the same song as "Girl From The North Country" with different lyrics. But that was such a good song, why not do it again? This time the lyrics aren't about missing someone the narrator has left, but anticipating the heartache that comes from leaving some, even if it is temporary. By singing both parts of the song, it's hard to say whether Bob is the leaver or the leavee here. He doesn't even take the obvious path of having the man abandon the woman here, and taking both roles downplays gender entirely making the song much more universal. Although I can imagine a great duet version of this song where one party takes the POV of the person about to sail, and the other plays the part of the one left behind who can see through their BS and knows that they're really going for good. Using the metaphor of finally giving into the acceptance of the gift of the titular boots to show a certain acceptance or at least awareness of the reality of the situation and the finality of the relationship is just a brilliant masterstroke. It's a wonderful, sad, heartbreaking song. Much like "Don't Think Twice, It's Alright" it paints a realistic portrait of a relationship that is ending without any acrimony or anger, but still lots of hurt and pain. There is no blame to be placed, but definitely, each party needs to take their own responsibility. There's not even a harmonica solo to break up the lovely fingerpicking and Bob's most plaintive singing. One of my all-time top Dylan songs.

When the Ship Comes In
(written by Bob Dylan)

Something in this song always felt like gloating or taunting. There's very little in here about how bad things are now before the ship comes in. In fact, so much of this song is focused or the torment of Dylan's oppressors, it almost feels like this song is some sort of revenge fantasy. There's a piano demo that is released on both *The Bootleg Series vol. 1* and *vol. 9*. That doesn't add much to the song. It's funny how little difference changing the only instrument makes. The guitar version is probably only preferable due to the audio quality. There's another harmonica solo that starts out primarily as just one note before breaking out tracing around the vocal melody. Bob's vocals don't sound particularly triumphant or jubilant, but luckily don't seem to have a lot of bitterness to them either. The guitar playing is strong throughout, even if it's just strumming the chords. This is a perfectly fine song, but not one I could ever get into too much.

The Lonesome Death of Hattie Carroll
(written by Bob Dylan)

This was initially released as very "news of the day" stuff. The incident in question happened on February 9th, 1963 and the conviction came down on August 28th while Bob was marching in Washington (the same march where Martin Luther King Jr delivered his historic "I Have A Dream" speech). Dylan wrote this song almost immediately thereafter, recording it on October 23rd, 1963 and releasing it on the album on January 13th, 1964 – less than a year since the titular death. Despite being so timely, the song is apparently timeless in Dylan's mind, having performed it as recently as May 2009, five months after the death of William Zantzinger. There are a few inaccuracies in the lyrics; like Zantzinger was actually booked on second-degree and not first-degree murder, but it doesn't blunt the impact of the song. The melody is surprisingly catchy while not being so jovial as to undercut the meaning of the lyrics. Having a memorable chorus helps make the changes in the lyrics of the final chorus that much more effective. The chords are pretty simple but played with a nice lilting waltz-feel. The tempo is played with a nice gravitas and solemnity, despite the occasional rushing of the tempo when Bob starts to get a little excited. It's not so rushed or sudden to be distracting and adds a nice human, organic feel to the song. Even Bob's harmonica solo is appropriately subdued. While the specifics of the case are no longer significant, there's still plenty of relevance in this story of the inequality of justice. As such, this is one of my favorites of Bob's quote-unquote "protest songs".

Restless Farewell
(written by Bob Dylan)

While Bob has recorded a crap-ton of Sinatra songs since the death of Frank, when Dylan was invited to perform at Sinatra's 60th birthday celebration, it was this somewhat obscure album track that the Chairman of the Board requested. While I'm not sure what this says about Frank's personal taste or how it fits in with the other songs being covered that night, it's hard to fault his choice. This is a great song, full of heartache and regret. The guitar playing does have some of that haphazard playing style that derailed "With God On Our Side", luckily it's not as indecisive or herky-jerky although it is a detriment to this song that is otherwise quite powerful. This is a song about the sadness of the anticipation of the end of a great series of friendships. While Bob does not express any ruefulness on having engaged initially in these relationships, his heart is still heavy knowing that their time is limited. Many listeners in retrospect, viewed this song as a farewell to his political finger-pointing songs and the activist scene that had Bob had ingratiated himself into during this period. While I doubt that Dylan meant that directly, he probably did feel himself being pulled from that smaller pool and had some sadness for those he was about to leave behind. Given that Bob also wrote the equal "Farewell" around this time, it would not surprise me. I'm not sure which of the two farewells is better, but this is a fantastic song.

Songs not on the album:
Percy's Song from *Biograph*
(written by Bob Dylan)

A song with all the earmarks of a protest song, but I'm not sure what the message is or who the bad guy is supposed to be. Sure, Bob is upset that his friend is going to prison, but this friend did apparently kill several people in some sort of automobile accident. Is the judge to blame for giving to harsh a sentence (although Bob does admit that some kind of punishment is warranted). He seems a little fishy the way that he "talks out the side of his mouth" but it does seem like there's nothing that the judge can do now that the case is sealed. I'm not sure where this is taking place that there is no appeals process in this or any case, but nothing is specified, and no particular law or system is being called out as the culprit. Ultimately, what makes this song so affecting and tragic, is it just seems like an accident. The deaths, the sentence, everything. Bob is not singing for the victims of the car crash or even for the victim of the harsh sentence, this is all about Bob who is losing a friend in what can only be summed up in a twist of fate. There are no seven curses to be called down on the judges head. In fact, he has nothing to do but to get up and go. Bob appropriately sings this song anger or malice. The fingerpicking on the guitar is intricate and lovely. Bob even manages to make his harmonica sound mournful. The refrain of "turn turn turn again", perhaps a foreshadowing of the Byrds is cleverly subverted when Bob finally does the only thing he can: sing. But even when he sings, it's still sad. This is a terrific track. It might've have undermined the more overtly political bent of the album had it been released on *The Times They Are A-Changin'*, but I think the album could've used its more balanced world-view.

Lay Down Your Weary Tune from *Biograph*
(written by Bob Dylan)

It's odd for a song to equate music with a burden, but this song feels weary. I'm not really sure what all the banjos and drums and strings are supposed to relate to here. These are not instrument Dylan has (yet) got involved with, so I'm assuming this is metaphorical and not about Dylan getting tired of being a musician already. While it certainly sounds like Bob is encouraging the listener to unload these musical millstones, there's no indication if he or someone else is offering to pick-up these burdens. Or if the listener needs to pick them up again after some rest. Or if they should merely abandon these musical albatrosses entirely. While the lyrical metaphor that holds the whole tune is somewhat confusing, there's no mistaking both the weariness and encouragement in Bob's performance. This isn't quite celebratory, Dylan realizes the depth of the anguish here. He just wants to help in his own small, simple way. As a result, this is one of the more optimistic tunes of Bob's protest period. Frankly, it's a far more encouraging sentiment than the title track, and would've made an excellent addition (replacement) for *The Times They Are A-Changin'*.

Paths Of Victory from *The Bootleg Series vol. 1*
(written by Bob Dylan)

One of the earliest Dylan piano songs. As such it is necessarily limited. Just three chords, but it at least shows that Bob could do more than just

"Black Crow Blues" or "Denise". The song is supposed to be an optimistic pre-victory anthem for those on Bob's side of the various civil rights struggles of the times, although it avoids getting into any specifics so as retain a more universal and timeless feel. This is definitely less of a revenge song than "When The Ship Comes In" which is far more concerned with the retribution that Dylan's enemies will face. The version on *The Bootleg Series vol. 9* is one of the few on that album that is actually superior to the original version. Bob is playing guitar on that version, and it sounds far more assured. Granted the guitar isn't doing anything particularly fancy or intricate, but Dylan sounds far more comfortable in this set-up. The song itself is uplifting without getting really under the skin. It's a nice sentiment, particularly for those who are weary of the fight, but its enthusiasm feels a bit premature making it hard to really give oneself to the joy offered in the lyrics. Certainly, there is more pedantic and less interesting stuff that Bob recorded during this time, but this isn't great either.

Only a Hobo from *The Bootleg Series vol. 1*
(written by Bob Dylan)

When Bob decided to add a few unreleased rarities to the *Greatest Hits, vol. II* package he opted to re-record these songs with Happy Traum rather than include the original archival outtakes (except for "Tomorrow Is A Long Time" which he tried to resurrect in the studio for the *New Morning* sessions but ended up including a live version from April 12th, 1963). But of the unreleased tunes he did record, three were culled from *The Basement Tapes* era, and only one came from earlier. It was this *Times* outtake that Dylan felt was worthy of trying, even if it didn't make the final cut on *The Greatest Hits, vol. II*. The song itself is nothing special. Another socially conscious song of Dylan's decrying the way the homeless are treated. The original *Times* version is pretty straightforward. The music is a little too jaunty for the rather harsh lyrics of the song. The banjo added the *Greatest Hits* version may seem even more callous, but it at least connects it to the more old-school traditional view of hoboes with bindles on their backs riding the rails alá Woody Guthrie's Bound For Glory. Note that Bob chooses the more antiquated and florid term "hobo" instead of something more politically correct or even current. It feels anachronistic. I think this hurts the song as it makes the problem seem like something that happened back in the olden days and not a problem that still requires addressing. While I agree with Dylan that it's a tragedy that so many homeless people are treated as less than human and their deaths are generally ignored, I don't know if this song is the most effective way of expressing that.

Moonshiner from *The Bootleg Series vol. 1*
(traditional, Arranged by Bob Dylan)

A traditional tune so thoroughly stamped with Bob's presence that is frequently mistaken for a Dylan original and is included on the *I'm Not There* soundtrack. This is one of Bob's most astounding vocal performances. He is just amazing here. The harmonica work is restrained and beautiful, mostly just long-held notes. Dylan shows off some really impressive if not flashy fingerpicking prowess. The lyrics are evocative without going into too much detail. It tells the self-aware tale of a bootlegger whose fondness for his own product is slowly but inexorably leading him to his own downfall. Words fail me on this song, it never fails to slay me. All I can say is, listen to it again.

Seven Curses from *The Bootleg Series vol. 2*
(written by Bob Dylan)

A devastating tale of a corrupt judge who did not honor the bribe he was given. Bob sings this with as much gravitas as "The Lonesome Death of Hattie Carroll" although I believe this is a fictional story. In fact, the naming of the character as O'Reilly and the frequent use of horses makes it sound like Dylan is trying to write a song that sounds like it was actually written during a much earlier time. This song is a painful and powerful as "Percy's Song" although the miscarriage of justice is for less muddied. True, O'Reilly's father did commit the crime. Whether or not he did deserve to die for that, it wasn't an unusual punishment for that particular crime. The fact that the judge refused the more traceable tangible material bribe that the daughter initially offered is probably more prudent than ethical. The father definitely wins points for encouraging his daughter not to give sexual favors in exchange for his freedom, not because he thinks the judge would go back on his word, but because it makes his skin crawl. Of course one wonders if the daughter had so much money on hand why the father was reduced to stealing a horse instead of asking for help from her. The real tragedy is that the judge not only abused his power and position but that he lied. The anger of the daughter is understandable as the unspecific "price" that was paid is accompanied with some imagery that implies just how horrible it was. In the end, the daughter is left with no recourse but the titular seven curses. It seems unlikely that the daughter is some sort of witch and that there is any substance behind these curses. In some ways, the curses outlined remind me of Wesley's threats at the end of *The Princess Bride* or Cat Steven's non-complaints in "Moon Shadow". Perhaps this and "Percy's Song" were left off of *Times* because they are fictional allegories about injustice rather than concrete current examples, but I think those are both some of the best songs Bob has even recorded.

Eternal Circle from *The Bootleg Series vol. 2*
(written by Bob Dylan)

What would be more appropriate than a Bob Dylan song about singing a comically over-long song? Better yet, this song itself is only a little over two-and-a-half minutes. The lyrics tell a quirky comic skit about a folksinger catching the eye of an attractive woman in the crowd, but due to the extreme length of the song, by the time the singer is done the mysterious woman has left the venue. Surprisingly for such a comedic conceit, "Eternal Circle" is played rather straight and somberly. In fact, if you're not paying close enough attention to the lyrics, you might not realize there even was a joke. Not that there's much of a punchline at the end and Bob mostly sounds resigned, but not surprised the woman in question abandoned him. Still, it doesn't dissuade the narrator as he picks up his guitar and starts the next song. For a such a richly funny idea, it's a little disappointing this song isn't as funny as "Talking World War III Blues" or "Motorpsycho Nitemare". A missed opportunity.

Suze (The Cough Song) from *The Bootleg Series vol. 2*
(written by Bob Dylan)
One of the first of Bob's tiny handful of instrumental tracks. The parenthetical subtitle arises from Bob's coughing whilst recording and subsequent note to producer Bob Johnston to "fade at cough." I have never heard anyone coughing into a harmonica before, but it sounds surprisingly musical. The song itself is a minor piece of ragtime-ish fingerpicking. Bob is apparently used to having a new set of lyrics to vary each verse and has a hard time coming up with new musical ideas, and so he repeats himself a bit despite the song's two-minute runtime. Still, it is brave for someone who, even at this point, is known primarily for writing lyrics to try and compose a vocal-less song. Dylan and Johnston's joy at the unusual accident which concludes this brief recording is infectious and the track ends up being funnier than some songs that Bob actually intended to be humorous. This is a personal favorite of mine.

Gypsy Lou from *The Bootleg Series vol. 9*
(written by Bob Dylan)
A fairly nondescript song about another one of Dylan's vagabonds and tramps. For a slight change of pace, Bob sings this song from the third person instead of trying to inhabit this (false) persona again. It's nice to have a song about this usual hobo stereotype applied to a female instead of the typical rambling man. Meanwhile, the narrator is merely overwhelmed and impressed by the length and breadth of her travels. The titular character doesn't seem to be actually doing anything unusual other than going places and crossing names off her list. The song aims for the upbeat goofiness of "Pretty Peggy-O" or "Freight Train Blues" but never quite achieves it. This may be why it was only recorded as a publishing demo and never attempted in a real recording studio. If Dylan had attempted a "real" version of this, he probably would've required another take to iron out some of the hiccups in this song. Not that we really needed that. This is a

pleasant but minor song at best.

Ain't Gonna Grieve from *The Bootleg Series vol. 9*
(written by Bob Dylan)

Somewhat similar to "Bound To Lose, Bound To Win" both in terms of length and feel. Unlike that tune, Bob doesn't state that there are more verses written out that he can't remember right now. It's hard to say for sure, but the way the song ends, it sounds like the tape just ran out, which would explain its rather brief runtime. It's a jolly little celebration of a song but didn't seem like listening to the next minute or three was going to give us a whole lot of new information, so perhaps it's no real tragedy that the recording ended the way it did. The choruses were already starting to become repetitive enough to be annoying. For whatever inadvertent technological reason, we ended up with just enough of this song.

John Brown from *The Bootleg Series vol. 9*
(written by Bob Dylan)

Something of an overwrought morality play in song form. Despite the fact the song wasn't released under his own name at the time, Dylan did perform it on 1995's *MTV Unplugged*. He did, however, release it under his common pseudonym "Blind Boy Grunt" for a 1963 compilation entitled *Broadside Ballads, vol. 1*. Not quite sure why this one has stuck with Bob (or whatever MTV executive picked out his set-list for the night) as it is a little heavy-handed and not particularly astute. The differences between the "Blind Boy Grunt" version and *The Bootleg Series vol. 9* demo are pretty negligible and mostly down to the quality of the recording equipment. The song tells the story of a young soldier who goes off to fight in a war, and the overly proud mother he left at home. Most of the song revolves around the mother and is told from her point of view; reveling in her hypocrisy of being so happy that her son is fighting in a good old fashioned war. When the titular John Brown returns from the unnamed front, he is severely maimed and disfigured. It grosses his mother out. John then tells his mom that the enemy soldiers were (to his surprise) also just human beings before giving her his medals. While I agree that all this jingoistic patriotism is unseemly and needs to be exposed, but I don't think that this song does a very good job of it. The characters (caricatures) are too broad and unrealistic. Nothing in this song has nearly the visceral impact of "Masters Of War", which has a similar message and is going for the same type of anger in the sound. The gory gross-out ending is only horrifying to those who specifically suffer from it and doesn't address the ravages of those who come home from battle without any actual physical scars. It's a good attempt, but something at which Dylan would get quickly and thoroughly better.

Guess I'm Doing Fine from *The Bootleg Series vol. 9*
(written by Bob Dylan)

There's a fine line between the optimism of the saying "count your blessings," and the pessimism of "things could be worse." The lyrics to this song straddle that line somewhat. Talking about how bad things are, but trying to be grateful for the good stuff you still have. The up-down feel of the chords implies that although Bob is playing this on the guitar, he probably wrote it on the piano. Dylan's performance here makes it hard to read whether this is meant to be cynical or grateful. Since this is intended as a demo for the publisher, it could be he is trying to play both sides, so that it could be interpreted either direction depending on who was covering this song. Perhaps this ambivalence is actually indecision on Bob's part which is why he never recorded the song for himself. In keeping with this theme of uncertainty, Bob seems a little unsure of how the chords go or how many bars come between each line during the penultimate verse, adding a surprising twist to the song. It doesn't sound deliberate like a middle eight or bridge or anything. It was obviously a mistake. Still, it adds a little more variety to this otherwise typical Dylan tune.

Farewell from the soundtrack to *Inside Llewelyn Davis*
(written by Bob Dylan)

Bob nearly biffs the first line of this song on the publisher's demo released on *The Bootleg Series vol. 9* almost singing "I'm sailing away my own true love" from "Boots Of Spanish Leather". It's possible that even Dylan was having a hard time distinguishing between this song and the similarly titled "Restless Farewell". Luckily the publisher's demo is not the only version officially available, as the studio take from the sessions for the album ended up on the soundtrack to the Cohen Brothers' film *Inside Llewelyn Davis*. While there are definitely similarities between the two songs, "Restless Farewell" is more about saying goodbye to a time and a group of friends that will never come again, "Farewell" is more about a singular parting between two lovers, who we are assured will meet again. Both songs are very touching and effective. "Farewell" is a slightly more optimistic and hopeful song. The sadness Bob feels here is more empathetic. He is not hurt by leaving as much as he feels guilty for the hurt he is causing his girlfriend by going away. While the guitar playing is pretty simple, it is moving. Unfortunately, this song's obscurity may be tied up with its closeness in title to "Restless Farewell", but really both songs are terrific and deserve to be counted amongst Dylan's best.

Bob Dylan's New Orleans Rag officially unreleased
(written by Bob Dylan)

The first song to be recorded to really feature Bob playing the piano. It would've been something of a revelation at the time, but after songs like

"California" and "Denise" and "Black Crow Blues" it becomes obvious that this sub-boogie woogie type of blues is about all Bob can play on the piano at this point. This song is at least alleviated by an odd narrative about some weird witchy woman that a friend of Dylan's suggested to make him feel better. I'm not sure if the woman in question is supposed to be a prostitute or a fortune teller or a therapist or what. Whoever it is, Bob never actually goes inside to meet her, since everyone who comes out of her door seems really messed up by the experience. As far as the funny, shaggy dog stories of Bob this one is no "Motorpsycho Nitemare". It's pretty weak overall. The jokes never really land because we're never really sure what Bob is complaining about or even what he's really even talking about. The song ends with Bob playing a glissando that throws him off forcing him to improvise an ending quickly. While I usually am in favor of Bob's funnier songs, I can't really get behind this one.

East Laredo Blues officially unreleased
(written by Bob Dylan)

An odd duck for sure. One of the very few instrumentals in Dylan's catalog. One the first times we hear Bob playing piano as well. As a piano song, it is thankfully not just another boogie woogie blues alá "California" or "Denise" or Black Crow Blues". This might be the first glimpse we get that Dylan can play anything else on the keys. The song itself feels sort of random. But not like a jam – it is certainly a composed piece. It just sounds random. There's not a melodicism to the main line, and the pounding on the chords is haltingly herky-jerky. As strange and interesting as it is, it doesn't really work for me. It feels too much like a warm-up than an actual attempt at a recording meant for an album. While it is mercifully short, it still starts to get a bit annoying after a minute or two. This is no "Suze (The Cough Song)". Bob certainly would have some great success with instrumentals in the future, but he wasn't quite here yet.

Rumored to have been recorded but unheard:
Tune J
(written by Bob Dylan)

I have no idea what this is, or what it sounds like, but I love the title – although it's probably just a working title for something else that I already know. Even if it is a separate song, I will most likely be as disappointed as I was with "East Laredo Blues".

"YOUR WEARY TUNES"

SIDE A:
1. Moonshiner
2. Boots Of Spanish Leather
3. Seven Curses
4. Suze (The Cough Song)
5. North Country Blues
6. Restless Farewell

SIDE B:
1. One Too Many Mornings
2. Percy's Song
3. The Lonesome Death Of Hattie Carroll
4. Lay Down Your Weary Tune
5. Farewell

Sure, the title tune is an undeniable American classic, but I think it raises expectations of the level of politics and protest on this record that undoubtedly can't be reached. Instead, I've swapped out this song, as well as the more overtly topical songs such as "Only A Pawn In Their Game" and "With God On Their Side". While I do agree with the sentiments expressed in the lyrics, these are not the best songs to me musically. Conversely, I have left "The Lonesome Death Of Hattie Carroll" on here because it is such a strong song. I'm not trying to deliberately neuter all the firebrand inclinations of this album. In fact, I think by making this record more varied in lyrical topics, songs such as that hit that much harder.

Ultimately the overall tone of this album is one of sadness. There are not "Talkin' Blues" or humorous asides on this album. Even if I wanted to add some, there just weren't really any recorded for this album. About all we have is "Suze (The Cough Song)" and that's just a short instrumental. So instead of focusing on the political, I turned more towards the theme of loss. A lot of these songs deal with losing something at some point, which is why I thought *Your Weary Tunes* makes such an apt title. While not nearly as fun as a lot of Bob's early acoustic albums, this does include some of my all-time favorite heart-rending tracks from this period.

ANOTHER SIDE OF BOB DYLAN

Produced by: Tom Wilson
Recorded: August 8th, 1964
Released: June 9th, 1964

Famous/Important/Popular Track(s):
- It Ain't Me Babe
- My Back Pages

My Personal Favorite Track(s):
- Motorpsycho Nightmare
- I Shall Be Free no. 10
- Ballad In Plain D

The main complaint leveled against *The Times They Are A-Changin'* is that the album is too political. It sounds like Bob himself agreed with this assessment, as this album is entirely devoid of anything that can be directly construed as a protest song. While Dylan had yet to thoroughly alienate the faithful folkies by plugging in and going electric, many already felt betrayed by this, his last acoustic album (until 1993).

Even the general tenor of the more romantic songs is utterly different. Instead of the sad songs from *The Times*, we've got songs that are far more angry and accusatory. Clearly, Bob has given up on trying to salvage his relationship with Suze and has moved on to the second stage of grief. Particularly in the brutal "Ballad In Plain D".

Unlike the previous two records, Dylan is no longer cultivating an album out of a series of sessions spanning months. Perhaps in an effort to help differentiate this album from the last two, Bob decided to record the entirety of the album in one long late night session. As a result, this is his acoustic album that sounds the most cohesive. Despite having almost no outtakes for this album, he still managed two leave to of his biggest hits on the cutting room floor ("Mama, You've Been On My Mind" and Mr. Tambourine Man").

While this is the last solo acoustic album Bob made, you can clearly see him chaffing against his self-imposed restrictions and chomping at the bit to try something new. While he was not actually playing rock'n'roll on this album, he is undoubtedly starting to write his first rock'n'roll songs. In no surprise that the nascent "folk rock" craze used so many songs from this album to launch their new hybrid sound: Cher had "All I Wanna Do", The Turtles had "It Ain't Me, Babe", The Byrds covered nearly a third of this album. While Bob hadn't plugged himself in yet, he was already opening up a socket for others to plug into him with this album.

Another big difference between this album and the last one is that Bob's funny, humorous side is back with a vengeance. While Dylan could always be funny, there is a surrealism added to tracks like "I Shall Be Free, no. 10" and "Motorpsycho Nitemare". Bob is no longer the plain-spoken ruffian of the first three albums. Whether funny or angry, you can always tell what Dylan was talking about on previous albums. Maybe it was the influence of the beat poets or the increased use of drugs, but Bob started being a lot less oblique beginning with this album. As a result, a whole cottage industry has sprung up around trying to decipher the literal meaning of Bob's lyrics. While allowing for personal interpretation does give the songs a more universal appeal, I do miss the days when Bob just said what he meant.

That is just one of my big disappointments with this album overall. It doesn't have nearly the impact on me as the first three Dylan LPs. For one thing, having all the songs cut in one night gives the album a very static sound. There's no real variety here, even with the debut of Bob's piano playing on "Black Crow Blues". Ultimately this album feels more tossed off and less intense to me, maybe because Bob had to restrain his performance a bit to maintain his vocal cords for an entire marathon recording session. Not that the album is bad, per se. But much like Dylan himself, I am impatient to get to what is next.

All I Really Want to Do
(written by Bob Dylan)

This is a goofy jaunt with a galloping guitar and silly falsettos. It's hard to say whether the singer is trying to assuage the fears of the person he's singing to that he will somehow take advantage of her. Or whether he is trying to get the object of this song to calm down and stop asking him for more than a friendship. A lot of this song's charm comes not from the writing but from Bob's half-drunk giggle in performing it. Lyrically it's just a list of things that rhyme that he will not do (other than be friends with you) which makes the fact that this was covered seriously and was a success for both the Byrds and a young Cher very surprising.

Black Crow Blues
(written by Bob Dylan)

There were the electric sessions that produced quickly retracted "Mixed-Up Confusion", but this is really the first time we've got to hear Bob accompanied by something other than his acoustic guitar. That alone makes this song really stand-out amongst Dylan's first four albums. Unfortunately, Bob's piano playing is rather rudimentary, particularly at this point. Dylan's piano abilities are mostly rooted in the boogie-woogie triplets he used while working as the keyboardist for Bobby Vee, making this song sound less like the blues and more like doo-wop. The lyrics are elliptical. The chord pattern is a standard 12 bar blues. The change in instrumentation is a godsend in terms of variety, but otherwise, this is not a terribly distinguishable track.

Spanish Harlem Incident
(written by Bob Dylan)

The lyrics are impressionistic, but it sounds like Bob likes whomever this girl is he's singing about. I'm not sure what Bob is talking about with the flashing feet and whatnot, but it sounds like a compliment. There are some fun, complicated chords in here although nothing too terribly sophisticated. It's a lovely melody and Bob is in good voice. Coming in under two-and-a-half minutes this never overstays its welcome despite having no real chorus or bridge or anything. There's not even a harmonica to break this up, but this song doesn't really need it. It doesn't sound like a stereotypical blues or folk song, but something wholly original to Dylan. Definitely the kind of song that The Byrds were made to cover; and they did.

Chimes of Freedom
(written by Bob Dylan)

Probably the closest thing to a "protest" song on *Another Side of Bob Dylan*. At least the word "freedom" seems relevant. The rest of the lyrics seem to be garbled beat-poetry. I'm not sure what exactly Dylan is getting at here, but it feels like it is a good thing at least for freedom chimes to flash. The melody here is pretty is a little cloying. The guitar playing is consistent (unlike "With God On Our Side") but not terribly interesting or exciting. At least Dylan's vocal performance is warm and robust. The song feels inordinately long for how little is going on. There are just the briefest bits of harmonica, not even a full solo. It doesn't add much. A perfectly perfunctory acoustic track.

I Shall Be Free No. 10
(written by Bob Dylan)

Clearly meant as a sequel of sorts of "I Shall Be Free". The title still doesn't mean anything, and I have even less of an idea why this is number 10. What happened to "I Shall Be Free nos. 2 - 9"? This feels like the most pop-culturally current song Bob ever wrote with references to Barry Goldwater, the space race, Mohammad Ali (back when he was still called Cassius Clay) and the Liz Taylor-Richard Burton romance. While some of these references are now past their time, you can always look them up and figure out what Dylan is singing about. The only thing I'm not sure of is what is the thing he learned in England. Is it that guitar riff? I am a little confused. The song is funny and light, and the music fits it perfectly. Bob, the comedian sells, the jokes in this tune perfectly. While fans tend to see Bob's goofier songs like this as inconsequential, I really enjoy it when Dylan gets to be outright funny like this.

To Ramona
(written by Bob Dylan)

Long before *Nashville Skyline*, Bob wrote this song that sounds like a perfect country pastiche, if not for the more surreal images in the lyrics. Dylan does a solo version at the 1969 Isle of Wight festival using his *Nashville Skyline* vocal style that makes it obvious just how "country" this song was meant to be. He even includes the phrase "cracked country lips" to help point to his objective. The lyrics are clearly just love song imagery juxtaposed with Bob's penchant for unusual images. Granted with the solo acoustic backing of *Another Side of Bob Dylan* this might not have been noticed when it was first released. It's a lovely, catchy little number if not one of the more exciting tunes Bob has penned. This first version does drag a bit as Dylan sometimes lets his guitar strum an extra beat or measure or two while he seems to be remembering or getting ready for the next line or verse. It certainly could've been sped up a hair to help emphasize the waltz-time feel of the song. The harmonica playing is nice but doesn't add much. Still, it doesn't overstay its welcome, which is good since as adorable as "To Ramona" is, it is at best a slight song.

Motorpsycho Nitemare
(written by Bob Dylan)

A farmer's daughter joke stretched out to full song length but saved by a dozen shrewd observations and pithy turns of phrase by Bob. A song that is only trying to be humorous lives or dies on whether or not you actually find it funny. A lot of people who don't like this song have probably just stopped laughing at the song after listening to it over and over (if they ever laughed). It doesn't have a lot of replay value if you don't like or get the joke(s). Of course, if it still gives you a chuckle, you are far more apt to overlook the song's more simplistic and repetitive nature. Me, I just enjoy the fact that Bob is even trying to be funny. It's not a side of him you get to see much as he gets older. Sure, some of the more timely references have become dated and now fly over my head, but I still appreciate it. For a song that is supposed to be a goof, it is a little slow. It almost reminds me of the first few bars of "Bob Dylan's 115th Dream" before Dylan realizes that the band isn't playing behind him. Musically, it's not more than just a two-chord shuffle with a couple of changes. There's no chorus or bridge or anything that actually repeats. This is not the kind of song you can really sing along to. Mostly it's just a shaggy dog story about trying to find something that would get him kicked out of a farm where our traveling narrator wound up just to avoid the even worse fate of being attacked by the *Psycho*-inspired farmer's daughter. It also has a nice message in the end about the importance of freedom of speech and how it saved his hide this one time. It's all silly, but good fun. Certainly not something the average listener who was only familiar with Dylan's biggest hits would expect from him.

My Back Pages
(written by Bob Dylan)

Another big hit for someone else as trendy (for the time) folk-rock number. The idea of being older then, but younger now is pretty clever. Unfortunately, that line is in the chorus, and so it gets repeated so often that it loses all of its impressiveness by the end of the song. I'm not sure exactly what the lyrics are about, but it sounds like Bob is just listing reasons why those he is scorning are so uncool, and then wrapping it up in a semi-obscure metaphor. He even makes a jibe about how bad it would be if he were to preach. Putting aside the irony this would have in future, the line itself is actually kind of preachy. Bob, however, sings this song with tremendous vigor and makes the song catchy despite being somewhat dull and stripped down. Ultimately this version is still better than The Byrds' more popular rendition, but this is not one of my favorite songs from Dylan's first acoustic period.

I Don't Believe You (She Acts Like We Never Have Met)
(written by Bob Dylan)

An upbeat anti-love song. The opposite of love is more likely to be apathy rather than hate so anyone can understand the hurt that would be caused by seeing a former lover pretending not to know who you are. Sure, some of the images in here are difficult to parse (mouth that is watery and wet), but the main thrust of the words is pretty hard to miss. It's not much of a surprise that this song was used during the first electric tours of 1966 as well as *The Last Waltz*. The only reason this was done initially on acoustic is because that was all Bob knew or had at this point; it clearly is aching for more of angry rock band arrangement alá "Positively 4th Street". Bob doesn't quite have that sort of sneer on this song, with the hurt underneath the bravado much closer to the surface in the more stripped down setting. Dylan almost gets the giggles at one point during this song. Bob tries to get angry during his harmonica breaks, but it doesn't have the necessary attack and comes off as a little futile. Despite this, it's still a pretty powerful song.

Ballad in Plain D
(written by Bob Dylan)

While many confessional singer-songwriters have followed in Dylan's footsteps, Bob himself is infamous for obscuring any personal information within his songs. Apparently, this is the one song where he didn't do that good of a job, and everyone was able to translate this story of Bob's relationship with Suze Rotolo (the girl on the *Freewhelin'* cover). However, even if you weren't familiar with the particulars of this relationship and its dissolution, one would be able to tell this was a very open and vulnerable song for Bob. As a result, Bob seems almost embarrassed by it, having never played this song live. Even when Dylan tried going autobiographical again on *Blood On The Tracks*, it was never again this direct or naked. There's still some cloaking of the specifics in the lyrics, despite being in plain D, but the particulars aren't important. You don't have to interpret every line here one-for-one to actual events in Dylan's life. You can tell what the portmanteau "scrapegoat" means to him, even if you don't have a literal meaning. You can clearly tell how he feels here. He feels hurt. He feels embarrassed that he hurt her. You can tell that he is genuinely sorry, but also that he accepts that the relationship is beyond repair so he will attempt to move on. It is one of the longest songs that Bob has written that I don't get bored by. The guitar playing is simple, none of the weird indecisiveness that can occasionally afflict Dylan as he isn't sure how to play the song. It's a shame that Bob never again got nearly this personal and open in his music. Or even in his interviews or autobiography or just casual conversation as far as I can tell.

It Ain't Me Babe
(written by Bob Dylan)

A song that Bob has returned to often, appearing on *The Bootleg Series vols. 5, 6, 10,* and *11,* as well as *Real Live* and *Before The Flood*. While it may have entered the public consciousness thanks to The Turtles folk-rock version, Dylan was probably more impressed that it was covered by Johnny Cash. Much like "Don't Think Twice, It's Alright" this is another song where Bob has to tell a potential (or current) lover that she should move along. He's not mad at her, but just unable to live up to her unrealistic expectations. It's not delivered with any venom or spite, at least not on *Another Side Of Bob Dylan*. He has sung it that way on occasion, but here he seems simply sympathetic to this woman who wanted more from him then he could possibly provide. It is possible to read the lyrics as Bob saying farewell to the folk audience who were expecting him to continue to write protest anthems for the rest of his life, but it doesn't add anything to your enjoyment of the song to read that into it. While I don't think this song is as powerful as "Don't Think Twice", it's still a lovely song performed directly and succinctly.

Songs not on the album:
Mama, You Been On My Mind from *The Bootleg Series vol. 2*
(written by Bob Dylan)

For an album with so few songs to choose from, it's surprising that this tune ended up on the cutting room floor. Especially since this song would go into be one of the more significant songs in Joan Baez's career (after flipping the gender, of course). In Bob's hands this is a somewhat melancholy love song. Rather than an over-the-top declaration of undying love, this is just a simple statement of "I was thinking of you". The vocal performance betrays a depth of feeling that is not directly addressed in the lyrics, however, nothing in the words makes the reason for this deception obvious. As a result, it is very stirring with a haunting melody. Bob's guitar playing has a bastion of economy and effectiveness. There's a piano version of this tune on *The Bootleg Series vol. 9* that is effective as a songwriter demo: you can hear all the lyrics and chords and melody. Emotionally, however, that version is entirely flat and formless. It's a shame that this didn't end up on *Another Side Of Bob Dylan* as this is one of Bob's best love songs. Dylan never is very convincing portraying over-the-moon mushy romanticism, and many of his quote-unquote love songs tend to be filled with bitterness or anger or scorn. This may be as close to a straightforward love song as Bob is likely to do. Definitely one of his best performances recorded on this night.

Mr. Tambourine Man released on *Bringing It All Back Home*
(written by Bob Dylan)

First attempted during *Another Side Of Bob Dylan*, this song might've fit in better there. That version featured Ramblin' Jack Elliott harmonizing on the choruses. He couldn't sing along during the verses because Bob refused to write them out for him. I'm not sure how good that version of the song is, but you know who did like it? Roger McGuinn. And so The Byrds were able to get their hit version of the song out before Bob even released his. This is a song Bob has sung and released on many live albums over the years. This first (second) official version is almost a solo acoustic version. However there is a second acoustic guitar in there plinking away through the whole song I find especially irritating (though not as much as on "It's All Over Now, Baby Blue"). I'm not sure why this bothers me so. Perhaps because I want the solo side of this album to be completely solo; or if he is going to have backup musicians he should go ahead and use the whole band. This just feels like an unnecessary compromise. All this curdles my already dismissive feeling about this song which is way too long for my taste. I have no idea who the tambourine man is or what all these lyrics mean. And frankly, I don't care. It doesn't get under my skin nearly as much as "Desolation Row" does, but given how overplayed this song is (both The Byrds' and Bob's), I can easily do without ever hearing this track again.

Denise officially unreleased
(written by Bob Dylan)

This song was left off of *Another Side Of Bob Dylan* because it sounds pretty much exactly like "Black Crows Blues". The piano on that song was a nice change of pace, but given how limited of a pianist Dylan is at this point another track with him tinkling the ivories is going to sound almost identical. The lyrics are about some woman named Denise I assume. I almost prefer this song to "Black Crow Blues" just because I haven't heard it as often. "Bob Dylan's New Orleans Rag" which is about the only piano tune to proceed these songs is also another 3-chord blues romp but taken at a little faster pace, so it doesn't drag as much. Ultimately splitting the difference between "Denise" and "Black Crow Blues" is almost as difficult as telling the difference between "Meet Me In The Morning" and "Call Letter Blues". By the time tracks like "California" or "I'll Keep It With Mine" come along Bob has learned enough about playing the piano to be able to record a few different kinds of songs, but there's no need for this track whatsoever.

"BOB DYLAN'S OTHER SIDE"

SIDE A:
1. Mama, You Been On My Mind
2. My Back Pages
3. It Ain't Me, Babe
4. Mr. Tambourine Man
5. All I Really Wanna Do

SIDE B:
1. To Ramona
2. I Shall Be Free no. 10
3. Motorpsycho Nitemare
4. I Don't Believe You (She Acts Like We Never Met)
5. Ballad Of Plain D

I have stacked Side A with all the songs that were transformed into "folk-rock" hits of the day. The second side has the more funny songs lumped together, although "All I Really Wanna Do" could certainly fit on either side. I chose to end the record with "Ballad In Plain D" even though it is not as funny (or even trying to be) as the rest of side two, but I think it's such a full, personal statement, that it is really the only proper way to end the album. There's not much left to say after you've said all that. I've skipped "Denise" or "Black Crow Blues" because I don't feel any of the piano songs are quite working yet. Just having one on their throws off the unity of the album, but having more than one is tricky since they are all so sonically similar. I also left off "Spanish Harlem Incident" since it neither feels like a folk-rock hit waiting to happen or a funny story-song for side two. As much as I dislike "Mr. Tambourine Man", I accept that it should be on one of these albums, and it makes more sense in the context of *Another Side* than *Bringing It All Back Home*. Plus, it adds a little extra variety to this album with "Ramblin'" Jack Elliott's harmony and doesn't have the annoying guitar noodling of the latter re-recording of this song. Ultimately though, there isn't much I can do to improve or even change the general feel of this album as it was done so quickly.

BRINGING IT ALL BACK HOME

Produced by: Tom Wilson
Recorded: January 13th – 15th, 1965
Released: March 22nd, 1965

Famous/Important/Popular Track(s):
- Subterranean Homesick Blues
- Maggie's Farm
- Mr. Tambourine Man

My Personal Favorite Track(s):
- On The Road Again
- Bob Dylan's 115th Dream
- It's Alright, Ma (I'm Only Bleeding)

The most common narrative in the popular consciousness is that Dylan is "the folkie who pissed everyone off by switching to rock'n'roll." For those who weren't really paying attention, it may seem like he transformed from Woody Guthrie to Keith Richards overnight. Still, those at the Newport Folk Festival July 25th, 1965 shouldn't have been surprised because *Bringing It All Back Home* had been released a little over four months earlier. The arrangement of "Corrina Corrina" on *Freewhelin'* should have tipped off astute listeners to Bob's ambitions. And if you managed to snag a copy of the deleted "Mixed-Up Confusion" single, you would have seen the writing on the wall since December 14th, 1962.

While "going electric" may have been a dramatic change, it was not as abrupt as it may have appeared. While die-hard purists may have come to boo Bob, they were treated to a full half of solo acoustic material beforehand. In the same way, half of *Bringing It All Back Home* is also acoustic. While plugging in May have been a bold, brave step, Dylan did hedge his bets a bit by entering the rock arena in this somewhat tentative and hesitant manner. Maybe this was a smart commercial move as the audience needed something familiar while they were readjusting, but it does undercut the audacity of this first electric record.

The boldest choice on the album was to put all the rock stuff on side A. Although that has the unintended consequence of making side B sound like an apology for the sins of the first side. Perhaps if the youth market didn't latch on to Bob's new direction, he could return to his folk roots quicker this way, writing off the whole band thing as a short diversion if a terrible mistake. Luckily Dylan gained a lot more new fans than he alienated, allowing him to keep pursuing his dream of backing Little Richard.

The way the electric and acoustic recording sessions were intermingled shows that this album was always planned on being half-and-half, not just one type of record that he re-thought half the way through. The second, acoustic side is really frustrating to me. It is definitely an extension of *Another Side Of Bob Dylan* with it long elliptical beat poetry lyrics. It's only four songs long; two of which are my all-time favorites and the other two I think are some of his most overrated.

The first half is a little more consistent, although it never reaches the highs of "Gates Of Eden" or "It's Alright, Ma (I'm Only Bleeding)". Dylan is still willing to be silly and funny, even with a band. It's nice to hear the humor from the last album continue, although this might be the last time he writes a song whose only aim is to get a laugh. Bob's not really comfortable or confident yet leading a full ensemble, but this naiveté and beginner's luck adds to the charm considerably. It is nice to see that Bob doesn't immediately assume that the softer ballads have to be the acoustic numbers, nor that you need a full band to really rock out.

There's some excellent stuff on this record, but I don't go back to it very often. I like having some diversity on my albums, but the way this straddles the line does it a disservice. I feel like Dylan is playing it too safe, here. This is a ground-breaking record, but not one of my favorites.

Subterranean Homesick Blues
(written by Bob Dylan)

One of my all-time favorite Dylan songs. This track has occasionally been pointed to as a sort of proto-rap. The musical backing is pretty garage-band simple, hanging on each of the three chords a little longer than expected to give Bob enough time to spit out all his words. It's very catchy despite having no chorus that repeats and words that go by too fast to really sing along with (at least not without a big breath and a good memory). The harmonica punctuations at the end of each verse are pretty simple – rarely more than a few notes – but are a great way of giving the song a little more space and interest. The lyrics themselves seem angry but not irritated. I'm not sure exactly what he's singing about or who he means he talks about the weathermen.

She Belongs to Me
(written by Bob Dylan)

Dylan going electric didn't mean that he had to rock-out on every number. This is the first example of Bob using the expanded palette of a band to tackle a slower type of song. It is an almost acoustic arrangement. The electric guitar is free of any distortion, and it sounds like an upright bass. There are drums, but they are not as propulsive to the song as the shaker. While the arrangement on this song is lovely, this is the first electric song that doesn't sound like it needs to be done with a full band, unlike say, "Subterranean Homesick Blues". Ultimately if this song were performed as a solo acoustic number, it wouldn't lose much. The words are oblique but clearly in praise (and awe) of some woman he loves. Despite the title, Bob doesn't seem very possessive of her; in fact, it's hard to tell from the lyrics how the object of his affections feels about him in return. Still, this is revered as one of Bob's best love songs as the words maintain an air of mystery without having any of the usual condensation or anger. Bob's more unalloyed love songs tend to be a little too lyrically simple and therefore don't resonate as well with Dylan fans.

Maggie's Farm
(written by Bob Dylan)

"Maggie's Farm" is nearly as angry as angry as "Masters Of War" but couched entirely in metaphors rather than blatant in its lyrical target. The opening acoustic guitar followed by the introduction of the remainder of the band sounds almost identical to "Subterranean Homesick Blues". Bob's vocals are almost more snide than irate, but he is clearly pissed off here. The music is pretty simple. Mostly just one chord for the whole verse, with only two extra chords sneaking in during the second to last line of each verse. While this has been a staple of Bob's live set since plugging in during the now infamous Newport gig, each tour he plays this on he constructs a riff to base the whole song around. However, the original recording here is all just chords and no real single note lines. It's no surprise that this song has endured. With the targets of his venom being neatly disguised it is easy for even a band like Rage Against The Machine to take up the banner and wave it in the faces of whomever is now the new enemy. Maybe not as good as "Subterranean Homesick Blues" but definitely cut from the same cloth. Another great song.

Love Minus Zero/No Limit
(written by Bob Dylan)

One of the more intriguing titles Bob has ever come up with; I have no idea what it means. The title may be one of the best things about this song. Not that it's bad at all. This is another attempt to do a slower acoustic-styled ballad while keeping the electric band on top of it. Unfortunately, this does not work nearly as well as "She Belongs To Me". The acoustic guitar on this song sounds a little harsh to my ears for some reason. The lyrics are even more oblique, making it hard to discern the love song underneath. The melody is a little less flowing. I hate to keep comparing this track to "She Belongs To Me", but they both sound so similar and seem to be going for the same general effect, that it is hard not to. And in that comparison, "Love Minus Zero/No Limit" inevitably comes out as the loser.

Outlaw Blues
(written by Bob Dylan)

A stomping rock number the skews closer to the traditional blues chord structure than "Subterranean Homesick Blues" or "Maggie's Farm". It even apes the lyrical repetition of a more standard blues tune, but the words are not your usual blues affair. While the line about not asking Bob about anything because he might tell you the truth does still have resonance, the majority of the lyrics are somewhat impenetrable. The playing is just as loose and natural as it is on the other electric songs on this album. Bob is clearly enjoying the freedom of singing without having to carry himself alone musically. This song tends to get a bit forgotten in comparison to some of the other tracks on this album, but it still a terrific song.

On the Road Again
(written by Bob Dylan)

Not the famous Willie Nelson, unfortunately. Instead, this is another 12-bar blues-rock number cut from the same cloth as "Outlaw Blues". The lyrics are just a tirade about the annoying, deranged or possibly criminal activities occurring at his girlfriend's family home. The most clever bit is the way the music stop at the end of each verse where one would expect to hear the title phrase repeated. Bob changes the line each time, so it is a different way of saying the exact same thing ("why do you stay here?"). There's some forceful, fun harmonica playing on this track. Bob has got a lot of songs during this period that are just as good, if not better; but this is still a great song.

Bob Dylan's 115th Dream
(written by Bob Dylan)

While Bob often peppered his acoustic albums with goofy songs Like "I Shall Be Free" or "Motorpsycho Nitemare" or "Talking World War III Blues" this is the only song in this vein that carried over into the electric period. Of course, the song almost ends up being a solo acoustic number. It sounds like Bob just starts playing the song without informing any of his backing band how it goes or even that he was starting. This leads to a great blooper at the beginning of the track. I love the fact that Bob decided to leave that flub in there. It makes the whole album seem that much more human, which in turn makes it all more impressive. The first song that Dylan's done electrically that isn't either a soft'n'slow love song or an out-and-out rock tune, Bob's band does a great job here playing the middle ground. And for much longer than your average pop-rock tune would take. The story, while filled with all sorts of absurdist moments and characters, is not just free-form psychedelia. It makes sense. It has a plot. And more than that it's got jokes. Lots of jokes. I love the line about pulling down his pants when asked for collateral. Quite risqué. Almost every verse ends with a punchline. Sure, some of them are funnier than others, but it is a great, goofy, good time. The chords are your usual I-IV-V, but this doesn't feel particularly bluesy. Bob's vocals seem almost as amused by the lyrics as the listener. The electric piano takes the place of the organ that usually dominates this era of Dylan recordings. While most people at the time probably took Bob's change in direction far too seriously (both positively and negatively) this track shows that Dylan was just trying to have a good time. This makes it one of my favorite songs from Bob's "electric period."

Mr. Tambourine Man
(written by Bob Dylan)
See entry under *Another Side Of Bob Dylan*.

Gates of Eden
(written by Bob Dylan)
There are few better examples in Bob's catalog than this song for showing how Dylan's vocal prowess can transform lyrics that are otherwise meaningless into something genuinely compelling. This song is stunning. The guitar playing is strident and hypnotic, with a driving 3/4 feel that never lets up. The harmonica is reduced to single blast punctuating the end of each verse. While I have no idea what Bob is saying here, he has a lot to say and has no time to waste. He spits out reams of images without stretching the length of the song out unnecessarily. Still, he's not doing his monotone, talking blues here. There is a real melody that Dylan is singing with venom and vigor. The cumulative effect is almost hypnotic. If this song had been done with the full band instead of being held for the acoustic side, it might've gotten tiresome by the end. It would've been interesting to hear him try. However, unlike many acoustic songs in Dylan's canon, this song has never been attempted in a more full band arrangement. Despite this, "Gates Of Eden" feels and sounds as much like a rock song as anything on Side A of *Bringing It All Back Home*.

It's Alright, Ma (I'm Only Bleeding)
(written by Bob Dylan)
As tremendous as "Gates Of Eden" is, this song manages to eclipse it. The images are still lacking in any literal sense, but are remarkable. Bob is clearly pissed off here, spitting out these words in a fury. Still, there's a bit of laconic coolness in the way he presents everything. Much as "Gates Of Eden", the harmonica is reduced to a single burst at the end of the chorus. The verses roll out in seemingly endless tension only to be resolved in the ever-changing chorus that references the title without ever exactly quoting it. The chords are a revolving series of variations on an otherwise simple progression that continually ratchets up the tension. Normally any seven-and-a-half minute song would start to chafe against my ADHD, but this track manages to maintain my interest and fascination throughout despite the simple solo acoustic guitar backing. While the song can be played in a variety of styles (check out the full band version on *At Budokan*), it doesn't need anything else. One of my favorites, this is one of the few tracks where I agree with the general Dylan fan-base on its worthiness as a masterpiece.

It's All Over Now, Baby Blue
(written by Bob Dylan)

After two stunning acoustic songs in a row, Bob ends this album with a song that is nearly as annoying as "Mr. Tambourine Man", a song saved only by the fact that is not as overplayed as that one. Once again the irritating slightly out-of-tune noodling lead guitar is back, undermining the intimacy of this song. The song itself is chirpy, which doesn't fit the lyrics or arrangement at all. There's more of Dylan's usual parade of mixed metaphors. Given its title, I would assume that this is about the ending of a relationship. Bob's vocals sound particularly strained and nasal on this. There's a couple of notes on here that he can't quite hit. Usually I would applaud someone for striving to hit those notes nonetheless, but it doesn't work here since the song makes no emotional connection to me. This is a song Bob clearly adores having it appear on *The Bootleg Series vols. 4, 5,* and *7*. He performs it as a solo acoustic track when he does it live on those albums, but maybe what this song needs is more of a full band feel. It was a minor hit for Van Morrison's first group, Them, although that version is mostly remembered for being sampled by Beck on the song "Jack-Ass". After having two of my all-time favorite acoustic solo numbers in a row, it's a shame that this is the track that Bob chose to end *Bringing It All Home* with.

Songs not on the album:
If You Gotta Go, Go Now A-side of a non-album single
(written by Bob Dylan)

One of the few funny songs Bob attempted after going electric. If you doubt how humorous this song is supposed to be, check out the solo live acoustic version of *The Bootleg Series vol. 6*. Dylan is killing with this song as everyone laughs at the double entendre and various innuendos. It falls a little flat in its full band studio incarnation as some of the jokes may go over the average teenager's head, and there's nothing to indicate any sort of winking at the audience. There was a brief time in 1965 when Bob was considered more of a possibly fading fad that needed cashing in on. During this period Dylan was seen as more of a singles-artist and the record company wanted to make sure that he was pumping out product at a steady clip lest he becomes passé. This single, much like "Can You Crawl Out Your Window?" are artifacts of this admittedly brief period in Bob's career. It might be this push to keep churning out hits that helped spur Dylan to use his '66 motorcycle crash as an excuse to drop out. As a piece of deliberately calculated attempt to replicate the traditional "Bob Dylan" sound is both hysterical and informative. The organ hasn't become his trademark yet, but there's plenty of electric piano here. The alternate take on *The Bootleg Series vol. 12* sounds like the same arrangement as the final version. There's some backing singers on here, somewhat buried in the mix. This would certainly not be the last time that Bob used backing vocalists. The lyrics are all about a woman who either needs to stop teasing him or put out already. While a tad selfish and misogynistic, Dylan makes each verse a nicely escalating build-up with the clever turn at the end that staying the night is something the girl in question has done previously. Maybe a little juvenile, but still pretty amusing. Definitely would've been a nice earthy change of pace to the more obtuse and obscure songs Bob was recording at the time. Unfortunately, the single didn't really take off, and this song was mostly forgotten because it wasn't included on any album.

I'll Keep It With Mine from *Biograph*
(written by Bob Dylan)

A song that did not make the final album, but did get released on *The Bootleg Series vols. 2, 9,* and *12* as well as the box-set *Biograph*. Despite the song's strength, it's easy to see why it was never included. Most of these versions are only solo piano run-throughs. The only full band version ended up on *The Bootleg Series vol. 2*, and that one the band itself is clearly learning the tune as the producer stops Bob briefly after the first line or two and asks Dylan to ask "what you were doing?" The rest of the band is understandably hesitant, coming in one by one as each figure out the chord progression. But by the end of that first take, they seem to have gotten something usable and would only need to go through the song one or two more times to have a finished product. By the time Bob is in Nashville, he has the studio musicians run-through like nine takes of the song that are purely instrumental and never get a Dylan vocal attached. Maybe he started to second-guess himself, and that's why one of the solo piano versions is what got released first. The backing they give here is not nearly as organic and lovely as the first band version, but would've worked quite well on that album, with some nice nylon string fingerpicking and tasteful drums that remind one a little of "4th Time Around". I love the way everything breaks down for the solo guitar figure. Who knows why Bob didn't feel like going back and finishing it. The idea of Bob recording a song without himself sing and playing along was unusual; especially for this time and Dylan just didn't feel comfortable singing along to a pre-recorded track. The solo piano versions of this song are simple, but a little barren. Any way you record it, it's a good song, but the solo versions don't add anything to it. While not quite as frustrating as "She's Your Lover Now" which didn't even make it all the way to the end of a full-band take, this is still disappointing.

Sitting On A Barbed Wire Fence from *The Bootleg Series vol. 2*
(written by Bob Dylan)

A song that Bob says in the lyrics is "just a riff." That is odd since the song actually has a pretty typical blues chord, but no prominent single-note riff anywhere in it. Still, you get the point that this song is not only tossed off but is self-aware about being tossed off. So it's surprising that there were so many takes recorded, with six takes ending up on the super-duper deluxe edition of *The Bootleg Series vol. 12*. Apparently, this song was in serious contention to be included on the album, even if it was meant to sound like it was just a goof. In fact, comparing the version on *The Bootleg Series vol. 2* and the one on *The Bootleg Series vol. 12* shows how little the song changed between takes other than the exact dollar amount that Bob opens the song with. In fact, a lot of lyrics are switched around for no discernible reason. The second take on *Vol.* 12 is slightly better as Bob lets out a surprising full throttled scream towards the end and even tells the producer to fade out at the end. It's a fun, simple, dumb song, typical of the era. The lyrics could be interpreted as deep, but it might be harder with this song than some of the other ones recorded for this album. If Bob hadn't cowered and compromised with an entire side of acoustic material, this would've been a worthy addition.

Farewell Angelina from *The Bootleg Series vol. 2*
(written by Bob Dylan)

Bob has recorded songs entitled both "Farewell" and "Angelina", but this one is completely separate from those. This is one of the solo acoustic songs recorded for side two of *Bringing It All Back Home*. Despite only being attempted once, it appears on both *The Bootleg Series vol. 2* and *12*. It's a song that Joan Baez later made her own and even titled her 1965 album after it. Dylan's version is much lengthier than Baez's. The attack of the guitar here is much more subdued than songs like "Gates Of Eden" or "It's Alright, Ma (I'm Only Bleeding)". The lyrics seem to be romantically inclined, even if the song is ultimately about leaving the titular Angelina. The words are a bit obscure, but Bob's voice indicates a mixture of sadness in regret in having to leave. Vaguely reminiscent of "To Ramona" this is lovely, touching, little song. If Bob had chickened out and released an all-acoustic follow-up to *Another Side*, this certainly would have been one of the stronger songs on it.

You Don't Have To Do That from *The Bootleg Series vol. 12*
(written by Bob Dylan)

A brief snippet of a song that Bob stops suddenly saying that he wants to do it at the piano instead. However, when he gets to the piano, he plays "California" instead, and the rest of this song is never heard again. It's a shame because it sounds quite promising. Something in the goofy lines of "Baby, I'm in The Mood For You" or "If You Gotta Go, Go Now". There are only two chords in the portion of the song we do have, but who knows where it might have gone from there (if anywhere). There's even a promising harmonica solo before Bob changes his mind and this song is lost forever. A shame!

California from the second volume of the *NCIS* soundtrack
(written by Bob Dylan)

Bob has not really learned anything new from "Black Crow Blues" or "Denise". The music and playing here is the same rudimentary barrelhouse version of the blues. The lyrics may be a west coast sequel to "Talkin' New York", but it doesn't have the nearly the humor. Bob does sing the verse about a black tooth that he would later use wholesale in the song "Outlaw Blues". Before this song was released on *The Bootleg Series vol. 12* where one would expect it, this track appeared on the extremely middlebrow TV show *NCIS* starring Mark Harmon. Who knows why, but there you go.

"SUBTERRANEAN OUTLAW BLUES"

SIDE A:
1. Subterranean Homesick Blues
2. She Belongs To Me
3. Outlaw Blues
4. On The Road Again
5. It's Alright, Ma (I'm Only Bleeding)

SIDE B:
1. Maggie's Farm
2. Bob Dylan's 115th Dream
3. Sitting On A Barbed Wire Fence
4. If You Gotta Go, Go Now
5. Gates Of Eden

Rather than hedging our bets with a whole album side of acoustic material, I have limited this record to one solo song at the end of each side. If the more band-oriented material on *Bob Dylan Make You Dance* had helped smooth the transition, we wouldn't need to be so tentative with this album. I was tempted to split these songs into two albums, with an entirely acoustic follow-up to *Bob's Other Side* that included the solo acoustic versions of "Bob Dylan's 115th Dream" and "She Belongs To Me" as well as "You Don't Have To Do That", and "Farewell Angelina" to complement the original side two of *Bringing It All Back Home*. It's not a bad listen, but it is pretty short, especially if you've already used "Mr. Tambourine Man" on the last (hypothetical) album.

However, the bigger problem with the idea is that it didn't leave enough electric songs to fill up a second album. It would've been nice to have a full electric record at this point, but where would the stand-out acoustic tracks "Gates Of Eden" and "It's Alright, Ma (I'm Only Bleeding)". I suppose I could've broken with chronology (as I have done from time to time) and just added those to *Bob's Other Side*. Actually, that's not a bad idea, since the last album was so weak, but those two songs would tower over the rest of that album and don't really fit in. So instead I've created this mish-mash of *Bringing It All Back Home* that features far more of the electric rock songs that were discarded when that was relegated to just half of the album.

Ultimately all I'm really doing to fix up this album, which was already pretty darn good, is replacing the two more annoying acoustic numbers with some material that I think fits the bold spirit of the album a lot better.

HIGHWAY 61 REVISITED
Produced by: Bob Johnston
(except "Like A Rolling Stone" produced by Tom Wilson)
Recorded: June 15th – August 4th, 1965
Released: August 30th, 1965

Famous/Important/Popular Track(s):
- Like Rolling Stone
- Positively 4th Street
- Ballad Of A Thin Man
- Desolation Row

My Personal Favorite Track(s):
- Tombstone Blues
- Ballad Of A Thin Man
- Jet Pilot

This is Bob's first fully electric album. It is also his second-to-last before the motorcycle accident, and everything went a little… wonky. Much like the previous album, there are a couple of overrated "classics" on here interspersed with some of my personal favorites. Ultimately, it sounds like the kind of record you would expect from listening just to the first side of *Bringing It All Back Home*. You think that Dylan would take advantage of the wider spectrum of possibilities that playing with a band would afford him. Sonically, there's only one track on here that doesn't sound like either an extension or a refinement of something on the last album. And that's my favorite song on here, "Ballad Of A Thin Man".

Sadly some of the charms that inexperience brought to the last album is missing on this one. While some of the lines on here are witty in their absurdity, there aren't any funny songs on here. While these humorous songs are occasionally hit-or-miss, they have been a fixture on each Dylan album up to this point (except *The Times They Are A-Changin'*). After this point, silly songs are pretty much absent from Dylan's discography which is a shame. It's always best when Bob doesn't take himself too seriously.

While I may have wished that *Bringing It All Back Home* was all-electric, I do slightly prefer that album to *Highway 61 Revisited*. It's not as fun or groundbreaking, and Dylan is starting some bad habits here that will undermine several of his albums going forward. Not that this record is bad or that I don't like it. I just think it's a bit overvalued in his canon.

Like a Rolling Stone
(written by Bob Dylan)

Whereas "Subterranean Homesick Blues" was scruffy, this song is stately. It's a little slower than you think it is for such an important "rock" song. The prominent organ makes this song sound like it's at home in a church as it is in a garage. One of the more famous tracks Bob ever cut; if it hadn't been released as a single and was just another album track buried on *Highway 61 Revisited*, it might become a personal favorite of the more hard-core fan, much like "Queen Jane Approximately", but it is doubtful that the average listener would've picked this track out as anything special. It's a fine track, but it is not as great as its reputation suggests. It certainly doesn't deserve an entire 286 book written about it by Greil Marcus.

Tombstone Blues
(written by Bob Dylan)

A sloppy rock track with a blues-funk feel that as good as it is doesn't need to be nearly six minutes long. It has some excellent lead guitar playing. It even has a catchy chorus – which is unusual for a Bob Dylan. Unfortunately, since the lyrics tell a story that makes no sense, there's really no reason why we have to have all twelve of them. Especially since there's no bridge or middle eight to break up this song. There's an interesting version of this song on *The Bootleg Series vol. 7* where the Chambers Brothers are attempting to sing back-up. While Bob would go through a couple of periods where Dylan would rely on female backing vocalists, this is about the only real instance of Bob attempting to sing along with other men's lower registers. It's a shame that this take was never really finished and Bob never tried that experiment again.

It Takes a Lot to Laugh, It Takes a Train to Cry
(written by Bob Dylan)

The first problem with this song: the title is way too long. Especially since it is not terribly related to the song itself. Sure there's a train involved in the lyrics, but this is almost as annoying as a Fiona Apple album title. I would've stuck with Bob's original title for this song: "Phantom Engineer". The version officially released on *Highway 61 Revisited* is a loping blues shuffle with nowhere to go. As such it's fine, but kind of boring. The more rocking alternate takes that ended up on *The Bootleg Series vol. 2, 7,* and *12* are less of a snooze; although for the most part, they are interchangeable. Still, I would agree with Al Kooper that this was the direction for this song, although I guess the slower version works as a nice change of pace. The lyrics are a jumble of typical nonsense from blues songs re-arranged till they make no actual sense. Definitely a lot of talks about trains. Sort of typical for this period, but a good song nonetheless.

From a Buick 6
(written by Bob Dylan)

Another fun mid-tempo blues-rock song. It's got the usual blues guitar and prominent organ. The lyrics are mostly gibberish. I have no idea why this is called "From A Buick 6" and not "She's Bound To Put A Blanket On My Bed". While this pretty standard boilerplate Dylan for this era, it is a fun song that doesn't overstay its welcome. It says something when even average Dylan is pretty damn good.

Ballad of a Thin Man
(written by Bob Dylan)

Not your usual blues based rock song, this is clearly Bob playing at the piano and using the chord progressions that one finds more naturally there. There are variations of a single chord while the bass note underneath descends. There's even a bridge that sounds very similar at first, using many of the same chords, but restructuring them enough that this feels like a separate part. The chords are for the most part minor, which is unusual for Dylan. The lyrics are nasty and accusatory. Many Dylanologists have tried to pend down who specifically Mr. Jones is, but it doesn't really matter. Whoever he is, he doesn't get it. That's all you need to know about the specifics of the lyrics. Everything else can be gleaned from the dismissive snarl Bob sings this song in. Clearly, Mr. Jones is a man to be pitied, but not associated with. This song stands out in Bob's electric period for not being either a pretty lovely song or an upbeat blues-rock number. There's something really different happening in this song. I just don't know what it is.

Queen Jane Approximately
(written by Bob Dylan)

A folk-rock piece of pop, one of the few songs that Dylan's written that doesn't fit the usual 12-bar blues chord pattern. This song is pretty close to the abbreviated version of such classic epics like "Sad Eyed Lady Of The Lowlands" or "Desolation Row" that I keep hoping for. Still a little long at five-and-a-half minutes, but much easier to sit all the way through. The lyrics are the usual Dylanesque gibberish. The organ is up in the mix, and the whole thing sounds like it wishes it were "Like A Rolling Stone". The tempo is mid-tempo without either dragging or exciting. The harmonica kicks the whole song up a notch. The raking of the guitar strings in a semi-autoharp fashion is really the only new twist here. Bob is singing in his usual accusatory tone, helping keep the meaningless lyrics from getting boring. Not one of the best tracks from this period, it still shows how much easier it is to swallow some of these songs with the benefit of an editor.

Highway 61 Revisited
(written by Bob Dylan)

Bob swaps out his harmonica for one of those toys that kind of sounds like a police siren when you blow into it. It sounds like that would be a really annoying idea, but surprisingly it makes the song. If you don't believe me, check out the version without the toy on *The Bootleg Series vol. 7*. The song itself is another one of Bob's great rocking versions of the 12-bar blues with some weird lyrics that are fun to sing but don't mean much. I'm not sure what it is was about this song that made Bob want to name the whole album after it, but it is still a great track. This song chugs along nicely and really help pick the pace back up after "Queen Jane Approximately". Much like "From A Buick 6" as good as this song is, there's not that much to say about it.

Just Like Tom Thumb's Blues
(written by Bob Dylan)

A mid-tempo song that isn't trying to be a sweet love song like "She Belongs To Me" of "Love Minus Zero/No limit" but also isn't trying to rock out like a "Maggie's Farm" or "Highway 61 Revisited". In fact, everything in this songs feels like it is trying to be medium. It really bugs me and manages to feel a lot longer than its already bloated five-and-a-half minute runtime. There's an alternate version on *The Bootleg Series vol.* 12 that is even slower, with drum supremely neutered that makes the song feel even more interminable. At least the version on *The Bootleg Series vol.* 7 isn't that bad, but it doesn't change or add much to the officially released version. The playing on the *Highway 61 Revisited* version is admirable with the piano adding a honky-tonk feel to the whole song. Bob's vocals fail to add any meaning or dimension to the already rambling meaningless lyrics. Ok, maybe it's not as bad as I'm making it out to be, but for some reason, this is an album cut that Dylan fans have inexplicably raised to the status of a modern classic when it should just be a relatively forgotten obscurity. At least it doesn't raise my ire nearly as much as the next song on *Highway 61 Revisited*.

Desolation Row
(written by Bob Dylan)

Not quite Side B of *Bringing It All Back Home*, this song is the acoustic finale to the album. The annoying lead acoustic guitar that tainted "Mr. Tambourine Man" and "It's All Over Now, Baby Blue" is back. This time it's joined by a bass, keeping it farther from being a solo performance while still lacking the drive of a full band showcase. To me, the alternate take first heard on *The Bootleg Series vol.* 7 would've been much better if it had only had drums. Without it, the song feels like an even more unsatisfying compromise. Not that drums would've saved the song from being too long, although a faster tempo might have helped. Just listen to the version on *MTV Unplugged*. Ultimately the song is just dull. There are some neat turns of phrase within the hodgepodge of images within the lyrics, but none of it feels very compelling. There's no chorus or bridge to interrupt this torrent of surrealistic gibberish. Bob's vocals feel flat and unemotional to me, which does not help matters. I know this is one of the favorites of many Dylan fans, but for me, this song is just a big old black hole that sucks up so much of the energy on *Highway 61 Revisited*.

Songs not on the album:
Positively 4th Street A-side of a non-album single
(written by Bob Dylan)
One of the few non-album singles that Bob has released in his career. Certainly the biggest of his career, anyone looking for the album this track comes off of will have to be directed to a compilation album. That is assuming that the average listener is able to determine the title of the song, as it is never sung or even referenced within the lyrics. Of the big Bob Dylan hits, I do prefer this to "Like A Rolling Stone". It's a similar snotty kiss-off track. The organ is once again way up in the mix as has become Dylan's trademark sound at the time. It is a surprising song to be so popular. Nothing is repeated anywhere in the song, it is just a continuous unfolding of verse after verse with no part repeating so you can sing along to it. Still, the utter bitterness pointed at the former love in this song is an emotion that almost everyone can sympathize with at some point in their life. There's a different take of this song on *The Bootleg Series vol. 12* that is not that different, but not nearly as forceful. This song is one of Bob's biggest, so there's not much else I can say about it except that I like it too.

Can You Please Crawl Out Your Window? A-side of a non-album single
(written by Bob Dylan)
Bob at his most willfully commercial. It almost sounds like a deliberate attempt to recapture the lightning in the bottle was "Positively 4th Street". This song was not nearly as big a hit, but considering how anti-crowd-pleasing Bob's reputation is, it's amusing to hear him try to consciously replicate the same sound that made him a pop star. Especially on the version on *The Bootleg Series vol. 12* with the tinkling celeste that sounds far more like The Hollies than Dylan's stubborn individualism. Who knows, if this song had become a hit and Bob had cranked out a string of similar singles, he might've ended up playing county fairs on the oldies circuit with Herman's Hermits and the like. Despite all his calculations, the song doesn't work to achieve its aims. As a result, the failed misfire becomes even more interesting. Sure, it's not a classic or a masterpiece, but it feels like a forgotten piece of average-60s Dylan. What you would expect him to sound like if you only heard his "hits" and weren't aware of his deeper catalog. Bob is even surprisingly self-aware of his public persona on this track, throwing out a callback to "Positively 4th Street" in an ad-lib towards the end ("You've got a lot of nerve to say you are my friend if you won't crawl out your window"). Perhaps because it is such a blatant cash-grab, it doesn't seem like a song of which Bob is particularly proud, having played it live only once. Maybe it's my perverse contrarian streak, but I really enjoy

this song.

Jet Pilot from *Biograph*
(written by Bob Dylan)

Maybe not a fully-written and finished song, this is a fun minute-and-a-half of Bob messing around with the musicians. For those who put a lot of importance into Dylan's lyrics, the way he tosses off these strange and meaningless phrases off the top of his head shows just how little effort and care he would sometimes put into them. There was nothing particularly special about these adlibs since Bob never came back to this song to finish it or even attempt another take. The joke at the end about how "she's no woman, she's a man" has not dated particularly well, but this is still overall a funny song. While not a particularly hilarious song, the idea of having jet pilot eyes from your hips on down is just strange enough to invoke chuckles. The music is the typical rock take on the three-chord blues structure that many of Dylan's tunes of this time were molded around. While Bob's electric period has a lot less amusement than his acoustic albums, little breaks like this would've certainly help relieve the tensions (and pretensions) of those albums.

I Wanna Be Your Lover from *Biograph*
(written by Bob Dylan)

Another attempt at a hit single along the lines of "Can You Crawl Out Your Window?" or "If You Gotta Go, Go Now" though this one wasn't actually released as a single. The title is clearly a cheeky reference to The Rolling Stones cover of Lennon & McCartney's "I Wanna Be Your Man". In a more broad sense, Bob is digging into and relishing the typical rock subject matter of teenage romance and expanding out from there into his usual cacophony of Dylan surrealism. He subverts the whole song, admitting that although he wants to be the lover of the woman he's singing to, he does have another girlfriend that he doesn't like nearly as much. The song is a simple rock tune in the style that Bob had been cranked out at the time. It's got a great chorus and is far livelier than most of the songs released around this time. It, unfortunately, was recorded in October 1965 somewhat between the end of *Highway 61 Revisited* in August of '65 and the beginning of *Blonde On Blonde* which didn't begin in earnest until Bob went to Nashville in February of 1966. As a result, the track languished in the can when it could've easily been a pleasant minor hit single to placate fans until Bob finished his next album.

Played live, but never recorded:
Long Distance Operator
(written by Bob Dylan)

A song recorded by The Band without Bob for the 1975 perversion of

The Basement Tapes. Dylan did write this one, but there are no studio recordings of him singing it, sadly. Bob didn't even write this during *The Basement Tapes* as this was actually performed by Dylan on-stage once on December 4th, 1965. Listening to the fuzzy bootleg of that song, it seems that the song seems pretty typical of the stuff Bob was doing at the time. It's a rock version of the usual 12 bar blues with some strange lyrics added. The Band version on the 1975 set is pretty straightforward, even if they don't copy the 1965 arrangement exactly. Not sure why this song got dropped by Dylan as it's pretty good. It's less of a surprise that The Band later picked it up and ran with it, although who knows why their version was included on this album.

Worked on in various hotels but not finished or recorded in a studio:
What A Friend I Have In Jesus
(traditional, arranged by Bob Dylan)
I Forgot More Than You'll Ever Know
(written by Cecil A. Null)
Remember Me (When The Candle Lights Are Gleaming)
(written by Scott Wiseman)
More And More
(written by Webb Pierce and Merle Kilgore)
Blues Stay Away From Me
(written by Alton Delmore, Rabon Delmore, Wayne Raney, and Henry Glover)
Weary Blues From Waitin'
(written by Hank Williams)
Lost Highway
(written by Leon Payne)
I'm So Lonesome I Could Cry
(written by Hank Williams)
Young But Daily Growing
(traditional, arranged by Bob Dylan)
Wild Mountain Thyme
(traditional, arranged by Bob Dylan)

The eighteenth and final disc of the super-duper deluxe edition of *The Bootleg Series vol. 12* features a bunch of hotel tapes. The first half of the songs come from May 1965 and the second half from May 1966. These tracks are not recording sessions nor live performances. They're not even rehearsals. These are just random jam sessions that happened to get recorded. The interesting thing about these songs is how they show where Bob's head was at and what his eyes were focused on for the future. "Young But Daily Growing" may be a throwback to his pre-songwriting folksinger days, but it is also a song that Dylan would attempt again during *The Basement Tapes* sessions. Another traditional song, "Wild Mountain Thyme" would re-emerge during Bob's solo acoustic portion of his 1969 Isle Of Wight performance. The Hank Williams songs covered here foreshadow Dylan's dalliance in country music on *Nashville Skyline*. Bob not only re-did "I Forgot More Than You'll Ever Know" for *Self-Portrait* but even released it at the time. Ultimately though it's "What A Friend I Have In Jesus" that is the more prescient, presage the born-again trilogy of *Slow Train Coming*, *Saved*, and *Shot Of Love*. Had anyone been paying close attention to these particular recordings at the time they may have been able to predict the next fifteen years of his career.

"HOW DOES IT FEEL?"

SIDE A:
1. Like A Rolling Stone
2. It Takes A Lot To Laugh, It Takes A Train To Cry
3. From A Buick 6
4. Highway 61 Revisited
5. Jet Pilot

SIDE B:
1. Positively 4th Street
2. Tombstone Blues
3. I Wanna Be Your Lover
4. Can You Please Crawl Out Your Window?
5. Ballad Of A Thin Man

Dropping the longer form songs like "Desolation Row" and "Just Like Tom Thumb's Blues" I have allowed this album to work as a more straight-forward, pop-oriented rock record. I've included all the singles instead of abandoning "Positively 4th Street" and "Can You Crawl Out Your Window?" as orphans. If you swap out the slower version of "It Takes A Lot To Laugh" with the faster take from *The Bootleg Series vol. 12* makes this an even snappier and fast-moving album. Better yet you can use the half-finished version of "Tombstone Blues" to add the sonic variety of the backing vocalists as well as cutting down the length of the song. Speaking of shorter song lengths, I love having the fragment "Jet Pilot" as a surreal appetizer between sides one and two. I suppose I couldn't avoid putting "Like A Rolling Stone" on here, although it's not one of my favorites. While most of the album is light and peppy, I think you have to close things with the apocalyptic funk of "Ballad Of A Thin Man". Really, it's the best way to end the album.

BLONDE ON BLONDE

Produced by: Bob Johnston
Recorded October 5th, 1965 – March 10th, 1966
Released: May 16th, 1966

Famous/Important/Popular Track(s):
- Rainy Day Women #12 & 35
- I Want You
- Just Like A Woman
- Visions Of Johanna

My Personal Favorite Track(s):
- Leopard-Skin Pill-Box Hat
- 4th Time Around
- Obviously 5 Believers

I realize that *Blonde On Blonde* is supposed to be one of, if not the best, Bob Dylan albums, but I don't get it. Everything that annoyed me about *Highway 61 Revisited* is just amplified here. There are some terrific songs on here, just as many as there were on *Highway 61 Revisited*; but the irritating tracks have increased in both length and number. All just to fill up what is an unnecessarily doubled album.

Switching from Mike Bloomfield and his usual cohorts to a bunch of Nashville studio cats (bypassing The Band almost completely), does change the sound somewhat, but not a lot. Much like *Highway 61 Revisited*, there's only one song on here that feels sonically different. And it's the first one. Everything else has the same instrumentation and arrangements as you would expect from the last two albums.

Once again, the outright laughs have been banished from the lyrics here. Bob is not trying to be funny anymore. At least not in a broad way that makes people laugh. The best we get are clever in-jokes that make you feel smarter than your friends because you pretend to get them. There's no "Motorpsycho Nitemare" or "Bob Dylan's 115th Dream" here. The best you can get is the fact that "stoned in "Rainy Day Women #12 & 35" can be taken both a Biblical form of capital punishment and slang for doing drugs.

My main complaints about the album are that the songs are generally too long and they lack variety. You would imagine with the broader canvass of a double-album Bob's would branch out and experiment more. That's the whole fun of a double-album is hearing the weird half-songs that usually get left off of a single disc. But there's no "Wild Honey Pie" here. Instead what we get are songs that are already too repetitive lasting longer and longer. And the similarities between the songs getting more and more apparent.

It may seem like I'm really ragging on this album, and I don't mean it to sound that way. These are minor complaints, only a level or two above nitpicking. But considering the near-universal acclaim that this album garners, I don't feel any need to add to that praise. Instead, I would prefer to be a counterweight, reminding folks that are a lot better albums in the Dylan oeuvre.

Particularly one double album that will be released only four years after *Blonde On Blonde*.

Rainy Day Women #12 & 35
(written by Bob Dylan)

Bob's rock records up to this point have been pretty stagnant in their instrumentation. Electric guitars – one usually playing lead lick throughout, bass, drums, both piano and a prominent organ, harmonica and maybe an acoustic guitar playing rhythm. Nothing very exciting or varied. This makes the faux-Salvation Army band sound on this track really stick out. We're hearing for the first time any sort of horns on a Dylan song. The lyrics are just an extended riff on the various places where one could get stoned. It doesn't even really matter if he is talking about getting stoned in terms of enjoying drugs or biblical punishment. Much like Dr. Seuss's Green Eggs & Ham all that matters is the different locations where this could happen. Still hearing Bob get this goofy (leading one to suspect the less lethal interpretation of "stoned") and trying out some new arrangement and instrumentation makes this a stand-out track.

Pledging My Time
(written by Bob Dylan)

A slow, sleazy, blues rock number. This could be a song of devotion to a loved one, except for the odd images of poison headaches and hobos stealing babies. The constant harmonica between each line is excellent. The half-sluggish swing tempo almost brings to mind the music that strippers would be undressing to at some old bump-n-grind. The harp takes a solo that is primarily just one long-held note. Bob's voice is almost exaggeratedly nasal. While this song is pretty standard for this album and this period, it's not bad. At least it comes in under four minutes and seems to be having a fun time in the process.

Visions of Johanna
(written by Bob Dylan)

A really long, slow, primarily acoustic number. There's a faster version on *The Bootleg Series vol. 7* that improves this somewhat, if only because this faster tempo shaves a minute of its seven-and-a-half minute runtime. The version (take 5) on *The Bootleg Series vol. 12* is almost frantic in its pace, but for some reason, that doesn't manage to change the length of this track at all. That version is far too busy to enjoy either. There are some nice organ swells and tasty country guitar licks on the officially released version.

However, given the stately speed at which this is taken coupled with lyrics, that are interesting but ultimately meaningless combines to make this track something of a chore for me to get through. Definitely one of Bob's more indulgent exercises on *Blonde On Blonde*. I realize that this one is a big favorite amongst Dylan-heads, but for me, this has always been a track I tend to skip over.

One of Us Must Know (Sooner or Later)
(written by Bob Dylan)

An organ-drenched mid-tempo number. It seems a lot longer than it really is, probably because the tempo could have been pushed up a hair or three. The piano playing is lovely. The lyrics seem to be circling around some sort of romantic discord, but it is not particularly comprehensible. The best parts of this song are the extended notes that Bob holds out at the end of the verse before going into the chorus. The harmonica solo that the song fades out on is surprisingly simple. It's a catchy enough song, but nothing about it particularly stands out.

I Want You
(written by Bob Dylan)

Another love song in the vein of "She Belongs To Me" or "Love Minus Zero/No Limit". While most of the lyrics are obscure, at least the chorus with its repetition of the title phrase are inarguable. The song is almost too chirpy. There's a bridge in there that doesn't add much, but does help break things up. Bob's vocals are so nasal it almost makes you question the sincerity of the lyrics, but there doesn't seem to be any undercurrent of deception going on here. The harmonica solo feels almost perfunctory, and one can almost get the impression that Bob is deliberately trying to write a commercial "Bob Dylan"-type hit single. It's not bad, but it doesn't feel particularly profound or heartfelt. As bizarre as the flute-led arrangement is on *At Budokan* that even feels more meaningful to Bob than this version.

Stuck Inside of Mobile with the Memphis Blues Again
(written by Bob Dylan)

Another fan favorite that I just don't get. At least it's taken at a much perkier pace than most of these overly long "classics". It's actually not that bad of a song for the first three or four minutes or so but has no reason to be over seven minutes long. Even the title seems way too long; at least it's actually sung in full during the song. Several times. Sure, there's something funny about the idea of someone's grandpa shooting a fire with their gun. But there's not enough coherence in these lyrics to make them compelling. Bob's vocals, while well-done, don't really belie any personal underneath either. As a result, by the time that Bob is getting chased for misplacing his ticket to some wedding, I have tuned out completely and am just looking at my watch. The faster version on *The Bootleg Series vol. 7* is still long. Bob himself even seems to disagree with my assessment of this song. It was included on *Greatest Hits vol. II* despite not actually being a hit. It wasn't even released as a single until the live version from the album *Hard Rain*. The single version is edited down to 3:35, so I may have to track that down and give it a shot. It's definitely a track I always skip when listening to *Blonde On Blonde*.

Leopard-Skin Pill-Box Hat
(written by Bob Dylan)

There's a weird version of this featuring a doorbell and car-horn on *The Bootleg Series vol. 12*. It sounds like an outtake from The Kinks' *Face To Face* album before they ditched the concept of linking all the songs together with appropriate sound effects; which seems appropriate considering that the subject of this song is a dedicated follower of fashion. With a few notable exceptions, all of Bob's recordings are just live performances captured on tape. For some reason, the actual possibilities available in the recording studio never appealed much to Dylan. This makes random experiments such as the sound effects version of "Leopard-Skin Pill-Box Hat" all the more intriguing. Unfortunately, this experiment didn't spur further attempts by Bob. While Bob doing something interesting and experimental is usually my favorite, this version hampers the flow of the song and was rightly discarded. It's certainly better than the extra slow version on *The Bootleg Series vol. 7* that nearly doubles the length of the song unnecessarily. Of course, it doesn't help that Bob attempts to ad-lib a couple of extra verses towards the end. This is a typical blues-rock song for Bob. It does have a pronounced descending turnaround over which the title refrain is sung. This is a nice twist on the otherwise standard 12 bar format. The lyrics are scathing, or at least Dylan's vocal performance lets you know that. Bob is even credited as playing lead guitar on this track. It's not as pronounced or as professional as the usual guitar solos, but knowing that it is Dylan himself hacking away at it adds to the sense of fun that it sounds like he's having while playing this song. *Blonde On Blonde* could definitely use more fun songs like this.

Just Like a Woman
(written by Bob Dylan)

I can't hear this song without think of Shelley Duvall's scene in *Annie Hall*. The way she recites the lyrics of the chorus makes the whole thing seem so ridiculous and pretentious. It's a good enough song with a lilting 6/8 feel and some lovely nylon string guitar arpeggios. I have no idea why this song stood out and became one of the big hits from *Blonde On Blonde*. Bob sings this like a sincere love song, but most of the lyrics come off as underhanded compliments if not direct insults. I will applaud the bridge section which does ratchet up the tension and excitement in this song far more than I would think it's capable of based on the first half of the song. The harmonica solo well-executed, but doesn't add much. The ending is a little more clunky and pat then you usually get from a Dylan tune. At least it has an actual finish instead of just fading out. Oddly enough the version on *At Budokan* is about the only one stick close to the original arrangement. "Just Like A Woman" is definitely an essential song in the Dylan oeuvre, and it's not a horrible song, but I don't get why this track is so highly regarded.

Most Likely You Go Your Way and I'll Go Mine
(written by Bob Dylan)

A great driving song with a weird two note hook that is played in tandem by the harmonica and a trumpet. It's nice to have the horn here, recalling the drunken brass band on "Rainy Day Women #12 & 35", adding a new dimension and color to this album. The drums have a neat martial snare drum pattern to them, and the rest of the band is smoking. The lyrics seem to be a joyous recounting of the break-up of a bitter relationship. Bob sounds righteously pissed on this track. For a long time, this track was sort of lost amongst the others in this highly regarded era. It did show up on the 1974 tour and subsequent live album with the Band, *Before The Flood*, but other than that had faded into obscurity. That is until the 2007 compilation album, uncreatively entitled *Dylan* came out. For some reason, to promote this compilation, DJ and producer Mark Ronson was employed to create a remix of this song that was released as a single and turned into a music video. While the resultant track is not nearly as horrific to listen to as it might appear on paper, it is still flitting somewhere between annoying and sacrilegious. It's nice that this track, which is one of my favorites on *Blonde On Blonde* was finally getting some recognition. It's just a shame that it came in such a manner.

Temporary Like Achilles
(written by Bob Dylan)

Originally entitled "Medicine Sunday" before a bit of a lyric re-write, I might remember what song this is if Dylan had titled it "Honey, Why You So Hard?" For an album recorded in Nashville, there's little that sounds country about *Blonde On Blonde*, but this is probably the closest on this album. Not overtly country, but with a definite feel being provided by the studio musicians with the piano sounding particularly honky-tonk. As such, it adds a nice change of pace to the usual soft ballads and hard rockers without being just a medium mediocrity. Despite being somewhat countrified, the chord structure is your typical 12-bar blues. Bob is not singing with that clear *Nashville Skyline* croon yet but is invested a lot more in the melody than usual. The lyrics seem to be a harsh warning to the new boyfriend of an old girlfriend, but with enough odd imagery and metaphors to keep the whole things mysteriously poetic. Along with "To Ramona" this is one of the songs that most presages the transition to full country that would come towards the end of this decade for Dylan. Not a great song, but still a pleasing diversion.

Absolutely Sweet Marie
(written by Bob Dylan)

A straight-forward rock number. Unlike many of Bob's more rocking songs of the era, he doesn't just rely on the usual 12-bar blues progression. In fact, it almost feels like a folk-rock song inspired by the pop singles by The Byrds or The Turtles or such that were initially inspired by Bob, to begin with. There's even a bridge section that switches things up nicely. The lyrics are almost a parody of Dylan's usual pastiche of surrealistic impressionism. The first take of this song was included on *The Bootleg Series vol. 12*, but it doesn't sound significantly different from the final version that ended up on *Blonde On Blonde*. The song is nearly five minutes long, but compared to the length of some of the other tracks on this album, this almost feels brief. Not one of the more exciting songs on the album, it was a surprising choice for George Harrison to pull out during the 30th Anniversary Concert at Madison Square Garden. Ultimately it's a pretty average song for this album.

4th Time Around
(written by Bob Dylan)

Theoretically Bob's answer to John Lennon's "Norwegian Wood". I'm not really sure how the two are related, but I like both of those songs. Both songs are in a waltz-time and have oblique lyrics that on the surface seem to be recounting semi-surreal yet utterly mundane encounters with a woman at her house. Sure, the words don't make a lick of sense, but it still captivating. Primarily due to the invested way that Bob sings this. There's some nice fingerpicked nylon string guitar on here. The musical is pretty much a two-chord alternating pattern that luckily switches up three-fourths of the way through each verse. There's no chorus or bridge here, so we are dependent on the words to keep us interested. Luckily the song bounces along quickly and the story, vague though it may be, hold my attention. While I often forget what song this is by the title, once it starts playing I remember that I do have a fondness for this particular track.

Obviously 5 Believers
(written by Bob Dylan)

By the third album of Bob's first rock period, it seems like Dylan is already getting sick of rocking. There seems to be a smaller percentage of out-and-out rock songs on *Blonde On Blonde* when compared to just the year previous on *Bringing It All Back Home* and *Highway 61 Revisited*. Luckily Bob had given it up entirely, and this is one of the hardest rock songs on this double album. There's a nifty little harmonica break that surprisingly was played by one of the studio musicians instead of Bob himself. I'm not sure if it's because the part required a certain consistency and polish that Dylan didn't think he could give or because it would occasionally overlap with the vocals. At this point in his career, Dylan was thoroughly opposed to overdubbing so there was no way he could do both. Whatever the reason, it does have more of a melodic than a blues-harp vibe. The music here is also primarily blues-based as most of his rockers are. The lyrics are about what you expect, random gibberish. This track may feel like a bit of a throwback on *Blonde On Blonde*, but really that album could've used more adrenalized numbers like this in my opinion. One of my favorites from this record.

Sad Eyed Lady of the Lowlands
(written by Bob Dylan)

Despite being three seconds shorter than "Desolation Row", this song gets a whole album side to itself. This smacks of arrogance and pretention, which hurts my ability to enjoy this song. I will admit that "Sad Eyed Lady" is slightly less monotonous than "Desolation Row" if only by virtue of having more instruments playing with which to create any sort of variation. The song itself has a nice little 6/8 feel to it and does at least have something definitely resembling a chorus to help break things up. Bob's vocals here are some of his most exaggeratedly nasal. The piano is playing really low in the register, so it becomes almost subliminal in the mix, but it really is the hero of the song. There's some nice organ playing and the drumming (especially the hi-hat) maintains such a steady, consistent feel it seems almost Olympic. The lyrics are apparently a paean to some woman Bob loved. According to "Sara" on *Desire*, Dylan wrote this for his bride-to-be, Sara Lownds. Of course, knowing Bob, who knows how much of it's true. If you are attempted to reconcile with your recently divorced wife, saying you wrote her an 11+ minute epic certainly can't hurt. This song doesn't irritate as much as some of Bob's longer epics like "Joey", "Tempest", or "Brownsville Girl", but rarely do I have the patience to listen to the whole thing. I usually shut it off after four or five minutes having gotten the gist and all that I need from this song.

Songs not on the album:
I'll Keep It With Mine from *The Bootleg Series vol. 2*
(written by Bob Dylan)
See entry under *Bringing It All Back Home*

She's Your Lover Now from *The Bootleg Series vol. 2*
(written by Bob Dylan)

A bit of a plodding mid-tempo ballad that unfortunately never quite gets a full take. There are some nice bits in here, but it is a little too long, so it's no surprise that the backing musicians finally get bored and throw up their hand so tantalizingly close to the end of the song. Apparently, of the 16 takes on the super-duper deluxe version of *The Bootleg Series vol. 12* only two are marked as complete – and neither of these is the version that got released in the more standard-issue *Bootleg Series*. Perhaps, the song sounds better as a theoretical possibility than it does as a real fact. *The Bootleg Series vol. 2* version is taken a slightly faster tempo and feels closer to a real take. There's far more possibility lurking there, and it's almost a shame when it breaks down just one verse from the finish line. *The Bootleg Series vol. 12* version is much more lumbering and far less of a disappointment when that one gives up the ghost. It's pretty typical of the songs during this period. The lyrics are a confusing mess of icons and imagery. Bob sings it well (depending on which take you're listening to). The band's playing is a little heavy-handed for such a light song. Clearly, Dylan was trying to get a good take of this song and felt strongly about it. Who knows why this one was given up on after such effort expended.

Lunatic Princess from *The Bootleg Series vol. 12*
(written by Bob Dylan)

Half of a song attempted once during the *Blonde On Blonde* sessions that for some reason was never finished or even tried again. It certainly holds some potential. It rocks out pretty well on the standard three chords with a catchy melody and the typical scrambled Dylan lyrics. I'm not sure why Bob stops sing mid-verse here, maybe he hadn't written anything past here. Perhaps he was making it all up on the spot. I'm not sure. It's a curious thing. Had it been finished it might've been one of the better tracks on this record, but not one that particularly stood out. However, as a brief but tantalizing tease, the song (or the idea of the song) takes on a life of its own.

Played live, but never recorded:
Tell Me, Momma
(written by Bob Dylan)

To help further alienate his audience, Bob would often kick off the electric portion of his 1966 concerts with this unknown and unfamiliar tune. I'm not sure why this song, which was so beloved by Dylan on tour, got shafted entirely in the studio. It might give one something of an impression of what a post-*Blonde On Blonde* album would've sounded like if it weren't for the motorcycle crash. It's a pretty typical rocking variation on the blues format with a few extra chords thrown in for fun, especially during the back-and-forth of the "I know that you know" part. While I would've preferred a studio version of this song, I think the live rendition on *The Bootleg Series vol. 4* gives you a pretty good idea of what this would've ended up sounding like. *Blonde On Blonde* could have used more muscular rockers like this song.

<u>Worked on in various hotels but not finished or recorded in a studio:</u>
When Will I Be Loved
(written by Phil Everly)
I Can't Leave Her Behind
(written by Bob Dylan)
On A Rainy Afternoon
(written by Bob Dylan & Robbie Robertson)
If I Was A King
(written by Bob Dylan)
What Kind Of Friend Is This
(written by Bob Dylan)
Positively Van Gough
(written by Bob Dylan)
Don't Tell Him, Tell Me
(written by Bob Dylan)
If You Want My Love
(written by Bob Dylan)

While I don't think there is a huge shift between the songwriting on *Blonde On Blonde* and *The Basement Tapes*, it is still interesting to theorize what Dylan's follow-up to *Blonde On Blonde* would have been had he not been diverted by that motorcycle crash in 1966. This handful of tunes started but seemingly never finished, are about the closest to a clue we have about that. The songs themselves are pretty skeletal at this point. "I Can't Leave Her Behind" is very pretty and has a lot of promise. "On A Rainy Afternoon" is a title gets re-used for a track recorded a year later for *The Basement Tapes*. It's hard to tell if the two songs share enough DNA to be the same song or if the re-used title was just a coincidence. "What Kind Of Friend Is This" is a blues thing that actually sounds better acoustic than as the rock song it would've morphed into had it been finished. "Positively Van Gogh" is pretty standard *Blonde On* Blonde stuff, but hearing the three different attempts to write/record the song is an insightful look into Bob's songwriting process. In fact, most of these songs aren't great, but are a fascinating listen as Dylan sort of teaches/helps Robbie Robertson learn how to write songs for himself. "Don't Tell Him, Tell Me" is a little more country-ish, with an almost pop sensibility in the lyrics and melody. With all of these songs, the sound quality is so bad that most of the words are unintelligible. This makes very little difference in one's appreciation of the songs Dylan was penning at the time. There are some nice bits scattered among these tatters and it a shame that Bob never went back and really finished any of these. Dylan's muse was running so hot and heavy at the time that he could nonchalantly leave little gems like this discarded on the side of the road without any fear that his inspiration may one day dry up. Ah, the folly of youth! Needless to say, this would not always be the case.

"TWO BLONDES, ONE RECORD"

SIDE A:
1. Rainy Day Women #13 & 35
2. Pledging My Time
3. One Of Us Must Know (Sooner Or Later)
4. I Want You
5. Leopard-Skin Pill-Box Hat
6. I'll Keep It With Mine

SIDE B:
1. Most Likely You Go Your Way And I'll Go Mine
2. Temporary Like Achilles
3. Absolutely Sweet Marie
4. 4th Time Around
5. Lunatic Princess
6. Obviously 5 Believers

Again, I have axed the longer epics like "Sad Eyed Lady Of The Lowlands" and "Stuck Inside Mobile With The Memphis Blues Again" to try and tighten this up into a streamlined single album. This record is far less daunting and much easier to digest than the monolith that is *Blonde On Blonde*. I have added "Lunatic Princess" since it is such a rocking little tune and I'm trying to create another upbeat album that would follow up *Highway 61 Revisited*. I have also added the version of "I'll Keep It With Mine" from *The Bootleg Series vol. 2* since I did cut so many of the slower songs on here and thought I should still have a few ballads. Other than that, it was mostly a matter of cutting some of the more extraneous material that was used to pad *Blonde On Blonde* up to double disc status so that "Sad-Eyed Lady Of The Lowlands" could have an album side all to itself. While this edit is much more to my liking, I still don't think this nearly as good as *Highway 61 Revisited* or *Bringing It All Back Home*. Ultimately those two records had more verve and bravery as Bob was still breaking out of his folk-music prison. By this point, Dylan had already proven that he was not crazy, and it all seems less vital or shocking as a result.

THE BASEMENT TAPES
Produced by: Bob Dylan
Recorded: March – October, 1967
Released: June 26th, 1975

Famous/Important/Popular Track(s):
- I Shall Be Released
- Quinn The Eskimo (The Mighty Quinn)
- You Ain't Going Nowhere
- Tears Of Rage
- This Wheel's On Fire

My Personal Favorite Track(s):
- I'm Not There
- Get Your Rocks Off
- Don't Ya Tell Henry

    This is a difficult album to talk about, primarily because it is not actually an album at all. Sure, it has been compiled and released officially (and unofficially) a couple of times, but *The Basement Tapes* is not an album as much as it is a series of home jam sessions that just happened to be recorded. These jams didn't even take place in a studio. No one was manning the mixing console. It sounds pretty darn good for an amateur recording, but that's all it is. I don't believe there was ever a plan to release this as an album while it was being made; and the random, aimless, wandering nature of these "recording" sessions bear this out.

    So, why did Bob record these songs? Sure, some of them might have been songwriting demos to give to other artists to collect publishing royalties while he stayed at home – but if that were the case why did he need a whole backing band on had to record with. He could've recorded them easily just by himself. In fact, they might have been easier to record that way. But even if that were the goal, why record all these covers? These clearly aren't meant as demos nor could they be used as such. If he was recording these for eventual release, then why is he just recording in the basement?

    Besides the technical limitations of this recording set-up, which may have appealed to his desire for a low-stress record making environment – but then why spend all this time goofing off? No was taking particularly good care of these tapes, so it's hard to imagine they would be delivered to the record company. Even when they were officially released, Bob always sort of treated these sessions that weren't meant for general release that somehow escaped his grip. So what was the goal here?

    I think Bob may have used the motorcycle crash initially as an excuse to get off the road and out of his touring commitments, but soon realized he didn't want to spend all his time 24/7 at home with his wife raising kids. He needed an excuse to get out of the house – not permanently, but for a couple of hours a day. Since Bob didn't have a 9-to-5 day job, he contrived these recording sessions as merely an excuse to give himself something to do every day.

Who knows how many other, equally intriguing, home jam sessions would've been just as legendary if only some enterprising bootlegger happened to be walking by Dylan's place at the time with the proper recording equipment? Whatever the reason this was recorded, it is a fascinating, behind-the-scenes, fly-on-the-wall glimpse into Dylan's headspace at this particular juncture in his development. While Bob's motorcycle accident did afford him an excuse to stop touring and slow down his lifestyle, it was not responsible for the "amnesia" that gripped Bob around this time.

Some fans think of Dylan's pre-crash recordings as infallible, but eye everything he did afterward with suspicion. But to me, most of the original songs on *The Basement Tapes* don't sound that much different from *Blonde On Blonde*, even if the recordings are not as professionally done. The lyrics are still surreal gibberish, although there is a more whimsical bent to these tunes. Ultimately, there is not as big of a change between these post-crash recordings and the ones that proceeded it as there are between these tracks and the ones on *John Wesley Harding*, even if some of *the Basement Tapes* in fact overlapped with that "real" album.

So, how best to listen to *The Basement Tapes*? Listening to all 139 tracks of the six-CD *The Bootleg Series vol. 11* is a bit overwhelming and hard to take in as a single piece of work. Going with the original 14 track acetate slots it in nicely as an album between *Blonde On Blonde* and *John Wesley Harding*. The only problem with limiting yourself like that is you not only miss several great originals ("I'm Not There", "All You Have To Do Is Dream") but you don't get any of those great improvisational joke songs like "I'm A Teenage Prayer" or "Baby, Won't You Be My Baby" much less any of the wide selection of covers.

Using the official 1975 release is ridiculous for the same reasons, but also is shackled with the historical revisionism of the inclusion of the Band tracks. Dylan's camp did not release the entirety of *The Bootleg Series vol. 11* on Spotify (in an attempt to get people to buy the thing) and instead limited the streaming service to a 15 track "sampler" playlist. These 15 tracks are a little more inclusive than the acetate or the '75 version – but as a result, leave off several songs that are important to the full Basement story.

Of course, each individual can pick their favorites and create a version of *The Basement Tapes* tailored only to them with as many or as few songs as they want, but this just gives you a skewed look into the work that tends to confirm the listener/compiler's pre-established prejudices about the work. Probably the best representation of this group of recordings is the 2-CD or 3-LP version of *The Bootleg Series vol. 11* (labeled "Raw" as opposed to

"Complete") These 38 songs give you a pretty good overview of the breadth and depth of this period in Dylan's recording career without bogging one down with too much minutiae.

For this book, I had to start somewhere, so I did decide to follow the track listing of the 1975 2-disc version, as it is the earliest officially released distillation of the period, and just go into the various songs left off from there. It does mean that I have to note (and skip over) each of the non-Dylan Band songs that ended up on the official album.

My personal opinion of this amorphous and nebulous album varies a lot. Certainly, the ratio of personal favorites to overrated claptrap is about the same as it was on the last three electric albums. As such, not having a consistent narrative about which songs would've ended up on the cutting room floor makes it difficult to tell how I really feel about the entire *Basement Tapes* experience. This may be why I have a hard time getting as excited about this period of Dylan's work as I would like. On the other hand, it prevents me from being as frustrated as I am about something like *Infidels*. While I do enjoy several songs recorded during these sessions, the lack of any feeling that Dylan chose to do any of this keeps me from getting too invested in this whole era of the Bob catalog.

Odds And Ends
(written by Bob Dylan)

This is a fun, upbeat tune, which is usually a great way to start out an album, but it's really odd to open with a song that is so short. This track doesn't even reach two minutes and as such serves more as an introduction to *The Basement Tapes* as a whole rather than a track unto itself. You get all the hallmarks of what to expect on the following record. Really impressive yet drunk sounding harmonies. Slightly over-done guitar solos. Lyrics that sounds silly and make no sense. Songs that just abruptly end as the tape runs out. In some ways, this is the perfect average basement song. One of the few good choices made on 1975's release of these recordings was opening with this.

Orange Juice Blues (Blues For Breakfast)
(written by Richard Manuel)

Non-Dylan track included on the 1975 *Basement Tapes*.

Million Dollar Bash
(written by Bob Dylan)

A bouncy little number with nonsense lyrics that prove to be more jovial than some of the foreboding surrealism of earlier Dylan songs. This song just sounds fun with The Band singing along on the chorus. The first take of this song even features some harmonica – something Dylan didn't do a lot of during *The Basement Tapes* sessions. This not a terribly strong or memorable number, so it was an unusual choice for the single. Still, it's pleasant and enjoyable and definitely doesn't overstay its welcome.

Yazoo Street Scandal
(written by Robbie Robertson)
Non-Dylan track included on the 1975 *Basement Tapes*.

Goin' To Acapulco
(written by Bob Dylan)
A plaintive, keening song with a lovely chorus. Despite the murky and muddy production, the beauty of this song comes shining through. The harmonies are glorious. I'm not sure what the lyrics mean exactly or who Rosemary is or why he has to see "soft gut." There sounds like there's a lot of sadness and regret in Bob's voice. Robbie gets off some surprisingly tasteful licks while Bob sings that long note on the word "yeah" towards the end of each chorus. Normally a song written as well as this would be a standout on any album, but given there is "Tears Of Rage" and "This Wheel's On Fire" covering the same emotional ground much better it's no real surprise that this was left off of the original fourteen song acetate that Dylan's company originally circulated as songwriting demos for other artists to cover. A good track, but there are better on this album.

Katie's Been Gone
(written by Richard Manuel and Robbie Robertson)
Non-Dylan track included on the 1975 *Basement Tapes*.

Lo And Behold
(written by Bob Dylan)
A primarily two-chord song with hints of country and blues in there. There are some sweet harmonies in there especially when Bob and the Band stop the song at the end of choruses. The lyrics are delightfully silly nonsense. There's an odd line in here about saving one's money only to rip it up. I'm not sure how one exactly goes about looking for a Lo and Behold unless those are the rather strange names for a pair of dogs or something. The first take of this song features Bob breaking down in laughter. After this, he has a problem getting the song back on track. Luckily there is another take with a more prominent piano that is complete. It is funny to catch Bob in an unguarded moment like that. A fun, goofy track that neatly encapsulates the more jovial spirit of *The Basement Tapes*.

Bessie Smith
(written by Rick Danko and Robbie Robertson)
Non-Dylan track included on the 1975 *Basement Tapes*.

Clothes Line Saga
(written by Bob Dylan)

The belatedly revealed subtitle to this song is "Answer To Ode". Knowing that this song was written in response to Bobbie Gentry's ubiquitous 1967 hit helps explain the deliberately uneventful exploits recounted in this song; even if none of this directly references that song. Written as a laugh, and taken at a moderate pace, this song is a hoot. Bob's comedic timing is in fine form with the pause before the revelation that his neighbor blew his nose. Sure nothing happens, but it all seems poised to have something exciting happen at any minute. It's another fun little song that doesn't merit further scrutiny.

Apple Suckling Tree
(written by Bob Dylan)

A folksy song led by Dylan's piano. There's some rather rudimentary drumming here that surprisingly get a couple bars to shine on its own at the end of each verse. The lyrics feel tossed off, but given the fact that there's harmony singing along with Bob throughout the song, the words must've been written out in advance. The lyrics almost sound like a parody of a lost love type of country song. The music is little more than a variation on the common I-IV-V chords. Despite the somewhat unsteady drumming, the song is almost funky. There's a tasty little organ solo in there. I don't even think I detect the presence of a guitar on this track. While not revelatory, definitely a worthwhile addition to *The Basement Tapes*.

Please Mrs. Henry
(written by Bob Dylan)

A song with a really catchy chorus. I love the little goofy organ bit at the end of the verses as the song re-starts itself. This may be the lustiest song Bob has recorded until "Lay Lady Lay". The lyrics are not very direct, which is probably a good thing. Bob even lets out a bit of a self-conscious giggle at one point. Bob is definitely begging here but is a little ashamed of being so needy, so he tried to play the whole thing off as a bit of a joke. Clearly, whatever he needs from Mrs. Henry, he doesn't feel much for her or even seems to respect her a whole lot. This may contribute to why he has to get down on his knees to plead for a little kindness from the titular woman. The music is goofy half-country as seems appropriate. The Band provides some pleasant backing vocals, especially as the song cuts off for the solo refrain about not having a dime. For all the important that *the Basement Tapes* have there a lot of deliberately slight songs on here. Maybe that is the secret to the success of this collection.

Tears of Rage
(written by Bob Dylan and Richard Manuel)

In addition to writing, ad-libbing, and covering a bunch of complete songs for *The Basement Tapes* Bob also would spend most mornings writing a bunch of lyrics at the typewriter with no real purpose at all. There's probably a bunch that remains unfinished and unseen. Another thirty or so got fleshed out by T-Bone Burnett's attempt to create his own Traveling Wilburys on their album *Lost In The River*. While Bob did give his blessing (and more importantly his lyrics) to the "New Basement Tapes" project it seems had little interest in it when it was done and never commented on it during or after its release. Only two of these words without music got finished off contemporaneously and got to be sung by Bob himself; "Tears Of Rage" and "This Wheel's On Fire" were given music and melodies by Richard Manuel and Rick Danko respectively. While I have been dismissive of The Band elsewhere in this book, I will admit that I really enjoy both of these songs. This is a lovely song full of hurt and regret. This was clearly a song Bob cared about at the time being one of the very few *Basement Tapes* songs to get three takes devoted to it, the only others were "Open The Door Homer" and "Nothing Was Delivered". The first take of "Tears Of Rage" is not horrible, but the musicians are still learning the song. The second take is incomplete; it sounds like Bob decided to switch the song into 3/4 time without informing anyone else and the result is a bit of a misfire. The final take is everything the song needed to be, and so Dylan moved on. It has no drums but some lovely high harmonies on there. I'm not sure what all the lyrics mean here, but Richard Manuel's music and Bob's singing a great sense of longing and loss here. Another great song from this collection that luckily did see release eventually.

Too Much Of Nothing
(written by Bob Dylan)

One of Bob's more surprisingly complex songs. The way the chords continually go up and up and up towards the end of each verse is more sophisticated than Dylan's usual I-IV-V progressions. There are two takes of this song; the first one feels a little tentative, making the super high falsetto harmony sound awkward and embarrassing. Luckily the second take is far more confident and assured with the harmonies in a more reasonable octave. I have no idea who or what Bob is talking about here. The general story surrounding *The Basement Tapes* is that Bob had too much of everything in 1966 and used the motorcycle crash and subsequent retreat from the public eye to get more nothing in his life. But it doesn't really matter what the words mean. Bob doesn't seem to be singing about himself here as he doesn't seem terribly hurt or upset by a lack of stuff (or abundance of nothing) in his life. He sounds more like he's giving friendly advice to someone who is about to provide a nothing-surplus to a third party, perhaps Vivian or Valerie. As a result, the song doesn't feel terribly urgent, yet lacks the goofy, carefree quality of some the sillier basement songs. It's obviously not just an impromptu jam, and would almost feel like filler if any of these recordings were actually meant to fill anything. It's catchy enough but not one of the more essential basement tracks.

Yea! Heavy And A Bottle Of Bread
(written by Bob Dylan)

For what seems like a frivolous bit of fluff that you would imagine was improvised, Bob actually took the time and effort to do two takes. Luckily he did, since the second take is much more cohesive if not exactly coherent. Either way, it seems like a small and trifling affair. The music is mostly just two chords. The quote-unquote chorus is just the last line of the preceding verse repeated four times with a bunch of Band members singing along. On the final note, one of the singers reaches down for a ridiculously low note that would've sounded funny even if had nailed it, which he doesn't. The lyrics seem like stoned silliness. I have no idea how you get bread in a bottle or what comic books have to do with this whole thing. The whole idea of a nose full of puss is just disgusting though. While clearly Bob and The Band are having a whole lot of fun, this forced whimsy is starting to get a little old. This seems like the kind of mild throwaway that would've been easily left off of any official release, but surprisingly it was included not only on the 1975 release but also the original 1967 songwriting demo acetate.

Ain't No More Cane
(traditional, arranged by Bob Dylan)

A traditional folk tune that Bob had been performing since his early days. The version originally released on the 1975 *Basement Tapes* was actually recorded by The Band without Dylan sometime later. Both takes of the real version were finally put out on *The Bootleg Series vol. 11*. It is a song that features harmonized humming/grunting at the end of each line, which actually sounds far better than that description may conjure. The version released (and possibly recorded) in 1975 features Levon Helm on lead vocals, although the erstwhile Band drummer did not return to the group in time to be featured on many – or possibly any – of the authentic *Basement Tapes* recordings. Their version is far more upbeat and sprightly with a jaunty accordion and mandolin. There's also some well-recorded drums belying the fact this recording does not fit. The original version with Dylan sounds far more world-weary and moving. While Bob's originals at the time tended to skew towards the goofy and lightweight, his choice of covers showed a lot of depth and seriousness being injected into these sessions, even if the sessions themselves were seemingly meaningless (in the best possible way). He cared enough about capturing this song that he insisted on doing two takes, although the differences between the two are slight. There was no alteration of the arrangement, just another attempt to get a suitable take. Suitable for what is hard to say, but it is an excellent recording nonetheless. The only cover song deemed worthy enough to have necessitated a second take was "Four Strong Winds". Make of that what you may, but it shows that simply recording songwriting demos for his publishing company wasn't Dylan's only objective in the basement.

Down In The Flood (Crash On The Levee)
(written by Bob Dylan)

I sure wish Bob would make his mind up whether this song is titled "Crash On The Levee" or "Down In The Flood". This is one of the basement songs that Bob seems most enamored of. It was one of the three tunes from here that he re-recorded with Happy Traum for *The Greatest Hits Vol. II*. He also re-recorded it and released this song on the soundtrack to his *Masked & Anonymous* movie. It's not a poor song, but I'm not sure why this particular tune stuck with Dylan more than so many others. With its references to floods of Biblical proportions, this definitely feels like Bob trying to write his own old-timey traditional folksong. The original *Basement Tapes* version is pretty heavy on the organ, with some great bass playing and the guitar being just an afterthought. Recording this song did require two takes, with the first take being a similar arrangement just lacking the confidence of the second attempt. The *Greatest Hits Vol. II* manages to be even more informal and casual than the basement take, but Bob's vocals are far more forceful here though. By the time we get to the *Masked & Anonymous* version from 2003, the song has become a straightforward rock number. This is the only studio version of this song that includes drumming, although when Dylan guested at The Band's gig at the end of 1971, that live version ended up as a bonus track on the re-release of their *Rock Of Ages* album. That live version is pretty similar to *The Basement Tapes* version with drums added and Robbie Robertson wailing away. I don't really like to confuse matters by spending too much time with live versions of any song. Sure, the *Masked & Anonymous* version may be considered a live track performed for a film crew instead of an audience. I do love the way Bob's growl adds some menace to the *Masked & Anonymous* version. This may be the most exciting of the three, but I think the Happy Traum take may be my personal preference. Still, either way, it's great, groovy little song.

Ruben Remus
(written by Richard Manuel and Robbie Robertson)
Non-Dylan track included on the 1975 *Basement Tapes*.

Tiny Montgomery
(written by Bob Dylan)

More circus freaks on display here. Not sure what is going on in the lyrics or why it's in Old Frisco. This is a fun little nothing song. The music is almost entirely just two chords. The Band responds with wordless aahs at the end of each verse. There's no chorus or bridge, just each verse ending with a salutation from the titular Montgomery. The only real variation here is the number of lines each verse has. Bob stretches this out each time around as he comes up with more Fellini-esque caricatures to add to the mix. Even for a *Basement Tapes* song, this isn't more than a trifle. While this doesn't sound improvised, I doubt a lot of time was spent writing it either. It appears that this was only attempted one time before everyone decided to move on to recording other songs. The organ sounds good here as does the walking bass, but there's not much to this song. Pretty typical stuff from this era.

You Ain't Goin' Nowhere
(written by Bob Dylan)

Of the three Basement songs re-recorded with Happy Traum for *Greatest Hits vol. II* this is the only one that was released on the official 1975 album. "I Shall Be Released" and "Crash On The Levee" were probably left off by Robbie Robertson under the guise of giving the people something new they haven't heard before (and also to make room for his Band songs), but for some reason, this one couldn't be ignored. This is probably because the majority of the audience weas more familiar with the version that The Byrds released on *Sweethearts Of The Rodeo* than the bonus track remake Bob did. Of course, Roger McGuinn managed to get one of the lyrics wrong, so Dylan threw in a little dig at him in that recording, but luckily it came off as friendly rather than irate. The song is very proto-Americana, predicted the future genre's low-key vibe and interests. This feel shines through on both *The Basement Tapes* and the *Greatest Hits* versions. Sure, the lyrics could be seen as a threat to someone who has been kidnapped, but it never comes across that way. The *Basement* version is jaunty and one of the few from these sessions to feature any drums, with some nice side-stick work during the choruses. The *Greatest Hits* version is even more casual and informal. The Byrds' version cranked up the country with some pedal steel and a traditional Nashville sound. The banjo on Bob's '71 version adds an even more back-porch vibe. There's even a bass that pops I here making the song fuller without ever crossing the threshold into feeling like an actual production. Both of Dylan's versions feature harmony vocals on the chorus, and it's tough to think of the song without that featured prominently. Sure, the song is an ode to laziness, but it is a first-rate well-done ode to laziness.

Don't Ya Tell Henry
(written by Bob Dylan)

Somebody's got a trombone, and they definitely don't know how to use it! This song sounds like a drunken mess, so it's no surprise that it was left off the 1975 collection. Much less forgivable it was swapped out for a later performance of this song by The Band without Dylan's involvement. The Band's version is a slick piece of work that sounds way too professional for *The Basement Tapes*. This is not the type of song that really thrives with more attention paid to it. The song itself is dopey fun, a well-worn blues pattern that even a novice trombonist could fake their way through. Fluffing this up with some prepared riffs and whatnot misses the point entirely. If you got a song this silly, playing it straight just makes you look foolish. The lyrics are typical basement nonsense; no idea if this Henry is related to the Mrs. Henry of the previous song. Most likely not as this is all just gibberish for fun and that was just a name that popped into Bob's head a lot at the time. As much of an intoxicated mess as this song is, it's still fun to listen to. Even the trombone which is getting close to sliding into obnoxious territory manages to remain charming throughout the two-and-a-half minute runtime. Compared to some of the really altered conscious rambles that are buried within these sessions, this is practically a masterpiece. It contains all the fun and humor of something like "All American Boy" or "I'm Your Teenage Prayer" while still being listenable as music. That's something of an achievement.

Nothing Was Delivered
(written by Bob Dylan)

A song that could also double as negative feedback on an eBay listing. It's incredible how literal and single-minded these lyrics are. Each verse is just about how something that was promised and it has not arrived. One of the few songs on *The Basement Tapes* to be deemed worthy of a third take, although that last take only lasts thirty seconds and is taken way to fast to be seriously considered. The first take has something of a light country feel. By the second take, those triplets on the piano have taken over, making the track sound something like a 1950 doo-wop type number. The song has a surprising amount of feeling and depth for what essentially is a one-star review on Amazon or Yelp. There are some lovely harmonies on the chorus that add a bizarre layer of heartache and loss. Obviously, this must be some sort of metaphor, but I have no idea what was supposed to be delivered here and why its loss is so staggering. I prefer the earlier version as the second take seems a little sillier without ever actually becoming funny. When Bob breaks down and speak-sings the last lines of one of the verses we see how much of a joke this song really is. Although really the difference between the two is slight and my preference does change often. The drumming on here is pretty stiff, and several of the fills lose the rhythm altogether, but it just adds to the charm of this song. In fact, this may be one of my favorite songs from this album.

Open The Door, Homer
(written by Bob Dylan)

It certainly sounds to me like Bob is singing the name "Richard" and not "Homer" during this song. I'm not sure why it was changed; perhaps out of deference to The Band's Richard Manuel. Maybe Bob didn't want to make him self-conscious. According to the official lyrics on bobdylan.com he is really singing about Homer. Of course, the fact there was a hit song back in the forties under the title "Open The Door, Richard" may have encouraged Dylan to re-title the song, although the two songs don't seem very related. I don't think the song is really about the Greek poet Homer either. This is one of the few songs that has three whole takes devoted to it. The first take is actually the best as its more upbeat. The second take doesn't even really get all the way through the song. They do finish a somewhat lethargic third take, but they seem to be having a hard time keeping a straight face during this song. The song itself isn't hilarious per se, but there are lots of weird characters floating this song, much like "Tiny Montgomery" or "Please Mrs. Henry". I love the line about flushing out your house, but I have no idea what it means. The song has some lovely harmonies on the chorus. It bops along quite merrily considering no drums are carrying this track. Certainly, one of the better originals that was actually written (and not ad-libbed) during *The Basement Tapes*. Not a grand artistic statement, but it is generally silly fun which is where these sessions really excel.

Long Distance Operator
(written by Bob Dylan)

See entry under *Highway 61 Revisited*.

This Wheel's On Fire
(written by Bob Dylan and Rick Danko)

A dark haunting song to end the album on. One of the few co-writes that Dylan has done at this point, you can see how Rick Danko honored the spirit of the lyrics with minor chords that Bob himself might not have thought of. I like the way the whole chorus builds up to the final word of "explode" where everything is let loose. Very apropos. I have no idea why there is a flaming tire here or why our memory might not serve us well, but this is a great song. Someone's playing drums here, which is nice even if they are a bit rudimentary. There are some great harmonies on the chorus, and the organ adds a bit of a dark circus vibe to the whole affair. I have even less of an idea why the cover of this song by Julie Driscoll and Brian Augur was used as the theme to *Absolutely Fabulous*. Maybe I'm missing something. Whatever it is, this is still one of the better *Basement Tapes* songs.

Songs not on the album:
Quinn The Eskimo (The Mighty Quinn) from *Biograph*
(written by Bob Dylan)
One of the first and biggest hits of the songs covered from *The Basement Tapes* that helped create the legend. Manfred Mann's 1968 version of this song reached #1 in the UK Single Chart. As such, this song's non-inclusion on the 1975 version of *The Basement Tapes* is somewhat surprising. I guess one could argue that the song was already released by Dylan on 1970's *Self-Portrait*, albeit in a live incarnation from the Isle Of Wight. However, Bob's inclusion of this otherwise unreleased song during his big festival comeback was probably due to the popularity of Manfred Mann's cover. Why the *Basement* tune "Minstrel Boy" was also debuted at the Isle Of Wight is harder to speculate. The live version is rough but amusing. Bob misses a lyric or two (I love the way he sings "Everybody's building .... boats") and the guitar solo begins with an ear-splintering squeal of feedback before being corralled into a manageable shape by Robbie Robertson. The *Basement* recording is also rough but amusing. The lyrics are silly gibberish that some have interpreted to be about Jesus, and others turned into a 1989 Denzel Washington movie. There are two versions on *The Bootleg Series vol. 11*. The first version is a little slower and more lifeless. The second version was the one that first appeared on the 1985 box-set *Biograph*. The music is mostly just two chords repeated over and over with a third thrown in for a change at the end of each verse. The chorus undeniable catchy, if challenging to decipher. The song swings gently without having any drums to propel it. It's a pleasant enough track, and a somewhat surprising song to have ended up as such a success.

I Shall Be Released from *The Bootleg Series vol. 2*
(written by Bob Dylan)
The other significant, startling omission from the 1975 version of *The Basement Tapes* this song was re-made and featured as a proto-bonus track on *Greatest Hits, vol. II* in 1970, but was first heard on The Band's 1968 debut, *Music From Big Pink*. The song had already been covered by Joan Baez, The Byrds, and Peter, Paul & Mary by the time *The Basement Tapes* came out in 1975, so you think they would've included it. Even Elvis Presley attempted recording a version. It is especially frustrating since it was presumably cut by Robbie Robertson to make room for the non-Dylan tracks on the double-album. Heck, a year later, during *The Last Waltz*, The Band saw fit to play this song with Bob, but couldn't make room for it on the official release of *The Basement Tapes*. This is one of the songs that even merited a second take during the original Basement sessions. Both takes feature some lovely high harmonies from one of The Band members that

are barely on this side of being annoying. The first take has Dylan stumbling on a few lyrics, which may be why there was a second run-through attempted with the same tempo and arrangement. It is a lovely anthem with a strong melody, and it is easy to see why this was the song on the original acetate that so many artists were drawn to cover from that initial batch of tunes.

Santa-Fe from *The Bootleg Series vol. 2*
(written by Bob Dylan)

While many fans were disappointed by the non-appearance of "Quinn The Eskimo" and "I Shall Be Released" from the original *Basement Tapes*, no one was really chomping at the bit to get an official release of this song when it made its debut on *The Bootleg Series, vol. 2*. It's inclusion at this early date may have had more to do with proving that the bootleggers hadn't uncovered everything rather than the actual quality of "Santa-Fe". Not that the song is annoying or anything, it's just given the quality of the stuff that hadn't been released from *The Basement Tapes* this was a surprising addition. The sound quality is one of the weaker of these songs. There's actual drumming on this song, which is nice even if it is just a snare that is audible. The lyrics are inscrutable as usual, but the melody is pretty catchy. The piano is sweet, even if the bass is over-playing for such a musically simple song. It doesn't really go anywhere, but it never offends while it is here. Just a hair over two minutes, it certainly doesn't overstay its welcome.

I'm Not There from the *I'm Not There* soundtrack
(written by Bob Dylan)

I would say this is the best song Bob ever wrote, except I'm not entirely sure he really ever wrote it. He certainly didn't finish writing it. What we have here sounds like Dylan was making it up on the spot, and giving another revision or two this could've been brilliantly transcendent or disappointingly neutered, depending. It's clear Bob hasn't settled on the chord pattern until the second or third verse through. The lyrics are mostly mumbles, which Dylanologists have spent more time attempting to transcribe than Bob has ever spent thinking about them. For a long time, when this song appeared on bootlegs, it carried the subtitle (1956) which still doesn't make any sense to me. Despite its relative obscurity (and the fact it was never released), this tune does make the perfect title track to Todd Haynes' impressionistic biopic. The song is heart-rending and full of hurt and sorrow and something that can't quite be pinned down or described. The bass does an amazing job keeping up with the ever-shifting chord structure while still being interesting and providing a melodic counterpoint. Given its half-formed nature, it's not a surprise that this wasn't on the shortlist of songs included on the 1975 release, but its inarguable quality has kept it legend alive until it finally saw official release.

This is a song that could never be replicated, and certainly seems like Bob never attempted a second take, or even finished writing it – although some have argued that the Bono co-write, "Love Rescue Me" is in fact derived from this original source. I don't hear it personally, which is good news, because I can't stand U2.

Minstrel Boy from *The Bootleg Series vol. 10*
(written by Bob Dylan)

The inclusion of the unreleased "Quinn The Eskimo" in the set-list for the 1969 Isle Of Wight Festival set-list and the subsequent release of the live track on 1970's *Self-Portrait* makes some sense. The song had been a hit in England for Manfred Mann. The addition of "Minstrel Boy" is far more startling. The song was not covered by anyone since it was not on the widely circulated acetate of *The Basement Tapes* or any of the bootlegs of the time. In fact, for a long time, there was some debate as to whether this song was technically a part of the *Basement* sessions or something newly penned for the event. While the number of classics overlooked by Dylan for official release in favor of relatively weaker tracks has plagued all of the premieres of *Basement* songs, the fact that this minor trifle was one of the first things we heard Dylan do in any legally obtainable fashion is baffling. Not that's there's anything wrong with this song, it's just that's there's nothing to it at all. I can't imagine what The Band thought when Bob brought it up in rehearsals for the show. Did they even remember it amongst all the other songs they blazed through during that summer? Most of the song is just a single acoustic guitar strumming while everyone harmonizes. When we get to the only verse, the bass begins to play along with the piano tentatively picking out a few notes before everyone drops back for the second chorus. The bass sounds ready to come back in for the second verse, but the second verse never happens. Luckily the live version isn't just one verse sandwiched between two choruses, and features far more instrumentation throughout, although it still opens nearly a cappella with everyone singing the chorus. We get two whole verses plus a guitar solo, that like several numbers from this set nearly succumbs to feedback. Who knows what the audience was thinking when they first heard this. Bob doesn't give it any sort of introduction. They probably just assumed it was a traditional folk tune that they weren't familiar with. The live version is taken at a much slower and freer tempo that the half-tossed off that finally saw release on *The Bootleg Series vol. 10*. There's nothing remotely contemporary in the lyrics, even if their meaning is somewhat obscure. Certainly, the whole concept of minstrels was already old-fashioned by 1969. There have been some suggestions that Lucky, the minstrel boy in the lyrics is a stand-in for Dylan himself. It's possible, but I'm not really sure if it's worth digging into it to find out. This is a perfectly pleasant but lightweight song. Any additional thought on the subject only gets in the way of the meager pleasures it has to offer.

I Don't Hurt Anymore from *The Bootleg Series vol. 11*
(written by Donald I. Robertson and Walter E Rollins)

Another pre-*Nashville Skyline* dip into country music. Without the usual pedal steel and fiddle to indicate the typical trappings of the genre, this almost comes off as an average blues rock number. Bob hasn't reverted to his Nashville croon style voice, giving this song a bit more edge. There's a harmony going throughout that doesn't seem 100% on all the lyrics. The lack of drums does threaten to have the song fall apart during the instrumental break, but somehow the Band pulls it through. Dylan's guitar is pretty out-of-tune, but it's more charming than distracting. Had people heard this when it was recorded, the country tendencies might've come as a shock. However, by this point, everyone is well aware of this facet of Bob's inspirations. As a result, there's not much else worth noting about this track.

Dress It Up, Better Have It All from *The Bootleg Series vol. 11*
(written by Bob Dylan)

While Bob may have written several great songs during *The Basement Tapes*, he also made up a bunch that are clearly not written in advance at all. This is pretty simple three-chord rock'n'roll that The Band can pull off without much effort. Luckily there are some drums here as the song doesn't have much else going on and needs that driving rhythm to keep it going. Despite being less than three minutes, there are plenty of solos, most of which are accompanied by some of Bob's stranger exhortations (play it for Bozo?). There's a couple of stop breaks in here, that make the song a little more tricky to play, although after the first one nearly fall apart, the Band gets a feel for them pretty quickly. I have no idea what Dylan is singing about here. I'm pretty sure that Bob also has no idea what he's singing here. While it is usually the slower songs that show of the strength of *The Basement Tapes*, it is good to have more rocking numbers like that to keep the whole project from getting too mopey or stale. It may not be a great song by itself, but within this context, it is elevated to the status of relief.

Johnny Todd from *The Bootleg Series vol. 11*
(traditional, arranged by Bob Dylan)

A traditional, old tune given a half-Calypso treatment despite the fact the lyrics reference Liverpool. The piano sparkles and the electric guitar does some nice picking behind the acoustic. It sounds like Bob is taking this song a lot more seriously than most of *The Basement Tapes* and this inspires The Band to try a little harder. There's a nice little guitar solo before the song quits just after two minutes. It's a pleasant enough tune, but hearing Dylan doing traditional folk is hardly surprising making this track far less remarkable than most of the random covers thrown during these sessions. Definitely, one that wouldn't hurt to skip.

Get Your Rocks Off from *The Bootleg Series vol. 11*
(written by Bob Dylan)

A dirty blues song, which is appropriate given the double entendre of the chorus/title. Much like "Please Mrs. Henry", the subtlety of the smuttiness depends a lot on whether or not your mind is in the gutter. While this sounds more thought-out than "All American Boy" or "I'm Your Teenage Prayer" we are still treated to the occasional bass voice interjections. There's not much to this song as it repeats itself musically, so your enjoyment depends a lot on how funny to find the punchline of "get your rocks off of me." The scenarios depicted in the verses are neither terribly explicit nor innocent, and in fact mostly just sound random. Bob starts laughing at one point, but the line "one man says to the other man" doesn't really reveal why this struck Dylan so funny at that moment. The slow groove of the song is great, but otherwise, this is probably more fun to record in the moment than to come back to and listen to over and over. Not to disparage the song; this is definitely the kind of silly humor that *The Basement Tapes* excels at. Surprisingly Both Manfred Mann's Earth Band and Coulson Dean McGuinness Flint in the early seventies. Both take the song way too seriously, burying whatever offhand pleasures the song initially had.

Silent Weekend from *The Bootleg Series vol. 11*
(written by Bob Dylan)

Another blues song – this one far less dirty. Even though the lyrics seem to be about a poor henpecked husband being given the cold shoulder by his wife, the music sounds almost celebratory. The narrator is looking forward to Monday, which he expects will brings some thawing in their relations, although where he gets this certainty is hard to say. Although this is a pretty straightforward three-chord blues for most of the song, there is a bridge that goes into some new territory. This change seems to surprise The Band almost as much as it does the listener. Musically, this is a more exciting and fast-paced version of "Get Your Rocks Off", but lyrically it is not nearly as amusing. Not a great song, but certainly a fun one.

All You Have To Do Is Dream from *The Bootleg Series vol. 11*
(written by Bob Dylan)

This is not the 1958 Everly Brothers hit, "All I Have To Do Is Dream". This is one of the later *Basement* recordings as we have someone behind the drum kit here. Bob actually attempted this song twice, with similar arrangements but in two differ rent keys. However, after these, the song seems to have been pretty much forgotten by Dylan. It is a lovely song, with some nice volume pedal use with the guitar solo by Robbie Robertson. I'm not entirely sure what the lyrics mean. You start by talking about "floor-birds" and the farmer with his silo, blah blah blah, I'm just going to tune out and enjoy the music instead. Still, this is one of the more thoroughly composed and thought-out of the *Basement* songs. The second take is taken at a little too fast of a tempo, with the last note of the chorus held out to an exaggerated length. Since this is one of the shorter songs, I actually prefer the slower feel of take one. Either way, though this song is easily as strong as the best of *The Basement Tapes* and deserves to be as enshrined as "I Shall Be Released", "Quinn The Eskimo", or "You Ain't Goin' Nowhere".

900 Miles From My Home from *The Bootleg Series vol. 11*
(traditional, arranged by Bob Dylan)

Not the song "900 Miles" by Woody Guthrie, but a different tune about that same amount of distance. This traditional song seems to have originated from a 1924 recording by Fiddlin' John Carson. This is the kind of plaintive proto-Americana with tons of harmony that would soon become The Band's stock-in-trade. Bob's version adds a bit of an island lilt, which is a nice touch. The drums are playing on this song, but are so low in the mix they might have been in the next room while they recorded this song. Neither organ or piano are terribly audible here, making this song a little more stripped down than some of the other Basement songs. Still, the song sparkles with a nice propulsive rhythm. It's a quick run-through of the song that ends with a cheeky cha-cha-cha ending. Maybe not the most striking of the covers from *The Basement Tapes*, this is still a lovely little gem.

One For The Road from *The Bootleg Series vol. 11*
(written by Bob Dylan)

A slow ballad with a little hint of blues. The prominent, if unimpressive piano leads on to surmise that it is Dylan himself on the keys. There's an electric guitar playing some arpeggios while a bass holds down the bottom simply. After about a minute, an organ and acoustic guitar join in. The song sounds like it's intended to be a tearjerker – or possibly it's merely a parody of a tearjerker. It's hard to tell precisely how sincere Dylan is here. I don't believe the song has been covered by any other artist who has either ignored or emphasized the potential irony here. While it is passably evocative, there's nothing particular special going on here. It seems like the kind of song that would be used as an encore by some un-self-aware Vegas hack, but never entirely comes across. It's perfectly perfunctory, but not terribly remarkable.

I'm Alright from *The Bootleg Series vol. 11*
(written by Bob Dylan)

A short piano-based blues tune. The harmonized chorus has some potential, but this song is far from finished. Bob is singing about a three-time loser, but seem optimistic nonetheless. Unlike anything else on *the Basement Tapes* for some reason, this song fades out at the end. Who knows how much more was written or finished of this song. It's pretty good, but it's no "I'm Not There" where the incompleteness is something of a frustrating tragedy. Certainly, Bob could've turned this into something special, but its hard to see what it would've been with just this fragment.

Folsom Prison Blues from *The Bootleg Series vol. 11*
(written by Johnny Cash)

While *The Basement Tapes* version of this song is the only one officially released, I am far more interested in the version attempted in a real Nashville studio in 1969. This song is possibly even more obvious and well-known than "Ring Of Fire" which was also tried during these sessions. I'm not sure whose idea it was to have the song end by speeding up to the point of falling apart, but it is one of the more unusual and strange turns in a Dylan recording. Bob was clearly putting in a good faith effort to record a straightforward, strictly commercial, middle-of-the-road type country album here. However, this wasn't Dylan's first trip to this particular rodeo. Bob had also attempted this song (along with several less well-known Johnny Cash songs) during *The Basement Tapes* sessions. That version is one of the more effective covers recorded in the basement that summer. While it would've been nice if they had a drummer while they were doing this song, it still rocks pretty hard. While I will give the nod to the country song that was actually recorded in Nashville, the basement version is pretty good. Dylan must've sympathized with the idea of being stuck someplace he didn't want to be and wishing he could be an anonymous train passenger. It's a shame that this song was left off *The Bootleg Series vol. 10*. Had it been included, this volume of the bootleg series would've been far more in keeping with the spirit of the original *Self-Portrait*.

Baby, Won't You Be My Baby? from *The Bootleg Series vol. 11*
(written by Bob Dylan)

While *The Basement Tapes* contain many drunken taking-the-piss-out types songs, most of these ("All American Boy", "I'm Your Teenage Prayer", etc.) did not make the cut for the two-disc "raw" version of *The Bootleg Series vol. 11* and instead were relegated to the 6-disc "complete" version. This is one of the more straightforward and listenable of these parodies and pastiches, so it's not surprising. There are not even any vocal asides from other Band members throwing the song into chaos or at least tangents. Instead, it's a type of satire of a rock song that seems like it was written by someone who doesn't understand it fully (like Allan Sherman or Stan Freberg). The repetition of the word "baby" in the chorus and title is mildly amusing, but not enough to build a whole song around. As a song, it's a minor song. As a goof, it's a toothless joke. It's not harmful or irritating or anything, but there's not much to it.

Sign On The Cross from *The Bootleg Series vol. 11*
(written by Bob Dylan)

Frequently cited by many as one of the best songs from *The Basement Tapes*, I don't get the appeal of this track at all. The song is not meant sincerely. We have plenty of evidence of what Bob sounds like when he's really preaching from '79-'81, and it doesn't sound like this. But if it's meant to be a joke, Dylan's not saying anything humorous or exaggerated or satirical in any way. It's a straight-faced and straight-laced parody. As an insincere facsimile of a sermon, it might've been enjoyable for a minute or two, but this stretches on for over seven minutes. There's no chorus or verse or bridge or anything repeated musically here; just a bed of faux-gospel music on top of which Bob rants on and on. While most of *the Basement Tapes* songs are merely tantalizing fragments, even the most complete of the songs rarely take more than four-and-a-half minutes. Yet here, Dylan feels comfortable here just letting the tape roll forever. It starts out boring at first and only grows more excruciating as it rambles on aimlessly. I know a lot of people love this, but this is one of my least favorite Dylan tracks.

Songs released on *The Bootleg Series vol. 11: The Basement Tapes – Complete* that were not included on *The Bootleg Series vol. 11: The Basement Tapes – Raw:*

Edge of the Ocean
(written by Bob Dylan)
Roll On Train
(written by Bob Dylan)
Under Control
(written by Bob Dylan)
I'm Guilty of Loving You
(written by Bob Dylan)
I'm a Fool For You
(written by Bob Dylan)
See You Later Allen Ginsberg
(written by Bob Dylan)
Big Dog
(written by Bob Dylan)
I'm Your Teenage Prayer
(written by Bob Dylan)
One Man's Loss
(written by Bob Dylan)

Lock Your Door
(written by Bob Dylan)
Try Me Little Girl
(written by Bob Dylan)
I Can't Make It Alone
(written by Bob Dylan)
Don't You Try Me Now
(written by Bob Dylan)
Bourbon Street
(written by Bob Dylan)
It Ain't Me Babe
(written by Bob Dylan)
My Woman She's A-Leavin'
(written by Bob Dylan)
Mary Lou, I Love You Too
(written by Bob Dylan)
What's It Gonna Be When It Comes Up
(written by Bob Dylan)

It's the Flight of the Bumblebee
(written by Bob Dylan)
Wild Wolf
(written by Bob Dylan)
Gonna Get You Now
(written by Bob Dylan)
2 Dollars and 99 Cents
(written by Bob Dylan)
Jelly Bean
(written by Bob Dylan)
Any Time
(written by Bob Dylan)
Down By the Station
(written by Bob Dylan)
That's the Breaks
(written by Bob Dylan)
Pretty Mary
(written by Bob Dylan)
King of France
(written by Bob Dylan)
She's On My Mind Again
(written by Bob Dylan)
On a Rainy Afternoon
(written by Bob Dylan)
I Can't Come In With a Broken Heart
(written by Bob Dylan)
Next Time On the Highway
(written by Bob Dylan)
Northern Claim
(written by Bob Dylan)
Love is Only Mine
(written by Bob Dylan)
Bring It On Home
(written by Bob Dylan)
The Spanish Song
(written by Bob Dylan)
Ol' Roison the Beau
(traditional, arranged by Bob Dylan)
Po' Lazarus
(traditional, arranged by Bob Dylan)
Kickin' My Dog Around
(traditional, arranged by Bob Dylan)
Young But Daily Growing
(traditional, arranged by Bob Dylan)
Bonnie Ship the Diamond
(traditional, arranged by Bob Dylan)
The Hills of Mexico
(traditional, arranged by Bob Dylan)
Down On Me
(traditional, arranged by Bob Dylan)
One Kind Favor
(traditional, arranged by Bob Dylan)
She'll Be Coming Round the Mountain
(traditional, arranged by Bob Dylan)
Hallelujah, I've Just Been Moved
(traditional, arranged by Bob Dylan)
Goin' Down the Road Feeling Bad
(traditional, arranged by Bob Dylan)
Come All Ye Fair and Tender Ladies
(traditional, arranged by Bob Dylan)
Mr. Blue
(written by DeWayne Blackwell)
Big River
(written by Johnny Cash)
Belshazzar
(written by Johnny Cash)
I Forgot To Remember To Forget
(written by Charlie Feather and Stanley Kesler)
You Win Again
(written by Hank Williams and Hiriam Williams)
Still In Town
(written by Hank Cochran and Harlan Howard)
Waltzing With Sin
(written by Sonny Burns and Red Hayes)
Bells of Rhymney
(written by Idris Davies and Pete Seeger)
Spanish is the Loving Tongue
(written by Charles Badger Clark)
Cool Water
(written by Bob Nolan)
The Auld Triangle
(written by Brendan Francis Behan)
Tupelo
(written by John Lee Hooker)
Four Strong Winds
(written by Ian Tyson)
The French Girl
(written by Ian Tyson and Sylvia Tyson)
Joshua Gone Barbados
(written by Eric Von Schmidt)
I'm In the Mood
(written by Bernard Besman and John Lee Hooker)

Baby Ain't That Fine
(written by Dallas Frazier)
Rock, Salt and Nails
(written by Bruce Phillips)
A Fool Such As I
(written by William Trader)
Song For Canada
(written by Pete Gzowski and Ian Tyson)
People Get Ready
(written by Curtis Mayfield)
Be Careful of Stones That You Throw
(written by Benjamin Lee Blakenship and Benjamin Lee Blankenship)
All American Boy
(written by Bobby Bare)
A Satisfied Mind
(written by Joe Hayes and Jack Rhodes)
Wildwood Flower
(written by A.P. Carter)
If I Were a Carpenter
(written by James Timothy Hardi)
Confidential
(written by Dorina Morgan)
Will the Circle Be Unbroken
(written by A.P. Carter)
Silhouettes
(written by Bob Crewe, Frank C. Slay, Jr., and Frank Slay)
My Bucket's Got a Hole In It
(written by Clarence Williams)

In addition to "Folsom Prison Blues", here we see the first appearance of several covers that Bob would return to over the years: "A Fool Such As I" was recorded during the 1969 Nashville sessions for *Self-Portrait* as was "Spanish Is The Loving Tongue" which got re-done a third time for the B-side for the "Watching The River Flow" single and a fourth time during the *Blood On The Tracks* sessions. Also, we have "A Satisfied Mind" which was re-done for *Saved* in 1980 and "People Get Ready" which was recorded for the *Feeling Minnesota* soundtrack in 1990. There are some great songs on here with Bob switching up and playing the autoharp and the electric piano. Unfortunately, these songs are all so poorly recorded they are difficult to enjoy and are really interesting from an academic viewpoint. There's a lot of good songs on here, some I even used for my personal *Basement Tapes* comp, but there are just a lot of songs here total. Some are real full-fledged songs, and some are half-formed jams that got taped to which titles got applied after the fact. It was just too gargantuan of a task to go through and find something new to say about all of these.

"TOO MUCH OF NOTHING WAS DELIVERED"

SIDE A:
1. Too Much Of Nothing
2. Nothing Was Delivered
3. Belshazzar
4. Odds And Ends
5. Clothes Line Saga
6. Song For Canada
7. Tears Of Rage

SIDE B:
1. Dress It Up, Better Have It All
2. Goin' To Acapulco
3. Tiny Montgomery
4. Yea Heavy And A Bottle Of Bread
5. Million Dollar Bash
6. Lo And Behold
7. Get Your Rocks Off

SIDE C:
1. Please Mrs. Henry
2. Auld Triangle
3. Santa-Fe
4. Wild Wolf
5. If I Were A Carpenter
6. Silent Weekend
7. She'll Be Coming 'Round The Mountain

SIDE D:
1. All You Have To Do Is Dream
2. Don't You Tell Henry
3. Big River
4. I'm Not There
5. Quinn The Eskimo (The Mighty Quinn)
6. People Get Ready
7. This Wheel's On Fire

Much like *The Freewheelin' Bob Dylan* there is enough material recording during these sessions to make at least three albums. And also, like *Freewheelin'* these songs can roughly be split into three categories: original songs, covers, and funny goofs. I had initially thought about making one whole side of this just silly throwaways:

1. I'm Your Teenage Prayer
2. See You Later Allen Ginsberg
3. Baby Won't You Be My Baby
4. The Spanish Song
5. All American Boy
6. It's The Flight Of The Bumble Bee
7. Silhouettes

I wasn't sure how much replayability there is in those songs – especially all massed together. I did make sure to include some of the more fun originals like "Don't Ya Tell Henry" and "Get Your Rocks Off" so that there would be a good example of some of the humor that went into making this album. I also wanted to make sure there were plenty of covers included to break up that long drought of non-original material between *Bob Dylan* and *Self-Portrait*. This might have helped people prepare, so they're not as surprised when *Self-Portrait* comes out. I also wanted to try and avoid songs that would end up re-recorded for other projects. This not only included the originals done with Happy Traum for *Greatest Hits, vol. II* but covers like "A Satisfied Mind", "A Fool Such As I", and "Folsom Prison Blues".

From there the biggest challenge was deciding whether to do a one-, two-, or three-record set. While there's a lot of good stuff in here – most of it tends to blend together if you create too long of an album. Unlike *The Freewheelin' Bob Dylan*, there are no clear chronological guidelines to help divide this up into separate pieces. All these songs sound of apiece so dividing them into different records didn't make sense. In the end, I went with a double album set since that most closely mirrored the original 1975 release of this material. Really, one LP would've been too short and left too much good stuff off. But a triple album is almost never a great idea (see *Triplicate*) as that would just get too overwhelming to listen to as a single piece of art.

When compiling a song list, there is a temptation to use only the songs and recordings that seemed the most complete, but I think that would've undermined that original intent of these off-the-cuff, goofing-off sessions. It's a trick finding the right balance. What was easy to decide was to ignore any and all of the latter-day recording by The Band alone. Even if I did like them, they wouldn't fit in here at all.

I tried to create a flow throughout the album, while not getting too bogged down in any one of the three categories of songs for too long of a stretch. However, the thought process behind which songs I picked or what order I put them in is a little indistinct and continuously in flux. Which I think is an appropriate way to look at *The Basement Tapes* period in general.

JOHN WESLEY HARDING

Produced by: Bob Johnston
Recorded: October 17th - November 29th, 1967
Released: December 27th, 1967
Famous/Important/Popular Track(s):
- All Along The Watchtower
- I'll Be Your Baby Tonight

My Personal Favorite Track(s):
- All Along The Watchtower
- The Wicked Messenger

Much as one would expect Bob to start *Bringing It All Back Home* with the acoustic side rather than the electric, one would've anticipated Dylan to have slowly dipped his toes into the world of rock'n'roll with arrangements closer to this: acoustic guitar and harmonica backed with bass and drums. Instead, we waited until after his quote-unquote electric period to finish before trying this halfway arrangement between the solo acoustic sound of his first four albums and the full-throttle sound of the next four.

Of course, Bob had initially intended to Robbie Robertson and Al Kooper to overdub organ and electric guitar on these songs. But Robbie and Al refused, claiming that it was unnecessary. Hearing the versions of "I Pity The Poor Immigrant" and "I Dreamed I Saw St. Augustine" live with the Band at the Isle of Wight festival, it is hard to disagree with them. Only "I'll Be Your Baby Tonight" doesn't sound trampled by the larger ensemble.

Then again, Dylan didn't just take the best tracks from his recently completed *Basement Tapes* project and re-do them in a professional studio with acoustic guitars for an official release. Listen to the tracks he recorded for *Greatest Hits vol. II* with Happy Traum for an idea how that might've sounded. But for whatever reason, Bob was not interested in doing that either. At least not yet.

What we get instead is one of the less drastic shifts in Dylan's career up to this point. This is no means like plugging in for *Bringing It All Back Home*. This is more like the subtle change that occurred between *The Times They Are A-Changin'* and *Another Side Of Bob Dylan*. And much like that slight pivot, the main difference is in the lyrics. On *John Wesley Harding*, the words are still just as abstract and confounding as ever, only now, instead of merely being a series of surreal lines, Bob is trying to tell a complete story here. There may not be a lot of concrete details or characterizations, but each song has its own plot and narrative through-lines. Bob has dabbled in songs like this before, like most of the "Talkin' Blues" and he would continue to write songs like this after such as "Lily, Rosemary, & The Jack Of Hearts". But this is the first time that Dylan has constructed an entire album around these parables and morality plays.

The sound of the album is very stark and austere, which kind of forces the lyrics to become the focal point. It is particularly telling that this album came out after *Sgt. Pepper* and the summer of love in the height of the psychedelic sounds of '67. But even without that context, it is hard not to hear this album as extremely economical and stripped down. Weirdly, it feels even less extravagant than Bob's first four solo albums, as the starkness of the instrumentation feels more like a deliberate choice, while those acoustic-guitar-only albums felt more varied in texture and were stuck in the solo mode more out of necessity than a desire to pare things down.

Unfortunately, this bleak sonic palette does make it harder for me to really get caught up in the experience of this album, and though I will admit I admire *John Wesley Harding* a lot, it's not a record I spin very frequently.

John Wesley Harding
(written by Bob Dylan)

First things first, the phrase "a gun in every hand"... I am assuming this guy only has two hands. If not, you have left a crucial detail out of this story, Bob. Of course, I know "every" has more syllables than "both," and Dylan needed that to fit in the lyrics, but it still is super-distracting every time I hear it. I'm not sure what it is that John did that was so noteworthy. He opened many a door, but we're not sure for whom. He took a stand, but he doesn't say for what. But whatever it was the situation was straightened out quickly. Whatever the situation was. He seems good. He's a friend of the poor, and he never hurts honest men. He doesn't make foolish moves, but what exactly does John Wesley Harding do? He is famous, but for what? He is often accused of stuff but is never convicted. Is that because he didn't actually do anything – or does he just have a good lawyer? It almost sounds like a story, but there's no plot. Nothing happens. It's just a description of the guy. It's all super vague. But it does quickly establish the sonic template for the album that follows. The only guitar is a single acoustic. There's a lot of harmonica and a burbling bass that is easy to pay attention to now that the instrumentation is so uncluttered. The drums are straight-forward. The vocals have much less rasp and far more warble.

As I Went Out One Morning
(written by Bob Dylan)

The phrase "I told her with my voice" is not nearly as weird and clunky (and presumably deliberate) as talking about having a gun in every hand, but it is close. The lyrics are trying to tell a story. Bob is out walking when he tries to rescue a woman who is presumably captured by someone named Tom Paine. Only it turns out the woman betrays him and attempt to harm our narrator. Bob turns the tables on her, and she offers to "secretly accept him" if he will let her go. All of this is scuttled once her captor Tom Paine returns to rescue the singer. Tom apologizes, and that is the end of the story. Maybe this all has some symbolism that I'm meaning, but it really feels like nothing more than a surreal parody of all those murder folk ballads that Bob loves singing. Plus it's not a very long song so you can enjoy the weird ride. Bob's acoustic guitar is very minimal here, so the bass steps up and tries to fill the space by being extra funky. There's no chorus or bridge or anything other than three verses alternating with short harmonica breaks. Overall a harmless but unremarkable track.

I Dreamed I Saw St. Augustine
(written by Bob Dylan)

There are a lot of harmonica notes played in rapid succession to open this somewhat laid-back country-feeling number. I don't know a lot about my saints, so I don't really understand the story or import of St. Augustine. It wouldn't surprise me to find that the Augustine referenced within these lyrics has little relation to any actual specific saints. It's more a song about regret for not standing up for what you believe... I guess. It aims to be touching, but nothing here really connects. The bass burbles along pleasantly. This is some of Dylan's most impressive if not impassioned harmonica playing, and there's about as much harmonica soloing as there is actual singing. It is pleasant, but nothing worth getting excited over.

All Along the Watchtower
(written by Bob Dylan)

This is the track that most people know this album for – and not even because of anything Bob did with it. Dylan never released this song (or any from *John Wesley Harding*) as a single but has kept it in rotation in his live set-list almost continuously since he returned to touring in the 1970s. It's not hard to see why, but even Bob will admit that his live performances of this song owe more to Jimi Hendrix's version than his own. Although we have all gotten used to that song as full band electric encore, it is always a little jarring to go back to the stripped-down acoustic original. Still, as incongruous as it is, this is the better version. It's exciting to go back and listen for the possibilities that Hendrix first heard in this recording. The chords are super simple; just three chords; practically begging this song to be covered by any aspiring garage band. Bob's harmonica wails, and while the acoustic guitar is merely strumming, the bass hints at the potential funk inherent in this song. Given the ubiquity of this song, it is hard to really hear this song with fresh ears and re-appreciate it. Luckily the *John Wesley Harding* version is always around to remind us of what this song can do.

The Ballad of Frankie Lee and Judas Priest
(written by Bob Dylan)

This is not exactly the kind of sound one associates with Judas Priest. The lyrics are odd, just on the verge of telling a coherent narrative. But some turns of phrase, just throw the whole thing off. Was Frankie Lee deciding how much money to borrow from Judas Priest or was there something specific about the serial numbers or some other reason why he had to choose between those dollar bills? Why would anyone call a home down the road with twenty-four women lined in the windows "paradise"? And if someone did, why should it bother anyone? Don't they have indoor plumbing or at least a well? If someone could die of thirst there, why didn't everyone? And how long did Frankie Lee spend picking money? Why would it take him long enough for someone to die of thirst? Or was Judas Priest already severely parched? This story was obviously meant to be metaphorical and not literal, but I have no idea what Dylan is trying to say. I almost get the feeling on this track that he is slyly making fun of anyone who is trying to decipher a deeper meaning out of his lyrics. Musically this song is just three repeating chords with no hook or chorus or bridge. It has a slight country tinge to the whole proceeding, but very folky too. It almost feels like a parody of a western. The backing is appropriately austere, as are most of the songs on this album. It's somewhat up, with a sly wink implied. To me, this is the *John Wesley Harding* song that comes closest to the style of *The Basement Tapes*.

Drifter's Escape
(written by Bob Dylan)

Oddly enough, this song isn't actually told from the POV of the drifter in question. It's hard to say who the narrator is in this case. The only mention of him is that he hears the drifter say "Help me in my weakness". So is the narrator the one who provided the lightning bolt that ending up freeing the drifter? Does that mean this song sung from God's point-of-view? Or Zeus's? Again a lot of questions are raised by a story that at first seems far more straight-forward than Bob's usual gobbledygook. What did the drifter do that was so weak and caused the town to put him on trial? Was the drifter framed? Is he innocent? Is the judge crying because he feels sorry for the drifter, or because of the crimes the drifter was accused of? Did the lightning cause structural damage to the courthouse? Are we talking about Hank Williams's alter ego Luke the Drifter here? Musically the song is relatively upbeat. The arrangement and instrumentation are standard *John Wesley Harding*; lots of harmonica solos, burbling bass, acoustic guitar, and drums. There is no chorus or even refrain repeated in this song. It clocks in under three minutes. Like many of the songs on this album, it is fine, but unremarkable. Especially if you don't get caught up in trying to unravel the plot.

Dear Landlord
(written by Bob Dylan)

The lyrics to this song are frequently interpreted to be about Dylan's manager, Allen Grossman. This may be true. I don't know what Bob's intent was here. However, there is nothing in this song that links it up specifically to anything autobiographical. Bob's voice seems to be wavering between forgiving and angry but mostly landing on pleading. Dylan trades his acoustic guitar for the piano on this song giving the whole thing a deeper and funkier texture than most of the *John Wesley Harding* tracks. It's interesting here that Bob is pleading for mercy, not from a divine figure or even magistrate of the court. Bob is trying to reason with a private citizen here, while this person is in a position of power in determining Dylan's fate, he has no real authority per se. It's an interesting twist on the usual "not going to work on Maggie's farm no more" dynamic. Bob is able to relate to the landlord in question as another human being like himself. He tries to show the landlord that they're not so different, but this realization comes as much of a surprise to bob as it does the song's subject. Ultimately though, this song does go anywhere beyond "please don't evict me, I need a few weeks to get together the rent". Not an exciting narrative, but a reasonably fun song.

I Am a Lonesome Hobo
(written by Bob Dylan)

Not surprising given Dylan's love of Woody Guthrie's <u>Bound For Glory</u>, but hoboes turn up a lot in Bob's songs. The standard *John Wesley Harding* template is in place, funky bass, acoustic guitar, and drums with plenty of helpings of harmonica. More of a character sketch than a full-narrative story. It sounds like a cautionary tale, but the fatal flaw that Dylan posits for bringing him to this lowly state is a lack of trust in his brother and suffering from petty jealousies, but nothing is spelled out that says how are why this took him down from having gold teeth and silk clothes. Even the moral of the song is kind of vague, so it's hard to take much of a lesson from it. Live by no man's code? Hold your judgment for yourself? These might be valuable lessons, but I don't really know what they mean. Given how much Bob generally lionizes hoboes, it seems that his comeuppance here is far more in the "lonesome" than in the "hobo" part of this song. I'm not sure why the protagonist here hasn't served time for begging on the street; is he too proud to stoop so low and would instead resort to a life of petty crime? Or has he just been lucky that he's never been caught (or convicted) of panhandling? All in all, a perfectly fine but unremarkable track from this album.

I Pity the Poor Immigrant
(written by Bob Dylan)

While I doubt the choice of the word immigrant here is meant to be taken literally, otherwise this song would be somewhat xenophobic. At least he seems only to be picking out one single immigrant and not all immigrants as a whole. It's interesting that Bob pities the immigrant here instead of condemning him. Everything that the immigrant in question here is doing seems to be upsetting to Dylan's moral code, but he is able to occasionally see past that to the reasons why this particular immigrant feels that he is forced to act in such a deplorable manner. The song is taken at a mildly rollick speed with a feel somewhere between 3/4 and 6/8. This is the *John Wesley Harding* song with the most steady and static bass-line, content to mostly play a variation of the usual I-V walking bass line. Bob's voice is the closest it gets to the more croon-y vocals that he would indulge on *Nashville Skyline*. While the less extensive range of instruments on this album does help it stand out from the previous Dylan releases, he is starting to run into the same issue he did on the first four albums. The restrictive option is tending to make all the songs begin to sound the same and otherwise worthwhile tunes are beginning to blend together. Still, this is a fine little song.

The Wicked Messenger
(written by Bob Dylan)

Up to this point, Bob was known almost exclusively for either fingerpicking or strumming chords and not playing single-note lead guitar lines. So it is a surprise to hear a song like this that is built almost entirely out of a pentatonic blues scale riff. As such, this song truly stands out, being heads and shoulder above everything else on *John Wesley Harding* with the possible exception of "All Along The Watchtower". The instrumentation isn't any different, but this song completely different from anything else on this album. Sure the lyrics the traditional *John Wesley Harding* type of narrative with a lot of weird characterizations and plot holes. The bass here just follows the guitar lick, leaving no chord or harmonic structure, just a never-ending driving riff. The harmonica solos are mostly just one or two long notes contrasting nicely. Even the vocal melody is just a shortened variation of that single guitar line. The only chord here is strummed at the end of each phrase. It's a fascinating change of pace for Dylan, surprisingly not attempted during the "thin wild mercury" years or during the tapings in the basement. It's a style of songwriting that Bob doesn't often employ, although he used it quite a bit on the album *Slow Train Coming*. As a result, this ends up being one of my all-time favorite Dylan tracks.

Down Along the Cove
(written by Bob Dylan)

For an album like *John Wesley Harding* with such a limited spectrum of instruments, you wouldn't think Bob would want to leave the two songs with Pete Drake on pedal steel for the very end. I would've mixed them up in there to try and add a little variation to the sound of this album. Of the two pedal steel songs, "Down Along the Cove" is less of a harbinger of things-to-come on *Nashville Skyline*. While more blues than country based in terms of the music, the lyrics stick out from the remainder of this album by being a straightforward pledge of devotion rather than a convoluted narrative of obscure meaning. That definitely foreshadows the aesthetic of the next album. The song itself is rather light and jaunty, and Dylan's vocal quality is much brighter to matched. Bob's playing piano again and the bass is all over the place. The pedal steel feels a little out of place like it was only brought in for "I'll Be Your Baby Tonight" and only thrown on here because he was already set-up and in the studio. If it had been placed earlier in the album, it certainly would've changed the character of *John Wesley Harding* completely. Having this song thrown in on the end makes it feel even more out of place. A pleasant song, but nothing special.

I'll Be Your Baby Tonight
(written by Bob Dylan)

While "Down Along The Cove" hinted at what was to come, this song tips Bob's hand completely. There's no blues or folk or even rock here, this is just country. You can shuffle this into the middle of *Nashville Skyline*, and this track would stand out far less than it does on the actual album it was recorded for. Bob's voice is completely in that smoke-free croon that characterized that next album. Sure the instrumentation is a little sparser, but not egregiously so. The lyrics are simplistic love song clichés. I can't imagine what listeners at the time thought of this abrupt left turn that ended this otherwise consistent album. If you didn't know *Nashville Skyline* was coming would you think this was an odd one-off experiment? With the benefit of hindsight, we can clearly see where this was going, but it must've been jarring at the time. In fact, it's still jarring now on this album. While I like this song, I have a hard time enjoying it in the context of the *John Wesley Harding* album. It's like that *Sesame Street* song "One Of These Things Is Not Like The Others". When I first heard this song on *Greatest Hits, Vol. II*, I assumed it was from that album. If you were going to pull a *John Wesley Harding* song as the B-side of "I Threw It All Away", this track would make more sense than "Drifter's Escape". Most of Bob's abrupt changes of styles like this do not have a warning shot at the end of the previous album, that's what makes this song so unusual. Imagine if *Another Side Of Bob Dylan* had ended with "Subterranean Homesick Blues" or if *Tempest* concluded with "Sentimental Journey". Still, it's just as good as most of the two albums it straddles between.

"HOBOS, DRIFTERS, IMMIGRANTS, & LANDLORDS"

SIDE A:
1. John Wesley Harding
2. As I Went Out One Morning
3. I Dreamed I Saw St. Augustine
4. All Along The Watchtower
5. The Ballad Of Frankie Lee And Judas Priest

SIDE B:
1. Drifter's Escape
2. Dear Landlord
3. I Am A Lonesome Hobo
4. I Pity The Poor Immigrant
5. The Wicked Messenger

There's not much I would want to change about this album. Which is good, because there are no other songs or even alternate takes floating around for this album. All I really did was lop off the two songs with Pete Drake on pedal steel. With such austere and minimal instrumentation, these two tracks ("Down Along The Cove" and "I'll Be Your Baby Tonight") really stand out. Not necessarily in an unpleasant way, but they do stand out. Besides, I may need them to flesh out my next re-made record…

I really wish there were some more options or outtakes or whatnot to work with here, but the album itself is pretty much all there is. At least until *John Wesley Harding* gets its own *The Bootleg Series* treatment. Assuming there even is anything in the vaults at all that hasn't been lost or destroyed.

NASHVILLE SKYLINE
Produced by: Bob Johnston
Recorded: February 12th – 21st, 1969
Released: April 9th, 1969
Famous/Important/Popular Track(s):
- Lay Lady Lay

My Personal Favorite Track(s):
- Nashville Skyline Rag
- Lay Lady Lay
- Country Pie

Dylan's solo acoustic period lasted four albums. His electric period took another three (four if you count *The Basement Tapes*). Bob's story-telling, acoustic trio phase came and went with only the one album, *John Wesley Harding*. Sadly, there wasn't even a tour following this album as I would've loved to have heard a three-piece version of some of his songs from both *Blonde On Blonde* and *Freewheelin'*.

The gap between the release of *John Wesley Harding* and *Nashville Skyline* (469 days) was nearly as long as the gap between *Blonde On Blonde* and *John Wesley Harding* (590 days). This would seem like an interminable delay in the early days of the sixties when bands would crank out two or three albums a year. And unlike the last lull, Bob wasn't recovering from a motorcycle accident (as well as recording *The Basement Tapes*. This kind of anticipation may have led many to overestimate the album on its first release when it clearly was the work of a man trying to distance himself from his spokesman persona. His next album (released 425 days later) would make this impossible for his disciples to ignore.

Turns out that *John Wesley Harding*'s "I'll Be Your Baby Tonight" wasn't a fluke, it was an omen. This is the sound of Dylan's trying to make music as a job, not a calling. Even though at this point he's a happily married family man, Bob's songs celebrating love found ("Tonight I'll Be Staying Here With You", "To Be Alone With You", "Peggy Day") sound no more intimate and personal than the songs lamenting love lost ("I Threw It All Away", "Tell Me That It Isn't True"). He's trying to emulate the Tin Pan Alley, Brill Building, and Nashville's Music Row School of songwriting: detached, pandering, and mechanical.

The thing that makes the album work is how bad he is at being this kind of songwriting hack. His earnestness at trying to write a good, commercial, popular song is almost enduring. Musically what can I say? I really don't like country music, but I don't mind it so much here. Probably because it is not very accurate or authentic, try as he might. The studio musicians employed didn't feel they were making a "country" album as much as they were doing their usual thing on a "folk" album.

The tune "Country Pie" is so off in its attempt to describe domestic bliss that it almost seems like one of Bob's weirder moments. As such, it's my favorite on the album. The big hit, however, is "Lay Lady Lay" with its unusual cowbell/bongo percussion. This odd instrumentation subverts the otherwise stereotypical country sound, helping make the track stand out all the more.

I know it's a far more popular stance to bag on "new" country while claiming to still enjoy the old stuff like Willie Nelson and Johnny Cash, but even that stuff I can't find my way into. I'm not sure what it is that keeps me from enjoying it. Maybe a lack of familiarity and being steeped in the culture makes it difficult for me to ascertain the subtle differences. As a result, it all feels the same to me, much like Hip-Hop and EDM and several other more rigidly defined genres that I just was not raised in and am not terribly familiar with. That being said, I do have a strange fascination with the albums where artists attempt to "go country" who probably shouldn't. Most of these are pretty bad to my ears (The Beach Boys *Stars and Stripes vol. 1*, Elvis Costello's *Almost Blue*, LaToya Jackson's *My Country Collection*, even The Byrds' *Sweethearts Of The Rodeo*). There's a couple I don't mind as much (Neil Young's *Old Ways,* Ringo Starr's *Beaucoups Of Blues*, Ween's *12 Golden Country Greats*). Of them all, *Nashville Skyline* is probably the one I return the most often. And not just because it is so short.

Girl from the North Country
(written by Bob Dylan)

You've got Johnny Cash in my Bob Dylan – you've got Bob Dylan in my Johnny Cash. It's the team-up that no one asked for or expected. The original is a lovely song with a beautiful message. This version sounds like it was far more fun to make than it is to listen to. Lyrics are mangled, and the band sounds hesitant and unprepared. Frequently Johnny and Bob are singing a different word at the same time, and one of them has to play chicken and switch to the other's choice of lyric. They juxtapose or even forget whole verses. There's no solo, they just run through the chords a few times at some point while they wait for the song to start again. Apparently, this is the most professional of the dozen or so sings that Cash and Dylan cut together. And listening to the bootlegs that float around, it's hard to argue with that. Really, if the album weren't already so short, none of these duets would've been officially released. However as a bold statement of what you're attempting to do, marching out front into the countryside with Johnny Cash by your side is a pretty bold move for a rock-star messiah in 1969.

Nashville Skyline Rag
(written by Bob Dylan)

Other than the unreleased "Suze (Cough Song)", this is the first instrumental track in Dylan's oeuvre. It's a simple, straightforward chord progression that allows each musician 16 bars to show off and solo. Since all of the musicians are studio pros, it does kind of making Bob's harmonica break pale a little in comparison. The best part though is they're each playing a different instrument. You don't have to hear a bunch of guitar solos, you get pedal steel, then dobro, then acoustic guitar, then piano. Thankfully there's no drum or even a bass solo since those almost always feel more like gifts to the players rather than something anyone really wants to listen to. At the end, each soloist gets another chance to shine with a closing riff. While this may seem like an inconsequential track used to pad the slim running time of *Nashville Skyline*, this is a song that bluegrass legend Earl Scruggs covered – once even performing it with Bob Dylan. I really wish Bob would record more instrumentals. It's also important to note that Bob opened this album with a retread of an old song and then followed up it up with this almost as if to say: don't look for important or meaningful lyrics here; that's not what this album is about or what it's for.

To Be Alone with You
(written by Bob Dylan)

A really rocking number featuring some heavy-duty chicken-pickin' guitar work. "To Be Alone With You" is easily the fastest song on *Nashville Skyline*. This is also an extremely short song – barely making it past two minutes. The lyrics are almost bawdy in their desire for some alone time with the one he loves, but nothing too terribly deep though. Definitely more of the "yeehaw" type country than the forlorn and lonesome sound one would expect. Still, it's not as much fun as "Country Pie" or even "Peggy Day".

I Threw It All Away
(written by Bob Dylan)

There's some nice lead work on a nylon string guitar for the introduction. This is also one of the songs that Bob went back to when he was goofing around in the studio with George Harrison in 1970. There's some nice organ on here, reminiscent of Dylan's early work, although not nearly as high in the mix. This is another simple love song, but this is supposed to be a tale of regret rather than joy. Despite this, Bob doesn't alter his vocal inflection, still going for that Jim Nabors-styled croon that he maintains throughout *Nashville Skyline*. This is a shame since the song itself is actually very pretty and effective, and had Bob sang it with some sincerity it would've been quite lovely. The studio musicians provide an able and sympathetic backing, but there is only so much they can do. Still, it's a lovely trifle. The bridge, in particular, is a nice touch that Bob doesn't often employ.

Peggy Day
(written by Bob Dylan)

A fun little country shuffle. The incongruity of meeting women named both Peggy Day and Peggy Knight seems silly, but the lyrics don't seem to be hinting that those are anything but their real names. It's kind of silly, but not really played as a joke. There's a lovely little bridge in here that used as the backing for the pedal steel guitar solo the second time around. The lyrics couldn't be more straightforward, and Bob quickly runs out of things to say. The band is cooking on this one, but ultimately this is just a mere trifle. The best part is the slowed down exaggerated ending Bob gives to this song.

Lay Lady Lay
(written by Bob Dylan)

The one song in Dylan's canon most defined by its percussion. The odd sounds there were apparently inspired as a vindictive demonstration of how unhelpful Bob and his producer's suggestions were in terms of what the drummer should play. In a weird bit of serendipity, the offhand but dismissive suggestions of bongos and cowbells were what the song needed, even if no one could have predicted it. As a result "Lay Lady Lay" stands out on *Nashville Skyline* for being one of the only songs that sounds like it is trying to be more than just a country song. The lyrics are lusty and bawdy, but Bob's new vocal affectations help disguise that enough to make the song palatable to middle America and a surprise hit. A song with no real chorus but two different bridge sections that start out similarly but each is unique. This a surprising song for Bob to attempt in Nashville and it's no wonder the drummer was unsure how to tackle it. Despite the song's more prurient subject matter, Dylan sings it lovingly and with real conviction. One of Bob's best songs.

One More Night
(written by Bob Dylan)

Before Bob was asking for "One More Weekend" on *New Morning*, he only needed one night to seal the deal. Of course, one more night can lead to one too many mornings, which requires one more cup of coffee. This is a simple, straightforward love song given the usual country polish by producer Bob Johnston and the studio musicians. There's some excellent dobro playing in this song, especially during the solo. Bob even goes up an octave for a bit during the repetition of the last verse. He doesn't quite nail it in his country croon, but it was impressive of him even to try. Bob is pretty cornball here; the saving grace is that he is doing it deliberately. Given the expectations Dylan was facing in 1969, you could even say he was doing it defiantly. This is one of the more pedestrian tracks on *Nashville Skyline* so your enjoyment of this song is primarily going to be based how much you like the sound of that album overall.

Tell Me That It Isn't True
(written by Bob Dylan)

The message of this song seems to be "ignorance is bliss, so do a better job of hiding your infidelities, babe". The narrator of this song appears deliberately willing to believe whatever lies his lover will feed me while somewhat worried that the woman in question doesn't even care enough to spare his feelings and lie to his face. It's an odd dynamic for a quote-unquote love song. Are we supposed to feel sorry for this guy? Are we supposed to believe that the rumors are untrue? How long can this relationship possibly last? Other than pleading to have these allegations denied (regardless of their veracity) this song doesn't say much. It certainly doesn't hint at what her response would be. It's all wrapped up in the typical trappings of *Nashville Skyline*, lots of pedal steel guitar and slick country playing. Bob's croon here betrays none of the possible insecurities that the lyrics clearly lend themselves to. Not much does happen in this song, but it slides by quickly in a blithe up-tempo manner, bothering no one in its wake. Not one of the better songs on this album, but certainly harmless.

Country Pie
(written by Bob Dylan)

This is so country it's got country in the title. It's also one of the hardest rocking songs on the album. There's an earlier take on *The Bootleg Series vol. 10* (one of only two selections from *Nashville Skyline* to be included on that particular volume) that completely lacks the necessary fire. Bob and the other musicians can tell too and don't even give that take a satisfactory ending. While the lyrics to most of the love songs on this album are deliberately trite, this song seems a little closer to the montage of abstract images that listeners of *Blonde On Blonde* would come to expect. Only Bob's vocal delivery makes it clear that these words have no profound significance, especially to him. In fact, the nursery rhyme, "Little Jack Horner"-vibe might make this song more comfortable on *Under The Red Sky* than any other album in his catalog. For a stridently inconsequential song, lasting only a minute forty is probably a good idea. In some ways, this song almost feels as defiant as some of the weirder tracks on *Self-Portrait*. Which, in the end, may be why I find "Country Pie" to be one of my favorite Dylan songs ever.

Tonight I'll Be Staying Here with You
(written by Bob Dylan)

Another straightforward country-flecked love song in the style of "To Be Alone With You" or "Tell That It Isn't True". It is the perfect sentiment for the album to end on; the narrator has won over the girl and now is going just to enjoy it. While he doesn't mention whether or not he is staying just for tonight or for good, it's still a victory both for the singer and for the object of his affections. It's another slight and typical *Nashville Skyline* song. While one of the main complaints leveled against this album is its brevity, I see this as a benefit, since having more songs (or minutes of music) in this same style would get a bit tedious if this were a forty-five to fifty minute album. Its efficiency and succinctness is one of this album's strengths. There's not much to say about this particular track that couldn't be applied to most of the songs here, so this is the perfect time to be wrapping this album up. If Bob were going to do another extra-long album, he was going to need more than just "going country" as a point of departure. Luckily, Dylan's next album was going to have a lot more than just Nashville sounds going on. A whole lot more.

Recorded with Johnny Cash:
One Too Many Mornings
(written by Bob Dylan)
Mountain Dew
(written by Bascom Lamar Lunsford and Scott Wiseman)
I Still Miss Someone
(written by Johnny Cash and Roy Cash Jr.)
Careless Love
(written by W.C. Handy)
Matchbox
(written by Carl Perkins)
That's All Right Mama
(written by Arthur Crudup)
Big River
(written by Johnny Cash)
I Walk The Line
(written by Johnny Cash)
You Are My Sunshine
(written by Jimmy Davis and Charles Mitchell)
Ring Of Fire
(written by June Carter and Merle Kilgore)
Guess Things Happen That Way
(written by Jack Clement)
Just A Closer Walk With Thee
(traditional)
Blue Yodel no. 1
(written by Jimmie Rogers)
Blue Yodel no. 5
(written by Jimmie Rogers)

<u>Rumored to have been recorded (with Johnny Cash) but unheard:</u>
Mystery Train
(written by Junior Parker)
How High The Water
(written by Johnny Cash)
Wanted Man
(written by Bob Dylan)
Amen
(written by Jester Hairston)

During the sessions for Bob's shortest album, he did manage to sneak off and record an entire second album's worth of material with Johnny Cash. One of the tracks, "Girl From North Country" did manage to be released on *Nashville Skyline*, while most of the rest were only issued on bootleg. The version of "One Too Many Mornings" recorded here is the only one that got partially released, with Dylan's vocals mostly left off and Johnny's vocals added to a new backing and vocals by The Avett Brothers. This Frankenstein creation was released on *Chimes Of Freedom – The Songs of Bob Dylan: Honoring 50 Years Of Amnesty International*. Most of the songs on here are pretty interchangeable. "Careless Love" stands out by virtue of lasting over seven minutes as Bob and Johnny keep trying to come up with the dumbest rhymes they can think of. I'm glad I'm not going to into each track individually as I would once again be struggling to come up with new ways to say the same things over and again.

I even toyed with the idea of curating a Dylan/Cash version of *Nashville Skyline II* for this book. Ultimately using Cash's backing band (including Carl Perkins) and recording in Nashville makes this project feel more like a Johnny Cash album with Dylan guesting more than a meeting of two equals. Still, Bob seems like the mastermind behind setting up this session. It sounds like one of Dylan's first attempts to re-create the informal, spontaneous feel he happened upon during *The Basement Tapes*, only with better recording equipment. The main problem is that he and Johnny Cash didn't have the shared experience to draw on. Plus the two of them only had one or two sessions instead of a whole summer together to goof off and occasionally hit record. The results are amusing but less than stellar. No new tunes were attempted, only songs that had been hits for one or the other – and then mostly Cash. Bob wrote only two of the 15-20 tracks recorded. While they a fascinating listen, ultimately it sounds 100 times more enjoyable for the musicians making it than it does for any potential audience. This would not be the last time Bob tried this with a famous friend. Just a year later, Dylan would host George Harrison for a studio session of old tunes and goofing around. Again there would be nearly an album's worth of songs, but nothing that really lived up to its potential.

<u>Recorded for the album, but unheard:</u>
Going Back To Chicago
(written by Bob Dylan?)

There was a tape auctioned off on eBay in 2008 which included eight takes of "Lay Lady Lay" in addition to a slow blues jam entitled "Going Back To Chicago" which probably wasn't so much written beforehand as it is made up on the spot. Not much is known about the song, but a brief excerpt of it was included with the eBay listing (while the seller inconveniently talked over it). While it doesn't sound like much, there are so few outtakes from *Nashville Skyline* that this is something of a find. Unfortunately, whoever did buy this tape hasn't disseminated it in any form that has made its way to me. I would like to really hear this song before passing judgment on it, but it seems like it would've been a nice addition to the already too-brief album. Besides it's fun to hear Bob Dylan improvising in his full *Nashville Skyline* croon with those studio session musicians providing ample support.

"COUNTRY PIE"

SIDE A:
1. To Be Alone With You
2. I Threw It All Away
3. Peggy Day
4. Tell Me That It Isn't True
5. Down Along The Cove

SIDE B:
1. Lay Lady Lay
2. Country Pie
3. One More Night
4. I'll Be Your Baby Tonight
5. Tonight I'll Be Staying Here With You

One of the first complaints most folks have about *Nashville Skyline* is its brevity. This was a short album. If Bob had released an album with "Highlands" on one side and "Tempest" on the other, it would be over three minutes longer than the official *Nashville Skyline*. But other than the half-hearted Cash duets and the missing "Going Back To Chicago" there's not much else we can add to this album. While *The Bootleg Series vol. 10* theoretically includes

Nashville Skyline along with *Self-Portrait* and *New Morning*. In its purview, the only songs from this album on the volume are the alternate versions of "I Threw It All Away" and "Country Pie". Luckily the two tracks I saved from *John Wesley Harding* fit much better on this country album than they did there. This did also mean that I could cut the Cash duet version of "Girl From North Country" (which I feel belongs on a Cash-Dylan album, if anywhere at all) and "Nashville Skyline Rag" (which I love, but want to save for an all-instrumental Dylan album). Ultimately this new theoretical album is still barely 25 minutes, but I think it holds together pretty well; not as a standalone album and as a preamble for what's coming next.

SELF-PORTRAIT
Produced by: Bob Johnston
Recorded: April 24th - May 3rd, 1969
& March 3rd – 30th, 1970
Released: June 8th, 1970

Famous/Important/Popular Track(s):
- Wigwam

My Personal Favorite Track(s):
- All The Tired Horses
- In Search Of Little Sadie
- The Boxer
- Wigwam

I will be honest: this may be my favorite Bob Dylan album. Not just in an ironic or campy way, like the way one might enjoy *Plan 9 From Outer Space* or *The Room*. But it's also not in a thoroughly straightforward or unabashed way either. Part of it might be my usual siding with the underdog, but I think it's more than that. I don't get too caught up in trying to figure out what Dylan's lyrics mean most of the time, but instead just accept them as they wash over me. As a result, I generally just sit back and listen to Bob without really getting involved in interpreting it. This is the only album of Dylan's that really challenges me and causes me to have to think.

Although Bob has definitely released albums that in popular and critical perception were worse than *Self-Portrait* (*Knocked Out Loaded*, *Down In The Groove*, even 1973's *Dylan* album) none have received the amount of ridicule and scorn that this one did. Why exactly? Of all of Bob's musical U-turns that could've turned into career suicides, this was the only one that didn't bring him far more fans that he alienated in the process. It was the first move he made that didn't seem wise in retrospect. Plus the title, *Self-Portrait*, may have promised a far more in-depth and personal view of the artist than it delivered.

I think the thing that still bugs Dylan fans about *Self-Portrait* is the big question that hovers over the entire album: Why'd he do it? Was recording an album almost entirely of covers a big F.U. to Albert Grossman who he was suing for control of his songwriting royalties? (Much like Lou Reed's *Metal Machine Music*). Or even a big F.U. to all of those rabid fans who were dissecting even the trite clichés of *Nashville Skyline* hoping for a deeper meaning? Much like the motorcycle accident, a way/excuse to slow down the star-making treadmill he was trapped on. Or had the "amnesia" set in and this was the best that Bob could do?

He has claimed that *Self-Portrait* was in his own way his "bootleg" record. What did he mean by that? It's not like this was previously unreleased (legally) material that he put out, like *The Bootleg Series* or even *The Basement*

Tapes, he deliberately recorded this to sound like a bootleg that didn't exist. Considering that the big Bob bootleg at the time was *The Great White Wonder*, which mixed 1961 Dinkytown recordings with 1967 Woodstock demos, he might have meant that *Self-Portrait* was just as jumbled, schizophrenic and incompatible with itself.

For those looking for something Bob's lyrics, this double album was undoubtedly a disappointment. He didn't even write two-thirds of the songs. And those he did write were either really sloppy live versions from the Isle of Wight Festival of previously released songs or songs with no words ("Woogie Boogie", "Wigwam") or only two lines repeated ad infinitum ("All The Tired Horses"). Really the only new lyrics on here belonged to "Living The Blues" and "Minstrel Boy".

While the title *Self-Portrait* may now, been seen as something of a joke, I'm not sure it really is. Don't think of this album as an accurate, in-depth look into Dylan's whole life. Rather see it as a blurry snapshot from a day in the life. Sometimes he is singing along to a couple of pop tunes on the radio that he kind of likes ("The Boxer", "Early Morning Rain"). Sometimes he is remembering some old tunes from his past growing up in the 50s ("Blue Moon", "Let It Be Me") as well as some older folk tunes that he discovered later and inspired him in the early days playing ("Copper Kettle", "Belle Isle", "Little Sadie", "Alberta #1" & "#2"). You can even see him trying to figure out the chords to one of those old tunes ("In Search Of Little Sadie").

Along with these random moments in the day captured on tape, we get Bob goofing around outside the studio making music, alá *The Basement Tapes* ("Woogie Boogie", "Minstrel Boy"). Other times he is trying to figure out some words ("Wigwam") or at least the next line ("All The Tired Horses") of some new songs he's just started writing. The double album also includes Dylan going to his day job: singing songs he doesn't really feel connected to anymore (the live versions of "She Belongs To Me" and "Like A Rolling Stone" with the forgotten lyrics).

It's possibly Dylan's most "recorded" record (at least until *Empire Burlesque*). Dylan albums up to this point (and most after) sound like they were recorded in under a week with a new group of under-rehearsed musicians learning the songs for the first time. This album features what is Bob's first vocal overdub when he harmonizes with himself (almost) on "The Boxer". While there are some obvious recording tricks and time taken on this album, there is still a certain amount of the usual sloppiness on the album (like the undeniable error that ruins the otherwise perfect "Days Of 49"). But it's like he's taken these little doodles on crumpled up napkins and put them into these ornate gilded frames. Much the same way Phil Spector's production transformed the Beatles' *Get Back* project into the perplexing *Let It Be*.

This album is definitely not what anyone wanted or expected at the time. In some respects, it was so weird, that every album that got decent critical or popular acclaim after it (*New Morning, Blood On The Tracks, Infidels, Oh Mercy, Time Out Of Mind*) were considered comebacks.

The issue is that *Self-Portrait* really is a mishmash of three distinct albums, that had they been separated out, would've had a much different impact if they had been released as is. The first album was recorded in Nashville, from April 24th to May 3rd, 1969. There had been some contemporary interviews where *Blue Moon* had been kicked around as the title for the next Dylan LP, so that's what I like to call this first album. There are eleven tracks recorded for this theoretical album. Six of these Nashville recordings ended up on *Self-Portrait* ("Blue Moon", "Let It Be Me", "I Forgot More Than You'll Ever Know About Here", "Living The Blues", "Take A Message To Mary" and "Take Me As I Am"). Two of them ("A Fool Such As I" and "Spanish Is The Loving Tongue") were officially released on 1973's *Dylan* album. The two Johnny Cash covers ("Ring Of Fire" and "Folsom Prison Blues") were never officially released, but are circulating among the hands of bootleggers. The only recording that is missing is labeled as "Running" and it is unsure who wrote it or what song it is, but it does look like anything by that title has been copyrighted by Bob Dylan. The other ten songs, however, hang together pretty well as a single LP. Other than "Living The Blues" (which is really a re-write of "Singing The Blues" written by Melvin Endsley) *Blue Moon* is made entirely covers. Coming off of *Nashville Skyline*, this album is slathered with even more country trappings. While *Nashville Skyline* is definitely country, it was a stripped-down, rugged, honest country. *Blue Moon* is even more MOR "countrypolitan" with string sections and backing vocals layered on. If this had been released in late '69/early '70 as a follow-up to *Nashville Skyline*, it might have surprised a lot of fans on its release, but it would've been a little less baffling. This would be seen as Bob's misguided and failed attempt to become an adult music pop star.

The second LP that makes up *Self-Portrait* could best be called *Live At The Isle Of Wight*. This is a recording of Bob and The Band playing at the Isle of Wight festival on August 31st, 1969. Those who have splurged for the 4-CD deluxe *The Bootleg Series vol. 10* got to enjoy an excellent recording of the entire concert. Since Columbia Records scrapped plans to release the October 26th, 1963 show they recorded at Carnegie Hall, when four

of these live tracks came out on *Self-Portrait* it was the first official release of any live Dylan. By the time of the Isle of Wight Festival, Bob had retired from performing live almost completely. All of Bob's few live appearances between his motorcycle crash and his return in 1974 have been recorded and released at some point (The 1968 Tribute To Woody Guthrie, The Concert For Bangla Desh, and his sitting in with The Band on January 1st, 1972), but The Isle of Wight festival is the only full set he performed during this time period. While not great, it is interesting to hear him take on some of his older material while still firmly ensconced in his *Nashville Skyline* voice and sound. Even the white suit he wore looks very "country singer." Generally I'm not a fan of live albums (if they're too close to the original, they're boring; if they stray too far, they're sacrilegious) this one is fascinating. It's the only live release (barring *Live At The Budokan*) of Dylan's that I regularly go back to.

The final album from which Bob drew his *Self-Portrait* was recorded in New York nearly ten months after the Nashville sessions that made up *Blue Moon*. These tracks are Bob and his friends David Bromberg and Al Kooper goofing around on a bunch of old folk tunes as well as some new songs (half of which will get re-recorded for *New Morning*) in addition to any other song that happens to float through Bob Dylan's brain. These sessions are no more focused or productive than the Johnny Cash sessions shortly before this or the George Harrison sessions shortly after this. In fact, they really feel like attempts to re-create the pointless but enjoyable atmosphere of goofing off from *The Basement Tapes*, only these are happening in an actual recording studio with real equipment and a professional engineer. (Boy I bet Columbia love paying for all this!) These sessions make up the majority of *Self-Portrait*. Of course, too fit in with those earlier sessions, these goofing-off tapes were flown to Nashville, so Bob Johnston can overdub strings and backing vocals and a rhythm section and whatever else he could. Had this been released on its own, and unadorned, it might've been greeted with some low-key respect as Bob was returning to both his acoustic and his folksong roots. But this is not what Bob was trying to do on *Self-Portrait*, and as a result, it is still one of the most baffling and reviled entries into his catalog.

In 2013, Columbia Records attempted a rehabilitation of *Self-Portrait*'s image. While most of the releases in the Bootleg Series focused on tours or albums that were popular and critically loved, *The Bootleg Series vol. 11* (subtitled "Another Self-Portrait") was not. But in trying to remake the original *Self-Portrait*, they were being a little bit dishonest. Notice that none of the Nashville sessions were included on this set despite the fact it contained of alternate takes from *Nashville Skyline*, outtakes from *The Greatest Hits, vol. II* and even the original *Basement Tapes* version of "Minstrel Boy". None of these really feel like they belong within *The Bootleg Series vol.*

11's purview. While alternate versions of "New Morning" and "Sign On The Window" from *New Morning* are included with extra overdubs, for the most part, the *Self-Portrait* tracks are presented in the same unadorned state as The Beatles' *Let It Be... Naked* and John and Yoko's *Double Fantasy: Stripped Down*. These alternate versions and additional outtakes make *Self-Portrait* seem like it was supposed to a be a fun light album that accidentally got far too much weight placed upon it.

The truth is, without the overdubs, the odd song choices and weird production, *Self-Portrait* (as portrayed by "Another Self-Portrait") is just boring. There's no mystery to solve anymore. What's the point of "Wigwam" without the horns or a non-jazz take on "If Dogs Run Free"? If they were being honest about the enigma that is *Self-Portrait* they would've included 1973's *Dylan* album in the box set. They could have at least put it on the deluxe version, instead of just another remastered version of the original *Self-Portrait*. With its mixture of unreleased tracks from both *Self-Portrait* and *New Morning*, 1973's *Dylan* could be seen as a lost disc off of *The Bootleg Series vol. 11*. Only this was assembled by Columbia (without Dylan's involvement) not to try and resuscitate *Self-Portrait*'s popular perception, but rather as revenge for Bob Dylan signing to David Geffen's Asylum label when their contract expired.

All the Tired Horses
(words and music by Bob Dylan)

If the Johnny Cash duet was a brave way to open *Nashville Skyline*, then "All The Tired Horses" is a gauntlet thrown in the face of anyone foolish enough to dare to listen to *Self-Portrait*. This does not sound like Bob Dylan... literally. He's opening with strings and backing vocals and minimal lyrics. More importantly, he's starting his *Self-Portrait* with a complete absence of himself. The drunken brass band on "Rainy Day Women #12 & 35" is a nice change of pace. The addition of the dobro and pedal steel *Nashville Skyline* didn't upset the apple cart too much. But this is a bold way to start an album. And much like putting the electric side of *Bringing It All Back Home* on first, this Bob saying you either need to get on-board with this fully or you should back out now. Unfortunately, this is also where a lot of people bailed, all the while snickering about how "riding" sounds like "writing," and so Bob must be having writer's block. But this isn't writer's block. This a piece that works more on orchestration and arrangement rather than traditional songwriting techniques. Despite the repetitive nature of the song, it builds up and then begins to ebb and flow before finally receding. While most of this is probably from the hand of producer Bob Johnston rather than Dylan himself, his decision to start his most controversial record in the fashion is fantastic. Not only that but the track itself, divorced from its surroundings and context, is still one of the most interesting complicated recordings that Dylan ever released.

Alberta #1
(revised melody and arrangement by Bob Dylan)
Of the three Albertas cut for this album this is the slowest, although none of them are really rocking. In fact, the differences between "Alberta #1" and "Alberta #2" have always been slight, so it was surprising when "Alberta #3" came along and split the difference between them. #1 does the lovely backing singers and some dobro overdubbed on top. The lyrics are just repeated pleas for the Alberta in question to both be nice and let her hair down. He even offers to bribe her for this. It's kind of odd. Why is her hair so important to him? It's not one of the more notable songs on the album – making the fact it appeared twice as bookends somewhat surprising.

I Forgot More Than You'll Ever Know
(words and music by Cecil A. Null)
This song starts with Bob singing in his most Jim Nabors croon accompanied by cheery backing vocalists, and a pedal steel guitar makes this far more country than anything unleashed on *Nashville Skyline*. Those vocalists and pedal steel continue to dominate throughout the remainder of the track. Taken at a leisurely pace in 3/4 time this recording is so sweet as almost to be sickly. Previously, Bob Dylan would have used this condemnation of an ex's new lover as a chance to eviscerate then, here he just sounds neutered. Not even resigned or remorseful. Maybe the fact that this is a cover rather than original keeps Dylan from making the words too personal. It's a very gentle song, despite the nature of the lyrics. This song manages to sound both beautiful and dull at the same time.

Days of '49
(written by F. Warner, J.A. Lomax and A. Lomax, revised melody and new music by Bob Dylan)
This is one of the hardest hitting songs on *Self-Portrait*, due in no small part to the drums and bass that were added later. Even better there's a bass harmonica added that sounds surprisingly like *Pet Sounds* for Bob Dylan. The version, without overdubs from *The Bootleg Series vol. 10*, is sadly naked and boring. The official version actually rocks. This is also the only track on *Self-Portrait* other than the live "Like Rolling Stone" that is longer than three-and-a-half minutes. About halfway through this song, Bob screws up, but everyone keeps going, and it is quite entertaining. While Bob has never been a big proponent of slick professionalism on his records, to hear such a blatant and obvious mistake on an officially released record is charming and endearing. For some reason, this is one of the few tracks that you average *Self-Portrait* hating Dylan fan will admit to liking. Perhaps only because of its length.

Early Mornin' Rain
(words and music by Gordon Lightfoot)

I'm used to thinking of Gordon Lightfoot as a very 70s singer-songwriter in the vein of Cat Stevens, Don McLean, or Jim Croce. I was surprised to learn that he was already respected enough to be on Dylan radar this early. The song itself is no "Wreck Of The Edmund Fitzgerald" or "Sundown" (both of which I would love to hear Bob cover). This is a simple, lilting song, and it's nice to see that Bob is only paying attention to obscure folk records, but also what was happening around him in the current pop music market. It is very of the late 60s folk moment, reminiscent of John Denver, so it's no surprise it was also covered by Peter, Paul, & Mary as well as Ian & Sylvia. Bob's vocals seem undecided if he is going to continue to sing like *Nashville Skyline* any more or not. He is not quite back into his traditional Bob voice, but it isn't quite as stylized as those songs. The harmonica playing on here is lovely as the little flourishes on the acoustic lead guitar. The drums are simple but effective in keeping this song rolling along nicely. Not nearly as brave a choice for Dylan to sings as Simon & Garfunkel's "The Boxer", but still fun to hear.

In Search of Little Sadie
(new music by Bob Dylan)

This is Bob in search of the correct chords and key for "Little Sadie". That in of itself would not be terribly interesting, although an odd choice to be released on an official album. What really makes this track stand out is the fact that Bob Johnston took this off-the-cuff that got accidentally recorded and got some Nashville studio musicians to try to follow Bob's wandering journey through the song. If you listen to the version without overdubs on *The Bootleg Series vo. 10* there is just a candid photograph of an artist at work. Add on the drums and bass valiantly trying to make sense out of the piece, and suddenly you have something fascinating. Perhaps it's fascinating in the same way as a train wreck, but it still one of the weirdest most experimental piece Bob ever added his name to. There are stories of the session musicians giving each other perplexed expressions while recording this. Their music sheets also included big up and down arrows penciled in to help them navigate the frequent changes in tempo. In a way, this song's tossed-off nature with the improbable overdubs is a microcosm of *Self-Portrait* itself. One of my all-time favorite Dylan tracks.

Let It Be Me
(written by Gilbert Bécaud, Pierre Delanoë, M. Curtis)

This is clearly a song that Bob has been particularly drawn to having recorded and released it twice, once on *Self-Portrait* in 1970 and again as the B-side of "Heart Of Mine" in 1981. The *Self-Portrait* version was recorded in the 1969 Nashville sessions and sounds very much of that period. Lots of backing singers and country production ladled copiously on everything. Bob is singing in his *Nashville Skyline* voice, which adds some distance between the singer and the already hokey lyrics. The version from the *Shot Of Love* sessions sounds more like a warm-up or rehearsal than the full production of the earlier version. There are still backup singers, but they sound rougher and more gospel than sickly sweet. The B-side version of "Let It Be Me" lacks any drums and with its prominent organ feels almost hymnal. Bob's singing on this version is a little more plaintive and as such feels a little more sincere. Still, I prefer the *Self-Portrait* version as it feels like it was completed and meant to be presented to the world. The *Shot Of Love* version feels a little like eavesdropping. While there's lots of potential there, it hasn't be realized yet, and so it feels a bit embarrassing. Either way though, it is fascinating to hear Bob attempt such a corny old pop song – in some ways it helps to point the way to the Sinatra fixation that would encompass Dylan in his later years.

Little Sadie
(revised melody and new music by Bob Dylan)

For those unfamiliar with the song that Bob was attempting to find in "In Search Of Little Sadie" Bob also includes a straightforward rendition for the listeners' reference. The overdub-less version on *The Bootleg Series vol. 10* is a little boring with the only flashes of interest being in the second acoustic guitar noodling around the edges. The song doesn't really kick in until you add the drums, bongos, bass, and mandolin. The stripped down version even robs us of the goofy "shave-and-a-haircut" ending. Still, even with the oomph that Bob Johnston's overdubs added to this song, it sounds pale compared to "In Search Of Little Sadie" That song is a brave wandering masterpiece. The actual "Little Sadie" is just another folk song with some nice singing and the traditional lyrics about killing your lover and going to prison. Only a double album like *Self-Portrait* would require (or have room) for both versions of this song. If you are having to choose between the two, this is not the one that makes the cut.

Woogie Boogie
(written by Bob Dylan)

If you don't count the unreleased "Suze (Cough Song)" this is only the second instrumental recorded by master lyricist Bob Dylan after "Nashville Skyline Rag". Much like that song "Woogie Boogie" sounds far more improvised than composed. It's just the standard 12-bar blues that most half competent musicians use to jam on when they don't have any better ideas. Unlike "Nashville Skyline Rag" this isn't a showcase for each player to show off their chops. Everyone seems to be going at the same time, and no one is taking turns. It's impossible to tell who to pay attention to. At least until the halfway point when a squawking sax butts in. It is turned up so high on the mix that it is impossible to notice anything once it starts. It's not even that great of a sax solo. Like many songs on *Self-Portrait*, this songs seems designed deliberately to confuse. There's no interpreting of what Dylan meant in the lyrics; because there are no lyrics. The question becomes solely why did Bob record this, much less release it. If you are going with the "Bob is deliberately trying to lose his audience" theory, this can be used as evidence of that. But this is not Dylan's first (nor his last) instrumental. He obviously took the time and meant to do this. Maybe he doesn't want his audience to get too complacent at this point and figured this would be an excellent time to show off all the curveballs he has at his disposal that he hasn't had a chance to deploy yet.

Belle Isle
(new music by Bob Dylan)

One of the songs with the most production overdubbed on it. Not only are there bass and drums added to gives this song something of a rhythm, but some of the most cloying, Muzak-style strings are plopped on top. In some ways, this song almost feels like "The Long And Winding Road" in this way. You can hear the original version of this song on *The Bootleg Series vol. 10*. That rendition of the song is unassuming, unadorned, and unremarkable. It's just Bob strumming with a second acoustic guitar filling in with lots of riffs. It's got the casual intimacy of a pair of friends jamming in your living room. The final polished version is a sweeping, majestic performance. Your preference between the two versions will depend on which Bob Dylan you want. It may be perverse and antithetical to most Dylan aficionados, but I always gravitate to the grandiose, as such gestures are few and far between in Dylan's catalog. Maybe if he did this kind of stuff all the time, I would find the un-overdubbed version more of a breath of fresh air. But as it is, I always pick the *Self-Portrait* release of this song.

Living the Blues
(words and music by Bob Dylan)

While this song is listed as one of the few originals on *Self-Portrait*, this song is mostly a re-write of Melvin Endsley's "Singing The Blues" that was popularized by Guy Mitchell. The biggest difference is in the bridge. Fans who were hungry for new Dylan profundity in 1970 were probably bitterly disappointed when the few new words released on this album were these half-cribbed clichés. The song itself was initially planned to be the single following the release of *Nashville Skyline* and Bob even made one of his few TV appearances on the Johnny Cash show promoting this song. The tune does feel like it would be right at home in the hands of someone like Leon Redbone, who did, in fact, cover this song on his 1985 album *Red To Blue*. Sure this song is a rip-off and deep as a puddle, but this is an undeniably fun track. Bob is clearly still in his *Nashville Skyline* voice, but the backing vocals certainly make this feel very cheesier than that album. The music feels a little more Dixieland or ragtime than the standard country. Bob is having a hoot playing up this bumpkin persona. This song clearly has the larger ensemble playing live rather than applied on later. As nothing more than another proud boast of "I have nothing to say" this song is almost up there with "All The Tired Horses". One of my favorites from *Self-Portrait*.

Like a Rolling Stone
(words and music by Bob Dylan)
See the entry under *Highway 61 Revisited*

Copper Kettle
(written by Albert Frank Beddoe)
Another traditional folk song in the mold of "Belle Isle". Without the syrupy strings, this is just another unimpressive bit of Bob singing an old tune with another acoustic guitarist playing licks. Al Kooper doesn't even show up on the organ until the song is half over. This version is now available on *The Bootleg Series vol. 10* with a surprisingly cheezy intro that this is "one of our old favorites." While that bit of spoken word is snipped off the official *Self-Portrait* version, it fulfills that promise of an over-the-top Vegas revue-style arrangement. The strings are full and lush. The backing singers are doing their best impression of a bell chiming. The end result is majestic and moving. Bob's still sort of singing in his *Nashville Skyline* voice, but on one or two notes lets a nice bit of grit through. The song's lyrics are instructional in regards to hiding one's whiskey bootlegging operation. For some reason, these are words that Bob really relates to, and he sings the hell out of them. The un-overdubbed take of this song sounds hesitant and unsure, particularly in the very beginning. The final version is stunning to me if surprising to the average Dylan fan.

Gotta Travel On
(words and music by Paul Clayton, Larry Ehrlich, Dave Lazar, and Tom Six)
There's some nice burbling bass and funky congas/bongos here. These along with the dobro were probably overdubbed later, but we don't have a stripped down version of this particular track on *The Bootleg Series vol. 10* to compare this to. Certainly, the backing singers were a latter addition. Despite being something of an old country song, this version has a feel that is half-folk, half-funk. The most notable version of this song by Billy Grammer from 1959 is something of a precursor to the rockabilly that would mutate into rock'n'roll. Luckily Dylan doesn't attempt the several key changes that Billy's version features. Bob isn't rocking as much as he is rollicking here. It's a fun song, but it doesn't quite stand out the way some of the more audacious or experimental *Self-Portrait* tracks do.

Blue Moon
(lyric by Lorenz Hart music by Richard Rodgers)

This recording is clearly closer to the *Nashville Skyline* period than the latter *Self-Portrait* tracks such as "Copper Kettle", "Gotta Travel On", or "Belle Isle". The fiddle scratching away at the end goes from pleasant to annoying and past that back to humorous. While *Nashville Skyline* was an attempt to apply a country sheen to what was still a Bob Dylan album, here Dylan is sublimating himself entirely in service of make a through-and-through country album. Even the choice of song, a Rodgers & Hart classic, is the sort of thing that a producer would foist on an unsuspecting country singer and not the kind of thing that someone like Bob, who had complete artistic control over his career, would pick. The result is delightfully unexpected. Bob is singing with great sincerity. Not that he genuinely believes the clichéd lyrics her is singing, but he thoroughly invested in giving a professional entertainment experience. The incongruity of the backing singers just helps push this further. When Bob was originally recording this half of the album in Nashville, *Blue Moon* was the tentative provincial title for the project. And this song really is the epitome of those early sessions. Cheezy, silly and a lot of fun.

The Boxer
(words and music by Paul Simon)

While most of the weird and wild songs were recorded in the first batch of *Self-Portrait* sessions in Nashville, the 1970 New York sessions weren't all half-remembered folk tunes that were later gussied up with inappropriate overdubs. He did record "All The Tired Horses" and "Wigwam" during these sessions, two of the songs most characteristic of the oddness of the whole *Self-Portrait* album. While most of the overdubs were overseen by Bob Johnston in Nashville without Dylan's input, he clearly had to be present for at least one of the overdubs for "The Boxer" as Bob is heard singing a duet with himself here. His old growly voice is now attempting to be Garfunkel to the *Nashville Skyline* voice's Paul Simon. The two different aspects of Dylan aren't even separated in the stereo spectrum, both sitting exactly in the center making them sometimes hard to distinguish from each other. The bass, drum, and dobro added in here clearly make this song feel of the same cloth as "Little Sadie" or "Gotta Travel On". Who knows if Bob thought of Simon & Garfunkel as equal influences to him as those traditional country and folk songs, or if this was just another song that Dylan half-remembered and wanted to run through. Most fans think this rendition is horrendous and comfort themselves by saying that Bob hated Paul Simon and deliberately made the song horrendous as a savage attack on his supposed rival. Of course, there's nothing in the song itself or Bob's later words or actions that would confirm any sort of animosity between the two. In fact, they even toured together in 1999 and would frequently duet this song on-stage. Even stranger than Dylan covering Gordon Lightfoot, whether the song was a toss-off or a sincere tribute, is the fact that Bob took the time and effort to try and add his own harmony as well as releasing the song officially in 1970 shows a lot of gall. More than just a curiosity, this is another one of my favorite Dylan tracks.

The Mighty Quinn (Quinn the Eskimo)
(words and music by Bob Dylan)
See the entry under *The Basement Tapes*

Take Me as I Am (Or Let Me Go)
(written by George Thompson and Edgar Battle)
Another track from the '69 Nashville sessions. This song could even be seen as the manifesto of *Self-Portrait*. Bob seems to be saying to the listener that either you have to accept him with all his flaws and eccentricities, or you need to just move along. Given Dylan's later re-casting of this album as a deliberate attempt to shed himself of his more fanatic factions of his audience, this song certainly seems to be a statement of that purpose. Either that, or it's just a corny old love song. With Bob, it could always be both. Or neither. This tune certainly has the same hallmark of the other songs recorded during these sessions: an over-the-top country touch with strings and syrupy backing singers. Bob is still in his *Nashville Skyline* voice, and alternating between that and his more recognizable Dylan vocal style adds to the general schizophrenic feel to *Self-Portrait*. The piano playing has a nice honky-tonk touch and really is the star of this track that does have both pedal steel and dobro on it. There are also both electric and acoustic guitars occasionally throwing in fills. It is a much fuller sound than *Nashville Skyline*. Bob had the money and cache to make this fuller (if MOR) production happen, even if no one thought he needed it. While not one of the great tracks from that set of sessions, it certainly fits in well there.

Take a Message to Mary
(written by Felice Bryant and Boudleaux Bryant)
This song opens with a super-cheezy intro from the backing chorus framing the song. Of all the '69 Nashville sessions, this is the one that fits closest with the '70 New York tracks. The lyrics feel like an old folk song with letters and prison-time and an abandoned fiancé. With the pedal steel and piano not entering the song until later it almost has the stripped-down then overdubbed feel of those songs. Ultimately though, it starts to come into its own as full-blown country production. The lyrics are almost "my wife ran off with my dog and my truck" type of over-the-top pathos. Bob's still singing in his Nashville croon. The intro is such a hokey device that it would have to come from these misguided attempts at middle America commerciality. While not as ridiculous as some of the tracks from these

sessions, this is still a great example of Dylan in the midst of what he later termed "the amnesia".

It Hurts Me Too
(written by Elmore James, new music by Bob Dylan)
One of the 1970 New York tracks that were released on *Self-Portrait* with the least amount of overdubbing. It's just a bass added to the dueling acoustics of Bromberg and Dylan making this one of the more stripped down tracks actually to see release on the album at the time. Surprisingly this is not recognized by most fans as a relief at this point on the record. In fact, it seems most fans have given up on *Self-Portrait* so thoroughly by this point on the double-record that no ever really talks about this song. When you stack this one up with the others recorded at this time and in this style, "It Hurts Me Too" does not stand out much. It's a country-blues song, with Dylan's interpretation far heavier on the country than the blues. The lyrics are relatively typical for a love song, which can be easily summarized by the chorus. While usually having such a starkly recorded track in the midst of so many lush productions would make a track like this standout, since *Self-Portrait* is so full of nothing but constant left turns, this tune gets left in the dust a little. It is not a huge shame, but it is a little bit of a disappointment.

Minstrel Boy
(words and music by Bob Dylan)
See the entry under *The Basement Tapes*

She Belongs to Me
(words and music by Bob Dylan)
See the entry under *Bringing It All Back Home*

Wigwam
(written by Bob Dylan)
The most *Self-Portrait*-y of all the *Self-Portrait* tracks, this was a surprising choice for the single from this album. And Bob's stature even managed to get this single a little commercial success back in the day. Everything most fans hated about this album on evident on this track: a lack of any new wisdom from Dylan's pen, an extravagant orchestral backdrop, an almost defiant desire to not be meaningful. The result is fascinating. The song sounds like it was just improvised on the spot with Bob singing nonsense in place of words and then an entire horn section was added later to play along with Bob's melody. If you listen to the un-overdubbed version on *The Bootleg Series vol. 10* you can hear that this is precisely what happened. That stripped down version is just a sketch of a song, but instead of going back and doing another proper draft, a gilded frame was affixed to the roughest

of rough sketches. It is amazing. Almost willfully self-destructive, yet ornate and beautiful on its own all the same. My jaw dropped to the floor the first time I heard this song. This may be my favorite Dylan recording of all time. And for years I thought I was alone in loving this somewhat obscure and forgotten album track. I didn't even realize until much later that its appearance in *The Royal Tenenbaums* movie had brought this lovely track back into the popular consciousness. It's a shame that Dylan has never pulled this one out live in concert.

Alberta #2
(new music by Bob Dylan)

The faster of the Albertas. This has piano bass and drum added to it as well as the backup singers and dobro. It's a definitely a more rocking way to close the album, but by the time this song rolls around, you probably have forgotten how "Alberta #1" was different and would be worried that your copy of *Self-Portrait* had become possessed and decided to start repeating itself without your permission. The strange circular nature of the two Albertas though is just one last mystery to throw onto the pile that is *Self-Portrait* before finally signing off.

Songs not on the album:
A Fool Such As I released on *Dylan*
(written by Bill Trader)

One of the two 1969 songs recorded in Nashville that ended up on the 1973 *Dylan* album. When the songs were released on CD in the select few territories that were allowed it, they switched the title from the vague and confusing *Dylan* to the more specific and memorable *A Fool Such As I*. It's not as random as it sounds, since this was the A-side of the only single released from the album and it did chart, if somewhat modestly. Dylan was still in the thrall of the country music capital he was recording when this was made, but he had in fact first attempted it two years early during *The Basement Tapes* sessions. Had that version came out at the time, maybe Bob's venture into country music would've been seen as less surprising. Of course, if that version had been released, more people would've been concerned with Dylan's inability to tune his 12-string guitar. Both versions are evidence of Bob's sincere affection for this type of music. The *Basement* version is clearly more of a rough run-through than a polished product. The Nashville version, on the other hand, is almost nothing but polish, which slick session pickers and full-throated backing vocalists. Even though he is still in his *Nashville Skyline* voice, Bob gives a rip-roaring vocal to this track. While some listeners might be put off by the more extravagant production choices on this take of the song and prefer the *Basement* version; for me that version doesn't sound like Dylan is trying. While the 1969 recording might be accused of trying too hard, personally that is what I would prefer.

Spanish Is the Loving Tongue released on *Dylan*
(lyrics by Charles Badger Clark, music by Billy Simon)

This is a song that Bob has attempted to record many times. The first version was during *The Basement Tapes* sessions in 1967. That didn't see an official release until 2014. The next time Bob tried it was during the 1969 Nashville sessions for *Self-Portrait*. That version did come out on 1973's *Dylan*. The first version to be released was actually the last one recorded, a solo piano version of this song ended up as the B-side of the "Watching The River Flow" in 1971. There were two takes recorded in this arrangement, and the first attempt was released on *The Bootleg Series vol. 10* in 2013. There has been some talk that this version includes a bass playing low in the mix, but if that's true, I can't hear it. Much like "A Fool Such As I", the 1967 version is too sloppy while the 1969 version is too produced. Much of the Nashville sessions featured an over-the-top country sound, but this song receives an arrangement like a Ramada Inn band aping a mariachi or Tejano style and then Americanizing it to make it as authentic as Taco Bell. It's a mess, but a beautiful and fascinating mess and I prefer it to the *Basement* version. The solo piano version is a lovely idea, although it is only available on the 1978 import compilation *Masterpieces*. It does straddle the difference between the under-done and over-done arrangements. The problem with stripping the song that bare, is that it is not really much of a song. The lyrics are very akin to The Monkees' song "What Am I Doin' Hangin' 'Round?" about the regrets of an American tourist who romanced an unsuspecting native while visiting Mexico and then abandoning her. Bob's piano playing is impressive, and it holds up well to Leon Russell's on the A-side. Overall, it's a pleasant, but awkward song in whatever version, although Dylan did continue to play this with his Las Vegas-styled band during the much-reviled 1978 tour following *Street Legal*, so clearly Bob felt there was something about this song that really spoke to him.

Pretty Saro from *The Bootleg Series vol. 10*
(traditional, arranged by Bob Dylan)

One of the less exciting traditional songs that Bob attempted during the '70 New York sessions. While Bob's singing on here is superb, this song was not included in the batch of tracks that were shipped back to Bob Johnston in Nashville to receive overdubs to be considered for *Self-Portrait*. While the song is done quite well, there's nothing particularly revelatory or exciting here, so it's no surprise that it was left off the album. It's also no surprise that when *The Bootleg Series vol. 10* was released to try and re-write the perceived wrongs of *Self-Portrait*, this was the track that was turned into a promotional video. The choice of material is about what you'd expect from Dylan's self-titled debut. It's a nice song, and it helps that it's short.

This may be one of the finest (and last) vocal performances Bob gave in his *Nashville Skyline* voice. A stunning performance really, but with *Self-Portrait*, I expect something much wilder, woolier, and experimental.

These Hands from *The Bootleg Series vol. 10*
(written by Eddie Noack)

A song about the virtues of simplicity and domesticity. As such this song fits in more with themes of *Nashville Skyline, New Morning,* and *Planet Waves* better than most of the old folk tunes that Dylan selected during these sessions. The song also has a bit of a religious component. While Dylan may be as sincere singing this as he did on "Gospel Plow" or "In My Time Of Dyin'" it's interesting to note that he's not uncomfortable with this material either. Perhaps the born-again phase ushered in on *Slow Train Coming* should not have been that big of a surprise. The song itself is actually a cover of a country tune that was first released in 1955 by Smilin' Jerry Jericho and later covered by Hank Snow, George Jones, and Johnny Cash. While Dylan was still buried in the grips of his country-mania during the 1969 Nashville sessions, the 1970 New York sessions were mostly devoid of tunes such as this. Of course with the song, Dylan and Bromberg can be forgiven for not realizing that this was a country standard and not another obscure folk tune. It's not a particularly striking performance, but pretty typical of these recordings prior to being overdubbed by Bob Johnston. If you're into that kind of thing, enjoy.

Thirsty Boots from *The Bootleg Series vol. 10*
(written by Eric Andersen)

While Eric Andersen is not nearly as big of a name as Paul Simon or Gordon Lightfoot, this is another fairly recent (at the time) song written by a contemporary/follower. The song is about the civil right movement, albeit thinly veiled, and was covered by Judy Collins, John Denver, and The Kingston Trio amongst other lighter folk acts. Eric's version is just a solo acoustic guitar fingerpicked with a very trained voice on top. Bob's got Al Kooper on the piano in addition to the usual soloing by David Bromberg. It's one of the few tracks with harmonica from these sessions. Bob, unable to match the clear, pure voice of Eric Andersen, sings this in his *Nashville Skyline* voice. Bob doesn't attempt to mimic Eric's fingerpicking and just strums his way through this. Perhaps if this song and/or this songwriter were more familiar to me, I would enjoy this track as much as I do "The Boxer" and "Early Mornin' Rain". Since they aren't, this track feels like just another anonymously penned traditional folksongs of the type that were recorded during these sessions.

Tattle O'Day from *The Bootleg Series vol. 10*
(traditional, arranged by Bob Dylan)

One of those folk songs that might have been considered back in the 1600s or whenever, but totally falls flat today. The lyrics are just a series of ridiculously impossible exaggerations. There's some mildly clever wordplay in here, but it is pretty dumb. I'm not sure if the joke is that the narrator is lying so baldly – or if we're supposed to be impressed by these obvious falsehoods. It feels a little like Dr. Seuss's And To Think That I Saw It On Mulberry Street. The song is done in the style of most of the 1970 NYC sessions, with a second lead acoustic guitar and piano accompanying Bob's simple strumming. Dylan's voice is in his post-*Nashville Skyline* half-croon before it reverted back to his more typically nasal growl. Perhaps if this track had been shipped off to Nashville for overdubs with Bob Johnston, it would've been more interesting, but as it is now, "Tattle O'Day" is just another unremarkable track justifiably left off the bizarre mishmash that is *Self-Portrait*.

Railroad Bill from *The Bootleg Series vol. 10*
(traditional, arranged by Bob Dylan)

A slightly bluesy folk tune from the 1970 NYC sessions. This song has more life and energy than many of the folk tunes covered during these sessions. Had it been added to *Self-Portrait* it is far more like it would've gotten bass and drums overdubbed as opposed to strings and backing vocals. Bob breaks out his harmonica here, and it sounds great. Everybody playing seems to be having a good time digging into a tune with a little more vitality to it. The song is jaunty and pleasant, but lacks the strangeness of *Self-Portrait* and was understandably omitted. While this may not be the specific song fans were hoping for from *Self-Portrait*, this probably would've been more palatable to the fan-base in 1970 than what they actually got.

House Carpenter from *The Bootleg Series vol. 10*
(traditional, arranged by Bob Dylan)
See entry under *Bob Dylan*.

This Evening So Soon from *The Bootleg Series vol. 10*
(traditional, arranged by Bob Dylan)

Dylan starts this recording by asking someone if he remembers Bob Gibson. I'll tell you that I don't remember Bob Gibson, or even know who he is. I'm assuming that Dylan is talking about the "holy ghost" of folk music and not the St. Louis Cardinals' pitcher. This is an old, traditional song that is often referred to as "Tell Ol' Bill". Luckily it is referred to as "This Evening So Soon" since Bob wrote a completely different, unrelated song titled "Tell Ol' Bill" in 2005 and that could've made things complicated. As it is, this is a pretty typical folk tune. The lyrics are about some cheating cad who winds up dead (or at least in a "hurry-up wagon") by the end of the song. It's no "Frankie & Albert" or "Lily Of The West" but definitely of a similar vein. Al Kooper's piano does a fantastic barrelhouse style run in here while David Bromberg is fiddling around all over with his acoustic guitar. This is a pretty typical unadorned recording from the 1970 NYC sessions. If Bob were doing a sequel to his debut, this would've been a perfectly fine addition, but not really anything that makes it stand out from the other traditional songs recorded here.

Annie's Going To Sing Her Song from *The Bootleg Series vol. 10*
(written by Tom Paxton)

Bigger than Eric Andersen, but not quite as well-known as Paul Simon or Gordon Lightfoot, is Tom Paxton. This an odd song about a guy who is apparently traveling with and dating a woman named Annie. This Annie has a particular tune that she sings that makes all the men weep and pine for her. The narrator has heard the tune ad nauseam and is a little jaded seeing it work on a new group of suckers night after night. In the end, however, the singer of this song admits that Annie's song (not John Denver's song called "Annie's Song") still moves him too. The particulars of the details between the Annie and the singer of this song are a bit vague. Not sure why they are occasionally parted or if his relationship with Annie is real or only in his head. I'm also not quite sure how that would change the length of the song, or how it's possible for one song to last the whole night. It is appropriate for Dylan to be covering a tune about a singer who, while not technically perfect, is still rather masterfully at connecting with an audience. The song he is a medium tempo shuffle and Bob does a fine job of singing it. Kooper and Bromberg's accompaniment is tasteful, and it feels like they are slightly more familiar with this tune than they are with some of the curveballs that Dylan threw at them during these 1970 New York sessions. Ultimately, this song suffers much the same fate as "Thirsty Boots" which while being somewhat contemporary feels like just another unremarkable traditional folk tune. Not that there's anything wrong with that, but it's no "The Boxer".

Ring Of Fire officially unreleased
(written by June Carter and Merle Kilgore)

A more recent vintage of song recorded by Dylan during the 1969 Nashville session. This song was only written a mere six years prior by June Carter Cash. In his attempt to assimilate country music into his sound, Dylan was willing to mix up songs from his boyhood by the likes of Hank Williams and Hank Snow with more recent fare. This thinking extended into his covering of contemporary singer-songwriters like Paul Simon during the 1970 NYC sessions. Bob gives the song a pretty straightforward rendition here, with lots of reverbed lead guitar. The backing vocalists seem to be mixed almost entirely out. Bob jumps the gun a bit getting into the second verse, but the session musicians are very professional and smooth everything out without missing a beat. There's a harmonica solo that is definitely not played by Bob as it has a clean and pure Nashville sound and not in Dylan's usual style at all. While this version still hasn't been officially released, Bob did go back and re-record this song for the soundtrack to the 1996 film *Feeling Minnesota*. This version was produced by Nile Rodgers of all people. This track is very much in the vein of *Down In The Groove* or the original Bromberg sessions for *Good As I Been To You*. Resorting to cover songs with backing vocalists and guest stars is the sort of thing that Bob was supposed to be getting away from post-*Oh Mercy* and to hear him still doing this type of recording just a year before starting *Time Out Of Mind* is surprising. This song is a little more obvious than Bob, who loves showing off the depth of his knowledge of obscurities, would usually gravitate towards. Maybe it is a bit cheezy and commercial, but that is definitely where Dylan's head was at in 1969.

Folsom Prison Blues officially unreleased
(written by Johnny Cash)
See the entry under *The Basement Tapes*

Rumored to have been recorded but unheard:
Running
(written by Floyd Tillman)
Dock Of The Bay
(written by Otis Redding and Steve Cropper)
Universal Soldier
(written by Buffy Sainte-Marie)
When A Fellow's Out Of A Job
(written by Grant Rogers)
Little Moses
(written by Bert A. Williams and Earle C. Jones)
Come A Little Bit Closer
(written by Tommy Boyce, Bobby Hart, and Wes Farell)

Of these unheard tunes, "Running" (probably "Running Away" by Floyd Tillman) was recorded in '69 in Nashville and was briefly considered for inclusion on the *Dylan* album. Why the track hasn't made its way into the hands of collectors is hard to say. The rest are one-offs recorded in New York in 1970 with Al Kooper and David Bromberg. Who knows how complete any of these are, or how seriously any of these titles were attempted. I would sure be curious to hear Dylan attempt to sing "Dock Of The Bay". Unfortunately when *The Bootleg Series vol. 10* was compiled the idea was to rehabilitate *Self-Portrait* by making it seem less weird, so none of these songs were included.

"SELF-PORTRAIT"

SIDE A:
1. All The Tired Horses
2. Belle Isle
3. Copper Kettle
4. Gotta Travel On
5. It Hurts Me Too
6. Thirsty Boots

SIDE B:
1. Alberta #2
2. The Boxer
3. Went To See The Gypsy
(demo version from *The Bootleg Series vo. 10*)
4. Early Morning Rain
5. This Evening So Soon
6. Days Of '49
7. In Search Of Little Sadie

Certainly one could build a pretty nice stripped down version of *Self-Portrait* from these sessions using the un-overdubbed versions of songs like "Belle Isle", "Copper Kettle", "Little Sadie" and "Days Of 49" from *The Bootleg Series vol. 10* and add those to the unreleased tracks "Pretty Saro", "Tattle O'Day", "Annie's Going To Sing Her Song", "House Carpenter", "Railroad Bill", "This Evening So Soon", "Thirsty Boots", and "These Hands". Those 12 tracks could form the *Let It Be... Naked* version of *Self-Portrait*. This might be quite popular if it were released at the time, a sort of update of Bob's debut album with David Bromberg adding some lead acoustic guitar.

Doing this would ignore the more weird and extreme songs that make this album such a strange and fascinating listen. I already excised some of the more unusual tracks, "Woogie Boogie" and "Wigwam" for the all-instrumental version of *Pat Garrett & Billy the Kid*, so losing outliers like "The Boxer" or "All The Tired Horses" or "In Search Of Little Sadie" really neuters this album. To avoid that, I went through and gathered all the stuff that definitely had overdubs on them from the 1970 New York sessions. The '69 Nashville tracks feel like a whole separate album which I actually cover in the next chapter. However there isn't quite enough from the fully tricked-out

NY tracks for a complete album, so I had to pad it out a bit with some of the unadorned recordings.

There was no way I could keep this as a double album, which is too bad. Ultimately, this compilation of mine is unusual in this book, as I think this is not nearly as striking as the original *Self-Portrait*. I think it was worth it to show off the variety of the album by breaking it into two separate, complete, and very different records. Hopefully, I have still honored the original quixotic intent of that double album in a single disc format.

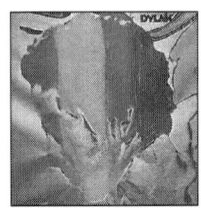

DYLAN

Produced by: Bob Johnston
Recorded: April 24th - May 3rd, 1969
& May 1st – June 30th, 1970
Released: November 19th, 1973

Famous/Important/Popular Track(s):
- A Fool Such As I

My Personal Favorite Track(s):
- Can't Help Falling In Love
- Mr. Bojangles
- Spanish Is The Loving Tongue

Forty years before *The Bootleg Series, vol. 10* Bob Dylan released an album of outtakes from *Self-Portrait* and *New Morning*. Or rather, Bob's former record company released this album. Dylan and Columbia weren't on speaking terms at this point, as Bob had signed with David Geffen's Asylum Label. While the continuing mystery of why *Self-Portrait* exists adds to the allure of that double album, *Dylan* doesn't exude the same aura. It's somewhat transparent why Columbia put this out behind Bob's back at the time: petty revenge. If Columbia had access to a bunch of more popular and commercial outtakes, they could have used for this album – like the entire *Basement Tapes* catalog, but instead, they chose to release these particular songs. The record contains no originals, but it's unclear if this is because Bob wasn't going give Columbia permission to use them or if Columbia wasn't going to do anything to increase Bob's publishing royalties.

At the time this album was widely ignored as a compilation of outtakes from what was considered his worst album at this point, the truth is only two of these nine tracks date for the *Self-Portrait* sessions. The majority of this album was recorded for *New Morning*. When recording for *New Morning* initially began, it was going to be a mix of originals, genre experiments, and mostly covers; much like its predecessor. Halfway through the recording sessions, *Self-Portrait* came out, only to be eviscerated by the critics and disparaged by the fans (who still bought it anyway). This may have caused Bob to lose his nerve and release an all-original album that was a lot closer to what audiences expected from him. Had he released a version of *New Morning* that had these *Dylan* tracks on it, Rolling Stone may have exclaimed "We've lost Dylan forever!" instead of "We've got Dylan back again!"

After Bob's tenure at Asylum turned out to be a bust and Bob crawled back to Columbia, this album has become something between a red-headed stepchild and exiled pariah. This album was quickly deleted on Bob's insistence upon returning. This is the only one of Bob's records to have such a fate. Later the album was issued on cassette, but it was never released on CD. At least not in North America, it did come out in Europe in Asia on compact disc, only with the title *A Fool Such As I*. As this was the only semi-legal way to obtain this album, import copies would show up on eBay demanding some ridiculous prices as well as on much cheaper bootlegs, often paired with the Johnny Cash duet sessions.

To complicate things (as well as to show how shunned the album was), Columbia released a best of compilation in 2007 that was also merely titled *Dylan*. However, the record started to receive a little bit of prodigal return when it was included in iTunes' *Bob Dylan: The Collection* set. It was released on August 29th, 2006 (and removed in December of 2009) although *Dylan* may have been included just to entice those who already had most of these songs to shell out $199.99 for this set of 763 songs. The album finally became available on CD in the USA in 2013, but only as part of the *Complete Album Collection Vol. One* (we're still waiting on Volume Two).

Since then, there has been a little less pretending that this album doesn't exist. It is available to purchase in MP3 form on iTunes and Amazon and is available to stream on Spotify, Tidal, and Deezer. At least for now. However, the album is still not fully accepted back. When *The Bootleg Series, vol. 10* came out, nothing from these sessions was included. The purpose of this volume of *The Bootleg Series* had a much different aim than *Dylan*. That collection was designed to rehabilitate rather than embarrass. Still, it would've been nice to make some nod towards it. Instead of including a remastered version of *Self-Portrait* with the deluxe version, they could've added this even more obscure entry that covers the same chronological ground.

Which is a shame, because this is a pretty good album. It's not nearly as wild or adventurous as *Self-Portrait*, but it is still pretty interesting. Perhaps *Self-Portrait* wouldn't have needed as much rehabilitation if Bob had stood by it with a follow-up that didn't feel like an apology the way *New Morning* does. Sure, the two 1969 Nashville tracks fit in as well with the *New Morning* material as it did with the overdubbed 1970 *Self-Portrait* NYC sessions. But that weird tonal clash is sort of the charm of these two records. I'm glad this album is at least somewhat readily and legally available since it is ripe for reassessment.

Lily of the West
(traditional, arranged By Bob Dylan)

An upbeat reading of the traditional song. There are some harpsichord runs throughout the song that sound so fast and high that I assume the tapes were slowed down when they were overdubbed, and then the tapes were returned to their normal speed. It's an odd effect that seems like it's both showing-off and cheating. Given Al Kooper's runs in "If Dogs Run Free" it could have actually been recorded at that speed. I don't know. It's an unusual instrumental flourish that is not repeated anywhere else during these sessions. The female backing singers are back answering Bob on the choruses. The lyrics tell a typical folk song story of the killing of a romantic rival by a jealous lover and subsequent hanging. As a straightforward folk tune, it would be unremarkable. But bouncing along in this upbeat arrangement at a brisk three and a half minutes, this is a fun but inconsequential way to start the *Dylan* album.

Can't Help Falling in Love
(written by George Weiss, Hugo Peretti, and Luigi Creatore)

Ok, maybe I'm a sucker for wacky juxtapositions, but I love hearing Bob singing a song so closely associated with Elvis Presley. The backing is very *New Morning*, with lots of female backing singers instead of the male ones from Presley's famous recording. Bob even opens with a harmonica solo, so there's no way to mistake this for a record by some other artist. While the song's melody may be a bit tricky for Bob's vocal range, he sings it sincerely and sweetly. This is not a joke to him. There's a lovely organ and acoustic guitar duet in the solo section. The tempo might be slightly slower than Elvis's version, but it's pretty close. This is one of my all-time favorite Bob Dylan recordings.

Sarah Jane
(traditional, arranged By Bob Dylan)

It's hard to believe that this is an old traditional folk song. Bob has ratcheted up the backing vocals and turned this into a fairly standard *New Morning* track. This feels like it was cut from the same cloth as "The Man In Me". The song is so buoyant that is bordering on giddy. The lyrics are a simple love song and Bob sounds absolutely overjoyed singing it. There's not much to this song, but it a lot of fun.

The Ballad of Ira Hayes
(written by Peter LaFarge)

A mawkish tale of the tragic misadventures of one the soldiers who raised the flag at Iwo Jima. I have no idea how accurate it is, but its combination of sappiness, patriotism, and doomed underdog story makes this the kind of material that Johnny Cash naturally gravitated towards. I'm not overly familiar with the author, Peter LaFarge, but it is definitely Johnny Cash who brought this song into the popular consciousness. For a song that is clearly meant to highlight the plight of the Native American, the frequent repetition of the phrase "the whiskey drinking Indian" makes the song a little harder to enjoy in these more enlightened times. Still, its heart is in the right place. It's hard to say whether this song places the blame for the downfall of Ira Hayes on his own alcoholism or simply the injustice of the treatment of the Pima tribe. The finger does seem to be pointed squarely at "the man," but it's hard to see how that caused Ira's inability to stay sober. Either way, the song is schmaltzy and designed to tug at the heartstrings. Bob sings it without a trace of irony. However, the sheen of the backing singers throughout the song tends to undercut the seriousness of the issue. The piano playing here has a lot of the free-form rhythm-less playing of "With God On Their Side" or "Only A Pawn In Their Game" but not as exaggerated. The song has to go on for a while in order to get all the facts of the story out there, but the song gets a little tedious by the end. This is one of my least favorite songs from the *Dylan* album.

Mr. Bojangles
(written by Jerry Jeff Walker)

One of the more surprising covers recorded during the *New Morning* sessions. Both this and "Big Yellow Taxi" show that even after Paul Simon's "The Boxer" and Gordon Lightfoot's "Early Mornin' Rain" on the last album, that Bob wasn't yet done with the idea of covering contemporaries (and some might say, followers). The song is a deliberately manipulative tear-jerker, as is almost any song that features a dead dog in the lyrics. Bob, however, treats these words without a trace of irony. The backing vocalists are still in attendance. The drums are rather subdued here, making this much less forceful than more famous version done by the Nitty Gritty Dirt Band. The slightly fictionalized story of an otherwise good man ending up in jail frequently because he is a drunk/alcoholic helps tie this song thematically with "The Ballad Of Ira Hayes". Bob misses the scansion of some the syllable here, betraying less familiarity with this tune that he shows when covering an old folk tune that he has known and sung for years. Still, Bob does everything he can to sell this tune. It's not nearly as jarring as hearing Dylan trying to cover "Can't Help Falling In Love", but it does have some of the same anachronistic feel to it. This is another great song that makes *Dylan* as essential as any other album in his catalog.

Mary Ann
(traditional, arranged By Bob Dylan)

A loping folk song done in the typical *New Morning* style. Lots of organ and backing vocalists with Dylan slowly getting over his *Nashville Skyline* voice. The song itself is stunningly simple, with only two or three chords. No real chorus as such, just the backup singers repeating the last line of each verse at the end. The lyrics are the typical love song mush, telling how great the object of one's affection is and how they will never ever hurt them. Bob sings this adequately but is not really connecting with the meaning here. One of the more dull and forgettable songs to have been given a second life on the *Dylan* album. Not nearly as exciting or surprising as "Big Yellow Taxi" or "Mr. Bojangles". No one is surprised when Bob sings a traditional tune. As such, this one tends to be one of the lesser covers from these sessions.

Big Yellow Taxi
(written by Joni Mitchell)

Of all the contemporary sing-songwriters that Dylan covered during this period (Paul Simon, Gordon Lightfoot, etc.) this might be one of the most surprising. Despite appearing at several stops during the Rolling Thunder Revue, Joni Mitchell's relationship with Dylan has always been at best stand-offish and occasionally even antagonistic. Bob's choice of material doesn't show a whole lot of depth in his understanding of Joni's career either; "Big Yellow Taxi" is one of her least obscure songs. Nothing in the way Dylan tackles this material shows why he's choosing to do it. While Bob has had no problem singing from the female point-of-view on "House Of The Risin' Sun" and "North Country Blues", he shies away from singing the line about his "old man", which necessitates a crass re-write of the line which ends up erasing the titular vehicle from the lyrics altogether and replacing it with the much more blunt "Big Yellow Bulldozer". The whole thing's got the usual *New Morning* sheen to it with backing vocalists and prominent organ. There certainly have been worse covers of this song (I'm looking at you Counting Crows), and I admire Bob's balls in covering this song. Ultimately though this song fails to charm in the same way that "Can't Help Falling In Love" or "Mr. Bojangles" does.

A Fool Such as I
(written by Bill Trader)
See the entry under *Self-Portrait*.

Spanish Is the Loving Tongue
(written by Charles Badger Clark)
See the entry under *Self-Portrait*.

"BLUE MOON"

SIDE A:
1. Living The Blues
2. Spanish Is The Loving Tongue
3. Take Me As I Am
4. A Fool Such As I
5. I Forgot More Than You'll Ever Know

SIDE B:
1. Let It Be Me
2. Ring Of Fire

3. Take A Message To Mary
4. Folsom Prison Blues
5. Blue Moon

This theoretical album would slot in between *Nashville Skyline* and *Self-Portrait*. It bridges that gap between the two. It maintains the country voice and instrumentation of the last record while pointing the way to the next album by being made up of covers almost entirely. Also, by separating the April/May 1969 tracks from March 1970 tracks, we are left with less of a conflicted hodgepodge and more of two distinct statements of purpose.

While a conflicted hodgepodge might be the thesis statement of the released version of *Self-Portrait*, this seemed to be Bob's original intention for this recordings back in 1969. *Blue Moon*, was even kicked around as a potential album title back in the day. This was going to be a quickly recorded follow-up to *Nashville Skyline* while that was still hot on the market, only featuring almost exclusively covers. The lead single was going to be "Living The Blues", and Bob even appeared on *The Johnny Cash Show* to promote this single and album that never happened. For some reason, Dylan got cold feet, and the tracks languished in the can for a year.

When Bob's 1970 NYC excursion with Al Kooper and David Bromberg didn't produce what he felt was an appropriate follow-up either, that's when the idea to mix the two sessions together came about. But if Bob had struck while his *Nashville Skyline* iron was hot and put out another credible, if deliberately mediocre, country album would've shored this up as Bob's latest career change instead of just making *Nashville Skyline* feel like something of a one-off.

Listening to the *Blue Moon* tracks as a separate piece, shows an interesting and fascinating conundrum in Dylan's life. He is trying to be middle-if –the-road, and yet he can't help but make things more weird and gothic than your usual Tammy Wynette or George Jones album. Frankly, as much as I enjoy the inscrutable oddness of the 1970 NYC sessions, I prefer these sunnier tracks.

NEW MORNING

Produced by: Bob Johnston
Recorded: May 1st – June 30th, 1970
Released: October 19th, 1970

Famous/Important/Popular Track(s):
- If Not For You
- The Man In Me

My Personal Favorite Track(s):
- Winterlude
- If Dogs Run Free
- New Morning

The heart of *New Morning* is a series of crowd-pleasing, middle-of-the-road love song. In many respects, it is very similar to *Nashville Skyline* just without all the country trappings on top of it. "Winterlude" is so defiantly pedestrian it may be too uncool for even Pat Boone or Andy Williams. But every now and then, around the edges, some of the experimental weirdness of *Self-Portrait* sneaks through. There are the two half-songs that conclude the album. More importantly, this album makes room for the spoken-word beat poetry of "If Dogs Run Free".

New Morning tries so hard to be normal (and domesticated), but there is something odd going on behind the scenes. The whole thing seems like Bob felt like he had to make an album, but wasn't sure why he wanted to. Perhaps he started this project thinking he was collaborating on a musical with Archibald MacLeish, but that motivation dissipated pretty quickly. Despite the somewhat warm reception to this album (mostly relief that this wasn't another *Self-Portrait*), Dylan wouldn't make another again unless he had a good reason to – even if that reason was just to score a western movie (*Pat Garrett & Billy the Kid*) or create some merchandise for his comeback tour (*Planet Waves*). This lack of clear vision or imperative added together to create an album that was unsure of what it wants to be.

Oddly enough, for an album with no purpose, this contains two of Dylan's most directly autobiographical songs since "Ballad In Plain D". Sure, some of the names are changed to protect the innocent, but these are not terribly obscured. "Day Of The Locusts" is clearly about a real incident where Bob accepted an honorary doctorate. "Went To See The Gypsy" is purportedly about a meeting between Dylan and Elvis, although Bob has staunchly maintained that this is not what the song is about and that he has in fact never actually met Presley in person.

As the album was initially being recorded, there was a lot more of *Self-Portrait*'s restless casting about and less of *Nashville Skyline*'s contented earnestness. Not only were there a bunch of covers records (the strangest of which ended up on 1973's *Dylan* and the safest of which graced 2013's *the Bootleg Series vol. 10*), but he was still messing around with overdubbing incongruous orchestration onto his songs, even if he ended up chickening out of releasing the horn-laden "New Morning" and the string-filled "Sign On The Window".

In the end, *New Morning* got a little too neutered as it was released, but luckily there are still too many of those confused and strange moments for this album to be completely believable as a paean to tranquility and settling down. While I enjoy this album quite a bit, it is hard not to be distracted by the much wilder record it could've been.

If Not for You
(written by Bob Dylan)

Here's a track that has been officially released in a number of different versions. In addition to the version that kicks of *New Morning*, there's an alternate take with George Harrison on guitar on *The Bootleg Series, vol .2*. There's also a version of this song with prominent violin released on *The Bootleg Series vol. 10* that also seems to be the same take with the fiddle replaced by a pedal steel guitar that was released on the compilation *Dylan, Cash and the Nashville Cats*. Oddly enough none of these takes seem to come close to what Bob described as his original vision for this song... Tex-Mex. Bob has claimed that he lacked the arranging and recording knowhow to get this song to sound that way, but I don't entirely buy that. I'm sure if he couldn't do it himself, he could've at least paid someone else to figure it out for him. I would be interested to hear Bob finally do this song in that style, but for some reason he never really pursued it.

Instead, the version that Bob put out is a little more straight-forward. It does have some sort of glockenspiel on it that a nice little touch and the intro has a really loud maraca on it that disappears once the singing starts. While the tune is paced a little quickly and performed urgently, there is a great little melody in there. The song has been covered by both George Harrison and Olivia Newton-John, both of whom slowed the song down a bit to bring out the romanticism of the tune. Neither of them took it at nearly the funereal pace that Bob's alternate take from *The Bootleg Series vol. 10* did though. The lyrics are nothing special. A straightforward devotion of love from a man to a woman, but whether played fast or slow, this is a nifty little track.

Day of the Locusts
(written by Bob Dylan)

One of the few instances of special effects on a Dylan record, this track starts with the sounds of crickets (which I presume are also kind of what locusts sound like). This is a surprisingly literally interpretation of the metaphorical title/chorus of the song which is otherwise a straightforward retelling of Bob Dylan going to Princeton to receive an honorary doctorate. Like many of the songs on this album, Bob is playing this on the piano.

After an introductory verse, the full band kicks in with backing singers, organ, guitar, and drums. It's a hummable song, but not a terribly memorable melody. It bounces along pretty well but doesn't ever stick. While most of the words are fairly direct, every now and then he references odd things like heads exploding or light filling the room. It's unsure if Bob was referring to the 1939 Nathanael West novel with the title or if he really was just hearing these particular insects singing to him while he was picking up his degree. One of the more minor songs on *New Morning*.

Time Passes Slowly
(written by Bob Dylan)

This song has been done in three very different arrangements. The version recorded with George Harrison and released *The Bootleg Series vol. 10* is one of the best tunes from this batch of recordings and features some of George's only vocals during these sessions. A second version released on *The Bootleg Series vol. 10* is far more bombastic with Al Kooper's organ to the fore. This reading of the song is quite dramatic, although bordering on melodramatic. Of course, the least interesting of the three versions of this song is the one that was officially released on *New Morning*. This version is far more laid-back and laconic. Mostly just piano, drums, and bass with an occasional bit of lead guitar. During the guitar solo, it sounds as if two different takes are just playing simultaneously. The piano playing on here is lovely. The lyrics seem to be evoking some pastoral idyll, but not really saying anything other than Bob's new life as a stay-at-home husband and father is beautiful. Despite this, you wonder how sincere Dylan really is. They say that time flies when you're having fun, but Bob seems to be singing the opposite. He's not quite complaining, but you can see some boredom starting to seep in around the edges.

Went to See the Gypsy
(written by Bob Dylan)

Initially attempted alongside all of the folk songs and covers of contemporaries during the second half of the *Self-Portrait* sessions. The legend has always had it that this song describes a meeting between Bob Dylan and Elvis Presley (with Priscilla Presley appearing as the dancing girl). Bob has refuted these claims, but more importantly, if this was about a Dylan/Elvis meeting the lyrics are so oblique as to take all the fun out of that interpretation. The first version is fairly typical for these sessions with Bob playing the song on an acoustic guitar with lots of lead guitar noodling between each phrase. This is a simple fun version that if it had been treated to overdubs by producer Bob Johnston might've fit nicely on *Self-Portrait*. Had it been released then it could have lessened the wrath of fans at the time who were only looking for original Dylan-penned material.

There's a different alternate version of this song that also first appeared on *The Bootleg Series vol. 10* that was actually recorded for *New Morning* that is almost as stripped down, but instead only features electric piano and bass. It is cool to hear Bob experimenting with a different set of colors on this recording, but eventually does get a little boring by the end.

The officially released version is the only one with any real pulse or life to it. It has drums keeping thing moving at a pace that keeps the song from dragging, although for some reason they stop playing for half a bar around the middle of the song for no reason. Perhaps there was a flub that was muted but never replaced. Or the drummer mistakenly assumed the song ended at one minute and sixteen seconds. It's a barely noticeable mistake, but interesting that he didn't go back and punch on those missing beats. Al Kooper's organ playing is fantastic, and the electric guitar has some fun throughout this song before starting to solo just as the track fades out.

Winterlude
(written by Bob Dylan)

When Bob recorded *Christmas In The Heart* in 2009, it's a shame he didn't attempt to write some new original carols to mix alongside the traditional classics. With its heavy waltz structure and winter imagery, this song is as close to a Christmas song as Dylan has ever written. It's a lovely adorable song, sweet and simple. It is practically dripping with cheese. Rarely has Bob appeared as un-ironic before. He is not revealing himself as a person in any way here, he is purely attempting to entertain. When Bob joked in December 1965 that he was a "song-and-dance man," these are probably the kinds of songs he was thinking about. While Bob starts by railing against "How Much Is That Doggie In The Window?" in the Martin Scorsese documentary, *No Direction Home*; clearly those songs he was inundated with as a Minnesota youth had an effect on him. You could almost imagine Pattie Page singing this song on *The Lawrence Welk Show*. The backing singers are so appropriate on this track. There's some nice quasi-flamenco guitar puttering around in the background. The drums are played with brushes which is a nice touch. This is one of my all-time favorite Dylan tracks. It's a shame that Bob doesn't challenge himself to get so nakedly schmaltzy ever again.

If Dogs Run Free
(written by Bob Dylan)

An experiment far more in line with *Self-Portrait* than *New Morning*. Bob is playing with jazz here. And not light jazz touches. He is going full-on beatnik reciting poetry over jazz replete with scat singing on top. There is an alternate version on *The Bootleg Series vol. 10* that strips the song of all those elements. Without the bebop affectations, this songs is just another monotonous three-chord shuffle praising the joys of staying home and raising your family. This doesn't seem to be Bob's original intention for the song as he has to add a couple extra lines at the end of each verse to make it fit with the new music. That version might've been less of a shock to *New Morning*, but ultimately makes the song pretty thoroughly forgettable. You need Al Kooper's flashy piano runs and Maeretha Stewart just going nuts on the scat vocals. If *New Morning* had been released with more oddities like this and "Winterlude", it might've reduced the album's stature as a comeback, but I think it would have also helped *Self-Portrait* seem like less of an anomaly. Heaven knows, with the overdubs that were left off and the covers that ended up on *Dylan*, there was more than enough material to make a worthy successor to *Self-Portrait* from these tracks.

New Morning
(written by Bob Dylan)

A rollicking fun song about the joys of living in the country, enjoying the outdoors, and a simple life of domesticity. If Bob Dylan and/or Bob Johnston had overdubbed some fiddles and pedal steel guitar on this, they would've had the perfect cornerstone for *Nashville Skyline II*. Instead, what they did was overdubs horns on the song, making this an attempt at Motown or the Beatles' "Got To Get You Into My Life". It was a nice fun change of pace for the album this song was named for. Unfortunately, after the critical drubbing *Self-Portrait* received, Bob lost his nerve and just put out the un-overdubbed version instead. While the original version is fine, with some nice organ work from Al Kooper and a violin somewhere in the mix, it can't hold a candle to the horn-driven version that finally saw official release on *The Bootleg Series vol. 10*. While the neutered version that was released was not as big of a disappointment as the next song, "Sign On The Window", it still shows Dylan backing away from the weirdness and making a truly worthy successor to *Self-Portrait* with *New Morning*.

Sign on the Window
(written by Bob Dylan)

The orchestral overdubs that elevated songs like "Belle Isle" and "Copper Kettle" on *Self-Portrait* are attempted again here. Unfortunately, Bob lost his nerve and released the stripped down version when *New Morning* was released on 1970. Al Kooper provided the charts here instead of Bob Johnston, and he does a lovely job of it, not nearly as chintzy. There's some really nice prominent harp on here. (That's an actual harp, and not just the word "harp" applied to a harmonica). The orchestral version expands everything with some real grandeur. The released version does retain the backing vocalist which help keep this from being too simplistic. Most of the song is just Bob alone at the piano, with the remainder of the band and vocalists waiting for the choruses to chime in. There's a neat little solo on the organ that almost sounds like a flute playing. However, the disparity between the number of instruments creates a weird lopsided arrangement that the overdubs do a fantastic job of correcting. The original sounds unfinished and it's a shame that the full version didn't get released until *The Bootleg Series vol. 10* in 2013. The lyrics are another paean to the joys of simple country living, raising your family, and keeping things simple and domestic. There's one of Bob's all-time best bridges where it reaches up to a completely unexpected key and elevates the entire song. Along with the title track, even if he had kept the original track list, Bob chickened out when it comes to releasing the genuinely magnificent and weird album that *New Morning* should've been.

One More Weekend
(written by Bob Dylan)

One of the nice things about Dylan's excursion into the country-sound is that he became much less reliant on the three-chord blues structure as a crutch. This song is his return to that mode of songwriting. While previously Bob had been able to bend and twist this musical cliché into some interesting songs, here he seems at a loss providing a sadly perfunctory and mediocre half-blues. The lyrics seem to be about getting away from the kids so he can have some time with his wife. It's a charming domestic situation of little import or tension. Particularly in the laid-back way Bob presents it. While Bob's previous blues forays have given him an excuse to really rock out, this band doesn't seem either capable or interested in that. In some ways, it sounds as sincerely bluesy as the version of "Spanish Is Loving Tongue" from *Dylan* is authentically Mexican. The continued use of the backing singers, which worked to the advantage of songs like "Winterlude", undermines the song here. He even throws in a bridge section, which normally I would view as a relief, but here it just shows how far away from a pure blues song "One More Weekend" is. Frankly, I'm surprised this song isn't a staple of all those dad-rock songs played by middle-aged men in garages by guys who should know better. Not that the track is unlistenable, it's just a little chintzy.

The Man in Me
(written by Bob Dylan)

A song that belatedly became something of a hit thanks to its inclusion in the soundtrack to *The Big Lebowski*. People who try to pin down the 1973 *Dylan* album as just outtakes from *Self-Portrait* need to only compare this song to most of the tracks on that album. The la-la-las from the backing vocalists are a dead giveaway. This is Bob trying again to write the type of straightforward love song that dominated *Nashville Skyline*. Only instead of just being about a single romantic relationship, this is also all about the joys of a settled life in the suburbs with a wife and 2 ½ kids. However as much as Bob is trying to convince the audience that he genuinely believes in this domestic bliss, it almost sounds like he's trying to convince himself even harder. And that undercurrent of doubt help keep this song from being too saccharine. Unfortunately, it's not quite enough, and the song ultimately fails, refusing to either be unabashedly cheezy or fully ambiguous. It's not bad by any stretch, but an odd choice for the Cohen brothers to use to open their movie.

Three Angels
(written by Bob Dylan)

While Bob had sung songs like "Gospel Plow" in the past, this is really the first time Dylan had turned his pen to matters of spirituality and theology. After this and "Father Of Night" Bob wouldn't really write about such matters again until the overtly Christian albums like *Slow Train Coming*. In this song it's hard to tell of the angels are literal or are just some residents still in their costumes from the Christmas pageant. There certainly is a gospel-ish tinge to the music; especially the prominent organ. Much like "If Dogs Runs Free", Bob does not sing this song as much as he recites it like beat poetry. The series of outlandish characters that Dylan chronicled passing in "A Hard Rain's A-Gonna Fall" are all clearly meant as some sort of metaphor. The people immortalized in "Three Angels" are supposed to be realistic. In fact, the whole thing seems deliberately mundane and dull. They are just quick vignettes from a sleepy suburbia, nothing grand or important here. Still, when the angelic choir comes in towards the end, you can't tell if Dylan is mocking their ordinariness or praising it. The song does an excellent job of setting the scene, but then it just ends before anything happens. It kind of feels interrupted like it's the introduction to a larger piece that never comes. Maybe part of the musical that Bob had been commissioned to work on at this time. Not that I'm complaining about it being too short since not much really happens, still it always feels a little abrupt.

Father of Night
(written by Bob Dylan)

In <u>Chronicles, Vol. 1</u>, Bob spends one of the five chapters detailing working with playwright Archibald MacLeish on a musical version of *The Devil & Daniel Webster* to be entitled *Scratch*. The project never got very far, but apparently, the first few songs for *New Morning* came from these writing sessions. While these idea and themes are not terribly evident in most of these tracks, this one definitely feels related. More of a spoken prayer than a sung melody, the song is even more explicitly religious than "Three Angels". An even shorter track than "Three Angles", it manages to feel less truncated because it has said all that it wants to say. Sure the lyrics seem to be addressing God, without actually asking for anything or saying anything to him. It's just a list of various things that he is a God of, grain, night, darkness, minutes, etc. Weirdly, it feels like the perfect coda to whatever was supposed to go after "Three Angels" but isn't there. It's an odd note to end *New Morning* on, but I can't imagine any way that something could really come after this song either.

Songs not on the album:
Lily of the West released on *Dylan*
(traditional, arranged By Bob Dylan)
See entry under *Dylan*.

Can't Help Falling in Love released on *Dylan*
(written by George Weiss, Hugo Peretti, and Luigi Creatore)
See entry under *Dylan*.

Sarah Jane released on *Dylan*
(traditional, arranged By Bob Dylan)
See entry under *Dylan*.

The Ballad of Ira Hayes released on *Dylan*
(written by Peter LaFarge)
See entry under *Dylan*.

Mr. Bojangles released on *Dylan*
(written by Jerry Jeff Walker)
See entry under *Dylan*.

Mary Ann released on *Dylan*
(traditional, arranged By Bob Dylan)
See entry under *Dylan*.

Big Yellow Taxi released on *Dylan*
(written by Joni Mitchell)
See entry under *Dylan*.

Bring Me A Little Water from *The Bootleg Series vol. 10*
(traditional, arranged by Bob Dylan)

Another traditional fold tune recorded during the *New Morning* sessions. Unlike "Lily Of The West" or "Sarah Jane" this was not included on the *Dylan* album. It's interesting to see that *Self-Portrait*'s renewed interest in recording these types of tunes continued through the next album. The song itself is more of blues work-song with the more gospel-ish elements emphasized by the backing vocalists. It's Bob once again pounding on the piano, with a little bit of electric guitar in the background. It's not entirely sure who Sylvie is in this song or how likely it is that she would be supplying our narrator with anything. Not a terribly exciting or interesting song, the fact that was included on *The Bootleg Series vol. 10*, while so many other more intriguing outtakes were left off, is a disappointment. Again it fits with the revisionist narrative of the particular volume which paints *Self-Portrait* as a casual jam session on some old folk songs and not the much broader and stranger project it really was.

Working On A Guru from *The Bootleg Series vol. 10*
(written by Bob Dylan)

A jam along the lines of "See You Later Allen Ginsberg" where Bob is verbal riffing on some phrases for the phonetics and not their literal meaning. This track comes from a session recorded with George Harrison along with a couple other studio cats. Bob is clearly enamored of George's guitar playing, encouraging him to take two solos, although maybe just because he doesn't have another verse ready off the top of his head. The music is pretty simple basic three-chord blues. It's hard to tell if the repeated references to gurus are a result of George's well-known devotion to Indian mysticism. It's probably not an insult or a dig as much as it is just a reason for this otherwise funny sounding word to pop into Dylan's brain. Like many of the more improvised tracks from these sessions, this song seems more fun to make than listen to. It sounds like George (or somebody) timidly tries to sing along with the "chorus" at one point, but doesn't get very far. This is the first draft of a song that Dylan never returned to, so unlike any of the other originals recorded during these sessions, this is the only option you have to hear this song. Ultimately it just a throwaway, but not a bad throwaway by any stretch.

Also recorded with George Harrison:
Yesterday
(written by John Lennon and Paul McCartney)
Da Doo Ron Ron
(written by Jeff Barry, Ellie Greenwich, and Phil Spector)
Ghost Riders In The Sky
(written by Stan Jones)
Cupid
(written by Sam Cooke)
All I Have To Do Is Dream
(written by Boudleaux Bryant)
Matchbox
(written by Carl Perkins)
Your True Love
(written by Carl Perkins)
Fishing Blues
(written by Henry Thomas)
Sign On The Window
(written by Bob Dylan)
If Not For You
(written by Bob Dylan)

Time Passes Slowly
(written by Bob Dylan)
Went To See The Gypsy
(written by Bob Dylan)
Song To Woody
(written by Bob Dylan)
Don't Think Twice, It's All Right
(written by Bob Dylan)
One Too Many Mornings
(written by Bob Dylan)
Gates Of Eden
(written by Bob Dylan)
Mama, You Been On My Mind
(written by Bob Dylan)
I Threw It All Away
(written by Bob Dylan)
I Don't Believe You (She Acts Like We Never Met)
(written by Bob Dylan)
Las Vegas Blues (Telephone Wire)
(written by Bob Dylan)
Honey, Just Allow Me One More Chance
(written by Bob Dylan)
Rainy Day Women #12 & 35
(written by Bob Dylan)
It Ain't Me Babe
(written by Bob Dylan)

If Bob Dylan was the guest star on the unreleased/unfinished album he recorded with Johnny Cash in 1969, then George Harrison is definitely Dylan's guest on this one. You only hear George singing on "Time Passes Slowly" and while there are a ton of old and new-ish Dylan compositions recorded here amongst the random covers, the only Beatles tune is "Yesterday", which George didn't write, sing or play on. I also toyed with the idea of putting these tracks together into a *New Morning II* for this book, but ultimately I these tracks also feel more tossed off than really recorded. Sure the one "new" song "Working On A Guru" could've been paired with tracks that would end up re-recorded for *New Morning* like "If Not For You". If I wanted to pull together an album from this session, I could've taken these as-yet-unheard tracks and picked another half an album from the bunch of covers recorded at this session. However, if we removed those four or five songs from the other albums, we would've really crippled them, especially considering how lackluster most of the recordings of these sessions really were.

It's been said that the officially released "Sign On The Window" comes from these sessions with George Harrison remaining uncredited on *New Morning* for contractual reasons. To my ear, I can't hear Harrison's guitar at all on this track, so I'm not really sure I believe it. Harrison has also been suggested as the guitarist on the officially released "Day Of The Locusts" and "Went To See The Gypsy". These seem a little more plausible to me, but it's harder to hear under the backing vocals and organ that Al Kooper overdubbed. This strikes at the heart of why it is hard to separate out a Dylan/Harrison album from these sessions. George clearly couldn't be clearly marked as a contributor at the time for legal reasons, and now we don't have any paperwork to verify things and are left to our own aural evidence. Really, if George Harrison weren't a Beatle and just the session musician he is treated like then these recordings wouldn't be any different from any of the other songs recording during the *New Morning* sessions.

In addition to the "new" songs recorded, like most sessions of this period, they devolved into a string of attempted covers. Certainly, Dylan's take on some of these tunes, particularly "Yesterday", rides a fine line between sincere tribute and mean-spirited parody. I suppose I could've also mixed these definitely Harrison tracks with the Johnny Cash sessions. Maybe instead of any covers or new originals, one could put together an album's worth of Dylan re-recording some of his old songs – but why would he do that, and why would anyone want to listen to that in 1969-1970?

Ultimately the two sets of super-star sessions are made with a very similar frame of mind and resulted in a very similar disappointment. A lot of old tunes that had already been recorded once being given an unnecessary second rendition in the studio along with half-remembered covers. In fact, the 1970 New York sessions for *Self*-Portrait also fall into this mold, although they didn't have nearly the wattage of star-power and therefore with lowered expectations were able to be released at the time. It would be a while before Bob would finally be able to recreate the "goofing off in the studio vibe" of *The Basement Tapes*. However, when he did, it would be with George Harrison for the Traveling Wilburys project in the late eighties.

Rumored to have been recorded but unheard:
Alligator Man
(written by Floyd Chance and Jimmy C. Newman)
Lonesome Me
(written by Don Gibson)
Kingston Town (Jamaica Farewell)
(written by Lord Burgess)
Long Black Veil
(written by Danny Dill and Marijohn Wilkin)
What's It All About
(writer unknown)
I Forgot To Remember
(written by Stan Kesler and Charlie Feathers)
Ahoooah (Owau)
(writer unknown)

There were also a number of other covers allegedly recorded during these sessions which haven't yet come to light. Maybe they're all in the Dylan Archive at the University of Tulsa. There are undoubtedly some titles that seem very odd for Dylan to be covering. Apparently "Alligator Man", which hasn't yet made its way into the hands of the collectors, was initially slated to appear on Columbia 1973 revenge album *Dylan*. I really want to know what a song titled "Ahoooah" could possibly be.

Written but unrecorded:
I Don't Want To Do It
(written by Bob Dylan)
I'd Have You Anytime
(written by Bob Dylan and George Harrison)

These two songs have never been recorded or performed live by Dylan and were composed sometime after the motorcycle crash while he was still living in Woodstock but before finishing *New Morning*. While most of the dirty hippies and potential acolytes who made the pilgrimage to Bob's home at that time were turned away with disgust, one was accepted (or at least tolerated) in the Dylan household: George Harrison. During this time the two collaborated on a song wherein George asked Bob to show him how he came up with all those lyrics, and Dylan asked Harrison some more of the fancier chords that he knew. The resultant tune was recorded by George for his 1970 post-Beatle breakthrough *All Things Must Pass* and does revolve primarily around a couple of major sevenths and is one of the best tracks on one of George's best albums. Bob also showed George a couple of new tunes he was working on. "If Not For You" managed to get recorded on both men's 1970 albums. The other song "I Don't Want To Do It" languished for a while, although George did record a demo of it in 1970. George finally covered it for the soundtrack of *Porky's Revenge* of all things. Dylan himself has never discussed the tune or attempted it on his own. There's a good chance he doesn't even remember writing it and would not recognize it as his own if you were to play it for him. Which is understandable. It's a perfectly fine but otherwise unremarkable song that would've fit in nicely with the rest of *New morning* had Bob deigned to include it.

"TOMORROW PASSES SLOWLY"

SIDE A:
1. **New Morning**
(version with horns from *The Bootleg Series vol. 10*)

2. Can't Help Falling In Love
3. Sign On The Window
(version with strings from *The Bootleg Series vo. 10*)
4. Big Yellow Taxi
5. If Dogs Run Free
6. Winterlude

SIDE B:
1. The Man In Me
2. Mr. Bojangles
3. If Not For You
(version with violin from *The Bootleg Series vo. 10*)
4. Tomorrow Is A Long Time
(unreleased version recorded during the *New Morning* sessions)
5. The Ballad Of Ira Hayes
6. Sarah Jane
7. Time Passes Slowly
(version #2 from *The Bootleg Series vol. 10*)

Here I'm trying to continue the weirdness of *Self-Portrait* instead of abandoning it altogether, as official *New Morning* did. I've included a bunch of cover songs as well as the more outlandish experiments from these sessions. Granted after the strangeness on *Self-Portrait* and *Blue Moon*, this may have been too much for the general audience, but each one of these odd records has its own distinct feel while being part of a larger period in Dylan's music.

That's why I used the version of "New Morning" with the horns and the version of "Sign On The Window" with strings. I'm definitely not going to use the less jazzy outtake of "If Dogs Run Free" from *The Bootleg Series vol. 10*. There are enough tracks recorded during these sessions for a double-album; but *Too Much Of Nothing Was Delivered* aside, I am generally trying to avoid those. Usually, there's just too much filler on a double-album. I also tried to avoid any of the songs from the George Harrison sessions, since those feel like part of a separate (and not very good) album. I did include the version of "Tomorrow Is A Long Time" recorded around this period since I think it really fits in with the album and was seriously considered for inclusion at the time.

I thought about putting all the covers on one side and leaving all the originals on the other, but I think it's important to see them all as part of the same experience, so I went ahead and pretty much just alternated between cover and original. Of all the possible versions of "Time Passes Slowly" out there, I thought it fitting to end the album with the most chaotic and overstuffed take. For "If Not For You" I had a tough time decided which to use. I love the version with George Harrison from *The Bootleg Series vol. 2*, but that didn't fit. The official album version is nice, put a little too pedestrian for what I was trying to accomplish with this album. Ultimately I used some audio software to create a version that has the violin take from *The Bootleg Series vol. 10* playing at the exact same time as the pedal steel take from *Dylan, Cash and the Nashville Cats*. This is the big hit single from the album and a great song all-in-all. I couldn't leave it out, so I had to use some audio trickery to make it fit. And I think it now fits beautifully.

Ultimately, this version I think feels right at homecoming after *Blue Moon* and *Self-Portrait*, instead of the hurried apology and refutation that *New Morning* finally became.

GREATEST HITS, VOL. II

Produced by: Leon Russell and Bob Dylan
Recorded: March 16th – November 4th, 1971
Released: November 17th, 1971
Famous/Important/Popular Track(s):
- Watching The River Flow

My Personal Favorite Track(s):
- George Jackson
- Wallflower

Just after going into seclusion following the motorcycle accident, Columbia released the first volume of Dylan's *Greatest Hits* to tide over record-buyers. In 1971, just as Bob was starting another period of fallow inactivity, his record company wanted a second volume to fill the gap. However, in order to entice a jaded public in buying another double album, they wanted Dylan to include a few previously unreleased tunes as an incentive. Now there were plenty of songs from the as-of-yet-unreleased *Basement Tapes* that could've filled this void nicely, but for some reason, the brass at Columbia Records didn't feel these tunes met their sonic quality standards and insisted that Bob re-record a handful of them for this compilation.

To satisfy their demands, Dylan brought fellow folk-singer Happy Traum to join him on acoustic guitar and banjo as he re-did three *Basement Tapes* songs in addition to *The Times They Are A-Changin'* outtake "Only A Hobo". While "Only A Hobo" didn't make the cut, these three *Basement* re-recordings appeared on side four of *Greatest Hits, vol. II*, alongside an outtake from his latest single and a live version of "Tomorrow Is A Long Time". "Tomorrow Is A Long Time" had been attempted during the *New Morning* sessions, so this was seemingly a song that Bob had suddenly a renewed interest in around '70-'71, but the live 1963 version was chosen over any of the studio attempts, perhaps to make the mixture of studio with a random live tracks from *Self-Portrait* feel like less of a one-off.

The double album compilation opens with "Watching The River Flow", which had been previously released as a single but was unavailable on any album. The rest of the rare material was tucked away on the final side of the last record. While the other three sides only have between 4-5 songs, these "bonus tracks" were not enough of side four, which opens with "If Not For You" and "It's All Over Now, Baby Blue".

While the most of the more obvious hits were already collected on *Greatest Hits, vol. I* and there are a couple of definitive tracks that hadn't been recorded yet that would have to wait for *Greatest Hits, vol. III*, ultimately this two-disc set if a pretty good sampler pack for getting into Dylan for a beginner. It touches on all of Bob's career phases up to this point and does a respectable job of presenting some lesser known deep cuts.

Normally, I wouldn't bother covering a greatest hits compilation in this book, but there are a number of songs recorded during this period that don't really fit in with either the album before it (*New Morning*) or the one after it (*Pat Garrett & Billy the Kid*), so it sort of required a chapter of its own. While Bob was definitely semi-retired by this point if you add together the bonus tracks recorded for this compilation with the two singles recorded in 1971 you almost have enough for a standalone album. Sure, there's not a lot of new material written during this period. All four Happy Traum tracks are re-recording of previously covered material. The B-side of "Watching The River Flow" is a cover that had already been covered, and the B-side of "George Jackson" is just "George Jackson" again. Still, it's interesting to look at the 1971 material as a whole and try to guess what Bob would've done had the muse not returned to him and he had to just eke out a living as a washed-up former rock-star now living the simple life of a family man.

The twin themes of restlessness and domesticity that were beginning to fight during *New Morning* are still waging here but in a slightly more unified fashion. Dylan is wrestling with his past legacy; what it means to him, what it means to his audience, and how he can utilize to his advantage while waiting to be inspired again. While these tracks may not have made for a coherent album in 1971, it is one of my favorite periods of lost Bob music.

Watching The River Flow A-side of a non-album single
(written by Bob Dylan)

One of two songs produced for Bob by Leon Russell. Understandably, this arrangement is led by the piano. One of the neat little tricks in this song is the way it slows down and falls apart after the first chorus on to pick itself up and pull itself together. I am guessing this was far more Leon's contribution than Bob's. There's a terrific electric slide guitar solo in the middle. The lyrics seem like a strident defense of laziness. I'm sure many fans at the time took it to be a commentary of his relative withdrawal from public life in the early '70s. It's a great fun track given an energetic reading by Leon's backing band. A lot of the seeds of the Rolling Thunder Revue can be found here with its oversized rock'n'roll band playing in a fun sloppy but majestic manner. This track and "When I Paint My Masterpiece" makes you with that not only had Bob written more material during this period but that he also let Leon Russell produce a whole album for him.

Spanish Is The Loving Tongue B-side of the "Watching The River Flow" single
(written by Charles Badger Clark)

See the entry under *Self-Portrait*.

George Jackson A-side and B-side of a non-album single
(written by Bob Dylan)
The only real obvious, straight-forward protest song between *The Times They Are A-Changin'* and "Hurricane". This song has not surpassed its topicality as those others have. It might be that there's simply nothing in the lyrics that explain why George Jackson was such a great guy. Sure, he was sent to prison on what seems like a small crime, and he wouldn't submit to authority once he was in jail, but it's never really stated why he wouldn't. Dylan claims that the prison guards are frightened of George's love, but no examples of that love are specifically given during the song. Sure he shouldn't have been imprisoned much less shot for a $30 theft, but its hard to see why Bob reveres him so much. While I'm sure fans were delighted to hear a new song with a political message in 1971, the fact that he couldn't even write enough material to fill both sides of a single must've been dispiriting. The "big band" version of the song doesn't come across as very angry or urgent in any way. In fact, it is almost chipper with its pedal steel and backing vocalists. The acoustic B-side works much better by evoking memories of an earlier Bob Dylan, and not from the actual performance. The song never did end up getting included on any compilation other than on *Masterpieces* a box-set released only in Japan, Australia, and New Zealand in 1978. As a result, this is one of the harder officially released Dylan songs to find on CD or MP3.

Wallflower from *The Bootleg Series vol. 2*
(written by Bob Dylan)
Recorded during the "George Jackson" sessions with the same "big band" backing him up as on the A-side, I have no idea what this was recorded for. Maybe a potential B-side? Or a demo? Either way, this version didn't see the light of day until *The Bootleg Series vol. 2*. I am pretty confident that the fact that Bob's son Jakob named his band The Wallflowers was merely a coincidence. There is a version of this song on the album *Doug Sahm and Band* released just a year or so after this was recorded with Bob providing the backing/harmony vocals. There is another version on *The Bootleg Series vol. 10* with just Bob on acoustic guitar and harmonica accompanied by a pedal steel guitar that makes more sense as a demo to show the song to potential artists to cover. The most noteworthy thing about that version is that it includes a key change in the middle. The songwriting here seems more overtly country than anything on *Nashville Skyline* from the waltzing time signature to the keening melody. While Doug Sahm's version naturally plays up the more Tejano elements and Bob doesn't do anything to signify its country-ness other than the pedal steel, it feels like that kind of song. The recording is a little garbled for some technical reason, but not enough to deter one's enjoyment of a straight-forward country-style love song from Bob Dylan.

When I Paint My Masterpiece from *Greatest Hits vol. II*
(written by Bob Dylan)

Another track produced by Leon Russell. Again this makes you wish that the two of them had worked together for a whole album. The backing certainly feels a lot more full and self-assured than the "big band" Bob put together for "George Jackson" and "Wallflower". The song itself seems to be treading the same lyrical territory as "Watching The River Flow" only Bob sounds a lot less patient for this writer's block to be over with. This is one of the very few songs that Bob has done with a key change in the middle of it. Usually, this is a cheap trick to keep the listener interested while not having to come up with any new parts for a song. It works well for that here. The Band's cover of this song was released before Bob's. The accordion in their version seems to enforce the more continental feeling of the song, especially with the lines about a pretty little girl from Greece, living in the Coliseum, and nights on the Spanish stairs. Very European! For a song written about not being able to write a song, this is pretty well-written. Not sure why this was left to be released as a bonus track on *Greatest Hits vol. II* instead of being the B-side of the "Watching The River Flow" single. The two definitely feel like two sides of the same coin.

I Shall Be Released from *Greatest Hits vol. II*
(written by Bob Dylan)
See the entry under *The Basement Tapes*

You Ain't Goin' Nowhere from *Greatest Hits vol. II*
(written by Bob Dylan)
See the entry under *The Basement Tapes*

Down In The Flood (Crash On The Levee) from *Greatest Hits vol. II*
(written by Bob Dylan)
See the entry under *The Basement Tapes*

Only A Hobo from *The Bootleg Series vol. 10*
(written by Bob Dylan)
See the entry under *The Time They Are A-Changin'*

"WATCHING MY MASTERPIECE FLOW"

SIDE A:
1. When I Paint My Masterpiece
2. Watching The River Flow
3. Wallflower
4. George Jackson (Big Band Version)

SIDE B:
1. George Jackson (Acoustic Version)
2. Only A Hobo
3. I Shall Be Released
4. You Ain't Goin' Nowhere
5. Down In The Flood

After the confusion of *Blue Moon*, *Self-Portrait*, and *Tomorrow Passes Slowly*, instead of retreating for several years, it would behoove Dylan to put out a more traditionally "Dylan" album. And so this is what I put together for 1971. Like *Bringing It All Back Home* there is an "electric side" followed by an acoustic side. Gone are the cover songs that plagued the last few albums. While the first two tracks have a definite Leon Russell piano vibe, the second half of the first side is pretty countrified, like the last few albums. However the inclusion of "George Jackson" as well as "Only A Hobo" marks a return to making political statements for Bob, which also would've curried favor amongst the critics and audience. While this theoretical album is something of a let-down after the last three weird ones, it is still a good solid album. It gives a good idea of what an early '70s sound from Bob would've been like. Something that, unfortunately, we didn't get a full album of at the time. It certainly would've made the wait between *New Morning* and *Pat Garrett & Billy the Kid* feel less excruciatingly long. That probably would've helped relieve the pressure of that soundtrack to live up to all these hopes and expectations in the minds of Dylan's increasingly impatient fans.

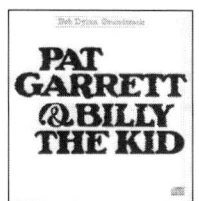

PAT GARRETT & BILLY THE KID
Produced by: Gordon Carroll
Recorded: January 20th – February, 1973
Released: July 13th, 1973

Famous/Important/Popular Track(s):
- Knockin' On Heaven's Door

My Personal Favorite Track(s):
- River Theme
- Turkey Chase
- Knockin' On Heaven's Door

When the Beatles spent over six months recording *Sgt. Pepper*, it had seemed extravagant at the time. Meanwhile, post-bike crash, Dylan was routinely taking over a year to release albums. But the anticipation during the three years that separated *New Morning* and *Pat Garrett* must've seemed astronomical in 1973. These days, we pretty much expect Bob (or anyone) to take that long between albums, particularly non-Sinatra cover albums.

While there was no way for any album to live up to that build-up, coming back with a soundtrack album was a convenient way to help defuse some of those expectations. Since most folks see Dylan primarily as a wordsmith, having a valid excuse to release a bunch of instrumentals was a natural way to ease himself back. (As opposed to *Self-Portrait*, where the lack of new original lyrics was meant to be deliberately off-putting). Still, I'm sure most people were disappointed that there were really only two new songs with lyrics on here (one of which was repeated several times). Even now, this album is mostly seen as an extremely long maxi-single for "Knockin' On Heaven's Door".

As much as I have argued that Bob's music is far more interesting than his lyrics, he's usually writing pretty simple three chord songs. It's not like he's got a "Rhapsody In Blue" hiding in him somewhere. But this is really our first chance to really see this facet of Dylan isolated. Sure there's "Nashville Skyline Rag" as well as "Wigwam" and "Woogie Boogie", but that's not much.

What we are left with is simple, but plaintive. It is appropriately evocative of the Old West. Since these instrumentals weren't designed to stand on their own, but rather accompany the film, it is easier to be a little forgiving of their somewhat humble charms. Overall though, this is a pleasant piece of mood music. Bob wouldn't attempt to score another movie until 2009's *My Own Love Song* and even then, he never actually released those instrumentals in an audio-only format. As a result, this is our only opportunity to really dive into Dylan, the composer rather than the songwriter/performer. As such, it is indispensable. I think it's a wonderful bit of mood music to boot.

Main Title Theme (Billy)
(written by Bob Dylan)

Our first time through the Billy theme. This version features a really prominent tambourine while one acoustic guitar plays the chords and the other solos about. About two and a half minutes in a bass fills out the sound, but the only percussion is still that never-ending tambourine which starts to sound a little like sleigh bells. If you hadn't heard the vocals versions of this song, you would have no idea what the melody is. This is an elegant, evocative instrumental that doesn't ever quite rise to the level of memorable. After about six minutes it fades out without coming to any sort of conclusion.

Cantina Theme (Workin' for the Law)
(written by Bob Dylan)

Another acoustic instrumental, only instead of tambourine, we get bongos. Certainly no sort of drum set yet for this album. The bass kicks in right away and this is much shorter, but again there is no real melody here, just chords with some soloing on top of it. There's even an electric guitar faintly in the background doing some finger-picking thing. Once again no ending has been written, and the track just fades out. Which makes sense, since this is a film soundtrack and Dylan wanted to make sure Peckinpah had as much or as little material as he needed while scoring this film.

Billy 1
(written by Bob Dylan)

You would be forgiven for initially assuming this was another instrumental. It's over a minute and a half of an introduction before the vocals begin. The lyrics are a simplified synopsis of the plot of the movie. There's no drums, just two acoustic guitars (one playing lead the other rhythm) and a very active bass in addition to Bob's harmonica. This version of the song is pretty straight-forward; lilting and evocative. It's an okay song if a bit on the nose. It certainly does not warrant this much repetition.

Bunkhouse Theme
(written by Bob Dylan)

A sweet little melody played on one acoustic guitar while the other plays some arpeggios around the chords. A very simple stripped down song with no drums, but there does seem to be somebody tapping their foot to keep time. It becomes very pronounced at various moments in the song. The whole thing has a very light feeling to it. It's also pretty short, just under two and a half minutes. Nothing consequential, but perfect filler for a soundtrack album.

River Theme
(written by Bob Dylan)

While "Wigwam" gets dismissed for being on a "proper" album, Dylan fans a far more forgiving to this song simply because it's on a soundtrack. It's supposed to be instrumental, so the vocals without words are perfectly fine. As a result, this song also tends to be a little more forgotten in Dylan's oeuvre. Sure it's not half as long and doesn't have the bombastic horns layered on top, but the two feel very similar. This is a much quieter song and is much more soothing. There's just a couple of acoustic guitars and a bass laying down the foundation. Bob has enlisted several friends to sing the la-la-la's along with him, but his vocals definitely dominate the mix. It is a sweet lovely melody that doesn't require any lyrics to convey its feelings of both sorrow and relief. One of my favorite tracks from this album.

Turkey Chase
(written by Bob Dylan)

One of the more fun and catchy instrumentals on this soundtrack. Led by some goofy banjo. Evidently, this song is meant to underscore a scene of comic relief. There's not much to it, but it is a lot of fun. Sort of brings to mind the version of "Nashville Skyline Rag" that Earl Scruggs recorded ,and Dylan guested on. The fiddle does a lovely job sawing away in the background. The acoustic guitar soloing is less of a surprise. It almost makes you wish that Bob would do a whole bluegrass album. Actually, I'm kind of surprised he hasn't by now. Not a terribly complicated song, it does have a nice descending bit in the intro that he repeats within the song. It's not just the usual three-chord blues work-out. It doesn't really go anywhere, but it creates a nice mood.

Knockin' on Heaven's Door
(written by Bob Dylan)

One of Bob's all-time most beloved songs. What people tend to forget is just how short it is. Only two verses, no bridge, just four chords. Usually, when it's performed live, Bob will come up with an extra verse just to pad the runtime out. Still, there's a reason why this show is such an evergreen. It is easy for other musicians to cover and put their individual stamp on. The chords are a great springboard for all kinds of instrumental soloing. Sometimes it's surprising to go back to the original and see how simple and stripped down it is. Kind of like "All Along The Watchtower", the song itself is much more famous than the original recording. Luckily this version does work very well. With the added benefit of the film itself, it is much easier to parse out the meaning of Bob's lyrics here. These are the dying regrets and laments of a gunfighter slain in the old west. There are no guitar histrionics on the original version. There's hardly even any drums. Just a strummed acoustic, a fingerpicked electric and a bass guitar.

And the background vocalists are going "ooh" and singing along with the chorus. Bob says what little he needs to say and gets out, quickly fading without ever ending. A surprising show efficiency on Dylan's part. "Knockin' On Heaven's Door" deserves all the accolades it gets.

Final Theme
(written by Bob Dylan)

A companion piece to "Wigwam" in some respects. The wordless vocals don't carry the melody throughout the whole so however, with a flute (or possibly recorder) taking the lead, instead the group chant/groan provides an occasional counterpoint. It's a sweet lovely song with minimal drums but the occasional cymbal crash punctuating the song. The main strummed guitar is acoustic, and the bass playing is fleet and nimble. There's a little fingerpicked electric guitar low in the mix. Sure, the song by itself can get a little repetitive within five-and-a-half minutes, but overall this is one of Bob's sweetest and most touching instrumentals. It's songs like this that really make *Pat Garrett & Billy the Kid* as an album and as a soundtrack. If you're into Dylan songs without lyrics, this is one of the best.

Billy 4
(written by Bob Dylan)

While each version of "Billy" may have a different line or even whole new verses, they don't feel so much like separate arrangements as much as merely alternate takes of the same song. I understand that as a soundtrack, having recapitulating themes is far more important than originality, but this does start to feel kind of samey. It is taken at about the same tempo, but this version nixes the long intro from "Billy 1" as well as the bass. In its place, we get lots and lots more verses describing various scenes in the film. There's still no chorus or bridge or any real change in the music until the last line gets repeated a few times shortly before fading out.

Billy 7
(written by Bob Dylan)

The most significant change in all of the "Billys". There's some electric guitar here, and the tempo has slowed down from evocative to dragging. There are some drums on here occasionally punctuating the proceedings with an unexpected roll. On the plus side, it is much shorter than "Billy 1" or "Billy 4". Once the drums really kick in towards the end, the song gets a boost, and if it started that way, this might be my favorite version. As it is, "Billy 7" is just another reinstatement of the main theme.

Songs not on the album:
Rock Me Mama officially unreleased
(written by Bob Dylan)

An unfinished song attempted during the *Pat Garrett & Billy The Kid* sessions that made its way onto various bootlegs. From there it was discovered by Ketch Secor of the Old Crow Medicine Show. Ketch decided to go ahead and finish the song off on his own, retitling it "Wagon Wheel" and only asking for Dylan's permission after the fact. It has since become a country hit for Darius Rucker, formerly of Hootie & The Blowfish. There's not much to Bob's version of it. He obviously didn't have any words for the verses, just a hummed melody. The only really finished lyrics are the chorus, with the title phrase being an old blues phrase that came either from Arthur Crudup or Big Bill Broonzy. It's unlikely that Dylan would've finished it off with the trite reminisces of growing up in the South the way Ketch, did; but it doesn't seem terribly out of character. Apparently the band here are still learning the tune while Bob is still writing it, but it is a catchy chorus, and you can see why someone would want it to get finished off, even if it wasn't Dylan.

Sweet Amarillo officially unreleased
(written by Donna Terry Weiss)

After the surprising success of "Wagon Wheel", Bob apparently sent Ketch Secor some more unfinished *Pat Garrett & Billy The Kid* outtakes to finish off. This time the collaboration was a little more intentional on Bob's part. The only problem is the "fragment" that Ketch finished off with his bandmate Critter Fuqua was not a Dylan original; even though Bob happily took his third of the songwriting credit. The song was actually written by Donna Weiss, and Bob should've known that since she played on the second leg of the Rolling Thunder Revue. Who knows if Dylan was being shady here, or just forgot. Either way, this "new" song was not as big of a hit for the Old Crow Medicine Show, though still very popular. The original fragment of this cover that Bob recorded that led to this whole shebang is pretty similar to "Rock Me, Mama". Bob only remembers the words to the chorus, just humming through verses. The backing musicians are slowly picking up the song and jumping in as the song picks up speed. There's plenty of spoken dialogue while the song is going on about how to play it. The lyrics are about a pillow thief or something, but it doesn't really matter. It has some tantalizing possibilities to it, but it sounds and feels very unfinished. Luckily it's little over a minute of Bob trying to remember the song, so it doesn't grate when treated as a completed track.

Goodbye Holly officially unreleased
(written by Bob Dylan)

One of the more direct and literal songs Bob wrote for the film *Pat*

Garrett & Billy the Kid. The soundtrack supervisor felt the song was too on the nose and made Bob go back and write a different song for the scene where Slim Pickens' character dies. Bob then came up with "Knockin' On Heaven's Door", which the supervisor also did not like. So much for taste. The song isn't quite complete, not being much more than a chorus with gang vocals and a single verse. It does have a bit of potential, and I wouldn't be surprised if Ketch Secor finished this one up at some point. It's a far more boisterous song than "Knockin' On Heaven's Door" and certainly would've downplayed the sadness of the moment on screen. Still, it's a catchy fragment, if not an effective bit of film score.

Pecos Blues officially unreleased
(written by Bob Dylan)

A simple instrumental with a trumpet following Bob's wordless vocal line. It reminds one of a smaller scale version of "Wigwam". There's not much to this song, but it's supposed to be in the background and not the center of attention. The drums play with a nice side-stick on the snare. It sounds like Dylan even corralled a couple of other singers to la-la-la along with him. It doesn't sound like the trumpeter knows the tune and is doing a pretty good job of following along and guessing where the melody is going. The whole thing has a very scruffy, unfinished feel to it, which makes sense since it was actually completed. You can even hear Dylan giving out some directions to the musicians in the recording. It may run on a little too long, but it is a lovely little bit of background music. If you're a fan of Dylan's instrumentals (like I am), you will need to get your hands on this track.

Billy Surrenders officially unreleased
(written by Bob Dylan)

Another instrumental Bob wrote and recorded for the film that didn't make the album. This is one of the more upbeat and rocking of these tunes. The lead melody is played by the organ and is a rudimentary part. There are some nice jangly acoustic guitars strummed throughout with a minimal drum backdrop. It's a nice little distraction of a piece, but you can't really pay attention to it all alone. It is the essence of background music and should be treated as such. While Bob doesn't know how to read or write music, you can hear him giving directions to the other musicians as to what to play. While each of the session musicians is contributing, Dylan isn't using them to come up with and write their own parts and then taking all the credit himself. He definitely has some sort of vision and is able to describe somewhat effectively. It's almost more interesting to listen to Bob teach the song than it is to listen to the actual song itself.

And He's Killed Me Too officially unreleased
(written by Bob Dylan)

Another song with a wordless vocal melody. However, you can clearly hear James Coburn saying the title phrase at the beginning of the track as the musicians were clearly playing along with the film. It's a pleasant little song with a fun acoustic guitar turnaround. The melody is only three or four notes that Bob is singing "aaah" over with a few friends. Towards the end, Bob attempts some vocal extemporizing to make the tune more complicated. It's not really Dylan's strong suit, but it is fun to hear him try. This track is a lot more rocking and less unobtrusive than some of the instrumentals Bob has written for this soundtrack. It's still not really meant to be examined on its own as a piece of music. It would be interesting for Dylan to do a whole album of instrumentals that weren't meat to accompany a film but are intended to be consumed on their own. Of all the strange and beguiling turns his career has taken it's a shame that he hasn't taken at least one album to try and prove himself just as a composer. But who knows, he might someday.

"PAT GARRET & BILLY THE KID"

SIDE A:
1. Main Title Theme (Billy)
2. Woogie Boogie
3. Pecos Blues
4. Billy Surrenders
5. Nashville Skyline Rag
6. Turkey Chase

SIDE B:
1. Workin' For The Law (Catina Theme)
2. Bunkhouse Theme
3. And He's Killed Me Too
4. River Theme
5. Wigwam
6. Final Theme

My instrumental Dylan album. I have used some wordless (if not necessarily vocal-less) tracks leftover from previous albums in order to swap them out for all the songs with words. I skipped "Suze (The Cough Song)" and "East Laredo Blues" since they felt far more tied to the period when they were done, some ten years before most of these instrumentals. I even considered putting the *Planet Waves* outtake "Crosswind Jamboree" on here since so many of these songs ended up on my re-configured version of that album. "Pecos Blues" is in the middle of side one, but I did put four songs in a row that have humming or "la-la-la"s or whatnot at the end of the album. I'm not sure how well some of this would've actually worked in the service of the film itself. But as an excuse to really dig into this less-known and less-loved side of Dylan's songwriting, I love the idea of an all-instrumental Bob Dylan album. There is a lot more versatility and sophistication in the arrangement than many people would assume.

PLANET WAVES
Produced by: Rob Fraboni
Recorded: November 2nd – 14th, 1973
Released: January 17th, 1974
Famous/Important/Popular Track(s):
- Forever Young

My Personal Favorite Track(s):
- On A Night Like This
- Going, Going, Gone
- Dirge

I've got to admit, I really don't like *Planet Waves*. For one thing, I'm not a big fan of The Band. I've not particularly liked any of the stuff they've done on their own as a group. Robbie Robertson always seemed like a smug, condescending, pretentious rock-star (like Sting, Bono, Springsteen or Bob Geldof). Back when they were just a band and not The Band, they were good for what Dylan was doing on tour in 1966, but there's a reason why he always ended up using the Nashville session players on his albums. (The fact that drummer Levon Helm was too chicken to endure the boos of Tour '66 is another stroke against them).

But it's not entirely The Band's fault that I don't like this album. On *Planet Waves*, Bob finally achieves what he was aiming for on *Nashville Skyline* and *New Morning*; he becomes a completely detached, uninvolved songwriter. But where those two discs were charming in the sincere ineptitude, this one actually pulls it off slickly – much to its detriment. As a result songs like "Tough Mama", "Hazel", "Something There Is About You", "You Angel You", and "Never Say Goodbye" are almost impossible to tell apart. It'll become a bad habit that'll pop up again and again in Bob's career.

The opening Zydeco of "On A Night Like This" promises more of the weird genre experimentation of *New Morning*'s "Winterlude" and "If Dogs Run Free", but never follows up on it. "Going, Going, Gone" is, in fact, a really strong song, but you can hardly tell over The Band's showboating.

"Forever Young" ends Bob's tradition of adding more than one version of the same song to the same album ("Alberta" and "Billy"). While the slower second version is pretty darn good (and proof that Rod Stewart is a thief), the fast version makes the song seem almost as forgettable as the rest of the album. Compare "Dirge" with the similarly arranged (just piano and acoustic guitar) "Blind Willie McTell" from *The Bootleg Series Vol. 1-3*, and see how distracting Robbie Robertson is in comparison to Mark Knopfler. His little scratching the string thing is all over here and really annoying.

Even without The Band, "The Wedding Song" sounds about as tacked on as it really was. Not that the album is painfully unlistenable or anything.

With a musician as talented as Bob Dylan, even when he's coasting, there's bound to be a certain amount of quality to endeavor. It's just that there's a real lack of anything interesting or risky going on here.

On a Night Like This
(written by Bob Dylan)

While Bob complained that he couldn't get "If Not For You" sounding Tex-Mex on *New Morning* it almost sounds like he got there with "On A Night Like This', although really this is far more Zydeco than Tex-Mex. If Bob had toured with Los Lobos's accordion player, David Hidalgo, this would definitely have to be one they would put in the repertoire. It's a fun, danceable song with a great harmonica solo that carries on through the fade out. The lyrics are nothing special, just about how much the singer loves his woman and how the weather that night reminds him of her and he wants to spend some time with her dancing. Certainly nothing about Jezebel the nun and Einstein's electric violin.

Going, Going, Gone
(written by Bob Dylan)

One of the darker songs in Bob's entire catalog, undercut somewhat by Robbie Robertson's scratchy guitar picking. It's a shame that Bob hasn't redone this song as its one of the best he has ever written. The lyrics seem to be hinting about a guy contemplating suicide. The minor chords bring a heaviness to the proceedings. Things try to escape to a major key in the bridge before falling apart. The chorus is simple but catchy. I am really torn on this recording. I really want to like it more than I do, but ultimately there's something unsatisfying about the execution. Maybe the performance and instrumentation are a little too jovial or even tossed-off than this song deserves. Only the organ seems vaguely mournful here. The live version on *At Budokan* doesn't even attempt to reach this level of pathos, turning the whole thing into some sort of weird showstopper. This is definitely a song ripe for rediscovery by the right artist.

Tough Mama
(written by Bob Dylan)

A real upbeat rocker that isn't nearly as funky as it thinks it is. This is the kind of song that is easier to dance to than to sing along to. Bob's harmonica playing is some the most manic he's ever unleashed. For a band as renowned for their singing as The Band, there is surprisingly little harmonizing on *Planet Waves*. The lyrics are semi-obscure paeans to the woman Bob loves. Unfortunately, it also contains the phrase "hotter than a crotch" which is just unpleasant. While this song is about a minute longer than it needs to be it doesn't get too old or repetitive. There's even a nifty little organ solo towards the end.

Hazel
(written by Bob Dylan)

A delicate slow ballad. This song sounds remarkably sad for a tune whose lyrics seem to suggest that this is a love song. Bob's singing doesn't give one much of an impression about whomever Hazel is – or even if Hazel is a real person. There's a neat bridge in this song, but The Band always seem like they want to be playing this song harder and faster and Bob is continually pulling on the reins, trying to get this to be a proper ballad. Bob has a lovely harmonica solo, but Robbie Robertson is trying to take a solo at the same time halfway through. It's kind of annoying. Overall this is one of the more mediocre tracks on *Planet Waves* which surprisingly was one of the few songs Bob played with The Bad for their inaccurately named *The Last Waltz*.

Something There Is About You
(written by Bob Dylan)

Another slow ballad. Coming right after "Hazel" does this song no favors. On an album loaded with forgettable tunes, this is one of the more mediocre ones. The lyrics seem to be about how much Bob loves his wife. There are a few autobiographical elements in this song, like bringing up Duluth, but that is followed up by the name Ruth, which is clearly inaccurate. Maybe Bob is trolling us. Or he just couldn't come up with a better rhyme. There's more harmonica playing here than any album since *John Wesley Harding*. The problem with this song (and *Planet Waves* in general) is its utter lack of distinction. I would much rather hear Bob try something ambitious and fail than to just have him dole out competent filler like this.

Forever Young
(written by Bob Dylan)

Sure, there were two versions of "Alberta" on *Self-Portrait*, but Bob has never seemed so indecisive as he does on this song which both closes side A and opens side B of *Planet Waves*. History and popular opinion seem to have chosen the slower more elegant version of this song, but it is worth noting that Bob originally didn't really hear it only as a ballad or an anthem. In fact it hard to tell how Dylan hear it at all. The demo version first released on *Biograph* doesn't really favor one arrangement or tempo over the other. Apparently, Dylan even tried it a couple of other ways with the band during the recording of this album that didn't get included. Sure, by the time Bob was playing this at the *Last Waltz* in just a couple years, he is favoring the slower version, this is also the take that was selected for *Greatest Hits vol. III*. The faster version is pretty funky, and despite only being half as long makes room for a couple of fun harmonica solos. The upbeat version also jettisons some extra repetitions of the title phrase, reducing the chorus to just a refrain. The only real drawback to the faster version is that it undercuts the words. These are some of Bob's most easily understandable lyrics, a paean to his young child and hopes that both he and his life turn out well. It's a touching sentiment with an undercurrent of fear for the future that most of Bob's treaties on domesticity during these years lack. As a result, the more pleading vocal on the slower version of "Forever Young" gives this song the edge. The theme here so universal and plainly stated that when Rod Stewart did his own song with the same title and subject, he had forgotten it had already been done before in nearly the same way and ended up giving Dylan a co-writing credit. There's some annoying mandolin running through the whole song, but otherwise, the playing very sensitive to the material and played with a hushed elegance that gains some energy during the choruses that the faster version cuts out entirely. This is not only the most famous song off of *Planet Waves* but also one of my favorites.

Dirge
(written by Bob Dylan)

A lovely slowly piano ballad that is nearly impossible to enjoy due to the hyperactive acoustic guitar that is continually trying to show off through the whole song. More than any other song, this is the one that makes me dislike Robbie Robertson. The melody itself is haunting. The lyrics even seem to be flirting with suicidal thought, and Bob sings it with real pain in his voice. Bob's piano playing, while never technically proficient, is always suitably simple. Meanwhile, there's a guitar constantly jumping up and down yelling "Look at me! Look at me!" like a kid with too much sugar. I'm always torn on this song because I really do like it. Sometimes I can tune the guitar out and really enjoy it. Other times it is so frustrating how the recording has been ruined, and it just makes me angry. It's not even necessarily the instrumentation. If you compare this to the piano with solo guitar arrangement of "Blind Willie McTell" that was released on *The Bootleg Series vol. 3* you can see how this kind of interplay could and should work. Hopefully, someday we will get an outtake or alternate version of this song that realizes its potential.

You Angel You
(written by Bob Dylan)

Not nearly as slow or dull as "Hazel" or "Something There is About You" but nearly as unremarkable. It tries to rock, but isn't as clunky as "Tough Mama". This song feels the most like boilerplate *Planet Waves*. The lyrics are another ode to Bob's wife. Although the sentiment is as trite as anything on *Nashville Skyline* or *New Morning*, it lacks even the clichés that make those love songs stick out in Dylan's oeuvre. Although I will admit that the metaphor of an angel for a loved one is pretty shopworn by this point. Luckily it's not as annoying or irritating as some of the songs on this album. It's got a nice, easy, middle-of-the-road feel to it. The organ work is nice, and Robbie's guitar isn't showboating nearly as badly. The melody is nice, without ever veering into being catchy or even memorable. At just under three minutes, "You Angel You" doesn't overstay its welcome. It's perfectly fine, but that's all.

Never Say Goodbye
(written by Bob Dylan)

Coming after "You Angel You" Does this song no favors in feeling very distinctive. This is one of the few songs on *Planet Waves* that takes advantage of The Band's vocal abilities, although the harmonies on the chorus are a little buried in the mix. There's a self-aware line in here about changing your last name, and few references to what may be Bob's home state of Minnesota, but nothing here really sticks, much less sticks out. Robbie Robertson's guitar tone maintains that annoying flange sound on it. It's a short enough song taken at a comfortable tempo. Harmless, but ultimately forgettable.

Wedding Song
(written by Bob Dylan)

Here we come to the first, but not last, of an unusual Dylan trope. Sometimes by the end of recording an album, Bob decided he doesn't like said album anymore and attempts to rescue it by quickly tossing off a solo acoustic number at the very end. Bob would do it again with "Dark Eyes" on *Empire Burlesque*. In fact, the whole *Good As I Been To You Album* is just a series of these songs after Bob decided to replace the full-band folk tunes he recorded with David Bromberg. The song itself has a desperation to prove that he sincerely believes this domestic-bliss ruse, and it comes off as flop-sweat. I think that someone less connected to this tune may be able to do a rendition of this that is un-ironic and sincere. Bob however is beginning to see the writing on the wall regarding his marriage and is desperately trying to convince her, or us, or himself, of the opposite. Not that the song is terrible, it's just trying too hard. For a tune that is supposed to be a celebration of a marriage, it is definitely in a minor key casting doubts on everything proffered here. The song feels hastily recorded; Bob is unsure of what the chord changes are or where they go, and he is faking his way through this. It adds a nice bit of intrigue as you don't know precisely where Dylan is going to land, but it never seems intentional. Bob would continue to have a solo acoustic section in his live shows for years and years to come, but he has rarely been able to re-create that transition seamlessly on record. While I may find The Band's plodding a bit annoying on this album, ignoring them completed undercuts *Planet Waves* as a whole.

Songs not on the album:
Nobody 'Cept You from *The Bootleg Series vol. 2*
(written by Bob Dylan)

The only real outtake from *Planet Waves*. Unlike most of the songs on this album, this tune got played during the 1974 tour that was ostensibly designed to support *Planet Waves*, with Bob trotting it out during his solo acoustic mini-set. As a result, the song's stature grew in its absence on the official album. Having been finally released on *The Bootleg Series vol. 2*, it's become clear that this is just another mediocre middle-of-the-road love song from this album. It's not necessarily bad, and maybe a better addition to the album than "Never Say Goodbye" or You Angel You" but is not a long-lost masterpiece. There's the usual oddly flanged guitar noodlings of Robbie Robertson. The organ work is nice, but the song itself is dull. There's no hook or chorus although the title phrase is used frequently throughout the lyrics. The words are supposed to be about how great the narrator's love is but given his dismissal of everything else in the universe the overall feeling is a tad nihilistic. Dylan's vocals are notably restrained giving the song more of a desperate feeling. It can't be very reassuring to the woman this song is sung at. Plus there's the heavy responsibility to be the only thing of any value in the world. Despite the preponderance of quote-unquote love songs on this album, in retrospect, it's no surprise that the marriage fell apart while Bob was on the road and the only follow-up that makes sense to *Planet Waves* is the divorce-soaked *Blood On The Tracks*.

Crosswind Jamboree officially unreleased
(written by Bob Dylan)

A sort of bridge between Pat Garrett & Billy The Kid and Planet Waves. This instrumental sounds like a cross between the sound of the latter and songs of the former. This could just be another jam to limber The Band up and to test levels, but unlike other instrumentals that have leaked out from these sessions, this one was a definite title (as opposed to the generic "Garth's Piano Tune" or "Instrumental/Country Tune"), so this seems a little more organized and intentional. In fact, Bob made sure that the tape box was corrected from the "Cross Fire" it was initially marked with. There are apparently two takes of this that were attempted, and Dylan even went to the trouble of having this song copyrighted. I'm not sure whether there are words to this that were never recorded and now lost to the sands of time, or if this was always meant to be instrumental, since Bob still used to writing those types of songs from the last album.

"CEREMONIES OF THE HORSEMEN"

SIDE A:
1. One A Night Like This
2. Goodbye Holly
3. Going Going Gone
4. Rock Me Mama
5. Sweet Amarillo

SIDE B:
1. Forever Young
   (slow version)
2. Billy 1
3. Dirge
4. Nobody 'Cept You
5. Knockin' On Heaven's Door

I have used all the songs with words and vocals from *Pat Garrett & Billy the Kid* in order to pad out this album after I took all the less exciting love songs from the mix. Maybe they don't fit together all that well, but I think it is a step up from the more mediocre monotony of the original *Planet Waves*.

This also gives a more rough and improvised feel to the overall album, which is odd since you would expect anything from Bob and the Band not too feel as slick and polished as *Planet Waves* ended up being. While the song "Love Minus Zero/No Limit" was not recorded for this album, he did toy with the idea of titling this album after that lyric from the nearly ten-year-old song for this album. It is as relevant as anything else on *Planet Waves*, so I have gone ahead and co-opting that title for this Frankenstein's monster of an album.

While I don't think this is not a great album by Bob, even with my attempts to fix it, anything with both "Knockin' On Heaven's Door" and "Forever Young" can't be all bad and probably would've been hailed as more of a full return to form after years out of the spotlight with only an instrumental soundtrack album in the last three years.

BLOOD ON THE TRACKS

Produced by: Bob Dylan
Recorded: September 16th – 19th, 1974
& December 27th – 30th, 1974
Released: January 20th, 1975

Famous/Important/Popular Track(s):
- Tangled Up In Blue
- Shelter From The Storm
- Simple Twist Of Fate

My Personal Favorite Track(s):
- Tangled Up In Blue
- You're A Big Girl Now
- Idiot Wind

Much like *The Freewheelin' Bob Dylan* and *Self-Portrait*, this album is the result of combining three different attempts to make a record. Unlike those other two though, there's not a whole lot of extra material here. Bob only recorded 12 titles, of which ten were selected for the final cut. Ultimately Dylan's indecision was on how this particular batch of songs should be recorded.

In September of 1974, Bob walked into his old studio in New York and laid down a solo acoustic version of *Blood On The Tracks*. The purpose of these recordings is not entirely clear. As professional and well-done as those recordings were, it doesn't look like they were ever seriously in contention to be released on the official album. However, they don't seem to be meant as demos either because when Eric Wasserman and his Deliverance band showed up in the studio the next day, Dylan seems to have actually done nothing to demonstrate the songs at all. This in addition to the weird open-E tuning meant that the band was flummoxed entirely in trying to follow along.

Instead of actually telling the studio musicians what he wanted or even what the chords were, Bob ended up firing everybody but the bass player and the occasional overdub from an organ or pedal steel. It was with this line-up that Dylan thought he had finished the album. This version of *Blood On The Tracks* was even starker and more stripped-down than *John Wesley Harding*, while still not being a complete retreat to the solo acoustic sound of his first four albums. From these sets of New York recording sessions, Bob commissioned album covers made, and liner notes to be written.

However before the album could be released, Dylan played the test pressing for his brother David while at home in Minnesota for the holidays. The two of them decided that the album was a bit too much, and ended up quickly rounding up a handful of unknown local musicians to re-record half of the tracks. These Minneapolis musicians were truly unknown as the covers had already been printed and they wouldn't get credit for their contributions for decades to come.

While the released half-Minnesota, half-New York album was a massive success for Bob, the existence of this test pressing (as well as its scarcity) elevated the New York sessions in the eyes of most fans as being far more honest and direct that the Minneapolis ones. Of course, Dylan himself waffled back and forth between full-band and acoustic a couple of times during the making of this album, and so the final decision to land somewhere between the two seems apropos. But the rarity of the New York sessions blinded some critics who felt that only the first sessions contained the full raw emotional power and that the later tracks were a downgrade that was a bit too nuanced and self-conscious. Of course the release of *The Bootleg Series vol. 14* whose deluxe version contains every last take from New York and absolutely nothing new from Minnesota only helped stoke this outlook, albeit unintentionally (apparently the session tapes from Minneapolis were lost... although that seems a little too convenient).

For years I couldn't tell the difference between the two sets of sessions and it was only for this book that I did the research to figure out which tracks were which. Having now listened to bootlegs of the original New York version of the album, I find it kind of dull and repetitive from a musical standpoint. It really made me appreciate the Minnesota tracks. I almost wish he had redone the entire album with them, although that might have gotten a little too repetitive too. Still, it would be interesting to hear what they would have done with "Buckets Of Rain" or "Simple Twist Of Fate".

This was an important album for Dylan. While *New Morning* might have been his first "comeback" album, this is the one that really cemented Bob's reputation as someone who you can't ever quite count out. If not for this album (and the critical and commercial support it received) it is likely that in the popular conception, Dylan would strictly be a sixties artist who never produced anything worthwhile outside of that decade. This pretty ridiculous, but who knows if there would have been an audience to grow impatient with Bob's further digressions if he hadn't made *Blood On The Tracks*. Instead, he'd just be in the country fair circuit in oldies packages with Peter Noone, Barry McGuire, and Donovan.

Tangled Up in Blue
(written by Bob Dylan)

I'm not sure how much thought Bob puts into the order of songs on his album, but it seems like he tends to frontload them with the biggest song first. "Blowin' In The Wind", "The Times They Are A-Changin'", "Like A Rolling Stone", "Subterranean Homesick Blues", even "If Not For You" are all track one on their respective albums. And this one is no different.

Nearly six minutes long with an acoustic backing band that harkens back to *John Wesley Harding* and *Pat Garrett & Billy the Kid*. The lyrics don't tell a full story, but rather a series of vignettes about two or three people. The ambiguous use of pronouns and tense makes it really hard to keep track of who's talking about who or when each of these verses takes place. There's no bridge or middle eight and the chorus, if you can call it such, is just a recapitulation of the title phrase at the end of each verse. The only real change or reprieve in this song is a harmonica solo over the verse chords that doesn't even kick in until five minutes into the song. While this should get old or repetitive throughout such a long tune, it is clear that Bob is heavily invested in this song and it comes through in his vocal delivery. While there are no big twists or changes in the song, it is a gripping work and one of Bob's best.

Simple Twist of Fate
(written by Bob Dylan)

A perfect follow-up to "Tangled Up In Blue" covering much of the same territory, but seemingly from a different angle. Stripped down to just bass and Bob's acoustic guitar and harmonica. Again the lyrics are a series of scenes that seem to point to a larger narrative without filling in all the gaps. There is a rueful resignation in the way Dylan sings these lines until he builds to that one note at the end of the second to the last line of each verse. Perhaps the narrator wishes he were able to affect more change in this story instead of being merely the victim of coincidences. Of course, that may just be his way of avoiding taking his portion of responsibility for the way things turned out, but he does sound very worn down and broken by it.

You're a Big Girl Now
(written by Bob Dylan)

The original New York version is laid back with just acoustic guitar, bass, and a little bit of organ and pedal steel coming in later. The main difference in the Minnesota version is the addition of drums that help propel the track forward. There's also a second acoustic guitar playing some licks and a piano part that feels almost subliminal. It's hard to say which version is better. Both have a lot to recommend them. As powerful as the New York version is, I think I prefer the Minnesota recording. Not just because that's what I'm used to, but without the drummer in there, this album does occasionally threaten to get a little sleepy and lapse into a feeling of sameness. Either way, this is one of my favorite *Blood On The Tracks* songs. There's lots of hurt and regret in Bob's voice. It's hard to say how sincere he is being with the compliment of the title phrase. It certainly comes off as a little infantilizing and derisive.

Idiot Wind
(written by Bob Dylan)

  This is often the prime example that Dylan fans use to point out how neutered the Minnesota tracks are in comparison to their New York counterparts. For my money, Bob not only sounds angrier but also more hurt on the fuller band recording that was released on the official version. If you want to hear an angry version with no compassion or remorse, check out the live version on *Hard Rain*. While this is a great song it goes on a bit long and having it taken at a slower tempo on the original NY version actually tends to tip "Idiot Wind" over to the boring side. Sure the lyrics about a man named Grey and a million dollar inheritance are complete fabrications, but you can tell how much Bob believes these words (or the meaning behind the words). It's a great stunning put-down. The lyrics are vicious, complaining that someone is stupid they forget to breathe is pretty harsh. But unlike songs like "Positively 4th Street", you can hear Bob admit to a certain amount of culpability here. He is taking responsibility here, if only for continually staying with some who was so bad for him. The piano adds a nice feel, while the organ stabs out in anger. All of it is held together by the drums. It all winds up with an excellent harmonica solo. Sure Bob's weird pronunciation of the "I" in "Idiot" into two syllables can be distracting; still, this is another terrific track.

You're Gonna Make Me Lonesome When You Go
(written by Bob Dylan)

  One of the more upbeat tracks recorded in New York, it's not surprising that Dylan saw no need to re-cut it later in Minneapolis. It's a love song in anticipation of the inevitable heartbreak at the end of the relationship. Still, he seems to be enjoying the moment, even if he knows that it won't last. It makes for a surprisingly positive song, that might even be convincing as a love song in the present sense if one ignored the possibility of the romance ending. While it is a nice jolt of sunshine, it kind of sticks out on *Blood On The Tracks* as a result. No wonder it is easily the shortest song on the album by over a minute. Perhaps it is a necessary palate cleanser before flipping the record over and get back into the weeds of Dylan's heartache and pain. In some ways, it would almost work best as a prelude to the album, kicking things off and pointing to where the rest of *Blood On The Tracks* will lead.

Meet Me in the Morning
(written by Bob Dylan)

  When people talk about how much more stripped down and acoustic the New York tracks are compared to the Minneapolis ones, they tend to forget that this song with it drums and fuzz guitar was actually cut during the original sessions. The lyrics at times here feel more like an entreaty to a new love than a plea to a lost love. The music is another 12-bar blues progression taking at a rollicking mid-tempo shuffle. There are several guitars playing around in the background, some of them pulling off some tasty licks and others just cluttering things up. By the time the really fuzzy guitar finally gets a solo and starts to take off, the whole song fades out. Since there's little breaking up this song, it tends to feel a lot longer than it really is. One of the lesser *Blood On The Tracks* songs, this could easily be swapped out for "Call Letter Blues" without effecting the overall album as a whole.

Lily, Rosemary and the Jack of Hearts
(written by Bob Dylan)

For an album whose lyrics are supposed to be personal and autobiographical and focused on heartbreak, this song just seems like a confusing story that would be more at home on *John Wesley Harding*. Perhaps there's a metaphor I'm missing implied within the narrative. The story itself is pretty compelling and clever. There was even the possibility of a movie based on this song kicked around for a while in Hollywood. The original version from New York is slightly slower, taking the runtime from nearly nine minutes to almost ten. That version is pretty much just Bob solo on acoustic with a little assistance from the bass player and a harmonica solo at the end. While Bob's singing is spot-on on the earlier version, there's not enough going on here to keep the listener's attention for that long. At least there's an actual narrative instead of just a collage, making it a little easier to digest than something like "Desolation Row". The Minneapolis version, on the other hand, is taken as an upbeat boom-chika-style country number that helps keep the song moving forward. The one-five bass line and brushed snare playing are very reminiscent of Johnny Cash's backup band, The Tennessee Two. There are large swaths of organ providing a nice contrast to Bob's jangling acoustic guitar. In fact, the song slowly increases tempo throughout its runtime in a way that may be too subtle to notice consciously but adds to the excitement. The remake certainly blows the original away. It almost makes you wish that Bob had re-cut all ten songs in Minneapolis. Who knows what impact that would've had. Sure, you could argue that the NY take is more intimate and personal, but with a disconnected story-song like this, that's not necessarily what you want. Maybe not one of the best *Blood On The Tracks* songs, but there's no need to make it any more boring.

If You See Her, Say Hello
(written by Bob Dylan)

The released Minneapolis version is not significantly heavier than the original New York version of this song. There's some mandolin on the second version which is pretty buried until the end. The percussion sounds more like a mapped maraca than a full drum set. There are some high, ghostly organ and gentle acoustic guitar soloing while the first version sounds like just bass in addition to Bob's harmonica and guitar. The lyrics are some of the most direct on this album about Bob's sense of hurt and longing over losing his wife. Both versions of this song feature some poignant vocals from Bob. Understandably, the second version sounds a little more resigned. In its way, that almost makes the track a little more hopeful about the possibility of healing. The song is definitely less angry and resentful than something like "Idiot Wind". While it is fun to hear Dylan be that bitter and vindictive, if that were the only emotion on display on *Blood On The Tracks* it would be a much less pleasant listen. Thankfully songs like this help balance things out.

Shelter from the Storm
(written by Bob Dylan)

One of the five New York songs that were spared a revamp later in Minneapolis. The song is sparse and minimal, just bass in addition to Bob's acoustic guitar. Still, the bass is prominent enough that it feels more like a full band track than a solo selection. There's an alternate take of this song that appeared on the soundtrack to *Jerry Maguire* of all places. That version is far more of a solo showcase, opening with a burst of harmonica and lacking the bass that helps give the released version its backbone. Ultimately though, there is not a significant difference between the two versions. The song itself is catchy if a tad repetitive. The hook at the end of each verse with a repetition of the title gives the song its structure. Despite being somewhat sparse, the tune is actually pretty jaunty. The harmonica solo towards the end is a welcome change of pace. The lyrics are a plea for some sort of solace, if thinly veiled. Bob sings this with far more optimism than resignation, adding a glimmer of hope to *Blood On The Tracks*. It's a fine track, and has definitely earned its place as one of more well-known tracks off this album.

Buckets of Rain
(written by Bob Dylan)

Another song with just acoustic guitar and bass. Bob's guitar takes more of a lead role here, playing leads and licks instead of merely strumming the chords. It's a nice effect, so it's easy to see why Dylan didn't feel the need to re-record this track in Minneapolis. For a song about crying copious amounts, it actually comes across as far more optimistic than most of *Blood On The Tracks*. It's not happy by any stretch, but at least comes across as more accepting than resigned. There's no sing-along chorus here, but a sweet little melody that gives the listener a glimmer of hope. Surprisingly, when Bette Midler decided to cover this song a year later on her *Songs For The New Depression* album, Bob himself came along to lend a hand and sing some vocals. He even authorized or authored the switch from "buckets" to "nuggets" of rain. It's kind of odd. Not one of the better *Blood On The Tracks* songs, but really one of the only ones you could end this album on.

Songs not on the album:
Up To Me from *Biograph*
(written by Bob Dylan)

One of the few outtakes from *Blood On The Tracks*. This song was left off the album for being a little too similar to "Buckets Of Rain". Certainly, one could swap this out for that track and make little difference to the record as a whole. Maybe it's not as hopeful of an ending lyrically. It's got the standard New York set-up of just acoustic guitar and bass. The most autobiographical line on this album comes here when he talks about having a harmonica around his neck. Most of the images here, however, are obviously metaphorical; I doubt Bob ever worked as a postal clerk, much less removed a wanted poster in his time on that job. While I love *Blood On The Tracks*, by this point the songs are started to feel a little samey. Particularly if you are listening to the original test pressing. It's probably for the best that this song didn't make it onto the album, it might've have made the whole thing too long and repetitive. This is an unfortunate habit Bob falls into frequently, and I am grateful that he sidesteps it here.

Call Letter Blues from *The Bootleg Series vol. 2*
(written by Bob Dylan)

I'm not really sure if this is a separate song from "Meet Me In The Morning". The lyrics are completely different and unrelated, but Bob sings it over the exact same backing track. Given how many of Dylan's song are, like this, just 12-bar blues there's probably a lot of Bob's songs that could be sung over this track without requiring any change at all. The rumors of an unreleased song from the *Blood On The Tracks* sessions would start most Bob-head salivating, so it was probably a little disappointing when this song appeared on *The Bootleg Series vol. 2* and wasn't a completely new song at all. Bob's singing on both this and "Meet Me In The Morning" are about the same, even if the lyrics are a little more dour and bitter. There's a couple of good lines about having to lie to his kids about where their mother is. Really though, these two are songs are pretty much interchangeable to me. Not sure why he picked one over the other, but it really doesn't matter much to me.

Spanish Is the Loving Tongue released on *The Bootleg Series vol. 14*
(lyrics by Charles Badger Clark, music by Billy Simon)
See the entry under *Self-Portrait*.

<u>Rumored to have been recorded but unheard:</u>
Bell Tower Blues
(written by Bob Dylan)
There Ain't Gonna Be A Next Time
(written by Bob Dylan)
Where Do You Turn (Turning Point)?
(written by Bob Dylan)
It's Breakin' Me Up
(written by Bob Dylan)
Ain't It Funny
(written by Bob Dylan)
Little Bit Of Rain
(written by Bob Dylan)

These are the titles of songs whose lyrics appeared in the little red notebook Bob was writing in during the making of this album. The fact that none of these tracks surfaced with the rather thorough release of the deluxe *Bootleg Series vol. 14* leads one to suspect that they were never recorded. Most likely they never even had music composed for them and were only lyrics, but we will probably never fully know for sure. "Bell Tower Blues" and "Little Bit Of Rain" may be nothing more than first drafts of what would become "Call Letter Blues" and "Buckets Of Rain". The fact that Dylan seemed to know which songs we wanted on this album seems to come in stark contrast to his indecisiveness on how those songs should sound.

"SHELTER FROM A SIMPLE TWIST IN BLUE"

SIDE A:
1. Tangled Up In Blue
2. You're A Big Girl Now
3. Idiot Wind
4. If You See Her Say Hello
5. Call Letter Blues

SIDE B:
1. Buckets Of Rain
2. You're Gonna Make Me Lonesome When You Go
3. Simple Twist Of Fate
4. Shelter From The Storm
5. Up To Me

With so few outtakes, there's not much to do here; although I suppose I could swap out some Minnesota tracks for various New York versions. Really the only switching I would want to do is to replace the stripped down NY version of "Simple Twist Of Fate" with one of the few full-band NY tracks.

Instead what I've done is put all Minnesota tracks on side one and moved the earlier New York tracks on the second side. Even then I moved "Call Letter Blues" (replacing "Meet Me In The Morning") to the end of side one so that the full band tracks are on one side and the acoustic stuff is on the flipside, replicating the feel of *Bringing It All Home*. I've dropped "Lily, Rosemary, & The Jack of Hearts", even though I really like its bounciness. Lyrically, it just doesn't fit as well with the rest of the album. Plus, given how long this album (especially side one is) I just didn't have the room. I did, however, find room for "Up To Me". I know a lot of people think it's too similar to "Buckets Of Rain", but I think opening side two with the latter and ending the album with the former makes for great bookends on the acoustic side of my slight re-configuration of *Blood On The Tracks*.

While we do have both Minneapolis and New York tracks to choose from for half the songs, ultimately I think Bob made the right choice here, and there's not much that needs to be done to make this album closer to my liking.

DESIRE
Produced by: Don DeVito
Recorded: July 3rd – 31st, 1975
Released: January 5th, 1976
Famous/Important/Popular Track(s):
- Hurricane

My Personal Favorite Track(s):
- One More Cup Of Coffee (Valley Below)
- Oh, Sister
- Abandoned Love

Bob Dylan is not really known as a collaborator. Up to this point, the only two songs that he co-wrote are "Tears Of Rage" and "This Wheel's On Fire" from *The Basement Tapes*. Even then these were lyrics that Bob wrote by his lonesome and then handed to members of The Band to write music to (Dylan apparently had enough music-less sets of words from this period that T-Bone Burnett was able to create an entire double album from them in 2014, as well as a podcast by Bear and a Banjo in 2019). Bob always wrote the words by himself, but something changed after *Blood In the Tracks*.

Perhaps he was embarrassed by how personal those lyrics had been. Or how personal they were seen as by everybody else. He wanted to make sure no one would mistake his new album as being about himself, so he hired himself a co-lyricist. Much like Brian Wilson turning to adman Tony Asher to work on *Pet Sounds*, Dylan ended up using playwright Jacques Levy to help him finish off the words for *Desire*. There was no way to see this album as a sequel to the intimate autobiography of *Blood On The Tracks*. Bob is writing about other people (Ruben Carter, Joey Gallo) and other places (Mozambique, Black Diamond Bay) here. Sure, there's a few story songs ("Isis", "Romance In Durango", "Oh Sister") that could be interpreted as self-referential the same way that "Lily, Rosemary, & The Jack Of Hearts" was, but given Levy's theatre background, it is easier to assume that these are purely works of fiction.

If making a deliberately non-personal album was Dylan's goal with *Desire*, he blew it thoroughly with the final song "Sara". There's no co-writing credit to hide behind here. People know that Sara is the actual name of Bob's wife, whose estrangement from "inspired" *Blood On The Tracks* (ironically that album was so good it apparently inspired Sara to give Bob another chance – it wouldn't last). Not only is using Sara's first name an unmistakable personal detail, but I think we can all assume that Dylan is the only person who can relate to a lyric about staying up all night in the Chelsea Hotel to write a song entitled "Sad Eyed Lady of The Lowlands".

Whatever Bob's motivations were lyrically, the album also has an entirely different sound from anything he had tried before. Whether it was folk or rock or country, Dylan's albums tended to stick to familiar instrumentation that hewed closely to the genre. Sure there were moments of experimenting with other textures on *Self-Portrait* and *New Morning*, but for the most part Bob generally just used what was standard. With *Desire* Dylan starts creating a new sound all his own. It's not a huge departure, but it is notable and consistent enough that nothing before (or after) this album sounds quite like it.

There are two key hallmarks of the *Desire* sound: Emmylou Harris's near-constant harmonizing and Scarlett Rivera's "gypsy" violin. This is a sound that is neither like the middle-of-the-road strings on *Self-Portrait* or the fiddle you would expect on *Nashville Skyline*, it has a sound and texture all its own. A lot of your ability to enjoy *Desire* depends a lot on whether you find that sound pleasant or grating because there is no getting away from it. Apparently, its appearance on the record is a complete fluke. Bob was just driving along and saw Scarlett walking down the street with a violin case and invited her to join the recording sessions without even really knowing if she could play. Dylan, in fact, asked a lot of people to these recording sessions but quickly found the huge band too unwieldy. Scarlett Rivera was one of the few people to make the cut alongside Emmylou Harris on vocals, Rob Stoner on drums, and Howie Wyeth on drums. It's not quite the full band sound of *Highway 61 Revisited* or *Blonde On Blonde* nor is it the stripped-down sound of *John Wesley Harding* or the NY half of *Blood On The Tracks*.

The timber of this particular ensemble makes any *Desire* outtakes easy to identify. I have mixed feelings about it. On the one hand, I love the uniqueness of the *Desire* sound in comparison to his other albums. On the other hand, this is not a particularly versatile sound, and so the within the album itself, the songs can start to sound a little samey. For me personally, *Desire* is a decidedly middle-tier Dylan album; neither an unabashed success or a complete disaster. As a result, it is not an album of his I return very often, or one I avoid when it comes up on shuffle.

Hurricane
(written by Bob Dylan and Jacques Levy)

This song continues to be one of Bob's most popular even though was (eventually) resolved. Part of its perennial status may be attributable to the fact that the issue at the heart of the lyric's tale, the treatment of minorities by the American police and justice system, is still sadly relevant 40+ years on. It also helps that it is still a compelling story told in a fascinating way. It probably helps that playwright Jacques Levy was on hand to help dramatize the plot, although Bob did an excellent job on his own making "The Lonesome Death Of Hattie Carroll" a fascinating listen.

For such a dark subject matter in the lyrics, the music for "Hurricane" is surprisingly upbeat. Unlike "George Jackson", his only other real "protest" song that Bob's recorded since plugging in, this song truly rocks as well as telling yet another story of the miscarriage of justice. There's a conga playing in the breaks and female backup singers that almost takes this song into disco territory if it weren't for the acoustic instrumentation. The bass playing by Rob Stoner is especially funky. Scarlet Rivera's gypsy violin is sawing away throughout the entire length of the song, so if that's a sticking point, you're not going to get any reprieve. It makes a nice contrast to the harmonica solo that the song fades out on. Much like the first song on *Blood On The Tracks* it saves the solo for the very end of the track. Unlike "Tangled Up In Blue", which is open to interpretation, "Hurricane" is definitely trying to be very clear about what happened and when. However, both songs work in the same way where you want to know what happens next. Even Bob dropping the n-word (which is pretty cringe-worthy) can't stop this song from being a good song about a sad subject.

Isis
(written by Bob Dylan and Jacques Levy)

Here is a song that in retrospect is unfortunately titled. The music is a heavy, hypnotic waltz with Scarlet Rivera's violin blurring the lines of precisely what continent or century this tale is supposed to take place in. It's just the same three chords over and over with no chorus or bridge, so it's a good thing that lyrics (and Bob's vocal presentation of them) are compelling. Unlike the evocative but elusive stories on *Blood On The Tracks*, we know the whole plot here, even if it seems far more metaphorical than factual. This tendency may be the result of working with Jacques Levy, a noted playwright. I'm not sure what the whole point of joining some random guy to find what turns out to be an empty tomb somewhere north, burying him, and then going back to his wife, Isis. The vocals make this all enchanting, however.

Mozambique
(written by Bob Dylan and Jacques Levy)

It's like a tour poster sprang to life and turned into a song. The arrangement does have a very "world music" flair to it, although I don't know how accurate it is. I would imagine Mozambican music sounds closer to the African rhythms of Paul Simon's *Graceland* than the more southwest, Tex-Mex flavor Dylan is going for here. The instrumentation is very in line with the remainder of *Desire*, dominated by Emmylou Harris's harmony vocals and Scarlet Rivera's gypsy violin. It's a fun, lightweight number. No mention is made of the politics of the titular country, just how lovely it is to visit and how friendly the people are. Unlike many of the songs co-written with Jacques Levy, there's no real story here or plot or characters. Just a description of the place. I'm sure the Mozambican Tourist Board thought this song was an unexpected godsend.

One More Cup of Coffee (Valley Below)
(written by Bob Dylan)

One of the few songs Bob wrote for *Desire* without Jacques Levy. This song continues in the globe-trotting vein of "Mozambique" or "Isis". We're not sure exactly where this takes place, but it definitely feels foreign. There are little flourishes in the melody that sound almost Hassidic or Arabic. It's not an inflection that Dylan often does. The only other song with this much vocal extemporizing would probably be "Jokerman", but that is far more in an R&B scale than this. Bob skips these completely from the live version on *At Budokan* completely anglicizing the song. There is some sort of finger-cymbal here that dominates the drums and other percussion and brings to mind belly-dancers. The lyrics are clearly dreading the leaving that is about to take place and is stalling as long as one can. I'm not sure what Bob is afraid of happening in "the valley below" but he is definitely dragging his feet on it. The women in question clearly seem to be gypsies or fortune-tellers of some kind, unschooled and illiterate. Perhaps the lack of Jacques is what gives Bob the freedom to not spell things out for as much on this song as he does on the rest of this album. It is a cool little bit of world music from Bob and definitely one of the stronger songs on *Desire*.

Oh, Sister
(written by Bob Dylan and Jacques Levy)

Similar in feel to "One More Cup Of Coffee", but not as exotically flavored. The pace here is a little turgid. The usual complement of gypsy violin and Emmylou harmony run through this song. It's a little slow, but the melody has a nice range to it. The lyrics seem to be a plea to someone's sister. I can only assume that the words are not meant to be literal since Dylan doesn't have a sister. Bob sings it with a real sense of entreaty in his voice. Seems genuinely baffled why this "sister" has rejected him. The imagery is almost biblical, talking about being re-born and mysteriously saved. Perhaps this is a precursor to Bob's born-again period. There's nothing new or exciting going on in this song. Luckily it's barely over 4 minutes long.

Joey
(written by Bob Dylan and Jacques Levy)

Dear lord, this song is interminable. Taken at a lugubrious pace, this song feels like a well-meaning documentary on the Biography channel that gives you all the salient points of a famous person's life but manages to ultimately fail at imparting anything that makes the celebrity in question interesting. This song has a much larger cast than the usual *Desire* songs.

There's even an actual accordion that comes in when Bob sings the line about an accordion. Everyone does a good enough job playing, but there's only so much you can do with three chords over the course of eleven minutes. The *Dylan & The Dead* version speeds this up enough to shave nearly two minutes off, and it is still way too long. Personally, I have a hard enough time getting into Bob's super-long songs like "Desolation Row" or "Brownsville Girl" even when they are well-executed. This doesn't even have that going for it. The lyrics are super-literal, although I imagine that the gangster in question is not nearly as pleasant and virtuous as this song tries to imply. Heck, having this song on *Desire* dilutes the impact of "Hurricane" who also was a real person and was an actual victim of a miscarriage of justice. This is one of my all-time least favorite tracks in the entire Dylan oeuvre.

Romance in Durango
(written by Bob Dylan and Jacques Levy)

Another song with a faux-international vibe. This time we're definitely south of the border opening with a line about hot chili peppers. There's even some lyrics in Spanish and a mariachi-style trumpet and accordion woven into the usual *Desire* mix. The electric guitar does this fast picking thing to mimic the sound of a mandolin. It's too bad the tune is taken at such a slow pace that it starts to get old by the time the song is over. The live version released on *The Bootleg Series vol. 5* still drags, but the live version that was released on *Biograph* comes closest to the feel I wish the studio version had. I'm not sure what the lyrics mean (particularly the Spanish ones) but it seems to involve some sort of adventure/romance between the narrator and some senorita named Magdalena. Bob and Emmylou do a great job of singing this, with Bob continuing his habit of adding little trills on some of the notes to evoke the exotic feel. It certainly feels like a dusty old western, just a little too languid to be a top-tier *Desire* track.

Black Diamond Bay
(written by Bob Dylan and Jacques Levy)

The only instance of Dylan crossfading one song into another is the beginning of this song. It's one of the most studio-specific (i.e., non-live) things Bob has ever done on record. This song's continues *Desire*'s international flair, albeit with a lot less specificity to the locale. The lyrics are another story of mystery and intrigue with playwright Jacques Levy giving it a little less plot and structure than some of the songs on this album. The song burbles along with the usual instrumentation at a medium pace. In order to get in the full narrative, the song does stretch out to nearly seven-and-a-half minutes. Any intrigue initially created by Scarlett's violin and Emmylou's harmonies have been blunted by its ubiquity by this point on the album. The bass is playing a very oom-pah figure that sounds almost like a polka or Johnny Cash. In addition to the drums, there are some prominent finger cymbals throughout the song. Bob's vocal delivery is pretty good, with some bits of acting adding a bit of theatricality to the proceedings. It's still not enough to get me to pay enough attention to the words to follow the convoluted story. There might be as much going on here as there is in "Lily, Rosemary, And The Jack Of Hearts" but I don't really know. There's no bridge to change things up, and the chorus is just the title being sung at the end of each verse. Had the song come a little earlier in the album, or it was a little more to the point, I might be able to really get into this one. As it is, this is just another *Desire* song to me.

Sara
(written by Bob Dylan)

One of the most autobiographical songs in Dylan's entire career, if only because it addresses his wife by name. It also one of the few to reference Bob's past work, referencing "Sad Eyed Lady of the Lowlands" makes this one of the most self-aware songs Dylan has ever penned. Given that after *Blood On The Tracks* one would assume that this marriage was over for good, this song feels like something of a last-ditch "Hail Mary" pass to try and keep the reconciliation from going south. Bob didn't have the time or luxury to disguise this song the way he usually would. This is one of the few *Desire* songs that wasn't co-written by Jacques Levy, such naked and personal a confession would've been difficult to collaborate on. The song itself is taken at a lovely stately tempo. The usual trappings of this album have grown well-worn and comfortable by this point. There's no Emmylou harmony here as Bob is truly on his own for this song, but Scarlet Rivera's violin continues to weave its spell in the background. It's got a nice rolling 6/8 feel without getting too portentous by dragging the tempo. Bob plays a lot of harmonica here, as if there was more he wants to say, but lacks the words (or courage). For such an intimate lyric, Bob's vocals aren't any more exposed then they were on songs about "Hurricane" Carter or the country of Mozambique. As thinly disguised as "Ballad In Plain D" is, Bob sounds far more connected singing that song. That may be the only other song in Dylan's catalog that comes as close as this to be directly addressing his actual life. As such, it becomes a fascinating track in Dylan's discography. However, if you didn't know that Sara was actually Bob's wife, and thought that the name was just plucked from the air like "Napoleon in rags" or "Dr. Filth," I wonder if the song would still have as much resonance.

Songs not on the album:
Rita May B-side of the "Stuck Inside Mobile With The Memphis Blues Again (live)" single
(written by Bob Dylan and Jacques Levy)

A song purportedly about Rubyfruit Jungle author, Rita Mae Brown, and Dylan's attempts to convince her to have a threesome with him and his wife. I cannot speak to the veracity of this rumor, although I will admit I find very amusing and hope that it is actually true. The song ended up being covered by fantastic musician and creepy human being, Jerry Lee Lewis. This version oddly enough ended up being released as the B-side for a single from the live *Before The Flood* album. It certainly feels like a far more lighthearted song than many of tracks on *Desire*, although Emmylou's harmonies and Scarlet's violin make it unmistakable which album this was recorded for. There's even a bridge section that threatens to get funky. It's significantly shorter than many of the mini-epics Dylan was writing with Jacques Levy at the time. While not the greatest song, there's not many tracks on *Desire* that this couldn't have been switched out with and the whole record would've been made much better.

Abandoned Love from *Biograph*
(written by Bob Dylan)

A less obviously exotic song than "Black Diamond Bay" or "Romance In Durango". There's still a bit of that international flavor here. The harmony vocals here don't sound like they're Emmylou Harris, but someone male. We've still got the gypsy violin of Scarlett Rivera though. This is a fun, jaunty tune, with lyrics a little more muddled and less theatrical than most of *Desire*. Not surprisingly, Bob wrote these words without Jacques Levy. The lyrics seem to be about a failed love affair, as the title would indicate. Perhaps some of these images are related to Bob's reconnection to his wife Sara, but it doesn't seem terribly optimistic about their long-term possibilities this second go-around. This song has earned a reputation as one of the great lost tracks that somehow got left off of a Dylan album. While it is a pretty good song, it is pretty standard *Desire* fare to me. It does, however, come in a lot shorter than most of the other songs, which helps a lot. Reportedly this song was left off the album in favor of "Joey" which is just ridiculous. As slight as "Abandoned Love" is, there is no question which is the correct choice there.

Golden Loom from *The Bootleg Series vol. 3*
(written by Bob Dylan)

With all of the gypsy violin from Scarlett Rivera on *Desire*, this is the only track where comes close to sounding like a country fiddle. The international exoticism of this album is placed in a more domestic locale on "Golden Loom". Not that the song is anywhere near the country leanings of *Nashville Skyline* or *Self-Portrait*. The congas in the background are just a hair away from being the clip-clop of a woodblock imitating horse's hooves. It's a charming, but slight, song. I have no idea what the lyrics are supposed to be about, but without Jacques Levy's input, they seem more like a series of images than a story with any sort of plot. Bob's vocals are almost laconic here. The harmonica playing is slightly bluesy. While not one of the great *Desire* outtakes, it is at least a lot short than several of the songs that were released and could've been swapped out to make the whole album a much swifter experience.

Catfish from *The Bootleg Series vol. 3*
(written by Bob Dylan and Jacques Levy)

Desire is an album almost entirely devoid of the sort of blues "Catfish" exemplified. There's some nice acoustic slide guitar on here. There's even a harmonica played by someone other than Dylan for a change. The lack of Emmylou's harmonies and Scarlett's violin make this track feel very out of place amongst these sessions. I'm not sure why the sudden change in instrumentation and tone. Not that I mind the change of pace, but this song kind of sticks out because of it. Whoever is playing the harmonica is doing a more traditional blues harp style and is sort of taking the place of the gypsy violin in the mix. The lyrics are about some baseball player. I have no idea if he was a current player at the time or started around the time of Doubleday or if he even exists at all. Ultimately it doesn't matter. Oddly enough the hero of this song is shown as walking away from his team to make more money elsewhere, it seems a little greedy and self-serving. It is a strange choice for idolization. The song itself is slinky and cool. Bob's vocals sound a bit detached on this number, perhaps because he's not much of a jock or sports fan. A pleasant little distraction from the *Desire* template, it wins points for being quick.

Sign Language from Eric Clapton's album *No Reason To Cry*
(written by Bob Dylan)

This recording perhaps belongs in a book about Eric Clapton more than this one, but Dylan does shadow Eric's vocals throughout, even if he is relatively lower in the mix. The task of matching vocals with Dylan is challenging, one that Emmylou Harris could barely keep up with and one that Clapton is utterly incapable of. The song is a nice little mid-tempo pop tune, although who knows how Bob would've tackled this if he had recorded it during these sessions. The lyrics are unusual. I'm assuming that the woman in question is actually using ASL to attempt to communicate with Dylan, but I'm not sure what the metaphor is trying to imply or what it has to do with the sandwich that he's eating. It's a short pleasant song, and one that I think could've fit in with the others on *Desire* had Dylan felt it was worth his time. If he was just throwing it away by giving it to Clapton, it was awfully nice of Bob to show up and duet on the song with him.

Played live, but never recorded:
Seven Days
(written by Bob Dylan)

Another song Bob wrote around this time but didn't bother to record for *Desire*. He did, however, give it to Rolling Stone Ron Wood for his solo album. It's a shame, based on the live version of this from *The Bootleg Series vol. 3*. It features a nice extended goofy riff over which Bob holds a single steady note which is a fantastic contrast. It's more rocking than a lot of the song included on *Desire*. The songs are about trying to be patient while waiting for the return of a lover, although apparently, she is his comrade from the north or something. I'm not sure what the relationship is or why she's gone or what will happen in a week. As is typical of Dylan, you don't want to ask too many questions. The ending is amusingly abrupt. While not the best song, I definitely think that this would've been a great asset to *Desire* if only Bob were able to capture it in the studio.

Rumored to have been recorded but unheard:
Money Blues
(written by Bob Dylan and Jacques Levy)
Footprints In The Sand
(written by Bob Dylan)
Wiretappin'
(written by Bob Dylan)
Patty's Gone To Laredo
(written by Bob Dylan)
What Will You Do When Jesus Comes?
(written by Bob Dylan)

The lyrics to "Money Blues" are floating around and available, but no recording has yet surfaced of what the chords or melody were supposed to be. Given the word "blues" in the title, it's probably another variation on the I-IV-V blues structure. The lyrics, co-written with Jacques Levy, are repetitive in the fashion of a typical blues song too. We only know that Levy co-wrote the song because that's how it was registered for copyright. "Money Blues" is, as one would expect, about how much it sucks to be poor. This feels like something that Bob wouldn't have had to deal with for thirteen years at this point, so it comes off as rather condescending. Maybe the recording would redeem this interpretation, but nothing that we've got so far makes it really worth searching out. This song was apparently recorded by Bob backed by Willie Murphy & The Bees in late 1975 along with "Footprints In The Sand". Who knows how many of these songs were co-written with Jacques Levy or seriously considered for *Desire*. "Wiretappin'" was recorded on the first day of sessions when everyone showed up (the same day that "Joey" was recorded) but apparently was too chaotic to use. It also includes the line "Wiretappin' / It can happen". "Patty's Gone To Laredo" and "What Will You Do When Jesus Comes?" are the names of songs you can hear a bit of in the background of *Renaldo & Clara*, so kind of hard to track down. The latter is based on an old gospel song and is taken in a sarcastic manner that Dylan would be disavowing in just a few years.

"HURRICANE"

SIDE A:
1. Abandoned Love
2. Rita May
3. Oh Sister
4. Sara
5. Catfish

SIDE B:
1. Isis
2. One More Cup Of Coffee (Valley Below)
3. Golden Loom
4. Hurricane

Dropping the eleven minute Joey from the list opened up a lot of space for great outtakes like "Abandoned Love" and "Golden Loom". As much as I enjoyed "Romance In Durango" and "Black Diamond Bay", I felt there were both too long. Instead, I used "Rita May" (which is fun) and "Catfish" (which is a nice change of pace. Since "Hurricane" is the song that really provided the impetus for the entire record, I felt you either had to open or close the album with it. In the end, I decided it was not only a good closer but a good name for the album too. If there was a studio version of "Seven Days" I probably would've added it here, but unfortunately there isn't (that I know of). While *Nashville Skyline* is often criticized for being too short, *Desire* can be a little long. Especially for a single disc, where the limitations of vinyl are shown when trying to put the entire 56+ minutes on there. This version of the album is much more compact, which is a good idea since the overall sound on this album is so consistent, it verges on becoming monotonous. This should help.

STREET LEGAL
Produced by Don DeVito
Recorded: April 25th – May 1st, 1978
Released: June 15th, 1978
Famous/Important/Popular Track(s):
- Changing Of The Guards

My Personal Favorite Track(s):
- Changing Of The Guards
- New Pony
- Señor (Tales Of Yankee Power)

This is the album that has most folks thinking "Dylan's gone Vegas!" This shows that either the listeners don't really understand Dylan or that Dylan doesn't really understand Vegas. I think there's a lot of truth to both of those options. Undoubtedly, the financial drain of both Bob's divorce from Sara and the cinematic flop, *Renaldo & Clara* had left Dylan with the need to refill his pockets. And while a big showbiz spectacle might be commercially appealing to someone like Neil Diamond, there's got to be a better way for Bob to make money than hiring the largest, slickest touring band of his career.

In some ways, this is just a mutation of the whole "Rolling Thunder Revue" thing from a few years earlier: only with the vagabonds and ragamuffins replaced with slick studio musician in matching sequined jackets. Emmylou's harmony vocals have now expanded into a trio of backing vocalists, and Scarlett Rivera's gypsy violin has been swapped out with a cheezy saxophone. It doesn't seem like Dylan was just trying to make money here. In fact, I don't think Bob knew what he wanted to do at all at this point. In some ways, it's like *Self-Portrait* where Dylan is throwing everything against the wall to see what will stick. The man difference is that Bob himself doesn't seem to care.

Despite having assembled his biggest backing band ever, *Street Legal* is recorded in a manner even more half-assed and haphazardly than *The Basement Tapes*. The end result is very muddy and murky. There might be a lot of cool stuff happening here, but it is almost impossible to discern one instrument from the next. This is probably the one album of Dylan's that has had the largest number of remasters and remixes over the years; not because it is a fan favorite, but because it needs it. Every technological advance is thrown at this album in an attempt to unbury *Street Legal*, and so far nothing invented has quite done it. In some ways, the one thing that I share most with Bob is a complete disinterest in being an audiophile. Neither one of us needs the highest tech gear with the latest advancements in sound reproduction technology. As long as everything is sufficiently audible, we both seem satisfied; but the recording of this album seems almost deliberately and perversely designed to keep the listener out.

This would be a more frustrating tragedy if it felt like there was something in there worth uncovering. The instrumentation is unique, but it lacks the personality of *Desire*. Bob's gone back to writing his lyrics alone, but it's hard to tell what he feels about them as he has to shout them in order to be heard over the huge band while refusing to wear earphones. The album isn't really Dylan being apathetic though. There's a couple of records in the 1980s where you can hear that, but this is Bob at his most uncertain. For an artist who made his reputation on boldly doing what he wanted regardless of the opinions of anyone else on the planet, it is interesting to hear him flailing like this.

But not that interesting, ultimately. This album does not even rise to the mid-tier level of its predecessor. Sure, there's a couple of really great songs on here, but ultimately, this album is just not a lot of fun for me to listen to.

Changing of the Guards
(written by Bob Dylan)

While fading out is a familiar trick on many Bob song, fading in is a little unusual. Especially for the first track on the record. It sounds like we missed something and we're coming in late. However given how quickly the song fades up, it's more likely there was a flub that was being edited out at the very beginning, but they had to hurry to get the song up to full volume before the vocals kicked in. There is no slow immersion into this new sound for *Street Legal*, we are immediately greeted with the backing vocalists and saxophone. This is one of the better songs on the album with verses alternating with turnarounds featuring the horn line. It is up-tempo and mixed far better than its reputation suggests. The lyrics are as vague as "Tangled Up In Blue" but less evocative. This could well be chalked up to Bob's comparatively less impassioned vocal delivery. As a result, this six and a half minute song feels a lot longer than it should. In the end, there's a run-through of the chords from the verse without anyone stepping up to take a solo, then we go back to that horn-laced turn-around while the tune fades out as abruptly as it faded in.

New Pony
(written by Bob Dylan)

This song is built almost entirely from a simple blues guitar lick along with the gospelesque backing vocals wondering "how much longer?" Bob's insistence on recording live in the studio with the full band and not wearing headphones limits his ability to subtly shade his vocal performance here (and throughout *Street Legal*) as he seems compelled to yell all the lyrics simply to make himself heard. There's some great conga work on this song, but you can hardly hear it in this mix. The guitar solo is perfunctory if not particularly noteworthy. The most interesting thing in this song – and really the only thing that changes within in the song – is the ways and times that the backup singers alter "how much longer?" In fact, at one point it sounds like one of them think they're doing the refrain twice while the other two stop at one. It's an amusing little mistake. The other interesting part of the song is the sax solo which sounds like it was flown in from "Woogie Boogie" of off *Self-Portrait*. While there was a sax part on "Changing Of The Guards" it was a static part of the arrangement, this here is a full-blown improvised sax solo – something that sounds conspicuously cheezy or Las Vegas-like. It is a surprise to hear that on a Bob Dylan album.

No Time to Think
(written by Bob Dylan)

The 6/8 time signature gives this song a swaying lilt. It would be a serviceable, cute little song at half the length. While the sax line at the end of each verse is nice, it unnecessarily pads this song out way too long. The lyrics seem to be pointing to some sort of anger, but Bob's voice is at his usual *Street Legal* shouting level, so there's no subtlety in the performance. There are only three chords in the whole song, and they repeat constantly. There's no chorus – just the title ending each verse. There are no solos or bridges or anything else to switch up the repetition, just that sax break after each verse. There could be a pretty strong song buried in there, but this offers almost no glimpse into that potential.

Baby, Stop Crying
(written by Bob Dylan)

Another mid-tempo rocker. There are the usual sax and backing vocalists. There's even another two saxophone solo, luckily both are brief. The organ is nice and high in the mix. The repetitive chorus is almost enough to make it catchy. Another song that could've had a minute or two shaved off of its runtime. Bob's vocals sound like they want to go softer on the verses, but he doesn't quite feel like he can afford to and still hear himself over the live band. The guitar playing is a sympathetic counterpoint to the melody. The bass playing is really wonderful from Jerry Scheff. Jerry was also a member of Elvis Presley's TCB Band in the '70s. More than anything that MOR era of Presley's work is what "Baby, Stop Crying" reminds me off. The lyrics are imploring a lover to stop crying, but it's never made entirely clear whether she should stop crying because there is nothing worth crying about or just because it annoys the song's narrator. This song lacks any real distinction. It's not bad, just sort of standard *Street Legal* stuff.

Is Your Love in Vain?
(written by Bob Dylan)

The only song from *Street Legal* to make it onto *At Budokan*, the live album that was ostensibly supposed to support it. The saxophone in the intro sounds as full as a whole brass section, so I assume it was doubled by a guitar or violin or something I can't quite detect. Despite the similarity in title to Robert Johnson's "Love In Vain" this is definitely not a bluesy song at all. It's got a full rolling chord structure with a bridge and a floating melody. As usual Bob's vocal delivery undercuts any power that the lyrics might have had, which may be for the best given how retrograde and misogynistic the words feel. Asking a woman if she can cook and sew (and make flowers grow) just feels kind of icky. The songs is aiming at an anthem-like quality with a full-bodied large band arrangement. It's really striving here, and I admire the ambition, but it just comes across as a little unpleasant.

Señor (Tales of Yankee Power)
(written by Bob Dylan)

This song has a cool, mysterious vibe to it. I'm not sure what the lyrics mean, but thanks to the subtitle, I'm assuming that it is some sort of "Ugly American" situation. Whatever it is, Bob's typical *Street Legal* vocal stylings don't derail it completely (although some more nuance might've helped make this song a classic). The saxophone is well-used here to add to the drama, it's far more subtle than blaring. The backing singers are far more minimal than many of the songs on this album. The mandolin and conga are nice little touches adding to the international flair to this song. The bridge takes an unexpected turn that really helps amp up the tension. It may not need all the solos, but the song isn't too long. Frankly, this is one of the better songs on *Street Legal*, it's too bad there's not more like it on this album.

True Love Tends to Forget
(written by Bob Dylan)

The rocks songs tend to fare a little better than the ballads on *Street Legal*. This is one of those slower love songs. It's certainly not the worst, by a large margin, but overall the song feels kind of mediocre. There's a nice slide guitar solo, and the sax playing is somewhat muted in the background. There's a strong bridge where's Bob shout-singing on this album really works well. I'm not really sure what the lyrics are about, but it seems like this is a song about love that is generally positive and un-ironic. The playing feels so live that you are almost surprised when the track ends and you don't hear any audience clapping. The song is not one of the longer ones on this album, which is nice. Not a song I would ever seek out, but not one I feel compelled to skip when it does come up.

We Better Talk This Over
(written by Bob Dylan)

One of the more metrically complicated songs Bob has ever written;

switching between 4/4 and 5/4 time to allow an extra beat every other measure. As a result, this becomes one of Bob's most musically compelling compositions. The lyrics are alright. As one would expect from the title, it is a plea from a scorned lover for another chance, although filled with Bob's usual obfuscation. He does ironically sing "you can't convert me" in this song. However, the constantly tripping up of where the ear expects the downbeat to later keeps one interested throughout. In this sense, it reminds me of the Toadies' 1995 hit "Possum Kingdom". The usual *Street Legal* backing vocal group is here, but there seems to be a surprising lack of saxophone on this track. The song is actually a little slow for as rushed as it feels. It's too bad that a song with such a nice catchy trick isn't taken with more vigor and fire. Bob's vocals are once again hamstrung by being sung without headphones. Despite all of this, the mere fact that Bob is trying something new with time signature makes this one of my favorite tracks on this album.

Where Are You Tonight? (Journey Through Dark Heat)
(written by Bob Dylan)

A song that sounds jubilant and exciting, this makes perfect sense to close out the record. However, the lyrics feel like they are supposed to be either hurt or lost or accusatory. Bob doesn't sing it that way though, and the song sounds quixotically triumphant. It opens with some nice conga work. The saxophone is more a part of the band than a featured soloist throughout; which is nice. It melds wells with the organ. The backing vocalists are again in full force. I have no idea what the subtitle means, and thought it was "dark heart" and not "dark heat" for the longest time. The song really feels like the final encore at the end of the convert. As such the extended soloing and runtime are not nearly as egregious, although my personal tastes still would've trimmed and edited this up a bit. It's not one of the better songs on *Street Legal*, but it is a perfectly good one to end on.

Songs not on the album:
Take It Or Leave It officially unreleased
(written by Bob Dylan)

A supposed original tune rehearsed during the sound-check of the New Haven stop of the 1978 tour. The song itself is pretty functional but unremarkable. It's no surprise that it wasn't revived either on stage or in the studio. Although given the somewhat mediocre quality of some *Street Legal* tracks, it would've fit in just fine, had it been deemed worthy enough for Bob to give it a real go in an actual recording studio.

Stop Now officially unreleased
(written by Bob Dylan and Helena Springs)

One of a bunch songs that Bob co-wrote with his backing vocalist

Helena Springs at this time. Most of these songs were not recorded, at least not recorded by Dylan, although most of them seem to have been available as possible inclusions for *Street Legal*. This is one of the few that Bob did end up recording. He in fact recorded two versions, one much faster coming in at 3:42 and a slower version lasting 5:37. Needless to the say, the faster, shorter version is my preference. The slower take is a bit of a drag, and one almost become impatient during the pre-chorus waiting for the song to resume. The slower version's arrangement feels like more of a rip-off of Muddy Water's "I'm A Man" than is necessary. It's surprising that it took two people to write this song which is mostly just a blues song with a chorus that consists almost entirely of the title repeated over and over. At least there is a bridge thrown in there which helps make the song seem a little more complicated. It certainly sounds like this was recorded for potential inclusion on the album with the full band playing, although the way Bob stops the singing one line to take over what would've been an overlapping vocal makes you think this might've just been a demo. Plus there's a bit of giggle that Dylan lets out halfway through and a nearly missed cue in returning to the chorus after a solo that makes it seem a little less professional and polished, unlike the rest of *Street Legal*. Of course, what *Street Legal* really could've used were some more moments of levity like this.

Coming From The Heart (The Road Is Long) officially unreleased
(written by Bob Dylan and Helena Springs)

A definitely gospel-flavored composition, surprising given that Bob was still a year out from becoming born again at this point. As poorly recorded as *Street Legal* is, this outtake is worse. The vocals are mixed too hot and occasional distorts the tape. I suppose I shouldn't complain since this tape was not meant (and still isn't available) for mass consumption. That would be far more frustrating if the song or the performance were particularly worth savoring. Instead, this is a pretty plodding and uninspired affair. The lyrics are your typical "woe is me" nonsense. Helena is not a talented or trained wordsmith like Jacques Levy, and her collaboration with Dylan here is rife with trite clichés. There's no sax on here, but the presence of the backing vocalists definitely ties this to the *Street Legal* period. Unlike "Stop Now", this does not need to be on the official album. And fortunately. it wasn't.

Other songs written by Bob Dylan with Helena Springs:
Afternoon
Baby Give It Up
Brown Skin Girl
Her Memory
(written by Bob Dylan, Helena Springs, and Kenny Moore)

I Must Love You Too Much
If I Don't Be There By Morning
Miss Tea And Sympathy
More Than Flesh and Blood
One More Time
Responsibility
Romance Blues
Satisfy Me
Someone Else's Arms
Take It Or Leave It
Tell Me The Truth One Time
The Wandering Kind
Walk Out In The Rain
What's The Matter?
Without You
Your Rockin' Chair

As iffy as Bob's collaborations with backing singer Helena Springs were, apparently the two of them wrote a whole album's worth of material together that never got recorded by Bob. A couple of these songs were recorded by others though so we can get something of an insight into what the Dylan/Springs album would've been, at least from a songwriting standpoint. Two of these tracks were recorded on Eric Clapton's album *Backless*. "Walk Out In The Rain" comes across as a trite mid-tempo rocker. Helena is no lyricist, and Bob doesn't seem to be up for helping her get better. It's a pleasant enough tune, as is "If I Don't Be There By Morning". Both are songs that supposed to be about the break-up of a relationship but neither seems particularly or heartbroken. The post-Robbie Robertson reconstituted Band recorded "I Must Love You Too Much" in 1996. I'm not sure if The Band dug this song out of Dylan's trash bin or if Bob specifically gave it to them, but either way, it does a lot about what Dylan thought of The Band trying to continue on past *the Last Waltz*. This song manages to have even dumber lyrics than either of the Clapton tracks. It's a sprightly undistinguished rocker of the type that any cover band might have thrown into their set-list as their sole original. "More Than Flesh And Blood" is a little better. Sure the lyrics aren't great, but they do a straddle the line between secular love song and gospel aspirations that Dylan's *Street Legal* era backing band give the recording. There's even the honking sax on here. Sure, it would've sounded weird for Dylan to be singing this, but while Helena Springs may be a great backup singer, she lacks the personality to make this song seem like anything other than an average late-70s R&B tune. I have not heard any of the other Springs/Dylan collaborations, but looking at the list none of these titles seem particularly inspiring to search out and interesting to listen to.

Played live, but never recorded:
Am I Your Stepchild?
(written by Bob Dylan)

A song that Bob Dylan gave Solomon Burke for his 2002 album *Don't Give Up On Me*, this was played live several times during the 1978 tour but never officially recorded in the studio. A simple blues-rock type of song alá "Stop Now" this would've been a nice addition to *Street Legal*. Solomon Burke's version is a little too slow but appropriate to his bluesier stylings – he does manage to give Bob a shout-out in his recording of the song. The live bootlegs of Dylan's take on this song in '78 do have some more of the gospel flavor to it, usually with some great sax playing. Sure, it's not some lost classic, but it is a pleasant rocking little tune.

Repossession Blues
(written by Roland James)

The 1978 tour was often derisively dubbed the "Alimony Tour" by critics. I'm not going to attempt to tackle all of the covers songs Bob has done live but not on record over the years (the sheer number of songs attempted during the Never Ending Tour would double the length of this book). However, I thought this one was worth noting as there are bootlegs of the rehearsal that sound very much like a *Street Legal* outtake. Sure, it's just Dylan doing another cover of another blues song, but it the fact that money woes were on his mind at the time is definitely very telling. This is a man at the end of his rope, and he is going to need something to throw him a lifeline and save him soon.

Rumored to have been recorded but unheard:
I'm Cold
First To Say Goodbye
Her Version Of Jealousy
You Don't Love Me No More
This A-way, That A-way
Legionnaire's Disease

In addition to the songs Bob co-wrote with Helena Springs, there were a number of other tunes rumored to be floating around at the time. "I'm Cold" is the only title remembered by musician Stephen Soles, who is one of the few people to have heard this particular batch of songs. Apparently after Dylan's divorce, but before starting *Street Legal*, Bob wrote a whole batch of extremely personal songs, which he played for a few friends around the piano and then promptly chose never to revisit again. Those who heard it swear it would've been a worthy successor to the naked heartache of *Blood On The Tracks*, but no one there recorded it and doubt Dylan even remembers this songs now, so we'll never know. The lyrics for "Legionnaire's Disease" are available on Dylan's website and his book of collected lyrics. The lyrics are not as metaphorical as one would assume from the title. Billy Cross was the guitarist for *Street Legal* and *At Budokan*, so one can assume his cover of "Legionnaire's Disease" from his 1981 album, *Up Front* does contain Bob's actual melody and not just his own personal extrapolation.

"TALES OF YANKEE POWER"

SIDE A:
1. Changing Of The Guards
2. New Pony
3. Stop Now
4. Señor (Tales of Yankee Power)

SIDE B:
1. Help Me Understand
2. True Love Tends To Forget
3. We Better Talk This Over
4. Where Are You Tonight? (Journey Through Dark Heat)

There's not much to work with here, but I've moved a few things around, dropped a couple of weaker songs and filled it out with the faster version of "Stop Now". It's still not a great album, but it goes down much easier. There's not a lot of outtakes to work with here. I was initially attempted to combine these tracks with those from *Slow Train Coming* since they are so musically similar, even if they are wildly divergent in terms of lyrical theme. While both *Street Legal* and *Slow Train Coming* feature the same mini-gospel choir and the single sax has been extended out to a whole horn section. Ultimately though, I just couldn't make it work. The muddy, murky mix of *Street Legal* sounds that much worse when stacked next to the slick sheen of *Slow Train Coming*.

I did, however, use the rehearsal version of Hank Williams' "Help Me Understand" to kick off side two, even though it was recorded during the tour between *Street Legal* and *Slow Train Coming*. Although it did not appear until *The Bootleg Series vol. 13* that is supposed to focus solely on Bob's religious period, sonically this fits here much better, lyrics aside. In fact, it may be recorded even better than some of the studio stuff on *Street Legal*. While Dylan could always deflect questions about its religious intent by stating that he didn't write it at the time, it is a potent signpost towards Bob's next musical phase.

SLOW TRAIN COMING

Produced by: Jerry Wexler & Barry Beckett
Recorded: April 30th – May 11th, 1979
Released: August 20th, 1979

Famous/Important/Popular Track(s):
- Gotta Serve Somebody
- Precious Angel

My Personal Favorite Track(s):
- Gonna Change My Way Of Thinking
- Do Right To Me Baby (Do Unto Others)
- When You Gonna Wake Up?

While *Street Legal* may not have been precisely apathetic or indecisive, it definitely felt uncertain. *Slow Train Coming* definitely does not have that problem. Whether or not you actually like or agree with what Bob's saying, there is no arguing that he means it. This confidence extends beyond just the lyrical content. While the instrumentation remains relatively consistent from the last album (horns and backing vocalists), Dylan has gone out of his way to record this as cleanly and pristinely as is possible in 1979. Bob has hired ace veteran producers, Jerry Wexler and Barry Beckett, to make sure you can hear everything on these songs, whether you want to or not.

For those who enjoyed the ambiguity of Dylan's lyrics and looked forward to each new album as a sort of puzzle to solve or at least endlessly analyze, this album must've come as a shock. This may have been more of a sticking point that the actual content of these "inarguable" lyrics. For someone like me who historically doesn't pay a lot of heed to Bob's words, the religious nature of these words is not a big hurdle to overcome. But I can understand why someone who is only looking for more poetic images and surrealistic clues would be put off by the relatively straightforward manner of this album.

Lyrics aside, this just sounds like another *Street Legal*, only recorded much, much better. Musically there is nothing that would hint that this was a religious album. This does not sound like gospel, it is "Christian rock." If you didn't speak the language, you would think this is far closer to *Street Legal* than *Saved*. It does sound terrific; maybe bordering on too slick and polished. For as much guff as *Street Legal* got for being "Vegas", this album is so much worse. Of course, critics at the time were too distracted by the change in philosophical direction to really harp on that. It even includes Bob's first ever "guest star" on an album since Johnny Cash lend a hand opening *Nashville Skyline*. While Dire Straits have since proven themselves to be an enduring staple of classic rock radio, in 1979 Mark Knopfler was still sort of a flavor-of-the-month addition; much like adding Rob Thomas to a Santana song in order to help an old dude score some cred with a younger audience unfamiliar with the fading legend.

I don't won't get too deeply into it, but this album makes it somewhat unavoidable. I am not a religious person. I'm not even one of those people who call themselves "not religious, but spiritual." While I lack the certainty of a Christopher Hitchens or Richard Dawkins, I certainly hope there is no God or afterlife or anything, because I agree with them that the overall effect that religion has had in the history of man has been almost entirely detrimental. All that being said; as much as I dislike organized religion (and Christianity specifically), I like Bob's born-again albums. They're not my favorites or anything, but they're pretty good. You can certainly hear how much conviction Bob has while singing this material.

With the benefit of hindsight, this first album is frequently cited as the best of the born-again trilogy. I can certainly understand that thinking, but personally, I don't think it's that much better than *Saved* or *Shot Of Love*. In fact, it generally doesn't feel that much different from *Street Legal* only much, much, much better recorded. I probably play (and enjoy) *Slow train Coming* almost the same amount as its predecessor.

Gotta Serve Somebody
(written by Bob Dylan)

This track starts off with an electric piano and bass that is both slinky and funky – sounding a 100 times more polished than anything on *Street Legal*, which despite all its pretense at showbiz schmaltz still had the ramshackle feel of the Rolling Thunder Revue which proceeded it. The lyrics are another one of Bob's list songs. This time its just a list of all the different things one could be, both good and bad, and how none of them exempt you from either following Jesus or Satan. There's even a bit in here that sounds like it was cribbed from hacky comedian R.J. Johnson about how "you can call him Ray or you can call him Jay." Other than the tie-up at the end of each verse about having to serve either the devil or the lord, there is nothing too terribly preachy or biblical here. It's a fun song, and the message can be ignored if you aren't paying too much attention, which is probably why this was the record company's choice for the first single off the album. However, the slick professional playing on this track does make it feel longer than it should for a five and a half minute song. While Bob's voice is clearly committed to the cause throughout the album, he doesn't seem terribly concerned if you are drinking whiskey or milk or whatever else he is listing off. Not a horrible track though.

Precious Angel
(written by Bob Dylan)

A far more laid-back song from the album opener. The pop music tradition of conflating of an ideal girlfriend with a heavenly creature gets even more complicated by adding actual religion to the mix. I'm not sure if Bob here is singing about an earthly woman who helped lead him to

Christianity or about a literal angel. Either way, he comes off as endearingly grateful, rather than simply lashing out at the nonbelievers. Although there still is plenty of scorn left for them. The song builds nicely with the horns waiting till the second verse and the vocals not coming in until the third. The acoustic guitar strumming throughout the song helps give it a personal feel that undercuts the more professional sheet the permeates the album.

I Believe in You
(written by Bob Dylan)

Lyrically, Bob's "born again" songs fall into one of two camps: Those about how we are all going to hell and those about how Dylan was saved. This song definitely falls into the second group. The lyrics are more of honest expression of devotion without getting into any specific dogma or theology. In fact, the "you" in the title is never explicitly named. If this had been written and recorded by George Harrison, one would assume it's about Sri Krishna. While this may be a song about personal salvation, Dylan still gets in a few digs about those in society who have scorned or rejected him because of his newfound beliefs. No matter what my own feelings about the existence of deities, Bob's singing here leaves little doubt how he truly feels. This is no "phase" or mask that Bob has put on here. He is extremely sincere; almost frighteningly so. This is another a slower song in the vein of "Precious Angel". This song is surprisingly free of backing vocals. The acoustic guitar is even more prominent here. Mark Knopfler's guitar playing is both tasteful and tasty. This is another song that feels like it could be taken by churches as an actual hymn without having to deal with any need to excuse or explain the more personal Bob Dylan-isms of it.

Slow Train
(written by Bob Dylan)

After a pair of slow ballads, we get another funky rock tune in the vein of "Gotta Serve Somebody". It's not nearly as cool or slinky as that track, but it grooves along nicely. Mark Knopfler's guitar playing is the star here. Sure we could've lost a couple of the solos and hopefully brought this song in under five minutes. Still, it doesn't get too boring for as long as it is. While the metaphor of the train for the second coming has been long established, Dylan doesn't name names on this track. He just assumes that everyone knows what kind of train he is referring to. The lyrics on the verses are litanies of various things about the modern world that disgust Dylan, and is thankful will soon be eradicated. While the things that he is complaining about and the solutions he is anticipating are much different, this song has a lot in common with tunes like "Blowin' In The Wind" and "The Times They Are A-Changin'". At least from a lyrical standpoint. Musically this is very professional sounding recording. There is a fire in the playing that is only mildly dulled by the smooth veneer that Jerry Wexler has applied on this.

Gonna Change My Way of Thinking
(written by Bob Dylan)

A song that Bob revisited with Mavis Staples on a tribute album to himself (*Gotta Serve Somebody – The Gospel Songs Of Bob Dylan*). Hearing Dylan do this song again in 2003 again confuses the issue of how devout Bob is in his Christianity now. Certainly, he sounds like he's having fun on that version stopping the song to do a little radio skit with Mavis about knocking off a chicken and reading "Snoozeweek." He also changes almost all of the lyrics, making it harder to discern just where Dylan's current religious allegiances lie. He does make a great juxtaposition of being "hungry as a horse" and being "hungry enough to eat a horse". The original, however, leaves no doubt as to what Bob believes. This is another harder rock song. As usual, when Bob is really trying to write a rock song, he ends up reverting to a I-IV-V 12-bar blues chord structure. This song usually a great little riff running through the whole song to propel it forward. The production is pretty minimal for the first third of the song, but eventually, the organ kicks in followed shortly by the horn section. The guitar playing's top-notch, but I don't know if we needed two whole solos. Could've cut the song down a bit in length. This is a strong, powerful, compelling song. Definitely one of the highlights of *Slow Train Coming*.

Do Right to Me Baby (Do Unto Others)
(written by Bob Dylan)

Rather than didactic in its condemnation or exultant in its praise, this is a song about the golden rule. Much like "Man Gave Names To All The Animals" it feels like it was pitched and youngster first going to Sunday school or bible camp rather than particularly adult. I wonder if Bob, in his first year of studying Evangelism had in fact endured these types of kids songs and was hoping to add to their number. While Bob has certainly played fast and loose with time signatures while playing solo, this is the first time he has really used that with the deliberateness necessary to convey these metric anomalies to a backing band. Every other line Dylan adds an extra beat to the measure to make room for the "not" in the second line that refutes the previous lyric. It's a clever little trick that makes what is on the surface a dopey repetitive song subtly interesting and compelling. Sure the message of the song is hard to argue with even without the Jesus connotations. But the way the beat is constantly being tripped up in addition to fun but dumb sing-along chorus takes this from being one of the more minor pieces on *Slow Train Coming* and makes it one of my favorites. It may be dumb fun, but it's still fun.

When You Gonna Wake Up?
(written by Bob Dylan)

A riff-based rock song along the lines of "Gonna Change My Way Of Thinking". I love the way the drums go into a double-time feel for the verses. There are some great lines being played by the horn section. The organ that comes in and takes a solo isn't quite a gospel organ, but close enough. Like many Dylan songs, this one could stand to be pruned by a minute or two. While not a funky a song as "Gonna Change My Way Of Thinking" this has a nice slinky feel. The whole song ends with a verse with no vocals that sounds like it was supposed to have a solo playing over it that never got recorded. The lyrics are once again beseeching (or condemning) the nonbeliever to change their ways. Bob sounds slightly threatening here; testifying of the hellfire that awaits those who don't follow him, rather than caring about their welfare. Still, there's no doubting his sincerity here. Pretty standard *Slow Train Coming* fare.

Man Gave Names to All the Animals
(written by Bob Dylan)

Another song, like "Do Right To Me Baby" that sound aimed more at a children's Sunday school class rather than to an adult audience. Lyrically this presages some of the nursery rhymes of *Under The Red Sky*. It's no surprise that some enterprising illustrator turned these lyrics into a kid's book (other children's books that Bob has unwittingly co-authored include "Forever Young", "If Not For You", "Blowin' In The Wind", and "If Dogs Run Free"). The feel of the music is very reggae, something that Bob is beginning to dabble within some of the arrangements on *At Budokan* and would continue with through the use of Sly & Robbie on *Infidels*. The lyrics are simple but dumb. It doesn't really teach any sort of moral lesson to the young ones or do much other than reinforce a literal interpretation of some of the more unrealistic aspects of the Bible. The most clever thing is the way, he leads everyone to expect the snake being named at the end of the song but then ending it early and withholding that. On the one hand, this is a nice change of pace from all the heavy subject matters throughout the rest of the album. On the other, this song is done with such professionalism and reserve that it is hard to really get into the fun of it. It sounds as polished and worked over as anything else on *Slow Train Coming* while a more slapdash production might've suited this stridently trivial song better. It almost feels like filler as Bob has run out of profound things to relate from his study of Christianity and now is just delivering the most banal of bible stories. It could almost make one hopeful that this would be the only born-again album in Dylan's discography, but clearly, Bob was going to find more to say on the subject.

When He Returns
(written by Bob Dylan)

While all of the songs on *Slow Train Coming* have a Christian emphasis to the lyrics, this is the first song on here that actually sounds like it is a Gospel tune from a musical standpoint. In a sense, this song points towards the sound of Saved and probably would've been a better fit on that album. This was recorded alone with just piano accompaniment; the playing is far too technical and full of flourishes to be the actual keyboard playing of Bob. This does rob the song of its intimacy and therefore some of its power. No matter how good the piano playing is, if Bob had played and sung this song by himself, directly addressing the audience with his newfound faith, it might have been less impressive but more affecting. Like "Wedding Song" or "Dark Eyes" the only place for a stripped-down, solo performance like this is at the end of the album. Dylan is wailing like a born-again preacher here, which is appropriate. The lyrics are hopeful, even if that hope is in the second coming. The song has a slow burn that never fully boils over into an ecstatic reverie. Had this been the end of Bob's born-again period, this would've been a great way to wrap all this up. Unfortunately, we've still got a ways to go before we are out of this era of Dylan's discography.

Songs not on the album:
Trouble In Mind B-side of the "Gotta Serve Somebody" single
(written by Bob Dylan)

Another riff-song in the mold of "When You Gonna Wake Up? Or "Gonna Change My Way Of Thinking". It's not nearly as catchy of a riff, so I can see why this was saved for a B-side instead of ending up on the album itself. In some ways, this song feels like a first draft for the song simply entitled "Trouble" that would end up on *Shot Of Love*. The song references Lot's wife, but instead of haranguing the audience for their faults, he seems to be asking the deity for help with his own flaws. It's a nice change of pace for there to be a bit of humility in the lyrics even if he still seems disgusted with himself and anyone else who isn't completely perfect. It's a fun, funky groove and frankly would've been a nice addition to the album in place of some of the more slow and sanctimonious songs on *Slow Train Coming*.

Ye Shall Be Changed from *The Bootleg Series vol. 3*
(written by Bob Dylan)

A mid-tempo track that neither rocks like "Gotta Serve Somebody" nor drags like "Precious Angel". It's the kind of song you can snap your fingers to, but not really dance along with. It's perfectly fine, but not terribly remarkable. It's not a surprise this was left off of the album. The lyrics all about Jesus as one would expect, although for some reason there's a line in the chorus about the dead arising and jumping out of their clothes that makes me think of some sort of zombie orgy. Ultimately this is a fairly workmanlike track. Unlike "Trouble In Mind", *Slow Train Coming* would not be substantially improved, or even changed, by the addition of this song.

Ain't No Man Righteous (No, Not One) from *The Bootleg Series vol. 13*
(written by Bob Dylan)

A blues-based song centered on a single riff, this song is pretty mild. The live version on *The Bootleg Series vol. 13* has a bit of a reggae lilt to it. However, the studio outtake has a much more boogie-woogie feel with prominent slide guitar from Mark Knopfler. Not surprising the reggae band Jah Malla ended up covering this track. This more like the fun of "Man Gave Names To All The Animals" or "Do Right To Me" in its less serious, more fun side. At least musically. The lyrics are still pretty dogmatic. In some ways, this feels as close as Bob has gotten to the Leon Russell songs from *Greatest Hits, vol. II*. While I would much rather have something like this with a pulse than some of the more dreary ballads, it makes sense why this was kept off the album.

Help Me Understand from *The Bootleg Series vol. 13*
(written by Hank Williams)

A Hank Williams song written under his preacher pseudonym of "Luke the Drifter". This is the heaviest waltz feel Bob has done since "Winterlude" or would do again until "Waitin' For You". The spoken recitation that Bob uses to tell the story of a broken family brings to mind the parody of a radio preacher that Bob employed on *The Basement Tapes*' "Sign On The Cross". With the prominent flute, backing vocals, and sax solo, this sounds the more like something from the *Street Legal/At Budokan* era than the slick production of *Slow Train Coming*. The lyrics are not particularly religious as much as it is a screed against divorce. Only the mention of "Heavenly Father" in the chorus seems at all related to any sort of faith. I know that a lot of churches consider this to be a sin, particularly in Hank Williams' day. These days, I think we've come to understand that it is much better for the child to have their parents break-up than to stick together if they are arguing and yelling and fighting all the time. Still, as an anachronistic piece cover, this is a fun cover you can imagine Dylan doing regardless of whether or not he is in the middle of his "born again" period.

Stand By Faith from *The Bootleg Series vol. 13*
(written by Bob Dylan)

When the Blind Boys Of Alabama covered this tune, they pointedly re-titled it "See By Faith". Ultimately that change does little to alter this song as the lyrics are almost entirely "how do we ____? / _____ by faith."

repeated over and over with any number of verbs placed in any random order. This is an amazingly simple song that you could teach to little kids at Bible camp. This has more of a gospel feel than the more rock tone of *Slow Train Coming*, but there's not much to this song either way. Maybe if there was a bridge or a change of some sort, it might work. Perhaps even a shocking or surprising twist in the final verb/verse. As it is this doesn't go anywhere, so it's no surprise it was abandoned.

<u>Played live, but never recorded:</u>
Blessed Is The Name from *The Bootleg Series vol. 13*
(written by Bob Dylan)

A song with a much more traditionally gospel sound that marks it as more *Saved* than *Slow Train Coming*. There's plenty of the traditional backing vocalists on here. The lyrics are almost entirely composed of the chorus repeated over and over. And those words are just the tile followed by "wisdom and might are his". While this is a fun and exciting song to play in the middle of a concert, I can see why this never got recorded in the studio. Its slightness and repletion would not have stood up on an album. Still, it's a fun little gospel track for when you're in the mood for that sort of thing.

See the entry on Page 243

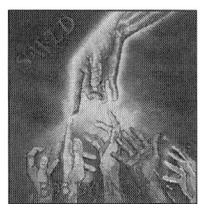

SAVED
Produced by: Jerry Wexler & Barry Beckett
Recorded: February 11th – 15th, 1980
Released: June 23rd, 1980
Famous/Important/Popular Track(s):
- Solid Rock

My Personal Favorite Track(s):
- Saved
- Solid Rock
- Are You Ready?

   This album took quite a beating when it came out, mostly because, after *Slow Train Coming*, most critics and fans were getting concerned that Dylan was only going to sing about Jesus from now until the end of days. Now, with the benefit of hindsight, where we know that this was just going to be a phase in Bob's career, the born-again trilogy is given a little more slack. Still, of the three albums, *Slow Train Coming* is always given the gold medal, with *Saved* and *Shot Of Love* competing for bronze.

   While this may be one of the quickest follow-ups Dylan has released since *New Morning*, the common consensus is that this album was not recorded quickly enough. Since he needed more material for an all-evangelical concert, Bob and his band had been playing these songs live for a while by the time they got to the Memphis studio, and as a result, they come off as little tired and underwhelming. Certainly, the sheen and polish from the last album here are missing, and the results feel rushed. Maybe Bob should've taken some more time to really re-think these tracks and how he was going to do them on vinyl as opposed to on-stage. Or perhaps he should've just released a live album of this material instead. Bob was chomping at the bit to get this material out there and suggested a live album called *Solid Rock* that Columbia ultimately nixed, although most of the concerts around this time were taped professionally, eventually leading to a treasure trove of concert recordings for *The Bootleg Series vol. 13*.

   Due to the fact the main lyrical thrust is the same, most folks tend to see this as just a lesser version of *Slow Train Coming*. Honestly, though, the previous album was just a rock album with gospel lyrics, *Saved* is Bob's attempt to write an honest-to-goodness gospel album. As a result, a looser, live, ragged feeling makes more sense than the spic-and-span studio polish of the last record. Sure, Dylan is not really practiced or well-versed at writing gospel music, but he has a pretty good handle on the basic concepts. The result is an album that feels and sounds religious, even if you don't pay attention to the lyrics.

   The end result is something of a curious beast. I enjoy Bob trying his hand at something new and experimenting, although by the end, it can feel a little repetitive. The vocals are still full of conviction, as well as fire and brimstone, but it is harder to ignore the religious elements if that is something that irks you. It scores points for not just being a retread of the last album and deserves more credit than it usually gets as the middle child of the born-again trilogy, but I don't end up listening to this record very often either.

A Satisfied Mind
(written by Jack Rhodes and Red Hayes)

Traditional gospel tunes were a part of Dylan's repertoire long before his "born again" period. And they continued to be sprinkled throughout his set long after. While Bob wrote a lot of new spiritual songs during this period, this is the only traditional gospel song he covered on record at this time. It's a short song, less than two minutes, and probably was as much of a warm-up as it sounds. The band is loose and taking their time entering the song. The theme of lyrics is, typical for Dylan, how those with power or money are going to pay for their iniquities. The song goes through a couple of verses before ever really kicking into high gear, but it is a nice appropriate way to begin this album.

Saved
(written by Bob Dylan and Tim Drummond)

Other than the extended collaboration with Jaques Levy for the album *Desire* this marks one of Bob's few credited co-writes until the mid-'80s. Written with Tim Drummond, the bass player in his band "Saved" turned out to be a one-off. While the lyrics are just as stridently Christian as they were on *Slow Train Coming*, this is the first song Dylan has done that really sounds like it could be played in a church and not just a Christian rock radio station. The backing vocals are no longer lush and mannered but are outright testifying in the background. The organ, long an essential instrument in Dylan's arsenal, now sounds at home laying down a strong gospel groove. Musically this might be the most religious thing Bob ever recorded. Lyrically he is preaching - not to the choir, but to anyone who isn't saved like he is. The hectoring of the heretics can feel a little caustic and condescending. However, Bob himself sounds truly grateful and even ecstatic to have seen the light on this track. It is hard to begrudge him that.

Covenant Woman
(written by Bob Dylan)

Lyrically a companion piece to "Precious Angel". Another poem of thanks to the woman who turned Bob on to the message of Jesus. It sounds a lot rougher and less polished than "Precious Angel". This roughhewn edge helps this song actually seem more sincere in comparison. The guitar playing is not as fluid and impressive as Mark Knopfler's work on *Slow Train Coming*, but it still works nicely. There's even an old-school styled gospel organ solo in the middle of this song. Bob's vocals are a little more hoarse, but that doesn't detract from the sincerity of his performance. The song is a little long and probably could've stood to be trimmed by a verse or two, but it is not terribly egregious. One of Bob's better love songs from his "born again" period.

What Can I Do for You?
(written by Bob Dylan)

The chorus effect on the guitar is very distracting. I'm not sure why, but it just rubs me the wrong way. This is another slow ballad with a tinge of gospel on top. Again the "you" in question is never explicitly stated, but given the cover of *Saved*, it's hard to come to any other conclusions who Bob is singing about here. Bob's voice is pleading and sincere. The harmonica sound on this album is much different than it is on any of Bob's other records. I think it might even be an electric harmonica of some sort since it sounds like there's a bit of distortion on it. Whatever it is, it has re-energized Bob's harp playing on *Saved*. The work of the backing singers on this track brings to mind the work of Prince. This song does go on a bit long, but it is heartfelt. While it is hard to overlook the religious intent of the lyrics, it's not a horrific song. You just got to be okay with that before you can attempt to enjoy it.

Solid Rock
(written by Bob Dylan)

We are definitely emphasizing the "rock" half of the title here. The most overtly gospel-sounding song after the title track. While not quite as successful as that song, this song is full of fire. Fire and brimstone even. Bob is singing his heart out here in an expression of thanks for the relative stability that his newfound spirituality provided – however briefly. This song was also supposed to supply the title for a live album that Bob had recorded during his gospel period, but the record company declined to release. Bob wrote lots of songs during this period that were performed live only but were never given a studio recording. While *Slow Train Coming* is still revered, *Saved* with songs like this and the title track rocks just as hard and feels even more fervent to me.

Pressing On
(written by Bob Dylan)

Another gospel-infused song. It starts with Bob alone at the piano for a verse before the singers join him. Then the drums and organ kick in, and the whole song slowly builds. This song seems deliberately created with the intent of whipping a congregation into a frenzy. It's a slow build, but one that does not relent throughout the entire song's runtime. The lyrics are about not giving up, but striving to the "higher calling of the Lord". There's no mistaking for how thoroughly Dylan believed these words when he recorded this song, even if the words seem to be just saying the same thing over and over and over. Sure, it presses on for a minute or two longer than it really needs to, but there's some nice work in here. 2/3 of the way through one of the singers lets loose this gospel yell that is just perfect for this kind of music. The only real disappointment in this song is that despite continuously building, it does come to any sort of climax. In fact, there's no ending at all, it just fades out. Still, this song is ample evidence that while *Slow Train Coming* is the first "born-again" Bob album, *Saved* is his only real "gospel" album.

In the Garden
(written by Bob Dylan)

Another song that slowly builds during of its runtime. Bob actually starts this song with just an organ instead of a piano. It's all very gospel with the attendant theatrics. It's almost a minute in before the bass and drums come in and start really moving this song. There's a lovely little organ solo in this song. There are a lot of key changes in this, continually ramping this song up higher and higher. In fact, it happens so often it almost feels like a joke. However, nothing in this song betray anything less than total sincerity from Bob. The lyrics here are a litany of pieces of evidence to Jesus's divinity followed by the general lack of acceptance by the populace at the time. It's nice that Bob is not directly hectoring the modern audience for a change, although the parallels are not drawn terribly subtly. Bob is again disgusted by society as a whole and people in general. In many ways, you could say Dylan's born-again phase is also his most misanthropic. This is just another typical *Saved* song, nothing in here that would possibly convert a nonbeliever.

Saving Grace
(written by Bob Dylan)

Putting all these songs of Bob starting alone at the organ (or piano) while the rest of the band take turns joining is not doing these songs any favors. After "Pressing On" and "In The Garden" the trick has gotten old and is starting to grate. Which is too bad, because there is nothing particularly wrong or bad with this song, it's just hard to get too excited about it at this point. The guitar playing is nice without being distracting (although the fast, mandolin-style playing is unnecessary). The organ is the real star here, even after the rest of the musicians have starting playing. The lyrics are supposed to be grateful, but Bob's delivery comes across as a little snide and condescending to those haven't been saved. Maybe re-arranging the order of the songs on *Saved* would've helped improve its reputation, but as it is "Saving Grace" is not one of my favorites.

Are You Ready?
(written by Bob Dylan)

While Bob wrapped up *Slow Train Coming* in a stripped down and direct fashion, albeit one marred by the flashy piano pyrotechnics, *Saved* concludes with a full band performance one of the more rocking tunes on the album. Again we've got a full Gospel sound here, but there's no building up. The whole band enters from note one. There's a terrific organ solo in here once again remind the listener that they should be in church. The only the instrumental element that doesn't sound like it belongs in the gospel milieu that is being presented is Bob's harmonica solo. Instead of necessarily hectoring the audience, he leaves the answer to the titular question up to the individual. Maybe some are ready, and others are not, but Bob's not here to judge. He's just here to remind you of someone else who is going to be doing a lot of judging. It's a big fun way to wrap up the album.

Songs not on the album:
Rise Again from *The Bootleg Series vol. 13*
(written by Dallas Holm)

When this was performed on tour in 1980, this was presented as a piano-based gospel song. On *The Bootleg Series vol. 13*, we are treated to a rehearsal that is just Bob alone on an acoustic guitar, accompanied only by a single backing vocalist. There are a few chords on here that are a little more complicated than your usual Dylan tune, and one the few covers included during these religious tours. It's another track where Bob lets one of his backing singers take the spotlight for a verse. The chorus is a little more pop-oriented than the more strictly gospel-ish verses suggested. The song aims for a kind of emotional uplift that never quite arrives. It's a beautiful song, with a lot more power than most of Dylan's slower Christian-era songs. The stripped-down version is such an amazing and stark contrast to the usual *Saved* repertoire, this one really stands out. However, even the live arrangement featured on some bootlegs of the era have nothing compared to the overly dramatic reading of the original version by Dallas Holm, which just sounds like bombast personified.

Making A Liar Out Of Me from *The Bootleg Series vol. 13*
(written by Bob Dylan)

A slow-burning ballad that was rehearsed, but never played in concert or recorded at an official session. This recording comes from a rehearsal, but apparently, the song was dropped from consideration even though it is a fully written song. Its tempo recalls something like "Every Grain Of Sand", but with an organ replacing the piano gives the song a real gospel feel that makes it fit in with *Saved*. The song itself is kind of drab and the melody is lifeless. The chorus is slightly more catchy than the verses, but the verses go on for quite a while before the chorus kicks in, and that is usually pretty short – just the title refrain. Despite this, Bob sings this song with fire and conviction. It's a shame that the melody is flat that there is really nothing for Dylan to sink his teeth into. Plus the song runs nearly six minutes long, getting no more exciting as it rambles on and on. Given the quality of some of the material Bob was writing around this point, it's no surprise that this got cast by the wayside.

Played live, but never recorded:
I Will Love Him from *The Bootleg Series vol. 13*
(written by Bob Dylan)

Since Bob was refusing to play any of his pre-born-again songs on his concerts he had to write a bunch of material to fill up his live set-lists. As a result, there are several songs Dylan wrote during this period that he never recorded in the studio, though some of them may have been on the planned but scrapped live album to be entitled *Solid Rock*. While I prefer critiquing recordings to live bootlegs, there's a number of these songs floating around that ended up on *The Bootleg Series vol. 13*. These songs are all similar in lyrical content. There is enough good material here that if Bob had taken his time to record *Saved*, he might've had enough for a double album. This tune starts out like more of a love song alá "Precious Angel" or "Covenant Woman" but quickly become frenetic gospel song. Live on-stage a lot of the nuances between this song get lost, and everything seems to end up in this same vein. I didn't pay much attention to the lyrics, assuming they were just about Jesus and stuff, but there's a line in there about "the state of Israel in 1948". I'm not really sure what the context is or how that fits in, but it did come as a bit of a surprise. The song is pretty solid and goes through the usual paces for nearly three minutes when an unexpected bridge shows up and throws everything off. It's a nice change. It's repetitive enough that Dylan can ask the audience if they know it well enough to join in and sing along. There's plenty of backing vocalists banging on tambourines to add the revival tent feel of this song. It's pretty standard *Saved* fare, but fun nonetheless.

City of Gold from *The Bootleg Series vol. 13*
(written by Bob Dylan)

This here is a pure gospel song, that was covered by the Dixie Hummingbirds, appropriately enough. That version even ended up on the Dylan-curated soundtrack to *Masked & Anonymous*. In some ways, this is closer to religious songs like "Gospel Plow" or "Sign On The Cross" that Bob was doing before he actually meant it. Not that it comes across as insincere, but it feels a little more deliberate and studied. It's one of the few songs that actually preaches of the great rewards that will come to the saved in the afterlife instead of harping on the tortures that are in store for the damned. It doesn't even come across as smug or holier-than-thou, it's just a friendly reminder of the supposed treasure that awaits the chosen few in heaven. As a song, it's a nit repetitive with no bridge or key changes or anything to interrupt the flow of the slow. Not bad, but at least it's short.

Cover Down, Pray Through from *The Bootleg Series vol. 13*
(written by Bob Dylan)

"Cover Down Pray Through" is a slinky, funky little number with lyrics that make their religious underpinnings a little more obscure, and may be one of the best songs of this batch. For a long time bootlegs mislabeled this as "Cover Down Breakthrough". Really if you give the lyrics as much thought as those bootleggers did, there's no reason not to love this song. Even having the correct lyrics, the chorus doesn't make a whole lot of sense. At some point in this song, Bob lets one of his backing vocalists take the lead. It doesn't seem as weird as it should. Sadly, this is no "All The Tired Horses". It's a shame that this song didn't make it on the official album, but when *the Bootleg Series vol. 13* finally came out, it is included twice on the eight CDs and once more on the DVD. This is one of the better "born-again" era songs.

Ain't Gonna Go To Hell For Anybody from *The Bootleg Series vol. 13*
(written by Bob Dylan)

This is a nice up-tempo gospel-ish number. Bob mentions that Ronnie Hawkins is in the audience before launching into this song. Kind of an odd juxtaposition before playing a purely religious song. The song starts out with a lone backing vocalist singing a cappella, before the other singers and the band joins in. It's a nice way to lead us into the song proper. Once the whole song really kicks in, things are far more predictable. It's kind of a weird sentiment. It comes off a sort of selfish. He doesn't care what anyone else wants or needs, he's going to avoid his own torture and punishment. What if the singer's going to hell would help save thousands of others? Would he go to hell for Jesus? He is singing proudly about how he wouldn't even do this for his own family. I know these are questions that aren't meant to be asked of the song, so it's best to ignore them and take this track for what it is, just another Dylan gospel tune.

"A SLOW AND SAVED TRAIN"

SIDE A:
1. Are You Ready?
2. When You Gonna Wake Up?
3. Slow Train

4. Saved
5. Gotta Serve Somebody

SIDE B:
1. Gonna Change My Way Of Thinking
2. Do Right To Me Baby (Do Unto Others)
3. Man Gave Names To All The Animals
4. Solid Rock
5. Trouble In Mind
6. Rise Again

Since both *Saved* and *Slow Train Coming* were recorded only 8 months apart and produced by the same team of Jerry Wexler and Barry Beckett. However, there is a big difference between the two albums. One is a slicker version of the blues/pop/rock of *Street Legal* with the lyrics changed to be about Jesus. The other is an attempt at a pure gospel album, both lyrically and musically. Still, there's not enough quality material for a record to be constructed from each that really stands on its own. Despite their differences, I have gone ahead and melded these two together into one super Jesus album. I have mostly gone ahead and replaced the slower songs from *Slow Train Coming* with the more up-tempo tracks from *Saved*.

Ultimately adding a little of the sloppier grittier tracks from the second born-again album helps dilute the too-polished sound of the first born-again album, making for a more varied yet cohesive listening experience. Frankly, there are so few songs I like on *Street Legal* that I loved, I thought about adding the three or four I did want to salvage onto this album. While it might've fit in musically I'm afraid the clash in terms of lyrical content made it too difficult.

Generally, I have eschewed live tracks on these reconfigured albums. There are a couple of songs that I really wanted to include on here that we just don't have studio versions of. Mostly "Cover Down Pray Through", but I ultimately found enough studio material to make this re-configuration work.

I don't think this album is going to convert anyone to Christianity... or even convince them to disregard their skepticism about Dylan's "born again" period, but it's still a pretty fun group of tracks to have as a one-off from this period.

SHOT OF LOVE
Produced by: Chuck Plotkin & Bob Dylan
(except "Shot Of Love" by Bumps Blackwell)
Recorded: March 26th – May 15th, 1981
Released: August 10th, 1981

Famous/Important/Popular Track(s):
- Heart Of Mine
- Every Grain Of Sand
- The Groom's Still Waiting At The Altar

My Personal Favorite Track(s):
- Shot Of Love
- Dead Man, Dead Man
- Trouble

Street Legal suffered from a general lack of purpose; something that Bob's conversion was useful in helping the next two albums avoid. But for whatever reason, by *Shot Of Love*, this was no longer enough, and Dylan was once again adrift. Not that he ever recanted or publicly stated that he had moved on from Christianity, but after several years and albums of a strictly religious focus, Bob started slowly and quietly moving past all of this. As a result, this is one of Dylan's most confused and uncertain albums. Not only in terms of the lyrics (half of which are still about the church the other half are casting about randomly looking for something to sing about); even the songs that are about Jesus are a little more ambiguous and open to interpretation that *Saved* or *Slow Train Coming*.

This album frequently gets lumped in together with the previous two as the final album in Bob's born-again trilogy. But just because there are some songs on here that reference religion, this album doesn't feel like part and parcel with the last two, even as far as the lyrics. None of the certainty that Dylan was going to heaven (and the rest of us are going to hell) is evident on even the most strident religious songs here. And his frequent digressions into love songs and paeans to "sick" Jewish comedians undercut the message even further.

The lack of direction also spilled over into the music as well. This is one of the least consistent sounding albums Bob had made since *Self-Portrait*. Not surprising since this was recorded with a couple of different producers in a couple of different studios backed by a couple different bands of musicians. Ringo Starr even shows up and doesn't get a whole drum set to play on (he's credited with just toms). No one really feels in charge here.

Whether or not you liked *Desire* or *Street Legal* or not, they at least held together sonically. This album feels like a patchwork compilation of several lost albums recorded during this period. The large number of outtakes from this album backs this idea up. While *The Freewheelin' Bob Dylan* was also thrown together similarly, that album at least had consistent instrumentation throughout to help smooth out the joints. *Shot Of Love* does not. This can be nice because we do get some variety on this album. Unfortunately, if we do start to get into a groove or sound that works, we also know it won't last.

As a result, it is hard to get a feel for this album or even really decide how if I like it. I certainly enjoy some of the songs, but even those songs don't feel related to each other. While I generally despair at the monotonous sound of some of Bob's records, when Dylan does choose to get a little more varied, it tends to be less consistent. This was not generally an issue with his albums in the past, *Self-Portrait* notwithstanding, but coming into the eighties there would be a couple of albums (*Knocked Out Loaded* and *Down In The Groove*) where this tendency would start to get out of hand. Having such a broad canvas to work with does make re-arranging the albums a lot more fun during this period, but does make it harder to really zero in on the officially released records as entities unto themselves.

Shot of Love
(written by Bob Dylan)

While the previous two albums would've made the love that Bob needs in this song more explicitly the love of God, here he leaves the source of this love ambiguous. As usual, Dylan seems more interested in condemning the worldly than in celebrating the divine. If this song were taking out of the context of this album and placed on *Desire* or *Street Legal*, you could be forgiven for assuming that the love he needs a shot of was coming from a woman and not a celestial being. However, it is a terrific track with a real rock feel and the backing vocalists stacking up with him on the title phrase in the choruses and bridge are great. Bob has not written an ending yet, and this song fades out after a little over four minutes.

Heart of Mine
(written by Bob Dylan)

One of the most musically gospel-tinged songs on *Shot Of Love*, this songs is not about Jesus but rather a love song. The definitively secular nature of the lyrics may have made this the obvious choice for the single. The words are odd addressing the narrator's heart and not the woman in question. Bob doesn't sound like he trusts his heart terribly and is trying to keep it from making the same mistakes again. Of course one could interpret this that since man's heart is wicked, the only salvation is to turn it over to Jesus. However, this is never explicitly stated, while there certainly would have been no doubt on the previous two albums. There's a lot of drums and percussion on this track leaving guest Ringo Starr with nothing to do but add some tom-toms. It gives the song an almost Calypso feel. Not a great track, but perfectly serviceable.

Property of Jesus
(written by Bob Dylan)

As Jesus-centric as these three albums are his name is very rarely sang in the lyrics. There's that one verse in "Gonna Change My Way Of Thinking" about Jesus at the well and one line in "Are You Ready?", but that's about it. This song has no such pussyfooting around whom it is that Bob has been worshipping and preaching about. However, instead of singing about Jesus directly, he takes on the POV of someone making fun of a believer in order to deliver one of his most withering put-downs since "Positively 4th Street". The temporary flirtation with calypso music on this album comes through in the clinking cowbell and other percussion added to this song. The honking sax here is actually reminiscent of *Street Legal*. This is one of the harder rocking songs on *Shot Of Love*, regardless of the message of the lyrics. Despite all the vitriol in Bob's voice here, this is actually one his most fun songs.

Lenny Bruce
(written by Bob Dylan)

The song most likely nominated for showing that Bob is moving past his "Christian phase." There's very little about Lenny Bruce that seems in line with any sort of Christian dogma. A Jewish comedian with a dirty mind and drug habit, he is not exactly the kind of person you would think would be idolized on one of Bob's earlier, and more hardcore, born-again albums. While the earthy and earthly nature of the subject of this song may have been heartening to those who were hoping Bob would get off this religious train, musically the song is a little disappointing. The melody is downright irritating and nasal in the same way as a child's taunting. The arrangement is somewhat faux gospel, led by the piano with the backing vocalists chiming in. The lyrics are simplistic. Lenny is admired for not cutting off any judges' heads. That's a low bar that almost everyone can pass. It does have the great line that rhymes the word "once" with the word "months." I have no idea why Bob put this out officially. The only person I think who could've really enjoyed this song is Lenny Bruce himself, and he was already dead. Definitely one of the weakest tracks on *Shot Of Love*.

Watered-Down Love
(written by Bob Dylan)

Is Bob talking to a potential paramour about dumping her loser boyfriend and getting with him? Or is he talking to the whole world, telling them to dump their materialistic ways and get with Jesus? It could be read either way I think. Dylan is seemingly torn between writing love songs and religious hymns right now and is playing trying to have it both ways. Regardless, Bob is again using the condescending sneer that he applied to "Property Of Jesus" to make fun of those who don't agree with him. The music is not nearly as harsh in tone as "Property Of Jesus" making for an interesting juxtaposition between the upbeat poppy rock song and Dylan's jeering scowl. The band is playing this as well as anything on *Saved* but is let down by a production and mix that dulls the punch of the song a bit. Much like "Heart Of Mine" this is sort of a typical, but unremarkable *Shot Of Love* track. Not bad, but there's better on this album... and worse.

Dead Man, Dead Man
(written by Bob Dylan)

While Bob has written a large number of great songs using three chords, he really proves himself here by right a great song using only two. This song is frequently lumped in with the more religious half of *Shot Of Love*. Maybe, I skipped that day at Sunday school, but the lyrics don't seem to be about anything, much less anything sacred. That being said, this is one of my favorite songs off of this album. The band gives this song a faux-reggae vibe that is applied to many of the songs on *Shot Of Love*. I love the way Bob stretched out that one note in the chorus. While I may not be able to make heads or tails of "A bird's nest in your hair," "the dust upon your eyes" or "The race of the Indian that overrules your heart," Dylan seems quite angry about all of this. There's great little squawking horn part in there that doesn't overstep its bounds and a truly menacing sound to the organ. Despite only having two chords, there's a lot of dynamic movement in the song. Bob even creates a whole new part repeating "ooh I can't stand it" at the end for the song to fade out on. Definitely a stunner.

In the Summertime
(written by Bob Dylan)

This sounds like a self-conscious attempt to write an anthem, much like "Every Grain Of Sand". It's not bad, just a little mawkish. The lyrics are little less fire-and-brimstone than some of Dylan's Christian songs. However, what he lacks in condemnation he does not make up for in anything. The words feel a little formless and unfocused. I'm not really sure if this song is about religion half the time. What exactly is the significance of the titular season in this song? I can't tell. However, this song shows Bob really re-discovering his love for the harmonica. It's all over this album and in this song, in particular, he plays some beautiful harp solos. Other than that, there's not much to distinguish this song. It's taken at a bit of a slow tempo, but there's little restraint in the playing of the backing band. Perhaps this song would've fared better with a more stripped down arrangement. It is generally forgotten by the time the album ends, and you have heard "Every Grain Of Sand" which is treading the same sort of ground but doesn't just slightly better. Otherwise, you could just easily swap the two of them for each other; you don't need both.

Trouble
(written by Bob Dylan)

While *Slow Train Coming* had songs like "When You Gonna Wake up?" "Gonna Change My Way Of Thinking" that were based around a single riff. *Saved* on the other hand, with its move from rock to gospel music doesn't have any such tunes. "Trouble" marks Bob getting back to this form of songwriting and it is quite effective. The whole song crackles with energy. There's a clicking noise that might be a cowbell thrown in there. Regardless of what the lyrics on *Shot Of Love* may be about, this is clearly Bob abandoning the traditional musical structures of gospel and rediscovering his love of rock'n'roll. Sure, the song doesn't do much except repeat that one riff, but it is a great riff. The lyrics are a little more obscure than the usual born-again fare. Bob and his backing vocalists are singing this with fury, however. Maybe, it's not as good as "The Groom's Still Waiting At The Altar", but it is a worthy companion piece.

Every Grain of Sand
(written by Bob Dylan)

There's a shorter, stripped down version of this song that appears on *The Bootleg Series vol. 3*. While I appreciate the brevity, there's too many vocalists and instrumentalists on this to really feel like we're peeking in on a personal confession. Instead, we just get a rough draft, that I know is preferred by many Dylan fans but doesn't quite do it for me. I don't mind the dog barking in the background, but Bob's vocals are far too pinched and nasal on this take. Sitting somewhere between the intimate "When He Returns" that closed *Slow Train Coming* and the full-bore "Are You Ready?" that concluded *Saved*, this is another attempt at an anthem. While it is pretty successful, you can still feel that this is what he is going for behind the scenes and doesn't feel as natural or inspired as some of his earlier born-again material. On the plus side, he is no longer using Biblical revelation to continuously badgering the listener. He's actually trying to help them feel better for a change, reminding them that even if they feel insignificant, they are still important and remembered. The song is in a 6/8 time that almost feels like it could be doo-wop. The pace is lethargic, blunting any optimism from the lyrics. This may be one of Bob's finest hours as a harmonica player. While this is not an instrument one normally associates with touching slow pop songs about Jesus, Dylan plays his heart out, making his harmonica seem even more heartbreaking than his vocals. While it never became the standard that Bob had clearly envisioned for it, "Every Grain Of Sand" is a great song.

Songs not on the album:
The Groom's Still Waiting at the Altar B-side of the American "Heart Of Mine" single
(written by Bob Dylan)
One of the more surprising omissions from a Dylan album also became one of the quickest retractions. When *Shot Of Love* was first released in 1981, this song was relegated to B-side status. By 1985 this song was added to the album at the beginning of the second side on every subsequent release of the album. While it might be some revisionist history, it's hard to argue with the logic. This song has a lot more fire and life (as well as popularity) than anything on the official album. Another one of the born-again songs built around a single recurring riff, this one is far less direct in its religious intent. In fact, if you didn't know what album this came off of and what Bob was usually singing about around this time, you would be forgiven for not realizing that this song was supposed to be about faith and church and whatnot. It's funky and hard rocking. There's a great slide guitar solo. Bob's vocals are full of condemnation instead of damnation, and you could easily think this was another song-length put-down of an unnamed former lover alá "Positively 4th Street". In fact, it is so much better than the rest of *Shot Of Love*, I find it easier to listen to the album without it otherwise it overshadows the rest of the songs and makes them harder to enjoy.

Let It Be Me B-side of the International "Heart Of Mine" single
(written by Gilbert Bécaud, Pierre Delanoë, M. Curtis)
See entry under *Self-Portrait*.

Caribbean Wind from *Biograph*
(written by Bob Dylan)
With all the reggae-ish island rhythms going on in this period, this is the only track that explicitly mentions the Caribbean. The backing vocals are doing this weird audible breath exhaling that almost reminds one of The Zombie's "Season Of The Witch". It's an interesting effect, but it's hard it threatens to get annoying. Sometimes when I listen to it, it doesn't bother me; but not always. Either way, this is a more upbeat and joyful song than most of the stuff that actually got released on *Shot Of Love*. The lyrics are an unusual combination of typical Dylan obscurities combined with attempts to preach the faith. In that way, it is almost the prototypical track from this album. The phrase "sniper-bait" is pretty disturbing. The guitar playing is nice and crisp, and the congas add a little flavor to this song that is not nearly as Caribbean sounding as some of the songs recorded during this period, especially "Don't Take Yourself Away". Many hard-core Dylan fans are disappointed that an earlier take (without the heavy breathing) wasn't issued on *Biograph* instead of this take since they feel it is far more

powerful. Personally, I think Bob's vocals on this earlier unreleased version are too nasal. The lyrics might be better, but it's not any more sensible. The mandolin on that version is nice, but the different melody that Bob sings on the chorus is far less catchy. The way Dylan stretches out the last notes of the chorus where he sings "nearer to the fire" sounds uncertain and unsure, but I do miss the weird riff break-down that the band plays at the end of each chorus. I may even prefer the earlier take, but it's pretty close and certainly not worth getting up in arms over.

You Changed My Life from *The Bootleg Series vol. 3*
(written by Bob Dylan)

The "you" of the title could either be a girlfriend or Jesus Christ. And if it is just an earthly paramour, the life-changing may be with romantic love or by leading the narrator to salvation. This sort of indistinct "is it religious or romantic" type of lyric is frequent in George Harrison's catalog, but given how strident and dogmatic Dylan's born-again period is, it is far more rare. This song is pretty boilerplate *Shot Of Love*. There's some nice propulsive snare work from the drummer here. A single backing vocalist is providing frequent harmonies instead of the mini-choir of backing vocalists that are often heard during these sessions. The chorus is actually pretty catchy, although Bob tries for a lower note at the end of the second to the last line of the chorus on the outtake on *The Bootleg Series vol. 13* that he never quite hits, and would sound funny even if he did nail it. It's certainly as good as a lot of the tracks that were released on the finished album, but it is hardly a stand-out. While several outtakes from these sessions were later added to *The Bootleg Series*, I'm not sure why this one made the cut of some of the others didn't. It is pleasant but unremarkable.

Need A Woman from *The Bootleg Series vol. 3*
(written by Bob Dylan)

A surprising song of romantic longing amongst these religious screeds. The song opens with Bob admitting that he's been having evil dreams lately. Unlike "Covenant Woman" or "Precious Angel" Dylan is no longer singing the praises of a good woman who brought him to Christ. Instead, he is speaking as a man of faith who is a little worried about jumping into the dating game. It's an unusual tact for a song to take, and Bob could've had some fun with this idea. Unfortunately, he forgoes any humor in the lyrics. Nonetheless, the song is a bright little pop tune. The chorus with its backing vocalists and answering guitar lick is pretty catchy. The song burbles along and a nice medium tempo with some nice organ work on top. Bob's vocals get a little nasal but are not horrendous. I like the way the whole song breaks down as Dylan sing the pre-chorus of "I... want... you... to...." Even though the song is titled "Need A Woman" he changes the lyrics to "Be That Woman" fairly quickly and doesn't change it back.

However, if he changed the title to that, it might have rubbed some people the wrong way. The Dylan of *Saved* wouldn't have cared how it appeared, but by *Shot Of Love*, he is clearly trying to make some concessions to try and win his audience back. This song would've been a nice but undistinguished addition to the album had it made the cut. Much like "You Changed My Life", there are worse songs on the official album and better outtakes that could've been added to *The Bootleg Series*.

Angelina from *The Bootleg Series vol. 3*
(written by Bob Dylan)

I don't know if this is the same Angelina that Bob was bidding farewell to in 1966. The song is another attempt at a ballad, and since "Every Grain Of Sand" worked out so well, it's no surprise that this track was left off of *Shot Of Love*. The lyrics are strange and difficult to parse in a way that most of the previous born-again records were not. Bob does a great job of finding all sorts of words that rhyme with the titular character's name. The song is a little too long and drags a bit. The band does a lovely job of slowly building up from the initial solo piano. However, once the song locks into its groove, and it never wavers or deviates from it. I start out supporting and rooting for this song, but I get bored and impatient before the halfway mark. Easily the weakest of the *Shot Of Love* outtakes that have been officially released.

Don't Ever Take Yourself Away from the *Hawaii Five-O* soundtrack
(written by Bob Dylan)

Bob's reggae obsession continues on this track. It's probably about as authentic as Jimmy Buffet song, but it is mildly enjoyable genre exercise. With its unspecified international feel, it almost sounds like something off of *Desire*. The lyrics are your usual devotional love song stuff. I suppose it is vague and generic enough that one could interpret as Bob pleading with Jesus not leave him, but it performed so perfunctorily with such a lackadaisical vocal commitment that seems unlikely that there is any deeper meaning to this song. It's a pretty straightforward song. The most unusual thing about it is that it did see release about thirty years after it was recorded, not on one of the Bootleg Series, but instead on the soundtrack to the utterly unnecessary reboot of the show *Hawaii Five-O*. It seems unlikely that Bob is a big fan of that particular show, but who knows? And if he isn't who knows how they ended up with this specific outtake. Theorizing about that may actually be more entertaining than the song in question itself.

Yonder Comes Sin from *The Bootleg Series vol. 13*
(written by Bob Dylan)

A song initially slotted for the first installment of *The Bootleg Series* before being vetoed by Dylan, this song took a while to get officially released finally. Apparently, Bob was nervous that the verse that dismissed his critics would be taken the wrong way at the time. This is one of the harder rocking songs of the *Shot Of Love* outtakes. Despite putting the word "sin" in the title and chorus, it can be little hard to suss out if the lyrics here are secular or religious. Either way, it's a fun little song. The bass part sounds suspiciously like The Rolling Stones' "Satisfaction" or Buffalo Springfield's "Mr. Soul". It's a driving and propulsive track with some fine organ playing. The interjections from the backing vocalists are not as distracting as one might expect. It's no "The Groom's Still Waiting At The Altar", but this is still a pretty good song.

Magic officially unreleased
(written by Bob Dylan)

There's something of a 1950's vibe to this song. The lyrics seem entirely romantic and non-religious although they are a little hard to pick out in this mix. This opens with Bob humming along with the main guitar riff that the rest of the band answers with a cha-cha-cha. The song is actually a little more tricky than a lot of Dylan's work. Nothing super-complicated, but a few more moving pieces than he usually employs. Despite this relative sophistication, it sounds like the song is quite done yet. There are several spots where it sounds like Bob hasn't gotten around to writing lyrics yet. Still, of the more than ample outtakes from *Shot Of Love*, this is one of the ones that are closer to be usable than most.

Is It Worth It? officially unreleased
(written by Bob Dylan)

Having Ditched Jerry Wexler and the Muscle Shoals studios for his latest "born again" album, Bob was at a bit of a loss as to where to record next. As a result, Dylan took his band up and down the California coast trying out numerous different studios to see which one(s) felt most comfortable in. Needing something to record during these auditions of studios, Bob and his musicians ran through any number of jams, half-finished songs, and covers. Some of these are certainly far more deliberate, if not exactly polished, than others. These outtakes do provide an interesting insight into Dylan's songwriting methods of the period. While "Yonder Comes Sin" and "Magic" feel complete, these titles seem to be far more in a state of gestation. "Is It Worth It?" opens with Bob teaching the band the central riff by singing it to them. They quickly pick up on it and launch into a song that is pretty cool. It certainly has a ton of potential and is almost usable even in this rough state.

High Away officially unreleased
(written by Bob Dylan)
This song is often listed on bootlegs with the subtitle "(Ah Ah Ah)" since that seems to be the sole lyrics of the chorus. I would assume that if Dylan had gotten around to finishing this song, those dummy lyrics would've been replaced by actual words. The song has a good rock groove, although the band is obviously still learning it, as the run through the meager material several times without stopping, making the song almost eight minutes long. For a long while, it seems like Bob only has the one musical idea for the song, but halfway through, he stops the band to deliver a slower, free-form break in the activities before leading the group back into the meat of the song. Maybe this was supposed to be the gospelesque intro to the song. This is another track with some definite unrealized potential.

Yes Sir, No Sir (Hallelujah) officially unreleased
(written by Bob Dylan)
This is another song revolving around a singular riff. For a song with a chorus of hallelujahs, this is a surprisingly spooky and menacing track. The pre-chorus rises for much longer than you would expect from a Dylan track. The whole thing has a really dark vibe that is missing from a lot of these tunes. This one is possibly one of my favorites from these unfinished songs.

You're Still A Child To Me officially unreleased
(written by Bob Dylan)
We're floating by on the same light reggae that informed "Don't Ever Taker Yourself Away From Me". In fact, this song may be an early draft of that latter one. No lyrics or any melody for most this song. Only after one-and-a-half of the song's two minutes have passed, do Bob and backing singers come in with a short, simple chorus. This one is far less finished than the last three.

Wind Blows On The Water officially unreleased
(written by Bob Dylan)
We've got another reggae-ish number. It's hard to tell how many lyrics Bob actually finished for this song since his vocals are pretty buried on this admittedly rough mix. It seems mostly like the only words are those within the title as they repeated by the backing vocalists almost constantly through this entire three-minute song. You can hear the cadence of the lyrics mutate via repetition, but other than that, nothing changes on this track. This is not one worth looking for.

All The Way Down officially unreleased
(written by Bob Dylan)

This is far more gospel sounding and feels like a part of *Saved* rather than *Shot Of Love*. The free-flowing intro with backing vocalists and organ sound like we're in church. Unfortunately, this intro is, in fact, the majority of this song. You almost get lulled into thinking that the introduction is the entirety of the song so it can be quite a shock when the band finally kicks into gear. However, that part doesn't last long, and soon the outtake is over.

My Oriental Home officially unreleased
(written by Bob Dylan)

"My Oriental Home" is probably not the title Bob had in mind for this instrumental, but who knows what he was going to call it. This doesn't seem a wholly composed piece as much as it is a jam centered around a riff that does have something of a faux-Hollywood approximation of Asian exotica to it. Had Bob gotten around to finishing this, it would've been a distinctive sound within his catalog. As it is right now, it is just tediously noodling.

We're On Borrowed Time officially unreleased
(written by Bob Dylan)

This, on the other hand, is much closer to a completed song. While not super-rehearsed, this doesn't sound like the band's first time playing this material. It's pretty much typical *Shot Of Love* type pop song with a driving rock edge. There's plenty of cowbell in here, but not much else happens.

I Want You To Know I Love You officially unreleased
(written by Bob Dylan)

This song has a shuffling train beat of an early Johnny Cash or Elvis Presley Sun Record. The lyrics are sung with the backing vocalists with a strange elongation of each line. Most of these are just a single one-syllable word punctuating the first beat of each bar until we get to the last half of the line when everything else tumbles out. It's a neat trick and produces an oddly anxiety-producing effect. Also, it means you don't have to write nearly as many words to fill up and entire song. It's not finished by any stretch, but there's a cool idea there.

On A Rockin' Boat officially unreleased
(written by Bob Dylan)

While this does have some gospel-ish flourishes, this is definitely a rock song. Clearly, the drummer is not awake for this song as we don't hear any percussion except the occasional thwack of a cowbell for the first two-and-a-half minutes. The electric guitar, bass, and piano are all playing like there is a full band here nonetheless. It sounds like Bob had some idea for this song, but ran out of ideas halfway through, although he does attempt to improvise a bridge near the end. There's definitely some potential on this track, even if it's not the greatest.

Movin' (On The Water) officially unreleased
(written by Bob Dylan)

Another rocking, nautically themed song. The jamming over a single chord for most of the song almost brings to mind the Talking Heads' *Remain In Light* album. The lyrics seem to be only made of the title – and even then it's just the first word over and over. Bob and/or the backing vocalists come in with that intermittently, but this is mostly instrumental. This is not a song by any stretch, it's just a groove. But it's a pretty good groove. Fun to jam to, but not much else is going on here. Certainly not one of the more memorable *Shot Of Love* outtakes.

Almost officially unreleased
(written by Bob Dylan)

This definitely seems far more pre-written that "Movin' (On The Water)" even if the lyrics for the chorus seem to mostly be just "aaahh" before turning into "aaahh-lmost." This song employs a relatively large number of chords for Dylan. While Bob seemed to have something a little more specific in mind for this track, it fizzles out after about two minutes. It's something of a power-pop ballad. Dylan's vocals are a little searching, although what he's searching for may just be the next line. By the second verse, he has hit on the idea of starting each two-word line with the word "almost." There's the germ of a beautiful, little ditty in here, but it certainly needs some more work. Still, as a glimpse into Bob mid-songwriting, it is fascinating.

Mystery Train officially unreleased
(written by Junior Parker)

We're jamming on a cover here to test out the acoustics of the studio and not trying to get a real releasable take. As a result, everyone plays spectacularly, knowing that the pressure's off. The tempo is taken at a much more sinister and threatening pace. A saxophone wonders in from what sounds like a *Street Legal* session. Everyone involved is having a grand old time. Bob's vocals, ghosted throughout by one of his backing vocalists, is thoroughly committed. With the ending of his Christian period, Dylan was clearly casting about for new things to write about. Eventually, his writer's block would lead him to admit defeat and start recording covers. If he had charged ahead proactively at this juncture and started taking his covers seriously (instead of treating them just as studio warm-ups) things might have worked out better for all of us.

Let's Keep It Between Us officially unreleased
(written by Bob Dylan)

The most gospel sounding track in the whole *Shot Of Love* sessions. Oddly enough the song is not about Jesus or anything religious. Instead it seems to be Bob pleading with a lover to keep things on the DL. It's not sure if they are just now getting together, or if they are just now breaking up. Maybe Dylan's just asking his lady friend not to blab about any secrets shared during their relationship. There's a nice mid-tempo R&B stomp. Someone with some real pipes could vocalize the hell out of this. Bonnie Raitt covered this song in 1982 and gave it a very urgent vocal feel. Bob, in contrast, seems to be taking this very laid-back. This vocal delivery is at odds with the music and works against it. I'm not sure how persuasive this song is, so it's probably for the best that its aims are small as opposed to apocalyptic. A couple of times Dylan sings about not letting people call the woman a slut. For some reason, it is weird to hear that word come from Bob. Otherwise, there is not much else to say about this track.

Played live, but never recorded:
Jesus Is The One from *The Bootleg Series vol. 13*
(written by Bob Dylan)

This song resists expectations and sounds more like a brother to the funky "Cover Down Pray Through" and is one of the few songs here I really wish had gotten a good studio recording back in the day. The bass sounds really distorted, which I'm assuming could've been fixed with a proper studio take, although you really do need the bass that high in the mix to keep the energy going on this song. I really like the way Bob is joined by one of the backing vocalists on the chorus while the rest answer him. The frantic percussion, including cowbell, gives this whole thing a very *Shot Of Love* vibe. This is one of the more frantic more songs from this era. Definitely a plus.

Thief On the Cross from *The Bootleg Series vol. 13*
(written by Bob Dylan)

"Thief On The Cross" comes across like more of a rock song than a gospel number, which is nice. It almost sounds like a Dire Straits song, which is odd since Bob was currently between visits from Mark Knopfler at the time. The slide guitar is pretty hot on this particular song. The song doesn't have a lot to say or do much musically, but it is something of a barn-burner. The song spends so much time on one chord, that any time it does decide to switch things up it feels very dramatic. There's an odd keyboard somewhere in the mix playing a cool riff throughout the song. This song in some ways points to the keyboard-heavy sound of *Empire Burlesque* that was to come in just a couple of years, mostly courtesy of Arthur Baker. Certainly one of the more rocking tunes from the whole "born-again" era.

Let's Begin from *The Bootleg Series vol. 13*
(written by Bob Dylan)
Something of a duet as one of the backing vocalists (Clydie King) sings along with Dylan throughout the entire song. This is a pretty typical mid-tempo love song. There's not nearly enough R&B or gospel flavor to this song, which could've used some of that to keep it from being too milquetoast. While this is not nearly Michael Bolton-level bad, it is seriously dipping towards that territory. Particularly with the late song key change up half a step to try and artificially induce some excitement to the song. The song ends after a competent but tepid guitar solo. This is definitely not something Bob needed to return to in the studio.

Rumored to have been recorded but unheard:
Fur Slippers
(written by Bob Dylan and Tim Drummond)
I Wish It Would Rain
(written by Bob Dylan)
Cold, Cold Heart
(written by Hank Williams)
Almost Persuaded
(written by Bob Dylan)
Reach Out
(written by Bob Dylan)
Bolero
(written by Bob Dylan)
The Girl From Louisville
(traditional, arranged by Bob Dylan)
It's All Dangerous To Me
(written by Bob Dylan)
The King Is On The Throne
(written by Bob Dylan)
I Wish It Would Rain
(written by Bob Dylan)

While "Fur Slippers" was covered by BB King of all people, most of these songs are unheard and unknown. Ron Wood recorded an instrumental by Dylan called "King Of Kings" for his 2002 album, *Not For Beginners*. Although there are no lyrics, the title suggests that it might have been composed at this time, although some have also indicated that it was written in either 1993 or 1996. There are some intriguing song titles in here, but until we actually get to hear them, there's not much that can be said. While *The Bootleg Series, vol. 13* is supposed to include *Shot Of Love* as one of the albums it is re-investigating, the emphasis is solely on the religious material, so any secular songs recorded around *Shot Of Love* were unfortunately disqualified from being considered for inclusion. Which is a shame, since there's definitely some interesting stuff recorded during this period as Bob was traveling from studio to studio looking for a new sound.

"CARIBBEAN WIND"

SIDE A:
1. Shot Of Love
2. Caribbean Wind
3. Yonder Comes Sin
4. Dead Man, Dead Man
5. Yes Sir, No Sir (Hallelujah)

SIDE B:
1. Trouble
2. Is It Worth It?
3. Don't Ever Take Yourself Away
4. The Groom's Still Waiting At The Altar
5. Every Grain Of Sand

There were a lot of songs recorded that wasn't quite written for this album. There's quite a bit of potential in some of them, most of them don't really feel done enough to swap out with any of the songs on *Shot Of Love*. I mostly used the more completed songs that have appeared over the years. And that still leaves me a plethora to choose from.

I went ahead and removed "Lenny Bruce", which in addition to being a mediocre song, also significantly muddied the waters of whether or not this was a "born again" album for Bob. Sure there are still a number of songs where the meaning is unclear (particularly when compared to the previous record), but nothing on here directly contradicts Bob's apparent faith now. Not even the more secular love songs, of which there are a few.

I have tried to emphasize the more rocking upbeat numbers over the ballads for this collection, although we do conclude with the masterful "Every Grain Of Sand". I have also tried to add as much island flavor to the sonic palette as well. These reggae leanings predated the Christian period by appearing in many of the arrangements on *At Budokan*. He would also continue this trend in the future, mostly while employing Sly & Robbie for the *Infidels* sessions. That's why I decided to re-name this album *Caribbean*

Wind.

I thought about adding "Let It Be Me" and/or "Mystery Train", as cover songs were going to be a large part of Dylan's discography from this point forward. While it was important to remind people that Dylan can be the interpreter of other people's material and to get them used to that, I just didn't feel like those tracks quite fit.

While this collection may not be as unrepentantly religious, I think it makes a good companion piece to *A Slow And Saved Train* as we see Dylan beginning to temper his zealotry without confusing the issue as to where he stood concerning spiritual matters at this time.

INFIDELS
Produced by: Mark Knopfler & Bob Dylan
Recorded: April 11th – May 17th, 1983
Released: October 27th, 1983

Famous/Important/Popular Track(s):
- Jokerman
- Blind Willie McTell

My Personal Favorite Track(s):
- I And I
- Foot Of Pride
- Blind Willie McTell

After the all-over-the-map mess of *Shot Of Love*, Bob has decided to go back to a more consistent sound for his next record. Perhaps realizing that he has lost some cultural cache after his sojourn in the "born again" wilderness, Dylan decides to try his hand at selling out. As usual for the eighties, Bob has no idea what is popular or what the audience wants for him, and so he ends up creating something rather strange that feels neither commercial nor authentic.

This is one of the most distinctive combination of personalities and instrumentation that Dylan has curated since *Desire*. Mark Knopfler has been brought back for the first time since *Slow Train Coming* and promoted to producer. Former Rolling Stone Mick Taylor is recruited to add even more guitar. But the bass and drums are provided by reggae all-stars Sly & Robbie. Sure, Bob has been flirting with reggae arrangements for a while now, but this is still odd. Even stranger, Sly & Robbie are hired and then not allowed to full-reign to do any real reggae on the album. One of the biggest disappointments of this album is that it doesn't sound like Dylan singing a Bob Marley/Dire Straits mash-up.

Of course, the real disappointment of *Infidels* are the songs that were recorded for the album but for some strange reason didn't make the cut. While no album should be judged by what isn't on the actual record, no disc in Dylan's catalog is more defined by what was left off of it than *Infidels*. But "Blind Willie McTell" alone may be more of a well-known, critic- and fan-favorite, than the eight songs on the album itself combined. And while I generally disagree with the public consensus about most things related to Bob, I will admit, they are probably right about this one.

At this time this was released, it was hailed as a comeback – mostly out of relief, the same way *New Morning* was greeted after *Self-Portrait*, but over the years, this album has not really held-up. With the benefit of hindsight (and the release of *The Bootleg Series vol. 3*), this album is mostly relegated to being thought of as a missed opportunity... when it is thought about at all.

The lyrics on the album eschew any sort of spirituality in all but the most oblique way. Instead, Dylan seems to be re-engaging with his political side for the first time (other than one-offs like "Hurricane" or "George Jackson") since before he plugged in. Unfortunately, he doesn't seem very angry or invested in this anymore. It's hard to tell where Bob stands anymore. Sure "Neighborhood Bully" is a pro-Israel allegory, but it has none of the depth or nuanced thought of "Only A Pawn In Their Game". "Union Sundown" demonstrated the very in vogue feeling that labor organizing had gone too far. This was a fairly common stance in Reagan's America but sounds weird coming from the man who was once so strongly associated with the likes of Woody Guthrie and Joe Hill. The *Infidels* outtake "Julius & Ethel" is unambiguous, but since the two of them had already been executed decades earlier, it's hard to figure out why Bob was bringing it up again.

In addition to leaving the Godly behind and trying to re-engage with the worldly, the love songs that first appeared on *Shot Of Love* have multiplied. Still, Dylan has really committed to this. At this point, Bob had married one of his back-up singers, but in his paranoid need to avoid having anyone know his about his private life, he hadn't mentioned it to anyone, and nobody really knew. So Bob couldn't really be out there openly singing songs of love or devotion. As a result, the romantic lyrics come across as impersonal and as calculated as anything he had tried since *Planet Waves*. This does not lead to terribly heartfelt or moving music.

I will admit that another one of my frustrations with this album comes from the fact that it only has 8 songs. Sure the songs are long (not necessarily a good thing), and vinyl was still the prominent medium at this point, so there was a limitation on how much music Dylan could cram on there. Still, even if there weren't a treasure trove of great songs left off of this album, the relative paucity of songs on *Infidels* feels like even more of a rip-off.

I do enjoy the overall sound of this album. There are some decent songs on here. I'm glad I don't have to try to ignore the sanctimoniousness of the lyrics anymore. But this is not an album, I return to often, either as released or with the half-dozen outtake added.

Jokerman
(written by Bob Dylan)

This song opens with a tom-tom fill that sounds very reggae before a burbling bass, and a sustained organ carry Bob as he begins to sing. Mark Knopfler's guitar doesn't kick in until halfway through the first verse. While the song "Shot Of Love" left its religiosity as somewhat vague, there is still no consensus as to how "born again" this track really is. The lyrics use a lot of biblical imagery, but that has always been Bob's stock-in-trade. They are not as clear and unambiguous as *Saved* or *Slow Train Coming*. While this song was chosen as the single and video from this album as well as appearing on many subsequent Greatest Hits compilations, I don't hear what all the fuss was about. Maybe people were just relieved at the time that it wasn't another "Property Of Jesus", but why it's endured is hard to say. It's not terribly catchy. The instrumentation, although interesting at first, gets old by the end of its 6+ minutes. Bob is trying really hard to sing this well, but the vocal extemporizing on the "whoah-whoah-whoah" before the title in the choruses is just painful to me. I mean it's not a horrible song, and better than a lot of things on *Infidels*, but this is not one I frequently go back to.

Sweetheart Like You
(written by Bob Dylan)
Opening with some odd lines about one's boss heading north, the remainder of this song is spent wooing some woman in a slightly condescending and insulting matter. I'm not sure what kind of dump the two of them have found themselves, but it requires being an important person. Still, he thinks that she is too good for this place. He also says she should be married and in the kitchen. I'm surprised this "sweetheart" didn't just slap Bob in the face. Musically, however, the song is lovely. The interplay between Mark Knopfler and Sly & Robbie is really tasteful, and the melody is beautiful. The tempo is slow without getting boring. Bob's vocals are committed and strong. This is a pretty typical track for *Infidels*.

Neighborhood Bully
(written by Bob Dylan)
While it can occasionally be hard to parse out the exact meaning in some of Bob's lyrics, there is almost no way to interpret this song as anything other than about the state of Israel. Maybe his Jewish roots are showing, or he is helping usher in the millennium/apocalypse/tribulations that his newfound beliefs are anticipating, but clearly, this song is pro-Israel. While the lyrics are meant to be ironic, it's hard to say why this "bully" is being treated so poorly or why he doesn't deserve the treatment. Sure, he's not polluting the stars, but is that something he is being accused of? Or is that even something anyone is capable of? I don't know. Unless it really is about some kid in the neighborhood who likes to pick on other kids. But that seems unlikely. This is one of the more hard-rocking songs on *Infidels*, and Bob's singing has an edge of anger to it. There's definitely a bit of funk in there. There's a lot more organ on this track than most of the others on this album. If you don't get too caught up in the politics in the lyrics, this is one of the best songs on the album.

License to Kill
(written by Bob Dylan)
I have no idea what Bob is singing about here. James Bond? Why is

touching the moon the first step to the doom of mankind (other than the fact it rhymes)? Despite all of this, Bob sings these words as if they were very urgent and we needed to heed them immediately. Despite the confusion this creates, I quite enjoy this song. A slower song, it's still taken with a lot of power. It's got a great bridge. The usual backing band is here, and they play with refinement. The harmonica solo that ends this song is one Bob's better ones. This song is just over three-and-a-half minutes, which helps a lot. It was an odd choice for Tom Petty second song during the *30th Anniversary Concert*, but I'm glad he gave this otherwise obscure track another chance to shine.

Man of Peace
(written by Bob Dylan)

While there may not be a lot of songs directly about Jesus or God on *Infidels* but we do at least get one about Satan. Here Bob is decrying the potential wolves in sheep clothing. Of course, Dylan could also be talking as much about politics as he is religion. This may not actually be about the literal devil as much as it is about lawmakers who present a façade of peacemakers while in fact working towards their own self-interest. I'm sure that a lot of people chose to interpret this song secularly merely because they were hoping for an end to Dylan's born-again period so badly, but for my money, I think this might actually be a song about Lucifer presenting himself in various guises in life. Either way, the thing Bob seems most concerned with here is the hypocrisy and duplicity of the alleged "men of peace" more so than any actual destruction such people cause. He'd probably be okay with them as long as they were up-front about their objectives. The music is fun upbeat rock shuffle with just a hint of reggae in there. It doesn't need to be six-and-a-half minutes, but it strolls along with a nice confident strut. There's a surprise acoustic guitar solo in here that is a nice change of pace. There's even a cheap sounding organ playing during the electric guitar solo that is genuinely goofy. Bob's vocals are pleasantly angry, but his three-note harmonica solo is ridiculous padding in a song that already has too much filler. When I'm making a mix tape of Bob's religious songs, this is one I always end up including.

Union Sundown
(written by Bob Dylan)

There is no question what the lyrics here are about. This can make the song hard to appreciate if you aren't on board with Bob's hypothesis here. Luckily this is one of the more rocking and fun *Infidels* song, so it is possible to ignore the words and just enjoy the track. Bob here seems to think that the unions have gotten too powerful and are now more of a hindrance than a help to the working man. He also seems to be against the globalization of manufacturing. He is worried about home gardens being legislated against and vegetables being grown on the moon. Despite describing all these problems and being generally upset at the path that modern unionization has taken, there are no alternatives or solutions presented here. This might be way Dylan's vocals here seem to be aiming for some sort of anger, but end up only delivering disappointment. Whether he's advocating for the disbanding of all unions or is just taking modern union leaderships to task for taking advantage of their position and hoping they will mend their ways. Regardless, this is still a funky rock track with some excellent slide guitar playing throughout. While the lyrics might make this song seem a little dated at first, I think there is still some real fire here. Definitely one of my favorite of the tracks actually released on *Infidels*.

I and I
(written by Bob Dylan)

Another cool slinky song. I haven't the foggiest idea what the words here are about. But Bob sings them with such emotion that you feel like there's some mystery in these words that is worth investigating. It's all just verse and chorus, with no bridge which can get a bit tiring for over five minutes, but the playing on here has enough variety and subtlety to captivate the listener. Both Mick Taylor and Mark Knopfler are constantly soloing through the song, but it doesn't become distracting or annoying as it does with some songs. The toms have a nice reggae sound to them, even if Sly & Robbie are keeping their Jamaican roots to a minimum. There's this weird synth that comes in occasionally and does this weird tremolo chord once or twice that adds to the general spookiness of the song. The version on *Real Live* can't hold a candle to this. Honestly, if this song had been left off the album, it probably would've been as revered as "Blind Willie McTell" or "Foot Of Pride"; however since it was actually released, it doesn't maintain the same coolness factor that those other songs have. A genuinely startling and dark track, one of my favorites on the album.

Don't Fall Apart on Me Tonight
(written by Bob Dylan)

An unremarkable love song in the mold of the ones that dominated *Planet Waves*. The musicians do an admirable job of trying to elevate this middling material. The number of classics left off of *Infidels* makes the mediocrity of this track that much more frustrating. There's nothing really wrong with this song, it's just forgettable. The tempo is stuck in a mid-tempo pulse that is neither exciting nor dramatic. The lyrics seem to be more about talking to a potential love interest out of embarrassing the narrator than it is about wooing that woman. There's no need for this song to be this long. At least there's a nice little turn in the bridge that helps keep the song from getting too monotonous. It's an especially baffling decision to end the album on this note. It's best not to think too much about it, it makes the song far more palatable that way.

Songs not on the album:
Tight Connection to My Heart (Has Anybody Seen My Love) *fka* Someone's Got A Hold Of My Heart released on *Empire Burlesque*
(written by Bob Dylan)

In its original incarnation as "Someone's Got A Hold Of My Heart", this song is just another one of the forgettable mid-tempo love songs from *Infidels* like "Don't' Fall Apart On Me Tonight" or "Sweetheart Like You". It's perfectly workable, but nothing worth paying much attention to. It's no surprise that it was left off of the album and didn't appear until *The Bootleg Series vol. 3*. However, redone as "Tight Connection To My Heart", the song finally comes into its own. It's not any faster but feels far more alive. The gospel-style backing singers that were banished from *Infidels* to prevent any reminders of the recently abandoned born-again period are back. Arthur Baker has not gone overboard with the synths or drum machines on this track, but they're still there. The lyrics are a little more obtuse and obscure. "Someone's Got A Hold Of My Heart" is just a straightforward song to a woman who has taken her love and left him. "Tight Connection" feels far more invested in the whole world. It's less personal and more political. The line about some being "shot later for resisting arrest" is pretty chilling, although I have no idea why anyone would wear a powder blue wig. It's still not a great song, but it is much grander in its *Empire Burlesque* incarnation.

Clean Cut Kid released on *Empire Burlesque*
(written by Bob Dylan)

Another song initially recorded for *Infidels* that was substantially improved by being re-done by Arthur Baker for *Empire Burlesque*. Unlike "Tight Connection"/"Someone's Got A Hold..." this song was recorded again from scratch instead of just taking the original Knopfler version and re-doing the vocals and adding a bunch of overdubs. The original "Clean Cut Kid" is taken ever so slightly slower with longer breaks between the verses, making the song over two minutes longer to its detriment. This is mostly a two-chord song so elongating it is not doing it any favors. The *Empire Burlesque* version features a very 80's sounding snare drum. It also has a lot more interjections from Dylan's harmonica and some backing vocalists filling out the sound. The *Infidels* version sounds pretty much like most of the songs from these sessions. The guitar playing is tight, and Robbie & Sly provide a surprisingly sympathetic backing if one that doesn't take advantage of their reggae roots. The song is often seen as an indictment of the treatment of veterans returning from the Vietnam War, but I'm not sure if I get that from the lyrics. Peter O'Toole gets name-checked though, so that's something. Bob gives this a lively, if not passionate, performance. It's not a great song in either incarnation, but I think Arthur Baker did a slightly better job with the track than Mark Knopfler.

Death Is Not the End released on *Down In The Groove*
(written by Bob Dylan)

The most explicitly religious song recorded for *Infidels*. If this track had been included on the album, it would've frustrated those listeners who were really hoping that Dylan was over his born-again period. By the time this actually came out on *Down In The Groove*, nobody really cared what Bob's religious convictions were and just wanted him to sing with any conviction at all. There are more backing vocals on this track that were probably added after *Infidels* to help this track fit in with the rest of Bob's work at this time. Oddly enough, the backing vocals are provided by not by Bob's usual singers, but Full Force, the hip-hop and R&B vocal group. Not that they do anything particular noteworthy with their vocals, providing just a gospelesque "no no" during the chorus and the occasional blocks of "oohs." The song itself, is not that in your face about what happens after death as much as it is about the fact that something does happen after death. It's the kind of song one would sing to mourners at a funeral to try and make them feel better. It's a pretty song but doesn't ever really connect as deeply as I think it would like it to. It could be that the pace is just too slow and I start to worry that death is not even the end of this song. Vital if you were putting together a more overtly Christian version of *Infidels* to follow up *Shot Of Love*, but not terribly memorable otherwise.

Angel Flying Too Close To The Ground B-side of the "Union Sundown" single
(written by Willie Nelson)

While several covers were kicked around during the *Infidels* sessions, this is the only one that saw official release. Even then it was buried on a B-side and hasn't been collected onto an official CD yet. Despite being a Willie Nelson song, this doesn't sound very country but has the standard Dire Straits-meets-reggae feel as the rest of the album. The snare drum is weirdly mixed, popping way out in the mix when it is hit directly at the end of each verse, but appearing more appropriate in the side-stick hits throughout the rest of the song. There's a female harmony vocalist throughout this song. Bob's harmonica solo does a great job of subverting the main melody. The song is taken at far too slow of a pace and starts to become wearisome by the end despite being brief. The lyrics are pure country love song drivel. As much as Dylan loves Willie, I'm not sure why he's covering this song, much less in this style. It's at least a little more excusable than some of the other middling love songs that did actually get released on *Infidels*.

Blind Willie McTell from *The Bootleg Series vol. 3*
(written by Bob Dylan)

The biggest song on *Infidels* is probably the one that was left off. When people argue that Dylan lost his mind during the eighties the non-inclusion of "Blind Willie McTell" is often presented as exhibit 1-A. Dylan's excuses and the reason for leaving the song off have never been terribly convincing and even producer Knopfler was surprised when he found it wasn't on there. The song itself is amazing, no doubt about it. There is some argument as to which is the superior take on the song: the full-band performance that is only available on bootlegs, or the solo piano and acoustic version released on *The Bootleg Series vol. 3*. Clinton Heylin argues that the solo version is vastly inferior. While I do agree that I like the full band rendition more, I don't think it's nearly that lopsided. Bob coughs during the first lines of the song, and it is very distracting to the song (why couldn't they have done another take?). Plus the solo version is not nearly that bad. It's certainly head and shoulder above "Dirge" which featured similar instrumentation. But if you are compiling your own version of *Infidels* (like most Dylan fans do) you will want the full band version as it fits in better. Perhaps you can even edit together the first verse of the piano version onto the remainder of the band version to create a complete performance that avoids that distracting cough. The song itself is ostensibly about the old blues singer Blind Willie McTell and even is modeled somewhat on the "St. James Infirmary Blues". From there it goes off in all sorts of tangents about slavery and other gruesome subjects. The song is haunting and harrowing, even if Mark Knopfler's production does seem at odds to that type of material. While I generally tend to be a contrarian, this is one of the few songs in the overlap on the Venn diagram between songs I like and songs other Dylan fans like. One of his best!

Foot Of Pride from *The Bootleg Series vol. 3*
(written by Bob Dylan)

While I agree that "Blind Willie McTell" is a masterpiece, I may actually like this *Infidels* outtake more. The verses are all based around a weird little one-chord riff. Each verse takes as long or little time as it needs to get through the odd numbers of lines. It's no surprise that Lou Reed chose to cover this track at the 30th *Anniversary Celebration* concert. The backing band can vamp as long as it needs for Lou to get through mumbling all of these words. I have no idea what the lyrics mean. Again there's a weird dig at women who dress like men thrown in there that I wonder how sincerely it was meant. I am familiar with the idiom of "feet of clay" but I have no idea whether the foot talked about here is an appendage at the end of a leg or a measurement of length. The short harmonica breaks at the end of each chorus almost remind me of the blasts in "Gates Of Eden" or "It's Alright,

Ma (I'm Only Bleeding)". The chorus is a killer and catchy as hell. Bob's sings these obscure lyrics with a real sense of venom in his voice. Despite being a little longer than I usually like my songs to be, the song continually builds upon itself, ramping up the tension. Frankly, an *Infidels* that included this song and "Blind Willie McTell" may have been one of my favorite Dylan records. Alas, it was not meant to be. Who knows what Dylan is thinking.

Lord Protect My Child from *The Bootleg Series vol. 3*
(written by Bob Dylan)

Despite the title, this song isn't particularly religious. While it does seem to be imploring to the Lord, Bob is not seeing his praises at all and is merely asking for a favor. In fact, he may as well be singing to his ex-wife more than any actual deity here. Oddly enough, Bob didn't have any small children at the time he recorded this song. He had separated from Sara for about seven years at this point, and their youngest was fourteen by the time he recorded this (he would have another kid, Gabrielle, two years after recording this track). However secular this song might actually be, it was probably left off of *Infidels* to keep the record-buying public from thinking this was another born-again Dylan record. This song aims for an anthem-like quality but fails to deliver. The antecedent that it most clearly wants to be is "Forever Young", but this songs never gets close to reaching those heights. Instead, we get just another power ballad with the standard *Infidels* sound of Mark Knopfler plus Sly & Robbie. Pleasant enough, but not one of the more fascinating outtakes from this album.

Tell Me from *The Bootleg Series vol. 3*
(written by Bob Dylan)

After years of writing only songs about hefty weighty religious topics, Bob seems like he was still trying to get comfortable getting back into the swing of writing a simple love song. This is an odd song to write about a romantic relationship. This is early in the courtship, before Dylan has entirely fallen for the woman in question, or is even quite sure how he feels about her. He just wants to get to know her better so that he can see if there is a spark or the potential for anything long-term there. The song has more of the reggae feel than many of these songs that have Sly & Robbie on them. It bops along in a relaxed but loping pace. Mick Taylor's slide playing is nicely prominent, while Mark Knopfler has mixed his own contribution into a surprisingly apt backing role. The backing vocalists definitely add to the more Jamaican vibe of this song. It's a pleasant enough song, possibly more enjoyable than some of the mediocre love tunes that did make it onto *Infidels* like "Sweetheart Like You" or "Don't Fall Apart On Me Tonight". However, unlike several of the unreleased tracks here, the lack of inclusion of "Tell Me" on the official album is no great tragedy.

Julius And Ethel officially unreleased
(written by Bob Dylan)

Not only was Bob having trouble writing love songs after his sojourn in the exclusively Christian era, but he was also dipping his toe back into trying to write about socio-political topics again. Other than "George Jackson" and "Hurricane", this was not something he had done since the early sixties, and his rustiness showed. Songs like "License To Kill" were too veiled while "Neighborhood Bully" wasn't veiled enough. "Union Sundown" came off as ham-fisted and lacked the subtlety and nuance of say "Only A Pawn In Their Game" or "The Lonesome Death of Hattie Carroll". This song revolves around the conviction and execution of Julius and Ethel Rosenberg for treason back in 1953. Kind of an odd topic for Dylan to be tackling nearly thirty years later. I'm not sure what his point or opinion on the matter is. He even sings that "some people say that hadn't been any crime" without ever stating either implicitly or explicitly what he thinks about it. The best he can come up with is that they were never convicted beyond a reasonable doubt. Mostly it's a very rough sketch of some of the main facts of the case without a lot of opinion or commentary. The backing is pretty high energy but in the usual *Infidels* style. The chorus flitters halfway between catchy and annoying. It's just the two names in the title repeated two times with a harmony vocalist. Lots of room in here for Knopfler to show off his guitar chops. It may not say much or go anywhere, but it is nonetheless a fun track, and certainly better to my ears than most of what actually did come out on the album, even if it's no "Foot Of Pride" or "Blind Willie McTell".

This Was My Love officially unreleased
(written by Jim Harbert)

Before jumping into the surprising "Sinatra period" in 2015, Bob had attempted this Frank Sinatra tune during the *Infidels* sessions. It has the usual hallmarks of those outtakes with plenty of organ dolloped on top of the usual Knopfler / Sly & Robbie mix. Despite how odd that sounds, it is actually a fairly straightforward rendition within that framework. Bob's voice is a lot more supple and less wizened than it would be for *Shadows In The Night*, et al. It certainly sounds more like a Frank song done in Dylan's style than the sort of repetitive Sinatra-aping of those late 2010s albums. Perhaps just one Sinatra cover per record for the next ten albums would've been a better way to dole out this quirky side of Dylan's catalog than five whole discs in a row. This is not an outtake that is going to make anyone rethink their positions of either *Infidels* or these latter-day Bob experiments, but it works much better as a love song than some of the boring fluff that did make the cut.

<u>Rumored to have been recorded but unheard:</u>
16 Tons
(written by Merle Travis)
Across The Borderline
(written by Ry Cooder, John Hiatt, and Jim Dickinson)
Aquarium
(written by Robbie Sly)
Back To The Wall
(written by Bob Dylan)
Choo Choo Ch'Boogie
(written by Vaughn Horton, Denver Darling, and Milt Gabler)
The Christmas Song
(written by Mel Tormé and Bob Wells)
Cold Cold Heart
(written by Hank Williams)
Columbus Stockade Blues
(traditional, arranged by Bob Dylan)
Dark As A Dungeon
(written by Merle Travis)
The Green, Green Grass Of Home
(written by J. Curly Putman)
Green Onions
(written by Steve Cropper and Lewie Steinberg)
Home On The Range
(written by Daniel E. Kelley and Brewster M. Higley)
I'm Gonna Wash That Man Right Out Of My Hair
(music by Richard Rodgers, lyrics by Oscar Hammerstein II)
I'm Movin' On
(written by Hank Snow)
Jesus Met The Woman At The Well
(traditional, arranged by Bob Dylan)
Lovers Concerto
(written by Sandy Linzer and Denny Randell)
Oh, Susannah!
(written by Stephen Foster)
Pledging My Love
(written by Ferdinand Washington and Don Robey)
Silent Night
(written by Franz Gruber and Josef Mohr)

In addition to covering Willie Nelson and Frank Sinatra during these sessions, the rumors are that Bob tried a lot of strange and different stuff during the *Infidels* sessions. Without the inspiration of the Lord to keep him focused, Dylan was apparently now willing to try and anything. Granted most of this stuff never saw the light of day. However, he did do "Across The Borderline" live at Farm Aid in 1986. And much as "This Was My Love" predicted the Sinatra period, the holiday tunes attempted here also pointed the way to *Christmas In The Heart*. There's a handful of titles here that one assumes are originals since no one has been able to identify them as anything else. The breadth and strangeness in the choice of tunes attempted here is stunning. It might be a sign of someone who is rudderless and looking for a new direction, but it still shows a lot of bravery and curiosity on his part. It would be interesting to hear some of these.

"SURVIVING IN A RUTHLESS WORLD"

SIDE A:
1. Man Of Peace
2. I And I
3. Blind Willie McTell
(unreleased electric version)
4. Foot Of Pride

SIDE B:
1. Union Sundown
2. Julius & Ethel
3. Neighborhood Bully
4. License To Kill
5. Death Is Not The End

Much like *New Morning*, there is enough material here for a double album; so that's what I went ahead and did at first. Each side of this double record even had its own theme. Initially side A continued the religious theme of the previous three records with "Death Is Not The End", "Man Of Peace, and "Lord Protect My Child" and concluding with Willie Nelson's "Angel Flying To Close To The Ground". That segued us into side B, which is comprised of love songs ("Sweetheart Like You", "Someone's Got A Hold Of My Heart", "Tell Me" and "Don't Fall Apart On Me Tonight").

In my original incarnation, the second disc kicks off with a whole side devoted to politics and the state of the union ("Clean Cut Kid", "Union Sundown", "Julius & Ethel", "Neighborhood Bully", and "License To Kill". Side D was then reserved for the more mysterious epics of this album ("Blind Willie McTell", "Jokerman", and "I & I") concluding with "Foot Of Pride" whose biblical imagery points the listener back to the religious themes at the start of the album, thus completing the cycle. This managed to use just about every outtake available, and I was initially satisfied.

The problem with this double-album concept is that there were too many songs in there I just wasn't excited about. The whole thing dragged in the middle, especially on the more romantic Side B. I ended up tightening it down to nine tracks that represent my favorite songs from these sessions. Nine songs may not seem like a lot, but they're all long songs, and the official album only had eight. While this version of *Infidels* might not be as thematic, I think it is far more palatable.

On this re-vamped, single disc version, I keep all of the more esoteric epics on side one, while putting the more political material on the second side. However, to prevent anyone from thinking that this is an album concerned with the material world, it both opens and closes with some of Dylan's more blatantly religious material from these sessions.

The title, *Surviving In A Ruthless World* was originally Bob's name for this album, but when someone pointed out to him that his last four albums (*Street Legal*, *Slow Train Coming*, *Saved*, and *Shot Of Love*) all started with the letter 'S', Dylan ended up re-naming the album to something that I think is far less evocative of the music contained within.

EMPIRE BURLESQUE

Produced by: Arthur Baker & Bob Dylan
Recorded: July 26th, December 6th – 22nd, 1984 &
January 15th – March 4th, 1985
Released: June 10th, 1985

Famous/Important/Popular Track(s):
- Dark Eyes

My Personal Favorite Track(s):
- Seeing The Real You At Last
- When The Night Comes Falling From The Sky
- Something's Burning, Baby

After the Christian era had passed, Bob's album eighties vacillated between two poles. On the one hand, there were the albums half-hearted thrown together out of habit (*Knocked Out Loaded*, *Down In The Groove*). On the other hand, were the albums where Bob was really trying to have a hit and become relevant again. Of those, one worked short-term (*Infidels*), one worked long-term (*Oh Mercy!*), and the third didn't work at all. *Empire Burlesque* is the third album. It is unusual and even slightly dispiriting to hear Bob trying so hard to sound hip. It's something that came so naturally to him as a young man and something he has shown no interest in as an old man. But it is something he desperately wanted as a middle-aged man.

Usually, the nicest thing anyone can say about *Empire Burlesque* is that the songs would've been pretty good without Arthur Baker's production. In fact, bootlegs of pre-Baker-ized tunes would fetch a pretty penny. But personally, I think the synthesizer-laden sound actually adds a lot to the album. Maybe it's just because I was ten years old and totally unaware of the record when it first came out, that I am able to see it as not so much of a crass commercial attempt to jump on the latest fad.

For me, the cheezy eighties production is no more anachronistic that his thin wild mercury sound. Of course, during the sixties, his aesthetic wasn't the dominant style of the period, especially the anti-psychedelic *John Wesley Harding*. But that's what makes this album so fascinating; never had Dylan tried so hard (and failed) to pander to his audience. Check out the Miami Vice threads on the cover. It definitely shows the most time and care spent in the studio since *Self-Portrait*. This isn't the boring, uninvolved Dylan who wrote the generic love songs of *Planet Waves* and *Infidels*. You can practically feel the flop-sweat as Bob is trying to connect to those teens who just wanted their MTV.

This is not nostalgia on my part. I didn't like most of the eighties music while I was living through it. It all felt soul-less and plastic to my young ears, which is why I gravitated towards artists like Dylan. True the feeling on this album is mostly desperation, but at least it's a feeling. As a result, I tend to truly prize *Empire Burlesque* over a lot of his other albums from this decade. Particularly the tracks where he (and producer Arthur Baker) really go for it full-throttle into that now-dated eighties sound.

Tight Connection to My Heart (Has Anybody Seen My Love?)
(written by Bob Dylan)
See the entry under *Infidels*.

Seeing the Real You at Last
(written by Bob Dylan)
There's some synthetic horns on here and a cowbell. This song rocks although it clearly betrays which decade it was recorded in. Despite the somewhat silly instrumentation, Bob seems to be having a good time rocking out with a full rock band again for the first time in a long time. No reggae, no gospel, just rock. He's straining his vocals a bit, but he lets out the occasional "unh" which is just fun. While lots of the "born-again" material was somewhat accusatory to those heathens who didn't follow the lord, Bob here seems to be turning his scorn towards a single romantic partner rather than the whole world. Furthermore, he comes across as far more sympathetic to the woman this song is directed towards than unusual. It's hard to say whether Dylan prefers the woman he now sees or the delusion he once had, but the disconnect between the two is throwing for a loop. However, she is not upset at her for being a hypocrite as much as he is being hard on himself for not seeing it sooner. Either way, he is not leaving her over it – but instead trying to come to terms with this new reality.

I'll Remember You
(written by Bob Dylan)
If it weren't for Bob's unique vocal presence, this song would sound like a power ballad from a hair metal band. You would almost expect it to be a duet with Cher. The lyrics are a rather straightforward declaration of love. Despite the somewhat dated production, this is a tune that Bob has returned to often even performing it during the 2003 movie *Masked & Anonymous* (although not included on the soundtrack album). Really, the sound isn't that dated other than the over-gated and loud snare drum sound. The organ actually sounds far more stereotypical Dylan than the synthesizers that dominate the rest of *Empire Burlesque*. It's a sweet touching song, and Bob's vocals do convey a little bit of sincerity even if they are a bit mannered.

Clean Cut Kid
(written by Bob Dylan)
See the entry under *Infidels*.

Never Gonna Be the Same Again
(written by Bob Dylan)

Another faux-power ballad for Bob's 80s album. The backing vocalists here sound more gospel than anything on *Slow Train Coming*. There are a few dollops of tinkling synths and cheap drum sounds on top of this track, but otherwise, it's a pretty straight-forward rock song. I love that the chime sounds keyboard is the last thing to fade out at the end. The lyrics are pretty decipherable, about the positive impact that meeting this one woman has on the narrator's life. Nothing too special there and Bob sings it amiably but without a lot of conviction. The song opens with a free-form verse without a very set tempo before the drums kick in an establish the full band sound. There's even a bridge in the middle of the song that helps keep the listener's attention from flagging. This is one of the better *Empire Burlesque* tracks.

Trust Yourself
(written by Bob Dylan)

A funky little tune with a nice groove. While the lyrics may be as deep as a Stuart Smalley aphorism, Bob sings it well – accompanied almost invariably by his backing vocals. Despite being a relatively short song, Dylan does give us a bridge to help keep the song from getting too repetitive. There's very little of the traditional *Empire Burlesque* synthesizers here, but there is some nice organ work courtesy of Benmont Tech. Both he and Mike Campbell from Tom Petty's Heartbreakers play on this track giving it a more organic feel than some of the songs on this album. If Bob had the guts to stick with these songs and Arthur Baker's production instead of adding some *Infidels* outtakes and an acoustic closer, people might've understood what this album was going for better.

Emotionally Yours
(written by Bob Dylan)

Empire Burlesque seems to be ping-ponging back and forth between the actual rock songs and the power ballads like this, "Never Gonna Be The Same Again" and "I'll Remember You". The lyrics are meant to be an exhortation of devotion. However, the specific emotions involved are not specified. If you want to interpret those as manic or emotionally unhinged, the song has a very different message. He could've just entitled it "Psychotically Yours", except that the sincere and sweet way Bob sings it implies that he means for these to be "good" emotions. Again there's a pleasant little bridge in here, and the title refrain at the end of each verse is nicely catchy is a smooth-R&B kind of way. Sure, Arthur Baker's synths and drum sounds are all over this, but it helps give some weight to this otherwise slight song. In fact, these touches work as well on the power ballads as it does on the rock songs, providing the track a bit of unintentional irony that adds to the impact of the song.

When the Night Comes Falling from the Sky
(written by Bob Dylan)

Almost everyone seems to prefer the version of this song with the E Street Band that was released on *The Bootleg Series vol. 3*. Perhaps it's my severe dislike for anything related to Bruce Springsteen, but I don't think that version can hold a candle to the officially released *Empire Burlesque* version. That version has all the cool synthetic drums and synthesizers you have come to expect from Arthur Baker. While those signposts might give some Dylan fanatics bad flashbacks, without all of those accouterments, this is just another long Dylan song attempting to seem epic. Now it has become a bizarre outlier in the Dylan discography, almost a dance remix version of your typical Bob Dylan song. It's even better if you check out the totally 80s video for this song. The song features a cool half-verse where everything drops out except the bass and all the bongos and congas fueling the tune. I have no idea what Bob is singing about here, but he's doing an adequate job of singing it. Especially considering that he has some woman shadowing his vocal throughout the entire song. It may seem silly at first, but by the time those fake horn blasts come in as a hair metal guitar wails away, I am thoroughly smitten with this song.

Something's Burning, Baby
(written by Bob Dylan)

This has a very definite march feel to the drums which open the song. Bob and his backing singer take the first verse with just this snare and tambourine with a light synth for accompaniment. This is another slow song but doesn't seem as dramatic as some of the earlier power ballads. This song has grander ambitions, trying to be some sort of epic classic like "Desolation Row" and failing. Instead, it creates something else entirely, and frequently far more compelling. It is very similar to the previous song, "When The Night Comes Falling From The Sky" in this manner, while not as good. It's shorter, which is a plus. The lyrics are the usual jumble of semi-apocalyptic images. The typical Arthur Baker synths are a little less egregious, which is disappointing; and there's no drum machine since the marching snare is so central to the arrangement. Bob is singing his heart out here, hitting a somewhat range-y melody with ease. He may be making sure to hit all those notes because he's got the harmony vocals shadowing him throughout the entire song, but whatever the reason, Dylan does a great job. There's a slide guitar that comes in at one point and bits of organ all over this song. It's not a cheerfully dated as some of *Empire Burlesque*, but this is still one of my favorites from this album.

Dark Eyes
(written by Bob Dylan)

The relief most Dylan find from the lack of synths and drum machines must've clouded their eyes from how unimpressive this track is. Not that the song is poorly written. It is an interesting tune with pleasant enough lyrics that could make an excellent recording. Unfortunately, all we get here is essentially a demo. Much like "Wedding Song" on *Planet Waves*, the stark nature of this recording makes the track sound like an apology for the entire album that proceeded it. It sours and invalidates all of the other tracks on *Empire Burlesque* by seeming to confirm everyone's worst fears about horrible Arthur Baker's production choices were. Bob sings this well enough, even if the lyrics seem like they are deliberately written to sound like a quote-unquote Bob Dylan song. I'm sure if this track had been given the same sheen as the rest of the album, no one would be rushing out to say it was the only good song on the album. Maybe in a different context, I would be able to separate my feelings about what this song does to *Empire Burlesque* enough to enjoy it on its own. But for now, I just feel like this song is something of a betrayal.

Songs not on the album:
Driftin' Too Far from Shore released on *Knocked Out Loaded*
(written by Bob Dylan)

A fun, upbeat song that never quite breaks into actual exuberance. Arthur Baker's touches help give the song some fun anarchistic touches, but the song itself is rather slight. The lyrics seem upset at something. Bob is talking about not having to call someone his whore and not wanting to make love to his servant in his father's house. If Dylan's vocals sounded sincere, it might have been off-putting, but luckily he doesn't seem terribly invested. I do like the line about not being on the wrong side, but actually being the wrong side. While it got lost in the mishmash of the released *Knocked Out Loaded*, this would've actually been a good substitute for "Dark Eyes" as it sounds far more of a piece with the *Empire Burlesque* aesthetic. On *Knocked Out Loaded* listeners were desperate for Dylan originals, especially ones that weren't co-authored. "Drifitin' Too Far From Shore" is too slight to withstand that type of scrutiny and helped torpedo listeners' perceptions of that album as it was officially released. It is a good song, but it is definitely a minor song. Perhaps one that Bob (or some other artist) should take the time to re-discover and revitalize.

Maybe Someday released on *Knocked Out Loaded*
(written by Bob Dylan)

A fun little 80s pop-rock tune. The drums are playing in half-time until nearly the end of the first verse when the drummer finally realizes what kind of song this is and start playing a more appropriate double-time pattern. It doesn't sound like a deliberate choice as it doesn't coincide with the end of the first verse. It's an odd choice, which I think helps humanize this song. The guitar solo gets a little buried under the synthesizer when it is time for it to shine, but given how repetitive and one note the solo is, that might be a wise decision. Much like "Drifitn' Too Far From Shore", this song's placement as one of the few solo originals on *Knocked Out Loaded* may have placed a level of scrutiny on this song that it's relatively minor status couldn't help but crumble under. Still, it's a fun little song that deserves better than it got.

Brownsville Girl *fka* **New Danville Girl** released on *Knocked Out Loaded*
(written by Bob Dylan and Sam Shepard)

A song written and re-written with Sam Shepard, the second playwright Bob has collaborated with. This was first recorded as "New Danville Girl" for *Empire Burlesque* and left off this album, much to the dismay of many fans. Bob took that backing track and re-wrote the lyrics and released it on *Knocked Out Loaded*, where it has become the only song anyone likes off of that album. Well... anyone but me. I've never gotten why this song is such a big deal. It is excruciatingly long, lasting eleven-and-a-half minutes. It's a story song where not much happens. It starts with Bob waiting in line for a Gregory Peck movie and then remembering a different Gregory Peck movie. From there we somehow get to talking about some guy named Henry Porter. I'm not sure how we get to talking about that, I usually nod off at this point. Even with Henry Porter, we don't actually meet the guy or find out anything about him, except that isn't his name. Sure the lyrics are all cool and evocative, but it doesn't need to go on this long. There are gunshots and a trial, but ultimately nothing of consequence happens. There are those who maintain that the original set of lyrics on "New Danville Girl" are better but they're still the same length. The music itself is a dull slog with little variation. It doesn't even have the amusing Arthur Baker touches like synth and drum machines. Arthur probably realized immediately that a song like this could never be a dance hit and didn't even bother trying to do anything on this track. The backing vocalists become almost oppressive here, commenting on everything Bob says. Luckily there is a separate chorus from the verse, so it's not completely repetitive like "Highlands" or "Tempest". I have no idea why so many people like this song, but if you are the type who does, it's understandable that you would hate everything else on *Knocked Out Loaded*. This, in turn, will make "Brownsville Girl" seem even better in comparison, and the whole thing becomes some sort of self-fulfilling cycle. But for me, this is one I almost always skip.

Freedom For The Stallion officially unreleased
(written by Allen Toussaint)
While Bob would really immerse himself in R&B covers during the recording of *Down In The Groove*, Bob has already started to play around with the idea here. The synths are appropriately corny on this track. Bob sings this with a passion that is sometimes lacking on his originals. This is taken at a pace just a notch or two faster than the power ballads on *Empire Burlesque*. Surprisingly there are no backing vocalists on here, although they may have been overdubbed on if the track had been selected for release on the album. The drums have some of the same marching snare feel as "Something's Burning, Baby". I'm not sure what the lyrics are supposed to be about, something like "Wild Horses" or "You Can't Tie A Mustang Down" I guess, using a horse as a metaphor for not being chained down or having to listen to society's rules. Who knows how critics would've reacted to Bob resorting to covers at this point in his career, but they were going to have to get used to it soon enough on the next album.

Straight A's In Love officially unreleased
(written by Bob Dylan)
Using the same metaphorical mixture of school and romance that was popular when rock was seen as strictly a teenager phenomenon, the lyrics here are vaguely reminiscent of Sam Cooke's "What A Wonderful World", the Monotones' "The Book Of Love" and Chuck Berry's "School Days". It's an odd choice for middle-aged Dylan to make in the 1980s. The song itself is somewhat vapid dumb fun. The synths here are vaguely organ-like, and the drums sound organic making this a little bit less dated than some of the *Empire Burlesque* tracks. The whole song breaks down halfway through for Bob to sing that the woman in questions has graduated with honors from the school of love. It's as deep as a rain puddle, but if it were taken seriously at all the song would be problematic and disturbing. The music is upbeat and vaguely reminiscent of those early rock songs. The drums even throw in a reference to Buddy Holly's "Peggy Sue" during the fills. While Bob would record a bunch of covers from this era during the *Down In The Groove* sessions, he writes a pretty passable pastiche of the period here. It's a shame this charming ditty still hasn't officially seen the light of day.

Always On My Mind officially unreleased
(written by Johnny Christopher, Mark James and Wayne Carson)
Continuing in the power ballad vein of half of *Empire Burlesque* comes this cover of the classic song that has a hit for both Willie Nelson and Willie Nelson. While a synth and drum machine rendition of this song might've been daring when Bob recorded it in 1985, two years later The Pet Shop Boys would actually take this song to the top of the charts again. Bob's rendition is not as 80s as it could have been, but it is definitely as far

away from its country roots as possible. The song starts somewhat abruptly as if not all the musician involved were clued into the fact that they were going to do a take but jumped in rather quickly. I can't tell if it's an excellent sounding jam or if it is a weak attempt at a releasable recording. Never one for half-measures, Bob sings this really well. Like "Freedom For The Stallion" this song fits in well with the R&B and early rock songs that Dylan would record around the time of *Down In The Groove*. Bob clearly needed to either buckle down and focus on doing a full record of these covers or stop being distracted by them so he could concentrate on writing new worthy originals. This back-and-forth half-and-half method was starting to bifurcate Dylan's attention as he gives a much more spirited vocal performance here than he does on many of the songs he actually finished and released.

Waiting To Get Beat officially unreleased
(written by Bob Dylan)

This song has not been formally released by Bob, but when *A Tribute to Bob Dylan in the 80s* came out in 2014, this song was covered by Tea Leaf Green. I don't know who they are, but I'm guessing this song was chosen more for its ability to impress with its obscurity rather than any genuine affection for the song. Dylan's version of this song is very much in the *Empire Burlesque* sound. Drum machines and synthesizers abound. The guitars are playing on the off-beat giving a slight reggae feel to the track. Once again we've got a female harmony vocal propping up Bob throughout the song. I'm not sure what the lyrics are about exactly. There is a line about getting dressed to get whipped, so maybe this song is actually quite literal; just about getting prepared for some sort of kinky bondage scenario. But somehow I doubt that. The bridge section goes into a double-time feel that provides more variety than many Bob songs. There's a hole in the song at one point, where I think someone was supposed to take a solo, but other than the stabbing chords of the synth trying to add an extra flourish or two at the end, nothing happens, and we just wait for the vocal to come back. It's an above average song for Bob, but no masterpiece. Mostly worthwhile as another example of the Arthur Baker sound from this album.

The Very Thought Of You officially unreleased
(written by Bob Dylan)

This is not a cover of the American Songbook standard that would've fit in well with *Shadows In The Night*. Instead, this is an original with the exact same title. This obviously was recorded at or near the same sessions as "Waiting To Get Beat" as it has the same reggae-lite feel and sound. In fact, it may well be the exact same backing track with just a different vocal (and melody and lyrics) overdubbed on top. It's not a bad song, by any stretch, but it just feels pretty redundant after "Waiting To Get Beat". You can easily switch out between the two somewhat indistinguishable tracks, but I would give the slight edge to "Waiting To Get beat" for at least having a more original title. Still, it would be a nice addition to *Empire Burlesque*.

Almost Done officially unreleased
(written by Bob Dylan)

Another of the more power ballad-y songs from these sessions. It sounds like the band is still learning the song before (or while) Bob is still trying to finish writing it. This is definitely a little rougher than some of the Arthur Baker productions as it doesn't sound like there's a full or complete take of the song. Still, there are some nice and interesting melodic ideas in there. If Dylan had come up with an ending for this track and had let Baker go to town on it, it might have really shone. However, this sounds like Bob trying to write the kind of song that would've been turned into an eighties hit, so him finishing later and recording it with Daniel Lanois or Jack Frost would've been a bust. As it stands now though, this is just unrealized potential and not really anything you can enjoy as is.

Go 'Way Little Boy officially unreleased
(written by Bob Dylan)

Certainly more finished than "Almost Done" but not as produced as "Waiting To Get Beat". The song hasn't been officially released although it was covered by the band Lone Justice as a B-side for their single "Sweet Sweet Baby (I'm Falling". Given the gender of the presumed irritant, it actually makes more sense for this to be sung by a woman. "Go 'Way Little Boy" a fairly straight-ahead blues-based rock song that lacks any of the more "modern" touches of *Empire Burlesque*. The Lone Justice version sounds a lot like the Dylan bootleg and may come from the same sessions with Ron Wood on lead guitar and Bentmont Tech on the organ. Nothing terribly special, but a perfectly serviceable rocker. It feels like it points the way to the more stripped down, less Arthur Baker-y sounds of *Knocked Out Loaded* and *Down In The Groove*.

Honey Wait officially unreleased
(written by Bob Dylan)

A half-written song that mostly consists of "honey wait for me" repeated followed by the occasional "oh yeah." There are a few more lyrics, but they sound half-remembered. It's only this chorus that has the strength of the backing singers joining Bob. It's not much more than a three-chord blues song. Not something particularly memorable or life-changing. Maybe if Arthur Baker had layered on his drum machines and synths, it would've turned into something, but right now it is just a jam. At one point both guitarists start soloing, leaving no rhythm part keeping the song in place and the track threatens to collapse, but somehow manages just to keep going.

Who Loves You More? officially unreleased
(written by Bob Dylan)

A slow-burning R&B torch song. This is a power ballad with a little more grit to it. There's a nice little guitar solo in here, and the song sounds fully fleshed out and realized. Who knows why this wasn't one of the tracks considered for overdubbing for *Empire Burlesque*. I'm not sure if it was Dylan's decision or Arthur Baker's, but I think it was the wrong decision. Bob's vocals are amazing on this track. While I love the songs like "Emotionally Yours" and "I'll Remember You" having a ballad with this kind of fire and passion on the album would be nice. The backing vocalists are limited to just let out some "Caribbean Wind" styled exhalations during this song. While this outtake is generally not well known, this may, in fact, be one of Dylan's best outtakes.

Dirty Lie officially unreleased
(written by Bob Dylan)

Employing the familiar chord structure that informed "Stray Cat Strut" and "Hit The Road, Jack" this song was rehearsed many times for the 1984 tour but never ended up getting performed live. There are however rehearsal tapes of this song that have ended up in the hands of bootleggers. This is a fully fleshed out song and not just a half-written jam. It's got a cool groove and nice slinky feel. It would've definitely held its own with the rest of *Empire Burlesque* had it actually gotten to the studio. It's a real shame that this one was never revisited by Bob. It was covered by The Secret Sisters on their 2014 album, *Put The Needle Down* which was produced by T-Bone Burnett.

I See You Around And Around officially unreleased
(written by Bob Dylan)

Another song rehearsed for the 1984 tour that never saw the light of day. Listening to the sub-one minute fragment that's out there, this song seems far less finished than "Dirty Lie". This is more of another power ballad attempt. There's a little potential here, but not much else to this fifty-second clip. It's starting to sound like a real song, but for some reason, it never quite came to fruition.

I Once Knew A Man officially unreleased
(written by Bob Dylan)

Another blues "original" by Dylan. This song was rehearsed with members of the LA punk band, The Plugz for Dylan's appearance on David Letterman's old TV show. Who knows what this song is for or why he was rehearsing it for the show, but we do have not just audio, but video of Dylan running through it. While the sound quality is poor, it's a fun little rocking number with some decent slide guitar. Nothing remarkable, but for a brief period of time it looked like Bob was going to eschew the MTV aesthetic and start hooking up with young punk rock bands. This, unfortunately, didn't pan out, other than the aforementioned appearance on *Late Night With David Letterman*.

> Rumored to have been recorded but unheard:
> **In The Summertime**
> *(written by Ray Dorset)*
> **I See Fire In Your Eyes**
> *(written by Bob Dylan)*
> **Look Yonder**
> *(written by Bob Dylan)*
> **Mountain Of Love**
> *(written by Harold Dorman)*
> **Queen Of Rock 'n' Roll**
> *(written by Bob Dylan)*
> **Rising Sun**
> *(written by Steven Hufsteter, Tito Larriva, Tony Marsico, and Chalo Quintana)*
> **Too Hot To Love**
> *(written by Bob Dylan)*
> **We Had It All**
> *(written by Donny Frittis and Troy Seals)*
> **When The Line Forms**
> *(written by Bob Dylan)*
> **The Girl I Left Behind**
> *(traditional, arranged by Bob Dylan)*
> **Help Me Make It Through The Night**
> *(written by Kris Kristofferson)*

Much like during *Infidels*, Bob was apparently open to trying anything during these sessions too. The main difference here between these two lists of titles is that the ratio of (presumed) originals to unexpected cover versions is much higher. The version of "In The Summertime" is not the *Shot Of* Love song that Bob wrote himself, but the similarly titled hit for Mungo Jerry from 1970. Clearly, as much as Dylan would like to go back to recording covers to fill out his albums, he was still too embarrassed to have to resort to that. At this point, Bob was still able to come up with more than enough original compositions. By the next album, *Knocked Out Loaded*, this would no longer be the case.

> Played live, but never recorded:
> **Enough Is Enough** officially unreleased
> *(written by Bob Dylan)*

This song may well be considered an outtake from the 1984 live album

Real Live. This original tune was never recorded in the studio but was performed a few times during the European tour of 1984, including the dates recorded for this particular live album. The inclusion of a song unavailable anywhere would've helped raise the profile of this little-loved live LP, for some reason Bob decided not to include it on the album. The song itself is a fun little rock'n'roll number with lyrics about "I'd rather be lucky than rich" and some nice start-stop bits, but it is nothing really spectacular in and of itself.

"THE EMPEROR'S NEW BURLESQUE"

SIDE A:
1. Waiting To Get Beat
2. Seeing The Real You At Last
3. Never Gonna Be The Same Again
4. Straight A's In Love
5. Trust Yourself
6. Emotionally Yours

SIDE B:
1. Maybe Someday
2. I'll Remember You
3. Driftin' Too Far From Shore
4. Something's Burning Baby
5. When The Night Comes Falling From The Sky

Removing the songs that were left over from *Infidels* and bringing back the songs that ended up on *Knocked Out Loaded*. We get a much more consistent sounding record. In order to maintain this consistency, I removed "Dark Eyes", much as I had left "The Wedding Song" off of *Ceremonies Of The Horsemen*, my version of *Planet Waves*. The end result is something a little more dark and apocalyptic, yet full of very 80s sounding drum machines and synthesizers. This is the most pop sounding, trend-chasing that Dylan has ever sounded, so why try to deny it? This collection is designed instead to emphasize that.

While a few covers were floating around from these sessions, I decided to keep this collection all-original. I think the *Knocked Out Loaded* tracks, "Driftin' Too Far From Shore" and "Maybe Someday" work better when surrounded by their fellow Arthur Baker-styled peers. However, I did keep "New Danville Girl" off here as it would throw everything out of whack. It creates an expectation from the rest of the songs that this album is not even trying to match. Furthermore, I just don't like it. Instead, I've added "Straight A's In Love" with its deliberately shallow, pop-oriented lyrics. I have also included "Waiting To Get Beat" and opened the album with it to continue the reggae fixation of Bob's starting from *Caribbean Wind*.

So, of course, I'm not only using the non-E Street Band version of "When The Night Comes Falling From The Sky", but I am also ending the album with it. It feels much more like a closer than the shrugged apology of "Dark Eyes". While this might not have been the MTV era mega-hit that Bob was going for, I think it shows the shameless ambition involved rather than trying to hide those commercial instincts under a fake veneer of artistic integrity.

KNOCKED OUT LOADED
Produced by: Bob Dylan
Recorded: April 28th – May 19th, 1986
Released: July 14th, 1986
Famous/Important/Popular Track(s):
- Brownsville Girl

My Personal Favorite Track(s):
- Got My Mind Made Up
- Band Of The Hand (It's Helltime, Man)
- The Usual

Popular conception generally holds *Knocked Out Loaded* in the same boat as *Pat Garrett & Billy the Kid*: namely one good song surrounded by a bunch of crap. Of course, "Knockin' On Heaven's Door" is one of Bob's 3 - 5 biggest songs, while the eleven minutes of "Brownsville Girl" will keep that song as a fan-favorite deeper cut at best. While the instrumentals on *Pat Garrett* are seen as inoffensive, but necessary for a soundtrack, the remainder of *Knocked Out Loaded* is treated as the worst of the worst to most Dylan fans. Only the hard-core completist listens to this album, and they all hate this album ... except for "Brownsville Girl". Considering that this one song is 31% of the album's 35:18 runtime, it keeps the record from being nearly as loathed as *Down In The Groove* or as angering as *Self-Portrait*.

No surprise however, I do not particularly care for the rambling narrative of Bob's one co-write with Sam Sheppard. So how do I view the remaining seven tracks of this "nadir"? It's not that bad. It certainly lacks the charm, or the cohesion, of *Infidels* or *Empire Burlesque*. This is mostly down to the lack of a clear hand steering the ship, like Mark Knopfler or Arthur Baker. The album is credited as produced by Bob Dylan, mostly out of default since no one really seems to be in charge. Later, Dylan would begin to take his managerial duties a little more seriously; but not until after he starts using the pseudonym of Jack Frost. The official album does include a number of leftover tracks from the last two albums, further diluting any personality or individuality *Knocked Out Loaded* may have had.

In a July 1986 story for *Rolling Stone*, Mikal Gilmore talks excitedly about the recording sessions for this album, but none of the energy he talked about seems to have actually made it onto the actual record. Maybe Mikal was caught-up in the moment and exaggerating about the strength of this tracks, or maybe Bob lost his nerve and all the good stuff got cut from *Knocked Out Loaded* before it was released.

This is an odd beast; aside from the outtakes from the last two albums, we get several songs that Dylan has co-written with a wide swath of random people: playwright Sam Sheppard, future Wilbury Tom Petty, schlockmeister Carole Bayer Seger. He even co-wrote a song apiece with Kiss bassist Gene Simmons and pop star Michael Bolton around this time, although he has never recorded his own version of either of those songs. Unlike his time with Jacques Levy, none of these collaborations seemed to have flowered into anything more long-term as Bob was casting around for a new direction or purpose.

Other than the one-off "A Satisfied Mind" on *Saved*, Dylan hadn't released any of the covers he had recorded since 1973's *Dylan*; and that wasn't entirely his decision. So the fact the three of the eight songs on this album weren't even co-written by Bob helped seal its fate in the minds of those who look to a new Dylan album as the latest dispatch from the oracle.

Even *Street Legal*, which felt rudderless and unfocused, didn't feel as tossed-off as the final layout of *Knocked Out Loaded* felt. But if you look at the new tracks recorded for this album, do we get a glimpse of what was going on in Bob's head. Clearly, he was bored. He had been doing this for like 25 years now. He just wanted to rock out. Play some old songs he loved and not worry about crafting the next masterpiece. As a result, everything feels rough and raw. Sometimes this translated to disinterested and half-assed as you can hear Dylan becoming bored himself halfway through some of these tracks (especially the outtakes).

It can be a slog through to get through sometimes, but there are some gems buried in here. Songs that probably wouldn't withstand real scrutiny, but charm when presented in such an offhand manner. Even thirty years on, this and *Down In The Groove* are still considered the bottom of the barrel in Dylan's discography. While I would argue there are plenty worse than these two, it was not a good time for Bob – or Bob fans.

You Wanna Ramble
(written by Little Junior Parker)

This may not actually rock, but it is definitely a very muscular shuffle. The backing vocalists are in full force. There's a section where it sounds like two different guitarists are unsure which one of them is supposed to be playing the solo. Both of them start simultaneously and then stop abruptly and tentatively wait for the other to finish their bit, but neither is turned up in the mix enough to take your attention. Towards the end of the song, there are a couple of stings from the synthetic horns. The lyrics are supposed to be an invitation to a fight, but Bob sings them not so much as a threat as it is an offhand suggestion. It's a little tepid, but more of a barn-burner than many of the tracks on *Knocked Out Loaded*.

They Killed Him
(written by Kris Kristofferson)

Two words: children's choir. Any other positive aspects this recording might have had are completely obliterated by the inclusion of the cloying children's choir on this track. One of the few Bob Dylan songs that are actively hard to listen to. Even without that atrocity, the song is still pretty bad. The lyrics mythologize and eulogize Jesus, MLK, and the Kennedys without going into a lot of details of why their particular murders were so tragic. The thing that seems to most link them together (and endear them to Dylan) was their respective refusals to bow to the pressures from authority. The melody is trying way too hard, and the instrumentation is 80s cheese without even the camp flair of much of the *Empire Burlesque* material. This wasn't an old Kris Kristofferson song that Bob had always known and loved. It was initially written in 1984, only two years before Bob recorded his version. As horrible as the children's choir is, it's not even an original idea for Dylan. He's just copying it from the arrangement on the Johnny Cash version of this song. When Kris Kristofferson finally released his own version of this song, he didn't include the children's choir. This song is just inexcusable.

Driftin' Too Far from Shore
(written by Bob Dylan)
See the entry under *Empire Burlesque*.

Precious Memories
(written by J.B.F. Wright)
Despite recording a whole album with Sly & Robbie, this sounds much more reggae than anything on *Infidels*. The steel drums almost take this into Jimmy Buffet parody territory. However, the prominence of the mandolin on the track gives the whole song as sort of Appalachian vibe which helps revert the song back to its roots as a traditional gospel hymn. The odd incongruity of the instruments makes this one of Bob's most experimental recordings. While the lyrics are supposed to be about Jesus, it is not terribly didactic in its tenor and as a result, did not spark much speculation about Bob's religion, particularly given the off-hand manner in which Bob sings this song. While "Precious Memories" is not a great song, it's a shame that Dylan doesn't have more strange songs in his catalog like this one.

Maybe Someday
(written by Bob Dylan)
See the entry under *Empire Burlesque*.

Brownsville Girl
(written by Bob Dylan and Sam Shepard)
See the entry under *Empire Burlesque*.

Got My Mind Made Up
(written by Bob Dylan and Tom Petty)
A song co-written by Tom Petty and performed by the Heartbreakers, this would have sounded in place on their album *Let Me Up (I've Had*

Enough). In fact, they released a version of it with Tom instead of Bob singing and no backing vocals but extra harmonica on their box-set *Playback*, and it sounds about the same. This is one of the better songs recorded around this time. Tom Petty & co. are still so enamored of Dylan that they play their hardest on this track. Musically the song is pretty simple, but it's played great. It does what songs like "You Wanna Ramble" and "Let's Stick Together" are trying to do but so much better. There's an acoustic slide guitar that takes a solo about two-thirds of the way through this song that is just amazing. The lyrics are pretty much gibberish, but just the mention of the country "Libya" makes the song feel current to its time and at least mildly aware of the politics of the world going on around it. Bob is having fun spitting out these non-sequiturs. Easily the best track officially released on *Knocked Out Loaded*. With this and "Band Of The Hand", I wish that Tom Petty had backed Bob on a whole album instead of just a couple of tours and these two songs.

Under Your Spell
(written by Bob Dylan and Carole Bayer Sager)

There's a line in there about dying of thirst two feet from the well that I always found heart-breaking. According to Carole Bayer Sager, she didn't contribute much to this song besides the title and was quite surprised that she was co-credited on the song when the album came out. It's kind of a power ballad of the mold of "Emotionally Yours" or "I'll Remember You" from *Empire Burlesque*; however it doesn't have Arthur Baker's touch. As a result, it sounds like a failed attempt at the usual 80s sound. Some may say that's better than a successful attempt, but I would disagree. It's an oddly slow song to end an album on. There are some odd lines that are whispered closely into the mic at one point in the song that I can't quite make out but does add to the intrigue of this song. The song is sort of mediocre in general. If it weren't for the unusual co-writing credit by the very pop songwriting titan who is more known for working with Burt Bacharach, Marvin Hamlisch, Neil Diamond, Barbara Streisand, and Christopher Cross, this song would be eminently forgettable.

Songs not on the album:
Band Of The Hand (It's Helltime, Man) from the *Band Of The Hand* soundtrack
(written by Bob Dylan)

This is the theme song to a mostly forgotten movie. Recorded with Tom Petty & The Heartbreakers while they were all on tour together in Australia. Despite not being officially released on any Bob Dylan, this song rocks as hard if not harder than anything on either *Knocked Out Loaded* or *Down In The Groove*. The backing singers add a R&B feel to this whole shebang. The band is rocking out here, as one would expect from a well-oiled machine like Tom Petty & The Heartbreakers. The song is not terribly deep. The lyrics are (I assume) something of a synopsis of the plot of the movie. The title gets somewhat wedged in by the back-up singer towards the end as it seems like Bob forgot the name of the movie he was supposed to be writing for and just came up with something called "It's Helltime Man". Bob's got some excellent harmonica playing in here and sounds righteously pissed sing this. While this may not be some long lost masterpiece, this is a song that is as good if not better than most of the stuff Dylan was putting out on his own album in the eighties.

The Usual from the *Hearts Of Fire* soundtrack
(written by John Hiatt)

A song written by John Hiatt that Bob covered for the soundtrack to the film he was starring in called *Hearts Of Fire*. In the movie, Bob plays an aging rock star and this song is supposed to be his one big hit from his younger days. Bob clearly didn't feel up to the challenge of writing a song that would actually fit this. It's strange in the movie, you are supposed to believe that this was an anthemic song of the 1960s, but nothing about this track feels terribly timeless or of that time. Taken out of the context of the film (which is easy to do since so few people saw it) this is a fun, upbeat rock track. Sure, some synths on here definitely timestamp it to the eighties, but Bob sings it with passion. I have no idea what the lyrics mean. Something about ordering the same thing at the same restaurant all the time I assume. The original from John Hiatt from his 1985 album, *Warming Up To The Ice Age*, is a little more muscular with a cheezy break-down towards the second half. Bob is not embarrassing himself here, skipping that section entirely. When the soundtrack for *Hearts Of Fire* disappeared into indifference, Dylan was going to rescue this song and put it on *Down In The Groove*. It ended up getting dropped, although other *Hearts Of Fire* songs were included. It's too bad as it is one of Dylan's best recording from this period.

Night After Night from the *Hearts Of Fire* soundtrack
(written by Bob Dylan)

This song is full of horns that may, in fact, have been created within a synthesizer. Ultimately it doesn't matter if the horns are "real" or not, they all sound part of the cheezy sound. The song is full of the reggae patios that Dylan flirted with on *Shot Of Love* and *Infidels.*, but less respectful – more like Jimmy Buffet or "Kokomo"-era Beach Boys. The lyrics are almost defiantly dumb. One almost feels like Bob wrote this song in character; the character he played in the *Hearts Of Fire* film, a washed-up former pop-star and not an actual, respected musician. This song sounds almost deliberately non-Dylan like. As such it is a hoot to hear Bob trying to play a part, even if he doesn't do it very convincingly. This may be one of the most trivial and minor works in the Dylan canon but as such as deserves almost a place of respect. Bob generally doesn't do filler. Even his biggest failures are attempts that don't live up to their ambitions. Maybe 80s Bob needed to spend more time being this frivolous instead of continually expecting himself to write another *Blonde On Blonde* or *Blood On The Tracks*. It may not have improved his commercial or critical standing during this decade, but it would've at least been less stressful.

Had A Dream About You, Baby from the *Hearts Of Fire* soundtrack
(written by Bob Dylan)

The only song from the *Hearts Of Fire* soundtrack to get released on an official Dylan album, sneaking out on *Down In The Groove*. It's another straightforward rock song with some simplistic love song lyrics. Given Bob's generally dismissive attitude towards dreams, this may not actually be as much of a compliment as it initially sounds. There's a nice twist in the bridge that takes the song into the dance club lyrically which probably helps tie it into the film's milieu and location. It's a short, fast song even if it is a little shallow. The *Hearts Of Fire* version of this song features a slightly more active bass and is about seventeen seconds shorter and ends straight-up instead of fading out. For those who are curious, yes that is Kip Winger of the band Winger playing on this song. And while there is no guitar solo or particularly fancy playing, it is Eric Clapton and the Rolling Stones' Ron Wood on guitar. Why? Who knows. Bob can get who we wants. And when he does, he does have to use them for anything interesting. But it is a surprise.

To Fall In Love With You officially unreleased
(written by Bob Dylan)

One of two outtakes Bob attempted to record for the *Hearts Of Fire* soundtrack. Ultimately, it sounds like Bob starting recording this song before he finished writing as some of the lyrics are just mumbled, and none of them are that great. Bob also tried this method of "songwriting" again in the sessions with a track labeled "Some Kind Of Way" which isn't even close enough to done to really talk about, although there is some funky slap bass there. With "To Fall In Love With You" seems like he's trying to sing a love song here, but isn't quite sure what his tack on the subject is this time around. Not that Dylan has to finish writing in order to get a great recording; just witness "I'm Not There" from *The Basement Tapes*. While Bob may not have gotten any lyrics settled on, the chord structure is actually one of Dylan's more complicated and winding. The melody is surprisingly assured and soaring. Despite (or perhaps because) Dylan doesn't know what he's singing about he gives quite a performance. Sure, it sounds like the band could use another take to really nail the performance, although they are probably holding back a bit knowing that this isn't a final version. Maybe with a completed lyric and another take this song could've really sparkled. It probably wouldn't have salvaged the *Hearts Of Fire*, either the film or the soundtrack, but it would've made it a lot more tolerable.

Old Five And Dimer (Like Me) officially unreleased
(written by Billie Joe Shaver)

Another cover Bob attempted during the *Hearts Of Fire* sessions. There's three takes currently circulating. Each one is vastly different from the next. The first version is a solo acoustic take that may exist just to teach the rest of the band the song. Or maybe it's supposed to be used in the scene in the film where Bob actually sings Shel Silverstein's "A Couple More Years". Since that song was filmed rather than recorded and done in character, it's hard to see how this solo studio take would work, but who knows? The second version is an upbeat take with an emphasis on a goofy riff running throughout the song. We've got the full band playing here and having a half-assed good time. The last version is taken at a much slower tempo closer to the first acoustic version, but again with the whole band playing along. They play in 6/8 time with a semi-1950s doo-wop feel. It's not as good as the second version, but the song itself is not that good or interesting. Bob is trying to get into the part of an aging rock star and is looking for songs that emphasize getting older as a theme. The original by Billy Joe Shaver in 1973 is neither a blues or a rock tune but is pretty much just country. Dylan doesn't attempt anything like that here. While Bob was having a hard time coming up with enough original material for his commitment to this film. And while the moviemakers were probably desperate for anything they could use, it's no surprise that the skipped over this track. Bob himself must've agreed since this song has not yet seen the light of day on any sort of official release.

Ride This Train officially unreleased
(written by Bob Dylan)

A half-hearted jam that never turned into a real dong from the *Hearts Of Fire* sessions. The bass is way too loud and sounds distorted, but such is the joy of bootlegs. The song itself actually has a cool groove and might've been worth something if it was finished. The lyrics are indecipherable and the melody is hard to pick out, but this is probably another mixing issue as the vocals are way too low. There's a couple of different parts to the song. It sounds like the band isn't sure where they come in, but when the changes arrive, they are familiar enough that they can switch pretty quickly. While Bob was in something of a dry spell as far as songwriting, finishing this up would've been nice. Nothing extraordinary, but certainly more muscular than a lot of the lightweight tunes he was penning during this period.

A Couple More Years officially unreleased
(written by Shel Silverstein)

This cover wasn't so much recorded as filmed. For a minute and a half in the movie *Hearts Of Fire*, Bob plays this song. Instead of lip-syncing to a previously recorded track, Dylan just plays it live. Even if it wasn't written for the film, the lyrics fit the character of an aging rock star pretty well. It's always interesting to hear Bob cover Shel Silverstein, although we don't really get a full performance. This brief moment may be better than most of the movie it is sitting within, but that's not saying much.

Played live, but never recorded:
Shake officially unreleased
(written by Bob Dylan)

This is pretty much Bob adding new lyrics to the song "Treat Her Right" by Roy Head. Still, in the midst of one Dylan's dry periods of songwriting, it was nice having him trying to write anything. This song was rehearsed a few times with Tom Petty & The Heartbreakers for their joint tour. It was also performed live during "Farm Aid" so, despite its relative obscurity, a lot of people got to hear this Bob semi-original. It's a fun grooving R&B rocker along the lines of "Got My Mind Made Up". It's a shame that there's no studio version of this since it is actually a lot better than a lot of stuff recorded around this time.

See the entry on Page 303

DOWN IN THE GROOVE

Produced by: Bob Dylan
Recorded: March 5th – June 16th, 1987
Released: May 30th, 1988

Famous/Important/Popular Track(s):
- Silvio

My Personal Favorite Track(s):
- Sally Sue Brown
- Ugliest Girl In The World
- Silvio

Everything fans hated about the last album without "Brownsville Girl" to placate them at all. Some people really hate this album, although it doesn't feel like the bile is very justified since Dylan himself isn't bothering to try on this album. By this point putting our records was a habit for Bob, but he had lost the reason why and this one came out almost on inertia. There's the handful of outtakes from the last few albums. It's padded out with six cover songs this time around. Dylan is still looking for co-writers, here hooking up with Grateful Dead lyricist Robert Hunter. At least this collaboration lasted more than one song (and would return with a vengeance on 2009's *Together Through Life*).

Looking just at the newly recorded songs and not the leftover tunes that got include, we can see that Bob has become even more nostalgic for his pre-fame adolescence listening to early R&B and rockabilly; especially in the outtakes from this album. Apparently, Dylan had joked at the time about recording *Self-Portrait II* and had toyed with the idea of doing a whole record of covers. The two folk albums of the early 90s are often considered a necessary respite while Bob got over his writer's block and eventually delivered *Time Out Of Mind*. Still *Down In The Groove* (and to a lesser extent *Knock Out Loaded*) doesn't get the same respect for helping pave the way for the comeback of *Oh Mercy!* In fact, the never-ending tour was initially set-up to promote this album, even if it has long since outgrown that purpose.

The production here is again fairly shaggy. Since both this album and *Knocked Out Loaded* were assembled piecemeal after the fact from a series of disparate recording sessions over the course of several months, the two records are very similar in feel. It had been a long time since Dylan had produced a follow-up that sounded so similar to the last album, even if it was hard to know what either album was entirely aiming for. There's no way to mistake a *Street Legal* track for something off of *Desire*, but these two are pretty interchangeable. Bob would do this a lot more in the future (*Good As I Been To You*/*World Gone Wrong* and *Shadows In The Night*/*Fallen Angels*) but it is never a good thing. Ultimately I think that is the biggest problem with these two albums: a lack of any sort of individuality or personality.

Despite what everyone says, there are worse Dylan albums than *Down In The Groove*; but that doesn't make it one of my favorites.

Let's Stick Together
(written by Wilbert Harrison)

This song feels a lot like the opening track to the last album, "You Wanna Ramble." It's another half-rocking cover that while better than most of the album, isn't all that great. While "You Wanna Ramble" was halfhearted in asking for a fight, this one is equally lackluster in pleading with his wife (or mother of his child) not to leave him. The guitars have too much reverb and chorus on them to be convincing as R&B. At least there's a couple of fun little harmonica solos. The song starts to fade out when it ends. It's kind of odd. They should've either kept it going while it faded out or left the ending on at full volume.

When Did You Leave Heaven?
(written by Richard Whiting and Walter Bullock)

There are some super-cheezy synths and ridiculously mixed drums to kick this song off. The pace is nearly glacial and not terribly steady, making these uber-80s drums sound even more silly. Bob is singing in unison with one of his back-up singers, and there's an electric guitar noodling about, but something seems to be missing in the arrangement. Maybe a bass? It feels weirdly off in a way that I can't quite put on my finger on. Bob is singing his heart out on this one. As short as the song is it also seems to fall apart and peter out towards the end. The drums give up and stop entirely after the vocals are done, but the guitar and synths don't take the hint right away and keep playing for several seconds before ending the song. The whole thing feels unfinished, so the fact that it was officially released is somewhat perplexing. However, it is not quite odd enough to be interesting, so this is a track I often skip.

Sally Sue Brown
(written by Arthur June Alexander, Earl Montgomery, and Tom Stafford)

So you got members of both the Clash and the Sex Pistols, and you have them play... this? It's just another blues-rock shuffle in the mold of "Let's Stick Together". Bob's reliance on the backing singers is becoming more pronounced as there's another singing along with him for the entire length of the song. There's also some male backing vocalists doing so odd "oh-whooms" that further neuters this track. The organ here almost sounds like a synth, but the rest of the instruments are typical rock, if not particularly distinguished. Nothing too terribly offensive or annoying about this track, but the missed opportunity of Bob trying to do some real punk is kind of disappointing.

Death Is Not the End
(written by Bob Dylan)
See the entry under *Infidels*.

Had a Dream About You, Baby
(written by Bob Dylan)
See the entry under *Knocked Out Loaded*.

Ugliest Girl in the World
(written by Bob Dylan and Robert Hunter)

Maybe not the funniest song in Bob's catalog, but possibly the one that is trying to be the funniest. On first glance, it's just a mother-in-law joke stretched out to full song-length. It's surprising that Dylan needed Grateful Dead's lyricist Robert Hunter's help to finish this song. Or that this is a subject matter that either one felt was worth exploring, but I'm glad they did. The redeeming quality of this song lies in the fact that none of these supposed knocks against the woman in question has any effect on the narrator's ardor. In fact, it almost feels as though both her quote-unquote ugliness and her resilience in the face of such opposition makes her more attractive to him. The music is another fun upbeat rock version of the 12 bar blues. It actually feels more spirited than "Sally Sue Brown" or "Let's Stick Together". The backing singers are chiming in with their commentary and Bob's harmonica playing is jubilant. Sure, the joke gets old and thin by the end (thankfully the song is only three-and-a-half minutes long), but it is still one of the best tracks on *Down In The Groove*.

Silvio
(written by Bob Dylan and Robert Hunter)

A song that Bob included for years in his live set-list despite never being a big hit. This is the second collaboration with Robert Hunter, and the Grateful Dead show up as backing vocalists, but not instrumentalists. The sound of this record is very acoustic with prominent mandolin. Despite this, "Silvio" is not a slow ballad. This is a rock song. Sure it's mostly an unending circle of three chords, but it's played with verve, and the backing vocals constantly shifting parts keeps this from getting monotonous. The chorus is super-catchy, but it fun enough to sing along to. The lyrics almost sound like Robert Hunter is making fun of Dylan by trying to write the most ridiculously Dylan-esque lines possible, but Bob either doesn't get the joke or thinks it really funny because he does a great job singing all this nonsense.

Ninety Miles an Hour (Down a Dead End Street)
(written by Don Robertson and Hal Blair)

The gospel-flavored rendition of a song traditionally associated with

Hank Snow. The lyrics are decrying an affair that neither participant seems able to end. The whole thing has the loose feel of the introduction to a song. However the band never actually kicks in, and the rest of the song passes by like that. I can't decide if I find it fascinating or annoying. Bob seems more invested in the singing of this than most of *Down In The Groove*. For a song about being out of control and going too fast the song is taken at a leisurely pace that feels very controlled. Even Hank Snow's version is far more rocking. This song is often cited by fans as one of the few bright spots on this album, but it has always been something of a dud to me.

Shenandoah
(traditional, arranged By Bob Dylan)

A traditional folk song, performed with an insistent throbbing bass, a tremolo electric guitar and a cadre of backing singers. Throw in a few slashes of a randomly played (and slightly out-of-tune) mandolin and a couple of harmonica solos, and you get "Shenandoah". We are nowhere near the reverent treatment that such songs would get on *Good As I Been To You* and *World Gone Wrong*. I have no idea what the lyrics are about here, maybe it's the story of Pocahontas. Bob is singing with vigor, but he does seem oddly disconnected from the test which one would suppose Dylan had loved for decades by now. The arrangement seems a little haphazard and ill-thought out. It feels like these were just the instruments and musicians who happened to be in the studio when Bob wanted to record this song rather than something he deliberately planned in advance. If you're going to have a rock arrangement of a folk song, there's nothing wrong with that – but where are the drums? If you want to do a more straightforward acoustic version, as the mandolin implies, then where is all the rest of this coming from? The backing singers, with their handclaps and tambourine at the end, seem to think this is a gospel song. The whole thing is a mess, which would be fine if it were an entertaining mess, but all-in-all, this cover doesn't do much for me.

Rank Strangers to Me
(written by Albert E. Brumley)

This song is often touted as "the best" (or "only even slightly good one") on *Down In The Groove*. Frankly, I don't get it. It's not bad. There's some top-notch fretless bass playing here, and Bob sings this well, but the song never really feels like it ever starts. The whole thing feels like a long intro to a more rocking song that never actually arrives. The instrumentation is pretty sparse, just Bob's acoustic guitar and a solitary backing vocalist harmonizing throughout. The song is about feeling lonely in the world, but Bob doesn't carry a whole lot of pathos in his voice. The song was initially popularized by the Stanley Brothers. Their version is not nearly as slow as Bob's, although this is too sleepy for bluegrass. It's certainly the kind of music that got re-popularized with the soundtrack to *O Brother Where Art Thou*, but Dylan doesn't give any life to this song. It's taken so slow and without pulse that you can't even tell it's in 3/4 time. Not that the song is bad necessarily, but it's hardly even one of the best on the somewhat low bar that is *Down In The Groove*.

Songs not on the album:
Pretty Boyd Floyd from *A Vision Shared – A Tribute To Woody Guthrie and Leadbelly*
(written by Woody Guthrie)

Considering how big of an influence Woody Guthrie was in Bob's formative years, it's surprising that the first cover of his that Dylan officially released wasn't until this 1988 tribute album. Bob had attempted Woody's "(As I Go) Ramblin' Round" for his debut album, but other than that, he never touched Woody's songs in the recording studio. Dylan played them a lot live during those days, check out "This Land Is Your Land" off of *The Bootleg Series vol. 7*, but hadn't really touched Woody's songs much since starting to write his own. The version here shows a lot of familiarity with the material but sounds oddly rushed off. Sure, the return to solo acoustic guitar and harmonica is appropriate here, but Dylan doesn't add much here. Perhaps he still has too much reverence for Woody Guthrie to do anything too terribly sacrilegious. Instead, we get a pleasant and straightforward recording that certainly would've been a bright spot on *Down In The Groove* but nothing as revelatory as one would hope from Bob finally tackling a Woody Guthrie tune on record.

Important Words officially unreleased
(written by Gene Vincent)

Initially Bob joked that *Down In The Groove* would be entitled *Self-Portrait II*. While the released album has none of *Self-Portrait*'s verve or daring, he probably was talking about the number of covers included. Many of the cover song recorded for this album are old R&B and early rock'n'roll songs. If he had stuck with that as an overriding theme for the album, it might not have made a real sequel to *Self-Portrait*, but it might have helped the album have some rationale for hanging together. Tracks like this would've at least given the whole exercise and excuse if not a reason to exist. Apparently, this song was under serious consideration for this album; it was on the original test pressing that accidentally got released as the album in Argentina of all places. Ultimately this is not a great lost track, however. It's a 50s song given a weak and watery treatment. Bob sings with familiarity and conviction but no fire. The song itself could be nearly any song from the era, and Bob's version doesn't add much to it, other than the incongruous harmonica solo towards the end. Dylan doesn't attempt to recreate Gene Vincent's original vocal gymnastics. The original may have been eclipsed over the years by heavier material, but Bob's rendition neuters whatever made the song exciting in the first place. It's faithful in tone and tempo but displays none of the passion that Bob must've felt when he first heard Gene Vincent. It's a respectful, but unnecessary, cover.

Got Love If You Want It officially unreleased
(written by Slim Harpo)
Ironically Bob does a better version of rockabilly with the blues song by Slim Harpo than an actual rockabilly song like Gene Vincent's "Important Words". This song is more of the watery blues-rock very similar to "Sally Sue Brown" with ample backing vocals pasted on. About 90% of the lyrics here are just the title phrase repeated over and over again. This would've been a perfect adroit if unremarkable addition to the *Self-Portrait II* concept if Dylan had followed that through to completion. Towards the very beginning of the song, one of the vocalists let's out with a loud "whooo!" that the energy of the actual track fails to match. There's a guitar solo in here that is hampered by sounding terribly hesitant. However, Bob's harmonica playing here is spirited, and his vocals are actually injected with some joviality that many of the *Down In The Groove* tracks lack. While not necessarily mind-blowing this song would've been an excellent substitution for almost anything that did get officially released on the album.

Sidewalks, Fences & Walls officially unreleased
(written by Maurice Gimbel & Jerry Williams Jr)
A cover of an R&B song initially released by Freddie North in 1971 that provided the title for Solomon Burke's 1979 album. It certainly fits in with the *Self-Portrait II* concept. Bob's take on this song is closer to "Emotionally Yours" from *Empire Burlesque* than any sort of authentic R&B. In fact, it sounds like it would've been a great B-side to Allen Toussaint's "Freedom For The Stallion" recorded during the *Empire Burlesque* sessions. That's a great breakdown in this version where the piano takes a bit of a solo. I'm not really sure what this song is about, maybe chalk graffiti. It does say that Solomon loves Mary over and over again. Oddly enough this isn't a Biblical reference, but rather an unintentional shout-out to Solomon Burke. When Freddie North sings the song, he says "Freddie loves Mary" and when Solomon covered it, he changed the name to his own. But when Bob covered this track, he kept that lyrical personalization as part of the song. If Bob had stuck with the all-cover idea, this song would've certainly been a stand-out.

Money Honey officially unreleased
(written by Jesse Stone)
Another early rock'n'roll/R&B song recorded during these sessions. Originally a hit first for the Drifters and later covered by Elvis Presley. The

song is a simple staple of many a cover band and this arrangement sound more like it was warmed up on the spot rather than thought about beforehand. The slide guitar is clearly taking the lead here. The first time through the little start-stop riff the band is all over the place, but by the end of the track, they've finally got it together. There's no clear ending planned out in advance, and so the tune tends to drag on repetitively towards the end, and probably would've been faded out if it had made the cut for the record. Bob is definitely singing through his nose, but he sounds like he is having a blast here. More evidence that this era was weighing heavily on his mind during this period. It could simply be that as Bob was getting older, he had no other examples of aging rockers to turn to and was, in turn, reverting to his childhood trying to reconnect with why he starting making music in the first place. It's another fine addition to the *Self-Portrait II* covers collection.

Willie And The Hand Jive officially unreleased
(written by Johnny Otis)

Even more half-assed and off-the-cuff is Bob's cover of "Willie And The Hand Jive". The bootlegs don't even sound properly mixed here with Dylan's vocals particularly buried. The bass is very 80s sounding, and the playing is too busy for what is essentially another cover of a simple early rock song. While the original version by Johnny Otis was a hit in 1958, I was far more familiar with Eric Clapton's 1974 cover. It's a simple song about a ridiculous dance/hand signal. Bob's version never sounds like more than a rehearsal, which is too bad, because it is amusing to hear this glorified wordsmith singing lyrics that at best are a code for masturbation. It's not worth the effort to seek out a bootleg with this track on it, but if you happen upon it, it is definitely worth a chuckle.

Twist And Shout officially unreleased
(written by Phil Medley and Bert Russell)

This Isley Brothers' song is already best known as a cover by The Beatles. It is a rudimentary three-chord song that most garage bands begin by learning. Those also happen to be the same three chords of many early garage rock warhorses, including Ritchie Valens' "La Bamba". This is where the Latin-ish feel for Bob's unexpected cover of this song comes from. This feels like another tossed-off jam of a song everyone already knows instead of a serious attempt to get a real take in the can for a prospective album, another cover from this early rock period that Dylan was so focused on at the time. Still, it is undeniably enjoyable to hear Mr. Voice-Of A-Generation sink his teeth into something so trivial and silly.

Just When I Needed You Most officially unreleased
(written by Randy VanWarmer and Tony Wilson)

A cover of the 1979 soft rock song by Randy VanWarmer. It was not a big hit, and Randy is pretty obscure. But that's not surprising, because the original is a horribly saccharine piece of fluff along the lines of say Bread. For some reason, Bob decided to cover this in an arrangement reasonably faithful to the original, although there is slightly more of an edge and a slight reggae feel. This isn't a song that isn't long-lodged in Dylan's brain from childhood, nor is this is quite an attempt to cash-in on something current. Who knows why this song was attempted, but the recording here shows a full-fledged take of the song and not just the rough run-through that "Twist And Shout" or "Willie And The Hand Jive" received. Weird.

Rumored to have been recorded but unheard:
Treasure Of Love
(written by Clyde McPhatter)
Chain Gang
(written by Sam Cooke)
If You Need Me
(written by Robert Bateman, Wilson Pickett, and Sonny Sanders)
Branded Mana
(written by Merle Haggard)
Making Believe
(written by Jimmy Work)
Just When I Needed You Most
(written by Randy Vanwarmer)
Rock 'n' Roll Ruby
(written by Johnny Cash)
Listen To Me
(written by Buddy Holly and Norman Petty)
You Can't Judge A Book By The Cover
(written by Willie Dixon)
Sugaree
(written by Jerry Garcia)

More random early rockabilly, rock'n'roll and R&B songs that Dylan alleged covered during these sessions. With a Grateful Dead tune thrown in for good measure. I'm not sure how many of these were serious attempts and how many were just musicians jamming and goofing around. It's a very thin line with Bob Dylan. I have not heard most of these, but it shows the kind of songs and sound Bob was going for on *Down In The Groove*, even if he failed to achieve it.

"KNOCKED DOWN AND OUT (LOADED IN THE GROOVE)"

SIDE A:
1. Night After Night
2. Silivio
3. Got My Mind Made Up
4. Ugliest Girl In The World
5. Band Of The Hand (It's Helltime, Man)
6. Had A Dream About You Baby

SIDE B:
1. The Usual
2. You Wanna Ramble
3. Sally Sue Brown
4. Let's Stick Together
5. Got Love If You Want It

Neither *Knocked Out Loaded* or *Down In The Groove* are the results of single artistic vision or even really a chronologically cohesive set of recording sessions. Therefore it is pretty easy to mix and match tracks from both of these two albums into a single record.

Much like Dylan had talked about in this period, I thought about putting together an entire album of covers here and calling it *Self-Portrait part II*. Instead, I just put all the covers on the second side. If I were going to do this, I would replace this Side A with "Freedom For The Stallion", "Sidewalks, Fences, And Walls", "Important Words", "Money Honey", "Shenadoah", and "Pretty Boy Floyd" and then switch the two sides. As tempting as it is to follow through with Dylan's original plan, there were too many originals that would be missed if I did that. But not enough to scrape together a second whole album out of them. In the end, I had to compromise and compile this half-originals (if co-written) and half-covers album concept.

While the album opens with something of a callback to the synths of *Empire Burlesque* with "Night After Night", the acoustic-rock sound of track two ("Silvio") shows the variety of this album as well as it re-focusing on quote-unquote "real" instruments. The songs here are all up-tempo rockers as Bob is trying to show off his muscle here and apologize for the more blatant pop leanings of the last album. It makes his turn playing a rock star in the movie *Hearts Of Fire* seem like less of an acting stretch.

While most Dylan fans try to ignore *Knocked Out Loaded* and *Down In The Groove*, I think they are looking for something that isn't really there. This is not Bob Dylan the genius, mercurial wordsmith. This is Bob, having a midlife crisis trying to relive the glory days of his teenage years. Let's not ignore that, but instead revel in the audacious awkwardness of it all.

OH MECRY

Produced by: Daniel Lanois
Recorded: February 28th – March 29th, 1989
Released: September 18th, 1989

Famous/Important/Popular Track(s):
- Ring Them Bells
- Everything Is Broken
- Most Of The Time

My Personal Favorite Track(s):
- Political World
- Everything Is Broken
- Man In The Long Black Coat

Bob Dylan was seen as infallible in the sixties. Every move that initially smacked of career suicide was quickly vindicated, both commercially and critically. It was only after 1970's *Self-Portrait* that Dylan made what was considered to be his first misstep. But this quickly paved the way for a new phenomenon in Bob's catalog: the comeback album. In the seventies, any miscalculation on Dylan's would eventually have a forgiving follow-up, whether it was *New Morning* apologizing for the lack of originals on *Self-Portrait* or *Infidels* making reparations for Bob's "born again" trilogy. Even *Blood On The Tracks* was seen as a "comeback" from the lackluster trio of *Planet Waves*, *Dylan*, and *Pat Garrett & Billy The Kid*.

But had never had as sustained a stumble as his mid-eighties work. *Empire Burlesque*, *Knocked Out Loaded*, and *Down In The Groove* were going to take a lot to forgive. It wasn't as if Dylan had made a poor choice in a new direction as everyone felt with the "religious" trilogy. It seemed more as if Bob wasn't trying anymore. And he didn't even care.

Someone of Bob's stature was expected to play arenas, but by the eighties, his star had fallen so far that he would require big name bands (The Grateful Dead, Tom Petty & The Heartbreakers) to back him up or there would be no way he could fill those sized venues. When he wasn't making some half-assed album and doing his summer stadium tours, Dylan didn't know what to do with himself. He even ended up sleep-walking through the Joe Eszterhas penned *Hearts Of Fire*, a rock-star vehicle that should be showcasing someone a little less enigmatic and less likely to know better.

It was an bizarre chapter in Bob's life – and one of the few that actually became a chapter in his autobiography. Dylan finally relented and agreed to start playing some smaller venues with a crackerjack, but anonymous, backing band (initially assembled by *SNL* alum G.E. Smith). Not only was he playing live with a purpose and vengeance again, but he was just playing a lot. This return to a decent solo show, alongside his appearance on *The Traveling Wilburys, vol. 1* helped raised Bob's profile in the public consciousness to the highest it had been since he quit berating his audience with fire-and-brimstone sermons. The time was ripe for his latest comeback.

But Dylan knew that recording wasn't really his strong suit. He had tried producing records on his own, but he lacked the focus or interest in the technical side to see the project through to any sort of satisfying conclusion. He needed someone like Mark Knopfler to guide him through the whole process and not just come in at the end like Arthur Baker to fix the mess he started. On the advice of Bono (*shudder*), Bob turned to producer Daniel Lanois.

More than just a sure hand at the mixing board was going to be needed. Dylan was going to have to start writing songs again, and not just relying on covers and co-writers. For whatever reason, Bob stepped up to the challenge and actually wrote more than enough material for a ten-track album. The result is Dylan once again feels energized and engaged with his content. Honestly, the difference is slight, but it was very effective, garnering Bob some of his best sales and reviews of the 1980s.

This is a difficult album for me to objectively view as it was one of the first ones I really got into. Having been a fan of the Wilburys, I soon discovered this record (or cassette to be honest) in my Dad's collection and first started getting into Dylan's discography. In retrospect now, it is a pretty good, but not great album. I can see why someone who was familiar with Bob's history and importance would find this to be such a relief. For my younger self, who had no context, this was all I knew of Dylan. I didn't like it as much as *Cloud Nine* or *Full Moon Fever*, but it was better than *Armchair Theatre*.

There's a lot of great songs on here. There are even a few good songs that are not on here; most of which got re-done for *Under The Red Sky*. Daniel Lanois' production is hard to ignore. It helps props up the more upbeat rocking material, although it does tend to overwhelm the slower, weaker material with the appearance of an importance that the song itself has not earned. While I don't return to this album often, it is one I know well and will always have a particular affection for in my heart.

Political World
(written by Bob Dylan)

In some way, this track keeps with *Down In The Groove*'s "Let's Stick Together" and *Knocked Out Loaded*'s "You Wanna Ramble" as semi-upbeat rock shuffle to open the album with. The most significant difference, at least on first glance, is this is a Dylan original and not an old cover. This song and pre-dates the more repetitive lyrics of *Under The Red Sky* with the same line being used over and over to open each couplet or verse, most of it leading to nothing. It still comes across as both paranoid yet accurate.

Daniel Lanois's swampy atmosphere helps elevate what is a rather simple I-IV-V song into a much more exciting opener for this album. There's no bridge or chorus or even an ending for this song. It's just verse after verse after verse with short breaks for soloing between. The song slowly slides in and gradually begins to build before it all comes together. Bob even starts singing before the drums come in. After the first verse, congas kick in, and it really kicks the whole song up a notch. We get several fun verses that reportedly illustrate how the world is political. You could rearrange them or even cut any one of them and have no overall effect on the lyrical meaning of this song. At least it doesn't overstay its welcome and fades out under four minutes.

Where Teardrops Fall
(written by Bob Dylan)

The 6/8 time signature and saxophone solo at the end gives this track something of a 50s doo-wop feel. However, the slide guitar seems to be trying to imitate a pedal steel guitar which provides the song with a slight country edge. The lyrics sound like they should be sad, but Bob's vocal here is a bit disengaged, making it hard to connect to whatever emotion he's trying to convey. I would assume this place that teardrops fall at is somewhat related to Elvis Presley's "Heartbreak Hotel", but it's hard to tell if Dylan is angry or sad or what here. It's a perfectly fine song, but not one of the more interesting ones on *Oh Mercy*.

Everything Is Broken
(written by Bob Dylan)

Another up-tempo rocker in the mold of "Political World". Based on a tried and true blues chord pattern, this has even more simple/repetitive lyrics, but at least is broken up every now and then by a short bridge. There's some terrific conga playing here. The bass plays this cool bass riff throughout the song that really makes the track jump. There are a couple of harmonica solos to make up for the fact that Bob couldn't come up with more for his list of things that are broken that rhyme. One *The Bootleg Series vol. 8* there's a different version of this song with the exact same backing track only with Bob singing an entirely different set of lyrics that also add up to nothing. I'm not sure why he needed to re-write these words – or even why he needed to write them in the first place. I do prefer Bob's performance on the official version better and not just because he has the harmonica instead of a weird tambourine solo.

Ring Them Bells
(written by Bob Dylan)

Another slow portentous (pretentious?) ballad in the vein of "Where Teardrops Fall". Are these bells the chimes of freedom? The lyrics are aiming for the implied depth of Bob's early 1960s work. While these words might mean as much to Bob as some of those old songs, this song doesn't connect nearly as well. The issue isn't inherent within the lyrics themselves, but rather Dylan's vocal performance gives no clues how we should feel about the bells in question here. This song feels like a self-conscious attempt to write an important tune that doesn't quite meet its objectives. The performance is good. It's mostly just Bob's piano with just enough tremolo guitar and organ in the background to keep this from feeling like a demo. The melody is strong, even if Bob sounds somewhat distracted singing it. There's a pleasant bridge to keep things interesting. Overall, I tend to prefer the upbeat songs on *Oh Mercy* to the ballads, and this is no exception.

Man in the Long Black Coat
(written by Bob Dylan)

One of my favorite Dylan songs. This song feels epic without having to last over eight minutes just to prove it. The crickets from "Day Of The Locusts" make their return appearance. There's some guitar noodling before the song slowly emerges from the sonic murk. I have no idea who the man in the long black coat is or what the words mean, by Bob's voice instills this song with a real sense of dread and trepidation. I love the idea that one's conscience is depraved, vile and not to be trusted. I'm not sure exactly what we're supposed to rely on to be our guide then. Not Jiminy Cricket. There's a bridge that extends the world of the song immensely. Everything in this song leads back to the title refrain as much as it feels like it's trying to escape. Bob's harmonica playing is especially lonesome on this track. I don't think this song gets nearly as much respect as it deserves in Dylan's canon. An exceptional, haunting performance.

Most of the Time
(written by Bob Dylan)

An expression of the faux-bravado following the end of the romance, with the real depth of the heartbreak being constantly hinted. This is one of Bob's strongest melodies. This recording is full of Daniel Lanois's usual textures: ghostly electric guitars in the background filling in all the cracks and space in the song. There's a delay on the drums that makes it sound like there are ghost notes being played filling the second half of some sort of snare drum marching pattern. There's a really strong bridge here that opens the song up in a good way. The lyrics are pretty simple to understand, with even the subtext being hard to miss. Bob sings this with a great weariness in his voice which is quite apropos. *The Bootleg Series vol. 8* contains two alternates for this song. One is clearly just an acoustic demo taken at a speedy a little too hasty for the message of the lyrics. It is nice to hear Bob's harmonica and old solo performer persona tackling this latter-day song, but it adds very little. The other version on *The Bootleg Series vol. 8* adds even less sounding almost identical to the released version. There might be some slight differences in the swampy textures that producer Lanois added to the song, but none of it make any significant difference to the song. One of the more intriguing versions of this song is the one used on the music video for this song. It starts with a bit of a jamming warm-up from the band, and it seems like this take is, in fact, a live-to-camera take of the song that for some reason Don Was got credit for producing. Bob even gets bored by the point where the song usually would've faded out and just train-wrecks the performance in order to end it. While the arrangement is pretty similar, it is stripped of Daniel's more ornate production choices. If you prefer the *Under The Red* Sky versions of the *Oh* Mercy outtakes, then you will like this. To my ears, it's not bad, but I still prefer the original. No matter how it's done, this is one of the best songs on *Oh Mercy*.

What Good Am I?
(written by Bob Dylan)

There's a lovely minute-and-a-half instrumental version of this song that Bob recorded for the soundtrack for the 2009 movie, *My Own Love Song*. The original version is heavily centered around tinkling piano, a spooky organ, and some lovely dobro playing. The song takes its time locking into a groove. There's a very soft kick drum buried in the mix maintaining something of a rhythm. The lyrics are just a list of potential failure that would invalidate one's existence. Dylan sounds slightly perplexed here and definitely disappointed in himself. When the bridge finally comes around Bob unleashes his most wrung out vocal, adding some real pathos here. While this is a good song, it is lacking something holding it together and propelling it forward. Perhaps some drums would make a big difference. It certainly helps on the covers of this song by Tom Jones and Simon Burke. Not one of the best songs on *Oh Mercy* but certainly not worth skipping.

Disease of Conceit
(written by Bob Dylan)

Another slow *Oh Mercy* ballad that sounds like it is trying to be an important Dylan statement that unfortunately just falls flat. Much like "Shooting Star" or "Ring Them Bells", these tunes drag down this album from being a good rock record. Much like "Dignity" the lyrics here are attempting to anthropomorphize a philosophical concept and then sketch a bunch of moments around that. While "Dignity" is difficult enough to understand in this setting, I at least know what dignity is. I have no idea what Bob is referring to with the phrase "disease of conceit". His vocal performance entrusts the words with a lot of pretention and faux-gravitas, but it is never clear what is being sung here. The music here matches in how seriously it takes these lyrics. It is done at a slow, deliberate pace that I assume was meant to be stately. Led by a prominent piano, there's no rhythmic backbone here. The drums are almost missing entirely Plenty of electric guitars playing up the profundity of the big ca-ching chord changes. The organ is nicely subtle, but the guitar solo is mawkish and overly dramatic; which fits the song. The best thing that can be said about it is that it runs by quickly. Not one of the better *Oh Mercy* tracks.

What Was It You Wanted?
(written by Bob Dylan)

Lots of spectral tremolo guitars and dobros typical of Daniel Lanois' production. The song has a slinky, sneaky groove. The lyrics are all various attempts to find out what the "you" is wanted. Sure, some the lines a little dunderheaded like "tell me again, I forgot" and "you can tell me, I'm back," but for the most part they managed to maintain the central mystery of the song without giving any more information about what is wanted. It really would be tiresome, except that Bob sings this with both a sense of curiosity and urgency. There's some atmospheric harmonica playing, and the whole sound of the song is tightly wound while still maintaining a spooky atmosphere. Nothing terribly important is going on here, but it's still a cool song.

Shooting Star
(written by Bob Dylan)

Another attempt to write a self-conscious masterpiece for *Oh Mercy*, this song fails much like "Ring Them Bells" or Disease of Conceit". The lyrics use seeing a meteor as a jumping off point for various meditations Bob has had. None of these thoughts feel very tied to each other or to that particular astronomical phenomena. As dull and plodding as "Shooting Star" is, it is almost saved by the bridge section that takes the whole track in a completely unexpected direction. Unfortunately, it doesn't last long as it isn't repeated. The song shows Lanois' usual atmospherics. Boy does that French-Canadian love his dobro. The song is taken at a stately and slow pace to try and amp up the importance that it doesn't actually manage to achieve. While most of *Oh Mercy*, is great it is songs like this that really keep it for being undeniably great. It's especially disappointing that this is the song that Bob decided to end this album on.

Songs not on the album:
Born in Time released on *Under The Red Sky*
(written by Bob Dylan)

This song was first attempted with Daniel Lanois for *Oh Mercy* before being re-recorded for *Under The Red Sky* with Don Was. Two of those original takes ended up on *The Bootleg Series vol. 8*. While both of those takes are superior to the Don Was version, they are not terribly different from each other, so I don't know why both were released. Maybe Bob couldn't tell which was better and decided to avoid the whole argument by leaving it off the original 1989 album. I think one may have a little more dobro than the other. By the time it was re-recorded by Don Was a slightly oriental-sounding synthesizer opening was added to the song. In the officially released version, Bob's vocals are far more pinched and nasal. This version has the unexpected addition of an accordion actually played by Dylan. In accordance to the superstar guest appearance ethos of that album, there's some piano played by Bruce Hornsby well as harmony vocals by David Crosby. In fact, this version isn't significantly worse or different from the *Oh Mercy* takes, just slightly less effective. From a songwriting standpoint, this track fits in far more with the deliberately serious tone *Oh Mercy* than the nursery rhymes and children's songs of *Under the Red Sky*. I'm not entirely sure what the lyrics are about, but they seem ponderous. It's a slower number, but not as mind-numbing as say "Ring Them Bells" or "Shooting Star". Maybe not top tier *Oh Mercy* material, but it certainly deserved a place on the album more than some songs that did get included.

God Knows released on *Under The Red Sky*
(written by Bob Dylan)

This up-tempo rocker isn't nearly as good as "Political World" or "Everything Is Broken" so it is no surprise it was left off of *Oh Mercy*. More surprisingly however it was re-recorded for *Under The Red Sky* and released there. While in its original version the song is an unrelenting barrage, the second version actually builds over the course of the song. In fact, so much of the song is devoted to this more sparse opening, it seems a little weird to consider it an intro. Really, the whole song doesn't really kick in with the drums until the song is almost half over. Really, you are lulled into the assumption that this free-form opening is the whole song and you can be quite stunned when the song actually turns into the rocker that it always was in its original incarnation. Even more strangely, the *Under The Red Sky* version of this song fades out while Bob is still singing new verses. You would think those who consider him a lyricist first and a musician a distant second wouldn't want those lyrical gems to end up cut off or hard to hear during that fade, but that's the direction the Was brothers decided to go in. I'm not sure which version I prefer. While the second version is full of surprises, it takes so long to really get going I start to get concerned. The *Oh Mercy* rendition that ended up released on *The Bootleg Series vol. 8* is far more consistent, but that also can get a bit dull and repetitive too. Either way, it's a decent song. Not one of the best from these sessions, but certainly one that deserves to be treated better.

Dignity from *The Greatest Hits vol. III*
(written by Bob Dylan)

Much like the equally pretentious "Disease Of Conceit" Bob extends a single metaphor out to the length of an entire song. This song was first recorded with Daniel Lanois, but everything was replaced except Dylan's vocals by Brendan O'Brien for inclusion on *Greatest Hits vol. III*. Later the original version came out on the soundtrack to the TV show *Touched By An Angel*. Most folks considered Brendan's version something of a hack-job, and this was the version subsequently released on various compilations. To me, the difference between the two versions is slight, and I actually prefer O'Brien to Lanois here. There's some nice banjo on here, and the organ playing is great on the *Greatest Hits* version. Maybe it wasn't Bob's original vision, but Dylan was obviously so disappointed with those results he left the song off of *Oh Mercy*. On *The Bootleg Series vol. 8*, two more variations on "Dignity" were released. One is an extremely straightforward version played alone on the piano. While it is a lovely performance, it still feels like a demo, which is what I think it was. The other version on *The Bootleg Series vol. 8* features some really prominent bass. It sounds very wonky and weird, with the severe upbeats threatening to throw the whole thing off track. It is an odd approach for a song that clearly was meant to be a serious anthem like "Shooting Star" or "Ring Them Bells". Despite having a plethora of officially released versions to choose from, this song never did much for me, and I'm not sure why so much time was spent on it. It's better than some of the songs that did make the cut on this album, but we're not missing anything amazing here.

Series Of Dreams from *The Bootleg Series vol. 3*
(written by Bob Dylan)

Another attempt at a "big statement" type anthem. The version of this released on *The Bootleg Series vol. 3* is annoyingly crossfaded with the previous song at the very beginning making it difficult to slot in various compilations. Luckily, another take was released on *The Bootleg Series vol. 8* that is nearly identical. The recording is taken at a rather slow tempo that allows enough room for the drums to do this intricate pattern on the toms. It's a weird dichotomy since the song itself feels slow and languid, but the drums are exciting and propulsive. I'm not sure if I actually like the effect, but it is interesting. The lyrics are, as the title suggests, just a series of random images without any real meaning or reality. Much like hearing anyone else describe their dreams, this might be interesting to Bob, but it is boring to anyone else. It doesn't help that Dylan has a lot of dreams in this series and the song goes on for a bit too long. The synths on here are the closest Daniel Lanois comes to the production styles of Arthur Baker although nowhere nearly as dated. Like "Dignity" this is not a horrible song, but I can see why it got cut from *Oh Mercy*.

People Get Ready from the *Flashback* soundtrack
(written by Curtis Mayfield)

Given Robbie Robertson's love of Curtis Mayfield, I believe that this song may have been first attempted during *The Basement Tapes* sessions at Robbie's behest rather than Dylan's. However, Bob did connect to this song as well, performing it during the 1975 Rolling Thunder Revue and releasing a rehearsal version on the very obscure promo EP *4 Songs From "Renaldo & Clara"*. On November 20th, 1989, Barry Goldberg produced a version of this song for Bob to do on the soundtrack to the Keifer Sutherland/Dennis Hopper comedy *Flashback*. The musicians are not listed or credited on this version. It has a much more organic sound and feel than Lanois' murky swamp blues, although it does feature a prominent dobro. There's even the re-appearance of the backing vocalists that mostly disappeared from Dylan recording by this point. It's a joyful gospel sound, although it does feel a little flat, it never comes off as forced. While Bob may not have felt comfortable writing his own religious material anymore, he still sounds thoroughly convinced on this track. The *Renaldo & Clara* version seems less certain in its beliefs. Scarlett Rivera's violin is pretty muted here as though she weren't sure what to play yet. The shouting male backing vocalist on the 1975 version is a stark contrast to the plaintive falsetto that accompanies Bob on the 1967 version. No surprise that Robbie knows this song and plays it well. While both of these earlier attempts at this song have some charm, I find the more polished sheen of the *Flashback* soundtrack version the most appealing.

Dirty World from *The Traveling Wilburys, vol. 1*
(written by the Traveling Wilburys)

The Traveling Wilburys proved to be something of a conundrum for me when writing this book. Bob is mostly known as a solo artist. One those rare occasions when he does collaborate, it usually pretty easy to tell whether he is providing back-up for someone else or if it is a project for himself. Rarely does he share the spotlight as evenly as he did with the Traveling Wilburys. On the one hand, should I include all of their songs since he (or at least his pseudonym) is at least credited with co-writing and playing every song? Or should I ignore the Wilburys all together, since they are not meant to be "Bob Dylan" projects at all? In the end, I decided to just focus on the songs on which Dylan sings the majority of the lead vocals by himself. While he has a line or two on several tracks, these three songs from the first album seem the most Dylan-y to me. I don't mind that Bob didn't pen these tunes all by his lonesome. There are several examples of covers and co-writes in this book. I just want to focus on Dylan as a recording artist, and these are the tracks that could easily be slotted into a Bob CD without apology or explanation. This process gets a little more tricky on the second Wilburys album as there are far fewer songs with only one lead vocalist. Reportedly Dylan did write and sing a majority of the lyrics on that album before some parts were swapped out to make *The Traveling Wilburys, vol. 3* seem more collaborative. The three Dylan songs on *Volume 1* are each modeled after a different disguise. On "Tweeter & The Monkey Man" Dylan is clearly spoofing Springsteen. With "Congratulations" Bob is clearly playing himself. For "Dirty World" the inspiration was apparently Prince. You may not know that from listening to the song, but only from anecdotes given by the various Wilburys in interviews over the years. From a musical or sonic standpoint, there is nothing here to remind you of the Purple One. However, the direct vulgarity of the lyrics is Bob's idea of what Prince sounds like. And it's hilarious. It's got a great feel like "Everything Is Broken" or "Political World" but is funnier than anything off of *Oh Mercy* The ending does sort of spoil the illusion that this is a solo-Dylan song; but hearing George Harrison, Tom Petty, Roy Orbison, and Jeff Lynne all just in at the very end is a great, unexpected treat. It's nice hearing Bob try to be funny again. Especially that last epilogue of a line where they sing the self-censored "it's a ____ing dirty world." One of my all-time favorites.

Congratulations from *The Traveling Wilburys, vol. 1*
(written by the Traveling Wilburys)

The Traveling Wilburys have a special place in my heart. In the late eighties, as a teenager, I was a huge Beatles fan (and still am). When this album came out, I bought it solely because George was my favorite. I didn't even know who the other four guys were. I loved that record, and from there I went on to discover more about the rest of the band. I bought *Armchair Theatre* by Jeff Lynne and *Full Moon Fever* by Tom Petty. It was from here that I also first began listening to Bob Dylan, leading me, thirty years later, to writing this book. It's no surprise I gravitated to Dylan, my two favorite tracks on the record were "Dirty World" and "Tweeter & The Monkey Man". On the flipside, I never got into Roy Orbison. "Not Alone Anymore" was my second least favorite track on the record. But the only song I would regularly skip over was "Congratulations" – the most Dylan-y sounding Dylan song on this record. It is the only Wilburys song that Bob has performed live in concert, but for some reason, it really bugged me. I'm not exactly sure why it bugged me as a kid. These days, I can hear it as the rest of the band trying to write a typical Bob song for Bob to sing, but at the time I think it was just too slow, too boring, too nasal, too something... While I have warmed to it a little over the years, it still is not a favorite of mine. It is interesting as an example of what a Jeff Lynne produced Dylan album would sound like (can you imagine?), but it is still not a track I come back to often.

Tweeter & The Monkey Man from *The Traveling Wilburys, vol. 1*
(written by the Traveling Wilburys)

I do not like Bruce Springsteen. At all. Ok, I like *Nebraska*, but otherwise can't stand the guy. I also accept that a lot of other people really do love Bruce Springsteen, including some people I do otherwise admire; including possibly Bob Dylan. I do not know if this song was meant as a kind-hearted tribute or nasty swipe at "the boss". However, knowing nothing about Springsteen at the time I first heard this, that all went over my head. I just knew that this was my favorite song on the album. Longer than any other track on *Traveling Wilburys, vol.1* by a good two minutes, I found the story of lyrics fascinated and funny, even if I couldn't literally decipher any of them. Certainly, all the Bruce allusions were lost on me. As much as I would like to think that Dylan despises Springsteen as much as I do, I doubt that is the case. Still, it makes me feel good to hear Bob mocking him so. But even without that component to the song, this is a great, fun track. While long for a Wilburys tune, it doesn't go on forever like some of Dylan's epics. The chorus is catchy, and the sound is great. Frankly, more than any other song, "Tweeter & The Monkey Man" can be directly blamed for the mere existence of this book you are currently reading.

"A DIRTY & POLITICAL WORLD"

SIDE A:
1. Political World
2. Man In The Long Black Coat
3. Everything Is Broken
4. Born In Time
5. Dirty World

SIDE B:
1. People Get Ready
2. Dignity
3. God Knows
4. What Was It You Wanted?
5. Tweeter & The Monkey Man

In keeping with the more "rawk" theme of *Knocked Down And Out (Loaded In The Groove)*, I have cut all the more pretentious ballads from *Oh Mercy* and replaced them with some Wilburys tunes and some fun outtakes. I have also added the version of "People Get Ready" to keep the thread of "cover songs" flowing through this record. What we're left with certainly grooves a lot harder, although it probably would've done less to rehabilitate Dylan's critical reputation by the late eighties.

Having some songs produced by Jeff Lynne or Barry Goldberg also keeps the more stylistic touches of Daniel Lanois fresh and unexpected instead of having that sound overwhelm the album and become drab by the end.

For "Dignity" I used the wonky full-band version from *The Bootleg Series vol. 8* instead of the demo version or the *Touched By An Angel* or *Greatest Hits, vol. III* This is the version that is more danceable and wonky, so it fits the album better. About the only slow and serious song I have left on this album is "Man In The Long Black Coat" because that song is so cool and dark and mysterious.

I end the album with the extended Springsteen parody of "Tweeter & The Monkey Man" to try and keep things light and undercut any of the seriousness that might've made *Oh Mercy* such a dour listen.

UNDER THE RED SKY

Produced by: Don Was, David Was, & Jack Frost
Recorded: January 6th – April, 1990
Famous/Important/Popular Track(s):
- Under The Red Sky
- Unbelievable

My Personal Favorite Track(s):
- Wiggle Wiggle
- Unbelievable
- This Old Man

Even today, some 28 years after it came out, there is no consensus on *Under The Red Sky*. It was definitely not the follow-up to *Oh, Mercy* everyone was hoping for at the time. However, it's not as disregarded as the *Down In The Groove* and *Knocked Out Loaded*. Today, there are those who like it and those who don't, but neither one feels that strongly about it. At the time, I'm sure people were relieved that Bob managed to write another whole album by himself but were disappointed that the record didn't even try to be as important and serious as Daniel Lanois' production made *Oh, Mercy* feel. The production feels a little too guest-star-heavy, but what really chapped fans' hides was how childish the lyrics came across.

In some ways this album has undergone a similar critical rehabilitation as Neil Young's synth-driven vocoder-laden 1983 album, *Trans*. Both albums were dismissed initially as slight and weird. However, as both *Trans* and *Under The Red Sky* were later revealed to be written primarily for their authors' young children, they have undergone a modest reassessment and are now seen as a little less heretical and more understandable. It might not make the albums more enjoyable, but at least more forgivable.

Producers David and Don Was are known for their ability to help older artists such as Bonnie Raitt or The Rolling Stones re-connect with their audience by going "Adult Contemporary," but they don't really have a distinctive sound like Daniel Lanois or Arthur Baker. There are a ton of guest stars on this album (Elton John, David Crosby, Bruce Hornsby, George Harrison, Slash) but none of them seem very well cast. I mean, if you're going to get Stevie Ray and Jimmie Vaughan to play on your song, you might want to pick something bluesy and not just whatever you happen to be recording that day.

A lot of strange decisions were made in the making of this record. Not enough time or thought was put into how this album should be assembled. Maybe with Bob's newly hectic touring schedule, there was a deadline to be met to get this album done. I'm sure the fact that Dylan was working on this album during the day and then schlepping off to work on the Wilburys second album at night didn't help.

Besides, 1990 was probably the last time that people expected (or wanted) Bob or any recording artist to put out a new album every year. After this point, it was not surprising if Dylan took three or four or even seven years between albums. The audience appreciated Bob taking his time to let the music marinate instead of rushing it, as I'm sure Bob did himself.

Ultimately the album suffers from this confusion and haste. The new songs that Dylan was working on felt extra inconsequential when stacked up with the *Oh, Mercy* outtakes that were re-recorded to fill out this album. If they had been allowed to live on their own, perhaps the charming, if child-like simplicity of Bob's lyrics on this album would've been less of a let-down.

There's a handful of tracks on here that I really like, but nothing is recorded with much investment, keeping this album from being one of my favorites. It's a bit of a missed opportunity as Dylan didn't fully commit himself to making a whole album for his child (and children everywhere) and also tried to pass this off as a major work and worthy successor to his successful comeback album.

Wiggle Wiggle
(written by Bob Dylan)

It's a Dylan dance song! There's a big hole in the middle where everyone is just strumming chords where you would expect a solo would go. Apparently, Slash was brought in and recorded a solo during that part. Dylan later came back and removed it saying it sounded too much like Guns 'n' Roses. I'm not sure what they were expecting, but instead, they forgot to put in anything else to fill in the gap. Still, it's a fun song and knowing that Bob was recording for his four-year-old daughter it is cute to imagine a bunch of kids dancing around and giggling to this song. The lyrics are pretty much nonsense, but definitely a lot of fun. However, you've got to wonder if a phrase like "wiggle till you vomit fire" would go over with the kindergarten crowd. It's a shame that doesn't get this silly that often because this is one of my all-time favorite Dylan songs.

Under the Red Sky
(written by Bob Dylan)

The opening keyboards bring to mind the synths that dominated *Empire Burlesque* and *Down In The Groove*, luckily this is quickly dispelled by George Harrison's slide guitar. There is, in fact, a lot of accordion on this song that one might mistake for an organ if you're not paying close enough attention. The song itself is a cute little nursery rhyme, but the production is just too cluttered and busy to make this track and effective lullaby. The lyrics are of the "dish ran away with the spoon" variety, but it's hard to find it very charming with this Adult Contemporary arrangement. George Harrison's guitar playing is lovely throughout, and there may be a good song here with a different mix that eliminates some of the extraneous instruments. This track is one of the least successful attempts at making a children's song on this album, so it is disappointing that Bob named the whole album after it.

Unbelievable
(written by Bob Dylan)

This song is more "Wiggle Wiggle" than "Under The Red Sky", which to me is a compliment. The lyrics are centered around disbelief in the modern world, something that makes Bob sound like a cranky old man. However, this does raise Bob's ire, and he delivers a much more intense vocal, even if most of the lyrics are a little vague about what is going wrong. There are some great organ bits in here that are almost long enough to be considered solos. A lot of the new songs on this album are fun and danceable making *Under The Red Sky* one of Bob's most upbeat albums, and "Unbelievable" is one of the best songs on it.

Born in Time
(written by Bob Dylan)

See the entry under *Oh Mercy*.

T.V. Talkin' Song
(written by Bob Dylan)

Ok, Bob has had a lot of three chords songs, and even a few two chord wonders; but the only chord in this song is A. The band just jams on that one chord for the whole song. It is almost impressive in its way. They actually do a pretty good job of getting a funky groove out of this when there's no movement inherent in it. Especially since the melody itself isn't particularly engaging and is probably closer to the talking blues format. The story itself is clearly meant to be an indictment of television – which adds to the impression on this album that Bob is a cranky old man yelling at whippersnappers on his lawn. Clearly, we're meant to sympathize with the British protester her who is railing against the advent of television. For an album that is dedicated to his 4-year-old daughter, I wonder if this is more of a warning to her; or an explanation of why she isn't allowed to watch as much *Sesame Street* as she would like. It's hard to say. This doesn't rock as hard as "Wiggle Wiggle" or "Unbelievable", but it's trying to.

10,000 Men
(written by Bob Dylan)

While this doesn't rock as hard as "T.V. Talkin' Song" it at least has two chords instead of just one. Definitely a very similar feel though. The repetitive lyrics sound like they're supposed to be a simple counting song for children, but starting at ten thousand seems a little ambitious. The various groups of 10,000 aren't really doing much or are related to each other. Halfway through Bob gives up on coming up with a list of things that could be that many and just sing "hey" instead. That leads to the assertion that Dylan could tell who your lover is by eating his head off. Disturbing and weird. I doubt it was meant literally. At least I really hope so. A simple, fun, silly song. There's no real dynamics or changes here, so it's relief that it doesn't last much longer than it does. 4:22 is already pushing it.

2×2
(written by Bob Dylan)

Another counting song, this one actually uses more numbers than just ten thousand. David Crosby does a great job of providing harmonies throughout this entire song. The piano is played by Elton John, and the bass is played by future *American Idol* judge Randy Jackson; not that either one really adds much personality to the proceedings. Elton does turn in a nice little keyboard solo, but it really could've been anyone. The lyrics are just a simple rhyming game and probably have no meaning. Unfortunately, Bob sings them like they have no meaning. In fact, Dylan is still singing new words as the song fades out. For a guy whose lyrics are sacrosanct, having the words become inaudible and then cut off completely is kind of surprising. However, there just wasn't any reason to keep the song going on any longer than it already is. We've all gotten the gust within three-and-a-half minutes. Like most of *Under The Red Sky*, this song is inconsequential but fun.

God Knows
(written by Bob Dylan)

See the entry under *Oh Mercy*.

Handy Dandy
(written by Bob Dylan)

A song often compared (unfavorably) to "Like A Rolling Stone", due in no small part to the similar chords structure as well as the similar sounding organ that is given a similar place of prominence in the mix. Unlike "Like A Rolling Stone" this song is substantially shorter but has a bridge section through in for variety. Bob also does a cute little stutter in there on the line "boy, you're t-talking crazy." The other big difference is that this is nowhere nearly as famous or well-loved. The lyrics are more of the goofy, nursery rhyme material that Bob is favoring on this album for his child. They don't mean much, but they are fun to sing. Bob certainly sounds like he's got a mischievous gleam in his eye while he sings this song. Bob certainly must know what comparisons this song is going to get when he records it like this, even adding Al Kooper to do the infamous organ part, but he doesn't seem to mind. It certainly doesn't feel like an attempt (successful or not) to relive his glory days and try to recapture his old commercial appeal. In fact, I think he enjoys the challenging, or at least the confounding, his fans with this weird re-tread. Maybe if it weren't so closely aligned to his biggest hit, Dylan fans would be able to appreciate it for the fun, if minor, work that it is. However for me, since I didn't notice the similarities at first until they were pointed out to me, I just like the song. It's not great, but it fits in really well with the remainder of *Under The Red Sky*.

Cat's in the Well
(written by Bob Dylan)

A fun rocker with some prominent accordion. As such it would almost fit in with *Together Through Life* and might be a harbinger of things to come there. The lyrics definitely feel like a nursery rhyme, something like "The Cow Jumped Over The Moon". Despite being a rather simple idea for a song, there's some nice twists and turns in there. I like the way the bridge subverts the more upbeat feel of the song. Sure, the lyrics are childish gibberish, but Bob sounds like he's having a good time. There's some superb guitar playing on here; not surprising since both Stevie Ray Vaughan and his brother Jimmy are playing, although it is the acoustic slide guitar that really steals the show. There's not much to this song, but it is a perfectly suitable ending for this goofy, fun album.

Songs not on the album:
Heartland from *Across The Borderline* by Willie Nelson
(written by Bob Dylan and Willie Nelson)

A song written and sung with country music legend Willie Nelson. The song is something of a return to the protest subject matter of Dylan's earliest songs. This song is a description of the plight of the American farmer without going into a lot of detail about how it came to be or what we should do about it. The song was initially attempted during the *Under The Red Sky* sessions, but that version is still unheard. The released version was clearly meant for Willie's album as it sounds very much in his style with Bob as just a guest vocalist. Bob and Willie's voices are both ragged in entirely different ways, but they make a surprising compliment to each other. Willie Nelson comes off far more sincere as Bob is nasal and a little uninspired here. It's a pleasant enough song that probably doesn't need as many solos as it has got. When the tribute album *Dylan Country* was released in 2004, this song was added to it without any concessions or alterations. "Heartland" is a somewhat rare track that is nice enough when you happen upon, but probably it is not worth buying the whole CD just for that one song.

This Old Man from *For Our Children – To Benefit the Pediatric AIDS Foundation*
(traditional, arranged by Bob Dylan)

The drums on this sound like the cheapest sounding drum machine preset available on an old Casio keyboard. Why this was used to keep rhythm on this track that is otherwise just Bob on acoustic and harmonica with an organ on top is hard to say, but it is a delightfully low-key touch. The whole thing feels very relaxed and un-worried over. While the approach is tossed off, Dylan is fully committed to singing this silly children's song. It certainly fits in with the whole *Under The Red Sky* ethos of singing songs for his four-year-old daughter, even if this wasn't recorded during those sessions. Bob gives a cheerful rendition, that is, unfortunately, a little buried in his catalog, only appearing on a benefit compilation album. Which is a shame, this a much more joyful cover than anything that ended up on *Good As I Been To You*. I'm not sure how much kids will actually like it, although they make think nothing of Bob's voice other than he sounds like a Muppet. Weirdly, this is a brave song for Dylan to cover, and not just because of the title. It may be a bit out of character, but I wish there were more examples of Bob having this much fun on record.

If You Belong To Me from *The Traveling Wilburys, vol. 3*
(written by the Traveling Wilburys)

Bob did recount in an interview with *Rolling Stone* that if he ever did write a sequel to his autobiography, Chronicles, vol. 1, featuring a chapter in regards the futility of recording the second Wilburys record at the exact same time as he was working on *Under The Red Sky*, working on one in the mornings and then recording the other during the evenings. Not nearly as commercially or critically enjoyed as the first Traveling Wilbury's album, the whimsically titled *Volume 3* may have been hurt by both the lack of surprise and the lack of Roy Orbison. Unlike *Volume 1*, this record features far more split team singing, so there's less obviously solo spots. Apparently Bob did most of the vocals himself since he wrote the lion's share of the lyrics and when Jeff Lynne and George Harrison took the tapes back to England to finish them off, swapped out a lot of Dylan's vocals for their own to make the record sound more like a band effort and less of a Bob solo outing. Still, there's two songs and one outtake on this album that are definitely Dylan's. The first of these occupies the "Congratulations" space on the record, being a typical or even stereotypical Dylan composition. There's some nice mandolin on here, and the backing harmonies are restricted to a line or two. The obtrusive Jeff Lynne styled synth pops in for a bit during the bridge but doesn't overstay its welcome. The lyrics are the usual soured love song that Bob has sung a dozen times, and he seems less excited to sing it than he does belting out lines like "she likes to stick her tongue right down my throat" or the goofy dance steps of "The

Wilbury Twist". Having fun was far more of a priority to Bob during 1990 than fulfilling his expected Bob Dylan persona. Still, this gives you a nice quick slice of what a Dylan album produced by Lynne would've sounded like without having to have the whole album actually exist.

Seven Deadly Sins from *The Traveling Wilburys, vol. 3*
(written by the Traveling Wilburys)

While on the previous Wilburys album Bob used Prince and Springsteen as inspirations, clearly Bob was modeling after a more generic 50s doo-wop on this track. One of the few Dylan solo vocals on the second album, he is shadowed throughout this track by a second vocalist, probably Jeff Lynne. It's unnecessary to keep him on key and kind of detracts from the giddy joy of hearing someone like Dylan attempt to sing this sort of song. Still, it is clearly written to be a stupidly simple sort of early rock'n'roll love song. It even features a period-accurate saxophone solo. The conceit of the lyrics is clever, a little like Elvis Costello's "Every Day I Write The Book". The first bridge lists the first four sins, but instead of having a truncated second verse, Bob just lists a different sin for sins #4 for the second bridge. With its counting structure, this song also feels definitely a part of the children's songs of *Under The Red Sky*. Like much of the Wilburys' second album, the fun here feels a lot more forced than the first go-around. Still, it's heartening to hear Bob trying to have any fun at all. And he is certainly having a lot of fun with this track.

Like A Ship from *The Wilburys Collection*
(written by the Traveling Wilburys)

One of two outtakes from *the Traveling Wilburys, vol. 3*. This song, along with the Harrison-sung "Maxine", were dusted off and given the Jeff Lynne polish when the two Wilburys records were re-released in 2007. Both of these songs would've been a fine addition to the album since they have more individual personality which of the second Wilburys record lacks. Listening to the original pre-doctored version of this song on bootlegs gives you a good idea of what Jeff Lynne had to work with for the whole project. On the one hand it lacks any fire and verve in this incarnation but is a lot more intimate and charming. It's hard to say whether Lynne improved or demolished this song, but his stylistic choices hadn't changed significantly from 1990 to 2007 as this fits pretty well within the sound of the rest of the album, only lacking George's slide guitar work. It's no great song, but it has a nice little chummy 1-2 oom-pah feel that Bob really leans into on his otherwise sloppy vocal. The lyrics are definitely silly, but at least deliberately silly, and even defiant. While not as obviously child-centric as many of the songs recorded during this period this does seem written for a younger and simpler audience. It's charming, if inessential.

Rumored to have been recorded but unheard:
Some Enchanted Evening
(music by Richard Rodgers, lyrics by Oscar Hammerstein II)
Shirley Temple Don't Live Here Anymore
(written by Bob Dylan, Don Was, and David Was)

There are two tracks recorded during these sessions that have yet to make their way into the hands of collectors. It's unknown how seriously "Some Enchanted Evening" was attempted or if it was just a jam. If more listeners were aware of this at the time, perhaps *Shadows In The Night* would've been less of a surprise when it was released. Although this might allegedly be an alternate title for the Dylan original "Night Of The Living Dread" which was recorded with NRBQ backing for the *Under The Red Sky* sessions. I'm not sure since it hasn't yet been leaked out. Even more surprising is the song "Shirley Temple Don't Live Here Anymore". The song was written by Bob with the Was Brothers that was meant to be recorded by Paula Abdul for her next album. Needless to say, Paula did not record this song, and Was (Not Was) ended up ret-titling the songs as "Mr. Alice Doesn't Live Here Anymore" and releasing the song on their 2008 album *Boo!* Listening to that recording, it's hard to imagine Dylan or Abdul singing it as it is a slice of post-modern funk with some heavy R&B. I'm curious as to how thoroughly the demo that Dylan recorded was built up. If it's got anything close to that full arrangement, then this is a song I definitely want to hear.

"FOR GABBY GOO GOO"

SIDE A:
1. Wiggle Wiggle
2. Handy Dandy
3. 2x2
4. Seven Deadly Sins
5. 10,000 Men
6. This Old Man

SIDE B:
1. TV Talkin' Song
2. If You Belonged To Me
3. Unbelievable
4. Like A Ship
5. Cat's In The Well
6. Froggie Went A-Courtin'

I did go a little out of strict chronology for this album. The closer, "Froggie Went A-Courtin'" was not recorded until the next album, *Good As I Been To You*. However, that song fits perfectly into my theme for this re-configured *Under The Red Sky*. While that album was dedicated to Dylan's four-year-old daughter, it is not quite kid's music like 1975's *The Johnny Cash Children's Album*. But there are plenty of songs like that recorded around this time. Why kids' band, The Wiggles, never covered "Wiggle Wiggle" is beyond me. Even the tune "Under The Red Sky" comes across like a nursery rhyme, although I didn't include that song because I thought it might be too slow for more restless kids. Maybe we can save that for the lullaby sequel.

I even put all the number songs ("2x2", "Seven Deadly Sins", "10,000 Men") all together on side one to help kids learn to count. Plus covers of well-known sing-alongs of "This Old Man" and "Froggie Went A-Courtin'". I doubt most kids would've actually enjoyed this CD in 1990, but then again most kids that age aren't picking out and buying their own music. So if the name on the cover (Bob Dylan) appealed to their parents, it might've been a best-seller. Not on the levels of Barney or Raffi, but it definitely could've warped a few young minds who would later go on to discover *Highway 61 Revisited* or *Blood On The Tracks*. While Rockabye Baby! Music has done lullaby rendition albums of everyone from Iron Maiden to Taylor Swift to Eminem to AC/DC, they have not yet attempted to cover Bob. Someone ought to get a hold of them and suggest it. It's got to do better than the *Lullaby Renditions of Nickelback*.

GOOD AS I BEEN TO YOU
Produced by: Debbie Gold
Recorded: July – August, 1992
Released: November 3rd, 1992
Famous/Important/Popular Track(s):
- Step It Up And Go

My Personal Favorite Track(s):
- Blackjack Davey
- Froggie Went A-Courtin'
- You Belong To Me

Prince has his *Black Album*. The Beach Boys have their *SMiLE*. Neil Young has dozens of records with names like *Chrome Dreams*, *Homegrown*, and *Toast*. Bob doesn't really have any complete albums just sitting in the vaults. Sure, there's plenty of outtakes sitting around for nearly every record he's made, complete with track-lists revised up to the last minute. But if Dylan starts a record, he will release it. The closest to an exception may be *The Basement Tapes* which wasn't really started as an album and did get an official release a mere eight years late.

The closest thing Bob may have in his catalog was recorded with David Bromberg in Chicago in 1992. This was the start of what eventually became *Good As I Been To You*, but none of these early tracks made their way onto the official album. Dylan had decided to take a little time crafting a follow-up to *Under The Red Sky* fearing that he would undo all the goodwill *Oh, Mercy* generated. However, even with two years to work on it, Bob had no new compositions to record. So instead, he took Bromberg's band and recorded a bunch of covers. The songs were allegedly mixed and ready to go when Dylan decided that a last-minute acoustic addition alá "Wedding Song" or "Dark Eyes" was needed. So Bob went home to Malibu to quickly lay down a few possible options alone in his home studio. Sometime during that process, Bob decided that these acoustic tracks were what he really wanted to do, scrapping all the Bromberg tracks and recording a whole new album of covers.

At some point, Dylan must've gotten cold feet; realizing that the only reason *Under The Red Sky* was not utterly reviled was merely because he had actually written a whole album again. Fearing that another covers record this soon after his "comeback" might drop his public standing back to *Down In The Groove* levels. If he was going to make another covers album, it would have to be special – or at least different.

So Bob decided to finally acquiesce to the demands of Pete Seeger and the folkies at Newport and go back to recording alone with an acoustic guitar. He hadn't done that since 1964's *Another Side* and hadn't done it with a bunch of folk tunes since his very first album. But there was a big difference between the 20-year-old who recorded *Bob Dylan* and the 51-

year-old who made *Good As I Been To You*. Despite his youth, Dylan had thoroughly, almost monomaniacally submerged himself in the old folk material. By 1992, the folk tune was just a couple of songs that were always slotted in during the newly birthed Never Ending Tour to give his backing band a breather. These acoustic mini-sets were eventually phased out of his concerts, but they were still a quick nod to the past that Bob felt compelled to include at the time.

As a result, Bob's first four and a half acoustic albums are gripping, intense, and interesting. *Good As I Been To You* (and its follow-up) are dull, drab and lifeless. In the overall scheme of Dylan's discography, with the benefit of hindsight, they are now considered an essential detour for Bob; a necessary respite while Dylan waited for his creative juices to rejuvenate, but not really something all that important to listen to on their own.

This album was "produced" by Debbie Gold, Bob's assistant. I'm not really sure what she did. This was recorded in Dylan's home studio, with just Bob, an engineer, and Debbie hanging around. Sounds like she was a surprised by her producer's credit as anyone else. The sound is clear, but there's really not much that anyone could've done to add (or subtract) much from these proceedings.

These may be important songs to Dylan personally, but it doesn't sound like he's really worked on them – or even thought about them much before trying them out in the studio. If I couldn't handle a solo album of acoustic folk tunes, I would have a hard time getting into Bob at all. But these two mid-nineties records can't hold a candle to anything from the first few acoustic entries. Even the debut, which is just as unoriginal, is so much more engaging than this album and the next one combined.

Frankie & Albert
(traditional, Arranged By Mississippi John Hurt)

Here we get to hear exactly how much and how little Bob Dylan has changed since his first album in 1961. His voice has grown a little wearier, much more nasal, and a lot less invested. His guitar playing has improved, but not significantly. This is an upbeat little number about the murder of a cheating lover. Bob is willing to let his guitar playing show a lot more than he was when he was 20. There are several breaks in this song, which has no harmonica, where Bob just lets his fingerpicking steal the show. Unfortunately, it's not much of a show to steal. While this is a thoroughly competent track, there is nothing in this performance to show how much love Bob reportedly have for this old songs.

Jim Jones
(traditional, arranged By Mick Slocum)

A traditional seafaring tale. Nothing terribly noteworthy or exciting about either this tune or this recording of this performance. It's pretty much a generic *Good As I Been To You* track. There's not even a guitar or harmonica solo. If you're not caught up in the story of the lyrics, there's not much else to pay attention to here. While inoffensive, there is nothing to make one come back to this track either. That's about all I have to say about "Jim Jones".

Blackjack Davey
(traditional, arranged By Bob Dylan)

A gripping tale of a woman who leaves her husband for a mysterious stranger. Of course, the term "woman" may be a bit much since she is only 15, but I guess that was far more common in the times this was written. Something about Bob's vocal delivery here fills this song with menace and dread. You can understand why a young girl would want to leave her stultifying life with a (presumably) much older man, even if she knows that she will inevitably be dooming herself in the process. Even the slip of the tongue from the servant that leads the husband to the interloping couple feels both inevitable and deeply tragic. I'm not really sure how the story ends – the husband finds her with the titular Davey, and then we go back in time to hear her being seduced into desertion. Despite abandoning her child, she has no regrets. I have no idea if he kills her or him or both of them die or if they escape or what. And for some reason, I don't mind. You know it's going to end badly; it's a folk song. What matters is the way Bob sings it. This is a mesmerizing performance. No harmonica or even really guitar solos. Just a dark, fascinating thrum. One of the best songs on either of Bob's 90s folk albums.

Canadee-i-o
(traditional, arranged By Bob Dylan)

A lovely melody with one high note that seems to be giving Dylan some trouble. It's your typical tale of a woman going in drag to sneak onto a boat. I think this was also the plot of *Mulan*. Bob gives this a well-intentioned reading but does nothing to really help distinguish this. The guitar playing is good, but not captivating. No harmonica here, although he does strum gamely through the chords of the verse to end the song. On an album like *Good As I Been To You*, with a limited instrumental palette, you have to work twice as hard to keep all the song from sounding the same. This track is not doing a lot to help that cause. While the Bromberg sessions may have been a bit of a bust, including at least a few of them would help stop all these songs from blending together.

Sittin' on Top of the World
(written by Walter Vinson and Lonnie Chatmon)

Bob's harmonica opens this blues song. It is so thoroughly "blues" that it almost feels like a parody. The lyrics are one of those "opposite day" type songs like "Oh! Susannah" you sometimes find in tunes of this vintage. The joke is of course that the singer feels really bad and does not think he's on top of the world. Bob sings this straight-laced and without any winking to the audience in his voice. This sort of undercuts the intentionally irony in the song and all we're left with is just a standard blues songs played alone on the acoustic guitar. Bob's playing is nimble but not very distinguished. This song might've felt more at home with more blues *World Gone Wrong* than the folk focused *Good As I Been To You*.

Little Maggie
(traditional, arranged By Bob Dylan)

A lot of the songs on this collection feature heroines who are taking the reins of their destiny despite being trapped in a time where such actions were undoubtedly frowned upon. I'm not sure if this was really deliberate on Bob's part, or if there just happens to be a lot of songs like this within the folk repertoire. It is unexpected for the time, which makes it an easy way to create drama or tension or interest in the listeners. The song itself is a respectable little up-tempo-ish tune with some nice minor chords and dexterous guitar work. It is definitely one of the shorter songs on here, which is nice. But it doesn't leave much of an impression. I'm not really sure who Maggie is or why she's drinking and carrying a gun, but it doesn't bother me too much either. Just another *Good As I Bee To You* song.

Hard Times
(written by Stephen Foster, arranged De Dannan)

The song has a little more personality and melody than your average folk song. Maybe that's because it really feels composed by a single auteur rather than passed down from generations of anonymous contributors. Not that Bob credited Stephen Foster when the album was first released. There's not a lot of fingerpicking on these acoustic albums, unfortunately, but Dylan does strum some of these chords in such a slow fashion that they almost turn into arpeggios. Unfortunately, they feel a little stiff and awkward. The lyrics are a complaint about one's life and an optimistic (desperate) plea for things to get better. Bob does better with this song as it has a more defined and specific melody. It could be a moving and depressing song if done right, but this version just feels like another unremarkable track on *Good As I Been To You*.

Step It Up and Go
(traditional, arranged By Bob Dylan)

One of the more fast-paced tracks on these acoustic folk albums. Bob almost cracks a smile here. The lyrics are pretty straightforward. Dylan does a respectable keeping up the energy on the guitar attempting a couple half-solos. He even lets out an occasional "woo" or "yeah" during these breakdowns. It's definitely a blues-based chord structure, but the melody is a little more folk-oriented. It's one of the shorter songs here, without a bunch of extra verses necessary to complete the tale. It's about as exciting as these two albums get, which still is a tad tepid, but it is nice to hear Bob enjoying himself a bit more. Not enough to change one's opinion of *Good As I Been To You*. In fact, the biggest drawback to the album is that none of the songs by themselves feel essential. You could remove any one of them, and the overall effect of the record would not change one iota.

Tomorrow Night
(written by Sam Coslow and Will Grosz, arranged by Bob Dylan)

While most of the songs on *Good As I Been To You* and *World Gone Wrong* fall into either the folk or blues category, this tune actually feels like one of those torch songs that pre-rock'n'roll singers used to croon before artists like Dylan rendered them obsolete. At the time, this might have seemed a little odd, but after a number of attempts to write his own torch ballad on *Love & Theft* and *Modern Times*, not to mention the whole Sinatra period, this song seems a little prescient. Granted it might be a little hard to discern under the acoustic guitar and harmonica trappings that makes this song sound like everything else on this album, but I think this may be Bob's inner Dean Martin finally coming out. Sure, he's attempted songs like "Some Enchanted Evening" or "This Was My Love", but none of these were ever under serious consideration to be officially released. All that being said, this is not a great song. It is different enough to add a bit of much-needed variety to *Good As I Been To You*. But given the similar template it's performed in, "Tomorrow Night" doesn't stand out that much. It's mostly only interesting for the way it illuminates recordings Bob would make in the next century.

Arthur McBride
(traditional, arranged by Paul Brady)

A lovely lilting folk waltz. The lyrics are about a guy and his cousin who went for a walk on Christmas and were accosted by a naval recruiter who was quite aggressive in his sales pitch. From here I'm not sure exactly what happens, but it sounds like things went badly, but there's pigs and a drummer involved. There's a lot of songs on this album about people joining the navy, which I guess happened a lot in folk songs. It's a perfectly adequate addition to this album, but like so much of *Good As I Been To You* as well as its follow-up, it all turns into a blur of folksy acoustic sameness.

You're Gonna Quit Me
(traditional, arranged By Bob Dylan)

A bluesy tune that probably sounds more like *World Gone Wrong* than *Good As I Been To You*, even though this is the song that gives that album its name. Bob is trying once again to impress with his guitar playing, trying to hold our interest while he plays the melody and the chords simultaneously while keeping his mouth shut. It doesn't add much to this song, although given how short this song is, it's not necessarily a bad thing. The "lord lord"s sung here are clearly meant as exclamatory and not religious. Who knows how the more didactic Dylan of *Slow train Coming* would've felt about this breaking of the third commandment. These are the things I think about while listening to this song because there's nothing in the song itself that really holds my attention. The lyrics are a typical "woe is me" song of love. Bob acquits himself nicely, but without distinction throughout. Luckily, we're getting close to the end of this album.

Diamond Joe
(traditional, arranged By Bob Dylan)

Not the traditional folksong recorded for the *Masked & Anonymous* soundtrack, but a whole different traditional folksong with the same title. Neither song is about "Diamond" Joe Quimby, the mayor character on *The Simpsons*. This "Diamond Joe" is about an extremely wealthy man who treats his workers very poorly, including the song's narrator. I'm not sure what line of work they're in (something about punching cattle), but he does sound like a horrible boss. While Bob sounded pissed off and outright defiant on "Maggie's Farm", here Dylan just sounds defeated and resigned to his fate. Again the song is just acoustic guitar and vocals, so nothing to really talk about there. It's pleasant enough track, but yet again, somewhat indistinguishable from the rest.

Froggie Went A-Courtin'
(traditional, arranged By Bob Dylan)

One of the more charming songs on *Good As I Been To You* is also the last. This is probably the only song on either of these albums that I was really familiar with. This song ties this album back to the children's songs and nursery rhymes of *Under The Red Sky*. Bob doesn't do anything fancy with this song other than sing through all nineteen verses of this song. This may include some of the best guitar playing on this album. When Bob finally wraps up with the verse about singing it yourself, he leaves plenty of space for the adventurous to do just that. Dylan manages to maintain the melody throughout that "solo" verse. This is the song with the most joy and humor on this album, something that Bob's previous all-acoustic album from the early sixties much more varied and exciting to listen to. No one is going to suspect Bob of doing a whole album like Raffi as his voice may actually scare small children. But if he did, I think it would be as warmly received as Pete Seeger's *American Folk Songs For Children*.

Songs not on the album:
You Belong To Me from the *Natural Born Killers* soundtrack
(written by Chilton Price, Pee Wee King, and Redd Stewart)

The best song recorded for *Good As I Been To You*, so of course it's not actually on the album. Perhaps, as I theorized, not being surrounded by a bunch of songs that sound the same helps make this track stand out. Of course, the tune is needless extended by Trent Reznor who copied and pasted some of Dylan's guitar playing and took out the vocals to make room for some dialogue from the film. But even this doesn't ruin the song. Heck, having something to change things up – even something as unrelated as Juliette Lewis and Woody Harrelson – helps liven things up. The song is still not very long, clocking in at just over three minutes. Bob's guitar playing is simple but evocative, and his singing is plaintive and carries some real longing. Why this track was cut is a mystery to me. Perhaps, unlike some of the other tracks on this album, Dylan would have a much harder time pretending that this was a public domain song, being a hit for Jo Stafford in 1952 as well as Pee Wee King. It's a shame that Bob left this off as it would've been a good substitute for almost anything else on the official album.

Miss The Mississippi from *The Bootleg Series vol. 8*
(written by Bill Halley)

Bob has re-configured his share of albums prior to release, re-doing half of *Blood On The Tracks*, etc. But rarely has he recorded an entire album only to throw it out completely to start again. The only real instance of that is the first version of *Good As I Been To You* recorded by David Bromberg with a full band. It was still going to be a collection of covers, although the inclusion of a couple of Bromberg originals makes this skew less to the strictly traditional folk template. There were twelve songs done and ready, most of which never got released. With hindsight, this might have been a smart commercial move overall. While the one-two punch of *Oh Mercy* And *The Traveling Wilburys, vol. 1* had garnered Dylan his best critical notices since he gave up Christianity, *Under The Red Sky* and *The Traveling Wilburys, vol. 3* had nearly undone all that goodwill. Had Bob released the original Bromberg album, which sounds and feels a lot like *Down In The Groove*, his late eighties comeback might have been seen as an anomaly and Dylan would've gone back to being written off. While the released version of *Good As I Been To You* may not have set the world afire, it was at least seen as an apology for that mid-'80s era instead of an extension of it. That being said, I like the few Bromberg tracks that have leaked out over the years. "Miss The Mississippi" is not a public domain song. It was written by Bill Halley (not Bill Halley of Bill Haley & The Comets) and first recorded by Jimmie Rodgers in 1932. This version starts off like a typical *Good As I Been To You* track with just a harmonica solo over Dylan's solo acoustic guitar.

After about thirty seconds, the band kicks in. We've got bass and drums, but the sound is still primarily acoustic. Most prominent in the arrangement is a lovely fluttering mandolin. Eventually, the dobro chimes in, and the overall tone for the first verse is somewhat reminiscent of *MTV Unplugged*. However, at this point, some lovely trombones begin wailing in the background sounding almost drunk. Unlike on *Shadows In The Night* they are not mixed to near inaudibility, although they don't do much by adding a little pad under the second verse before disappearing. This is a lovely little arrangement, showing off the ability to do a full band version of a folk album without resorting to the usual rock sound. It certainly adds more variety to the *Good As I Been To You* sound without betraying the album's intent or vitality.

Duncan And Brady from *The Bootleg Series vol. 8*
(traditional, arranged by Bob Dylan)

While "Miss The Mississippi" is full-banded yet acoustic, "Duncan And Brady" is definitely electric. Sure, there are acoustic guitars in here, but the lead slide guitar is what you remember. The organ stabs bring to mind those early-60s Dylan recordings. Those stop-time breaks with the kick drum keep things pummeling along nicely. The lyrics are similar to "Frankie & Albert", once again telling a story of cheating and murder. The pace may be a little too fast for Bob to truly invest the lyrics with as much emotion as some of the acoustic *Good As I Been To You* songs, but this is far more energetic and exciting. Maybe Bob was right, and a whole album like this would've been too much, and it needed to be cut with an acoustic track or two. But I think a balance could've been achieved rather than the dreary solo acoustic album we got. While we don't have a full release of all the Bromberg songs if they are all of similar quality it would be a terrific album. Considering this is one of the only two that were deemed worthy of release by Dylan & Co., so it's possible the rest are not nearly this good. Still even in the liner notes for *The Bootleg Series vol. 8*, author Larry Sloman calls for an official release of the rest of the Bromberg sessions.

Polly Vaughan officially unreleased
(traditional, arranged By Bob Dylan)

Another Bromberg session song with the more mandolin-led acoustic sound of "Miss The Mississippi". The appearance of the electric slide guitar is so loud as to be startling. Hopefully, that would've been mixed properly if this were officially released. The trombones that adorned "Miss The Mississippi" re-appear here, making one wonder if they were going to be a prominent feature of the entire Bromberg album. Again, they're not doing much by adding color; but oh what a lovely color! The lyrics tell the tale of some hunting accident where the ghost of the woman who accidentally mistaken for a swan and killed comes back to testify on the hunter's behalf in court. So, the usual folksong weirdness. Unfortunately, in order to get all this story told (as well as making room for several solos) extends this song slightly beyond the point of tedium. Still, it has a nice sound and feel to it. *Good As I Been To You* certainly would've benefited from more moments like this.

Sloppy Drunk officially unreleased
(written by Jimmie Rogers)

While the trombones sounded inebriated on "Miss The Mississippi", they are downright sloshed here. While we have the usual acoustic band with mandolin and slide guitar, this track manages to be quite funky. Perhaps some of the reason that Dylan decided to ditch the Bromberg version of *Good As I Been To You* is that he felt that arrangements like this were somewhat disrespectful to his beloved folk songs. Still, this song is so much more fun than the entire album as it was released put together. Sure, the word "sloppy" in the title is an appropriate description for the playing on this track, but I think that adds to this song immensely. It's a shame that we don't have a cleaned-up, legally available version of this recording because it is dynamite.

Catskills Serenade officially unreleased
(written by David Bromberg)

The longest and slowest of the Bromberg songs I've heard, it's not surprising that this is my least favorite. The horns are even more subliminal than ever on this track. This song is mostly dominated by the organ. There's also a melodica or something playing. It almost sounds like a harmonica, but given the fact that Bob is singing while it is playing, it must be something else. There are some nice flourishes on the mandolin, but it is also pretty sidelined on this song. Bromberg plays lead guitar without the slide. The song opens with just Dylan on harmonica and acoustic guitar. It even ends with what sounds like the band coming to the song's natural conclusion, but no one told Bob, so he keeps playing on harmonica by himself for nearly another verse after the song otherwise feels over. The lyrics apparently tell the story of a Rip Van Winkle character, but it seems kind of out-of-place amongst the more traditional folk tune recorded for this song. The 1976 original by David Bromberg is pretty sleepy yacht rock that still rocks harder than Dylan's version. It was generous of Bob to record a couple of songs from his producer's own pen for the original *Good As I Been To You*, but this just doesn't work. Still, it's more exciting than a whole album of Dylan alone in the nineties.

Other songs recorded with Dave Bromberg that are not circulating:
Nobody's Fault But Mine
(written by Blind Willi Johnson)
The Lady Came From Baltimore
(written by Tim Hardin)
Casey Jones
(traditional, arranged By Bob Dylan)
World Of Fools
(written by David Bromberg)
I'll Rise Again
(traditional, arranged By Bob Dylan)
Hey Joe
(written by Billy Roberts)
Northeast Texas Woman
(written by Willis Alan Ramsey)

These are the reported titles that Dylan and Bromberg recorded together in the early nineties. There's another Bromberg original included in there along with a couple of traditional tunes as well as some early blues and country numbers. I'm not sure if the "Casey Jones" here is the 1970 Grateful Dead song written by Jerry Garcia and Robert Hunter, or if it is "The Ballad of Casey Jones", the traditional song written around 1900. Either way, it's about a railroad engineer. The song "Hey Joe" is probably best known as being covered by Jimi Hendrix, even though it wasn't written by him. Much like "All Along The Watchtower". If Bob was planning on (belatedly) repaying Jimi's tip-of-the-hat, he certainly could've picked a song Hendrix wrote himself. Maybe Dylan is just more familiar with the original version. There's also a Tim Hardin song included here, albeit one that was also covered by Johnny Cash. Covering songs by lesser contemporaries like Tim Hardin and David Bromberg marks some of a return to *Self-Portrait*, where he covered Gordon Lightfoot and Paul Simon. Not only would the addition of a full band made for a more varied version of *Good As I Been To You*, but this also would've featured a lot broader spectrum of songs as opposed to only folk tunes that Bob could try to claim as public domain. Who knows what all these arrangements sounded like or how many of these tracks featured trombones, but I'm guessing that overall, the Bromberg version would have been a much less critic-pleasing, but more personally exciting album.

See the entry on Page 342

WORLD GONE WRONG
Produced by: Bob Dylan
Recorded: May 1993
Released: October 26th, 1993

Famous/Important/Popular Track(s):
- Blood In My Eyes

My Personal Favorite Track(s):
- Love Henry
- Broke Down Engine
- Delia

What is there to say about *World Gone Wrong* that wasn't already said about *Good As I Been To You*? Bob had figured out a new way to avoid writing any new material or spending much time in the studio and still be able to crank out product for the record-buying public. They ate it up (or at least accepted it with minimal fuss) last time, so why not just do it again?

There are those who are more familiar with this material who can tell you that this album has more blues and fewer folk songs than the last one, but the point is pretty moot since they both sound the same. At least *Good As I Been To You* had surprise or novelty on its side. There's not even the scrapped Bromberg session to talk about here. The two pluses on *World Gone Wrong*'s side is that it is shorter, having only ten songs instead of 13; and it features some hilarious, inaccurate rambling linear notes by Dylan, while *Good As I Been To You* had not notes or credits at all really.

This is the last album Bob produced under his own name, although apparently, Debbie Gold was still on hand providing as much "production" as she had on *Good As I Been To You*. I'm not quite sure why the change in producer credits.

This is a tough album to write about because it feels like there's so little to say and I've already had to say it so often with the last entry. While the mid-80s period often gets lambasted for being half-hearted and tossed-off, for my money there's a lot more interesting moments on *Knocked Out Loaded* or *Down In The Groove* than are to be found on either of these two albums.

Oh well. Let's get this over with.

World Gone Wrong
(traditional, arranged By Bob Dylan)

A surprisingly slow-paced song to kick off an album. This track is noticeably more blues than the folk of *Good As I Been To You*. The guitar playing is even stiffer this time around, but it definitely sounds like he's not trying to impress as much as he was with the last album. He usually fluffs the little run he throws in at the end of each verse. Otherwise, this song is mostly pretty much strummed. His vocals seem even less invested this time around. Not a particularly encouraging start for this album.

Love Henry
(traditional, arranged By Bob Dylan)

It's the age-old story: "Girl meets Boy. Boy spurns girl for another love and then goes to sleep. Girl murders boy before he can return to his other girlfriend. Girl attempts to bribe her pet bird to keep it silent." You know, that old tale. When Dylan and others talk about the murky strangeness of the traditional folksongs, it is lyrics like this that they are referring to. For as many strange turns of events as there are in this song, Bob sings this with real sympathy and sadness. It is a surprisingly effective recording. The guitar playing is nice with a solo that is half single note melody and half strumming through the chords of the verse. There's no harmonica here. It's a relatively short song. One of the best on *World Gone Wrong*.

Ragged & Dirty
(traditional, arranged By Bob Dylan)

A quick upbeat blues song, with Bob doing a great job holding together the central lick throughout the song although he does botch it once or twice. The lyrics are your typical "woe is me" stuff. Dylan does a pretty good job of singing this, but it doesn't really connect with me. Still no harmonica playing, which seems like it would be a natural fit for Bob Dylan playing a blues song. While there's not much to this song, it wins points for its lively pace and for being relatively brief.

Blood in My Eyes
(traditional, arranged By Bob Dylan)

Another blues song, this time at a much slower pace. It almost brings to mind "It Takes A Lot To Laugh, I Takes A Train To Cry". While most of the song revolves around the same circular chord sequence, Bob does throw in a bit of bridge at some point to help and even switch from just strumming the chords to an attempt at a single note solo to try and break things up. The song is a little stiff in places, but it is a brave and sincere attempt on Dylan's part. Overall though this feels like just another *Good As I Been To You*/*World Gone Wrong* track, even though for some reason a full-blown music video has actually filmed and released for this particular song. If you like watching Dylan in black & white wander around some city while wearing a top hat and gloves while occasionally lip-syncing, this is the video for you.

Broke Down Engine
(written by Blind Willie McTell)

Bob is finally recording Blind Willie McTell, the songwriter not the song. This is a fast little blues number. Despite the limited options of just acoustic guitar and voice, Bob throws in some actually knocking on his guitar to accompany the line about knocking on his door. It's funny how big of a difference that one little gesture makes. In a pair of albums with only a limited spectrum, every little bit counts. Bob sings this song well and plays it superbly. It also helps that this is not a very long song. While definitely still the blues, this song is a lot more jovial an upbeat than most of the tracks on *World Gone Wrong*. More fast numbers like this might've helped liven up this record.

Delia
(traditional, arranged By Bob Dylan)

One of the more folky, less bluesy, songs on this album. The refrain running through this song is "all the friends I ever had are gone" which is a pretty bleak statement. Once again, some poor girl gets shot to death for some reason. Bob sings this song with sadness in his heart that it helps this song stand out a little. Not a lot, but it's something. Bob plays another guitar "solo" that isn't much more than the chords of verse without singing on top of them. I was not surprised to learn that Johnny Cash recorded a version (or four) of this song. It seems right up his alley. Bob does fine with it, but this song tends to blend in with the rest of these songs.

Stack A Lee
(traditional, arranged By Frank Hutchison)

A song about killing a man over a hat. Seriously. I don't think there's any way that I am misinterpreting these lyrics. Weird. This song also seems to be stepping away from the more blues-centric matrix that most of *World Gone Wrong* is working in. As a result, it's almost a nice change of pace. The harmonica on here is almost jolly. Bob, however, fails to inject any humor into these obviously silly lyrics. He mostly just growls. It's kind of disappointing. This song could certainly be done with a sense of humor or at least a gleam in the eye. Instead, Bob takes this as seriously as all the other dour tracks on this album. The song is done at a nice clip, although once or twice Dylan falters to keep up with the unrelenting pace of the guitar. Better than a lot of *World Gone Wrong* songs, but that's not saying much.

Two Soldiers
(traditional, arranged By Bob Dylan)

This song has a pleasant 3/4 feel to it. The melody is strong and heartbreaking. Bob's voice cracks on occasion adding some poignancy to the entire performance. The lyrics are the usual affair of tragic death and the grief of those left behind. Separated out of *World Gone Wrong* this song might've been able to generate some resonance. It's just after several songs in this milieu (especially if you listened to *Good As I Been To You* just prior to this album) it blunts the potential impact this song might have. Of course, Bob released several songs of nothing but acoustic guitar and voice to start his career and didn't begin to suffer this kind of fatigue. Perhaps I just don't love traditional folk songs as much as Dylan, and so they all start to blend together to me. Bob's originals at least had some personality and diversity to them that helped keep things from feeling too stagnant. I really tried to like this song, but I just got worn down. In this way, it is emblematic of Dylan's early 90s folk period in miniature.

Jack-A-Roe
(traditional, arranged By Bob Dylan)

A much darker minor-key song than most of the 90s folk albums. Bob's vocals are spine-chilling. It's a creepy cool song, that would be a nice change of pace if it weren't stuck in the middle of a bunch of other songs that are just acoustic guitar and voice. As such, it becomes just another *World Gone Wrong* track. Bob attempts his most complicated guitar solo yet and almost pulls it off. It's another tragic tale of forbidden love, sailors, murder, fathers and daughters. Sadly, by this point in the album, I'm too burned out to pay enough attention to figure out what is really going on in the plot. The words just envelop me in a wash of typical folksong phrases. There are some songs from these two albums that I do enjoy when they pop up randomly on shuffle. Divorced from its context, this might be one of my favorite tracks from this period. Maybe I simply lack the ability to appreciate the subtlety and nuance here, but I'm starting to get burned out from these songs.

Lone Pilgrim
(written by Adger M. Pace, B.F. White)

A song about a guy who goes to a cemetery and hears a ghost telling him that he doesn't mind being dead. There's no indication as to whether the pilgrim in question is a good or bad person or if he's in heaven or what. There's little religion here although he does mention that his "master compelled him home." Dylan of '79-81 would've definitely emphasized the life-after-death theme. Instead the lesson this song seems to be that "don't worry about death, it's no biggie". Kind of an odd note for this album to go out on, although putting this song anywhere else on the album makes it very hard for any song going after to carry any heft since death itself is inevitable and somewhat trivial. Bob clearly is singing far more from the ghost's perspective than that of the guy who stumbled upon his tomb. Oddly enough the pilgrim's message is not even meant for the guy hearing it as much as it is for his wife and kids whom he left behind. It's an adequate song, surprisingly tender and thankfully brief. If the whole 90s folk album period had been cut down to a single EP of 4 to 6 songs, it might've kept all the tracks from running together, but here at the end of it all, it's hard to remember anything specific that we just heard.

Songs not on the album:
32-20 Blues from *The Bootleg Series vol. 8*
(written by Robert Johnson)

The songs of Robert Johnson are far more individually composed and wrapped up in the persona of the songwriter than the average quote-unquote traditional tune from these two albums. Even songs by Blind Willie McTell or Stephen Foster seem far more public domain than those of Robert Johnson. It may be because of this that "32-20 Blues" was left off of *World Gone Wrong*. Which is a shame, because this does of individuality is what those two records lacked and sorely missed. While nowhere as good as Bob's unreleased version of "Milk Cow Blues" from *The Freewhelin' Bob Dylan* sessions, this is a nice change of pace. Bob doesn't have a tenth of Robert Johnson's technical virtuosity on the guitar, but he plays its pretty straight here avoiding embarrassing himself too much. The lyrics here are far more cold-blooded and gruesome in a way that all the murders described in the traditional tunes can't achieve. While the addition of this track would not have changed my overall opinion of the album substantially, it is a shame that it had to wait until *The Bootleg Series vol. 8* to finally see release.

Mary And The Soldier from *The Bootleg Series vol. 8*
(traditional, arranged by Bob Dylan)

Another outtake from *World Gone Wrong*. This one is far more folk than blues. As usual, the lyrics concern the story of a military man. The chords and tune are bright, but Bob's voice sounds a bit melancholy here. I'm not quite sure why this song got passed over. There is plenty of room for it; *World Gone Wrong* only had ten songs while *Good As I Been To You* could accommodate thirteen. Not that I'm overly upset, both albums feel too long with their repetitive soundscapes, but I don't see the logic behind Dylan's decision to exclude it. It's not better or worse or even noticeably different from the rest of the album. Certainly, other tracks would need to be cut and replaced with "32-20 Blues" if Bob wanted this to be an all-blues collection. Whatever his reasoning, I'm glad to be done with Dylan's solo-acoustic '90s retreat.

Boogie Woogie Country Girl from *Till The Night Is Gone: A Tribute To Doc Pomus*
(written by Jerome "Doc" Pomus and Reginald Ashby)

After doing two albums of traditional folk tunes, Bob wasn't quite done in the studio covering other's material. Here he recorded a somewhat obscure track for a tribute album to early rock songwriter Doc Pomus. The song itself is not terribly complicated, being just a 12 bar blues played in a rock format with some ridiculously simple lyrics. Still, it's nice to hear Bob recording with a band again. I think this is one of the first instances of Bob recording with his backing band from the Never Ending Tour. This is the kind of song these musicians could play in their sleep. Luckily they're at least half awake for this. This is one hundred times more exciting than anything off of *World Gone Wrong* or *Good As I Been To You*, but is not all that memorable. Bob doesn't have nearly the attack of Big Joe Turner's or Mickie Muster's versions. There's no boogie-woogie or rockabilly on display here. Still, it's a step up from another acoustic song.

My Blue Eyed Jane from *The Songs Of Jimmie Rodgers - A Tribute*
(written by Jimmie Rogers)

One of the only album released on Bob's Egyptian Records label was this tribute to Jimmie Rogers. Needless to say, Dylan recorded a track for this compilation. It's a charming country trifle. While not going overboard with the country music trappings as he did on *Nashville Skyline* it's nice to hear an older, ragged voiced Dylan take on this type of material. There's another take of this song circulating with a mystery female vocalist on it that less dark, dreary, and portentous, although the arrangement on both takes is relatively similar with some prominent pedal steel playing. Either way, this song is much livelier and more cheerful than most of the blues covers recorded for *World Gone Wrong*. This song was recorded at the same sessions that produced "Boogie Woogie Country Girl". Both were always intended as tribute album contributions, but Dylan did also run through Gordon Lightfoot's "I'm Not Supposed To Care", Elvis Presley's 1959 hit "One Night Of Sin", and Barbecue Bob's old folk-blues song "Easy Rider (Don't Deny My Name)". Perhaps a more full-band country-and-rock flavored follow-up was initially planned after *World Gone Wrong* but was eventually scrapped, due to the underwhelming response to Dylan's second record of covers in a row. Or maybe these songs were all intended for tribute albums which never materialized. Either way, this batch of songs would've made for an fascinating sequel to the *Self-Portrait II* that Bob considered recording before ending up with *Down In The Groove*.

Any Way You Want Me officially unreleased
(written by Aaron Schroeder and Clyde Otis)

Recorded September 30th, 1994 for an Elvis tribute album that never materialized. With prominent slide guitar, the track feels very similar in texture to the David Bromberg sessions for *Good As I Been To You* although it was actually produced by Don Was. The song itself is pretty typical of the slow-burning 6/8 ballads that Elvis cut. The instrumentation is simple and stripped down, but Bob gives a fierce vocal performance. It's not as bizarre or fascinating as Dylan's attempts to do Elvis on the 1973 album *Dylan*. Still, it's nice to hear Bob revert to his childhood self in an effort to emulate one of his earliest heroes. It makes a good companion to "My Blue Eyed Jane" and "Boogie Woogie Country Girl". It's too bad that when

Bob finally did his whole reverting to his youth album, it was "all Sinatra, all the time." I think a Dylan rockabilly album would have been fascinating to hear. Maybe he will still do that someday.

Lawdy Miss Clawdy officially unreleased
(written by Lloyd Price)

Another song from the session that produced "Any Way You Want Me" for the aborted Elvis tribute album. The version that has leaked out on bootlegs sounds badly mixed as if we're missing some elements of the tapes. This is a much more up-tempo song than "Any Way You Want Me" although Bob tackles it with the same slower 6/8 ballad feel. Still, Dylan really snarls through the lyric and gives a great performance. Although the track falls apart before really finishing, with less than two-and-a-half minutes we almost get a worthy successor to the Bob-doing-Elvis of "Can't Help Falling In Love". It's a shame we don't have a fuller sounding complete take of this song.

"GOOD AS THE WORLD GONE WRONG"

1. Duncan And Brady
2. People Get Ready
3. You Belong To Me
4. Polly Vaughn
5. Boogie Woogie Country Girl
6. Broke Down Engine

SIDE B:
1. Miss The Mississippi
2. Blackjack Davey
3. Ring Of Fire
4. My Blue Eyed Jane
5. 32-20 Blues
6. Sloppy Drunk

For me, *Good As I Been To You* and *World Gone Wrong* are pretty interchangeable, so mashing the two of them together is no big surprise. However, by limiting oneself to just those two albums, you end up with the same problem of a monotonously consistent tone. To keep from just having another solo acoustic album long after Bob lost his ability to make such things varied and interesting, we need to start including other tracks recorded around this time. Luckily or not, Dylan was in the midst of a writer's block at the time, so there's really no way to compile this album without making it all covers. One place to start are the sessions recorded by David Bromberg in Chicago that were initially supposed to be the meat of the first album. From those I've included four of the five known outtakes, skipping "Catskills Serenade".

However, just using that quartet along with the cherry-picked best of the two released folk albums adds up to a jarring, uneven listen. I've also included a bunch of songs from the various tribute album Bob contributed to in the nineties. This definitely adds to the variety of the record.

As for the acoustic numbers, I have just included one from each (*Good As I Been To You*'s "Blackjack Davey" and *World Gone Wrong*'s "Broke Down Engine") in addition to my two favorite outtakes (*Good As I Been To You*'s "You Belong To Me" and *World Gone Wrong*'s "32-20 Blues"). I toyed with the idea of bifurcating the acoustic songs to side two and the band songs on band one, as I had on *Shelter From A Simple Twist In Blue* and *Watching My Masterpiece Flow*, but even half-an-album of these particular acoustic tracks ends up sounding sort of samey. Instead, I decided to place the tracks every third song or so. I think it all flows pretty well.

While recording an album like this might not have charged up Dylan's songwriting batteries as much as what he did end up releasing, I think this is a far more enjoyable listen. Goofy, but enjoyable. Others might condemn it as something of a throwback to the *Self-Portrait part II* sounds of the *Down In The Groove* era, but for me, this is what I'm looking for.

TIME OUT OF MIND
Produced by: Daniel Lanois
Recorded: January 1997
Released: September 30th, 1997

Famous/Important/Popular Track(s):
- Make You Feel My Love
- Love Sick
- Not Dark Yet

My Personal Favorite Track(s):
- 'Til I Fell In Love With You
- Cold Irons Bound
- Dreamin' Of You

Bob may have found a more effective way to tread water with his mid-90s folk albums without alienating his audience like *Knocked Out Loaded* and *Down In The Groove* did. However, he was still going to need another *Oh Mercy* type of comeback if he wanted to remain seen as a current artist and not just a nostalgia act. So he went back to the *Oh Mercy* drawing boards and plucked the two most important lessons: write the whole album yourself and get Daniel Lanois to produce it. And boy howdy, did Lanois produce this. It's no wonder that this was the last album where Dylan let an outsider produce his own record. From here on out, Bob was going to have to take self-producing seriously, even if it did mean using the silly alias of Jack Frost.

In some ways, this album is just a cynically commercial as *Empire Burlesque*, the main difference being that *Time Out Of Mind* actually succeeded in its ambitions. The reason for this may be that *Empire Burlesque* sounds like a record that should've been a hit at the time, no matter who recorded it; while *Time Out Of Mind* sounds like an album that should be a hit for Bob Dylan no matter when it was recorded.

Of course, the other thing that really helped push this album to "comeback" status was a complete accident on Dylan's part: nearly dying. I'm not sure how serious the incident was – or if it was merely over-dramatized much like the '66 motorcycle accident, but it did have journalists and pundit began prematurely penning Bob's obituary. And you just can't buy hype and goodwill like that.

As for the album itself, the fact that many of the lyrics seemed morbid or at least about death probably helped sales as well, even if it was a complete coincidence.

Ultimately what you get is an album that sounds like it's trying just a little too hard to sound like what fans would want from a "Bob Dylan" album. It clocks in at only a minute shorter than *Blonde On Blonde*, but because this is the era of the compact disc, it comes at you in one single piece of plastic instead of being broken up into four sides of vinyl.

Everything on this album sound designed to remind you of how big and important Dylan is. Or was.

I guess that's my biggest problem with this album, it's a little too eager to please. Much like *Oh Mercy*, it is an album I feel like I generally enjoy in total, but when I look too closely at it, there's only a handful of songs that really stand-up for me.

Still, it's an essential album in Dylan's career. After this album (and attendant death scare) critics were far too wary ever to pan another Bob album, lest it turns out to be his swan song. Over the following years, Bob has occasionally hidden behind this critical blank check to coast a little, while occasionally abusing this goodwill to make a few more experimental pieces (the Christmas album and the Sinatra trilogy) that still managed to get grudgingly positive reviews despite occasionally testing the patience of the record-buying public.

Love Sick
(written by Bob Dylan)

This song starts out with nothing but stabs from an organ and Bob's heavily processed vocals. A few guitar fills organically grow out around this. The bass shows up to help the organ realize that it's time to change chords. By the second verse, the instrumentation has grown much fuller – there are even some drums buried in the mix towards the end of this verse. By the time chorus hits, there's a driving electric guitar which retreats once the verse returns. Despite the overdone filters on Dylan's vocals, you can still hear the hurt and frustration in his voice. The swampy sounds and production instantly bring to mind Lanois's work on *Oh Mercy*. There's a solo section where nothing is really turned up enough in the mix to feel like it's taking the lead. While the pace is languid, there is a real sense of anxiety and menace to this track that makes it an ideal opener for *Time Out Of Mind*. The song ends with a half-verse that encapsulates all of Bob's frustration and resignation on this track.

Dirt Road Blues
(written by Bob Dylan)

One of the shorter *Time Out Of Mind Tracks*. The organ on this track is charmingly cheap sounding. Bob's singing is excellent, but there's an effect on his voice that makes it sound like it's being broadcast from somewhere else. Other than that Lanois really dials back the atmospherics on this track. That's a good call since this song doesn't really need that kind of gloom and murk, nor would it really be able to justify it. The lyrics are very typical standard blues; as is the simple three-chord structure of the music. There seems to be some confusion as to which guitarist is supposed to be taking the solo, so you end up having two going on simultaneously, neither one of which quite commanding our attention. It's a minor piece, but on an album filled with apocalyptic epics, it's a nice change of pace. However coming second it seems a little early for a reprieve. This is the kind of up-tempo blues song that Dylan's touring band could probably do in their sleep by now, and this track probably has far more of them than Lanois' usual studio musicians.

Standing in the Doorway
(written by Bob Dylan)

A sad, slow song that verges on being whiny. The swirling organ holds the piece together like glue, while there's some riffing from a couple guitars. Bob's voice is extra phlegmy here. But that works quite well for this song. The lyrics are again focused on regrets and disappointments. Like most of the songs on this album, it runs a little long. There's no real change of pace here. There's a couple of holes in the song between a few of verses that sound like invitations for someone to take a solo, but no one ever does, and eventually, Bob returns to singing. The biggest surprises are how he's going to finish the last line of each verse that starts with the title. It doesn't even end, it just sort of fades out as the band is finally getting to play around with the only real chord change in the song. It's just a little too sleepy and a little too long for an album that already has plenty of songs with those tendencies.

Million Miles
(written by Bob Dylan)

A creepy mid-tempo blues song with a hint of shuffle. The lyrics are typical blues fare. I do like the line about looking for a janitor to "sweep me off my feet". Sure, this could stand to be edited down by a minute or two, but isn't annoying as some of the *Time Out Of Mind* songs. There's not even an ending to this song, it just fades out. The guitars and organ never stop fiddling away in the background, never rising to the point of being either adding or detracting from the song. Just part of the usual Daniel Lanois fog laid on all his songs. When one of the guitars finally does take a solo at center stage than choose to confine themselves to only a few repeated notes. I would much rather herear this semi-original blues song with a full band than anything off of *World Gone Wrong*.

Tryin' to Get to Heaven
(written by Bob Dylan)

If Bob doesn't get to heaven before they close the door, will he have to knock, knock, knock? This song almost feels like one of *Empire Burlesque*'s power ballads only without Arthur Baker's production to save it. This is kind of a boring, slow song. The lyrics seemed to be concerned with an impending mortality. These are words that should be inspiring a fierce vocal performance from Bob, but he just sounds phlegmy here. The harmonica solo is a nice change of pace from the otherwise standard playing here. The organ sounds good here but isn't doing much. The slashes from the electric guitar are a little distracting. Nothing much happens in this song. Not one of the stronger *Time Out Of Mind* songs.

Til I Fell in Love with You
(written by Bob Dylan)

Another blues pastiche with lots of Daniel Lanois's touches. There's some very tremolo-guitar on here as well as some half-funky electric piano. The song is the usual, "loving you makes me sad" type of blues. Bob could do this kind of song in his sleep, which is almost what it feels like he's doing here. It's not bad, per se; just nothing happens. There's little-to-no variation going on here. It's got a nice feel to it, but no matter how great the groove is, it's bound to get old. Especially with a song as slow and long as this one. The only real exciting part is the keyboard solo that comes at the very end and gets faded out on. Overall, *Time Out Of Mind* feels like a great album, but when you actually take the record apart and look at the songs individually, there are just too many songs like this one that just pads out the already overlong running time of this album.

Not Dark Yet
(written by Bob Dylan)

Before "Make You Feel My Love" was championed by Garth Brooks, Billy Joel, and Adele, this was the big song off of *Time Out Of Mind*. It's another song taken at a glacial pace. The acoustic guitar sounds nice and bright in here. The lyrics could be seen as centering around thoughts about one's imminent demise. Thanks to the health scare that predated and promoted this album, that was a subject matter most critics and fans wanted to hear on *Time Out Of Mind*. Truth is Bob probably wasn't thinking about that, but that does help justify Dylan's super-weary vocal approach. The song is pleasant enough, but lack the liveliness to be any sort of anthem. As usual, the solo seems to be composed of several instruments timidly throwing out riffs simultaneously since no one has actually been designated as the soloist. The yawning bowed upright and held organ chords give this song a nearly droney feel. The drums sound very muted and powerless here. The swampy production is definitely in full force here. I think the song could've been tightened up quite a bit, but right now feels a little blah. Not bad, just hard to get excited about.

Cold Irons Bound
(written by Bob Dylan)

Along with "Love Sick" and "Not Dark Yet", this is one of the big songs that was pushed from *Time Out Of Mind*. Feel to it. Bob's ragged vocals sell this song. The track has a nice swampy groove courtesy of

Daniel Lanois. Bob himself may have seen this song as more of a straightforward rocker. The live in-studio version that Bob re-did for the soundtrack to his movie *Masked & Anonymous* strips away the layers of murk and reveals an even more muscular recording of this song. That version is a lot more fun, but I miss the mystery and slinkiness of the original. The two versions aren't really that different ultimately, although Bob sounds more feisty in 2003 than he did when he first recorded it. Sure the song doesn't need to be over seven minutes, especially with an intro that is mostly studio noodling before the bass kicks in. It is the surprising funky bass that is the hero of this song. It's a lot faster of a song than it seems at first. The lyrics are again about the futility of love as well the futility of trying to avoid love. While critics would like to see this album as a meditation on mortality in the face of a near-fatal incident, this song is one of the most focused on romantic themes (and the breakdown of such relationships) since *Blood On The Tracks*. Who knows why this was so much on Bob's mind at this point, but it does add an extra layer of urgency to many of the best *Time Out Of Mind* tracks. And this is one of the best tracks on that album.

Make You Feel My Love
(written by Bob Dylan)

Despite trying to push "Not Dark Yet", "Love Sick", and "Cold Irons Bound" as the big songs from this album, it is this unassuming little ballad that broke out from *Time Out Of Mind*. Much like the Dylan of old, this song rose to prominence, not because of Bob's original recording but rather the covers that have appeared in its wake. In some ways, this song is an anomaly on the album. A straightforward pop ballad with a positive spin on romance in the lyrics as opposed to the dirge-y cantankerous heart-broken songs that fill the remainder of the album. It is a well-written song, even if it doesn't really fit here. The arrangement here is piano-based with an organ filling in these on the top and a minimal bass swooping around the bottom. The melody is so strong, you can see why it immediately started attracting singers whose vocals weren't as phlegmy as Dylan's. Much like the folk-rock hits of the 60s though, Bob's original trumps any later cover of the song. Adele, Garth Brooks, and Billy Joel sing this too sweetly, too sincerely. While the lyrics are hopeful that the singer can prove his love to the object of his affection, Bob's voice makes it clear that he has already tried and failed in this endeavor many times. This dark, frustrated undercurrent is what keeps this song from being pure pabulum. Still, it is an oasis of optimism compared to its surroundings. While this should provide something of a palliative to the overwhelming gloom of the rest of the record, it ends up coming off as a little insincere. Not that I think Bob was being deliberately calculating in trying to write the kind of pop standard that this song unexpectedly became, but it does feel very out-of-character. Not only for *Time Out Of Mind* but for Bob Dylan himself.

Can't Wait
(written by Bob Dylan)

Despite the title, this is a song about frustration and not anticipation. Bob has released three different studio versions of this song, one on *Time Out Of Mind* and two more outtakes on *The Bootleg Series vol. 8*. The version in B-flat is pretty cool, cocky and rocking. The fact that Bob offhandedly announces what key he wants to try it in right before launching into the tune certainly adds to its coolness factor. That version is led by the piano and the electric guitar providing a nice counterpoint. It sounds like Daniel Lanois hasn't quite added all of his usual production to this, although there is a subtle, slow maraca played by someone on here. The other version on *The Bootleg Series vol. 8*, is so much slower that it takes the running time from 5:45 to seven-and-a-half minutes. This version of "Can't Wait" is super-spooky and spectral. Usually a longer, slower version of any Dylan song annoys the heck out of me, but I really like the feel of this take. It almost has the dread of a scene from a classic David Lynch movie. The officially released version is taken at about the same tempo as the first version, coming in just three seconds longer, but retains some of the creepiness from the second unreleased version. It is a good compromise, although I wish Bob weren't so indecisive. The song is basically another in the three-chord blues matrix, although there is a bridge where an acoustic guitar sneaks in on the first version. It may not be particularly unusual, but it's got more of a gleam in its eye than many of the *Time Out Of Mind* tracks. This may not be a masterpiece, but this is one of the few tracks where the usual *Time Out Of Mind* strengths manage to overwhelm the many faults of this album. Of course, deciding which version you prefer may be a tough decision.

Highlands
(written by Bob Dylan)

The longest Dylan song ever! Astute readers can probably surmise how I would feel about this track by now. I am not a fan. The whole interaction with the waitress could be entertaining by itself in a deliberately mundane slice-of-life sort of way, but it takes forever to get there, and I don't even remember what all goes on before or after it. The song is tedious. There's a cool (albeit cheap) sounding organ in there that I like. The same musical phrase is repeated indefinitely for sixteen-and-a-half minutes. There's no real melody here, Bob just reciting verses in a rhythmic manner. Neil Young and Erica Jong get named-checked here as does Billy Joe Shaver. It almost feels like a John Cage experiment or Andy Warhol's 8-hour film of the Empire State Building, but not as daring. It's not even really supposed to experimental. Dylan obviously thinks someone would want to listen to all this. And he's right, a lot of people do. But I am not one of them. Even if you were to cut ten minutes from this song, it still wouldn't be terribly interesting to me.

Songs not on the album:
Mississippi released on *Love & Theft*
(written by Bob Dylan)

A song recorded (and recorded and recorded) for *Time Out Of Mind* before being left off. It was re-recorded four years later, by which time Sheryl Crow had released her version on the album *The Globe Sessions*. In this way, it is reminiscent of the how that "Mr. Tambourine Man" was a hit for The Byrds before Bob could get his own recording of this out there. On *Time Out Of Mind*, this song sticks out like a sore thumb. For many fans, it's their favorite on that 2001 album, but for me, it always seemed out of place, neither a jazz-inflected torch ballad or a blues-based rock tune. Clearly, Dylan and Lanois weren't sure how to approach the song in 1997. Of the three versions included on *The Bootleg Series vol. 8* none of them stand out as the definitive version. Some are a little more acoustic, others have more atmospherics applied, but they all are about the same. They are all taken at about the same tempo with the same lazy off-hand approach. One lacks drums, the other has a particularly prominent upright bass part. By the time of *Time Out Of Mind*, the song is played with more of a jaunty swing. More strummed guitars and certainly a perkier tempo. All of this helps to alleviate the sense of boredom and portentousness that invade the unreleased versions of the song. The lyrics are aiming for a sort of "I'm a rambler, I'm a gambler" vibe without any of the specific to indicate why returning to this particular state was a bad idea. Is there a warrant out or are there bad influences he is likely to fall back in with? Nothing is stated for sure. While the song does ramble on a bit, it is certainly less aimless than some of the stuff that did make the cut for *Time Out Of Mind*. On that album "Mississippi" is a winner; on *Love & Theft*, it's a drag.

Ring Of Fire from the *Feeling Minnesota* soundtrack
(written by June Carter and Merle Kilgore)

Before Bob had wholly given up on a career as a cover artist and started writing songs for *Time Out Of Mind*, he did head into the studio and record a new version of this song for the otherwise forgettable Keanu Reeves vehicle *Feeling Minnesota*. This is nothing like the country fried version Dylan attempted in Nashville for *Self-Portrait* before decided to leave it off. This really shows where Bob was headed before he decided to step back up to the plate with *Time Out Of Mind*. The production here is pretty sterile, although there is a sweet acoustic guitar solo. The backing vocalists who have plagued all his recording since *Street Legal* are back in evidence after being MIA for the acoustic folk albums. Bob's vocals come off a little wheezy, if sincere. Of all the Johnny Cash songs that Dylan has recorded over the years, he has tended to pick the bigger, more obvious hits. This is definitely a song that has already been done to death, but Bob seems like he's having a much better time singing this than he is on anything off of *Time Out Of Mind*. It may not be worth the effort it takes to track down this soundtrack, but if you happen to run into it at a used CD store at a reasonable price, it is worth picking up.

Red River Shore from *The Bootleg Series vol. 8*
(written by Bob Dylan)

Another long and languid track from the *Time Out Of Mind* sessions. This song drags a bit but isn't nearly as annoying as "Standing In The Doorway". Two versions of this song eventually sneaked out on *The Bootleg Series vol. 8*. One version is about what you would expect with echo-y electric guitars and the usual Lanois production touches. That version has some nice organ in it that feels almost like an accordion. However, the second version definitely features a very prominent accordion. With its half-Tejano feel, it almost could be slotted into the accordion-heavy *Together Through Life*. Other than that, the two versions are pretty similar, with the accordion version winning out just by dint of novelty. The song itself is okay. There's a bit of the faux-international feel of *Desire* on this track. The lyrics are convoluted, but Dylan's singing doesn't convey anything extra to their meaning. I'm assuming it's about a woman he used to know and is now missing, but what do I know? Maybe if it were a little shorter or faster, this would be a much stronger contender for the album, although there are definitely worse songs that did make the cut. It certainly would've helped increase the quotient of variety on *Time Out Of Mind*.

Dreamin' Of You from *The Bootleg Series vol. 8*
(written by Bob Dylan)

The "single" from *The Bootleg Series vol. 8*. It's easy to see why this was chosen. It's even harder to understand why it was left off of *Time Out Of Mind*. A slinky cousin to "Love Sick" and "Cold Irons Bound", *Time Out Of Mind* could've used a lot more songs with this kind of excitement and energy. The lyrics feel somehow simultaneously ominous and romantic. I'm not entirely sure what Bob is singing about here, but there's always some random line that sticks out each time I listen to it. The song has the usual Lanois murk to it but is livelier than expected. Sure, at nearly six minutes, the track could've used some editing; especially since a couple of the solo sections have competing guitars playing at the same time, feeling more like filler or padding than an essential part of the song. Still, this is much more exciting than most of what did make it onto the album. Its exclusion is inexcusable.

Marchin' To The City from *The Bootleg Series vol. 8*
(written by Bob Dylan)

An outtake included twice on *The Bootleg Series vol. 8*. One take is six-and-a-half minutes long. It is a slow bluesy song that starts out almost like one of the piano-led gospel tunes from *Saved*. The other version is an upbeat version that gets the point across in under four minutes. That version has an organ that sounds almost accordion-like punctuating the off-beats. The verse melody is so similar to "Can't Wait" I can see why it was left off, but personally I enjoy it as much if not more. The melody in the chorus is completely different, so it doesn't bother me a bit. Both versions are good, but given how many slow dragging numbers were recording around *Time Out Of Mind*, I definitely prefer the faster take. However, neither rendition feels at all like a march. Too bad.

Rumored to have been recorded but unheard:
Shake Sugaree
(written by Elizabeth Cotton)

I wonder how this record would've been received it had contained any cover songs. It certainly seems to be a dog whistle that irritates a lot of Dylan fans and critics. However, Bob wussed out and not only kept this song off of *Time Out Of Mind* as well as any of the subsequent *Bootleg Series*. So far, I don't believe this recording has made its way to even the most rabid collectors.

"MARCHIN' TO THE RED RIVER SHORE"

SIDE A:
1. Love Sick
2. Marchin' To The City
3. Can't Wait
4. Red River Shore

SIDE B:
1. Cold Irons Bound
2. Mississippi
3. Million Miles
4. Dreamin' Of You

Much like *Desire* or *Infidels*, the average song length on this album is so excessive, it's hard to pare this down to a single LP and not end up left with an eight- or nine-song album. Usually, any album with less than ten songs on it feels like a rip-off, but there's not much I can do here. Of course, excising "Highlands" helps a lot. I have also returned the sore I feel it fits in much better.

For this album I have used the shorter version of "Marchin' To The City", the one that only appeared on the bonus disc of the deluxe edition of *The Bootleg Series vol. 8*. Even though it's slower and longer, I did use the bonus disc version of "Can't Wait". There are a lot of Dylan albums where the best songs are left on the cutting room floor. Even for *The Bootleg Series vol. 8* it seems like all of my favorite takes are on the bonus disc and not the standard edition. That is also where you can find my preferred version of "Red River Shore" with the prominent accordion. In fact "Mississippi" is the only outtake where I preferred the non-bonus disc edition. Of the two takes of this song on the standard edition, I used the more upbeat one marked version #2. It just feels far more like *Time Out Of Mind* than *Love & Theft*.

Of the few songs from the officially released album, I have only kept "Cold Irons Bound", "Love Sick", and "Million Miles". That may not seem like a lot, but considering there are only eight tracks on this hypothetical LP, that's fine. While *Infidels* has the reputation as the album that had the best stuff left off of it, with the release of *The Bootleg Series vol. 8* it appears that *Time Out Of Mind* is as much a culprit. At least in my eyes. And apparently also in the eyes of Columbia Records chairman, Don Ienner. When Bob accepted the Grammy for Album of the Year, he mentioned that Don Inner also felt that his favorite songs weren't on it.

LOVE & THEFT
Produced by: Jack Frost
Recorded: May 2001
Released: September 11th, 2001

Famous/Important/Popular Track(s):
- Things Have Changed
- Tweedle Dee & Tweedle Dum

My Personal Favorite Track(s):
- Summer Days
- Lonesome Day Blues
- Honest With Me

"The best since *Blood On The Tracks*" is a phrase that gets bandied about a lot in the latter half of Dylan's career. While I may personally argue that the logic of this dichotomy is flawed, if there is an album that this superlative pertains to, I think it's *Love & Theft*.

While Bob may have achieved his aim of a comeback with *Time Out Of Mind*, something about the process of making that record irked him, even if he was pleased with the results. If he wanted to make albums the way that he wanted to, he was going to have to do it himself and not rely on some other producer. However he couldn't just let the album happen on it own either, that obviously didn't work for *Knocked Out Loaded* or *Down In The Groove*. As much as he hated the cold, technical aspects of the recording studio, Dylan was going have to take producing seriously or else continue to be swamped by outsiders like Daniel Lanois.

And so Bob created his own, strict but simple recording philosophy. Do it quick, streamlined, with minimal fuss or interference. No headphones. No overdubbing. No fancy tricks. Minimal microphones even. Very old school. No hiring of slick studio professionals or big-name guest stars. Dylan would just use his fine-tuned crackerjack touring band.

This would mean that from this point forward, there would be very little experimenting from Bob in the recording studio, particularly in regards to instrumentation. Sure, there would be an accordion on *Together Through Life* and a small choir (plus sleigh bells) on *Christmas In The Heart*, but for the most part, all of these later Jack Frost-produced records would sound the same.

Not that this consistency in sound meant that the songs themselves would have to be repetitive in style. Dylan's backing band is very versatile when given a chance. And there isn't a bigger example of this than on *Love & Theft*. Roughly half of the album is giving over to blues-rock tunes, the type he had done many times before. Perhaps with more vigor in his youth, but nothing outside of his wheelhouse. The other half of *Love & Theft* would be devoted to Bob's new love of crooning over old school, jazz-tinged, torch ballads. It's like someone finally taught Dylan some ninth chords and he was going to use every last one.

In some ways, *Love & Theft* is to *Time Out Of Mind* what *Under The Red Sky* is to *Oh Mercy*: a fun, goofy follow-up to a dark, murky, serious Daniel Lanois produced comeback. While Bob has not penned a strictly humor-only saw since "Bob Dylan's 115th Dream" some of the line in these lyrics on this album are the funniest and silliest he's done since *Another Side Of Bob Dylan*. Luckily, the death scare the accompanied *Time Out Of Mind* still loomed on critics minds ,and they were far more hesitant to dismiss a silly Dylan in 2001 than they were in 1990, afraid that any album Bob put out could be his last, and they didn't want to look like jerks in retrospect.

Of course, also adding to the depth and weight of this album is another coincidence that really had as much to do with *Love & Theft* as Dylan's heart scare had to do with *Time Out Of Mind*. Though there's no way he could've known or predicted what would happen, this album was released on 9/11. That may have given the otherwise light and fun record a certain gravity that it might not have carried had it been released on an average, ordinary day.

For whatever reason, the more whimsical side of Bob was received warmly this time around. Which is a good thing, because this is one of Bob's best sets of songs ever. Sure the record itself is a little perfunctory, if professionally, recorded. But these are some of my favorite tunes Dylan's ever written. There's a lot of really great songs on here, and the only real weak link on the album is the track that was actually a reject from *Time Out Of Mind*. That says something.

Tweedle Dee & Tweedle Dum
(written by Bob Dylan)

While *Time Out Of Mind* is stately and slow and stark, *Love & Theft* instantly announces how its different with one of Dylan's most rocking songs, "Tweedle Dee & Tweedle Dum". Like "Changing Of The Guards" on *Street Legal*, this album starts by fading in. This, however, feels less like an attempt to hide a mistake and more like a car pulling into town bringing this music with it. From a musical standpoint, it's not a terribly complicated song. Pretty much just a variation on the usual 12 bar blues. Unlike Daniel Lanois murk instrumentation, Dylan's touring band bring a stark crispness to the proceedings. You can tell when someone is soloing and when they're just playing around. The lyrics are pretty condemning of the titular idiots – although it seems even more damning of the people around them who are continually being duped by them. However since there's no real indication of who Tweedle Dum and Tweedle Dee are specifically supposed to represent, it's hard to tell where Dylan's venom is pointed. However, Bob's vocal delivery makes it clear that he is far more bemused than angry at the whole situation.

Mississippi
(written by Bob Dylan)
See the entry under *Time Out Of Mind*.

Summer Days
(written by Bob Dylan)
Another up-tempo blues-rock stomper. This one has a bit more off jazz and swing to it, although it still is rooted thoroughly in the usual 12 bar blues pattern. The lyrics are nothing but silly fun, and despite Bob's grizzled voice, it sounds like he is having a blast singing them. There's an intro lick that the band stops and plays on occasion during this song, but it doesn't really stop Bob from singing throughout the song although there are a couple of verses that are left for guitar solos. This is really one of the hardest rocking things Bob has recorded since the mid-60s electric days. Songs like this are what make *Love & Theft* one of my favorite Dylan albums.

Bye and Bye
(written by Bob Dylan)
Bob's first real foray into the 40s croon that would soon overtake his work, this is a lovely swinging jazz-styled tune. While Bob covered a lot of Sinatra, if Frank were going to sing Dylan this would be right up his alley. There are some fun little interjections from the organ, and some swanky jazz-guitar chord voicings that are more complicated than anything Bob's done since "If Dogs Run Free". It even has a great little bridge part it returns to a couple of times, despite being a somewhat shorter song for Bob. There's also half of a guitar solo in there that is just delightful. The lyrics are pretty silly, including a dad joke about sitting on his watch so he can be on time. Bob doesn't wink at the joke, and it can pass by unnoticed if you are not looking for it. I'm not really sure what the words are about, but Bob sounds like he's smiling through the whole song. Another great song.

Lonesome Day Blues
(written by Bob Dylan)
A fun, upbeat blues song with a real swing feel. It probably doesn't need to be six minutes, but I still like it. It's got a hypnotically simple riff that answers just about every line. Unlike Daniel Lanois's production, there is a clear delimitation here between when the instruments are supporting the singer and when they are taking a solo. The lyrics are not nearly as fun or funny as "Summer Days" but Dylan is still growling them with gusto. I do like the admonition that "you can't make love all by yourself" as well as the assertion that "things you have the hardest time parting with are the things you need the least." It's a great track that tends to get a little

overshadowed by the other great tracks on *Love & Theft*.

Floater (Too Much to Ask)
(written by Bob Dylan)

A less overtly jazz song than some of the swooning torch songs on this album. The chords are generally missing the sevenths and ninths one would expect from a true swing pastiche. There's some nice violin on here helping change up the sound here. It almost feels like a slowed down jump blues, but it's got that bridge making this far more complicated than that. Bob's is adding a little more rasp here than he usually applies to his crooning. There are some great lines in there involving various Shakespeare characters. This song doesn't jump out of the speakers as vivaciously as many of the *Love & Theft* songs but still is a fun little number. Not great, but enjoyable.

High Water (For Charley Patton)
(written by Bob Dylan)

Hey look, it's a banjo. While the song itself is just an acoustic blues, the addition of the banjo here almost gives the impression that this song is somehow far more country than it really is. It also sounds like there might be an accordion on here, shades of *Together Through Life* that is yet to come. The song is mostly based around a single chord, with the occasional chromatic turnaround at before and after the title line. This is not a bad song, but compared to the genuinely rocking songs that come before it, this feels a little flat. There are no drums during most of the song, just these occasional timpani-like rolls adding a weird sense of drama to the song that otherwise doesn't really go anywhere. The lyrics are fun, but not nearly as funny as many of the other *Love & Theft* songs although it does include the phrase "throw your panties overboard." This song is not quite an out-and-out dud, but something of a miss for me.

Moonlight
(written by Bob Dylan)

Another faux jazz ballad. There are some really cool chord progressions in here, and probably more syllables per line than is typical for this type of song. Still, I'd rather Bob get all these words out rather than either slowing the song down or adding an extra three verses. Really Dylan is singing almost as fast here as he was on "Subterranean Homesick Blues" without ever getting tripped up. The lyrics are not terribly important but seem to centered around a romantic rendezvous. He's hopeful but not desperate. He actually comes off as quite charming and enticing here. There are some lovely tremolo guitars here, and the brushed snare drum keeps things pumping along at nice swinging pace. This is one of my favorite songs on *Love & Theft*, certainly the best of his torch ballad attempts.

Honest with Me
(written by Bob Dylan)

Alternating the jazz ballads with the blues rockers is part of *Love & Theft*'s ability to maintain the listener's interest. This is another song along the lines of "Lonesome Day Blues" or "Summer Days". The lyrics are nonsense for the most part, with the refrain pleading for some honesty from some woman who doesn't know what Bob's gone through. There are some goofy images here including a baseball bat in hell and Bob going hunting bare. Dylan is enjoying the hell out of singing these words. While the majority of the song is a 12-bar blues chord structure, there's a nice little exchange in the intro that is occasionally thrown in between verses that helps change things up without extending the song too ridiculous lengths. While Bob may not be the young punk of "Subterranean Homesick Blues" anymore, it's nice to see him really rock out again. Another great song.

Po' Boy
(written by Bob Dylan)

What I can only assume is a song about a sandwich. This is a much folksier version of the torch ballads that bob has been experimenting with on this album. It is one of the only songs with acoustic guitars on it; certainly, the lone track with them pushed to such prominence. It is a nice little change of pace for the song. There are some more goofy one-liners in the lyrics here, including a goofy "room service" pun and an honest-to-goodness knock-knock joke. Bob is smiling slyly to himself throughout these songs. The lyrics probably don't have any big deeper meaning, but that's okay. It's whimsical and fun all the same. It's a great little track, and while there may be some similar tunes on *Love & Theft*, it doesn't feel old or repetitive yet. It may not be as grand or surprising as say "Moonlight", but its devilish offhandedness is part of its charm.

Cry a While
(written by Bob Dylan)

Other than the inclusion of a re-recording of "Mississippi", up to this point, *Love & Theft* has been a nearly perfect album. While the last two songs aren't terrible by any stretch, they do ruin this streak a bit. The conceit of this song is interesting, constantly switching between half-time and double-time (I'm not sure which is the standard tempo) every couple of lines. Unfortunately, the song itself is just another blues-based song that doesn't rock nearly as hard as "Lonesome Day Blues" or "Summer Days" or "Tweedle Dum & Tweedle Dee". Appearing on the same record as those monsters makes this track seem a little limp in comparison. If this had appeared on *Planet Waves* or *Street Legal*, this would've been one of the best of the bunch. Perhaps the alternating tempos are undercutting any momentum that this is song starting to build up. Normally I would applaud

Bob trying something so musically complicated, something in the execution here feels off. It's one of the few tracks on here that doesn't fit into either the rocking blues or jazz ballad columns that the rest of the album is divided between. Unfortunately, it seems like it wants to fit into the harder rocking category and just fails to reach it. Not horrible, but one of the lesser *Love & Theft* tracks.

Sugar Baby
(written by Bob Dylan)

It's unfortunate that the two weakest tracks on *Love & Theft* are also the two last. It leaves one with the impression that the album wasn't nearly as good as it really was. This is a slow portentous song. It is not quite the deliberately pretentious track that many of Dylan's album closers are, it is still far from engaging the way much of the album before it was. Neither a smoky torch song or a rocking blues barnstormer, this is more of a power ballad. It's not even as amusingly out-of-character as the tracks from *Empire Burlesque*. It's about the only song on here without any sort of drumming. The chord sequence is a little more complicated than typical Bob. There's what sounds like an accordion somewhere in the mix along with a nice mix of electric and acoustic guitars. The lyrics are free from any of the goofy one-liners that peppered the rest of the album. It sounds more like "Mississippi" than any other track on this album, and I sort of wonder if this song was also written long before the rest of *Love & Theft*. It's not enough of a blemish to end up torpedoing this album, but it an unfortunate way to cap off what is one of Dylan's all-time greatest masterpieces.

Songs not on the album:
Things Have Changed from the *Wonder Boys* soundtrack
(written by Bob Dylan)

Bob's Oscar-winning song. For years after, Dylan would leave his academy award (or a replica) just sitting on his guitar amp on-stage. This is the other side of "The Times They Are A-Changin'". Bob is bitter that things have a-changed, but for the better. Bob's half-angry, but far more disappointed. The song is a medium-fast blues shuffle with prominent acoustic guitars throughout. Coming shortly before *Love & Theft*, this song gives a good indication of what to expect from this album. This song tells you all you need to know about the difference between a Daniel Lanois production and a "Jack Frost" production. This is uncluttered and clean, nothing fancy about it. The song was something of a surprise hit, now being far more remembered than the Michael Douglas vehicle it was penned for. While it doesn't rock as hard as "Summer Days" or "Honest With Me" this has a lot of energy. The lyrics are elliptical but clever. The chorus is catchy. If it hadn't gotten so much attention via the Oscars, Bob might've recycled it for *Love & Theft*. Or more likely it would have just languished in obscurity along with the songs Dylan did for *Gods & Generals, Lucky You, North Country* or *The Divine Secrets Of The Ya-Ya Sisterhood*. I'm not sure why Bob was suddenly doing so much soundtrack work. Maybe since singles aren't really a thing anymore, this is a way for Bob to release a song without waiting for the rest of the album to be written. Who knows?

Return To Me from the second volume of *The Sopranos* soundtrack
(written by Carmen Lombardo & Danny Di Minno)

While Bob had written numerous pseudo-torch ballads for *Love & Theft*, this is his first foray into recording a cover of one of these standards. At the time it seemed like a goofy one-off that was relegated to a TV soundtrack for good reason. Who knew how deep down this particular rabbit hole Dylan would be venturing in just another ten years or so. Even if this was initially a hit for Dean Martin and not Frank Sinatra, this would be a harbinger of things to come. Bob sings one of the verses in the original Italian, which adds to the novelty aspect of this song. But Dylan is playing it very straight and sincere here. The sound is far more acoustic than *Shadows In The Night, Fallen Angels*, or *Triplicate* would turn out to be. There's an accordion and even drums on here. It's utterly charming and in fact much more enjoyable than most of Bob's Sinatra period. I'm not sure a whole 5 discs worth of Dean Martin would be preferable to what we would end up getting, but this is a disposable, adorable, little track.

I Can't Get Her Off Of My Mind from *Timeless – A Hank Williams Tribute*
(written by Hank Williams)

While a tribute to Dean Martin might have been a surprise from Bob, especially in 2001, a cover of Hank Williams song is much less unexpected. Again it makes you long for the elder Dylan to tackle a full *Nashville Skyline*-style return to country music. There's a surprising amount of accordion on this track that you wouldn't hear again until *Together Through Life*. Bob's voice is ragged, but he does attempt a few yodel-like octave jumps that are utterly charming. The band plays this with finesse, but you can tell it's not their forte. Luckily Bob picked a more upbeat number rather than some dour country weeper. If you're familiar with this song and the album *Love & Theft* this song sounds about the way you would expect it to. It's a charming addition to the Dylan canon, but pretty disposable. More and more Dylan is segregating his covers from his originals. At this point, covers are only reserved for tribute albums and soundtracks. He hasn't released an album with both covers and originals since 1988, and it doesn't look like he ever will again. This is a shame as I think the mixture helps to highlight and show off where Dylan is coming from when he sings these new songs. A song like this might've made a lovely little addition to *Love & Theft*.

A Red Cadillac And A Black Moustache from *Good Rockin' Tonight: The Legacy Of Sun Records*
(written by Lily May and Willie Bea Thompson)

While Bob still has not recorded his rockabilly album, here's another track from that era. When submitting a tune for the Sun Records tribute, Dylan expectedly went obscure, eschewing Elvis or Orbison or Jerry Lee or Johnny Cash. Instead, he chose a song by Warren Smith. While this could come off as pretentiously showing off his in-depth knowledge of the Sun Records catalog, given Bob's vintage, he probably came to this obscurity rather organically. While Dylan takes his version at about the same speed as the original, but Warren's sounds as amped as energetic as it could for the period. Bob, on the other hand, sounds laid back and relaxed. He's more disappointed than upset that his girl has been fooling around on him. Dylan doesn't even seem that jealous of the titular vehicle. As for the mustache, by this point Bob has grown out his own version of the Vincent Price/John Water facial hair; a look which he has inexplicably maintained to this day. There's nothing too terribly illuminating or extraordinary about this recording, but it is nice to hear Bob going back to his pre-folk rockabilly roots.

Waitin' For You from *The Divine Secrets Of The Ya-Ya Sisterhood* soundtrack
(written by Bob Dylan)

While *Love & Theft* splits the difference between rock and jazz, the country side of Dylan gets pretty ignored on the album. This song is a return to that. This song sounds far more country than the Hank Williams or Johnny Cash tributes that Bob released around this time. It has a prominent fiddle and pedal steel. The 3/4 waltz time is even more undeniable than "Winterlude". While the song may seem relatively simple, it is oddly bifurcated. What sounds like the first two verses turn out to be an extended intro, before going into a different section. While the two parts are very similar, it never goes back to that same chord pattern from the first half of the song. However, if you're not paying close attention, you might think that the whole song is all operating over the same musical progression. While it's a bright little song, it illustrates the main issue with this song. There is just not enough of a change going on. It all seems kind of samey. It's nice to hear Bob of this era stretching out and going back to the country sound, it's just not a big enough departure.

Train Of Love from *Kindred Spirits – A Tribute To The Songs Of Johnny Cash*
(written by Johnny Cash)

A recording of a live-in-the-studio spot from a televised Johnny Cash tribute special. While Bob has undeniably played plenty of Johnny Cash in the past, most of it hasn't gone released. In the past Dylan has picked to cover some of Johnny's more well-known tracks such as "Ring Of Fire" and "Folsom Prison Blues", for this tribute, he decided to get a little more obscure. Possibly because several other bigger artists already called dibs on those more famous songs. Bob opens the song by apologizing to Johnny for being unable to attend the event in person, but offers as an explanation only that "that's the way it is". From there Dylan and his touring launch into a fairly expected version of "Train Of Love". Bob mentions that he used to play this song before he ever wrote a song himself. This is one of the few instances where Bob lets any of his bandmates sing along with someone adding some ragged harmony to the choruses. Despite the pedal steel, the song is taken with far less of a country flavor than "Waitin' For You". The song is done well, although it's ultimately unremarkable. Dylan clearly has an affection for the material in his voice, but this is just another cover from the Never Ending Tour to come and go as all these songs must.

"LONESOME SUMMER DAYS"

SIDE A:
1. Tweedle Dum & Tweedle Dee
2. Summer Days
3. Lonesome Day Blues
4. Honest With Me
5. Things Have Changed

SIDE B:
1. Bye & Bye
2. Floater (Too Much To Ask)
3. Moonlight
4. Po' Boy
5. Return To Me

While this album doesn't have the clear division between acoustic and electric as *Bringing It All Back Home*, I did re-arrange this album so all the harder rock songs are on side one, while the softer, jazzier tunes ended up on side two. I already used "Mississippi" for the last album, so I had to cut it from this album along with a couple of my less favorite tracks.

For this re-imagining, I have gone ahead and added the contemporaneous "Things Have Changed" since it's both an Oscar-winner and a song I really liked. It makes a good conclusion for the harder side one. As for side two, I have added the authentic torch song "Return To Me" to wrap things up. It's been a while since we've had a cover song on one of these albums. It not only fits in well with the originals here but is a good head's up for the direction that Dylan was going to steer (crash?) into starting in 2015.

While *Love & Theft* is already a pretty perfect album, these little tweaks help it fit in better with the flow of my previous hypothetical Dylan platters.

MODERN TIMES

Produced by: Jack Frost
Recorded: February 2006
Released: August 29th, 2006

Famous/Important/Popular Track(s):
- Someday Baby
- Thunder On The Mountain

My Personal Favorite Track(s):
- Rollin' And Tumblin'
- Someday Baby
- 'Cross The Green Mountain

Love & Theft is not a great record. It's a great set of tunes ably and well-recorded, but it's not that much different from a really well-recorded bootleg with all the audience noises magically removed. The reason it works so well as an album is that the songs themselves were so good. If you were to take that same no-frills approach to recording and apply them to a batch of songs that are over-long and in severe need of an editor, you would end up with a very irritating album indeed.

And that's pretty much what *Modern Times* is. The Jack Frost production (or lack thereof) remains consistent, but the songs themselves just aren't as good. I'm not sure exactly what the difference is, but the songs all feel indulgent as they ramble on. It's not just that there are one or two overblown tracks like "Highlands" or "Brownville Girl", even the shortest song on here is barely under five minutes. It all gets so boring. *Love & Theft* is eleven minutes shorter and has twelve songs instead of ten.

Much like the last album, we are mostly listening to either more slow jazz ballads and rocking blues tunes. Only this time around, the rock songs don't rock as hard; and the torch songs are a lot less of a surprise.

There's not a lot to say about the overall sound and feel of this album. It's just the sound of Dylan's band in a room recorded well. However, the critics were still possibly concerned about Dylan's frail health and therefore lavished heaps of unearned praise on this album. Especially given the five years between this album and the last one, I think people were just glad that Bob was doing anything at all. Frankly, given how little time or thought was given to the actual recording of this album, it might've benefited from being rushed out a little sooner after the release of *Love & Theft*. Maybe then, Dylan wouldn't have had time to write verses five through thirteen for every track.

At the time, people saw Dylan as being on a roll post-*Time Out Of Mind*. The fact that he wasn't flooding the market any more helped. The time between releases stoked anticipation for each new album that would blind critics to how hastily done it really was. Bob could do no wrong in many fans' and critics' eyes at this point, with this album seen as the third part of a trilogy encompassing *Time Out Of Mind* and *Love & Theft* that could finally hold its own against Dylan's original electric albums.

Even Bob himself, dismissed this idea at the time, noting that *Time Out Of Mind* with its Lanois production didn't fit well with the other two. It would be a while yet before Dylan would take advantage of this recent return to public goodwill before he would start really experimenting again. And for me I think this is the biggest flaw of *Modern Times*; Bob isn't trying anything new. This is what people expected from Dylan in 2006, and he's happy to give it to you because it comes so easy for him at this point. But he's not really as engaged or energized as he was when he was doing something so utterly un-Bob Dylan like going Christian or even retreating to his folk roots.

This is just average Bob. And I would much rather have bad Bob than average Bob any day of the week.

Thunder on the Mountain
(written by Bob Dylan)

This is another rock-shuffle opener in the vein of "Let's Stick Together" or "You Wanna Ramble?" only this is not a cover. While *Love & Theft* had all sorts of energy and adrenaline on its fast numbers, this song is pitched somewhere between laid back and just plain lazy. Frankly, it would be pretty unremarkable if it weren't for the name-checking of young R&B star Alicia Keys. However, these lyrics are just more of the general mishmash of meaningless blues clichés and psychedelic imagery of this song. This song goes on far too long for as little as it says. There's another well-done but forgettable guitar solo after every verse or two, extending this song far longer than it has any need to be. Sadly, this is one of the more exciting and energetic songs on this album.

Spirit on the Water
(written by Bob Dylan)

Another torch ballad to croon along to in the vein of "Bye & Bye" or "Moonlight" from the last album. But while those tracks try to mimic the economy of the old songs it emulates, this one stretched to nearly eight minutes. This is a shame because I really like this song at first, but it does tend to get old long before it is over. The only reason to stick with this song that long kicks in at six minutes: there's a harmonica solo, which sounds so out of place on all these lovely jazz guitar chords. I love the juxtaposition. Plus we haven't heard Bob's harp at all on *Love & Theft*. The lyrics are a jumbled mess of images that don't really add up to much. It's hard to tell from Bob's vocal inflections how he feels about all of this, but he sounds lovely singing it. I do love the line "You ever seen a ghost? No. But you have heard of them" as well as off-handedly mentioning he killed a man in paradise. Maybe someday someone will edit this down, and I can begin to enjoy it, but right now my enthusiasm for this song always curdles long before we get to the end.

Rollin' and Tumblin'
(written by Bob Dylan)

A rocking shuffle played over the usual I-IV-V blues chord progression. There's not much to this song, but it far livelier than most of *Modern Times*. The lyrics are of the "don't tie me down, I'm a rambler" sort. Despite this being one of the most fun songs on this album, Bob doesn't sound nearly as gleeful as he did on *Love & Theft*. Like just about everything on this album, it is about two minutes too long (at least). If Bob's going to insist on his songs being this length he's got to start writing more parts for them as they tend to get boring by the end. There are some nice guitar solos on there, but nothing that really sticks out. Certainly nothing worth padding out this song. Despite all of this, "Rollin' And Tumblin'" may be one of my favorite tracks off of *Modern Times*.

When the Deal Goes Down
(written by Bob Dylan)

Everything I said about "Spirit On The Water" is also applicable here. There are very few differences. On the plus side, the song is barely over five minutes instead of being over seven-and-a-half. On the negative side, we don't get a harmonica solo here. There is some lovely jazz guitar soloing here. The song's got a nice waltz feel to it with the 3/4 time signature that helps distinguish this from "Spirit On The Water" as well as "Beyond The Horizon". Songs like those three, plus "Bye & Bye", "Moonlight", and "Po' Boy" definitely should've hinted at the Sinatra period to come, but nothing could've possibly that prepared one for just how long that period would last.

Someday Baby
(written by Bob Dylan)

One of the more rocking numbers on *Modern Times* this is still more gently rocking back and forth than aggressively rock-and-rolling. In terms of construction, this is just another 12 bar blues. It's a got a great riff running throughout the whole thing. The fact that the guitar solo is done with a slide is a nice little change of pace. The repeated lines at the end of each verse let us know that this song is about the narrator looking forward to getting over a failed romance. Bob sings this with a sense of triumph and cockiness with little no hint of the heartache underneath that inspired this posturing. Coming in just under five minutes is still a bit long, but better than a lot of track on this album. By not being too ambitious or dramatic this song winds up being one of the best on this album almost by default. There is a different take of the song on *The Bootleg Series vol. 8* that takes everything a much statelier pace and eliminates the central guitar riff. All this conspires together to reduce the already limited stature of this song while increasing its length by a full minute. As a result, this song now feels more akin to the remainder of *Modern Times*; when what that album definitely needed the change of pace the released version of "Someday Baby" provides.

Workingman's Blues #2
(written by Bob Dylan)

While most of *Love & Theft* is divided between rocking blues numbers and faux-crooning torch ballads, *Modern Times* tries to stretch out from this trying a few songs that don't really fall into either category. While normally I would applaud these types of exercises, most of these songs just feel formless and lacking in any particular character. This song is definitely one of them. This is not a country like one would expect from a sequel to Merle Haggard's "Workingman's Blues". Instead, we just get a generally mediocre medium-tempo song with a weak melody and little interest or change in the chord structure. Bob's voice feels extra croaky here and gives me no clue as to what these lyrics are supposed to me. Some of it sounds like an update to the politics of "Union Sundown" but large swaths of the words seem to be involved in the machinations of a simple story about a guy missing his family or girlfriend or something. I don't know. If the song weren't so long, it might not need two different songs worth of lyrics in there. A little violin pops in at the very end, but it's far too little, too late. It doesn't get a chance to do much, and you can be forgiven for missing it entirely before the song finally fades out.

Beyond the Horizon
(written by Bob Dylan)

We're back in "Spirit On The Water" / "When The Deal Goes Down" territory here. There are some subtle cellos and pedal steel here, but this is dominated by some jazz guitar. Bob is singing his best here, but I'm not sure what he is trying to tell me about these lyrics. These are a lot more complicated chords than is usual for a Dylan song. This song doesn't drag like "Spirit On The Water" however the novelty of Bob writing and singing this type of song is starting to wear thin. I think it was starting to get old to Dylan too. There's nothing on *Together Through Life* or *Tempest* that is as blatantly paying homage to this era of songwriting. However, if he had grown weary of writing songs such as these, he certainly was going to jump into singing these "Great American Songbook" standards with both feet. Maybe Dylan has been wracked with guilt in later years, feeling as though singer-songwriters such as himself had destroyed this American institution; and in retribution, it was up to him to bring that type of music back singlehandedly. Who knows? It's definitely become more than a quirk that arises on occasion, but a full-fledged facet that has to be reckoned with in an attempt to understand Bob's art.

Nettie Moore
(written by Bob Dylan)

Look, I realize that the word "o'er" is a common poetic contraction for "over", but Bob's reliance on it to ensure he has sufficient rhymes for the chorus of this song is distracting. This is another track that slips between the cracks of the jazz ballads and the blues rockers on *Modern Times*. I just wish that it were a more successful attempt to branch out. This song is mostly a monotonous kick drum and bass thud that never varies or wavers with occasional bits of guitar arpeggios to let us know where we are. It only lets up for the choruses. As is usual for this album, this song is about twice as long as it needs to be. Bob's vocals are worn-out giving no clue as to how he feels about these lyrics. The effect of this arrangement isn't as hypnotic as it wants to be; it's a little more like listening to a tuned metronome. While applaud Bob stepping out and trying something a little different for this track, this just gets annoying long before the song wraps up. It is different enough to keep from being one of the worst *Modern Times* tracks, but there's not much to recommend about it either.

The Levee's Gonna Break
(written by Bob Dylan)

We've got another jump-blues type of rock-shuffle here. The lyrics are again worried about the safety of levees and fears of a Noah-style flood. While this is more energetic than most of *Modern Times*, it doesn't hold a candle to the rockers on *Love & Theft*. Songs like "Summer Days" or "Lonesome Day Blues" have a real fire to them. This feels much more lackadaisical and indifferent. Which is a shame because a real barn-burner or two would've really turned this album around. The drums here are played with brushes, and the bass is definitely an upright. All of this saps the energy from the song. The music is just another 12 bar blues, with no variation or dynamics. The lyrics feel like blues clichés, and Bob doesn't invest them with much vocal intensity. While not as ludicrously over-long, it certainly could've lost a verse or two in order to bring down a nearly six-minute runtime. None of the guitar solos break out to make much of an impression, even if it's a bad impression. Typical of this album, the song is perfectly suitable, but dispiritingly bland.

Ain't Talkin'
(written by Bob Dylan)

Much like "Nettie Moore" this song is neither fish nor fowl, neither blues-rock or torch ballad. As such it initially stands out as something new and different and interesting. However, by the end of over eight-and-a-half minutes, any novelty has long since worn off. At least there's a nice prominent acoustic guitar doing some cool finger-picking here. The alternate version of this on *The Bootleg Series vol. 8* has some nice banjo in its place as well as playing at a quicker pace and being substantially shorter. Unfortunately, this all actually undermines whatever differences between this song and many of its *Modern Times* brethren, so this takes is not quite a good replacement for the official version. For an album where most of the songs are in the six- to nine-minute mark, this one still feels like it's the track that is aiming for epic-ness. It doesn't quite succeed, but you at least can admire its ambition. Not much happens here, there's little in terms of variation in the parts or even dynamics within the constantly repeated musical passages we do have. The lyrics are aiming for some post-apocalyptic depth, but the only thing that stands out is the complaint about a toothache. Bob's flat growl continues here, with little inflection. Despite all of this, "Ain't Talkin'" may end up being one of my favorites of this album. Its heart is in the right place, and at least it's trying to do something else.

Songs not on the album:
Diamond Joe from the *Masked & Anonymous* soundtrack
(traditional, arranged By Bob Dylan)

While it has the same name and the same public domain copyright, this is an entirely different song from the track recorded for *Good As I Done To You*. I'm not sure if this is a coincidence or deliberately. A lot of *Masked & Anonymous* is confusing, not the least of which is the screenplay which Dylan co-authored. The soundtrack album is not any more coherent. Half of it is not recorded by Dylan, but rather an odd international smorgasbord of various international covers of Bob Dylan songs. Bob, on the other hand, couldn't even be bothered to write new material for his own movie. Instead, he contributes a couple of remakes of some previously recorded tunes ("Cold Irons Bound" and "Down In The Flood") in addition to two newly recorded traditional covers with his touring band. Everything on the soundtrack is also performed by Bob live to film in the movie. There's no real explanation for why he's doing these songs or if they're part of his character's repertoire or what. This "Diamond Joe" includes the director saying "action" at the very beginning. It features some prominent banjo and the drummer just playing with brushes on a box. I'm not sure if this supposed to be a scene of the band just relaxing and jamming or if this is something that they are rehearsing for the big concert at the end. In the end, this becomes far more country than anything Bob's recorded since the *Nashville Skyline / Self-Portrait* days. Really though with the harmony vocalists and the quick tempo, this is probably closer to bluegrass. It's certainly less annoying and pretentious than anything on *Modern Times*. And at two-and-a-half minutes, it's much more merciful as well.

Dixie from the *Masked & Anonymous* soundtrack
(traditional, arranged By Bob Dylan)

While not nearly as offensive as the confederate flag, I still have a hard time enjoying this song as it is so enmeshed in America's history with slavery. Given the muddled themes of the *Masked & Anonymous* movie, it could be that this is a subversive choice for Bob Dylan's character to play; that he is making a statement here. Or could be that this is something that his character would play in earnest in this alternate timeline of America where Mickey Rourke is president. Most likely those this is just an old song that Bob likes, and there was no more thought put into it than "Diamond Joe". Unfortunately, Bob and director Larry Charles don't make it clear or obvious what the motivation is behind including this song in both the movie and the soundtrack album. Whatever the reason is, this song still leaves a bad taste in my mouth, no matter how well Bob may perform it.

'Cross The Green Mountain from the *Gods & Generals* soundtrack
(written by Bob Dylan)

Another Dylan mini-epic. This song clocks in at over eight minutes. Bob also did a video for this song (in fake beard and wig) that is barely over three minutes. That edit may be preferable, as the various vignettes in the lyrics are not terribly connected and you can lose almost any verse without making any difference to the song as a whole. Unlike many soundtrack songs that Bob was doing at this time, this one seems far more tailored to the subject matter: war, more specifically the Civil War. Dylan's various snapshots show the various cruelties and casualties of a large-scale battle such as this. There are some truly gruesome or heart-wrenching scenes in here. A well-loved commander betrayed by his own men, a letter from a soldier who doesn't realize that by the time his mother reads it he will have died, all sorts of stuff. The song is slow and lugubrious, with a period-appropriate fiddle throughout. There are some bridges in this song, though they're very slight variations of the verse, so they don't change things up as much as you would expect. The song does a good job of creating the pulse that "Nettie Moore" and "Ain't Talkin'" are trying for but don't quite succeed at. It's almost good enough for its length to be overlooked. If it weren't for the video edit which acknowledges how bloated the song is. Still, it's better than most of the songs on *Modern Times*.

Tell Ol' Bill from the *North Country* soundtrack
(written by Bob Dylan)

While modern technology along with Dylan taking the production reigns has really limited the number of modern studio Dylan recordings that have made their way into the hands of bootleggers. But for some reason, the session for this one-off soundtrack song somehow made their way to the public. As a result, many fans found there was a minor key version of this track that was not released that they preferred to the jaunty song that did appear on the *North Country* soundtrack. Perhaps as a result of this fan demand, the minor key alternate take was officially released on *The Bootleg Series vol. 8* while the originally released version has languished without any release on an official Bob Dylan album. It's kind of a shame; even though I prefer the minor key version, the *North Country* take of this song is a lovely, charming, country-ish recording. The minor key version is done at the same up-tempo pace which is nice and has a little more depth and pathos. The upbeat take has some bucolic fiddling on it, while the minor key version has some tasty electric guitar. Listening to the whole session, which you can find on YouTube or elsewhere, gives you a good idea of how much exploring and experimentation in terms of key and feel and tempo Bob engages in while in the studio these days. The song itself is pretty trifling, and you can see why Dylan tossed it off for a movie soundtrack. Really the best part of this song is comparing and contrasting the different available versions.

Huck's Tune from the *Lucky You* soundtrack
(written by Bob Dylan)

A shorter, less epic version of "Cross The Green Mountain". It's a gentle waltz with a country feel. It's not nearly as gleeful as "Waitin' For You". There's some astounding rhythmic organ buried in the mix here. There's no fiddle, but lots of pedal steel guitar. This is not a very memorable or remarkable tune, but it is also complete innocuous which is a step up from some of the tracks Dylan was recorded around this time. I have no idea who the Huck in the title is. I don't think he's mentioned at all in the lyrics. Maybe it's the name of one of the characters from the movie, *Lucky You* from which soundtrack this song first appeared. Or perhaps it's Huckleberry Finn, I really don't know. Unlike a lot of soundtrack songs that Bob recorded at the time, this one was rescued from obscurity and placed – without alteration – on *The Bootleg Series vol. 8*. It's a charming little tune, but definitely slight, which helps it stand out amongst its more pretentious contemporaries, but is not a classic by any stretch.

Do Re Mi from *The People Speak* soundtrack
(written by Woody Guthrie)

Despite Bob's well-noted obsession with Woody Guthrie, this one of the few recordings we have of him singing one of Woody's songs. Recorded live in the studio for the 2009 PBS documentary based on the books of Howard Zinn, this song features the rather odd band of Van Dyke Parks on piano and Ry Cooder on electric guitar. While Van Dyke is known for his ornateness, he gives a somewhat restrained performance here that is perfectly simpatico with Dylan's simple delivery. It is, in fact, a lovely and touching little performance. Bob's voice is ragged and does the song no favors, but the interplay between the piano, acoustic, and electric guitars is sumptuous. While this may not be a revelatory as one would have hoped from Dylan covering Woody, it is a gentle and beautiful performance. While it lacks the fire of anger that one would expect from a song protesting the mistreatment of the poor, is one of the prettiest hidden gems in the Dylan catalog.

Can't Escape From You from *The Bootleg Series vol. 8*
(written by Bob Dylan)

A song with an almost doo-wop feel in 6/8 time. Bob wrote and recorded this song in 2005 for a film that never actually got made, which is kind of weird. I'm not sure what kind of movie this was supposed to be, but given how tangentially related so much of Dylan's soundtrack work was at this time, there is very little we can infer about the movie from this song. The song itself is ludicrously simple. It's not quite boring, but it is getting pretty close. Nothing much changes in the song, it just rolls on and on and on. It mostly just feels like a lesser re-write of "Every Grain Of Sand". Bob's vocals are husky and disinterested. At a little over five minutes, it is slightly shorter than some of the stuff Dylan was doing around this time. Towards the very end, it sounds like a cello comes in to take a solo, but doesn't really. Even if it did, it would be too little, too late to save this track.

"CROSS THE MOUNTAIN & BEYOND THE HORIZON"

SIDE A:
1. Rollin' And Tumblin'
2. Tell Ol' Bill
3. Someday Baby
4. A Red Cadillac And A Black Mustache
5. The Levee's Gonna Break
6. 'Cross The Green Mountain
   (video edit)

SIDE B:
1. Do Re Mi
2. Diamond Joe
3. When The Deal Goes Down
4. Huck's Tune

5. Beyond The Horizon
6. I Can't Get Her Off Of My Mind

This has never been one of my favorite albums; however, it doesn't fit in really well with either *Love & Theft* or *Together Through Life*, so I wasn't able to construct a hybrid album to deal with the few tracks here I like properly. Instead, I am left to sift through the hodgepodge of stray tracks recorded by Bob during this period. This does mean there are a few more covers on here than Bob was usually including on his albums at the time. While nothing from this period rocks as hard as side one of my version of *Love & Theft*, I did try to front-load this album with the more danceable tunes, even if it ends with the softer "'Cross The Green Mountain".

The album is a little long, coming in at just over fifty minutes. I have tried to pick the shorter songs from this period. For "'Cross The Green Mountain" I would recommend using the shorter video edit of this song. I actually went with the major key version of "Tell Ol' Bill" from the soundtrack to *North Country*, instead of the minor key version on *The Bootleg Series vol. 8*. While the minor version might be cooler, this album is already downbeat enough and needs more fun songs.

There are only two of the torch ballads included here, because as good as "Spirit In The Water" is it just goes on too long. The same goes for "Ain't Talkin'" which has a cool creepy vibe but just keeps going and going.

This re-working isn't going to change my mind about *Modern Times*, but it does help make it a lot more enjoyable. At least for me personally.

TOGETHER THROUGH LIFE

Produced by: Jack Frost
Recorded: December 2008
Released: April 28th, 2009

Famous/Important/Popular Track(s):
- Beyond Here Lies Nothin'

My Personal Favorite Track(s):
- Beyond Here Lies Nothin'
- Forgetful Heart
- It's All Good

After the disappointing sameness of *Modern Times*, anything that was at all original and interesting would have been greeted by me with open arms. And when the opening track, "Beyond Here Lies Nothing" was previewed weeks before this album's release I was excited. And while *Together Through Life* is undoubtedly a step up from *Modern Times*, it was not nearly as revolutionary as I had first hoped. Mostly it is a surprising return to some of the mid-'80s habits that one would've assumed he had forgone completely. But now, once again he is playing with members of Tom Petty's Heartbreakers (Mike Campbell) and co-writing with the Grateful Dead lyricist Robert Hunter.

The main difference between this album and past ones was the accordion supplied by Los Lobos member Dave Hidalgo. While at first, this marks a nice new surprise, by the end of the album the accordion is so obsequious and omnipresent that you even forget it was ever there to begin with. Otherwise, it's just the general sound of Dylan's backing band that we've had for the last two albums. And while the overall feel is much better than *Modern Times* due to a relative dearth of slower torch ballads ("Life Is Hard" may be the only one that falls into that category), the songs on this one generally aren't very exciting. Songs like "Shake Shake Mama", which sounds like it should be a fun update of Dylan dance songs like "Wiggle Wiggle" and "The Wilbury Twist" winds up being just another up-tempo 12-bar blues number.

The only song on the whole album that comes close to reaching the promise of that opening track is sadly the closing track, "It's All Good". The title phrase is just another of the now expected anachronisms that pop-up on Bob's otherwise pre-1960 retro world-view. And while it is just a single lick repeated infinitely with some clever/repetitive lyrics over it alá "Political World" or "Everything Is Broken", this track displays far more fun and energy that the rest of the album put together. Not that it is horrible, just not terribly interesting. When it was first released this album received the usual "Sure glad Dylan isn't dead" hype and praise, but quickly fell from favor amongst critics and fans.

Originally this album was inspired and started as the soundtrack to the otherwise forgettable movie *My Own Love Song*. Dylan did write a number of instrumental cues that are in the film. If these tracks had been released as an album (and they still haven't) as opposed to *Together Through Life*, it would have made for a much more memorable, distinctive and enjoyable listening experience for me. Although, everyone else probably would have hated it.

Beyond Here Lies Nothin'
(music by Bob Dylan, lyrics by Bob Dylan and Robert Hunter)

Now, this contains more of that *Love & Theft* energy. This song sounds like the Tejano cousin of the Zydeco "On A Night Like This". Much like "Rainy Day Women #12 & 35", the addition of some brass to the instrumentation does wonders in keeping things from getting too stale. More importantly, the accordion makes its presence felt right away and creates a wonderful little world within this song. And Mike Campbell's lead guitar work is far less timid than Dylan's usual touring band's. This track has tons of swagger. The lyrics are the typical meaninglessness, but they're not distracting. I was so psyched when this was released as the first song before the rest of *Together Through Life*. Unfortunately, nothing else on the album comes close to it.

Life Is Hard
(music by Bob Dylan, lyrics by Bob Dylan and Robert Hunter)

The song initially commissioned for *My Own Love Song* that started the whole *Together Through Life* project. The film soundtrack includes an instrumental version of this song, a solo guitar version of this song, and a version sung by the film's protagonist, portrayed by Renee Zellweger. This was meant to be a centerpiece of both of these projects. It's an okay song with a lovely melody and a winning message in the lyrics. It's not quite the jazz ballad like "Moonlight" or "Spirit On The Water", but neither is it the three-chord blues that the previous two albums have been almost entirely composed of. It's got some nice mandolin playing on it that gives it in a strangely non-specific, but foreign, feel instead of invoking the Americana that a mandolin usually implies. This is one of the least accordion-heavy songs on *Together Through Life*. The lyrics are a lovely little paean to how much the narrator needs the object of his affection – although they are now apparently separated. It's nice to hear Bob stretching out into something a little different musically here, but it's not quite up to the standards that a tent-pole song for a film soundtrack would need to be. Still, it's a pretty song; one of the best on this album.

My Wife's Home Town
(music by Willie Dixon, lyrics by Bob Dylan and Robert Hunter)

A rip-off of "I Just Want To Make Love To You" so blatant that Bob just gives Willie Dixon a co-writing credit. Another mother-in-law joke expanded to an entire song, similar to "The Ugliest Girl In The World", also written with Robert Hunter. While that song was able to get past some of the meanness of the lyrics by having the narrator admit to still being into said "girl." This song feels akin to one of the more misogynistic rants of Al Bundy from *Married... With Children* and as such curdles the whole track. No one is sure why the singer of this song is staying with his wife (other than fear of her demonic powers). Sure, it's a little cleverer than just saying "My Wife Is Satan", but it still comes off a little hateful. The music is ably played though. If you want to hear Bob sing a Muddy Waters song with an accordion taking the lead, this is what you're looking for. The accordion kick ass here and the whole things struts along with a cocky self-assurance. However, given how unoriginal the music is and how mean the words are, it's hard to get past that and enjoy the performance.

If You Ever Go to Houston
(music by Bob Dylan, lyrics by Bob Dylan and Robert Hunter)

A pretty typical three-chord blues structure, the introduction tricks you by starting with the IV and V chords before resolving to the I and keying the listener into what key this song is in. Unfortunately, other than that trick, the song is pretty unimaginative. The accordion is still front and center. There's some nylon string guitar in there, but it's pretty buried in the mix. The steady one-two sound of the chord-riff gets irritating after a while. It sounds like they might have been going for a sort of southwest Tejano feel, but didn't quite commit fully to it. The lyrics don't mean much and Bob doesn't do much with them. While it might be a cool little track at three minutes, it wears out its welcome long before it is over. The pace is steady, but not exactly pulse-pounding. Nothing in the song varies from the template established by the end of the first verse.

Forgetful Heart
(music by Bob Dylan, lyrics by Bob Dylan and Robert Hunter)

This is about as bluesy as an accordion can get. There's some banjo plunking around in the background that I could've used more of. The song is another one of Bob's rewrites of the standard 12 bar blues format. Mike Campbell take a tasty slide guitar solo, and Dylan's growl seem appropriate to these disparaging lyrics. However, instead of the anger we would find on something like "Positively 4th Street" or "Property Of Jesus", we just get a feeling of resignation. I'm not sure if it is a sign of maturity or of just getting old and tired, but Dylan seems to have accepted the fact that all woman are going to be mean to him and treat him bad. It sounds like he's used to it by now. This song is a nice change of pace, but not nearly as big of a change of pace as *Together Through Life* really needed.

Jolene
(music by Bob Dylan, lyrics by Bob Dylan and Robert Hunter)

No. Not the Dolly Parton song. Too bad. Instead, we get an up-tempo blues song with a nice little swing to it. The song is really centered around that riff that is infinitely more catchy than the vocal melody itself. In fact, if you just ignore the lyrics to this song and whistle along to the riff, the song is a lot more fun. The words are in praise of a somewhat evil woman that Bob is utterly enamored with. Although Dylan keeps reiterating that he is the king, you can tell by the way he sings it that the queen outranks him here. Bob's gravelly rasp is perfect for this kind of blues song. Not quite dumb enough to be dumb fun, but still a bright addition to *Together Through Life*.

This Dream of You
(written by Bob Dylan)

The only song on here written without Robert Hunter. I have no idea why he was not used for just this one track, but overall it doesn't sound out of place. Given the faux-international feel and violin playing, this song almost feels like something from *Desire*. Clearly, the accordion here is supposed to make you feel like you're dining al fresco at some Parisian sidewalk café. At least Bob isn't trying some Pepé LePew accent here. The lyrics are about the longing for a long-lost lover. Bob's voice is too rough to really express this sort of world-weary regret. There's a nice Mike Campbell slide solo that could stand to be turned up in the mix. There's some mandolin (or mandolin sounding guitars) in here at to the continental feel of the song. The song is festive if a bit too long. Another nice addition to an album that can feel a little samey at times.

Shake Shake Mama
(music by Bob Dylan, lyrics by Bob Dylan and Robert Hunter)

While "Wiggle Wiggle" and "The Wilbury Twist" were fun because one does not expect Dylan to be recording dance tunes, this song is a little disappointing. This is another variation on the same blues chords that Bob has been relying on a lot. The central riff is pretty bland and forgettable. The lyrics are not as goofy as you would hope from a song titled "Shake Shake Mama". Indeed the words aren't so much extorting the listener to dance as much as they are the usual "woman done me wrong" blues trope. The song is far more rocking and upbeat than a lot of tunes on *Together Through Life*, but even musically it doesn't really feel like it would cause anyone to shake. It's almost more disappointing because of what it could've been, but definitely is not: another addition to the small pool of great Dylan dance tracks.

I Feel a Change Comin' On
(music by Bob Dylan, lyrics by Bob Dylan and Robert Hunter)

Many folks saw this song as about Barack Obama. I somehow doubt that Bob would ever address something so pedestrian in his lyrics. If "Things Have Changed" is the dark follow-up to "The Times They Are A-Changin'" then this song is the final sequence in that trilogy. Whether the latest change Bob feels is coming is a change for the better or a change for the worse, Dylan leaves up to the listener. This is one of those songs where it seems like Bob is self-consciously and deliberately trying to write his next anthem or masterpiece, which is a formula that usually leads to failure. Not that this is a horrible song. It's got a more interesting chord structure than any of the other songs on *Together Through Life* without resorting to the jazz stylings of songs like "Moonlight" or "When The Deal Goes Down". Bob's line about how dreams never worked for him reminds me of the bit about "in order to dream you've still got to be asleep" from "When You Gonna Wake Up?" It's a surprisingly anti-encouraging statement that Bob has apparently held fast to all these years. The song has nice upbeat shuffle feel without ever trying to really rock out. The accordion continues to glue everything together on this record. The melody has a few hooks and is pleasant if not super-catchy. While this might not be the stand-out track from this album that Dylan initially envisioned, it's a good song.

It's All Good
(music by Bob Dylan, lyrics by Bob Dylan and Robert Hunter)

While it may be a little embarrassing for a musician of Dylan's vintage to try and incorporate a trendy catchphrase like the title here, the sheer audacity and incongruity of the moment makes the whole exercise joyful. Sure, the phrase "it's all good" went from hip to passé within the timespan of a few short months, the fact that Bob has immortalized this bit of slang is precious. Of course, it helps that the song itself is infectious and danceable. Sure the lyrics are pure drivel, but coming from Dylan's grizzled rasp, they take on a whole new dimension. The music is all based on a single chord-riff, but the band actually injects this tune with some dynamics, taking things down at certain points and bringing it to a boil later. It may be as a deep a puddle of water, but it's a good time. At the end when the accordion and the slide guitar stop playing in unison and start echoing that main riff back and forth to each other is just excellent. Sure, the song didn't need to be five-and-a-half minutes long, but it is still one of my all-time favorites from *Together Through Life*. It's certainly the closest the album comes to fulfilling the promise of the opening track, "Beyond Here Lies Nothin'".

Songs not on the album:
Sweeping The Floor from the unreleased soundtrack to *My Own Love Song*
(written by Bob Dylan)

An upbeat blues swing with the upright bass turned way up in the mix. It only lasts a minute, but it is a fun little bit of incidental music that for some reason I imagine accompanying a low-stakes car chase in the film (which I admittedly have not yet seen).

Bumble Bee from the unreleased soundtrack to *My Own Love Song*
(written by Bob Dylan)

This is just a couple of spaced-out chords on the mandolin (or a guitar really high up on the neck) with some odd reversed echoes firing off in between each of these chords. Not really a song or even music as much as a sound effect that provokes a mood or emotion that I assume matches the scene.

Jane's Lament from the unreleased soundtrack to *My Own Love Song*
(written by Bob Dylan)

Some semi-flamenco type of fiddling around on a nylon string guitar. Tasty but not long enough to leave much of an impression on its own. It's a nice little treat.

Joey's Theme from the unreleased soundtrack to *My Own Love Song*
(written by Bob Dylan)

This is just "Forgetful Heart" without the vocals laid on top of it yet. Nothing too special.

Driving South from the unreleased soundtrack to *My Own Love Song*
(written by Bob Dylan)

A brief snippet of some blues guitar. It doesn't sound like it was borrowed from a specific song off of *Together Through Life* but doesn't really stand on its own either.

Back Alley from the unreleased soundtrack to *My Own Love Song*
(written by Bob Dylan)

This is a short run-through of "Beyond Here Lies Nothin'" only lacking both the vocals and the trumpet. It's nice to hear how cool the accordion part is in semi-isolation, but nothing worth saving.

Snow Falling from the unreleased soundtrack to *My Own Love Song*
(written by Bob Dylan)

Some banjo picking (or a guitar that really sounds like a banjo). It doesn't do much or go anywhere, but it creates a cool little mood for whichever scene it was meant to accompany in the film.

Billie #30 from the unreleased soundtrack to *My Own Love Song*
(written by Bob Dylan)

This sounds like a different mix of an instrumental snippet of "This Dream Of You" It mostly emphasizes the strummed acoustic guitar which has some nice rakes on it, but this doesn't really stand out or standalone either. The title almost sounds like a parody of Bob's work on the *Pat Garret & Billy The Kid* soundtrack, which I appreciated.

Road Weary from the unreleased soundtrack to *My Own Love Song*
(written by Bob Dylan)

A boogie-woogie type of blues guitar line that sounds like it was isolated out from "Beyond Here Lies Nothin'". Bereft of its original context, it's a little hard to place the riff at first. A fun little bit of track deconstruction, but nothing essential.

Click Clack from the unreleased soundtrack to *My Own Love Song*
(written by Bob Dylan)

A bit of an accordion-led Tejano shuffle that at least doesn't sound like it was recycled from a song off of *Together Through Life*. While it may have been written for the film, "written" may be too big of a word for it. It's just a single chord and a feel, but Bob's band plays it wonderfully.

Robbie Robert's Lament from the unreleased soundtrack to *My Own Love Song*
(written by Bob Dylan)

A bit of electric guitar soloing that sounds like it was recorded from very far away. No heavy metal heroics here, but it is doubtful that Bob played it himself or indicated any specific notes of melody played here. It slowly gets closer to the listener over its one-minute duration.

New Orleans Drums from the unreleased soundtrack to *My Own Love Song*
(written by Bob Dylan)

As the title implies, this is just drums. It's not a drum solo per se as much as it is merely 70 seconds of a drum pattern. It's quite possible this was lifted from one of the actual songs on *Together Through Life*, but I can't quite place it, I think it might be "Beyond Here Lies Nothin'". In isolation, this simple but funky drum track is surprisingly evocative.

Jane's Step from the unreleased soundtrack to *My Own Love Song*
(written by Bob Dylan)

A couple of chords strummed on an acoustic guitar. Of all the songs here, it is most likely that this was actually played by Dylan himself. Nothing too terribly spectacular or exciting here, but a pleasant little palate cleanser.

Blues Club from the unreleased soundtrack to *My Own Love Song*
(written by Bob Dylan)

Just some faint blues guitar playing. This one, unfortunately, is too hard to hear to give much of an impression.

Swingin' from the unreleased soundtrack to *My Own Love Song*
(written by Bob Dylan)

Some electric blues slide guitar. Doesn't feel very "composed" as much as it is just the kind of improvising that most guitarists fiddle around with while waiting for other musicians to set-up. However, since this was played by Mike Campbell (or possibly one of the guys in Bob's band), it sounds a lot better than your average guitar player.

East Texas from the unreleased soundtrack to *My Own Love Song*
(written by Bob Dylan)

Just a minute and a half of "This Dream Of You" without the vocals. Not particularly worth seeking out in this format.

"MY OWN LOVE SONG: TOGETHER THROUGH LIFE"

SIDE A:
1. Beyond Here Lies Nothin'
2. New Orleans Drums
3. Swingin'
4. Life Is Hard
5. Jane's Lament
6. Click Clack
7. Snow Falling
8. Forgetful Heart

SIDE B:
1. Driving South
2. Robbie Robert's Lament
3. Jolene
4. Bumble Bee
5. This Dream Of You
6. Sweeping The Floor
7. Jane's Step
8. It's All Good

Since no official soundtrack was released for *My Own Love Song*, I have used this album as an excuse to finally release some of these snippets from the cinematic graveyard where they were buried. Ultimately I just lopped off the *Together Through Life* songs I think didn't work and replaced them with some choice soundtrack cuts. Since these tend to be so short I usually have two of them paired together between each of the full songs. This may not make for a true sequel to the soundtrack for *Billy The Kid & Pat Garret*, I think it helps elevate this album from being what was starting to become a run-of-the-mill post-millennial Bob Dylan album.

I did end up decided to nix "I Feel A Change Comin' On" even though it has some potential. Ultimately it wasn't quite up to snuff. Cutting tracks like "Shake Shake Mama", "If You Ever Get To Houston" and "My Wife's Home Town" was a much easier decision. Maybe some people will find the instrumental snippets a distraction from the flow of this record, but for me, I appreciate the new and more intriguing direction of this re-working of *Together Through Life*.

CHRISTMAS IN THE HEART

Produced by: Jack Frost
Released: October 13th, 2009

Famous/Important/Popular Track(s):
- Must Be Santa

My Personal Favorite Track(s):
- Here Comes Santa Claus
- O' Come All Ye Faithful (Adeste Fideles)
- The Christmas Song

For the first time since 1970, Bob has released two studio albums in one year. And it is my favorite since 1970's *Self-Portrait*. For an artist whose career was once defined it's left-turns and radical re-inventions, this was the weirdest thing Bob had done since he recovered from Christianity. And even stranger is how completely straight he plays it. He sings one verse of "Adeste Fidelis" in the original Latin. He doesn't even try to write or re-write any new carols to add to the canon (unfortunately). It just sounds like a traditional Bing Crosby holiday record from the fifties, with the only really incongruous element being Bob's ragged voice. From the first moment with the sleigh bells and the choir on "Here Comes Santa Claus" you know this is a Christmas record. Even if you had never heard any of the songs before (which is nigh impossible) and didn't know what the lyrics meant, it still sounded Christmas-y.

This definitely the most "produced" of all the (aptly-named) Jack Frost productions. This is what you'd expect a Bob Dylan Christmas record to sound like if you ever expected a Bob Dylan Christmas record. In fact, the only really unsuccessful song on the album is the one closest to Dylan's usual milieu, "Christmas Blues".

For those wondering if Bob had given up Christianity, or had just given up talking about, this album offers plenty of evidence for both sides: he sings passionately and sincerely about the baby Jesus ... and Santa Claus. He even wraps up the album with a traditional "amen" coda; something he didn't try on the trio of born again albums.

Even when it is seasonably inappropriate, this CD finds its way into my player frequently. It may be easier to appreciate this album when you are not being bombarded so constantly by other renditions of "Silent Night" and "Winter Wonderland" that any version of such fare is bound to grate.

In some ways, this album is a bridge between the two eras of covers before and after it. The more traditional hymns bring to mind the folk songs of *Good As I Been To You* or *World Gone Wrong*, while the more Bing Crosby inflected "modern" songs presage the Sinatra period of *Shadows In The Night*, *Fallen Angels*, and *Triplicate*.

Here Comes Santa Claus
(written by Gene Autry and Oakley Haldeman)

You want Christmas?!? Here's your goddamn Christmas!! There's no mistaking this for any other Dylan album as the very first sound you hear are sleigh bells solo for several measures followed by a choir of "oohs." However, once Bob's vocals kick in, there is also no mistaking this for a lost Bing Crosby record either. This song has a much faster up-and-down melody than Bob usually rights for himself, but he tackles it with aplomb. The instrumentation would be cheezy if it weren't so steadfastly retro. There even is a guitar solo that does nothing be to reiterate the melody. The perfect "Up With People" style choir trades lines with Bob's wheezy rasp throughout the song creating all sorts of dissonance that is just magical. Bob is not going to ease you into the Christmas spirit. He is going to dunk you into 100 proof eggnog on the very first track. You should be able to tell instantly from this song whether you are going to be in or out with *Christmas In The Heart*.

Do You Hear What I Hear?
(lyrics by Noël Regney, music by Gloria Shayne Baker)

A stately recording of this Christmas chestnut. There's some lovely violin in here, once again showing that this album has a far greater instrumental palette than your average Jack Frost-produced record. The drums are keeping up a gentle marching pattern that is just perfect for this song. Bob tone is a little gravelly, but he hits all the notes with aplomb. His tone is as warm as a sweater on a December morn. While not as big of a shock as "Here Comes Santa Claus", this is defiantly continuing that path. Bob isn't even going to shy away from the more overtly religious carols in the Christmas canon. He even throws in a key change in this song; just because that's the kind of thing that these old recordings would do.

Winter Wonderland
(lyrics by Richard Smith, music by Felix Bernard)

The sleigh bells are back. As are the Andy Williams-style singers. While not as bodacious as "Here Comes Santa Claus" we are firmly ensconced in *Christmas In The Heart* by this point, and we don't need to define the sound as much here. There's some plucked violin in the mix here and well as a brief upright bass solo at the end that all adds to the variety and gaiety of this track. The pedal steel guitars here sound far more Hawaiian exotica than the C&W style that Dylan uses the instrument for on other records. Bob does trade some of the lines with his backing vocalists but sounds more than up to the task of singing this melody. It's great little track that does squeak in under two minutes. A delightful Xmas treat!

Hark the Herald Angels Sing
(lyrics by Charles Wesley, music by Felix Mendelssohn)

Bob is trading back and forth one secular and then one religious song so far. There are lots of strings here. Maybe not a whole string section but more than one violin. Plus the upright bass is being bowed as well. This gives the arrangement here more of a symphonic sound while still staying within the confines of his usual backing band. After the first verse, everything strips down for half a verse sung by the backing singer and accompanied almost entirely by a softly tinkling celeste. I think I can even detect orchestral bells faintly in the background. While a more somber and serious carol, there is still a lot of joy imparting not only in the vocals but in the audacious use of instruments in this track. This one may not stand out at first, but upon repeat listens Bob's "Hark The Herald Angels Sing" really grows on you.

I'll Be Home for Christmas
(lyrics by Buck Ram and Kim Gannon, music by Walter Kent)

While Dylan would soon be knee deep in a severe Frank Sinatra fascination, on this album, it seems like his main inspiration is Bing Crosby. Bob opens this song mostly accompanied with only a chorus of male singers going "ooh." The band does eventually kick in, and Bob decides to let his backing singers take the lead on every other line in thanks for their service. This is certainly the song and arrangement that most bridge the gap between songs like "When The Deal Goes Down" and "Bye & Bye" that preceded *Christmas In The Heart* and later albums such as *Shadows In The Night*, *Fallen Angels*, and *Triplicate*. In the context of this holly jolly yuletide, these kinds of torch ballads make complete sense, and Dylan sings it wonderfully.

The Little Drummer Boy
(written by Harry Simeone, Henry Onorati, and Katherine Davis)

It's your usual song about giving the gift of a drum solo to a newborn. There was always something odd about this song. Why would a baby want to hear that? Maybe giving a kid a drum would make sense, if he were a little bit older, but I doubt that an infant who just wants to sleep (along with his mother) would have any use for a drum solo. Unlike a lot of modern arrangements of this song, Bob does not overly emphasize the titular percussion. In fact, it is given a respectful distance which is nice. Bob and the accompanying mini-choir do a lovely job of singing what is a sad melody, considering the subject matter. The playing is generally stately and restrained. The backing vocalists get half a verse to themselves to shine. Not one of the more exciting tracks from this album, but it is a nice respite from the more "jolly" tunes here.

The Christmas Blues
(written by David Jack Holt and Sammy Cahn)

Surprisingly, the Christmas song that works the least on this album is the blues song. You would've thought that would be right up Dylan's alley. Unfortunately, this doesn't work. Maybe because it's not really a blues song, but rather a pop-oriented attempt at aping the tropes of a blues song. It's got some harmonica on it, which is always lovely as that tends to be a rarer occurrence in later Dylan records. The song is pretty ghastly, but Bob can't seem to decide whether or not to lean into the growl that would be thematically appropriate here or continue to try and croon with clarity as he has for the remainder of this album. I wish he had either doubled down on the blues on this track or discarded them entirely and played it up like he had with "Here Comes Santa Claus" or "Winter Wonderland". Even the harmonica solo is just playing the melody instead of improvising on a pentatonic scale. Personally, this is the only song I this album I regularly skip.

O' Come All Ye Faithful (Adeste Fideles)
(traditional, arranged By Bob Dylan)

Bob sings the first verse in Latin. What else do you need to know? There are some lovely winds playing in the intro and an undercurrent of cello and accordion. This song is taken with the utmost seriousness and solemnity. Bob's pronunciation of the Latin may betray a lack of understanding of the language, but he still sings every syllable of this with conviction. After the second verse in English, the backing vocalists take the lead for the first half of the third verse. There are no drums played here, or needed. Everyone knows this song. There's no need to add more to this song than Bob already does. It's not stripped down by any stretch, just served with reverence. Another Xmas classic!

Have Yourself a Merry Little Christmas
(written by Hugh Martin and Ralph Blane)

This can be one of the more melancholic Xmas carols ever written. Bob, however, doesn't mine this tune for pathos, instead choosing to emphasize the jolly and light feel of the rest of this album. This song starts in a more standard fashion, no chirpy backing singers, no sleigh bells or trumpets or violins. Just lovely interplay between the piano and an electric guitar with the tremolo turned up. It's kind of a nice refreshing change of pace. About two minutes in, Bob cedes the singing to the backing singers who take the lead on two lines and then disappear again. It's an odd choice. The backing vocalists do return with some oohs before the whole thing is over, but this is one of the more stripped down solo-ish tracks on *Christmas In the Heart*. As amazing as I think this album is, it does threaten to get repetitive. Luckily, there are tracks like this that offer just enough variation to keep this album from getting as monotonous as *Good As I Been To You* or *Shadows In The Night*.

Must Be Santa
(written by William Fredericks and Hal Moore)

The big "hit" from the album is actually one of my least favorite tracks on here. It's always fun to hear Bob do a rambunctious polka, but other than the lyrical content, this song feels like it belongs on a different album. The arrangement is clearly nicked from the Brave Combo's version of this song. I love the way Dylan throws in the names of the last few presidents for no good reason too. It just all this jolliness feels a bit forced. The other up-tempo songs on this record feel like Christmas songs you've heard a million times before, this feels like Bob trying to show off his musicology by digging out some obscure folk or blues tune and making you feel bad for not being familiar with it, to begin with. The only other songs as close to obscure as this are "Christmas Island" and "The Christmas Blues". Which may be why other listeners were far more willing to accept Dylan's vocals on this track than on something they are used to hearing sung in a specific and "pretty" way. While the rest of this album comes across as very sincere and reverential, this is the only track on here that feels like a drunken uncle at a holiday party that most reviewers compared this album to. Ultimately it's a fun little change of pace with a specific genre twist like the exotica of "Christmas Island", but doesn't work nearly as well.

Silver Bells
(written by Raymond Evans & Jay Livingston)

One of the slower and sadder of the secular carols recorded here. The arrangement here starts with a piano and some faint mandolin. There's a nice bit of pedal steel guitar once the whole band kicks in as well as some fine fiddling. Bob sings this track alone without any assistance from the backing vocalists. If you listen carefully you can almost hear a tuba playing oompah-pah in the background. I don't know whether it's actually in there or if it's just my imagination. Even for an album that plays it pretty straight, this is not one of the more radical re-interpretations. There are no solos here, keeping the song to just about two-and-a-half minutes. While not nearly as touching and compelling as the more religious carols, this is still a lovely number, fit for any holiday celebration.

The First Noel
(traditional, arranged By Bob Dylan)

I don't know if the "ah-noel" is a traditional ending alá "amen" or if it's just something that Bob made up. This is the religious carol that is probably treated closest to the frivolity of the secular material. The song opening with an a cappella round. The backing vocalists even take the lead at one point. Later the whole song breaks down just leaving Bob singing over a pump organ (or possibly an accordion). There's some love chimes and/or bells on this song. This is what of the more intricate instrumental arrangements on this album. The snare drum is playing a bunch of rolls and marching patterns, but it is taken very softly. With so much going on here, the song covers a lot of ground within its two-and-a-half minutes. By this point on *Christmas In the Heart*, it is not a surprise, but it is still a lovely little package of joy.

Christmas Island
(written by Lyle Moraine)

Nothing confirms the 1950s template for this album like this throwback to the brief exotica/tiki lounge fad of the time. Finally, the pedal steel guitar returns to the state of its birth, not Texas but Hawaii. You can practically hear the fake grass skirts and coconut bras on the hula dancers here. Sadly I don't think there's any ukulele involved. The song itself is dopey but appropriate. It's one of the more obscure tracks on this album that tends to feature more well-known carols. Only "Must be Santa" and possibly "The Christmas Blues" are less likely to be sung at a children's holiday recital. Unlike the faux-blues styling of "The Christmas Blues" this song thrives on inauthenticity. If there were any actual concession to the traditional sounds of Oceania, it would have undercut the not-entirely-true fantasies of an island getaway that this song represents. And this is recording is actually in praise of artifice. While Dylan is often seen as a paragon of authenticity, don't forget that when he came on the scene, his portrayal of his background to the media was as made-up as Vanilla Ice's. In a weird way, the deliberately fake "island" sound here is authentic to Robert Zimmerman if not Bob Dylan. While not as sincere as the more religious carols on here, this is just as important to *Christmas In The Heart*

The Christmas Song
(written by Mel Tormé and Bob Wells)

Bob Dylan sings Mel Tormé! If the Dean Martin cover "Return To Me" was our first hint of what Dylan would be doing 2015-2017 then this is the second. The clunkily titled "The Christmas Song" is better known by its opening line "Chestnuts roasting on an open fire", although Dylan restores the often-forgotten introduction to this song. The song is performed with the same sincerity and reverence as a track like "Beyond The Horizon" or "Spirit On The Water". The brushed drums bring to mind the Vince Guaraldi Trio's work on *A Charlie Brown Christmas*. The pedal steel even has a nice little solo. This is one of the few songs on here without backing vocalists. Although the lyrics are definitely secular, Bob's voice is dripping with reverence. It, in fact, may be one of the saddest songs on the album, despite nothing to indicate that in the lyrics. While I do tend to prefer and remember the more obviously jolly tunes like "Here Comes Santa Claus", this song does provide a nice counterpoint and some variety to the mood of this album. Another stand-out!

O Little Town of Bethlehem
(traditional, arranged By Bob Dylan)

Another reverent rendition of a religious carol to finish things off. We've had some fun with the lighter, more secular tunes, but Bob definitely wants to end this album with a reminder of "the reason for the season." The track kicks off with some lovely a cappella oohs. The instrumentation here is mostly church organ and piano, with some shimmering electric guitar to keep this version too church-bound. After the first verse, there is a traditional key change. Bob's vocal is at his gruffest, and by the end of the second verse, he lets the backing vocals take over for a couple of lines. Not even particularly apropos lines, leaving one to wonder, if he couldn't do those last few or if he screwed them up and just had the backing vocalists cover for him. One of the shorter songs on the album; after just two verses and an "amen" ending, Dylan wraps up his jolliest, warmest, most unexpected yuletide gift.

Songs not on the album:
'Twas The Night Before Christmas from the B-side of the "Must Be Santa" single
(written by Clement Clarke Moore)

Not so much a song as it is a recitation of the well-known poem, with some cheap, public-use Christmas music tinkling in the background. This was not originally meant to be released, but was rather just a bit performed by Dylan for his satellite radio show "Theme Time Hour". For some reason this was taken and used as the B-side of the "Must Be Santa Single" but it is not any more of a song than "Last Thought On Woody Guthrie" from *The Bootleg Series, vol. 1* is. However, it is a fascinating look at Bob as an orator. He may not be much of an actor, nor is he ever cast in movies that really require much acting from him (*Hearts of Fire* and *Masked & Anonymous*). This recording might be some of what limited thespian skills he does have. His speaking voice has a lot of character. Apparently, Bob was initially offered the guest role of the "Space Coyote" in an episode of *The Simpsons*. Dylan passed on the part, and it was given to Johnny Cash. It's too bad though because listening to his "'Twas The Night Before Christmas" makes one think that Bob really could've knocked that role out of the park.

"CHRISTMAS IN THE HEART"

SIDE A:
1. Here Comes Santa Claus
2. Winter Wonderland
3. I'll Be Home For Christmas
4. Have Yourself A Merry Little Christmas
5. The Christmas Song
6. Christmas Island
7. Silver Bells

SIDE B:
1. Do You Hear What I Hear?
2. Hark The Herald Angels Sing
3. The Little Drummer Boy
4. O' Come All Ye Faithful (Adeste Fideles)
5. The First Noel
6. O Little Town Of Bethlehem

One of the harder albums for me to re-configure. Not only are there nearly no (known) outtakes from this album, but I love almost every song that is on this album. I did go ahead and cut "Must Be Santa" since its rambunctious spirit felt at odds with the rest of the album. From there I tried to divide all the more upbeat and secular song to side one, while the slower religious carols on side two. But this album doesn't cleave cleanly or evenly along those lines. Ultimately, this line-up is more of a thought experiment than any sort of improvement in my eyes. Really, there is no way to improve on *Christmas In The Heart.*

TEMPEST

Produced by: Jack Frost
Recorded: January – March 2012
Released: September 10th, 2012

Famous/Important/Popular Track(s):
- Duquesne Whistle

My Personal Favorite Track(s):
- Narrow Way
- Scarlet Town
- Tin Angel

On March 9th, 2012 *The Aspen Times* published an interview with Los Lobos accordionist David Hidalgo. Hidalgo, who played on *Together Through Life* and *Christmas In The Heart* casually mentioned that he had just finished working on a new Dylan record. This was a big scoop since no one else in the public knew that Bob was working on anything new at the time. In the interview he mentioned that Dylan was interested in some of the more exotic instruments that he played, such as the tres, stating that the new album would have something of a Mexican sound and that each song had a completely different approach to it.

Unfortunately, when *Tempest* came out, this was not the case at all. The songs all ended up sounding the same, with very similar arrangements and instrumentation to *Modern Times* and no trace of anything vaguely Mexican. Furthermore, it sounds like David Hidalgo isn't on the album at all. Now I don't think this is not because David was lying to *The Aspen Times*. Rather it seems that Bob was hurt that David betrayed his confidence and broke the news of his new album.

While Dylan is not necessarily opposed to pre-release publicity to generate excitement for his albums, he does like to tightly control the flow of information about himself that comes out, and I imagine that Bob saw this interview as a breach of trust. Dylan wants to control the narrative that surrounds his album so he can't put out possibly spurious assertions like that *Tempest* was initially meant to be a religious record.

I think it is far more likely that, instead of a version of *Tempest* that is a sequel to *Slow Train Coming*, there is an iteration of the album that has more of what there is far more exciting and varied before Bob either mixed Hidalgo out, or re-recorded the songs, or just chose the least "Mexican" sounding takes and tracks. But who knows? We may not hear these outtake until *The Bootleg Series vol. 29* or until after Dylan's dropped his grudge against Hidalgo. Which may not happen until after his death. I don't think that Bob has worked with, or even talked to, Hidalgo since the news leaked.

Which is a shame because *Tempest* is one of Dylan's least interesting albums. If the comments in *The Aspen Times* are accurate about what

Tempest was supposed to sound like, I would've been really excited for this record. As it is, this is a mess.

We have gone from one of my favorite Dylan albums to one of my least. Much like *Together Through Life*, and pretty much everything since *Time Out Of Mind*, this album was greeted with nothing but near-universal praise. However, unlike *Together Through Life* this adoration has not waned after the initial joy of getting a new Dylan album wore off. And I don't understand what all the big fuss is about. The first few bars of the opening track, "Duquesne Whistle", do start to offer the same sort of hope that "Beyond Here Lies Nothing" did for that album – but that optimism doesn't even manage to last through the whole song. The generic 3 chords of the previous blues songs and the slow tedium of the torch ballads have been merged together into one consistent style that lasts the entire album - a style that has none of the blues tunes' rock energy or any of the ballads' interesting jazz chords.

Fans and critics go on about how bloody and murder-filled the lyrics are, but if you're not really listening to the words you would have no idea as these are mostly pretty sedate tunes. While the co-writing credit for Robert Hunter on "Duquesne Whistle" indicates it was a leftover from the *Together Through Life* sessions, only the 12-bars blues with accordion draped on of "Early Roman Kings" manages to capture what little spark that last Dylan album of originals had.

Given how much I loved *Christmas In The Heart* and how much this album was a throwback to the things I didn't like about *Modern Times*, I really would've preferred that Bob stopped writing new material and just stick to recording albums of covers. Many people compared this album's title to the final work by Shakespeare and assumed that Dylan was retiring after this album. Of course, no one in 2012 could've predicted what the future of Dylan's discography was going to hold. Who knows what the public reaction would've been had we had any idea what was coming next.

Duquesne Whistle
(music by Bob Dylan, lyrics by Bob Dylan and Robert Hunter)

The song kicks off with a swing piece that sounds oddly faint for no discernible reason. After 42 seconds of that, the drums kick in, and everything becomes louder. This is a swing tune with a walking bass line that promises a lot more fun than *Tempest* ever manages to deliver. The music is a little more jazzy and complicated than Dylan usually works with. Perhaps all that time playing Bing Crosby numbers for *Christmas In The Heart* taught Bob some new chords. It's still just a rather medium-level shuffle that starts to get old two minutes before it's over. However there is a little musical bit at that point that at least gives us something new to listen to for a bit, but there's no need for the solo as the songs fades out padding out the run-time. After the stately croon on the last album, Bob's voice sounds especially ragged on phlegmy here. The lyrics are, as usual, inscrutable. However Dylan's vocal delivery is not doing a convincing job of conveying how he feels about these words, so it is hard for the listener to be too terribly investing in figuring out what they mean.

Soon After Midnight
(written by Bob Dylan)

While there are no out-and-out ballads like "Moonlight" or "Spirit On The Water" on *Tempest*, this may be as close as we get. It's not a standard 12-bar blues. It even has a bridge section. It's a mid-tempo pop tune served at a medium heat with nothing terribly distinguishing about it other than the fact it's shorter than most things on this album. There's an adequate pedal steel solo. The lyrics with all their talk about midnight and fairy queens seems like it should invoking some sort of Cinderella fairy tale, but is in fact just a boilerplate Dylan love song. Not much to say about this one.

Narrow Way
(written by Bob Dylan)

This song is nothing but a simple blues riff repeated over one chord for the entire verse. It only gets to the IV and V chords for the choruses. This sounds like it would've fit in with the more up-tempo numbers on *Modern Times*. Bob's voice sounds especially bored on this track, and not as an affectation. Nothing in there makes me particularly want to pay attention to the lyrics. Which is a problem since this track is seven-and-a-half minutes and there is nothing else going on. There is no bridge or middle eight or anything. The guitar solo is almost just a simple pair of note pasted on top of a vocal-less verse. The choruses never manage to be catchy no matter how often they are repeated. One of the least successful tracks on *Tempest*.

Long and Wasted Years
(written by Bob Dylan)

A lot of pedal steel on this track. The chord structure sounds a little more complicated than Bob's usual blues rip-off. There's a simple six-note descending riff that opens each verse that helps keep the listener's attention. Again, there's no bridge or chorus or anything else going on here. Not nearly as inventive or jazzy as some of the cuts on *Love & Theft* or *Modern Times*. The lyrics seem to be about regret; maybe even a lost love, but Dylan's singing doesn't imbue them with much ruefulness. Bob does reference "Twist & Shout" in the lyrics, presaging the Beatles-quoting "Roll On John". This song is a little too slow to be exciting or even interesting, but runs a merciful 3:46 so it doesn't become too grating.

Pay in Blood
(written by Bob Dylan)

Many have remarked that *Tempest* has a lot more violence, bloodshed, and even gore than one would expect from a Bob Dylan album. Personally, the most disturbing image in here is actually the politician who is "pumping out the piss". The lyrics for the chorus/refrain are clever, playing off the expectations of whose blood someone would be paying with. I'm assuming that the words here are meant as a threat, although to whom or what I'm not sure. Bob's vocals sound so close to feeble that it is hard to be intimidated by them, but you got to admire his bravado here. The most noteworthy part of the song is how he goes to the minor VI chord for a funky breakdown in the second half of each verse. It feels strange and unexpected. Unfortunately, it is not quite enough to make the song itself interesting, especially when Dylan repeats it so often. Maybe if it were just an occasional bridge in the song, it wouldn't dull the impact. Not a great song, but one of the better ones on *Tempest*.

Scarlet Town
(written by Bob Dylan)

The banjo makes another appearance along with the violin. Neither one is particularly prominent in the mix or given much to do, but it does help change things up a bit. The song is obviously trying to melancholic, with a haunting melody. Unfortunately, Bob's blown vocal cords strip this song of any poignancy it might have had. The lyrics are a series of sad tableaus, but they don't feel particularly applicable or like they add up to anything. Bob does manage to sing the phrase "flat-chested junkie whore" which may be even more surprising than hearing him reference Alicia Keys. The song goes on for over seven minutes despite only being just a three-chord pattern with no variation. The song is primarily acoustic, so it is something of a surprise when the electric guitar pops up takes a solo midway through. It feels a little dampened though and lacks real punch. While not a great song, there are a lot worse on *Tempest* and as such this track tends to stand out in comparison.

Early Roman Kings
(written by Bob Dylan)

The only song on here with the accordion that dominated the previous album *Together Through Life*. With a simple blues structure and a riff ripped off from Muddy Waters' "Mannish Boy" this song feel far more at home on that album than it does on *Tempest*. I have no idea what the lyrics are talking about. I thought early Rome was more involved with senators and triumvirates. I certainly never got the impression in history class that it was ever a monarchy, although I will admit that history is not my forte. It's probably a metaphor for something, but I have no idea what. Maybe the mafia. Whatever the accuracy of the lyrics, Bob's gravelly voice sounds super-appropriate here. As a fun song with an upbeat feel, this actually helps stand out on *Tempest* and inject some life into the whole affair. Not a major song, but there's nothing wrong with it.

Tin Angel
(written by Bob Dylan)

A tragic tale of infidelity and murder worthy of any folk song. Whatever action may be taking place within the narrative of the lyrics is thoroughly undermined by the music. This song runs over nine minutes and only has one chord. It's a cool groove, with an undercurrent of banjo and some sweet glissandos on the upright bass. But no matter how cool it is, it will get irritating after being so relentless played without any change in the tempo or dynamics or any sort of bridge or chorus or middle eight. There's a bit of melody, which is about all that makes this an actual song instead of just a recited poem over a looping background. If this weren't Bob, I would be convinced that this was only two or four bars of music that were copied and pasted in ProTools to create the illusion of a whole song. Knowing Dylan however, I'm sure this was in fact played live by real musicians all the way through. But if they're not given anything else to do, then what is the point of wasting the band's time playing the same thing over and over and over again? The lyrics are dark and mean-spirited and gruesome. Bob's growl may be scary or intimidating at first, but the longer it goes on, the more it sounds like he is just a feeble old man unable to make good on any of his threats. I would almost just rather read Bob's lyrics off of the page than listen to this track again.

Tempest
(written by Bob Dylan)

The song starts off with a nice faux-Irish feel with a prominent fiddle. From there we settle into a 3-chord verse in 6/8 time. I sure hope you like it because we're not going to get anything else for the rest of the song. At fourteen minutes, this is the second-longest song Bob has yet released, only behind "Highlands". Nothing changes in this song. There are no bridges, no choruses, no dynamic, no change in the arrangement or the tempo, no instrumental soloing except for the occasional blank verse to allow Bob time to catch his breath. The only thing is the never-ending series of incidents on the Titanic that are listed here. Most of these are apocryphal. In fact, many references to Leo, the sketchbook artist, seem drawn more from James Cameron's movie than any historical record. There's a watchman mentioned a couple of times that seems to be the closest thing to some sort of overreaching theme that unites all these rambling couplets. We hardly get to know any of these characters, making this song in some ways a sequel to the shallow characterizations of Jim Carroll's "People Who

Have Died" or "88 lines about 44 Women" by the Nails. Bob's growl gives no indication of whether or not he feels these people deserved their fate or if it was just bad luck or what. Even Gordon Lightfoot's "The Wreck Of The Edmund Fitzgerald" was more compact and concise and exciting. Ultimately it doesn't matter. Nothing in this song matters. It just keeps going on and on. This is easily one of my least favorite Bob Dylan tracks ever. Of course, Bob decided to name the album after it. Yet despite its self-importance, Dylan doesn't even end the album with this impossible-to-follow-up song.

Roll on John
(written by Bob Dylan)

Bob Dylan has met John Lennon. While not super-close, the two did know each other. There is photographic evidence of that. I have to remind myself of that fact because this 32-year belated tribute Lennon feels completely out-of-touch with who he was as a person or even what it was that made him famous in the first place. If it weren't for the occasional ham-fisted references to Beatles song within the lyrics, one would assume that this song is actually about some random Irish slave who came to America in the 1800s or something. Dylan has never been one to let historical accuracy to get in the way of a good song, but considering how famous John Lennon was, ignoring whole swaths of his life to go into a rambling faux-folk tale is just inexplicable. Not only are the lyrics misguided, but nothing in the music itself seems terribly related to anything John liked or wrote. There's at least a chorus in here, but that's about the only concession to Lennon's typical songwriting. Not that a tribute to Lennon needs to sound like a Beatles-clone, but this song is just turgid and dull. As hard as Bob has fought over the years not be seen as a 60s-only artist, writing a song like this instantly paints him as someone whose best days have been behind him for several decades. This is unfortunate as it's not true and there's nothing in here about how Dylan actually felt about Lennon or how his death might've affected someone who was in a similar position as he was.

Songs not on the album:
Things We Said Today from *The Art Of McCartney*
(written by John Lennon and Paul McCartney)

While Bob couldn't muster a compelling tribute to John Lennon, he surprisingly also recorded a tribute to Paul McCartney around the same time that worked far more effectively even though Bob is clearly more aligned with John than Paul of the two Beatles. While Dylan did perform "Something" by George Harrison live on occasion, he has not yet recorded a tribute to the one member of the band he actually spent the most time with. I think this was actually recorded with McCartney's backing band, making one of the few times Bob has recorded without his touring band in the last twenty or so years. Whoever the group is, they play this song fairly straight and faithful to the original arrangement. There's a bit more electric piano played on this, and I wonder if that was actually Bob providing some of the instrumental backing on this track as it sounds a little more out of place. The major difference is really the lack of someone doing Lennon's harmony vocal from the original which really helped elevate the song on *Help!* Luckily instead of picking one of Paul's bigger hits, this choice of a relatively obscure album track fits Bob perfectly. While he may not have this song steeped in his bones as thoroughly as something by Woody Guthrie or Blind Willie McTell, he still attacks this song with verve and vigor. It is a surprising triumph on a tribute album that tends a little too much to the bland.

The Love That Faded from *The Lost Notebooks Of Hank Williams*
(lyrics by Hank Williams, music by Bob Dylan)

While T-Bone Burnett was putting together a super-group to put music to unfinished lyrics from Bob's *Basement Tapes* days, Bob himself was rounding up superstars to write music for a recently uncovered set of poems by his hero Hank Williams. Some of the participants in this album project tried to skew their songs closer to Hank's personal style, while others used it as a basis to write another song that was more typical of their own sound. In addition to spearheading the project, Bob co-wrote and sang one tune, "The Love That Faded". Bob's version of a Hank Williams tune is definitely far more straight-ahead country than anything he's recorded since *Nashville Skyline*. Dylan hasn't penned a lyric this non-cryptic since *Planet Waves* in 1974, and it's nice to hear Bob playing it so understandable. Dylan writes an appropriately short tune to accompany these words. No one would mistake this for an authentic Hank Williams song, or even a Bob Dylan cover of an authentic Hank Williams song, but he obviously took the task very seriously. Despite being appropriately humble, he also seems far more excited and invested in this track that he did on anything on *Tempest*. It clearly meant a lot to Dylan being one of the few releases on his own Egyptian Records label. He even was gregarious enough to allow his son, Jakob, to write and record a tune on here too, being one of the only examples of Bob acknowledging his progeny (who had his own musical career by this point) in any sort of public and professional way.

"LONG & WASTED YEARS"

SIDE A:
1. Duquesne Whistle
2. Soon After Midnight
3. The Love That Faded
4. Long And Wasted Years
5. Pay In Blood

SIDE B:
1. Narrow Way
2. Early Roman Kings
3. Things We Said Today
4. Scarlet Town

Much like *Time Out Of Mind*, the songs here are all so long, that it is hard to get up to ten without making the whole album too long. However, unlike *Time Out Of Mind* there aren't even a large number of outtakes to work with. This might be because there has been no official volume of *The Bootleg Series* that covers this period (yet). I don't think anything has leaked out into the hands of collectors. Mostly I just excised the longer, more boring tracks ("Roll On John" and the title track) and added the few tribute album cuts that came out around this time to try and add more excitement and variety to this album. It's still not great, but for this record, my hands were tied. I definitely couldn't conflate it with the next album. But if you want a quick, *Reader's Digest*-style edit of *Tempest*, this is the way to go.

SHADOWS IN THE NIGHT
Produced by: Jack Frost
Recorded: February - Early March 2014
Released: February 3rd, 2015
Famous/Important/Popular Track(s):
- The Night We Called It A Day

My Personal Favorite Track(s):
- Autumn Leaves
- Some Enchanted Evening
- That Lucky Old Sun

It seems like the kind of project I would love: Bob Dylan, the man known for songwriting and not singing, sings the songs of Frank Sinatra, the man known for singing and not songwriting. Certainly, it's the type of project critics would've torn apart in the past. However since *Time Out Of Mind*, critics have been hesitant to say anything negative about Dylan for fear that each album might be his last one – they even found a way to say nice things about *Christmas In The Heart*. While this seems like the kind of weird, idiosyncratic record I am always looking for from Dylan, I was somewhat disappointed by this one. Dylan has been crooning torch songs since *Love & Theft*, so this wasn't as big of a surprise as it initially seemed.

Furthermore, the instrumentation has remained consistent from 2001 once again using his anonymous touring band. There are some horns on there, but they are so buried in the mix, you'd think that Bob was almost embarrassed by them (perhaps they reminded him too much of Rod Stewart's never-ending "Great American Songbook" albums).

There aren't even the backing vocals that enlivened *Christmas In The Heart* or the accordion that helped make *Together Through Life* sounds at least partially different. The starkest difference in instrumentation is the lack of any sort of drums on the record. There is none of the faux-scat singing from "What's It Gonna Be When It Comes Up?" from *The Bootleg Series vol. 11* or even the Italian lyrics from Bob's rendition of Dean Martin's "Return To Me" from the second *Sopranos* soundtrack.

You can't snap your fingers to any of these tunes – they just don't swing. As a result, the songs all tend to blend into each other becoming one large monochromatic bore. Still, this and *Christmas In The Heart* seem to matter far more to Dylan than *Tempest* or *Together Through Life*, which Dylan seems to only write/record/release to stay in the good graces of either his audience or record label and therefore he is granted the indulgence of doing these more personal covers albums. This is definitely a nice trait to see Bob still indulging in even his twilight years, it's just too bad this record is such a snooze.

If *Self-Portrait*'s defiant manifesto was "Take Me As I Am (Or Let Me Go)" the more resigned theme for *Shadows In The Night* is expressed in

"Why Try To Change Me Now?"

The "Standards" album is a trope for aging rockers almost a pervasive as the Christmas album. You have Ringo Starr's *Sentimental Journey*, Paul McCartney's horribly titled *Kisses On The Bottom*, Willie Nelson's *Stardust*, Harry Nilsson's *A Touch Of Shmilsson In The Night*, and Jeff Lynne's *Old Wave*. Linda Ronstadt released a trio of them in the mid-eighties, Carly Simon has released them intermittently over the years, and Rod Stewart's *Great American Songbook* series threatens to overwhelm the entire rest of his career.

I'm a Fool to Want You
(written by Frank Sinatra, Jack Wolf, and Joel Herron)

One of the few songs that Frank Sinatra got credit for as a co-writer. This is a super-slow song – kind of an odd choice to open an album. No drums. A very muted guitar. Mostly just upright bass and a prominent steel guitar. At about 1:45 some horns kick in, but they don't jazz things up at all. They are turned down so far in the mix as to be practically subliminal. And the parts they are playing are mostly just some chord pads, so it's not like we're missing much. The upright bass goes from plucked to bowed at some point, but still, all you can really hear in this song is Bob's voice (which is warm and wonderful) and the pedal steel guitar.

The Night We Called It a Day
(written by Matt Dennis and Tom Adair)

An appropriate choice for Bob to play on David Letterman's second-to-last show. There are some very subtle horns in there, but they're not adding much. There's even a bit of a trumpet solo, but it's mixed so low after the guitar solo it's easy to miss entirely. The tempo is taken at a snail's pace. Bob's original crooner tunes like "Po' Boy" or "Beyond The Horizon" at least felt like they had some life to them; this sounds utterly uninteresting. Bob sings it well, which is almost too bad. If he had done a particularly lousy job singing something like this the juxtaposition might've been interesting. As it is, this track is just boring.

Stay with Me
(written by Jerome Moross and Carolyn Leigh)

The lyrics here could have just as easily felt at home during Bob's "born-again" trilogy. The opening even feels somewhat hymnal. I had no idea Sinatra covered songs with this kind of lyrical content. However, musically this sounds pretty much of a piece with the rest of *Shadows In The Night*. There's nothing terribly remarkable here. No drums or horns on this track to help give it any sort of momentum. Mostly you are just hearing the pedal steel guitar and bowed upright bass. If the arrangement had been a little more acoustic, it certainly would've felt like a puritan folk hymn. As it is, there's not much here except fodder for speculation as to Bob's current religious beliefs.

Autumn Leaves
(written by Joseph Kosma, Jacques Prévert, and Johnny Mercer)

We start with some lovely pedal steel guitar playing an intro before the song settles into place. This is the song with the most elastic tempo and phrasing on *Shadows In The Night*. There are no drums on this recording, and everything is just flowing languidly here. Luckily this song is relatively short, and Bob doesn't try to extend it unnecessarily; otherwise, this might become tortuous. As it is, is a lovely quick mood piece. This is the first song I recognized from this album, having only the most surface acquaintance with Sinatra's catalog. That might help me enjoy this version better as I don't feel like a chump who doesn't know his Frank when listening to this track.

Why Try to Change Me Now?
(written by Cy Coleman, Joseph McCarthy)

Another lumbering jazz ballad. The steel guitar is once again leading the way. Certainly, the lyrics here could've been sung defiantly here. Instead, Bob takes this with nothing but resignation in his voice. He doesn't even seem all that thrilled to be the way he is now, he's just too tired to do anything about it. So in this song, he's given up. Only the last two or three notes of the bridge have any sort of life in them. It's a perfectly fine rendition of this song (that I am unfamiliar with), but it doesn't add much.

Some Enchanted Evening
(music by Richard Rodgers, lyrics by Oscar Hammerstein II)

One of the few songs I was aware of previous to Bob Dylan's version. Again the pedal steel dominates the track. The lack of drums or percussion on this track makes it feel a lot slower than it really is. However, much like "Autumn Leaves" these track benefits from my familiarity with it, although if I try to sing along, I am always rushing the beat. Given it's more familiar nature and almost up-tempo feel, you would almost expect this song to be on *Fallen* Angels and not this album. Not that it takes much for a song to vault to the upper echelon on *Shadows In The Night*, but this is one of my favorites from this album. Barely.

Full Moon and Empty Arms
(written by Buddy Kaye and Ted Mossman)

The first track released from *Shadows In The Night*. When this first appeared on Bob's website without explanation or context, it was quite a surprise. Only later was it announced that this was from Dylan's upcoming album and that this record would be a tribute to Frank Sinatra. This definitely was not a song I had heard of before, so I had nothing to compare it to when I first heard it. Now, in the context of five discs of Sinatra material, this song seems like a pretty bland and unremarkable choice for an introduction to this new period of Dylan. Of course, that also makes it a somewhat appropriately representative choice. Another slow song with no drums, a swooping melody, and distinctive pedal steel guitar. Pretty standard *Shadows In The Night* material.

Where Are You?
(written by Harold Adamson and Jimmy McHugh)

Another Sinatra song I am completely unfamiliar with. Again taken at a super-slow pace with no drums to push it along, but lots of pedal steel on it. Bob is singing to a lover that at first I assumed was hypothetical until he gets to the bridge where he talks about her leaving. I think I would've liked it better if he was looking for an ideal mate that he hadn't actually met yet. There's not much to say about this track without repeating what I've said about most of the songs on *Shadows On The Night*. I would almost welcome an egregiously painful song at this point in the album just to shake things up a little bit. Unfortunately, that's not coming. Damn competency!

What'll I Do?
(written by Irving Berlin)

We're coming down to the homestretch on this album, and it's becoming clearer and clearer that Bob is not going to be throwing us any curveballs. Hope starts to die as the listener sits through another pedal steel-led, drum-less slow ballad. The pace is almost sleep-inducing, and nothing is done to help make this song stick out from the pack. No matter how great the songwriter may be, this song leaves your memory before it's even finished playing. Luckily, giving up hope, also makes the album a little less frustrating at this point. But it never becomes engaging. We're just biding our time on this track.

That Lucky Old Sun
(lyrics by Haven Gillespie, music by Beasley Smith)

A song I am mostly familiar with because of Brian Wilson's 2008 album of the same name. This is the track on *Shadows In The Night* with the most distinctive and prominent horns. Granted they're not doing much, but it's more than the chords pads that have been laid down throughout the rest of the album. The lyrics are about envying an inanimate object because it doesn't have to find gainful employment. The song is treated with grave importance instead of the idle daydreaming that would seem more appropriate. It has all the flair and dramatic weight of a finale, which does help it stand out from the other songs that all seem far more preoccupied with romantic entanglements. There's also a sense of relief that the album is over when hearing this song that might help elevate it a little. I am definitely glad to be done with *Shadows In The Night* by now.

Songs not on the album:
Stormy Weather released on *Triplicate*
(music by Harold Arlen, lyrics by Ted Koehler)

This song was apparently not recorded during the *Triplicate* sessions, but rather during the making of this album. How you can tell, I daren't say, but that's the rumor. This has a rather dramatic opening alá "September Of My Years" that would appear on that later album, before settling into a more traditional arrangement. This is a song I was familiar with because of its appearance on fellow Traveling Wilbury, Jeff Lynne's solo album *Armchair Theatre*. The horns are still sound muted in the mix, but are far more active than they were on say "That Lucky Old Sun". The track is almost creepy, but not that different from many of the songs on this album. If it stuck with that ominous feel of the intro throughout the song, it might've helped this track stand out a bit more. Luckily it does end with a recapitulation of that motif, which helps remind you of one of the few distinguishing marks on this otherwise typical *Triplicate* track.

Rumored to have been recorded but unheard:
Didn't He Ramble? Officially unreleased
(written by Bob Cole and J. Rosamond Johnson)

In addition to the entirety of *Fallen Angels* (which I didn't bother to include in this chapter, for clarity if not consistency) apparently, this track was also recorded. I can't imagine why this was never released, and everything else was, but here you go.

See the entry on Page 419

FALLEN ANGELS
Produced by: Jack Frost
Recorded: February - Early March 2014
Released: May 20th, 2016
Famous/Important/Popular Track(s):
- Melancholy Mood

My Personal Favorite Track(s):
- Young At Heart
- It Had To Be You
- That Old Black Magic

Even with the similarities that *World Gone Wrong* had to its predecessor, there is nothing to compare to the near carbon copy that is *Fallen Angels*. At least *World Gone Wrong* was recorded during different sessions a year after Bob did *Good As I Been To You*. *Fallen Angels* consists solely of outtakes from the same recording sessions that produced *Shadows In The Night*. Really these recordings could've stayed in the can until the release of *Bootleg Series Vol. 63: Another "Shadows In The Night"*.

Granted there are some slight differences between the two, but they are mostly in terms of song selection rather than production, arrangement or instrumentation. *Fallen Angels* does come a little bit closer to the finger-snappin' swing that was so missing from *Shadows In The Night*. Some of the tracks even have audible drums and "That Old Black Magic" even comes close to actually having a pulse. There's a hint of faux-Orientalism to the arrangement of "On A Little Street In Singapore" that brings it a little too close to seeming racist, although I suppose it is authentic to the period in which it was written.

The second big difference between *Shadow In The Night* and *Fallen Angels* is that Bob seems a little less stressed about showing off his impressive knowledge of Sinatra's catalog here. Some of these songs ("Young At Heart", "It Had To Be You") might even be familiar to people who have never purchased one of Frank's albums. Still no "New York, New York" or "My Way" though, sadly.

The strangest song inclusion, however, has to be Hoagy Carmichael's "Skylark", a song that Frank never recorded (although it certainly is in his style and from his time). The inclusion of this song brings up the question: was the fact that 21 of the 22 songs on these two albums were recorded by Frank Sinatra a coincidence? Or did Bob mistakenly think that "Skylark" had been covered by him? The latter seems like an egregious mistake and one that Dylan would've corrected. The former just seems.... odd. If it wasn't for the Sinatra connection, why were these songs chosen? He had to have realized how many were recorded by Frank. Why include "Skylark" then? Or at least cover some other standards that were also untouched by the Chairman?

These questions might be the most interesting thing about this re-tread of *Shadows Of The Night*. It may be a slightly more upbeat collection, but do we really need a second dose of this? Between the two Sinatra discs, I doubt I can even find enough worthwhile material to cobble together my own ten song playlist that I would actually enjoy. With "Autumn Leaves" and "Some Enchanted Evening" from the first and "Young At Heart" and "That Old Black Magic" from the second being the only tracks from either I like, it barely makes for a decent EP.

The best thing about *Fallen Angels* is that it has to signal the end of Dylan's Sinatra period. Right?

Right?

Young at Heart
(written by Johnny Richards and Carolyn Leigh)

A more up-tempo and familiar number than anything on *Shadows In the Night*. The arrangement is still the stripped down western swing combo. If there are any drums on here, they're inaudible, but this does have a little bit of life to it. Of course, saying it's more exciting than *Shadows In The Night* is damning this song with faint praise. At least the original song here is familiar enough to me that the incongruity of Bob singing it can at least keep me amused. Nothing great, but certainly a step up from the last album.

Maybe You'll Be There
(written by Rube Bloom and Sammy Gallop)

We got the violin (or is it a fiddle?) in the intro helping give this song a slightly different instrumental palette. The usual, muted wash of horns are felt but not really heard in the background. The drums are completely missing in the mix – and maybe weren't playing at all. The slower pace and relative obscurity makes this feel more like the *Shadows In The Night* outtake than this song really is, instead of something distinct and independent. The most interesting thing about it is the general lack of pedal steel which can get overwhelming during some of these sessions.

Polka Dots and Moonbeams
(written by Jimmy Van Heusen and Johnny Burke)

The guitar is acoustic rather than the arch-top style electric guitar that was used on most of these tracks. That is a nice little change of pace. There's still the pedal steel that takes the second solo of the song before the vocals even begin. One and a half minutes of this song's three and a half minutes have transpired before Bob starts singing. This song shuffles along with a little more liveliness thanks to some brushed snare drum. The melody has a bit of range to it, but Bob handles them okay. The surrealism of the title images may have appealed to Dylan's more bizarre sense of lyrics, so he has no problem pulling off this song. A good enough addition to these songs.

All the Way
(written by Jimmy Van Heusen and Sammy Cahn)

There are drums here, but as usual, it is creeping along too slowly to pay much attention to. The lyrics are another declaration of unadulterated love. Bob seems far too intent on hitting all the notes in the melody to invest the words with much passion. The playing is, as always, tasteful but that's not surprising by the point. This is one of the longer songs on here. While nothing compared to some of the epic length songs that Dylan has written himself, this still starts to drag by the time the song breaks down a bit before Dylan leads everyone back after taking a bit of a vocal showcase. I really want to think that *Fallen Angels* is more upbeat than *Shadows In The Night*, but songs like this keep proving otherwise.

Skylark
(written by Hoagy Carmichael and Johnny Mercer)

Again there's some violin on here helping alleviate the boredom from having the same instruments on each track. The acoustic guitar solo reminds me a little of Woody Allen's film *Sweet & Lowdown* which is a nice touch too. There's even some softly brushed drums helping keep this song afloat. The lyrics are about a bird, which is a metaphor for love, I think. Bob sings it ably. As the sole non-Sinatra cover on this collection, this song inherently grabs a little bit more attention. Which is good because otherwise, this track does tend to blend in with all the other songs on *Shadows In The Night/Fallen Angels*. It's not horrible by any stretch, just average.

Nevertheless
(written by Harry Ruby and Bert Kalmar)

I'm not sure if it's a hi-hat or a brushed snare, but there's at least a little bit of drums on here. I kind of wonder how the drummer in Bob's band feels about this whole Sinatra excursion. Is he hurt that he isn't being used for much? Is he bored? Or is he enjoying the fact that he is pulling in a full paycheck for doing so little? I don't know. There's a nice little jazz guitar solo in here, but most of the chords work here is covered by the pedal steel. It's a pleasant little song, maybe a bit more lively than most of the slow ballads on *Shadows In The Night*, but not even rising to the level of memorable. As far as aural wallpaper goes, this is one of the less offensive tracks here, but nothing much you can really say about this song.

All or Nothing at All
(written by Arthur Altman and Jack Lawrence)

The song opens with a guitar riff that gets your hopes up for a song that really jumps but as soon as the band joins in, it someway has been dropped into a lower gear. It's still more hopping than most anything on *Shadows In The Night*, but that's not saying much. There's some mandolin strumming in here helping change things up a bit, as is the apparent lack of pedal steel on this track. The minimal drums help juice this up a bit. The lyrics are typical pop music cleverness of this era. Bob sings them well but doesn't ring any additional emotion from the song. The song itself is pleasant without leaving any impact. It's a pretty standard standard.

On a Little Street in Singapore
(written by Peter DeRose and Billy Hill)

There is just the slightest pulse of a heartbeat on this track, which comes across as quite a relief. There is some Hollywood-styled "orientalism" inherent in this track, that was not nearly as disturbing back in the day in which it was written. Luckily Bob's arrangement doesn't play up any of these potentially awkward elements. Instead, we get a short little ditty with some of a march feel to it. There are some drums here – not loud or forceful – but definitely present. This song is such a palliative within *Fallen Angels* that it is easy to overlook how unremarkable the track really is. Within the context of this album, the song stands out; on its own this song is nothing special. But it is definitely brief. A quick little palate cleanser to help differentiate one song from the next on *Fallen Angels*.

It Had to Be You
(written by Isham Jones and Gus Kahn)

One of the more familiar songs covered on *Fallen Angels*. Even if Bob does include an extended intro that most people have forgotten about entirely. Once the real song kicks in, it's taken a loping snail's pace. Certainly, some more drums (which may or may not be audible) would've helped this song which is drifting perilously close to elevator muzak. Still, it's got some nice smooth jazz guitar, and the pedal steel is pushed into a far more complementary role which is a relief. The solo is a minor delight, but not terribly surprising. This is one of the longer songs on *Fallen Angels* but luckily is still not too over-taxing. In fact, it may be one of the better songs on the album, it's just hard to tell when so many of these songs sound the same.

Melancholy Mood
(written by Walter Schumann and Vick R. Knight, Sr.)

There's a snare drum played with a brush giving this track more of a pulse than anything on *Shadows In The Night*. In attempting to replicate the original arrangements, there is over a minute of introduction that here is reduced to merely an arch-top style guitar playing the melody for an entire verse. Bob's singing doesn't seem particularly melancholic on this track, but he does an excellent job. Despite the long intro and the short duration of this song, it does make time for half of a guitar solo at the end that doesn't add much to the song but does make it long enough to keep from feeling extraordinarily short.

That Old Black Magic
(written by Harold Arlen and Johnny Mercer)

This is what we were missing. Some life, some verve, some drums! This song swings in ways that nothing on either *Shadows In The Night* or *Fallen Angels* can even touch. There are no horns here, but this still feels like a bit of big band. The electric guitar dominates the pedal steel for a change, and the whole thing coalesces around the ride cymbal that takes us between verses. Sure, if this song weren't preceded by a bunch somnambulant snoozers, this might be tossed off as a mild curiosity. However, in the context of this album, this song is a godsend. Was Dylan afraid of embarrassing himself by doing more material of this enthusiasm? Did he really think that two whole albums of Sinatra tunes that avoided it would be better accepted? Who knows? I'm just glad this is on the record. Easily the best track on *Fallen Angels*.

Come Rain or Come Shine
(written by Harold Arlen and Johnny Mercer)

It may be the penultimate track on the album, but "That Old Black Magic" did raise my hopes for *Fallen Angels*. "Come Rain Or Come Shine" immediately dashed those hopes. This is a very average song for this album to go out on. It may even be slightly above average with some brushed drum work helping this song achieve a bit of excitement. But not nearly enough to help it rise above the general feel of spinning one's wheels that I have while listening to this album. While this album of outtakes is slightly better than the album it was originally recorded for, the differences here are slight. And this track is emblematic of that. Sure there's marginally more life in these tunes, but other than "That Old Black magic" all of these songs are pretty much interchangeable. But this has got to be the end of the whole "Sinatra period." Right? Please.

See the entry on Page 419

TRIPLICATE

Produced by: Jack Frost
Recorded: February 2016
Released: March 31st, 2017

Famous/Important/Popular Track(s):
- I Could Have Told You

My Personal Favorite Track(s):
- Stormy Weather
- There's A Flaw In My Flue
- Sentimental Journey

Ugh!

Maybe Dylan wants to continue to confound expectations. The only problem is now everyone expects Dylan to be continually changing, and the only way to surprise anyone is to stay exactly the same. Love or hate the Sinatra songbook period, this is overkill. The "electric" period only lasted 4 discs (3½ if you don't count the second side of *Bringing It All Back Home*). The finger-pointin' period only lasted four discs as well. The born-again period was only 3 discs (2½ if you don't count the secular songs on *Shot Of Love*). Bob has never stretched anything out for this long. Whether you count the three discs on *Triplicate* as three different albums (since they each have their own "title"), that is still a lot of discs for one type of music. Sure, there are 6 discs of *The Bootleg Series vol. 11* and 18 discs of *The Bootleg Series vol. 12* – but those are archival, and only that many discs in the deluxe editions. There are even 36 discs of *The 1966 Live Recordings*, but that seems like something that was released by the record company, but these five albums are all Bob's idea. Even if it was 5 discs of something I like – say *Christmas In The Heart* – that would still be too much for me. Of course, repeatedly referring to this as a 5-disc set is a bit disingenuous; these 52 songs could easily fit onto 2 CDs.

I wasn't the only one who was getting sick of Dylan's Sinatra kick by this point, *Triplicate* was the first album of Bob's not to reach the top 10 since before he made his comeback with 1997's *Time Out Of Mind*.

Granted these recordings are not from the exact same sessions that produced *Fallen Angels* and *Shadows In The Night*, but they sound incredibly similar. And like *Fallen Angels*, only one of the tunes included ("Braggin'") wasn't recorded by Frank Sinatra; once again raising the question of how or why these particular covers were selected.

I Guess I'll Have to Change My Plan
(music by Arthur Schwartz, lyrics by Howard Dietz)

I thought I knew what to expect from a Dylan Sinatra album after having endured two of them, but I am immediately surprised here. This sounds like swing music. The arrangement is big band and not just Bob's usual touring group's approximation of such. Oddly enough, I think this is what everyone was fearing they would get when *Shadows In The Night* was first announced. I bet a lot of the critical praise that the first Dylan Sinatra album received resulted mostly from it not sounding like this track. But this is what I was disappointed the last two albums didn't give me. The horns are now in your face instead of being subliminal. There's even an old school key change in this song. If the whole album had sounded like this, it still would've gotten old by the end but would've held my attention a lot longer than another *Fallen Angels / Shadows In The Night* retread.

The September of My Years
(music by Jimmy Van Heusen, lyrics by Sammy Cahn)

There's a creepy dramatic opening to this song. However once the singing kicks in, we start to understand that "I Guess I'll Have To Change My Plans" was more of an anomaly than a harbinger of what *Triplicate* would have to offer. The only real difference between this and the last two albums is the prominent bowed upright during the first verse. Again we've got lots of pedal steel and jazz guitar with no real drums or rhythmic pulse. The song is slow and melancholy. While Bob's worn voice might be more suited to this material than the jump, jive, and wail of the last track, there is no revelation to his performance here. The lyrics here are more concerned with aging and the encroachment of one's inevitable demise than the usual romantic entanglements of many of these tunes. Not an optimistic start to this record, especially knowing we have a long way to go from here.

I Could Have Told You
(music by Jimmy Van Heusen, lyrics by Carl Sigman)

Led by the pedal steel guitar, this is another slow jazz standard. There are no drums or any other percussion audible on this track. The melody is not terribly range-y, and Bob sings it with aplomb. However, no matter what you think of Bob's vocal abilities – particularly at this age – it doesn't sound like Dylan really means these words. He is not invested in the lyrics – they could have been about anything really, and he would've sung them the same way. An odd choice for the first taste off of this album – but a representative example of what *Triplicate* is all about.

Once Upon a Time
(music by Charles Strouse, lyrics by Lee Adams)

I guess it was brave of Dylan not to open *Triplicate* with this song. There are some lovely guitar arpeggios during the intro. The pedal steel has an unusually wonky feel answering some of the lines in the verse that makes this song a little more charming. This song has a little bit of pulse with the drums, but then the drums cut out for the bridge section and the bottom of this song just falls out. It's a charming little record, and would even be a lovely addition to any collection of lullabies. But if you're not trying to fall asleep, this gets a bit old.

Stormy Weather
(music by Harold Arlen, lyrics by Ted Koehler)
See entry under *Shadows In The Night*.

This Nearly Was Mine
(music by Richard Rodgers, lyrics by Oscar Hammerstein II)
The song starts with a bowed upright bass buzzing like a didgeridoo. It's not really that noticeable, but you are forced to look deep on these tracks to find anything that helps tell them apart. This is not a song I was aware of before this album. The theme of the lyrics is, once again, lost love. Bob's singing is particularly robust here. Once again the lack of percussion undermines any vitality this might've had. Sure – not all songs have to be exciting and upbeat, but after the tease of the opening track, the continuously slow and somnambulistic feel of these songs starts to really get old.

That Old Feeling
(music by Sammy Fain, lyrics by Lew Brown)
I worry about being too repetitive during the rundowns of all these songs. Meanwhile, Bob is having no such qualms about repetition. No wonder he called this *Triplicate* and not "Threesome" or "Triptych" or "Triad" or something. This is just another slow love song that Dylan is doing his Bing Crosby-karaoke over. There is nothing in this song that helps it stand out from the other tracks on this album – or the previous two albums. There's a nice little guitar solo here that sounds more interesting and imaginative than anything Bob is doing here. This song certainly does give the listener that old feeling.

It Gets Lonely Early
(written by Gordon Jenkins)
The strange, creepy intro that was done with such a grand effect on "Stormy Weather" and "September Of My Years" is attempted again here; only much less successfully. It's not even enough to help elevate this track to the level of memorable. Another song whose lyrics mix the theme of growing old with that of losing romantic love. Bob sounds particularly forlorn sing this song, although you can't help but think about Bob as a senior citizen getting his early bird dinner at 4:00 and going to bed by 6 o'clock. Still no drums on this track. We don't even have the wash of horns to liven things up. This first disc is subtitled "Till The Sun Goes Down", but other than the first track, this all feels very much it is past Dylan's bedtime and he's half-asleep.

My One and Only Love
(music by Guy Wood, lyrics by Robert Mellin)

This song starts with the horns and a bowed upright giving one the impression that this track will feature more of an orchestral instrumentation than it actually delivers. The horns are muted as usual, but one of the trumpets is even playing some nice little lines on occasion. Sadly these are not only mixed low but sound really far away. Instead, we get the standard western swing band playing throughout the song. Jazz guitar, pedal steel, upright bass, and minimal drums. Bob sings better than you'd expect on this one, but this still isn't something you'd expect Bob to sing.

Trade Winds
(written by Cliff Friend and Charlie Tobias)

Instead of playing up the faux-exotica as he did on "Christmas Island" this track falls into sounding pretty much like almost every other track on *Triplicate*. Finally, the drums return, and we get a little oomph to this song. Sure it's pretty breezy, but it's better than nothing. For once the pedal steel sounds particularly apropos. Still, you long for Bob to go full-on with the island sounds with some ukulele and hula girls or something. The song keeps threatening to reach the level of interesting, but never quite gets there. At least it's not an infuriating mess of squandered possibilities, just a little disappointing. It's charming and lightweight, but not quite enough to salvage the first disc of *Triplicate*.

Braggin'
(written by Artie Manners and Jimmy Shirl)

Ok, so apparently Bob is just saving all the good, horn-driven swing numbers to open each of the discs. This may not quite be as good as "I Guess I'll Have To Change My Plans" but it still a breath of fresh air. The song almost sounds more like proto-rock'n'roll than the usual jazz standard. It's not a song I'm familiar with. You'd almost expect a Brian Setzer solo on here, although the guitar playing is nice and tasty. The lyrics are an admonition to cool it with the self-aggrandizing. The music itself however struts and swaggers in such a way to completely contradict that sentiment. You may not get up and dance to this song, but you'll at least bop your head or tap your toes. There's a couple of lines in here that Bob delivers so mush-mouthed as to render the lyrics unintelligible. Frankly, if this song were just one disc made up of songs with this type of playing and arrangement I might look at the whole Sinatra period a lot less harshly.

As Time Goes By
(written by Herman Hupfeld)

Here's another song I actually recognize. The first verse is done as a free-flowing introduction. Funnily enough, once the band kicks in, the tempo actually goes down instead of up as you would expect. Once again we're back in the typical snooze-inducing territory of Dylan's Sinatra period. There are drums on here, but they're not helping much. The pedal steel glosses over everything. There's a tasteful little jazz guitar solo. My familiarity with the material makes it a little easier for me to endure this track, but it doesn't add much to me. I almost wish he had done the whole song alone with a single electric guitar as he did during the first verse. It would've at least helped this track stand out more.

Imagination
(music by Jimmy Van Heusen, lyrics by Johnny Burke)

This is another song in the same vein as "Trade Winds", up-tempo, but not quite swinging. You can at least snap your fingers along to it, which already makes it better than anything off of *Shadows In The Night* or *Fallen Angels* (except "That Old Black Magic"). In some ways, the extraordinary length plays in *Triplicate*'s favor. Having to come up with enough material to fill three discs, Bob has stretched out and added a few curveballs into the mix. It's not great by any stretch, the album could undoubtedly use some pruning, but if you were to take the best handful of songs from this triple album they would certainly wipe the floor with the same number of curated songs from the first two Sinatra albums. And songs like this are a large part of the reason why. I'm not familiar with the original, but that's okay. The pleasure from this song doesn't derive from its familiarity and incongruity. This song is super-peppy, while not manic. The lyrics sound like they'd feel at home on a Disney soundtrack. It's another love song, but this one is a little hopeful than many of these tracks. The electric guitars overpower the pedal steel for a change. The drums are brushed but are propulsive. It's a sunny change of pace from all the gloom that permeates this whole period of Dylan's career.

How Deep Is the Ocean?
(written by Irving Berlin)

Whatever respite "Imagination" granted the listener is quashed by this track. Pretentious and ponderous, this song drags along. There are a few bits of nice jazz riffing on the guitar, but nothing really catches the ear. It's another lovelorn song dripping with clichéd metaphors for longing. The slide guitar solo is adequate, but surprisingly amateur sounding. (Is the pedal steel? Hard to say.) Not much going on here: bowed bass, no drums, the usual. The reason medium-level songs like "Imagination" seem to pop so much is the preponderance of lethargic tracks such as this. This one is an easy track to skip.

P.S. I Love You
(music by Johnny Mercer, lyrics by Gordon Jenkins)

Not the Lennon-McCartney song, but rather an even older oldie. This song was covered by Nellie McKay on the ukulele for the soundtrack to the Gerard Butler/Hilary Swank rom-com of the same name, so I actually know this tune. Bob's version restores the introduction that Nellie left off. While her version is charming and winsome, Dylan's falls into many of the same old traps of this period. The acoustic guitar on here is a nice change in the texture. The conceit of the lyrics is that this is a rather banal recounting of events with the twist of the admission of love in the postscript. As such, the song is naturally inclined to feel trivial. Bob's performance here doesn't have enough layers to keep this from happening, although he sings with grace. There's an oddly disturbing line in here about the author doing his best to obey all the recipient's wishes. It can come off as a little like old-fashioned misogyny when sung by a female voice but just seems weird when Bob sings it. This is a song that would've benefitted from a much more invigorated arrangement. It's not nearly as annoying as some of the tracks on *Triplicate*, but it doesn't stand out in that rather crowded field either.

The Best Is Yet to Come
(music by Carolyn Leigh, lyrics by Cy Coleman)

This is the only full-horn section song on this album that isn't placed at the beginning of the particular disc it's on. The arrangement sounds like an actual big band; nothing super crazy, but closer to Tony Bennett's backing band than Bob's. There's a full set of woods and brass here. The drums percolate nicely, and there's a great little riff from the upright bass during the intro. Sure, Bob's voice is still out of place – but now it is charming and fun like it was on *Christmas In The Heart*. If the rest of the Sinatra sessions were closer to this, I'd be thrilled. Definitely one of the best on *Triplicate*.

But Beautiful
(music by Jimmy Van Heusen, lyrics by Johnny Burke)

Here we come crashing back to the expected tempos and textures of *Triplicate*. There's some life to this song, with the softly brushed drums, but nothing compared to the (relatively) high energy of "The Best Is Yet To Come". The lyrics are another paean to love, albeit a lost love. While Bob's usual oblique surrealism could get wearying, having to listen to so many songs that were composed during an era when a lyricist's available range of subject matter is beginning to wear down on me. The song is beautiful but unremarkable. While *Triplicate* is throwing in a few monkey wrenches to keep the listener from dozing off completely, it is songs like this that makes tunes like "Braggin'" or "The Best Is Yet To Come" stand out so much.

Here's That Rainy Day
(music by Jimmy Van Heusen, lyrics by Johnny Burke)

The arrangement here is decidedly simple, with all the instruments playing the same rhythmic figure together throughout the entire first verse. It's hard to say if it is daring or lazy, but once the more traditional and nuanced band playing comes into play, this song is far less memorable. In fact, by the end of the tune, you have forgotten the semi-weird way this track opened, and it feels like just another *Triplicate* track. All the usual culprits are here: no drums, ample pedal steel, bowed upright bass, and Bob's sincere croon. It's another dark and lovelorn lyric. Not much happens here, so we'll just move on to the next song.

Where Is the One?
(music by Edwin Finckel, lyrics by Alec Wilder)

Hey, guess what? This is yet another indistinguishable *Triplicate* track. Tracks like this feel like filler. Definitely would've been cut if this were released as *Duplicate*. Bob's not doing anything we have gotten very used to by this point. Again we are missing the drummer. There are no horns on here either. The jazz guitar is well-played, but who cares? It almost feels like Bob is personally trying to attack me, and I'm having a hard time coming up with something new to say about all of these tracks. Sigh.

There's a Flaw in My Flue
(music by Jimmy Van Heusen, lyrics by Johnny Burke)

A song that Frank Sinatra allegedly recorded to see if anyone was actually paying any attention to the words. I'm not sure how accurate that story is. Sure, the central metaphor in this song is far more convoluted and tortured than most of the songs of this vintage. There are some amusing phonetics involved, but otherwise, this is just another lonely, lost love lyric. Bob's diction is on point here, but he doesn't do anything to emphasize the humor here except drawing out the line "smoke gets in my nose." If you ignore the somewhat unusual lyrics, however, this is just another fairly typical *Triplicate* song. Steel guitar, no drums, slow tempo, blah, blah, blah. You've heard it all before. Moving on.

Day In, Day Out
(music by Rube Bloom, lyrics by Johnny Mercer)

Here it is, the first track on disc three, and we're back to the more swinging sounds of "I Guess I'll Have To Change My Plans" or "Braggin'". There are some great sounds from the woodwind section and a nice beat on the drums. Sure, the novelty of hearing Dylan singing this type of music is starting to wear thin, even on these more traditional sounding big band numbers. Still, it is a relief to see any sort of life or joy on *Triplicate*. I do like this song, but I'm not sure how much of this is Stockholm syndrome at this point. I'm just grateful and relieved not to be hearing what 90% of this album has become that I am willing to overlook how weak this track might be. It may not be as good as the other disc-openers or "The Best Is Yet To Come", but this still is pretty good for *Triplicate*.

I Couldn't Sleep a Wink Last Night
(music by Jimmy McHugh, lyrics by Harold Adamson)
This song opens with a slightly adventurous diminished chord intro, but that quickly ends, and we end up in another typical *Triplicate* song. Again the lyrics paint this as another forlorn love song. The guitar solo is restrained, and nothing on this song approaches playful. As slowly as this song is played, nothing about it seems to imply exhaustion or even the sense of being tired. That would've at least made sense, but even that gets missed. The song ends with more of that slightly surprising diminished chord stuff, but it's not enough to keep this song from fading like a dream as soon as one wakes up.

Sentimental Journey
(music by Bud Green, lyrics by Les Brown and Ben Homer)
This is the essence of elevator muzak – they kind you find the house band playing in the bar of a cheap nowhere Howard Johnson's in the 1970s. You almost expect Murph & The Magic Tones from *The Blues Brothers* to be playing this sort of song. By amping up the cheese factor, Bob almost makes this song work. Unfortunately, this song is still taken at such a snail's pace it's hard to enjoy the camp value of it. There are some moments in the bridge that are a touch outside of Bob's range. It is charming to hear him strive (and almost reach) those notes. The horns are providing some padding here, but nothing too extravagant. If Bob is going to do lounge songs – he should really commit in the arrangements and really do lounge songs.

Somewhere Along the Way
(music by Jimmy Van Heusen, lyrics by Sammy Gallop)
There are some lightly brushed drums here, which does make this a notch more exciting than two-thirds of *Triplicate*. By this point in the album, there's not much Bob could do to try and surprise us, but he's not even trying to do that. There's a gentle little guitar solo in here to break things up a bit, but this is pretty much more of the typical *Triplicate* tripe.

When the World Was Young
(music by Philippe-Gérard, lyrics by Johnny Mercer)
An overly dramatic opening to this song that kicks into the slowest gear possible when it finally does get going. It may have the lowest BPM of any song in the entire Dylan discography. The song is so slow you can barely

tell it's in 3/4 time. It a strange way, making this song even more languid and lugubrious helps it stand out from the rest. It repeats the free-flowing rhythm of the introduction halfway through the song. This is the type of arrangement that is designed to showcase a singer with a particularly strong technical voice, so hearing Bob singing it and trying to sing it well is almost brave. If more of these songs were that willing to fail, I might at least applaud the guts it took to sing these standards.

These Foolish Things
(music by Jack Strachey, lyrics by Eric Maschwitz)

A sleepy little number. One of the longer tracks on *Triplicate*. There's some pleasant drumming; too bad you can barely hear it in the mix. Like most of the lyrics here, this is just another love song. This is also one of the few songs that has a full solo in the middle instead of just an exaggerated into. This song might've worked as a nice change of pace if there weren't already so many songs at this pace on this triple album.

You Go to My Head
(music by J. Fred Coots, lyrics by Haven Gillespie)

We're getting near the end here. The last half of the last disc. The pedal steel is a little subdued here, comparatively. Instead, the star is the twinkling and tinkling electric guitar. The upright bass cuts off at the end of each verse, making the track twice as quiet for these brief passages. It's a bit of a shock, but only if you're paying enough attention to notice it. While the title sounds familiar to me, I don't recognize this song at all. One of the least memorable songs on a (triple) album full of them.

Stardust
(music by Hoagy Carmichael, lyrics by Mitchell Parish)

This recording focuses on the jazz guitar riffs with the pedal steel muted more towards the background than it has been on some of these tracks. As usual, there are about 40 seconds of intro before the vocals kick in. Some drums are being played with brushes in there, matching the upright bass so closely they almost become inaudible. Bob's voice is generally pretty warm with some straining on the higher longer notes, but not embarrassing or even remarkable.

It's Funny to Everyone But Me
(written by Jack Lawrence)

This is yet another slower melancholy ballad. This one at least seems to have a bit more oomph to it. The pedal steel is still draped over everything, but the electric guitar gets some nice jazz riffs out there. The drums are again rather minimal, but at least they're there. Bob's vocal performance does show that these songs are definitely not funny to him. Which may overall be my main complaint about this period in Dylan's career.

Why Was I Born?
(music by Jerome Kern, lyrics by Oscar Hammerstein II)

The best thing that can be said about this track is that it's the last one on here. It's also about the only interesting thing about this song. By this point, I think I definitely can state that while I may not know precisely why Bob Dylan was born, I can assure you that he was not born to record the songs of Frank Sinatra. I assume the song is meant to be melancholic if not heart-breaking, but the only effect it has is boredom. I could go into detail about whether there were soft drums or no drums, or if there was more electric guitar than pedal steel, but the specifics don't matter – it has all dissolved into an indistinguishable mishmash of general *Triplicate* dullness. Oddly enough, it was at this point that I wondered why I hadn't heard any real piano or organ or keyboards of any kind on the Sinatra albums? Bob had long given up playing the guitar on-stage by this point, preferring to retreat behind his keyboard. And this type of cocktail music is so closely associated with the piano. Yet somehow I cannot think of a single moment that actually had any keyboards in it. Was Dylan playing them during the recording and they are just buried in the mix? Did he not play them at all, and if so, why didn't he hire someone to come in and cover the piano part. Maybe that was what was missing on all these albums. Although I doubt the addition of a keyboard would've really salvaged these songs or my opinion of them. It just would've been nice to have one more thing to help distinguish these 52 tracks from each other.

Songs not on the album:
He's Funny That Way from the EP *Universal Love – Wedding Songs Reimagined*
(music by Neil Moret, lyrics by Richard Whiting)

Released on a surprise EP created by MGM hotels in support of gay marriage (and the hotel's ability to host these types of weddings), Bob added one of the six songs on this EP. The concept behind the EP is pretty clever, having artists sing covers with the gender pronouns swapped out. For those hoping that Dylan would return to the political arena, his appearance on this CD was good news. Other than "George Jackson", "Hurricane", and a couple of tracks on *Infidels*, this was the most overtly socially conscious thing Bob has done since before going electric. However, for those hoping Dylan would start writing his own songs again – or at least stop covering Sinatra – were going to be disappointed. This song was written in 1929 and was recorded by Frank as "She's Funny That Way". Of course it had also been recorded by Billie Holliday with the masculine pronouns, so it's not that big of a shock – but the fact Bob doubles down on singing a song about being in love with a man is a far cry from his rewriting the line about having "an old man" from his cover of Joni Mitchell's "Big Yellow Taxi" on *Dylan*. Of course, the change in genders makes it obvious that this wasn't recorded during the *Triplicate* sessions, but that would also be obvious just listening to this track. Dylan's usual backing band seems to be completely absent; there's no pedal steel to be found. While there are a few period-appropriate touches of big band horns on a couple of *Triplicate* tracks, this is Bob's first real use of an orchestra during the Sinatra years. While he did do a one-off live performance in Japan with a full orchestra in the nineties, this is the first time he has recorded with one since the rejected version of "Sign On the Window" from *New Morning* in 1970. It is far more authentically vintage than most of the stuff recorded during this period. The song starts with a string section intro but quickly reverts to just voice and piano. This shows much a real pianist would've helped albums like *Triplicate*. Soon all the other parts of the orchestra join in while Bob gives a sincere and completely non-ironic reading of these slightly surprising lyrics. While this doesn't swing as hard as "Day In, Day Out" or "Braggin'", this feels far more a part of those less anachronistic recording than the sleepy stripped-down tracks that make up the majority of the last three albums.

"THE IMPORTANCE OF BEING FRANK"

SIDE A:
1. The Best Is Yet To Come
2. Day In, Day Out
3. I Guess I'll Have To Change My Plans
4. Braggin'
5. That Old Black Magic
6. As Time Goes By
7. Sentimental Journey

SIDE B:
1. Stormy Weather
2. Autumn Leaves
3. Young At Heart
4. Some Enchanted Evening
5. It Had To Be You
6. Stardust
7. That Lucky Old Sun

Since four of the five discs from this period only had ten songs on them, I initially considered having my Sinatra songs compilation have a total of ten songs too. Given my general distaste for this period, it seemed fair. That would be two tracks from each disc. The four songs from *Triplicate* with an actual swing band on them were an obvious pick. You add to "That Old Black Magic" to that, and you got a terrific five-song stretch for the up-tempo side one. However, when it came to picking the remaining five for the softer side two, I was surprised to find how many songs I wanted to include. Pretty much everything that I recognized or seemed familiar. This ended up meaning I was taking three instead of two from each disc. This isn't a lot of the possible songs, but it is a much higher percentage than I expected, given my feelings about this material. Even at fourteen songs, this is still only about 42 minutes long.

I ended up adding a couple of less rocking songs at the end of side one. Both songs revolve around nostalgia and memory, which makes a fine lead-off to the second side. For side two, we open with a couple of dark meteorological songs and end with a pair of more optimistic astronomical tunes to complete the journey from a dark and stormy night to the hopeful dawn.

Of all the hypothetical albums I have cobbled together, this one is the biggest surprise to me. I was pretty down on all three records from this period, however, when I cut away the dross, I found the weird, goofy collection that I expected when I first heard that Dylan was doing Frank.

Not that I want him to start recording *Quadruplicate*. Unless it includes a duet with Jakob Dylan on "Something Stupid". And he uses the Sid Vicious arrangement of "My Way". And he adds some tracks from 1980's *The Future: Reflections on the Future in Three Tenses, further enumerated as A Musical Fantasy in Three Tenses for Frank Sinatra, Philharmonic Symphony Orchestra, and Mixed Chorus*. Hey, maybe I am onto something...

While this might not have changed my mind about these CDs completely, I am starting to have the same sort of doubts that accompanied those who initially dismissed many of Bob's prior left-turn swerves. Almost every Dylan critic is later forced to eat their words. Maybe I was wrong. And in retrospect, what if Dylan was right about this whole Sinatra thing?

Scary.

The Never Ending Bootleg Series:

While it is evident that Dylan doesn't have much interest in constant reliving the past, his record does. That's because Columbia Records knows that the past is where the real money is in Dylan's career. So seeing which time periods are considered most ripe for the raiding of the Dylan vault it is instructive to look at their series of official "bootlegs." While the first three volumes came out as a single piece of 3 CDs, the rest have all been issued in with 2 CDs in the standard version (although deluxe versions exist for almost all of them ranging from 3 discs to a whopping 18). Why the first set is volumes 1 thru 3, while the two CDs of *Live 1966* aren't considered volumes 4 & 5, etc. is just part of the mystery of Columbia Records' math. That means of the 21 discs in the series, 16 of them are chronologically invested in the sixties, only the first of the five+ decades of Dylan's career. Not only that, but there have been a number of archival releases of live recordings (*Live at The Gaslight 1962*, *Live at Carnegie Hall 1963*, *In Concert – Brandeis University 1963*, and *The Real Royal Albert Hall 1966 Concert*) all of which are confined to the sixties. Why these particular releases were not given the appellation of "Bootleg Series" I do not know. Of course, there is also less stuff both recorded during the subsequent years, but it does highlight how the industry sees Bob Dylan: as a relic from a bygone era to be repackaged and marketed to baby boomers.

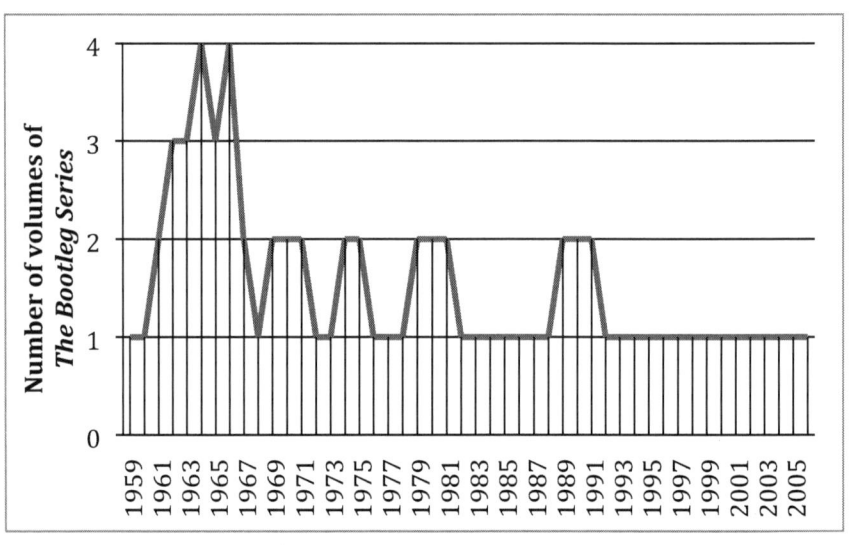

1 - 3	Rare & Unreleased	1961–1991
4	The "Royal Albert Hall" Concert	1966
5	The Rolling Thunder Revue	1975
6	Concert at Philharmonic Hall	1964
7	No Direction Home: The Soundtrack	1959-1966
8	Tell Tale Signs	1989–2006
9	The Witmark Demos	1962–1964
10	Another Self Portrait	1969–1971
11	The Basement Tapes Raw	1967
12	The Cutting Edge	1965–1966
13	Trouble No More	1979–1981
14	More Blood, More Tracks	1974

The Bootleg Series

- **Vol. 1–3:** Rare & Unreleased
- **Vol. 4:** Live 1966 The "Royal Albert Hall" Concert
- **Vol. 5:** Live 1975 The Rolling Thunder Revue
- **Vol. 6:** Live 1964 Concert at Philharmonic Hall
- **Vol. 7:** No Direction Home: The Soundtrack
- **Vol. 8:** Tell Tale Signs
- **Vol. 9:** The Whitmark Demos
- **Vol. 10:** Another Self Portrait
- **Vol. 11:** The Basement Tapes Complete
- **Vol. 12:** The Cutting Edge
- **Vol. 13:** Trouble No More
- **Vol. 14:** More Blood, More Tracks

DYLAN in COMPILATIONS:

One easy way to try and determine which Dylan songs are the most important is to look at which ones have been included on a compilation album. According to bobdylan.com, there are six recognized official compilations: 1967's *Greatest Hits vol. I*, 1971's *Greatest Hits vol. II*, 1994's *Greatest Hits vol. III*, 2005's *The Best Of Bob Dylan*, and 2007's 3-CD *Dylan*. Also included is the 2 disc compilation *The Essential Bob Dylan*. This is where things get kind of complicated. *The Essential Bob Dylan* was first released in 2000. It came out again in 2009 with a third bonus disc that included six extra songs thrown in for good measure. It was then re-released in 2010 and again in 2014. Both of those times some songs were cut to make room for new songs to be added. Also in 2000 when the album was released in Britain and Australia, the track-list was slightly different. I've decided to ignore the international version and notate which of the variations of *The Essential Bob Dylan* the track appeared on.

I'm not including the box-set *Biograph*, since that was only one-third "greatest hits" another third is deep cuts, and the rest are unreleased rarities to try and induce the hardcore fan who already had the rest of these songs to buy the set.

Looking at which songs are included in nearly every compilation gives a more unanimous selection of what was considered a "greatest hit." Of course, some songs weren't recorded until after certain compilations were released, so inevitably that can't start appearing on compilations until afterward. Also, some songs initially recorded during *The Basement Tapes* were re-recorded by Bob with Happy Traum for inclusion on *Greatest Hits vol. II* when these songs are included in subsequent compilations sometimes it's the basement version and sometimes it's the Happy Traum version. For simplicity's sake I have not divided out the two, but rather included them all under the heading of *The Basement Tapes*.

Bob Dylan
- Song To Woody
  (Dylan)

The Freewheelin' Bob Dylan
- Blowin' In The Wind
  (Vol. I, The Best of, Dylan, Essential '00, Essential '10, and Essential '14)
- Masters Of War
  (Dylan)
- Don't Think Twice, It's All Right
  (Vol. II, Dylan, Essential '00, Essential '10, and Essential '14)
- A Hard Rain's A-Gonna Fall
  (Vol. II, Dylan)

The Times They Are A-Changin'
- The Times They Are a-Changin'
  (Vol. I, The Best Of, Dylan, Essential '00, Essential '10, and Essential '14)

Another Side of Bob Dylan
- All I Really Want To Do
  (Vol. II, Dylan)
- My Back Pages
  (Vol. II, Dylan)
- It Ain't Me, Babe
  (Vol. I, Dylan, Essential '00, Essential '10, and Essential '14)

Bringing It All Back Home
- She Belongs To Me
  (Vol. II)
- It's All Over Now, Baby Blue
  (Vol. II, Dylan, Essential '00, and Essential '14)
- Subterranean Homesick Blues
  (Vol. I, Dylan, Essential '00, Essential '10, and Essential '14)
- Mr. Tambourine Man
  (Vol. I, The Best of, Dylan, Essential '00, Essential '10, and Essential '14)
- Maggie's Farm
  (Vol. II, Dylan, Essential '00, Essential '10, and Essential '14)

Highway 61 Revisited
- Just Like Tom Thumb's Blues
  (Vol. II)
- Like A Rolling Stone
  (Vol. I, The Best Of, Dylan, Essential '00, Essential '10, and Essential '14)
- Positively 4th Street
  (Vol. I, Dylan, Essential '00, Essential '10, and Essential '14)

Blonde on Blonde
- I Want You
  (Vol. I, Essential '10)
- Stuck Inside Of Mobile With The Memphis Blues Again
  (Vol. II)
- Rainy Day Women #12 & 35
  (Vol. I, The Best of, Dylan, Essential '00, Essential '10, and Essential '14)
- Just Like A Woman
  (Vol. I, Dylan, Essential '00, Essential '10, and Essential '14)
- Most Likely You Go Your Way And I'll Go Mine
  (Dylan)

March 27th, 1967
***GREATEST HITS, VOL. I* released**

The Basement Tapes
- Down In The Flood (Crash On The Levee)
  (Vol. II)
- Quinn The Eskimo (The Mighty Quinn)
  (Vol. 2, Essential '00, and Essential '14)
- You Ain't Goin' Nowhere
  (Vol. II, Dylan, Essential '00, Essential '10, and Essential '14)
- I Shall Be Released
  (Vol. II, Dylan, Essential '00, Essential '10, and Essential '14)

John Wesley Harding
- I'll Be Your Baby Tonight
  (Essential '00, and Essential '14)
- All Along The Watchtower
  (Vol. II, The Best of, Dylan, Essential '00, Essential '10, and Essential '14)

Nashville Skyline
- Tonight I'll Be Staying Here With You
  (Vol. II)
- Lay Lady Lay
  (Vol. II, The Best of, Dylan, Essential '00, Essential '10, and Essential '14)

Self Portrait
- *none*

Dylan
- *none*

New Morning
- If Not For You
  (Vol. II, Dylan, Essential '00, Essential '10, and Essential '14)

November 17th, 1971
GREATEST HITS, VOL. II released

Pat Garrett & Billy the Kid
- Knockin' On Heaven's Door
  (Vol. II, The Best of, Dylan, The Best of, Essential '00, Essential '10, and Essential '14)

Planet Waves
- On A Night Like This
  (Dylan)
- Forever Young
  (Vol. III, The Best of, Dylan, Essential '00, Essential '10, and Essential '14)

Blood on the Tracks
- Shelter From The Storm
  (Essential '00, and Essential '10)
- Tangled Up In Blue
  (Vol. III, The Best of, Dylan, Essential '00, Essential '10, and Essential '14)
- Simple Twist Of Fate
  (Dylan)

Desire
- Hurricane
  (Vol. III, The Best of, Dylan, Essential '00, Essential '10, and Essential '14)

Street-Legal
- Changing Of The Guards
  (Vol. III, Dylan)

Slow Train Coming
- Gotta Serve Somebody
  (Vol. III, The Best of, Dylan, Essential '10)
- Precious Angel
  (Dylan)

Saved
- *none*

Shot of Love
- The Groom's Still Waiting At The Altar
  (Vol. III, Dylan, Essential '00, Essential '10, and Essential '14)

Infidels
- Jokerman
  (Vol. III, The Best of, Dylan, Essential '00, Essential '10, and Essential '14)
- Blind Willie McTell
  (Dylan, Essential '09 and Essential '10)

Empire Burlesque
- Dark Eyes
  (Dylan, Essential '09)

Knocked Out Loaded
- Brownsville Girl
  (Dylan, Vol. 3)

Down in the Groove
- Silvio
  (Vol. III, Dylan, Essential '00)

Oh Mercy
- Ring The Bells
  (Vol. III)
- Dignity
  (Vol. III, Essential '10)
- Series Of Dreams
  (Vol. III)
- Everything Is Broken
  (Dylan, Essential '00, and Essential '10)

Under the Red Sky
- Under The Red Sky
  (Vol. III, Dylan)

Good as I Been to You
- You're Gonna Quit Me
  (Dylan)

World Gone Wrong
- Blood In My Eyes
  (Dylan)

<u>**November 15th, 1994**</u>
***GREATEST HITS, VOL. III* released**

Time Out of Mind
- Not Dark Yet
  (Dylan, The Best of, Essential)
- Make You Feel My Love
  (Dylan, Essential '09, Essential '10)
- Mississippi
  (Essential '09, Essential '10 and Essential '14)

<u>**October 31st, 2000**</u>
***THE ESSENTIAL BOB DYLAN* first released**

Love and Theft
- Summer Days
  (The Best of)
- Things Have Changed
  (Dylan, The Best of, Essential)
- Highwater (For Charlie Patton)
  (Dylan)
- Po' Boy
  (Dylan)

November 15th, 2005
THE BEST OF BOB DYLAN **released**

Modern Times
- Someday Baby
  (Dylan)
- When The Deal Goes Down
  (Dylan, Essential '10 and Essential '14)
- Thunder On The Mountain
  (Essential '09 and Essential '10)

October 2nd, 2007
DYLAN **RELEASED**

Together Through Life
- Beyond Here Lies Nothin'
  (Essential '09 and Essential '10)

August 18th, 2009
THE ESSENTIAL BOB DYLAN **RELEASED AGAIN**

Christmas in the Heart
- *none*

October 1st, 2010
THE ESSENTIAL BOB DYLAN **released yet again**

Tempest
- Duquesne Whistle
  (Essential '14)

March 25th, 2014
THE ESSENTIAL BOB DYLAN **released one more time**

Shadows in the Night
- *none*

June 10th, 2016

THE ESSENTIAL BOB DYLAN released for the last time (so far)

<u>Fallen Angels</u>
- *none*

<u>Triplicate</u>
- *none*

"GREATEST HITS, VOL. IV"

1. Things Have Changed
2. Make You Feel My Love
3. The Night We Called It A Day
4. You're Gonna Quit Me
5. Mississippi
6. Duquesne Whistle
7. Must Be Santa
8. When The Deal Goes Down
9. I Could Have Told You
10. Blood In My Eyes
11. 'Cross The Green Mountain
12. Melancholy Mood
13. Dreamin' Of You
14. Beyond Here Lies Nothin'

It's been 23 years since Bob Dylan's *Greatest Hits, vol. III*. While there have been a number of compilations since then, they all start from scratch, allowing Columbia to include the huge hits of the sixties again and again. However, if they had resisted that urge and instead waited to release a *Greatest Hits, vol. IV*, in the vein of the past three. I decided to hypothesize what kind of album this would be. I tried to replicate the general feel of *Volume III* by only having one track per album and limited myself to 14 songs. I also decided to focus on the songs that were either released as "singles," or as music videos, or at least compiled on 2007's Dylan 3 CD set instead of just picking my favorites. I'm not sure how well it would sell or what the market for it would be...

DYLAN on LIVE ALBUMS:

While one could certainly look at Bob Dylan's live set-list and calculate which songs he himself thinks are most important (and believe me, people have); looking at the list of songs that were released on contemporary (as opposed to archival) live recordings gives one a glimpse into what tunes Columbia Records deems most important. I curated these from 1974's *Before The Flood*, 1976's *Hard Rain*, 1979's *At Budokan*, 1984's *Real Live*, 1989's *Dylan & The Dead*, and 1995's *MTV Unplugged*. It is an odd segment of time where the record company felt like a new live album was a worthwhile investment from Bob Dylan every 2 to 5 years.

Knockin' on Heaven's Door
(Before The Flood, At Budokan, Dylan & The Dead, Unplugged)
All Along the Watchtower
(Before The Flood, At Budokan, Dylan & The Dead, Unplugged)
Ballad of a Thin Man
(Before The Flood, At Budokan, Real Live)
Like a Rolling Stone
(Before The Flood, At Budokan, Unplugged)
Maggie's Farm
(Hard Rain, At Budokan, Real Live)
Lay Lady Lay
(Before The Flood, Hard Rain)
Rainy Day Women #12 & 35
(Before The Flood, Unplugged)
It Ain't Me, Babe
(Before The Flood, Real Live)
Don't Think Twice, It's All Right
(Before The Flood, At Budokan)
Just Like a Woman
(Before The Flood, At Budokan)
It's Alright, Ma (I'm Only Bleeding)
(Before The Flood, At Budokan)
Blowin' in the Wind
(Before The Flood, At Budokan)
Shelter From The Storm
(Hard Rain, At Budokan)
The Times They Are A-Changin'
(At Budokan, Unplugged)
Tombstone Blues
(Real Live, Unplugged)
Most Likely You Go Your Way (And I'll Go Mine)
(Before The Flood)
Highway 61 Revisited
(Before The Flood)
One Too Many Mornings
(Hard Rain)
Stuck Inside Of Mobile With The Blues Again
(Hard Rain)
You're A Big Girl Now
(Hard Rain)
I Threw It All Away
(Hard Rain)
Idiot Wind
(Hard Rain)
Mr. Tambourine Man
(At Budokan)
Love Minus Zero/No Limit
(At Budokan)
One More Cup Of Coffee (Valley Below)
(At Budokan)

I Shall Be Released
(At Budokan)
Is Your Love In Vain?
(At Budokan)
Going, Going, Gone
(At Budokan)
Oh, Sister
(At Budokan)
Simple Twist Of Fate
(At Budokan)
I Want You
(At Budokan, Dylan & The Dead)
All I Really Wanna Do
(At Budokan)
Forever Young
(At Budokan)
Highway 61 Revisited
(Real Live)
I And I
(Real Live)
License To Kill
(Real Live)
Tangled Up In Blue
(Real Live)
Masters Of War
(Real Live)
Girl From The North Country
(Real Live)
Slow Train
(Dylan & The Dead)
Gotta Serve Somebody
(Dylan & The Dead)
Queen Jane Approximately
(Dylan & The Dead)
Joey
(Dylan & The Dead)
Shooting Star
(Unplugged)
John Brown
(Unplugged)
Desolation Row
(Unplugged)
Dignity
(Unplugged)
With God On Our Side
(Unplugged)

DYLAN on STAGE:

There's a big difference between Bob's personal favorite songs and his most well-known recordings. Dylan himself can be something of a contrarian, sticking up for what he likes in complete disregard for the desires of his audience. Of course, Bob has a lot more freedom in picking what he wants when it comes to the songs he chooses to add to his set-list and play live. When it comes to the tracks selected for his various compilations and live albums, Dylan does have to answer to his record company. Sometimes during his career, he seems somewhat disinterested in that side of the business and lets Columbia do whatever they think best, even if ultimately Dylan has the final veto power.

But when it comes to the songs that Dylan chooses to play, he is utterly his own man (for better or for worse). I have gone ahead and pulled this data from Dylan's official website. I cannot verify its accuracy, but it's probably a pretty good starting point. Since the "Never Ending Tour" is still living up to its name, these numbers are continually changing. I compiled this information at the end of the year 2018, so take this all with a grain of salt.

Certainly songs and albums that are older will have higher numbers in general, just because there have been more opportunities, but here is where the albums stand in terms of times played:

Highway 61 Revisited	6,844
The Freewheelin' Bob Dylan	4,705
Love & Theft	4,643
Blonde On Blonde	4,216
Bringing It All Back Home	3,588
Another Side Of Bob Dylan	3,286
John Wesley Harding	3,259

Album	Count
Blood On The Tracks	3,194
Time Out Of Mind	2,589
Tempest	2,258
Modern Times	2,122
The Times They Are A-Changin'	1,900
Slow Train Coming	1,476
Oh Mercy	1,411
The Basement Tapes	1,030
Saved	1,017
Nashville Skyline	939
Together Through Life	913
Infidels	786
Shadows In The Night	733
Planet Waves	668
Greatest Hits, Vol. II	642
Down In The Groove	642
Empire Burlesque	631
Under The Red Sky	614
Shot Of Love	586
Street Legal	521
Desire	487
Pat Garrett & Billy The Kid	461
New Morning	427
Fallen Angels	350
Good As I Been To You	251
Bob Dylan	183
Triplicate	160
Self-Portrait	114
World Gone Wrong	43
Knocked Out Loaded	12
Dylan	2

Sadly, the album *Christmas In The Heart* has never had any of its songs played live at any time ever, although he did cover Dick Farina's "Xmas Island" once on January 14th, 1963. Meanwhile, three of the top six tunes all come from *Highway 61 Revisited*, easily boosting it to the top spot.

Below is a list of the top 25 songs played live. Bob has played a number of songs live that he hasn't recorded. "Things Have Changed" has been performed 869 times despite never having appeared on any of his official albums. Bob has even played Buddy Holly's "Not Fade Away" 138 times despite never having been officially recorded. That's more times than *Self-Portrait*, *World Gone Wrong*, *Knocked Out Loaded*, and *Dylan* combined.

All Along The Watchtower	2,268
Like A Rolling Stone	2,048
Highway 61 Revisited	1,959
Tangled Up In Blue	1,685
Blowin' In The Wind	1,558
Ballad Of A Thin Man	1,237
Don't Think Twice, It's All Right	1,070
Maggie's Farm	1,051
It Ain't Me, Babe	1,033
Rainy Day Women #12 & 35	963
Things Have Changed	943
Mr. Tambourine Man	903
Love Sick	887
Summer Days	885
Masters Of War	884
Just Like A Woman	871
It's Alright, Ma (I'm Only Bleeding)	772
Simple Twist Of Fate	763
Stuck Inside Of Mobile With The Memphis Blues Again	748
High Water (For Charley Patton)	712
Honest With Me	699
Thunder On The Mountain	698
The Times They Are A-Changin'	633
Silvio	594
Desolation Row	581

There's also a bunch of songs that Dylan has recorded and released that he has never bothered to perform live even once. Breaking this out by album shows which songs were completely neglected... so far. Some songs take a while to show up in the set-list. 1969's "Country Pie and 1970's "If Dogs Run Free" didn't make their live debut until 2000.

BOB DYLAN
(183)

Song To Woody	53
Pretty Peggy-O	52
This Land Is Your Land	32
Man Of Constant Sorrow	22
Baby, Let Me Follow You Down	22
House Of the Risin' Sun	8
See That My Grave Is Kept Clean	3
Dink's Song	3
Talkin' New York	2
Highway 51	2
He Was A Friend Of Mine	2
Fixin' To Die	1
Gospel Plow	1
Man On The Street	1
No More Auction Block	1

THE FREEWHEELIN' BOB DYLAN
(4,705)

Blowin' In The Wind	1,558
Don't Think Twice, It's All Right	1,070
Masters Of War	884
Girl From The North Country	546
A Hard Rain's A-Gonna Fall	457
Tomorrow Is A Long Time	69
Bob Dylan's Dream	50
Talkin' World War III Blues	15
Talkin' John Birch Paranoid Blues	13
Who Killed Davey Moore	8
Hero Blues	5
Honey, Just Allow Me One More Chance	3
Walls Of Red Wing	3
Rocks and Gravel	3
Talkin' Bear Mountain Picnic Massacre Blues	2
Sally Gal	2
All Over You	2

The Ballad Of Donald White	2
Long Time Gone	2
Oxford Town	1
Corrina, Corrina	1
Wichita (Going To Louisiana)	1
Let Me Die In My Footsteps	1
Quit Your Low Down Ways	1
Worried Blues	1
The Death Of Emmett Till	1

THE TIMES THEY ARE A-CHANGIN'
(1,900)

The Times They Are A-Changin'	633
Boots Of Spanish Leather	298
The Lonesome Death Of Hattie Carroll	296
One Too Many Mornings	237
Ballad Of Hollis Brown	211
John Brown	170
With God On Our Side	29
Only A Pawn In Their Game	8
When The Ship Comes In	3
Eternal Circle	3
North Country Blues	2
Restless Farewell	2
Bob Dylan's New Orleans Rag	2
Seven Curses	2
Percy's Song	1
Lay Down Your Weary Tune	1
Only A Hobo	1
Farewell	1

ANOTHER SIDE OF BOB DYLAN
(3,286)

It Ain't Me, Babe	1,033
To Ramona	381
I Don't Believe You (She Acts Like We Never Have Met)	349
My Back Pages	260

Mama, You Been On My Mind	201
All I Really Want To Do	102
Chimes Of Freedom	56
Spanish Harlem Incident	1

BRINGING IT ALL BACK HOME
(3,588)

Maggie's Farm	1,051
Mr. Tambourine Man	903
It's Alright, Ma (I'm Only Bleeding)	772
It's All Over Now, Baby Blue	556
She Belongs To Me	491
Love Minus Zero/No Limit	365
Gates Of Eden	217
Subterranean Homesick Blues	120
If You Gotta Go, Go Now	9
Bob Dylan's 115th Dream	6
Outlaw Blues	1

HIGHWAY 61 REVISITED
(6,844)

Like A Rolling Stone	2,048
Highway 61 Revisited	1,959
Ballad Of A Thin Man	1,237
Desolation Row	581
Positively 4th Street	359
Just Like Tom Thumb's Blues	243
Tombstone Blues	169
It Takes A Lot To Laugh, It Takes A Train To Cry	168
Queen Jane Approximately	76
From A Buick 6	2
Long Distance Operator	1
Can You Please Crawl Out Your Window	1

BLONDE ON BLONDE
(4,216)

Rainy Day Women #12 & 35	963
Just Like A Woman	871

Stuck Inside Of Mobile With The Memphis Blues Again	748
Leopard-Skin Pill-Box Hat	535
Most Likely You Go Your Way And I'll Go Mine	315
Visions Of Johanna	216
I Want You	214
Absolutely Sweet Marie	181
One Of Us Must Know (Sooner Or Later)	60
Obviously Five Believers	40
Fourth Time Around	37
Pledging My Time	21
Tell Me, Momma	15

THE BASEMENT TAPES
(1,030)

I Shall Be Released	491
Crash On The Levee (Down In The Flood)	176
This Wheel's On Fire	121
You Ain't Goin' Nowhere	108
Tears Of Rage	81
Folsom Prison Blues	19
Confidential	12
Quinn The Eskimo (The Mighty Quinn)	6
Big River	3
You Win Again	2
Yea! Heavy And A Bottle Of Bread	2
Will The Circle Be Unbroken?	2
Ain't No More Cane	2
Million Dollar Bash	1
Minstrel Boy	1
People Get Ready	1
Silhouettes	1
Po' Lazarus	1

JOHN WESLEY HARDING
(3,259)

All Along The Watchtower	2,268
I'll Be Your Baby Tonight	444

Drifter's Escape	256
The Wicked Messenger	125
Down Along The Cove	83
I Dreamed I Saw St. Augustine	39
The Ballad Of Frankie Lee And Judas Priest	20
I Pity The Poor Immigrant	17
Dear Landlord	6
As I Went Out One Morning	1

NASHVILLE SKYLINE
(939)

Lay, Lady, Lay	407
Tonight I'll Be Staying Here With You	144
Country Pie	136
To Be Alone With You	126
Tell Me That It Isn't True	76
I Threw It All Away	48
One More Night	2

SELF-PORTRAIT
(114)

I Forgot More Than You'll Ever Know	54
Gotta Travel On	17
Blue Moon	12
Wild Mountain Thyme	10
Early Mornin' Rain	8
The Boxer	7
Let It Be Me	3
Living The Blues	1
Railroad Bill	1
Spanish Is The Loving Tongue	1

DYLAN
(2)

Sarah Jane	1
Mary Ann	1

NEW MORNING
(427)

The Man In Me	155
If Dogs Run Free	104
If Not For You	89
New Morning	79

GREATEST HITS, VOL. II
(642)

Watching The River Flow	500
When I Paint My Masterpiece	142

PAT GARRETT & BILLY THE KID
(461)

Knockin' On Heaven's Door	460
Billy 1	1

PLANET WAVES
(668)

Forever Young	493
Going, Going, Gone	79
Tough Mama	44
Something There Is About You	26
Wedding Song	9
Nobody 'Cept You	8
Hazel	7
You Angel You	2

BLOOD ON THE TRACKS
(3,194)

Tangled Up In Blue	1,685
Simple Twist Of Fate	763
Shelter From The Storm	376
You're A Big Girl Now	212
If You See Her, Say Hello	88
Idiot Wind	55
You're Gonna Make Me Lonesome When You Go	12
Meet Me In The Morning	1
Lily, Rosemary And The Jack Of Hearts	1

Buckets Of Rain   1

DESIRE
(487)
One More Cup Of Coffee (Valley Below)   151
Joey   82
Oh, Sister   67
Isis   46
Romance In Durango   38
Hurricane   33
Sara   33
Seven Days   18
Mozambique   17
Black Diamond Bay   1
Rita May   1

STREET LEGAL
(521)
Senor (Tales Of Yankee Power)   265
Changing Of The Guards   68
Am I Your Stepchild?   53
Baby, Stop Crying   39
Where Are You Tonight? (Journey Through Dark Heat)   33
Is Your Love In Vain?   31
We Better Talk This Over   15
True Love Tends To Forget   14
Repossession Blues   2
Coming From The Heart (The Road Is Long)   1

SLOW TRAIN COMING
(1,476)
Gotta Serve Somebody   463
I Believe In You   259
Man Gave Names To All The Animals   155
When You Gonna Wake Up   148
Slow Train   127
Gonna Change My Way Of Thinking   85
Precious Angel   73

Do Right To Me Baby (Do Unto Others)   73
When He Returns   47
Blessed Be The Name   43
Ain't No Man Righteous   3

SAVED
(1,017)

In The Garden   329
Solid Rock   162
Saving Grace   103
What Can I Do For You?   93
Saved   83
Pressing On   65
Covenant Woman   57
Ain't Gonna Go To Hell For Anybody   46
Are You Ready   30
Cover Down, Pray Through   27
City Of Gold   19
I Will Love Him   2
A Satisfied Mind   1

SHOT OF LOVE
(586)

Every Grain Of Sand   185
Lenny Bruce   103
Shot Of Love   76
Dead Man, Dead Man   48
Heart Of Mine   46
Watered-Down Love   41
In The Summertime   26
Let's Keep It Between Us   19
Let's Begin   18
Jesus Is The One   10
Trouble   7
The Groom's Still Waiting At The Altar   5
Caribbean Wind   1
Thief On The Cross   1

INFIDELS
(786)

Blind Willie McTell	226
I And I	204
Jokerman	157
Clean Cut Kid	68
License To Kill	46
Man Of Peace	41
Union Sundown	30
Tight Connection To My Heart (Has Anyone Seen My Love)	14

EMPIRE BURLESQUE
(631)

Seeing The Real You At Last	242
I'll Remember You	226
When The Night Comes Falling From The Sky	61
Never Gonna Be The Same Again	26
Trust Yourself	25
Emotionally Yours	19
Driftin' Too Far From Shore	14
Enough Is Enough	9
Dark Eyes	8
Brownsville Girl	1

KNOCKED OUT LOADED
(12)

A Couple More Years	4
Shake	4
Precious Memories	3
Got My Mind Made Up	1

DOWN IN THE GROOVE
(642)

Silvio	594
Rank Strangers To Me	26
When Did You Leave Heaven?	10
Had A Dream About You, Baby	4
Shenandoah	3

Sally Sue Brown 2
Pretty Boy Floyd 2
Money Honey 1

OH MERCY
(1,411)
Man In The Long Black Coat 286
Everything Is Broken 284
What Good Am I? 241
God Knows 188
Shooting Star 126
Born In Time 56
Dignity 53
Most Of The Time 36
Disease Of Conceit 32
Ring Them Bells 31
Political World 28
What Was It You Wanted 22
Where Teardrops Fall 14
Series Of Dreams 10
Congratulations 3
People Get Ready 1

UNDER THE RED SKY
(614)
Cat's In The Well 299
Under The Red Sky 148
Wiggle Wiggle 105
Unbelievable 29
T.V. Talkin' Song 20
Heartland 7
2 X 2 4
10,000 Men 1
Handy Dandy 1

GOOD AS I BEEN TO YOU
(251)

Duncan And Brady	81
Tomorrow Night	58
Jim Jones	31
You're Gonna Quit Me	31
Hard Times	30
Blackjack Davey	18
Little Maggie	1
Hey Joe	1

WORLD GONE WRONG
(43)

Two Soldiers	24
Delia	9
Ragged & Dirty	3
My Blue Eyed Jane	3
Blood In My Eyes	2
Jack-A-Roe	2

TIME OUT OF MIND
(2,589)

Love Sick	887
Cold Irons Bound	423
Make You Feel My Love	274
Tryin' To Get To Heaven	247
'Til I Fell In Love With You	194
Can't Wait	187
Not Dark Yet	152
Million Miles	75
Mississippi	75
Standing In The Doorway	58
Highlands	9
Shake Sugaree	8

LOVE & THEFT
(4,643)

Things Have Changed	943
Summer Days	885
High Water (For Charley Patton)	705
Honest With Me	699
Tweedle Dee & Tweedle Dum	488
Lonesome Day Blues	160
Cry A While	157
Waiting For You	157
Sugar Baby	130
Moonlight	101
Floater (Too Much To Ask)	87
Bye And Bye	78
Po' Boy	41
Red Cadillac and a Black Moustache	3
Return To Me	2

MODERN TIMES
(2,122)

Thunder On The Mountain	698
Spirit On The Water	547
Workingman's Blues #2	267
When The Deal Goes Down	148
Nettie Moore	142
Ain't Talkin'	118
The Levee's Gonna Break	73
Beyond The Horizon	58
Rollin' and Tumblin'	57
Dixie	7
Huck's Tune	7

TOGETHER THROUGH LIFE
(913)

Beyond Here Lies Nothin'	428
Forgetful Heart	234
Jolene	162
If You Ever Go To Houston	32

I Feel A Change Comin' On	22
My Wife's Home Town	20
This Dream Of You	12
It's All Good	3

TEMPEST
(2,258)

Early Roman Kings	457
Pay In Blood	436
Soon After Midnight	375
Duquesne Whistle	350
Long And Wasted Years	327
Scarlet Town	311
Roll On John	2

SHADOWS IN THE NIGHT
(733)

Autumn Leaves	203
Why Try To Change Me Now	167
Stay With Me	68
I'm a Fool to Want You	63
What'll I Do	58
The Night We Called it a Day	47
Full Moon and Empty Arms	42
Stormy Weather	35
That Lucky Old Sun	30
Where Are You?	18
Moon River	2

FALLEN ANGELS
(350)

Melancholy Mood	175
All Or Nothing At All	122
That Old Black Magic	45
Come Rain or Come Shine	8

TRIPLICATE
(160)

I Could Have Told You	62
Once Upon a Time	59
The September of My Years	20
How Deep Is the Ocean?	7
That Old Feeling	6
This Nearly Was Mine	4
Where Is the One?	2

DYLAN in DIGITAL & STREAMING FORMAT:

Here are the top 10 tracks from Spotify on Dec. 31st, 2018. Why they are not in order of the most streams to least, I cannot possibly say:

1. Knockin' On Heaven's Door — 92,341,227
2. Like A Rolling Stone — 122,117,944
3. The Times They Are A-Changin' — 88,325,411
4. Hurricane — 70,752,826
5. Blowin' In the Wind — 52,098,731
6. Must Be Santa — 14,672,638
7. Girl From The North Country — 50,902,003
8. Don't Think Twice, It's All Right — 36,799,580
9. Shelter From The Storm — 30,022,412
10. Mr. Tambourine Man — 35,690,229

Below is the list of "Top Songs" from iTunes on Dec. 31st, 2018. Since several of these songs can be found on a multitude of albums, sometimes the same song can show up two or three times. It looks like most iTunes users are getting their MP3s from compilation albums rather than the original recordings. Of course, iTunes doesn't give us the actual number of downloads, so I can't add the numbers of downloads together.

1. Knockin' On Heaven's Door — *Greatest Hits, vol. III*
2. Like A Rolling Stone — *Greatest Hits, vol. I*
3. Shelter From The Storm — *Blood On The Tracks*
4. The Times They Are A-Changin' — *The Essential Bob Dylan*
5. Mr. Tambourine Man — *Greatest Hits, vol. I*
6. Lay Lady Lay — *The Essential Bob Dylan*
7. Tangled Up In Blue — *Blood On The Tracks*
8. Blowin' In the Wind — *Greatest Hits, vol. I*
9. Hurricane — *The Essential Bob Dylan*
10. A Hard Rain's A-Gonna Fall — *The Freewheelin' Bob Dylan*
11. Don't Think Twice, It's All Right — *The Freewheelin' Bob Dylan*
12. Like A Rolling Stone — *Highway 61 Revisited*

13.	Simple Twist Of Fate	*Blood On The Tracks*
14.	Positively 4th Street	*Greatest Hits, vol. I*
15.	Girl From the North Country	*The Essential Johnny Cash*
16.	Subterranean Homesick Blues	*Bringing It All Back Home*
17.	Ballad Of A Thin Man	*Highway 61 Revisited*
18.	Girl From The North Country	*The Freewheelin' Bob Dylan*
19.	Visions Of Johanna	*Blonde On Blonde*
20.	The Times They Are A-Changin'	*Greatest Hits, vol. I*
21.	Highway 61 Revisited	*Highway 61 Revisited*
22.	You're A Big Girl Now	*Blood On The Tracks*
23.	It's All Over Now, Baby Blue	*Bringing It All Back Home*
24.	If You See Her, Say Hello	*Blood On The Tracks*
25.	Just Like A Woman	*Blonde On Blonde*

In contrast here are the top 25 songs according to the Tidal streaming service on the same day:

1. Like A Rolling Stone
2. Have Yourself A Little Christmas
3. Blowin' In The Wind
4. Hurricane
5. Tangled Up In Blue
6. Don't Think Twice, It's All Right
7. Man In The Long Black Coat
8. Girl From The North Country (w/ Johnny Cash)
9. Little Drummer Boy
10. The Times They Are A-Changin'
11. Girl From The North Country
12. Here Comes Santa Claus
13. Knockin' On Heaven's Door
14. Must Be Santa
15. Lay, Lady, Lay
16. The Man In Me
17. Shelter From the Storm
18. I Want You
19. Just Like A Woman
20. Make You Feel My Love
21. Visiona Of Johanna
22. Mr. Tambourine
23. Simple Twist Of Fate
24. Most Of The Time
25. Desolation Row

STREAMING SAMPLERS:

While I can understand not putting the entire Deluxe editions of each volume of *The Bootleg Series* available on streaming to try and encourage hardcore collectors to pay the exorbitant price tags, Columbia Records has taken it a step further. For the last few volumes, they withhold even the whole two disc standard edition. They don't want to lose out on the revenue or publicity of streaming services entirely, so the record company creates what amounts to a single disc sampler platter for these albums. Even the streaming version of *The Bootleg Series vol. 14* featured the exact same songs as the physical copy on CD but used completely different takes of each song. While it's odd, it is interesting to see what songs are (and are not) selected for each.

The Bootleg Series, Vol. 10
- Went To See The Gypsy - demo
- Only A Hobo - unreleased, *Greatest Hits, vol. II*
- Working On A Guru
- In Search Of Little Sadie - without overdubs
- Pretty Sar-O
- Bring Me A Little Water
- Minstrel Boy - unreleased, *The Basement Tapes*
- Highway 61 Revisited - live with The Band, Isle of Wight 1969
- Time Passes Slowly #1 - alternate version
- Annie's Going To Sing Her Song
- This Evening So Soon
- If Not For You - alternate version
- Belle Isle - without overdubs
- Tattle O'Day
- When I Paint My Masterpiece - demo

The Bootleg Series, Vol. 11
- Odds And Ends - take 1, alternate version
- Million Dollar Bash - take 1
- You Ain't Going Nowhere - take 1
- Ain't No More Cane - take 2, alternate version
- One Too Many Mornings
- Dress It Up, Better Have It All
- Too Much Of Nothing - take 2
- Lo And Behold! - take 2
- All You Have To Do Is Dream - take 2

- Nothing Was Delivered - take 1
- Folsom Prison Blues
- Don't Ya Tell Henry
- 900 Miles From My Home
- I'm Your Teenage Prayer
- I Shall Be Released - take 1

The Bootleg Series, Vol. 12
- She Belongs To Me - take 1, solo acoustic
- Subterranean Homesick Blues - take 1, alternate take
- Like A Rolling Stone - take 5, rehearsal (short version)
- It Takes A Lot To Laugh, It Takes A Train To Cry - take 8, alternate take
- Desolation Row - take 2, piano demo
- Just Like Tom Thumb's Blues - take 3, rehearsal
- Highway 61 Revisited - take 2, alternate take
- Queen Jane Approximately - take 5, alternate take
- Visions Of Johanna - take 5, rehearsal
- She's Your Lover Now - take 6, rehearsal
- Leopard-Skin Pill-Box Hat - take 8, alternate take
- Stuck Inside Of Mobile With The Memphis Blues Again - take 13, alternate take
- Absolutely Sweet Marie - take 1, alternate take
- Pledging My Time - take 1, alternate take
- I Want You - take 4, alternate take

The Bootleg Series, Vol. 13
- Slow Train [Live in London]
- Precious Angel [Live Nov. 16, 1979]
- Gotta Serve Somebody [Live Nov. 15, 1979]
- When He Returns [Take 2]
- Solid Rock [Live Nov. 29, 1979]
- Gonna Change My Way of Thinking [Live Jan. 31, 1980]
- Ain't Gonna Go to Hell for Anybody [Live Apr. 24, 1980]
- When You Gonna Wake Up? [Live July 9, 1981]
- Covenant Woman [Take 3]
- Shot of Love [Outtake]
- Making a Liar Out of Me [Rehearsal]
- City of Gold [Live Nov. 22, 1980]

- Yonder Comes Sin [Rehearsal]
- Caribbean Wind [Rehearsal with pedal steel]
- Dead Man, Dead Man [Outtake]

Triplicate
- The Best Is Yet To Come
- These Foolish Things
- It's Funny To Everyone But Me
- When The World Was Young
- I Could Have Told You
- Sentimental Journey
- That Old Feeling
- My One And Only Love
- Stardust
- Once Upon A Time

DYLAN'S BIGGEST HITS
As covered by others

Bob Dylan has never really been known as a "singles" artist. Infamously Bob is one of the most famous musicians never to have actually recorded a #1 song of his own. However, many other artists have had great chart success with Bob Dylan's songs. That helps play into the myth that Bob Dylan is a great songwriter and a lousy singer. A lot of Bob's fame and notoriety from cover versions by other artists. There's not a particularly good resource for finding all the "hit" cover versions of Bob's songs. I have done my best to compile as complete a list as I could, accompanied by the chart position (and which chart it appeared on). That may also give an idea of which songs are Bob's biggest.

Song	Artist	Chart
Mr. Tambourine Man	by The Byrds	#1 US Billboard Hot 100
Jammin' Me (written by Tom Petty, Bob Dylan and Mike Campbell)	by Tom Petty & The Heartbreakers	#1 US Billboard Album Rock Tracks
If Not For You	by Olivia Newton-John	#1 US Billboard Easy Listening
Wagon Wheel (written by Bob Dylan and Ketch Scolar)	by Darius Rucker	#1 Hot Country Songs
Make You Feel My Love	by Garth Brooks	#1 Hot Country Songs
Blowin' In The Wind	by Peter, Paul & Mary	#2 US Billboard Hot 100
If You Gotta Go, Go Now	by Manfred Mann	#2 UK Singles
Forever Young (written by Jim Cregan, Kevin Savigar, Bob Dylan and Rod Stewart)	by Rod Stewart	#3 US Billboard Hot Adult Contemporary Tracks
It Ain't Me, Babe	by Johnny Cash & June Carter	#4 Hot Country Songs
Make You Feel My Love	by Adele	#4 UK Singles
This Wheel's On Fire (written by Bob Dylan and Rick Danko)	by Brian Auger, Julie Driscoll & Trinity	#5 UK Singles

Steel Bars *(written by Michael Bolton and Bob Dylan)*	by Michael Bolton	#7 US Billboard Adult Contemporary
It Ain't Me Babe	by The Turtles	#8 US Billboard Hot 100
Blowin' In The Wind	by Stevie Wonder	#9 US Billboard Hot 100
Don't Think Twice, It's All Right	by Peter, Paul & Mary	#9 US Billboard Hot 100
Make You Feel My Love	by Billy Joel	#9 US Billboard Hot Adult Contemporary Tracks
The Mighty Quinn	by Manfred Mann	#10 US Billboard Hot 100
Don't Think Twice, It's All Right	by The Wonder Who? (The Four Seasons)	#12 US Billboard Hot 100
Forever Young	by Joan Baez	#13 Adult Contemporary
It's All Over Now, Baby Blue	by Them	#13 German charts
This Wheel's On Fire *(written by Bob Dylan and Rick Danko)*	by Siouxie & The Banshees	#14 UK Singles
All I Really Wanna Do	by Cher	#15 US Billboard Hot 100
Knockin' On Heaven's Door	by Guns 'n' Roses	#18 US Billboard Album Rock Tracks
All Along The Watchtower	by The Jimi Hendrix Experience	#20 US Billboard Hot 100
Si Tu Dois Partir (If You Gotta Go, Go Now)	by Fairport Convention	#21 UK Singles
I'll Be Your Baby Tonight	by Robert Palmer & UB40	#24 US Billboard Hot Modern Rock Tracks
My Back Pages	by The Byrds	#30 US Billboard Hot 100
Die Antwort Weiss Ganz Allein Der Wind	by Marlene Dietrich	#32 German charts
She Belongs To Me	by Rick Nelson	#33 US Billboard Hot 100
Too Much Of Nothing	by Peter, Paul & Mary	#35 US Billboard Hot 100
Knockin' On Heaven's Door	by Eric Clapton	#38 UK Singles
All I Really Wanna Do	by The Byrds	#40 US Billboard Hot 100
You Ain't Going Nowhere	by The Byrds	#74 US Billboard Hot 100

Nashville Skyline Rag	by Earl Scruggs	#74 Hot Country Songs
Love Is Just A Four Lettered Word	by Joan Baez	#86 US Billboard Hot 100
When The Ship Comes In	by Peter, Paul & Mary	#91 US Billboard Hot 100
Just Like A Woman	by Manfred Mann	#101 US Billboard Hot 100
A Hard Rain's A-Gonna Fall	by Leon Russell	#105 US Billboard Hot 100
Mr. Jones (Ballad Of A Thin Man)	by The Grass Roots	#121 US Billboard Hot 100

DYLAN on CASSETTE:

Back in the mid-'80s Columbia Records re-released Bob's catalog on the now demonized format of cassette tape. By the time I started getting into Bob in the mid-'90s these were all relegated to the 3-for-$10 clearance bin at the Tower Records by the Cherry Creek mall. Now, since LPs were square and cassettes were rectangular, reproducing the album covers left a white margin on the bottom for the record company to do with as they want. Now some cassettes, such as *Saved* and *Shot Of Love,* just had the UPC bar code in that spot. Others, like *Planet Waves* and *Infidels,* only featured the full track listing for the cassette. But most of Bob's cassettes had affixed there was a list of five (or in one case six) songs that the marketing department wanted to highlight from each album. I'm not sure who was in charge of selecting these songs, or what their criteria was, but looking at the list of "suggestions" from each tape gives one an easy and interesting way to thin out the Dylan discography into a more manageable size. Although I just gave my cassettes up to the ARC Thrift Stores a year or two ago, thanks to the good people at the Searching For A Gem website I was able to recreate this odd list for the Dylan novice, albeit one that stops at *Slow Train Coming.*

BOB DYLAN:
She's No Good
In My Time Of Dyin'
Man Of Constant Sorrow
House Of Risin' Sun
See That My Grave Is Kept Clean

THE FREEWHEELIN' BOB DYLAN:
Don't Think Twice, It's All Right
Bob Dylan's Dream
Masters Of War
A Hard Rain's A-Gonna Fall
I Shall Be Free

THE TIMES THEY ARE A-CHANGIN'
The Times They Are A-Changin'
One Too Many Morning
The Lonesome Death Of Hattie Carroll
Ballad Of Hollis Brown
North Country Blues

ANOTHER SIDE OF BOB DYLAN:
It Ain't Me Babe
Chimes Of Freedom
All I Really Want To Do
My Back Pages
I Don't Believe You

BRINGING IT ALL BACK HOME:
She Belongs To Me
Maggie's Farm
Mr. Tambourine Man
It's All Over Now, Baby Blue
It's Alright

HIGHWAY 61 REVISITED:
Desolation Row
From A Buick 6
Tombstone Blues
Like A Rolling Stone
Queen Jane Approximately

BLONDE ON BLONDE:
Rainy Day Women #12 & 35
Just Like A Woman
Visions Of Johana
Stuck Inside Of Mobile With The Memphis Blues Again
I Want You

GREATEST HITS, VOL. I
Rainy Day Women #13 & 35
Subterranean Homesick Blues
Like A Rolling Stone
Positively 4th Street

THE BASEMENT TAPES:
Please, Mrs. Henry
Tears Of Rage
Crash On The Levee (Down In The Flood)
Tiny Montgomery
Nothing Was Delivered

JOHN WESLEY HARDING:
The Ballad Of Frankie Lee And Judas Priest
Drifter's Escape
I Dreamed I Saw St. Augustine
All Along The Watchtower

NASHVILLE SKYLINE:
I Threw It All Away
Nashville Skyline Rag
Girl From The North Country
Lay Lady Lay
Tonight I'll Be Staying Here With You

SELF PORTRAIT:
Wigwam
Copper Kettle
Little Sadie
Early Morning Rain
Days Of '49

DYLAN:
The Ballad Of Ira Hayes
Mr. Bojangles
Big Yellow Taxi
Sarah Jane
Lily Of The West

NEW MORNING:
Sign On The Window
If Not For You
Went To See The Gypsy
If Dogs Run Free
Three Angels

GREATEST HITS, VOL. II
Watching The River Flow
Don't Think Twice, It's All Right
Lay Lady Lay
Stuck Inside of Mobile With The Memphis Blues Again
If Not For You

PAT GARRETT & BILLY THE KID:
Knockin' On Heaven's Door
Billy 7
Cantina Theme (Workin' For The Law)
Bunkhouse Theme
Turkey Chase

BLOOD ON THE TRACKS:
Idiot Wind
Lily, Rosemary And The Jack Of Hearts
Tangled Up In Blue
Simple Twist Of Fate
Shelter From The Storm

HARD RAIN:
Maggie's Farm
Idiot Wind
You're A Big Girl Now
Shelter From The Storm
Lay, Lady, Lay

DESIRE:
Hurricane
Mozambique
Isis
Romance In Durango
One More Cup Of Coffee
Sara

STREET LEGAL:
Baby Stop Crying
Is Your Love In Vain?
No Time To Think
True Love Tends To Forget
Where Are You Tonight? (Journey Through Dark Heat)

AT BUDOKAN:
Like A Rolling Stone
I Shall Be Released
Just Like A Woman
All Along The Watchtower
Knockin' On Heaven's Door
Forever Young

SLOW TRAIN COMING:
Gotta Serve Somebody
Precious Angel
Do Right To My Baby (Do Unto Others)
Gonna Change My Way Of Thinking
Man Gave Names To All The Animals

DYLAN on 45 (or cassingle or MP3...):

Of course, it's one thing to see what the record company execs thought were the most important songs from each album with the benefit of hindsight. It's something else altogether to see Columbia Records try to predict what tracks would be the most popular at the time. Below is a list of every 7-inch 45rpm vinyl single that was released by (or for) Bob Dylan. I have included the US Billboard Hot 100 chart position, if applicable, to show how well the record company guessed at the audience's taste. I have limited this list to the USA as Bob Dylan is an American artist at the primary tastemakers in popular music is still centered in the USA. That almost every song Bob's written has been released as a sing somewhere in the world. Including all of that would just become unwieldy and useless.

While the 12" LP format remained popular enough for all of Bob's albums to be released on that format, the last single to be released on vinyl was 1988's "Silvio". And the next single, 1989's "Everything Is Broken" – released on cassette – was the last commercially available single released by Bob in any format in America until the "Independent Record Store Day" promotions started in Apr 2009. Trying to determine what was the "single" released starting with *Under The Red Sky* becomes much trickier. Sometimes there were promo singles released on CD; sometimes there are single songs released as download-only prior to the release of the album.

BOB DYLAN
none

THE FREEWHEELIN' BOB DYLAN
- **Mixed-Up Confusion** b/w Corrina, Corrina *withdrawn single*
- **Blowin' In The Wind** b/w Don't Think Twice, It's All Right

THE TIMES THEY ARE A-CHANGIN'
none

ANOTHER SIDE OF BOB DYLAN
none

BRINGING IT ALL BACK HOME
- **Subterranean Homesick Blues** b/w She Belongs To Me *(reached #39)*

HIGHWAY 61 REVISITED
- **Like A Rolling Stone** b/w Gates Of Eden *(reached #2)*
- **Positively 4th Street** b/w From A Buick 6 *(reached #7)*
- **Can You Please Crawl Out Your Window?** b/w Highway 61 Revisited *(reached #58)*

BLONDE ON BLONDE
- **One Of Us Must Know (Sooner Or Later)** b/w Queen Jane Approximately *(reached #119)*
- **Rainy Day Women #12 & 35** b/w Pledging My Time *(reached #2)*
- **I Want You** b/w Just Like Tom Thumb's Blues [LIVE] *(reached #20)*
- **Just Like A Woman** b/w Obviously 5 Believers *(reached #33)*
- **Most Likely Go Your Way (And I'll Go Mine)** b/w Leopard-Skin Pill-Box Hat *(reached #81)*

THE BASEMENT TAPES
- **Million Dollar Bash** b/w Tears Of Rage

JOHN WESLEY HARDING
none

NASHVILLE SKYLINE
- **I Threw It All Away** b/w Drifter's Escape *(reached #85)*
- **Lay Lady Lay** b/w Peggy Day *(reached #7)*
- **Tonight I'll Be Staying Here With You** b/w Country Pie (reached #50)

SELF-PORTRAIT
- **Wigwam** b/w Copper Kettle *(reached #41)*
- **Wigwam (unreleased demo)** b/w Thirsty Boots
- **All The Tired Horses** *promo 7" vinyl*

DYLAN
- **A Fool Such As I** b/w Lily Of The West *(reached #55)*

NEW MORNING
- **If Not For You** b/w Tomorrow Is A Long Time [LIVE]

GREATEST HITS VOL. II
- **Watching The River Flow** b/w Spanish Is The Loving Tongue *(reached #41)*
- **George Jackson (big band version)** b/w George Jackson (acoustic version) *(reached #33)*

PAT GARRETT & BILLY THE KID
- **Knockin' On Heaven's Door** b/w Turkey Chase *(reached #12)*

PLANET WAVES
- **On A Night Like This** b/w You Angel You *(reached #44)*
- **Something There Is About** b/w You Tough Mama *(reached #107)*

BLOOD ON THE TRACKS
- **Tangled Up In Blue** b/w If You See Her, Say Hello *(reached #31)*

DESIRE
- **Hurricane (Part I)** b/w Hurricane (Part II) *(reached #33)*
- **Mozambique** b/w Oh, Sister *(reached #54)*

STREET LEGAL
- **Baby, Stop Crying** b/w New Pony
- **Changing Of The Guards** b/w Señor (Tales Of Yankee Power)

SLOW TRAIN COMING
- **Gotta Serve Somebody** b/w Trouble In Mind *(reached #24)*
- **Man Gave Names To All The Animals** b/w When You Gonna Wake Up?
- **Slow Train** b/w Do Right To Me Baby (Do Unto Others)

SAVED
- **Solid Rock** b/w Covenant Woman
- **Saved** b/w Are You Ready?

SHOT OF LOVE
- **Heart Of Mine** b/w The Groom's Still Waiting At The Altar

INFIDELS
- **Sweetheart Like You** b/w Union Sundown *(reached #55)*
- **Jokerman** b/w Isis [LIVE]

EMPIRE BURLESQUE
- **Tight Connection To My Heart (Has Anybody Seen My Love?)** b/w We Better Talk This Over *(reached #103)*
- **Emotionally Yours** b/w When The Night Comes Falling From The Sky

KNOCKED OUT LOADED
- **Band Of The Hand (It's Helltime, Man)** b/w *the b-side is a non-Dylan song*

DOWN IN THE GROOVE
- **Silvio** b/w Driftin' Too Far From Shore

OH MERCY
- **Everything Is Broken** b/w Dead Man, Dead Man [LIVE] *cassette only*
- **Most Of The Time** *promo CD single*
- **Series Of Dreams** *promo CD single*
- **Dignity** *promo CD single*

UNDER THE RED SKY
- **Unbelievable** *promo CD single*

GOOD AS I BEEN TO YOU
- **Step It Up And Go** *promo CD single*

WORLD GONE WRONG
none

TIME OUT OF MIND
- **Love Sick** *promo CD single*
- **Dreamin' Of You** b/w Down Along The Cove [LIVE]

LOVE & THEFT
- **Things Have Changed** *promo CD single*
- **Tweedle Dee & Tweedle Dum** b/w Bye And Bye *promo vinyl 7"*
- **Honest With Me** *promo CD single*

MODERN TIMES
- **Someday Baby** *promo CD single & MP3 download single*
- **Rollin' And Tumblin'** *promo CD single*

TOGETHER THROUGH LIFE
- **Beyond Here Lies Nothin'** *MP3 download single*

CHRISTMAS IN THE HEART
- **Must Be Santa** b/w 'Twas The Night Before Christmas *promo vinyl 7"*

TEMPEST
- **Early Roman Kings** *MP3 download single*
- **Duquesne Whistle** b/w Meet Me In The Morning

SHADOWS IN THE NIGHT
- **Full Moon And Empty Arms** *MP3 download single*
- **The Night We Called It A Day** b/w Stay With Me

FALLEN ANGELS
- **Melancholy Mood** *MP3 download single*
- **All The Way** *MP3 download single*

TRIPLICATE
- **I Could Have Told You** *MP3 download single*
- **My One And Only Love** *MP3 download single*
- **Stardust** *MP3 download single*

DYLAN on MTV/YouTube

Below is a list of all of the songs for which Bob (and/or his record company) has shot a music video. Some of these are good. Some of these are really bad. Most of these are kind of weird. A few don't even have Bob Dylan in them. Most, but not all of them, were released as singles. I'm not sure why they would make a video for a song that wasn't being released as a single.

- **Subterranean Homesick Blues**

  One of the earliest progenitors of the "music video", this is possibly the best known of Bob's on-camera work. It's just a short film that was used to open D.A. Pennebaker's documentary *Don't Look Back*. No explanation or context for this "video" is provided within the rest of the film. Some of the filmmaking decisions (too shoot it all in one take and in B&W) may have been less artistically-driven at the time then it would seem in the heyday of MTV. Still, the director's idea not to rely on Bob's admittedly limited ability to lip-sync and mime guitar playing was very astute. In a lot of ways, this quote-unquote video crystalized who Bob Dylan is in the minds of the public... even to this day.

- **Like A Rolling Stone**

  From one of the earliest innovations in music videos to one of the latest. For no good reason at all (other than to show off their new technology), an interactive web video was created for this song in 2013. It's a pretty neat concept, while you flip through the virtual "channels" of the fake TV, the song continues to play unabated while which random scene we see lip-syncing to the video is controlled by the viewer. There are some TV shows where they got the actual performers to play along (Drew Carey on *The Price Is Right*, *The Property Brothers*, Marc Maron's podcast) and others where we get actors faking a satirical version of QVC or a local news broadcast. It is interesting and funny but gets old pretty quick. While the technology on display is impressive – it didn't usher in a new wave of interactive filmmaking, and this one-off has already been pretty much forgotten.

- **Most Likely Go Your Way (And I'll Go Mine)**

  For the 2007 compilation, *Dylan*, Mark Ronson was hired to remix this track from *Blonde On Blonde*. Part of the promotion included a video for this new remix. Dylan himself did not appear to be involved at all (in the video, the remix, or the compilation). What we see here may be a more thorough or factual representation of Dylan's actual life story than we got in the entire feature film *I'm Not There*. Instead of anyone lip syncing, we follow our Dylan surrogate from behind as he seems to find his way through visual clues from Bob's entire career. We've got the cover from *Freewheelin'*; we've got the big brass bed from "Lay Lady Lay". It's a clever sort of Where's Waldo full of clues for the Bob aficionado. Inessential, but fun.

- **Pretty Saro**

Even though MTV stopped showing music videos a long time ago, at some point in the 2010s Columbia started commissioning videos to help promote their latest volumes of *The Bootleg Series*. As with most things involving *The Bootleg Series*, Dylan himself seems pretty uninvolved. For some reason, this video made up almost entirely of vividly colorful photographs from the Farm Security Administration archive at the Library Congress interspersed with a few brief snippets of home movie footage of the same vintage. It's hard to say when exactly these photographs were taken. Everyone looks like they belong in an era before color photography was even an option. Ultimately it is lovely to look at but completely detached from the Dylan song it is supposed to be promoting.

- **Tangled Up In Blue**

Much like "Subterranean Homesick Blues" this is not technically a music video so much as it is a clip from a film that features an entire song that was taken out of context and used as a video much after the fact. This time the movie is the Dylan-directed *Renaldo & Clara*. Given how the movie has pretty much disappeared since it was released in 1978, this clip is all most people have seen of it. It doesn't give much of an idea what the film is about. All we get here is an extremely tight close-up of Bob's make-up smeared face and hat, while he performs a solo acoustic version of the song. Not nearly as iconic as "Subterranean Homesick Blues", it's still pretty well-known.

- **Sweetheart Like You**

Starting with *Infidels* in the early eighties, Columbia Records accepted the fact that MTV was going to be a real driver in terms of the commercial success of their artists and was able to pressure Dylan into making a few of these new-fangled "videos". One of the first Bob deigned to do was this clip for "Sweetheart Like You". Oddly enough, the cover photograph for *Down In The Groove* comes from this video shoot. The video features Dylan and a cast of extras pretending to be his back-up band playing in an empty venue/restaurant. There's just an old lady cleaning up for their audience. Most of the video is black with very stark lighting. Bob doesn't seem terribly comfortable but doesn't embarrass himself too much. Other than the overuse of the eyeliner.

- **Jokerman**

    This *Infidels* video required far less work from Dylan. What we get would now in the era of YouTube be called a "lyric video." We get all the words to the song shown on the screen, while seemingly random images appear behind them in the background. We get pictures of Jesus, flag-clad coffins, ancient statues, Adolph Hitler, a-bomb test, the moon landing. I have tried, but I cannot find any connection between what particular lyric is being sung and the image that is shown. We do eventually see the Joker from the Batman comics, which is funny. It's mostly static, but there are some bits of animation, or at least the camera moving on the frozen image. Then, around every chorus or so we get a medium close-up of Dylan in an all-white ensemble, playing his guitar and lip syncing. Weird, but ultimately meaningless.

- **Tight Connection To My Heart (Has Anybody Seen My Love?)**

    You know how hideously dated the album cover for *Empire Burlesque* looked? Imagine that album blown up into an entire full-length video. It's soooo super-eighties. We've got women with big hair and suit jackets with big shoulder pads. Bob wears a Hawaiian shirt, and that is not the worst of his fashion faux pas. He is also seen on stage wearing a leather jacket half unzipped to show that he is wearing no shirt and topped off with a trucker's baseball hat. Scary! This is Dylan's biggest video production to date. It requires him to act as he is arrested in a Japanese hotel by masked military mean, questioned and eventually put in jail. It ends with Bob and two Japanese women doing some sort of Motown-styled choreographed dance. I'm not sure what any of this has to do with the song. But as a time capsule of the 1980s and how badly Bob fit into this period, you can't beat this video.

- **Emotionally Yours**

    Despite being shot in black-and-white, this is a far less ambitious video than "Tight Connection To My Heart". The only truly regrettable bit of clothing Bob is wearing is a single dangling earring. This seems to take place in the same abandoned venue as "Sweetheart Like You", only the rest of the band is gone, and the old cleaning lady has been replaced by a young spinning lady. During the bridge, we get a flashback (?) to

Bob in the sunshine saying something to the young lady who was hanging onto a rope from the tree. Whatever Bob said to her has made her run off, and that is why Bob is so sad in this video. I think. Towards the end, a second guitarist just appears on the bench with Dylan to play the guitar solo. Music videos were weird back in the day.

- **When The Night Comes Falling From The Sky**
  This video is also in black-and-white. It opens with Dave Stewart of Eurythimics getting on a bus and teaching the song to Bob's band. Then we even get a remix of the song with a great new drum (machine) fill to open the song that manages to shave like three minutes off of the song. Bob's lip-syncing is, as to be expected, half-hearted. Half of the video revolves around Bob and his "band" playing in some nightclub or warehouse. It's the middle of the day because the video frequently cuts to a bunch of random teens trying to work their way up to the windows to look in and watch Bob play. There are brief bursts of solarization during the video as Bob and the band pose in choreographed motions with their guitars. At least Bob is playing for a full house and not a single audience member. Bob's backing singer looks a lot like Tina Turner. There's not much of a plot here. Maybe with some more garish colors, this might've worked, but as it is, it's just drab.

- **Band Of The Hand (It's Helltime, Man)**
  Another Bob Dylan video with no apparent input from Bob Dylan himself. Instead, we get the theme song of *Band Of The Hand* playing over clips from the movie, with a couple of dated video toaster effects thrown in. I've not seen the movie. And nothing in this video makes me tempted to watch it. I'm not sure what it's about exactly. Lots of 80s gang members that are hard to take seriously as threatening given the neon and pastel color palette of the era. Nothing on screen feels at all related to the song, as though the clips were grabbed at random. I can't imagine this was played a lot on MTV in 1986.

- **Most Of The Time**
  Bob is not terribly comfortable as a video star. In an attempt to work around this, instead of forcing Dylan to lip-sync to a pre-recorded track, he and his band simply play the song live for the cameras. The arrangement is not drastically different from the version on *Oh Mercy*, but it is definitely not the album version. Once again Dylan is performing in some sort of weird empty auditorium. The whole video is rather dimly lit. It's possible that the necessary lights were hurting Bob's eyes as he keeps his sunglasses on. There are some odd bits of scaffolding in the background and the occasional tiny TV monitor also

showing Bob, for the most part, this is a pretty straight by-the-numbers "performance" music video.

- **Political World**

    This video was actually directed by musician John Mellencamp. Once again, Bob is on stage where he feels most comfortable. Instead of playing for an empty house though, Dylan is performing for a dinner party of slinky models and older actors playing various random power players. Dylan's performance is obviously secondary to all of the goings on around the dinner table. Bob seems to be backed by a single band member playing lap slide. The characters in the party are very cool and aloof. By contrast, Bob seems like a bit of a goof dancing around more animatedly than he has for any previous video. Bob is wearing a white half-sleeved sweatshirt with a light turquoise T-shirt over it. It's a weird look. This is certainly a less embarrassing and retro-looking video than the stuff Dylan did for *Infidels* or *Empire Burlesque*. It's probably for the best that none of the singles from *Down In The Groove* or *Knocked out Loaded* did well enough to justify the video treatment.

- **Series Of Dreams**

    Long before the video for Johnny Cash's cover of "Hurt" there was this. Another montage of earlier clips of the artist as a younger man. Only this time everything's blended together with a visual style that takes the video for A-Ha's "Take On Me" to the nth degree. Everything cuts so quick and moves around so fast, that any time it holds for a little longer it is a relief. Occasionally the lyrics for the song will flash on the screen, reminding one of the video for "Jokerman". Most of the clips are either from *Don't Look Back* or *Renaldo & Clara* mainly because that's where Columbia had the most film footage to work with. Even then we still get bits of Bob's 80s videos in there as well. It even uses the "Subterranean Homesick Blues" video but replacing the lyrics on the cards for this new song. Luckily it doesn't go to that very often, because while that video is a classic, this one is a bit of a mess.

- **Unbelievable**

    Another video directed by John Mellencamp. The video is divided into two fairly unrelated halves. One features a very 1950s looking male model in a bright red convertible going to a bar and picking up Molly Ringwald before getting into a fight with some toughs. The two escape and the hunk takes Molly Ringwald to a motel. After spending the night together, Molly steals the guy's wallet, belt, and car. Distraught the guy tries to hook up with the hotel desk clerk but ends up hitchhiking.

There on the road at night, he is picked up by a car that is not his but does have his wallet and belt on the passenger seat. We don't know who is driving the car. It could be Bob Dylan. Did I mention Bob Dylan is in this video? He plays a limousine driver who is driving around a literal pig. I'm not sure how this connects to either the other half of the video or the song itself. But there you go.

- **Blood In My Eyes**

A black-and-white clip featuring Bob trying to be inconspicuous while wandering the streets of London despite the fact that he is A.) wearing a silly top hat with gloves and B.) Bob Dylan. Bob is seen lip syncing, but not playing the guitar (although at one point it seems like some street musician is accompanying him. Bob even attempts to juggle some fruit at one point. There's plenty of shots of Bob leading a ragtag group of bystanders across a bridge. In general it shows Dylan as far more comfortable and happy in public and amongst people than his reputation generally suggests. Again, the visuals seem completely unrelated to the song at hand, but it's a fine little slice of life. It is surprising that, while no singles were issued from *World Gone Wrong*, this song did get a music video nonetheless.

- **Not Dark Yet**

A pretty straightforward performance video. Half of it in black-and-white and the half in color seems distorted like it was a reflection that was filmed. Now and then we get blue-bleached shots of a house or a trainer or a road. As usual, nothing we see correlates to the song, musically or lyrically. We get lots of close-up of Bob's band member's hands while playing, while Dylan's face is frequently obscured. It's pleasant enough, but given how disinterested MTV was in playing Dylan videos (and music videos in general) at this point, it's understandable how half-hearted this comes off. Given how few other outlets there were for music videos in these pre-YouTube days, the fact that Columbia Records spent the money for this at all can be seen as something of an extravagance.

- **Dreamin' Of You**

Another video that wants to show young Dylan and avoid current Bob as much as possible. I can understand that. Bob is no longer a sex symbol at this age, so instead, we get, lost of archival photographs, etc. However, if you didn't want to show a craggly old man in your video, maybe you should have it star Harry Dean Stanton. Here the venerable, wizen actor seems to be playing a curator of Dylan concert posters going to his garage to pour through artifacts and pull together *The Bootleg Series, vol. 8*. Harry Dean Stanton is a goddamn national treasure! Here he orders coffee from a waitress at a diner. He does lip sync a line or two, and we do see him play a little guitar, but mostly he's just going through old files and photos of Dylan. While none of it is terribly pertinent to the song at hand, it does do a great job of advertising the latest offering from Columbia Records.

- **Things Have Changed**

Since this song is from the soundtrack to *Wonder Boys*, we manage to get stars Michael Douglas, Tobey Maguire, and Robert Downey Jr, although their scenes were filmed separately from Dylan's. We get Bob occasionally taking the character's place in the film. Sometimes we get the actors taking Dylan's place singing the song. We get Dylan flirting with Katie Holmes. We get Dylan on one knee playing guitar as if he forgot his guitar strap. We even get Dylan singing to his hamburger. Bob is even less interested in an accurate lip-sync than usual. I've not seen the movie, so I can't say how well this relates to it, but this video is probably more relevant to the film than the song.

- **'Cross The Green Mountain**

Another video where we are given the impression that Bob is interacting with the characters from the film whose soundtrack this is promoting. However, it is obvious that these scenes with Bob we all filmed separately. Dylan did shock the audience of the 2003 Newport Folk Festival by showing up in the fake beard and wig he wore in this video. No idea why he wore it there, he just feeling weird that day. This video may require the most "acting" of Bob since "Tight Connection To My Heart" as Bob wanders around and reacts to the Civil War battleground he finds himself in. The best thing about this video is that it gave us an edit of the song that is far more endurable than the original album version.

- **When The Deal Goes Down**

If you're looking for an actor to star in your video instead of Dylan, going with Scarlett Johanssen makes more commercial sense than Harry Dean Stanton. What we get here is a lot of shaking hand-held faux-home movie footage of Scarlett in some non-specific past time period. Probably, late fifties or early sixties. We see Scarlett visiting relatives and watching a manatee at the aquarium. Given how old fashioned the song is, this at least seems somewhat related to at least the feel of the song. The period details are all very well done, although not much is explained in this video. You could've switched this out with "Spirit On The Water" and not changed anything about this video.

- **Beyond Here Lies Nothin'**

    An expertly filmed fight scene made somewhat unpleasant by the fact that it seems to be either a hostage or domestic violence situation. This is made somewhat bearable by the fact that the woman gives as much punishment as the guy. As a short, wordless film, this would be interesting. As a scene in a larger narrative, it could be pivotal. As a music video, it is just confusing. No idea what the song has to do with all of this violence, no matter how well choreographed. While there's no spoken dialogue, there are plenty of diegetic sound effects that occasionally threaten to drown out the song itself. At this point, who knows why Bob was still making music videos, but this is the video he wanted to make. Or did mind being applied to his song, since Bob is again nowhere to be seen in this video.

- **Must Be Santa**

    Bob returns to appearing in his own videos in a big way here, and to wearing silly wigs. The time period here is somewhat vague but could be either contemporary or late fifties. Bob is wandering around a ribald Christmas party singing and dancing with the guests. The long wig may have been chosen to try and hid half of Dylan's face as he poorly lip-syncs. Then, inexplicably a man runs down the stairs chased by several other men. Glasses are thrown, and eventually, the man jumps out the window. While not nearly as violent as "Beyond Here Lies Nothin'" the focus here is on stunt work. Despite the Christmas setting, this feels a little disconnected to the song itself. Although Santa does pop in for a cameo at the end, looking as confused as Dylan as the strange man runs off into the night.

- **Little Drummer Boy**

    After the chaos of the last *Christmas In The Heart* video, what we get here is far more seasonally appropriate. What we get are animated drawings of various family members getting together and enjoying each other's company. The whole thing looks (and probably is) roto-scoped. Very little of the footage is Christmas-specific, but certainly, nothing in here couldn't actually (or even likely) be happening during the holidays. There's even a little boy who is playing a drum, making this possibly the most tied in that a Dylan video has been to its song.

- **Duquesne Whistle**

    Another amazing short film that just happens to have a Dylan song playing under it. An amusing twist on the usual rom-com tropes with the persistent wooing of the protagonist suitor is seen for the creepy stalking it really would be in normal life. As with most of Dylan's latter-day videos, this soon turns graphically violent. The happy ending is revealed to by a delusion from our lead character's concussed mind. It's all very well-done and funny. While none of this seems horribly related to "Duquesne Whistle", it has even less to do with the shots of Dylan (not lip syncing) but walking down the streets at night with a random assortment of gangsters, hookers, and some guy dressed like Gene Simmons from Kiss. I'm not sure who or what these more recent Bob videos are for, but somebody is spending some time and money making them.

- **The Night We Called It A Day**

Another short film masquerading as a Dylan video. What we have here is a straight-up film noir pastiche, replete with mobsters, showgirls, double-crosses, and gunplay. Unlike many of these videos, Bob not only appears here but does some acting. The plot is a little convoluted, and perhaps some dialogue, whether spoken or a silent movie title cards might've helped straighten things out. In the end, it looks like Bob's character got away with murdering the girl in the elevator. But ultimately, the plot is not the point. It's all about the feel, and it does evoke the feel of the forties pretty well. While the song choice is completely random and any other *Shadows In The Night* track in the background would've had the same effect. Still, it's nice to see that Bob is still pretty ambitious with his videos.

DYLAN on LP:

Even at the nadir of vinyl's popularity, Bob Dylan's albums were always released on as actual records, perhaps as a consideration to Bob's core group of baby boomer fans. This interesting thing is once CDs became the prominent musical medium is where the side breaks are placed. Even more interesting is the number of vinyl LPs that are needed for Bob's latter-day releases. While 1997's *Time Out Of Mind* is only one second less than 1966's double album *Blonde On Blonde*, so it's not surprising that this album was released on 2 records with the epic final song sitting alone on side D for both. 2001's *Love & Theft* is a total running time of 57:25 does make it a little difficult to fit onto a single disc, but splitting it up into two discs does allow them to charge a bit more for the record. It does also leave only 2-3 tracks per side, making for a very choppy vinyl listening experience. While both that record and its follow-up's nearly hour-long runtimes does tie the record company's hands a little bit, when *Together Through Life* came out it can only be greed that necessitated it being released as a 2 record set. It's only 45:33 – several other records, including *Another Side of Bob Dylan*, *Highway 61 Revisited*, and *Blood On The Tracks* are all between 51 and 52 minutes and were all released on one disc. Perhaps because that was more in the style of the time. In fact, *Desire* runs a 56:13 that Columbia squeezed onto a single disc. However in the 2000s, as vinyl became more fetishistic token for hipsters and a point of pride for audiophile snobs, Bob's records are almost always released as 2-disc sets – in part for the higher fidelity. But only for Bob's albums of originals. The smaller market for Bob's albums of covers are a harder sell, and so they tend to be put onto a single LP to keep them from being priced out of the hands of the more casual fans. Still, it's interesting to see how and where these records are broken up.

BOB DYLAN
Release Date: March 19, 1962
Duration: 36:11

SIDE A
1. You're No Good   1:40
2. Talkin' New York   3:20
3. In My Time Of Dyin'   2:40
4. Man Of Constant Sorrow 3:10
5. Fixin' To Die   2:22
6. Pretty Peggy-O   3:23
7. Highway 51   2:52

SIDE B
1. Gospel Plow   1:47
2. Baby, Let Me Follow You Down 2:37
3. House Of The Risin' Sun 5:20
4. Freight Train Blues   2:18
5. Song To Woody   2:42
6. See That My Grave Is Kept Clean 2:43

THE FREEWHEELIN' BOB DYLAN
Release Date: May 27, 1963
Duration: 50:13

SIDE A
1. Blowin' In The Wind   2:49
2. Girl From The North Country 3:23
3. Masters Of War   4:38
4. Down The Highway   3:32
5. Bob Dylan's Blues   2:28
6. A Hard Rain's A-Gonna Fall 6:53

SIDE B
1. Don't Think Twice, It's Alright 3:40
2. Bob Dylan's Dream   5:02
3. Oxford Town   1:50
4. Talking World War III Blues 6:27
5. Corrina, Corrina   2:44
6. Honey, Just Allow Me One More Chance 2:00
7. I Shall Be Free   4:47

THE TIMES THEY ARE A-CHANGIN'
Release Date: January 13, 1964
Duration: 45:30

SIDE A
1. The Times They Are A-Changin' 3:12
2. Ballad Of Hollis Brown 5:03
3. With God On Our Side 7:05
4. One Too Many Mornings 2:38
5. North Country Blues 4:33

SIDE B
1. Only A Pawn In Their Game 3:30
2. Boots Of Spanish Leather 4:38
3. When The Ship Comes In 3:15
4. The Lonesome Death Of Hattie Carroll 5:45
5. Restless Farewell 5:32

ANOTHER SIDE OF BOB DYLAN
Release Date: August 8, 1964
Duration: 51:17

SIDE A
1. All I Really Want To Do 4:02
2. Black Crow Blues 3:12
3. Spanish Harlem Incident 2:22
4. Chimes Of Freedom 7:09
5. I Shall Be Free No. 10 4:45
6. To Ramona 3:50

SIDE B
1. Motorpsycho Nitemare 4:31
2. My Back Pages 4:20
3. I Don't Believe You 4:20
4. Ballad In Plain D 8:15
5. It Ain't Me Babe 3:30

BRINGING IT ALL BACK HOME
Release Date: March 22, 1965
Duration: 47:14

SIDE A
1. Subterranean Homesick Blues 2:17
2. She Belongs To Me 2:48
3. Maggie's Farm 3:51
4. Love Minus Zero / No Limit
5. Outlaw Blues 3:00
6. On The Road Again 2:30
7. Bob Dylan's 115th Dream 6:29

SIDE B
1. Mr. Tambourine Man 5:25
2. Gates Of Eden 5:42
3. It's Alright, Ma (I'm Only Bleeding) 7:30
4. It's All Over Now, Baby Blue 4:13

HIGHWAY 61 REVISITED
Release Date: August 30, 1965
Duration: 51:30

SIDE A
1. Like A Rolling Stone   5:59
2. Tombstone Blues   5:53
3. It Takes A Lot To Laugh,
   It Takes A Train To Cry   3:25
4. From A Buick 6   3:06
5. Ballad Of A Thin Man   5:48

SIDE B
1. Queen Jane
   Approximately   4:57
2. Highway 61 Revisited   3:15
3. Just Like Tom Thumb's
   Blues   5:08
4. Desolation Row   11:18

BLONDE ON BLONDE
Release Date: May 16, 1966
Duration: 1:14:23

SIDE A
1. Rainy Day Women
   #12 & 35   4:35
2. Pledging My Time   3:55
3. Visions Of Johanna   7:30
4. One Of Us Must Know
   (Sooner Or Later)   4:55

SIDE C
1. Most Likely You Go Your
   Way And I'll Go Mine   3:26
2. Temporary Like Achilles   5:03
3. Absolutely Sweet Marie   4:50
4. 4th Time Around   4:40
5. Obviously 5 Believers   3:31

SIDE B
1. I Want You   3:10
2. Memphis Blues Again   7:07
3. Leopard-Skin
   Pill-Box Hat   3:50
4. Just Like A Woman   4:52

SIDE D
1. Sad Eyed Lady Of The
   Lowland   11:23

THE BASEMENT TAPES RAW
Release Date: November 3, 2014
Duration: 2:01:17

SIDE A
1. Open The Door Homer — 2:52
2. Odds And Ends — 1:48
3. Million Dollar Bash — 2:52
4. One Too Many Mornings — 3:23
5. I Don't Hurt Anymore — 2:15
6. Ain't No More Cane — 1:57
7. Down In The Flood (Crash On The Levee) — 2:05

SIDE B
1. Tears Of Rage — 4:14
2. Dress It Up, Better Have It All — 2:52
3. I'm Not There — 5:12
4. Johnny Todd — 2:04
5. Too Much Of Nothing — 2:53

SIDE C
1. Quinn The Eskimo — 2:16
2. Get Your Rocks Off — 3:46
3. Santa-Fe — 2:08
4. Silent Weekend — 3:00
5. Clothes Line Saga — 2:59
6. Please Mrs. Henry — 2:34
7. I Shall Be Released — 3:55

SIDE D
1. You Ain't Goin' Nowehere — 2:48
2. Lo And Behold! — 2:53
3. Minstrel Boy — 1:39
4. Tiny Montgomery — 2:56
5. All You Have To Do Is Dream — 3:23
6. Goin' To Acapulco — 5:36
7. 900 Miles From My Home

SIDE E
1. One For The Road — 4:49
2. I'm Alright — 1:45
3. Blowin' In The Wind — 6:35
4. Apple Suckling Tree — 2:50
5. Nothing Was Delivered — 4:26
6. Folsom Prison Blues — 2:46

SIDE F
1. This Wheel's On Fire — 3:54
2. Yea! Heavy And A Bottle Of Bread — 2:16
3. Don't Ya Tell Henry — 2:30
4. Baby, Won't You Be My Baby? — 2:52
5. Sign On The Cross — 7:21
6. You Ain't Goin' Nowhere — 2:43

JOHN WESLEY HARDING
Release Date: December 27, 1967
Duration: 37:55

SIDE A
1. John Wesley Harding 2:58
2. As I Went Out One Morning 2:49
3. I Dreamed I Saw St. Augustine 3:53
4. All Along The Watchtower 2:31
5. The Ballad Of Frankie Lee And Judas Priest 5:35
6. Drifter's Escape 2:52

SIDE B
1. Dear Landlord 3:16
2. I Am A Lonesome Hobo 3:19
3. I Pity The Poor Immigrant 4:12
4. The Wicked Messenger 2:02
5. Down Along The Cove 2:23
6. I'll Be Your Baby Tonight 2:34

NASHVILLE SKYLINE
Release Date: April 9, 1969
Duration: 27:10

SIDE A
1. The Girl From North Country 3.44
2. Nashville Skyline Rag 3:14
3. To Be Alone With You 2:10
4. I Threw It All Away 2:26
5. Peggy Day 2:05

SIDE B
1. Lay Lady Lay 3:21
2. One More Night 2:25
3. Tell Me That It Isn't True 2:43
4. Country Pie 1:39
5. Tonight I'll Be Staying Here With You 3:23

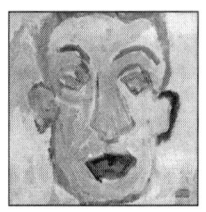

SELF-PORTRAIT
Release Date: June 8, 1970
Duration: 1:13:15

SIDE A
1. All The Tired Horses   3:11
2. Alberta #1   2:55
3. I Forgot More Than You'll
   Ever Know   2:22
4. Days Of 49   5:42
5. Early Mornin' Rain   3:31
6. In Search Of Little Sadie   2:26

SIDE B
1. Let It Be Me   2:58
2. Little Sadie   1:58
3. Woogie Boogie   2:06
4. Belle Isle   2:28
5. Living The Blues   2:41
6. Like A Rolling Stone   5:14

SIDE C
1. Copper Kettle
   (In The Pale Moonlight)   3:32
2. Gotta Travel On
   (Done Laid Around)   3:04
3. Blue Moon   2:26
4. The Boxer   2:45
5. The Mighty Quinn
   (Quinn, The Eskimo)   2:54
6. Take Me As I Am
   (Or Let Me Go)   2:59

SIDE D
1. Take A Message To Mary 2:44
2. It Hurts Me Too   3:16
3. Minstrel Boy   3:29
4. She Belongs To Me   2:42
5. Wigwam   3:08
6. Alberta #2   3:20

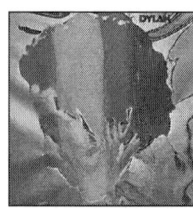

DYLAN
Release Date: November 19, 1973
Duration: 33:22

SIDE A
1. Lily Of The West   3:44
2. Can't Help Falling In Love
3. Sarah Jane   2:43
4. The Ballad Of Ira Hayes   5:08

SIDE B
1. Mr. Bojangles   5:31
2. Mary Ann   4:172:40
3. Big Yellow Taxi   2:12
4. A Fool Such As I   2:41
5. Spanish Is The Loving
   Tongue   4:13

NEW MORNING
Release Date: October 21, 1970
Duration: 35:17

SIDE A
1. If Not For You   2:42
2. Day Of The Locusts   4:00
3. Time Passes Slowly   2:35
4. Went To See The Gypsy   2:51
5. Winterlude   2:22
6. If Dogs Run Free   3:40

SIDE B
1. New Morning   3:58
2. Sign On The Window   3:40
3. One More Weekend   3:10
4. The Man In Me   3:08
5. Three Angels   2:07
6. Father Of Night   1:31

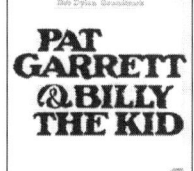

PAT GARRETT & BILLY THE KID
Release Date: July 13, 1973
Duration: 35:19

SIDE A
1. Main Title Theme (Billy)   6:00
2. Cantina Theme (Workin' For The Law)   2:50
3. Billy 1   3:51
4. Bunkhouse Theme   2:10
5. River Theme   1:32

SIDE B
1. Turkey Chase   3:20
2. Knockin' On Heaven's Door   2:28
3. Final Theme   5:18
4. Billy 4   2:01
5. Billy 7   4:57

PLANET WAVES
Release Date: January 17, 1974
Duration: 42:12

SIDE A
1. On A Night Like This   2:57
2. Going, Going, Gone   3:25
3. Tough Mama   4:17
4. Hazel   2:52
5. Something There Is About You   4:46
6. Forever Young   5:00

SIDE B
1. Forever Young   2:51
2. Dirge   5:40
3. You Angel You   2:51
4. Never Say Goodbye   2:55
5. Wedding Song   4:50

BLOOD ON THE TRACKS
Release Date: January 20, 1975
Duration: 51:42

SIDE A
1. Tangled Up In Blue 5:40
2. Simple Twist Of Fate 4:18
3. You're A Big Girl Now 4:36
4. Idiot Wind 7:45
5. You're Gonna Make Me Lonesome When You Go 2:58

SIDE B
1. Meet Me In The Morning 4:19
2. Lily, Rosemary And The Jack Of Hearts 8:50
3. If You See Her, Say Hello 4:46
4. Shelter From The Storm 4:59
5. Buckets Of Rain 3:29

DESIRE
Release Date: January 5, 1976
Duration: 56:13

SIDE A
1. Hurricane 8:33
2. Isis 6:58
3. Mozambique 3:00
4. One More Cup Of Coffee (Valley Below) 3:43
5. Oh, Sister 4:05

SIDE B
1. Joey 11:05
2. Romance In Durango 5:50
3. Black Diamond Bay 7:30
4. Sara 5:29

STREET LEGAL
Release Date: June 15, 1978
Duration: 50:18

SIDE A
1. Changing Of The Guards 6:36
2. New Pony 4:28
3. No Time To Think 8:19
4. Baby Stop Crying 5:17

SIDE B
1. Is Your Love In Vain? 4:30
2. Señor (Tales Of Yankee Power) 5:42
3. True Love Tends To Forget 4:14
4. We Better Talk This Over 4:04
5. Where Are You Tonight? (Journey Through Dark Heat) 6:16

SLOW TRAIN COMING
Release Date: August 20, 1979
Duration: 46:19

SIDE A
1. Gotta Serve Somebody   5:23
2. Precious Angel   6:30
3. I Believe In You   5:08
4. Slow Train   5:57

SIDE B
1. Gonna Change My Way Of Thinking   5:27
2. Do Right To Me Baby (Do Unto Others)   3:52
3. When You Gonna Wake Up?   5:28
4. Man Gave Names To All The Animals   4:25
5. When He Returns   4:31

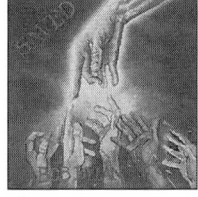

SAVED
Release Date: June 23, 1980
Duration: 42:39

SIDE A
1. A Satisfied Mind   1:57
2. Saved   3:58
3. Covenant Woman   6:01
4. What Can I Do For You?   5:51
5. Solid Rock   3:54

SIDE B
1. Pressing On   5:09
2. In The Garden   5:57
3. Saving Grace   5:01
4. Are You Ready   4:39

SHOT OF LOVE
Release Date: August 10, 1981
Duration: 40:15

SIDE A
1. Shot Of Love   4:18
2. Heart Of Mine   4:29
3. Property Of Jesus   4:33
4. Lenny Bruce   4:32
5. Watered-Down Love   4:10

SIDE B
1. Dead Man, Dead Man   3:58
2. In The Summertime   3:34
3. Trouble   4:32
4. Every Grain Of Sand   6:12

INFIDELS
Release Date: October 27, 1983
Duration: 41:39

SIDE A
1. Jokerman 6:12
2. Sweetheart Like You 4:31
3. Neighborhood Bully 4:33
4. License To Kill 3:31

SIDE B
1. Man Of Peace 6:27
2. Union Sundown 5:21
3. I And I 5:10
4. Don't Fall Apart On Me Tonight 5:54

EMPIRE BURLESQUE
Release Date: June 10, 1985
Duration: 46:24

SIDE A
1. Tight Connection To My Heart (Has Anybody Seen My Love) 5:19
2. Seeing The Real You At Last 4:18
3. I'll Remember You 4:12
4. Clean Cut Kid 4:14
5. Never Gonna Be The Same Again 3:06

SIDE B
1. Trust Yourself 3:26
2. Emotionally Yours 4:36
3. When The Night Comes Falling From The Sky 7:18
4. Something's Burning, Baby
5. Dark Eyes 5:04

KNOCKED OUT LOADED
Release Date: July 14, 1986
Duration: 35:18

SIDE A
1. You Wanna Ramble 3:20
2. They Killed Him 4:08
3. Driftin' Too Far From Shore 3:42
4. Precious Memories 3:16
5. Maybe Someday 3:21

SIDE B
1. Brownsville Girl 11:06
2. Got My Mind Made Up 2:59
3. Under Your Spell 4:03

DOWN IN THE GROOVE
Release Date: May 30, 1988
Duration: 32:10

SIDE A
1. Let's Stick Together 3:08
2. When Did You Leave Heaven? 2:14
3. Sally Sue Brown 2:28
4. Death Is Not The End 5:10
5. Had A Dream About You, Baby 2:54

SIDE B
1. Ugliest Girl In The World 3:33
2. Silvio 3:06
3. Ninety Miles An Hour (Down A Dead End Street) 2:56
4. Shenandoah 3:38
5. Rank Strangers To Me 2:57

OH MECRY
Release Date: September 18, 1989
Duration: 38:46

SIDE A
1. Political World 3:43
2. Where Teardrops Fall 2:30
3. Everything Is Broken 3:12
4. Ring Them Bells 3:00
5. Man In The Long Black Coat 4:30

SIDE B
1. Most Of The Time 5:02
2. What Good Am I? 4:45
3. Disease Of Conceit 3:41
4. What Was It You Wanted 5:02
5. Shooting Star 3:12

UNDER THE RED SKY
Release Date: September 10, 1990
Duration: 35:21

SIDE A
1. Wiggle Wiggle 2:09
2. Under The Red Sky 4:08
3. Unbelievable 4:05
4. Born In Time 3:38
5. T.V. Talkin' Song 3:01

SIDE B
1. 10,000 Men 4:23
2. 2x2 3:38
3. God Knows 3:00
4. Handy Dandy 4:02
5. Cat's In The Well 3:21

GOOD AS I BEEN TO YOU
Release Date: November 3, 1992
Duration: 55:31

SIDE A
1. Frankie & Albert 3:50
2. Jim Jones 3:52
3. Blackjack Davey 5:47
4. Canadee-I-O 4:20
5. Sittin' On Top Of The World
6. Little Maggie 2:52
7. Hard Times 4:31

SIDE B
1. Step It Up And Go 2:54
2. Tomorrow Night 3:42
3. Arthur McBride 6:20
4. You're Gonna Quit Me 2:46
5. Diamond Joe 4:273:14
6. Froggie Went A Courtin' 6:25

WORLD GONE WRONG
Release Date: October 26, 1993
Duration: 43:51

SIDE A
1. World Gone Wrong 3:53
2. Love Henry 4:23
3. Ragged & Dirty 4:07
4. Blood In My Eyes 5:04
5. Broke Down Engine 3:21

SIDE B
1. Delia 5:38
2. Stack A Lee 3:51
3. Two Soldiers 5:44
4. Jack-A-Roe 4:59
5. Lone Pilgrim 2:43

TIME OUT OF MIND
Release Date: September 30, 1997
Duration: 1:12:50

SIDE A
1. Love Sick 5:21
2. Dirt Road Blues 3:36
3. Standing In The Doorway 7:43
4. Million Miles 5:52

SIDE B
1. Tryin' To Get To Heaven 5:21
2. 'Til I Fell In Love With You 5:17
3. Not Dark Yet 6:29

SIDE C
1. Cold Irons Bound 7:15
2. Make You Feel My Love 3:32
3. Can't Wait 5:47

SIDE D
1. Highlands 16:31

LOVE & THEFT
Release Date: September 11, 2001
Duration: 57:25

SIDE A
1. Tweedle Dee & Tweedle Dum — 4:46
2. Mississippi — 5:21
3. Summer Days — 4:52

SIDE B
1. Bye And Bye — 3:16
2. Lonesome Day Blues — 6:04
3. Floater (Too Much To Ask) — 4:59

SIDE C
1. High Water (For Charlie Patton) — 4:04
2. Moonlight — 3:22
3. Honest With Me — 5:49

SIDE D
1. Po' Boy — 3:05
2. Cry A While — 5:05
3. Sugar Baby — 6:40

MODERN TIMES
Release Date: August 29, 2006
Duration: 1:03:04

SIDE A
1. Thunder On The Mountain — 5:55
2. Spirit On The Water — 7:42

SIDE B
1. Rollin' And Tumblin' — 6:01
2. When The Deal Goes Down
3. Someday Baby — 4:55

SIDE C
1. Workingman's Blues #2 — 6:07
2. Beyond The Horizon — 5:36
3. Nettie Moore — 6:52

SIDE D
1. The Levee's Gonna Break — 5:43
2. Ain't Talkin' — 8:48

TOGETHER THROUGH LIFE
Release Date: April 28, 2009
Duration: 45:33

SIDE A
1. Beyond Here Lies
   Nothin'   3:50
2. Life Is Hard   3:39
3. My Wife's Home Town   4:15

SIDE C
1. Jolene   3:50
2. This Dream Of You   5:54
3. Shake Shake Mama   3:37

SIDE B
1. If You Ever Go To
   Houston   5:48
2. Forgetful Heart   3:42

SIDE D
1. I Feel A Change Comin'
   On   5:25
2. It's All Good   5:27

CHRISTMAS IN THE HEART
Release Date: October 13, 2009
Duration: 42:21

SIDE A
1. Here Comes Santa Claus   2:35
2. Do You Hear What I Hear?
3. Winter Wonderland   1:52
4. Hark The Herald Angels
   Sing   2:30
5. I'll Be Home For Christmas
6. Little Drummer Boy   2:52
7. The Christmas Blues   2:54
8. O' Come All Ye Faithful
   (Adeste Fideles)   2:48

SIDE B
1. Have Yourself A Merry Little
   Christmas   3:024:06
2. Must Be Santa   2:48
3. Silver Bells   2:35
4. The First Noel   2:30
5. Christmas Island   2:542:27
6. The Christmas Song   3:56
7. O' Little Town Of
   Bethlehem   2:17

TEMPEST
Release Date: September 10, 2012
Duration: 1:08:31

SIDE A
1. Dusquesne Whistle   5:43
2. Soon After Midnight 3:27
3. Narrow Way   7:28

SIDE B
1. Long And Wasted Years 3:46
2. Pay In Blood   5:09
3. Scarlet Town   7:17

SIDE C
1. Early Roman Kings   5:14
2. Tin Angel   9:05

SIDE D
1. Tempest   13:54
2. Roll On John 7:25

SHADOWS IN THE NIGHT
Release Date: February 3, 2015
Duration: 35:17

SIDE A
1. I'm A Fool To Want You   4:51
2. The Night We Called It A
   Day   3:25
3. Stay With Me   2:56
4. Autumn Leaves   3:02
5. Why Try To Change Me
   Now?   3:38

SIDE B
1. Some Enchanted Evening 3:28
2. Full Moon And Empty Arms
3. Where Are You?   3:37
4. What I'll Do   3:21
5. That Lucky Old Sun   3:39

FALLEN ANGELS
Release Date: May 20, 2016
Duration: 37:50

SIDE A
1. Young At Heart   2:59
2. Maybe You'll Be There   2:56
3. Polka Dots And
   Moonbeams   3:20
4. All The Way   4:01
5. Skylark   2:56
6. Nevertheless   3:27

SIDE B
1. All Or Nothing At All   3:04
2. On A Little Street In
   Singapore   2:15
3. It Had To Be You   3:39
4. Melancholy Mood   2:53
5. That Old Black Magic   3:04
6. Come Rain Or Come
   Shine   2:37

TRIPLICATE
Release Date: March 31, 2017
Duration: 1:33:42

DISC 1: 'Til The Sun Goes Down (31:48)

SIDE A
1. I Guess I'll Have To Change My Plans — 2:27
2. September Of My Years — 3:25
3. I Could Have Told You — 3:36
4. Once Upon A Time — 3:37
5. Stormy Weather — 3:05

SIDE B
1. This Nearly Was Mine — 2:48
2. The Old Feeling — 3:38
3. It Gets Lonely Early — 3:10
4. My One And Only Love — 3:21
5. Trade Winds — 2:40

DISC 2: Devil Dolls (32:07)

SIDE C
1. Braggin' — 2:44
2. As Time Goes By — 3:22
3. Imagination — 2:34
4. How Deep Is The Ocean? — 3:23
5. P.S. I Love You — 4:17

SIDE D
1. The Best Is Yet To Come — 2:57
2. But Beautiful — 3:22
3. Here's That Rain Day — 3:27
4. Where Is The One? — 3:14
5. There's A Flaw In My Flue — 2:47

DISC 3: Comin' Home Late (31:47)

SIDE E
1. Day In, Day Out — 3:01
2. I Couldn't Sleep A Wink Last Night — 3:15
3. Sentimental Journey — 3:11
4. Somewhere Along The Way — 3:18
5. When The World Was Young — 3:47

SIDE F
1. These Foolish Things — 4:11
2. You Go To My Head — 3:06
3. Stardust — 2:30
4. It's Funny To Everyone But Me — 2:38
5. Why Was I Born? — 2:50

ORIGINAL or CANCELLED ALBUM LINE-UPS:

Just so you don't think I'm crazy, I'm not the only one who has a habit or re-ordering and re-structuring Dylan's discography. Bob himself (or his record company) have been guilty of that often enough in the past. As evidence of that, I present a handful of albums with the song-list with which they were almost released. Some came closer to being actually released than others – in fact, a few of these actually did make their way out into the marketplace despite being recalled. Some are slight variations. Others are wholesale revamps. Either way, it is a fascinating look at the somewhat lost art of assembling an album.

The Original Test Pressing of *The Freewheelin' Bob Dylan*

SIDE A
1. Blowin' In The Wind
2. Rocks And Gravel
3. Let Me Die In My Footsteps
4. Down The Highway
5. Bob Dylan's Blues
6. A Hard Rain's A-Gonna Fall

SIDE B
1. Don't Think Twice, It's Alright
2. Gamblin' Willie's Dead Man's Hand
3. Oxford Town
4. Corrina, Corrina   6:53
5. Talkin' John Birch Blues
6. Honey, Just Allow Me One More Chance
7. I Shall Be Free

The Original Acetate of *The Basement Tapes*

SIDE A
1. Million Dollar Bash
2. Yea, Heavy And A Bottle Of Bread!
3. Please, Mrs. Henry
4. Down In The Flood (Crash on the Levee)
5. Lo And Behold!
6. Tiny Montgomery
7. This Wheel's On Fire

SIDE B
1. You Ain't Going Nowhere
2. I Shall Be Released
3. Too Much Of Nothing
4. Tears Of Rage
5. The Mighty Quinn (Quinn the Eskimo)
6. Open The Door, Homer
7. Nothing Was Delivered

The Original Running Order for *Self-Portrait*

SIDE A
1. Alberta
   Not sure which "Alberta"
2. I've Forgotten More
3. Days of '49
4. Early Morning Rain
5. Take A Message To Mary
6. It Hurts Me Too

SIDE B
1. Gotta Travel On
2. Blue Moon
3. The Boxer
4. The Mighty Quinn
   Live at Isle of Wight
5. Take Me As I Am
6. Copper Kettle

SIDE C
1. Let It Be Me
2. In Search Of Little Sadie
   Listed as "Ball & Stripes"
3. Woogie Boogie
   Listed as "Boogie Woogie Boogie"
4. Living The Blues
5. Belle Isle
6. Like A Rolling Stone
   Live at Isle of Wight

SIDE D
1. Minsrel Boy
   Live at Isle of Wight
2. She Belongs To Me
   Live at Isle of Wight
3. Wigwam
   Listed as "New Song #1"
4. Alberta
   Not sure which "Alberta"
5. All The Tired Horses

The Original Running Order for *New Morning*

SIDE A
1. Mr. Bojangles
2. The Ballad Of Ira Hayes
3. The Man In Me
4. One More Weekend

SIDE B
1. New Morning
2. Father Of Night
3. Sign On The Window
4. Tomorrow Is A Long Time
5. If Dogs Run Free

The Original Running Order for *Dylan (1973)*

SIDE A
1. Mr. Bojangles
2. The Ballad Of Ira Hayes
3. A Fool Such As I
4. Spanish Is The Loving Tongue
5. Mary Ann

SIDE B
1. Running
2. Sarah Jane
3. Lily Of The West
4. Alligator Man

Theoretical Running Order for *Infidels* (unconfirmed)

SIDE A
1. Jokerman
2. License To Kill
3. Man Of Peace
4. Neighborhood Bully

SIDE B
1. Don't Fall Apart On Me Tonight
2. Blind Willie McTell
3. Sweetheart Like You
4. I And I
5. Foot Of Pride

The first test pressing of *Down In The Groove*

SIDE A
1. Let's Stick Together
2. When Did You Leave Heaven?
3. Got Love If You Want It
4. Ninety Miles An Hour (Down a Dead End Street)
5. Sally Sue Brown

SIDE B
1. Ugliest Girl In The World
2. Silvio
3. Important Words
   This was replaced by "The Usual" on the second test pressing.
4. Shenandoah
5. Rank Strangers To Me

The original track list for *Greatest Hits, vol. III*

1. Jokerman
2. Hurricane
3. True Love Tends To Forget
4. Tangled Up In Blue
5. Gotta Serve Somebody
6. Forever Young
7. Dignity
8. Silvio
9. Ring Them Bells
10. Tight Connection To My Heart (Has Anybody Seen My Love)
11. The Groom's Still Waiting At The Altar
12. Brownsville Girl
13. Under The Red Sky
14. Knockin' On Heaven's Door

Songs removed from *The Bootleg Series vol. 1-3* when it was reduced from a 4 CD set to a 3 CD set

1. Dink's Blues (December 1961 Hotel tape)
   Released on *The Bootleg Series, vol. 7*
2. I Heard That Lonesome Whistle (*The Freewheelin' Bob Dylan* outtake)
   Still unreleased
3. Guess I'm Doing Fine (Witmark demo 1964)
   Released on *The Bootleg Series, vol. 9*
4. It's All Over Now Baby Blue (alternate take)
   Released on *The Bootleg Series, vol. 7*
5. Positively 4th Street (alternate take)
   Released on *The Bootleg Series, vol. 12*
6. She's Your Lover Now (solo piano version)
   Released on *The Bootleg Series, vol. 12*
7. Silent Weekend (*The Basement Tapes* outtake)
   Released on *The Bootleg Series, vol. 11*
8. You're Gonna Make Me Lonesome When You Go (alternate version)
   Released on *The Bootleg Series, vol. 14*
9. No Man Righteous (No Not One) (*Slow Train Coming* outtake)
   Released on *The Bootleg Series, vol. 13*
10. Ain't Going To Go To Hell For Anybody (live, Toronto 1980)
    Released on *The Bootleg Series, vol. 13*

SONG INDEX

(I Heard That) Lonesome Whistle 42
'Twas The Night Before Christmas 389
10,000 Men 319
2 × 2 320
32-20 Blues 340
4th Time Around 94
900 Miles From My Home 115
A Couple More Years 294
A Satisfied Mind 238
Abandoned Love 215
Absolutely Sweet Marie 94
Ain't Going To Go To Hell For
 Anybody 243
Ain't Gonna Grieve 58
Ain't No Man Righteous (No, Not One)
235
Ain't No More Cane 105
Ain't Talkin' 368
Alberta #1 144
Alberta #2 152
All Along the Watchtower 124
All I Really Want to Do 63
All or Nothing at All 407
All Over You 36
All the Tired Horses 143
All the Way 406
All The Way Down 255
All You Have To Do Is Dream 114
Almost 256
Almost Done 282
Always On My Mind 280
And He's Killed Me Too 191
Angel Flying Too Close To The Ground
267
Angelina 252
Annie's Going To Sing Her Song 156
Anyway You Want Me 341
Apple Suckling Tree 103
Are You Ready 241
Arthur McBride 330
As I Went Out One Morning 123
As Time Goes By 412
Autumn Leaves 401
Baby, I'm In the Mood For You 29
Baby, Let Me Follow You Down 12

Baby, Please Don't Go 40
Baby, Stop Crying 221
Baby, Won't You Be My Baby? 116
Back Alley 379
Ballad For A Friend 18
Ballad in Plain D 66
Ballad of a Thin Man 83
Ballad Of Donald White, The 40
Ballad of Frankie Lee and Judas Priest,
 The 125
Ballad of Hollis Brown 49
Ballad of Ira Hayes, The 162
Band Of The Hand (It's Helltime, Man)
290
Belle Isle 147
Best Is Yet to Come, The 414
Beyond Here Lies Nothin' 375
Beyond the Horizon 367
Big Yellow Taxi 164
Billie #30 380
Billy 1 186
Billy 4 188
Billy 7 188
Billy Surrenders 190
Black Crow Blues 63
Black Diamond Bay 213
Blackjack Davey 328
Blessed Is The Name 236
Blind Willie McTell 268
Blood in My Eyes 337
Blowin' in the Wind 23
Blue Moon 149
Blues Club 381
Bob Dylan's New Orleans Rag 59
Bob Dylan's 115th Dream 74
Bob Dylan's Blues 24
Bob Dylan's Dream 26
Boogie Woogie Country Girl 340
Boots of Spanish Leather 51
Born in Time 310
Bound To Lose, Bound To Win 36
Boxer, The 149
Braggin' 412
Bring Me A Little Water 173
Broke Down Engine 337

Brownsville Girl	279
Buckets of Rain	205
Bumble Bee	379
Bunkhouse Theme	186
But Beautiful	414
Bye and Bye	356
California	79
Call Letter Blues	206
Can You Please Crawl Out Your Window?	85
Can't Escape From You	372
Canadee-i-o	328
Can't Help Falling in Love	162
Can't Wait	349
Cantina Theme (Workin' for the Law)	186
Caribbean Wind	250
Catfish	216
Cat's in the Well	321
Catskills Serenade	334
Changing of the Guards	220
Chimes of Freedom	64
Christmas Blues, The	386
Christmas Island	388
Christmas Song, The	388
City of Gold	242
Clean Cut Kid	266
Click Clack	380
Clothes Line Saga	103
Cold Irons Bound	347
Come Rain or Come Shine	408
Coming From The Heart (The Road Is Long)	224
Congratulations	314
Copper Kettle	148
Corrina, Corrina	27
Country Pie	134
Covenant Woman	238
Cover Down, Pray Through	243
Cross The Green Mountain	370
Crosswind Jamboree	198
Cry a While	358
Dark Eyes	278
Day In, Day Out	415
Day of the Locusts	167
Days of 49	144
Dead Man, Dead Man	248
Dear Landlord	126
Death Is Not the End	267
Death Of Emmett Till, The	35
Delia	338
Denise	68
Desolation Row	84
Diamond Joe	331, 369
Dignity	312
Dink's Song	17
Dirge	196
Dirt Road Blues	345
Dirty Lie	283
Dirty World	313
Disease of Conceit	309
Dixie	370
Do Re Mi	371
Do Right to Me Baby (Do Unto Others)	232
Do You Hear What I Hear?	384
Don't Ever Take Yourself Away	252
Don't Ya Tell Henry	108
Don't Fall Apart on Me Tonight	265
Don't Think Twice, It's All Right	25
Down Along the Cove	128
Down In The Flood (Crash On The Levee)	106
Down the Highway	24
Dreamin' Of You	351
Dress It Up, Better Have It All	113
Drifter's Escape	125
Driftin' Too Far from Shore	278
Driving South	379
Duncan And Brady	333
Duquesne Whistle	392
Early Mornin' Rain	145
Early Roman Kings	394
East Laredo Blues	60
East Texas	381
Emotionally Yours	276
Enough Is Enough	284
Eternal Circle	56
Every Grain of Sand	249
Everything Is Broken	307
Farewell	59
Farewell Angelina	78

Father of Night	172
Final Theme	188
First Noel, The	387
Fixin' to Die	11
Floater (Too Much to Ask)	357
Folsom Prison Blues	157
Fool Such as I, A	152
Foot Of Pride	268
Forever Young	195
Forgetful Heart	376
Frankie & Albert	327
Freedom For The Stallion	280
Freight Train Blues	13
Froggie Went A-Courtin'	331
From a Buick 6	82
Full Moon and Empty Arms	401
Gates of Eden	75
George Jackson	182
Get Your Rocks Off	114
Girl from the North Country	23, 131
Go 'Way Little Boy	282
God Knows	311
Goin' To Acapulco	102
Going To New Orleans	42
Going, Going, Gone	194
Golden Loom	215
Gonna Change My Way of Thinking	232
Goodbye Holly	189
Gospel Plow	12
Got Love If You Want It	300
Got My Mind Made Up	289
Gotta Serve Somebody	230
Gotta Travel On	148
Groom's Still Waiting at the Altar, The	250
Guess I'm Doing Fine	59
Gypsy Lou	57
Had A Dream About You, Baby	292
Handy Dandy	320
Hard Rain's a-Gonna Fall, A	25
Hard Times	329
Hard Times In New York Town	14
Hark the Herald Angels Sing	385
Have Yourself a Merry Little Christmas	386
Hazel	195
He Was a Friend of Mine	15
He's Funny That Way	418
Heart of Mine	246
Heartland	321
Help Me Understand	235
Here Comes Santa Claus	384
Here's That Rainy Day	415
Hero Blues	37
High Away	254
High Water (For Charley Patton)	357
Highlands	349
Highway 51	12
Highway 61 Revisited	83
Honest with Me	358
Honey Wait	282
Honey, Just Allow Me One More Chance	28
House Carpenter	16
House of the Risin' Sun	13
How Deep Is the Ocean?	413
Huck's Tune	371
Hurricane	210
I Am a Lonesome Hobo	126
I and I	265
I Believe in You	231
I Can't Get Her Off Of My Mind	360
I Could Have Told You	410
I Couldn't Sleep a Wink Last Night	416
I Don't Hurt Anymore	113
I Don't Want To Do It	177
I Don't Believe You (She Acts Like We Never Have Met)	66
I Dreamed I Saw St. Augustine	124
I Feel a Change Comin' On	378
I Forgot More Than You'll Ever Know	144
I Guess I'll Have to Change My Plan	409
I Once Knew A Man	283
I Pity the Poor Immigrant	127
I See You Around And Around	283
I Shall Be Free	28
I Shall Be Free No. 10	64
I Shall Be Released	110
I Threw It All Away	132
I Wanna Be Your Lover	86
I Want You	91

I Want You To Know I Love You......255	Joey's Theme 379
I Was Young When I Left Home 18	John Brown 58
I Will Love Him.......................................242	John Wesley Harding 123
I'd Hate To Be You On That Dreadful Day 37	Johnny Todd 113
I'd Have You Anytime............................177	Jokerman...262
I'll Keep It With Mine 77	Jolene..377
I'm Alright 116	Julius And Ethel.....................................270
I'm Not There 111	Just Like a Woman 92
Idiot Wind 203	Just Like Tom Thumb's Blues 84
If Dogs Run Free....................................169	Just When I Needed You Most..........302
If Not for You 167	Kingsport Town 32
If You Belong To Me 322	Knockin' on Heaven's Door................187
If You Ever Go to Houston................376	Lawdy Miss Clawdy..............................342
If You Gotta Go, Go Now....................76	Lay Down Your Weary Tune 54
If You See Her, Say Hello 204	Lay Lady Lay 133
I'll Be Home for Christmas.................385	Lenny Bruce 247
I'll Be Your Baby Tonight 128	Leopard-Skin Pill-Box Hat....................92
I'll Remember You 275	Let It Be Me...................................145, 250
I'm a Fool to Want You 400	Let Me Die in My Footsteps..................30
Imagination..413	Let's Begin 258
Important Words....................................299	Let's Keep It Between Us 257
In My Time of Dyin' 11	Let's Stick Together...............................296
In Search of Little Sadie 145	Levee's Gonna Break, The...................368
In the Garden..240	License to Kill..263
In the Summertime 248	Life Is Hard 375
Is It Worth It?..253	Like a Rolling Stone 81
Is Your Love in Vain?...........................221	Like A Ship...323
Isis...211	Lily of the West......................................161
It Ain't Me Babe 67	Lily, Rosemary and the Jack of Hearts 204
It Gets Lonely Early..............................411	Little Drummer Boy, The 385
It Had to Be You....................................407	Little Maggie..329
It Hurts Me Too 151	Little Sadie 146
It Takes a Lot to Laugh, It Takes a Train to Cry 82	Living the Blues 147
It's All Good...378	Lo And Behold 102
It's All Over Now, Baby Blue 76	Lone Pilgrim..339
It's Alright, Ma (I'm Only Bleeding) 75	Lonesome Day Blues 356
It's Funny to Everyone But Me..........417	Lonesome Death of Hattie Carroll, The 52
Jack-A-Roe 339	Long Ago, Far Away 34
Jane's Lament..379	Long and Wasted Years.......................393
Jane's Step..380	Long Distance Operator........................86
Jesus Is The One 257	Long Time Gone......................................37
Jet Pilot 86	Lord Protect My Child.........................269
Jim Jones..327	Love Henry...337
Joey 212	Love Minus Zero/No Limit 73

Title	Page
Love Sick	345
Love That Faded, The	397
Lunatic Princess	96
Maggie's Farm	73
Magic	253
Main Title Theme (Billy)	186
Make You Feel My Love	348
Making A Liar Out Of Me	241
Mama, You Been On My Mind	67
Man Gave Names to All the Animals	233
Man in Me, The	171
Man in the Long Black Coat	308
Man of Constant Sorrow	11
Man of Peace	264
Man on the Street	15
Marchin' To The City	352
Mary And The Soldier	340
Mary Ann	163
Masters of War	24
Maybe Someday	289
Maybe You'll Be There	405
Meet Me in the Morning	203
Melancholy Mood	407
Milk Cow Blues	41
Million Dollar Bash	101
Million Miles	346
Minstrel Boy	112
Miss The Mississippi	332
Mississippi	350
Mixed-Up Confusion	28
Money Honey	300
Moonlight	357
Moonshiner	55
Most Likely You Go Your Way and I'll Go Mine	93
Most of the Time	308
Motorpsycho Nitemare	65
Movin' (On The Water)	256
Mozambique	211
Mr. Bojangles	163
Mr. Tambourine Man	68
Must Be Santa	387
My Back Pages	66
My Blue Eyed Jane	341
My One and Only Love	412
My Oriental Home	255
My Wife's Home Town	375
Mystery Train	256
Narrow Way	393
Nashville Skyline Rag	131
Need A Woman	251
Neighborhood Bully	263
Nettie Moore	368
Never Gonna Be the Same Again	276
Never Say Goodbye	197
Nevertheless	406
New Morning	170
New Orleans Drums	380
New Pony	220
Night After Night	291
Night We Called It a Day, The	400
Ninety Miles an Hour (Down a Dead End Street)	297
No More Auction Block	20
No Time to Think	221
Nobody 'Cept You	198
North Country Blues	51
Not Dark Yet	347
Nothing Was Delivered	108
O' Come All Ye Faithful (Adeste Fideles)	386
O Little Town of Bethlehem	389
Obviously 5 Believers	94
Odds And Ends	101
Oh, Sister	212
Old Five And Dimer (Like Me)	293
On a Little Street in Singapore	407
On a Night Like This	194
On A Rockin' Boat	255
On the Road Again	74
Once Upon a Time	410
One For The Road	115
One More Cup of Coffee (Valley Below)	212
One More Night	133
One More Weekend	171
One of Us Must Know (Sooner or Later)	91
One Too Many Mornings	50
Only a Hobo	55
Only a Pawn in Their Game	51
Open The Door, Homer	109

Outlaw Blues	73
Oxford Town	26
P.S. I Love You	414
Paths Of Victory	54
Pay in Blood	394
Pecos Blues	190
Peggy Day	133
People Get Ready	313
Percy's Song	53
Please Mrs. Henry	103
Pledging My Time	90
Po' Boy	358
Political World	306
Polka Dots and Moonbeams	405
Polly Vaughan	333
Poor Boy Blues	18
Positively 4th Street	85
Precious Angel	230
Precious Memories	289
Pressing On	239
Pretty Boyd Floyd	299
Pretty Peggy-O	11
Pretty Saro	153
Property of Jesus	247
Queen Jane Approximately	83
Quinn The Eskimo (The Mighty Quinn)	110
Quit Your Low Down Ways	31
Ragged & Dirty	337
Railroad Bill	155
Rainy Day Women #12 & 35	90
Rambler, Gambler	17
Rambling, Gambling Willie	31
Rank Strangers to Me	298
Red Cadillac And A Black Moustache, A	361
Red River Shore	351
Repossession Blues	226
Restless Farewell	53
Return To Me	360
Ride This Train	293
Ring Of Fire	156, 350
Ring Them Bells	307
Rise Again	241
Rita May	215
River Theme	187
Road Weary	380
Robbie Robert's Lament	380
Rock Me Mama	189
Rocks and Gravel	41
Roll on John	396
Roll On John	39
Rollin' and Tumblin'	366
Romance in Durango	213
Sad Eyed Lady of the Lowlands	95
Sally Gal	34
Sally Sue Brown	296
Santa-Fe	111
Sara	214
Sarah Jane	162
Saved	238
Saving Grace	240
Scarlet Town	394
See That My Grave Is Kept Clean	14
Seeing the Real You at Last	275
Señor (Tales of Yankee Power)	222
Sentimental Journey	416
September of My Years, The	410
Series Of Dreams	312
Seven Curses	56
Seven Deadly Sins	323
Shake	294
Shake Shake Mama	377
She Belongs to Me	72
She's Your Lover Now	96
Shelter from the Storm	205
Shenandoah	298
Shooting Star	310
Shot of Love	246
Sidewalks, Fences & Walls	300
Sign Language	216
Sign On The Cross	117
Sign on the Window	170
Silent Weekend	114
Silver Bells	387
Silvio	297
Simple Twist of Fate	202
Sittin' on Top of the World	328
Sitting On A Barbed Wire Fence	77
Skylark	406
Sloppy Drunk	334
Slow Train	231

Snow Falling	379
Solid Rock	239
Some Enchanted Evening	401
Someday Baby	366
Something There Is About You	195
Something's Burning, Baby	277
Somewhere Along the Way	416
Song to Woody	14
Soon After Midnight	393
Spanish Harlem Incident	64
Spanish Is the Loving Tongue	153
Spirit on the Water	365
Stack A Lee	338
Stand By Faith	235
Standing in the Doorway	346
Standing On The Highway	19
Stardust	417
Stay with Me	400
Step It Up and Go	329
Stop Now	223
Stormy Weather	403
Straight A's In Love	280
Stuck Inside of Mobile with the Memphis Blues Again	91
Subterranean Homesick Blues	72
Sugar Baby	359
Summer Days	356
Suze (The Cough Song)	57
Sweeping The Floor	379
Sweet Amarillo	189
Sweetheart Like You	263
Swingin'	381
T.V. Talkin' Song	319
Take a Message to Mary	150
Take It Or Leave It	223
Take Me as I Am (Or Let Me Go)	150
Talkin' Bear Mountain Picnic Massacre Blues	30
Talkin' Hava Negeilah Blues	31
Talkin' John Birch Paranoid Blues	33
Talkin' New York	10
Talkin' World War III Blues	27
Talking Devil	39
Tangled Up in Blue	201
Tattle O'Day	155
Tears of Rage	104
Tell Me	269
Tell Me That It Isn't True	134
Tell Me, Momma	96
Tell Ol' Bill	370
Tempest	395
Temporary Like Achilles	93
That Lucky Old Sun	402
That Old Black Magic	408
That Old Feeling	411
That's Alright, Mama	42
The Very Thought Of You	281
There's a Flaw in My Flue	415
These Foolish Things	417
These Hands	154
They Killed Him	288
Thief On the Cross	257
Things Have Changed	359
Things We Said Today	396
Thirsty Boots	154
This Dream of You	377
This Evening So Soon	155
This Land Is Your Land	20
This Nearly Was Mine	411
This Old Man	322
This Was My Love	270
This Wheel's On Fire	109
Three Angels	172
Thunder on the Mountain	365
Tight Connection to My Heart (Has Anybody Seen My Love)	266
Til I Fell in Love with You	347
Time Passes Slowly	168
Times They Are a-Changin', The	49
Tin Angel	395
Tiny Montgomery	107
To Be Alone with You	132
To Fall In Love With You	292
To Ramona	65
Tombstone Blues	82
Tomorrow Is A Long Time	35
Tomorrow Night	330
Tonight I'll Be Staying Here with You	135
Too Much Of Nothing	104
Tough Mama	194
Trade Winds	412

Train A-Travelin'	40	When the World Was Young	416
Train Of Love	361	When You Gonna Wake Up	233
Trouble	249	Where Are You Tonight? (Journey Through Dark Heat)	223
Trouble In Mind	234	Where Are You?	402
True Love Tends to Forget	222	Where Is the One?	415
Trust Yourself	276	Where Teardrops Fall	307
Tryin' to Get to Heaven	346	Who Loves You More?	283
Turkey Chase	187	Why Try to Change Me Now	401
Tweedle Dee & Tweedle Dum	355	Why Was I Born?	418
Tweeter & The Monkey Man	315	Wichita (Going To Louisiana)	41
Twist And Shout	301	Wicked Messenger, The	127
Two Soldiers	338	Wiggle Wiggle	318
Ugliest Girl in the World	297	Wigwam	151
Unbelievable	319	Willie And The Hand Jive	301
Under the Red Sky	318	Wind Blows On The Water	254
Under Your Spell	290	Winter Wonderland	384
Union Sundown	264	Winterlude	169
Up To Me	206	With God on Our Side	50
Usual, The	291	Woogie Boogie	146
Visions of Johanna	90	Working On A Guru	174
Waitin' For You	361	Workingman's Blues #2	367
Waiting To Get Beat	281	World Gone Wrong	336
Walkin' Down the Line	33	Worried Blues	32
Wallflower	182	Ye Shall Be Changed	234
Walls of Red Wing	33	Yea! Heavy And A Bottle Of Bread	105
Watching The River Flow	181	Yes Sir, No Sir (Hallelujah)	254
Watered-Down Love	247	Yonder Comes Sin	252
We Better Talk This Over	222	You Ain't Goin' Nowhere	107
We're On Borrowed Time	255	You Angel You	196
Wedding Song	197	You Belong To Me	332
Went to See the Gypsy	168	You Changed My Life	251
What Can I Do for You?	239	You Don't Have To Do That	78
What Good Am I?	309	You Go to My Head	417
What Was It You Wanted	310	You Wanna Ramble	288
What'cha Gonna Do?	38	You're Still A Child To Me	254
What'll I Do	402	You've Been Hiding Too Long	43
When Did You Leave Heaven?	296	Young at Heart	405
When He Returns	234	You're a Big Girl Now	202
When I Got Troubles	16	You're Gonna Make Me Lonesome When You Go	203
When I Paint My Masterpiece	183	You're Gonna Quit Me	330
When the Deal Goes Down	366	You're No Good	10
When the Night Comes Falling from the Sky	277		
When the Ship Comes In	52		

Printed in Great Britain
by Amazon